GREECE AND THE COLD WAR

Diplomat-, stem of Latin *diploma* 'a state letter of recommendation' [...] from Greek *diploma* 'a licence, a chart', originally 'paper folded double', from *diploun* 'to double, fold over', from *diploos* 'double'.

Online Etymological Dictionary, 2017.
https://www.etymonline.com/word/diplomatic

What starts to cause resentment is when one thinks how the Greeks in charge are dealing with Anglo-American competition in the Mediterranean and the Middle East. I am afraid they behave as though they don't see it (or, when they happen to, they react pedantically). The tragedy is, unfortunately, that this antagonism, thanks to the glorious Greek Rally, has been entangled in our domestic politics. And so, in the heads of those in charge, who care first about their domestic interests and then about external affairs, the confusion is total; and when this state of affairs reigns in their heads, the technical advisers (the diplomats) have nothing else to do, if they are wise, but to stay quiet [...]. The vicious circle is back. I don't know who will break it. Mercy!

George Seferis, *Political Diary II*, 5 May 1952, p.131–2.

GREECE AND THE COLD WAR

Diplomacy and Anti-Colonialism in the Aftermath of Civil Conflict

Alexander Kazamias

BLOOMSBURY ACADEMIC
LONDON • NEW YORK • OXFORD • NEW DELHI • SYDNEY

BLOOMSBURY ACADEMIC
Bloomsbury Publishing Plc
50 Bedford Square, London, WC1B 3DP, UK
1385 Broadway, New York, NY 10018, USA
29 Earlsfort Terrace, Dublin 2, Ireland

BLOOMSBURY, BLOOMSBURY ACADEMIC and the Diana logo are
trademarks of Bloomsbury Publishing Plc

First published in Great Britain 2022
This edition published 2024

Copyright © Alexander Kazamias, 2022

Alexander Kazamias has asserted his right under the Copyright,
Designs and Patents Act, 1988, to be identified as Author of this work.

For legal purposes the Acknowledgements on p. ix constitute an
extension of this copyright page.

Series design by Adriana Brioso
Cover image: General Alexandros Papagos, Greece, 1951.
(© David Seymour / Magnum Photos)

All rights reserved. No part of this publication may be reproduced or transmitted
in any form or by any means, electronic or mechanical, including photocopying,
recording, or any information storage or retrieval system, without prior
permission in writing from the publishers.

Bloomsbury Publishing Plc does not have any control over, or responsibility for,
any third-party websites referred to or in this book. All internet addresses given
in this book were correct at the time of going to press. The author and publisher
regret any inconvenience caused if addresses have changed or sites have ceased
to exist, but can accept no responsibility for any such changes.

A catalogue record for this book is available from the British Library.

Library of Congress Cataloging-in-Publication Data
Names: Kazamias, Alexander, author.
Title: Greece and the Cold War : diplomacy and anti-colonialism in
the aftermath of civil conflict / by Alexander Kazamias.
Description: London ; New York : Bloomsbury Academic, 2022. |
Includes bibliographical references and index.
Identifiers: LCCN 2022000462 (print) | LCCN 2022000463 (ebook) |
ISBN 9781848859999 (hardback) | ISBN 9781350205505 (pdf) |
ISBN 9781350205512 (epub) | ISBN 9781350205529
Subjects: LCSH: North Atlantic Treaty Organization–History–20th century. |
Nationalism–Greece–History–20th century. | Cold War. | Greece–Foreign
relations–1935–1967. | Greece–Politics and government–1935–1967.
Classification: LCC DF850 .K38 2022 (print) | LCC DF850 (ebook) |
DDC 327.495009/045–dc23/eng/20220601
LC record available at https://lccn.loc.gov/2022000462
LC ebook record available at https://lccn.loc.gov/2022000463

ISBN: HB: 978-1-8488-5999-9
PB: 978-1-3502-0549-9
ePDF: 978-1-3502-0550-5
eBook: 978-1-3502-0551-2

Typeset by Integra Software Services Pvt. Ltd.

To find out more about our authors and books visit www.bloomsbury.com
and sign up for our newsletters.

CONTENTS

List of illustrations	vi
List of tables	viii
Acknowledgements	ix
Introduction	1
1 CONCEPTUALIZING THE DUALISM OF GREEK FOREIGN POLICY	7
2 HEGEMONY, DEPENDENCE AND THE US POLICY REVIEW OF 1952	29
3 THE DOMESTIC STRUCTURES OF THE POST-CIVIL WAR POLITICAL SYSTEM	53
4 FROM DEPENDENCE TO DUALISM: CYPRUS ENTERS GREEK FOREIGN POLICY	83
5 DEPENDENT NATIONALISM: 'OPERATING BETWEEN TWO NOTIONS'	113
6 THE SEMI-INTERNATIONALIZATION OF THE CYPRUS QUESTION: THE UN APPEAL	145
7 THE DUALIST ASPECTS OF FOREIGN ECONOMIC POLICY	179
Conclusion	211
Notes	222
Bibliography	283
Index	301

ILLUSTRATIONS

1. Prime Minister Alexander Papagos and Mrs Maria Papagos with shipowner Stavros Niarchos and wife Evgenia Livanos aboard the tanker S.S. *World Harmony*, Phaleron Bay, September 1954. Photographer: Antonis Patsavos. Antonis Patsavos Collection, ELIA-MIET Photographic Archive — 17
2. Field Marshal Papagos's resignation letter from the leadership of the armed forces, dated 28 May 1951. It says: 'Mr President, I have the honour to submit, for health reasons, my resignation from the post of Field Marshal of the armed forces. All Yours, signature'. Sophocles Venizelos Papers, Benaki Museum Historical Archive — 66
3. Alexander Papagos speaking during an election campaign rally at Klafthmonos Square, Athens, 2 September 1951. To his right (far), Panayiotis Kanellopoulos, and to his left (near) Spyros Markezinis. Karamanlis Foundation Photographic Archive — 79
4. The Greek Rally enters Parliament for the first time as the official opposition party. Seated in the front row, Alexander Papagos (middle), Stefanos Stefanopoulos (right) and Panayiotis Kanellopoulos (left). First session of the new Parliament, 10 October 1951. Karamanlis Foundation Photographic Archive — 80
5. Swearing-in of the Papagos Government in Parliament, 12 December 1952. Right to left: Alexander Papagos, Emmanuel Tsouderos, Panayiotis Kanellopoulos, Spyros Markezinis, Stefanos Stefanopoulos, Constantine Karamanlis. Karamanlis Foundation Photographic Archive — 82
6. President Dwight Eisenhower inspects a Greek bronze helmet of the fifth century BCE, a gift from Greek Coordination Minister, Spyros Markezinis, centre, and the Greek Ambassador to the United States, Athanase Politis. Other gifts brought by Markezinis and Politis included a gold medal, making the president an honorary citizen of Athens; an eighth-century BCE earthenware wine flask and a necklace of ancient Greek coins for Mamie Eisenhower. White House, Washington, 7 May 1953. Associated Press — 88
7. Prime Minister Papagos with French Prime Minister Joseph Laniel during his official visit to France, 19 January 1954. Karamanlis Foundation Photographic Archive — 129
8. Clashes between students and police guards during a protest over the Cyprus question, 1954. United Photoreporters Agency-Greece, ELIA-MIET Photographic Archive — 149

9	Members of the Greek Delegation to the Ninth Session of the UN General Assembly awaiting the opening of proceedings, New York, 30 September 1954. Left to right: Alexis Kyrou, Director General of the Greek Ministry of Foreign Affairs; Constantine Karanikas, Economic Counselor of the Greek Embassy in Washington; and Christian Xanthopoulos-Palamas, Greece's Permanent Representative to the UN. United Nations Photographic Archive	154
10	Minister of Economic Coordination, Spyros Markezinis, announces the devaluation of the drachma in his historic radio speech of 9 April 1953. ELIA-MIET Photographic Archive	194
11	Prime Minister Alexander Papagos (middle), with his two Deputy Prime Ministers, Stefanos Stefanopoulos (right) and Panayiotis Kanellopoulos (left). 22 December 1952. Karamanlis Foundation Photographic Archive	212

TABLES

1	Results of the Greek legislative elections of 5 March 1950	36
2	Results of the Greek legislative elections of 9 September 1951	55
3	Results of the Greek legislative elections of 16 November 1952	56
4	Foreign economic and military aid to Greece, January 1945–July 1949	182
5	US economic assistance to Greece, 1948–55	183
6	US military aid to Greece, 1947–56	183
7	The Greek balance of trade, 1948–56	184
8	Comparison of the projected cuts in US economic aid to Greece in *The Varvaressos Report* and actual reductions, 1950–5	189
9	Comparison of inflation rates in Greece and nine main trading partners, 1952–6	195
10	Percentage of annual change in prices in the Greek economy, 1951–5 (Consumer Price Index)	201
11	First addendum of tariff increases submitted to the GATT by Greece, 26 March 1954	204
12	The trade deficit of Greece, 1951–63	208
13	Agricultural products and ores as a percentage of total Greek exports, 1952–62	208
14	Change in the structural composition of Greek GDP, 1950–61	209

ACKNOWLEDGEMENTS

This book is the product of long years of research, conducted across different countries, where I was fortunate to receive the generous support and advice of excellent scholars and researchers. Others were kind enough to facilitate access to the numerous archives I visited or invite me to speak in seminars and guest lectures, where thought-provoking questions helped me rethink certain arguments in the book. I wish to take this opportunity to express my heartfelt thanks to all these individuals.

I am particularly indebted to Martyn Rady, Kieran Williams, Mark Wheeler, Catherine Hoskyns, Tudor Jones, Michael Smith, Brian Hocking, Neil Forbes, Hazel Barrett, Ken Matthews, Alex Thomson, Lisa Carter, George Kazamias, Marilyn Booth, Venetia Apostolidou, Riki Van Boeschotten, Titika Dimitroulia, Effi Gazi, Vangelis Karamanolakis, Gonda Van Stean, Dimitris Papanikolaou and Costas Skordylis for their valuable ideas, comments and encouragement at different stages of working on this manuscript.

During the earlier part of my research, I was privileged to receive excellent motivation and advice from the former prime minister of Greece, George Rallis; Professors Constantine Svolopoulos, Argyris Fatouros and Panos Moullas; the prominent journalists and historians Spyros Linardatos and Sofianos Chrysostomidis; and the editor of *Anti* magazine, and dear friend Christos Papoutsakis. As they have all departed from this world, I wish to pay tribute to their memory.

My work for this book has taken me to numerous places where I received excellent friendly and professional assistance. I wish to thank the staff at the Hellenic Parliament Library, the Historical Archive of the Ministry of Foreign Affairs, the Hellenic Historical and Literary Archive (ELIA), the Constantine Karamanlis Foundation, the Historical Archive of the Central Bank of Greece, the British National Archives at Kew Gardens, the Dwight Eisenhower Foundation, the National Library of Greece, the Firestone Library at Princeton University, the Bodleian Library, Oxford and the Lanchester Library at Coventry for enabling me to use key archival, bibliographic and photographic material.

Last but not least, I wish to thank Anastasia Stouraiti for our ever-interesting conversations, and our children, Maya and Stefanos, for their sharp sense of humour and the joy they bring to our lives. This book is dedicated to them, and to my parents, Stefanos and Marguerite Rose.

INTRODUCTION

The aim of this book is to provide a reassessment of the ways in which we think about nationalism in hegemonic world orders. Its main focus, the relationship between Atlanticism and nationalism in the first decade of the Cold War, remains a largely unexplored area, in both the field of diplomatic history and the discipline of international relations. Until the late 1980s, the prevalent view held that European nationalism was a declining phenomenon during the Cold War, partly because of its damaging association with the atrocities of Nazism in the 1930s and 1940s and partly because after 1945 it was thought to have ceded its place to the conflicting global ideologies of Western liberalism and Soviet communism.[1] However, even after the end of the Cold War, historians like Mark Mazower held on to this notion, stating in his acclaimed *Dark Continent* (1998) that the 'panoply of national cultures, histories and values' which dominated Europe in the 1990s 'hardly mattered in the Cold War, as Europeans on both sides of the Iron Curtain [had] surrendered the initiative [...] to the superpowers'.[2] Similarly, international relations scholars, like John Mearsheimer, whose realist perspective is otherwise sensitive to nations and 'national interests', also subscribe to the view that 'nationalism has been contained during the Cold War'.[3] According to this perception, the upsurge of nationalism in the 1990s in areas like the Balkans must be explained as a revival of an older phenomenon which, according to William Pfaff, was 'frozen between 1945 [...] and the collapse of Communism in 1989'. As another historian recently put it, after 1945 'nationalism began to lose some of its former political influence within European societies [...]. The end of the Cold War, however, also contributed to a new surge of nationalist movements'.[4]

The present study questions these assumptions. It argues that, even in the deeply frozen climate of the Cold War, nationalism still mattered a great deal to many Europeans, not only in larger states like Italy (which became embroiled in the Trieste dispute from 1946 to 1954) or France (following General de Gaulle's return to power in 1958), but also in some of the most superpower-dependent and strategically vulnerable Balkan states, like Greece. Taking Greek foreign policy as its focal point, the present book shows that far from having dissipated or ossified, nationalism continued to play a crucial part during the Cold War as both an ideological and a political force.

In proposing this alternative reading, a vital distinction must be drawn between the new form that nationalism acquired during the Cold War and the chauvinist ideologies which prevailed across much of Europe and the Balkans in the interwar period. In the case of Greece, both the Civil War of the 1940s and the onset of the Cold War resulted in a blending of interwar nationalist ideas and practices (crystalized under the Metaxas Dictatorship of 1936–41) with the emerging principles of liberal Atlanticism under a new official discourse that bore the name of *Ethnikofrosyni* (national mindedness).[5] Strictly speaking, the *Ethnikofron* citizen of the 1950s was no longer an unqualified nationalist, like the dedicated supporter of General Metaxas in the 1930s, whose ideological aspirations could be fulfilled within an isolated and inward-looking Greek state.[6] The *Ethnikofron* subject and the post-war Greek state which embodied his/her ideals were marked by a new dual loyalty: on one hand to the nationalist ideals of Hellenism bequeathed by the Metaxas regime and other pre-war political traditions; and on the other hand, to the unity of Western political systems under the Cold War liberal principles championed by the United States. In this respect, the alternative interpretation offered here differs not only from the 'frozen phenomenon' thesis mentioned above, but also from the traditionalist theory advocated by Anthony D. Smith, which holds that a strong element of continuity connects interwar and post-war European nationalism.[7] In contrast to the latter conception, the present book maintains that since 1945, European nationalism has undergone a significant transformation in its endeavour to remain influential in the new Cold War climate. Consequently, for reasons that will become apparent below, it will be argued that after 1945, nationalism, in both the Balkans and other parts of Europe, could not persist as an influential movement except in an impure form which I shall call thereafter *dependent nationalism*.

To properly account for this phenomenon, the present study adopts a methodology that is Janus-faced, looking on one side to the empirical techniques of diplomatic history and on the other to the theoretical concepts of international relations and foreign policy analysis. This choice is motivated by the belief that, if we are to capture the metamorphoses of nationalism during the Cold War, we need a diplomatic history that is armed with the theoretical tools of the discipline of International Relations. This synthesis arises from the deeper conviction that neither diplomatic history nor foreign policy analysis can develop beyond certain epistemological limits unless they break down the barriers that have traditionally set them apart and borrow extensively from each other's methods and techniques. In this regard, the present study embraces the principle advocated by Greece's eminent twentieth-century historian, Nicos Svoronos, who considered the rivalry between historical empiricism and theoretical investigation as 'a false dilemma'. As he put it, 'this apparent contradiction is resolved when one accepts the circular [...] function whereby observation leads to general concepts and these, in turn, become instruments for guiding empirical research.'[8]

The revision of established norms always carries the hazard of overstating the alternative viewpoint to underline its hitherto overlooked importance. In our case, the main pitfall would be, in an attempt to reinstate the overlooked role of Greek nationalism after 1945, to slide in the opposite extreme and portray it as a more powerful force than the Cold War itself. Indeed, such a revisionist tendency[9] has developed in the historiography on modern Greece since the early 1980s, beginning with semi-autobiographical accounts of leading politicians and diplomats who sought to defend their record in office from the critique of radical historians who depicted them as lackeys of American imperialism. A key work in this tradition is *History of Lost Opportunities* (1981) by former Foreign Minister and conservative opposition leader, Evangelos Averoff-Tositsas, which forms one of the pillars of Greek ethnocentric historiography on the Cyprus question. Its nationalist overtones can be seen in statements, such as 'no matter how many political shocks we suffered, we steadily continued to struggle for Cyprus, striving to protect [...] the sacred aspirations of Hellenism', etc.[10] Another influential work in the same tradition is *Ten Years of the Cyprus Question* (1980) by the senior diplomat Angelos Vlachos, which depicts Greek foreign policy in the 1950s as a struggle between radical and moderate strands of nationalism in which the latter is supposedly vindicated.[11] In recent years, this narrative has formed the basis of several scholarly accounts which present Greek foreign policy in the 1950s as allegedly independent from the United States and NATO and essentially gripped by the supreme nationalist aspriration of achieving *Enosis* (union) between Cyprus and Greece.[12]

This book does not embrace these revisionist arguments, nor does it intend to take us back to the neo-Marxist and *Marxisant* historiography which forms the orthodox narrative on post-Civil War Greece.[13] Although it shares some concerns with Greek ethnocentric historiography about the neglected role of nationalism after 1945, it questions the manner in which these historians have tried to address this key question. In particular, the present study is sceptical of the ethnocentric historians' tendency to treat nationalism in essentialist/trans-historical terms, as an unaltered substance that passed from the interwar to the post-war period without undergoing substantial change. Moreover, it is critical of their attempt to tone down the impact of external factors on Greek foreign policy, particularly the dominant role of the United States since the promulgation of the Truman Doctrine in 1947. Finally, in contrast to this narrative, the present study seeks to reinstate nationalism's neglected role during the Cold War from a standpoint that is non-ethnocentric.

The alternative theoretical approach adopted here is rooted in a perspective whose objective is to overcome the systemic bias of neo-Marxism and the positivist/ethnocentric tendencies of realist approaches. Critical International Relations (IR) theory[14] sets out from a third standpoint, whose aim is to conceptualize foreign policy as a process operating at the interface between global and national politics in a manner that is not determined by either. According to Andrew Linklater,

> critical-theoretical approaches deny that the interests of insiders naturally take precedence over the interests of outsiders; they reject the supposition that in the event of a conflict between duties to fellow citizens and duties to humanity, the former inevitably come first.[15]

Critical IR theory conceptualizes foreign policy in holistic terms as a practice involving politico-strategic, socio-economic and ideological factors that carry equal importance in the decision-making process. This perspective rejects the tendency of realist and (to a lesser extent) pluralist approaches to hierarchize foreign policy issues into 'high' and 'low politics'. At the same time, it differs from neo-Marxist approaches in that it avoids reducing politico-strategic relations to socio-economic factors.[16] According to its leading proponent, Robert Cox, critical IR theory 'contemplates the social and political complex as a whole'.[17] Following Cox, the present study adopts a conception that stresses the open-ended dialectical relationship between state power and socio-economic forces.[18] Finally, as some scholars have noted, Cox's approach seeks 'to move beyond [the] "static sense of history" and disappointing conception of change' often encountered in Marxism and embraces a method that underlines 'the historicist and agency-oriented aspects of Gramsci's political sociology'.[19] As Adrian Budd remarks, this perspective has 'demonstrated a willingness to develop concepts dynamically' through 'rejecting the transhistorical essentialism that Cox argues characterizes both Realism and structural versions of Marxism'.[20]

On this basis, the present study opens the possibility for a post-revisionist analysis of Greek foreign policy. What distinguishes this approach from those dominating the scholarship is, above all, its attempt to circumvent both the overemphasis of Marxist and *Marxisant* analyses on Greece's dependence, and the inflated role ethnocentric historians accord to post-war Greek nationalism. Instead, a post-revisionist analysis focuses on the dynamic interaction between dependence and nationalism. Insofar as critical IR theory is primarily concerned with the study of relations between the world system and its constituent parts, its significance for a post-revisionist analysis of Greek foreign policy is vital. Equally important is the theory's adherence to a non-reductionist conception which holds that states, social forces and world orders interact through an open dialectic in which none enjoys primacy over the others.

While global US hegemony and the local nationalist movement for *Enosis* with Cyprus defined Greek foreign policy in the early years of the Cold War, critical theory suggests that we can analyse the complex interaction between them without assuming that one always determines the other. Because critical theory treats relations between states, social forces and world orders as marked by an open-ended dialectic, its method is essentially historicist. This means that, to explain why world orders sometimes influence domestic national politics and why, on other occasions, the opposite occurs, it is necessary to always examine the specific historical context that favours one outcome over the other. In this respect, critical theory offers fertile ground for analyses seeking to combine the conceptual tools of International Relations with a rigorous historical investigation.

A practice closely linked to the phenomenon of *dependent nationalism* is foreign policy dualism. In its basic form, foreign policy dualism refers to the process of co-articulating two distinct and conflicting objectives within a single policy as though both were compatible and complementary. Although the concept has not received systematic treatment, Stanley Hoffmann has used it in *Gulliver's Troubles* (1968) to denote the tendency of the United States to mix realist and idealist objectives within the same foreign policy. According to his sketchy (and clearly inadequate) definition, dualism refers to 'a deep tension between two ways of dealing with political issues'.²¹ More recently, Gabriel Gorodetsky deployed the term to account for contradictions in early Soviet foreign policy, when Moscow both promoted world revolution and sought stable diplomatic relations with the very Western governments it was working to overthrow. Although Gorodetsky, too, did not subject the term to systematic treatment, he notes its oversight by the scholarship and stresses its great analytical potential. As he put it, there is an 'overwhelming tendency in both Western and Soviet historiography [...] to overlook the dualism of Soviet foreign policy',²² a criticism that is equally relevant to the scholarship on modern Greece. Gorodetsky maintains that foreign policy dualism has been overlooked chiefly because historians avoid examining 'under the same spotlight' phenomena which are typically thought as opposites, like revolution and realpolitik.²³ With regard to post-war Greece, a similar observation would be appropriate in relation to the seemingly incompatible notions of dependence and nationalism.

The core argument of the present work could be summarized around three key points. First, Atlanticism and nationalism are two ontologically distinct and contradictory political doctrines²⁴ whose combination in the Cold War was largely encouraged by their shared fear of and hostility towards communism. Second, a proper synthesis of the two doctrines can never be attained because their intrinsic incompatibility undermines any positive connections that could develop between them. As a result, their combination in the foreign policies of states like Greece locks them into a negative dialectic whereby Atlanticism grows in large part through undercutting nationalism and *vice versa*. Third, the co-articulation of both doctrines leads to the emergence of a dualist foreign policy that lacks the coherence and consistency of either Atlanticism or nationalism. In its endeavour to balance out what it sees as the best elements of both, this policy ends up producing self-contradictory decisions whose effects in the 1950s undermined both Greece's relations within the Atlantic Alliance and the struggle of Cypriot independence.

In his acclaimed book, *The Irony of American History* (1952), Reinhold Niebhur drew an interesting distinction between 'the tragic' and 'ironic' elements in human history. He maintained that both relate to 'incongruous' behaviour, either by individuals or by states. The ironic element, he said, arises from actions whose 'hidden defects' are not known to their perpetrators, while the tragic element results from contradictory actions that are knowingly carried out. Irony 'prompts some laughter', he continued, but tragic action elicits 'admiration and pity for the hero who is willing to [...] incur guilt for the sake of some great good'.²⁵ This typology led Niebhur to present post-war American 'hegemony' as a series of unintended contradictions, driven by 'illusions of childlike innocence'.²⁶ In the case of post-Civil War Greece, both irony and tragedy were equally at play. *Dependent nationalism* started out in 1952 as an ironic aspiration by a Greek government which, initially, could not foresee to what lengths the powers of the 'Free World' would go to maintain colonialism in Cyprus. But when this gradually became apparent, the same government held on to its self-contradictory policy in ways that were less heroic, but still as tragic as those described by Niehbur. This book tells the story of how these ironic aspirations turned into a tragic policy.

1

CONCEPTUALIZING THE DUALISM OF GREEK FOREIGN POLICY

The widely held view that Greek foreign policy during the early decades of the Cold War was wholly dependent on the United States and the interests of the Atlantic Alliance is a reductionist thesis that contradicts key historical evidence.[1] Equally simplistic, however, is the opposite view which overstates the tensions between Greece and its Western allies over the Cyprus question to argue that, since 1952, the country's foreign policy pursued a predominantly independent course.[2] Apart from a few accounts which have opted for more nuanced analyses, these two perspectives have dominated the historiography on post-war Greece and continue to polarize it around two opposed and conflicting approaches: the dependence and the ethnocentric narratives.

The differences between both perspectives range from their contradictory empirical assessments to their divergent methodologies and underlying theoretical assumptions. Caught up in the polarized climate of the Cold War and the legacy of the Greek Civil War, each developed its own self-styled approach without seeking to establish a common understanding with the rival narrative. Worse still, apart from some half-hearted attempts, like John Iatrides's edited volume *Greece in the 1940s* (1981) historians on both sides have been reluctant to even engage in a proper debate to clarify the points of difference between them.[3] Instead, they remain preoccupied with their self-justifying analyses, leaving behind a substantial gap that calls for more synthesizing studies.

So deep is the divide between both narratives, that on key empirical questions, such as the rise of Field Marshal Alexander Papagos to power in 1952, they adhere to two utterly disconnected versions of events. For proponents of the dependence approach, Papagos was installed as prime minister by the US embassy and the Greek army, whereas for ethnocentric historians his rise to power resulted from his landslide election victory on 16 November 1952. A corollary of this disagreement is the growth of a wide interpretative gulf over the nature of the Greek post-Civil War regime and its institutions. While the dependence narrative portrays the Greek state from 1949 to 1967 as primarily supported by a dark 'parastate' consisting of the army, the police, the security forces, the Secret Service (KYP) and certain far-right civil society groups, Greek ethnocentric historians dismiss this assessment as 'extremely simplistic' and claim that parliamentary institutions usually held the upper hand.[4] Fundamental differences can be equally found over questions of methodology and theoretical approach. By and large, neo-Marxist and *Marxisant* works, which form the basis of the dependence narrative, are over-theorized and rely on the contemporary opposition press, whereas ethnocentric historians are usually under-theorized and rely on official and semi-official sources which they seldom analyse in a sufficiently critical fashion. A further area of contention is the difference over the nature of the Greek political system itself. Most studies adhering to the dependence narrative tend to conceptualize post-war Greece as a peripheral/underdeveloped society with an authoritarian state, while ethnocentric historians treat it as a Western pluralist system with strong parliamentary institutions and a deserved place in NATO, the OEEC and the Council of Europe.[5]

To arrive at a better understanding of Greece's position in the early Cold War, it is necessary to reexamine these interpretative assumptions. In so doing, it does not suffice to simply conflate arguments from both narratives in the hope of attaining some Solomonic happy medium. This method has been already attempted, but predictably, without success. One study from the 1990s, for example, claims that 'on the theoretical level' it stands on the 'antipodes of the theories of dependence', but when we turn to its empirical argument we find that it replicates most of the core assumptions of that theory, including the thesis that the US embassy and the Greek army were the dominant power centres in post-war Greece.[6] Another historian, in an attempt to explain Papagos's rise to power as an outcome of both US intervention and an independent, democratic development, resorted to the following conclusion: 'Despite the preference of the American and British embassy for a "Papagos solution", both Washington and London still retained serious reservations'.[7] As a result, we never learn if Papagos ultimately rose to power because Britain and the United States 'preferred' that outcome or whether he was democratically elected because their 'serious reservations' prevailed. A longer list could be provided, but these examples should suffice to show what contradictions can arise when one attempts to bridge the gap between the two main narratives by simply adapting or conflating their positions.

To arrive at a more fruitful alternative, what must be stressed from the outset is that both the dependence and ethnocentric narratives are marked by strong reductionist and deterministic bias as they seek to drive their analyses towards predetermined ends.[8] With regard to neo-Marxist and *Marxisant* approaches, determinism usually takes the form of a tendency to deny any autonomy for the post-Civil War Greek state and thus attribute most of Greece's ills to the 'Great Powers' and their allegedly sinister motives. Conversely, in the case of Greek ethnocentric historiography and the realist assumptions on which it usually rests, determinism takes the form of exaggerating the autonomy of the Greek state and attributing secondary importance to domestic social forces and the dominant world order.[9] These criticisms apply equally to some of the most recent works. For instance, one study from the perspective of dependence argues that, after the Truman Doctrine, 'no power approached the United States in terms of influence vis-à-vis internal political developments', not even 'the Greek government' itself.[10] Meanwhile, another study from an ethnocentric perspective argues that 'in the

1950s the supreme objective of the Greek side was *Enosis*,[11] a statement implying that all other foreign policy aims, like NATO membership, the alliance with the United States and the fight against international communism, were supposedly less important. A more productive investigation, however, requires an alternative perspective that stresses the limits of both approaches and offers new analytical tools to overcome them.

The relevance of Critical Theory

Since the 1980s, a new theory of international relations began to develop around the work of Robert Cox which has since gained a notable influence.[12] Critical IR theory is primarily concerned with the way in which a given historical context gives rise to particular forms of action in world politics. Its aim is to explain international relations through examining the way in which different parts of the world system (i.e. states, international organizations, transnational movements, etc.) interact with the whole.[13] In contrast to neo-Marxist and positivist/realist approaches, critical theory rejects the tendency to consider international relations as an activity defined by unidirectional causality. It therefore rejects both neo-Marxist/dependency theory that holds that the dominant world order ultimately determines state action and the neorealist notion that 'international structure emerges from the interaction of states'.[14] Instead, critical IR theory analyses the relationship between states and world orders from a non-reductionist perspective that focuses on the 'dialectical' relationship between them, an approach that goes back to one of the theory's original founders, the Frankfurt School philosopher, Max Horkheimer, and his core principle that dialectics constitutes a precondition of any 'rounded knowledge that deals with historical reality'.[15]

From these foundational propositions, Cox went on to develop a theoretical model that conceptualizes world politics as a history of how world orders are formed, reproduced and transformed. According to this model, international relations is constituted through an intersected dialectic operating concurrently at three levels: (a) the dominant *forces in society*, (b) the main *forms of state* and (c) the established *world order*. All three levels, according to this theory, interact continually, while none possesses ontological primacy over the others. This implies that change at one level either produces alterations in the other two or is met with resistance and is ultimately reversed. Although critical theory opens the possibility of studying world politics from a non-deterministic historical perspective (and that is why it is often called 'historicist'), it should be stressed that its aim is not to reduce International Relations into a branch of global history. In analysing international relations historically, critical theory adopts a specific research programme which, as Cox pointed out, focuses on 'understanding the contradictions and sources of conflict within existing structures'.[16] In this respect, the theory should be understood as providing 'a method of identifying the crisis in which conflict is actual or potential'.[17] In highlighting contradictions, incongruities and crises, critical IR theory does not merely seek to expose the failings of world politics. As Linklater and others have remarked, its ultimate purpose is to highlight possibilities which 'might lead to a change of the system'.[18]

Critical theory and foreign policy analysis (FPA)

Despite opening new pathways for general IR theory, critical theory has had a limited impact on middle-range IR theory and empirical research. In 2010, Steven Roach remarked that after twenty-five years as an established paradigm in IR, many scholars still propound that critical theory needs 'a policy-relevant' approach.[19] This omission is probably nowhere more obvious than in the absence of a critical theory of foreign policy, a type of middle-range theory that could give rise to a whole new spectrum of empirical research on the foreign policies of different states, international organizations and transnational actors. Indeed, the development of such a theory has been expected for quite some time by scholars like Valerie Hudson, who predicted some years ago that critical theory will provide fertile ground to a new generation of foreign policy analysts. In her book *Foreign Policy Analysis* (2007) she observed that

> FPA theory, because of its comparative marginalization within IR over the last several decades, has not intersected very much with critical theory. Surely the next generation of FPA scholars will not only see critical theory interface with FPA, but hopefully they will be a part of bringing such an interface to pass.[20]

Recent theoretical studies have also highlighted the higher interpretative value of 'dialectical approaches' over 'monocausal' and 'dualistic' models of FPA,[21] a conclusion that privileges critical theory as a perspective that places dialectics at the heart of its enquiry.

In the following paragraphs, a brief outline of how critical IR theory can be used to analyse foreign policy will be provided. In sketching out such a model, the aim is not to construct a fully fledged theory of FPA. A task of such magnitude would require more systematic groundwork and greater elaboration. What is intended here is to simply provide a model that will guide the empirical analysis of the ensuing research.

On this basis, a critical theory of foreign policy can be said to be primarily concerned with the ways in which a given historical context gives rise to the sum total of decisions and non-decisions defining the relationship of a particular actor with its international environment. In contrast to behaviourist approaches, which privilege the role of policy-makers, the main focus of critical FPA is the relationship between decision-makers and their international and domestic contexts. In an essay co-authored with Harold Jacobson, Cox emphasized the importance of this distinction when analysing decision-making from a critical perspective: 'What goes on within particular agencies', they wrote, 'can be a small part of the total process'. Therefore, what is required is a wider understanding of what they call 'the environmental variables relevant to decision making'.²² In a similar vein, others have identified the difference between critical and non-critical approaches in relation to the former's focus on 'the socio-economic context' in which decisions are made.²³

The above does not imply that critical theory regards foreign policy as a chain of passive/adaptive responses to the pressures exerted by the domestic and international environments. Critical theory stresses that decision-makers imagine and creatively construct policy in ways that may run counter to or go beyond the structural constraints set by their environment. In recent years, several scholars have highlighted the importance of recognizing the 'creative dimension' in decision-making from a constructivist theoretical perspective.²⁴ In contrast to social constructivism, which focuses mainly on the role of agency and its creative input, critical theory maintains that the imaginary element in decision-making cannot be detached from the numerous constraints placed upon it by a given context. In this regard, the dialectical relationship between the decision-makers' ideas and the contextual limits placed upon them is viewed as an on-going struggle in which the former either adapt to their environment or resist it and seek to transform it. Under no circumstances does critical theory assume that decision-makers 'imagine' or 'create' policy outside a tightly structured context.

While other foreign policy analysis models, like pluralism, have lately acknowledged the importance of 'non-decisions',²⁵ critical theory has always highlighted the centrality of this parameter. Following Bachrach and Baratz, who first introduced the concept in the 1960s, Cox and Jacobson have argued that one of the ways in which structural pressures affect decision-making is through the mental images of power decision-makers create. These images, they argue, regardless of how relevant they are to reality, tend to lead decision-makers to eliminate certain options from their agendas during a 'pre-decision' stage, because the implications of including them are considered likely to provoke undesirable reactions.²⁶ Despite several criticisms,²⁷ the concept of 'non-decisions' has survived as a valuable analytical tool which can be applied to explain key aspects of decision-making without resorting to speculative assumptions and theories.²⁸

A critical theory of foreign policy is also premised on a distinctive conception of the decision-making environment. Using Cox's triadic model, a critical perspective should conceptualize foreign policy as the product of a dialectic relationship between: (a) a set of domestic social forces, (b) a dominant form of state and (c) a prevailing world order. Although other models, particularly pluralism, have also deployed a similar triadic perspective to analyse foreign policy,²⁹ critical theory holds different assumptions about what lies inside each of these levels. Because it perceives power as fragmented and dispersed across a number of competing actors, pluralism views the foreign policy environment as a loosely structured and potentially malleable 'arena', whereas critical theory conceptualizes it as a field in which power assumes a more centralized and tightly structured form. Consequently, critical theory does not perceive the domestic and external foreign policy environments as wide open spaces ('arenas') populated by autonomous or semi-autonomous 'actors' that are connected through diverse hierarchical and non-hierarchical 'linkages'.[30] Except in periods of crisis, when such fragmentation could occur, critical theory conceptualizes the external environment as hierarchically structured around a global hegemonic order and views domestic contexts as equally structured around a domestic hegemonic bloc of socioeconomic and political forces.[31]

Furthermore, critical theory conceptualizes the state from a distinctly neo-Gramscian perspective. This sees it as a complex social construct possessing relative autonomy from its internal and external environments, but still drawing power from both the domestic hegemonic bloc of social forces and, externally, the hegemonic world order. As Mark Rupert remarks, 'states, for Cox, are historically constructed (and continually reconstructed) in the nexus between global and domestic social relations'.[32] Consequently, the main function of the state is not to provide security or arbitrate over domestic conflicts, but to make the dominant alliance of social forces, i.e. the hegemonic historic bloc, exercise effective hegemony. Insofar as critical IR theory takes account of both the domestic and external attributes of statehood, the role of the state as consolidator of hegemony operates concurrently at both the national and international levels. As John M. Hobson explains, 'Cox not only attributes a moderate degree of domestic autonomy or agential power to the state, but also grants it moderate international agential power to shape the international system'.[33] This means that the state is viewed as an institution capable of wielding a certain degree of power (both internally and externally) to adjust the national hegemonic bloc with the structures of the world order (without, however, managing to harmonize them).[34] In this regard, the state is constantly caught up in the midst of a dialectical relationship between an internal and external hegemony.

Finally, a critical theory of foreign policy rests on a firmly historical approach. As a perspective primarily concerned with change and its various possibilities, critical theory does not conform to the a-historical models which have dominated foreign policy analysis since the 1960s. At the same time, it can be neither reduced to traditional diplomatic history, with its overemphasis on the role of 'great men' and its empiricist bias towards official archival sources. As a result, the application of a critical method to the study of foreign policy is possible only through a synthesis that brings together the analytical tools of foreign policy analysis with the research methods of diplomatic history. The new and essential element of this synthesis is a critical narrative that avoids discussing the routine aspects of foreign policy, but focuses on the conditions that produce conflict, crisis and a prospect for change. As Cox and Jacobson remarked, the main concern of critical approaches is to highlight 'the points of conflict within the system that seem to suggest a potential for structural transformation'.[35] In this regard, the task of reconnecting foreign policy to its historical context is aimed primarily as a means of locating the elements of irregularity that pave the way for change.

Greece as a semi-peripheral society

If critical theory provides the basis of a non-reductionist approach to foreign policy analysis, the concept of the 'semi-periphery' offers a useful analytical category for the study of post-war Greece. Although the term has its origins in the neo-Marxist dependence theory of Immanuel Wallerstein (who also applied it to Greece),[36] most studies on modern Greece that use a dependence theory perspective, ironically, avoid it. This paradox is linked to both methodological and ideological factors. Methodologically, many works on post-war Greece tend to apply key concepts without subjecting them to rigorous treatment. For instance, one influential study, entitled *Problems of Greek-American Relations: Confronting Dependence*, offers the following unreferenced definition of the key concept featuring in its title: Dependence, it says, 'varies from the negative form of slavery and subservience to the positive form of harmonious interdependence'.[37] Besides other flaws, this definition reveals a marked inability to grasp the crucial fact that 'dependence' is a highly asymmetrical and submissive relationship while 'interdependence' is based on mutuality and non-submissive relations. There are also ideological reasons behind the avoidance of the term 'semi-periphery', especially among neo-Marxist and *Marxisant* scholars of modern Greece. Under Wallerstein's definition, a 'semi-peripheral' country acts 'in part [...] as a peripheral zone for core countries and in part [...] as a core country for some peripheral areas'.[38] Such a conception, however, implies that Greece is less dependent on the 'core' than 'peripheral' countries are, a position that potentially undermines the view of several neo-Marxist and *Marxisant* scholars that Greek dependence on the United States was almost complete. Consequently, save a few exceptions,[39] most of the works using a core/periphery analysis of postwar Greece have treated the country as part of the capitalist 'periphery'.[40] Indeed, some have even adopted the untenable position that Greece should be treated as a 'third world' country.[41]

Analysing Greece as a 'semi-peripheral' society, however, does not presuppose adherence to neo-Marxism or dependency theory. Realist scholars like Barry Buzan have used the terms 'centre' and 'periphery' to denote disparities in 'power, wealth, organization and stability' in the world system, while Mouzelis has applied the concept to Greece from an essentially Weberian perspective.[42] Following similar attempts from the standpoint of critical IR theory,[43] the present analysis uses the concept of the 'semi-periphery' to refer to societies like Greece, whose position lies between the 'core' and 'peripheral' countries of the world system. As Wallerstein and others have argued, another key feature of 'semi-peripheral countries' is the increased autonomy of the political sphere, particularly in relation to socio-economic structures. Christopher Dunn has pointed out that 'the state in the semiperiphery is more crucial than in core or peripheral areas',[44] while from an historical sociology perspective, Mouzelis has asserted that the Balkans and Latin America developed an overgrown state because they adopted Western-style political institutions before experiencing the social effects of advanced industrialization.[45]

A corollary of the pronounced autonomy of the political, according to Wallerstein, is the tendency of semi-peripheral countries to periodically resort to nationalist policies that run counter to the structures of global dependence:

> To summarize the politics of 'non-socialist' semi-peripheral countries during times of world economic downturn: there tends to be an increase in 'economic nationalism', but most likely the sort that favors the indigenous upper strata, and hence leaves largely intact the cohesion of the capitalist world-economy.[46]

Despite the concept's analytical potential, Wallerstein's 'semi-periphery' is imbued with all the limitations of his neo-Marxist world systems theory. First, although he acknowledged that non-socialist 'semi-peripheral' countries experience a sharp growth of nationalism, in a deterministic fashion he ruled out the possibility that this nationalism could unsettle the dependence chain between the semi-periphery and the core countries. In other words, under his theoretical system, dependence is predestined to prevail over all nationalist outbreaks in the semi-periphery. Second, Wallerstein's concept is suffused with an economistic bias that is evident in his view that, despite the autonomy of the political sphere, nationalism can only take the form of an 'economic nationalism'. As a result, what is given with one hand (the increased autonomy of the political) is taken back with the other (a nationalism that is, after all, 'economic'). Third, in Wallerstein's theory, the actions of semi-peripheral countries are mechanically determined by 'long-term cyclical shifts' in the world system. In other words, politics in the 'semi-periphery' acquires autonomy only 'during times of economic downturn'. In times of economic expansion, as in the period 1945–67, 'semi-peripheral' states are thought to be adopting a passive role, devoid of any bargaining power vis-à-vis the hegemonic world order. As one empirical study of Greek foreign policy based on Wallerstein's theory has argued, 'semiperipheral states tend to become satellites of hegemonic power in the expansion periods of the world-economy'.[47]

However, if we approach the concept of the 'semi-periphery' from the perspective of critical IR theory, we can relieve it from the burdens of determinism and economism. To begin with, because critical IR theory stresses the dialectical nature of the relationship between states, social forces and world orders, it is no longer unthinkable for semi-peripheral nationalism to challenge the dependency link. Whether or not semi-peripheral nationalism will eventually disrupt dependence, for critical IR theory, is an open question to be determined by the historical circumstances of each case. Second, in contrast to Wallerstein's economistic conception, for critical IR theory, the prominent role of politics in the semi-periphery is no longer nominal but begins to gain real substance. As Hobson remarks, 'the relatively autonomous state forms an important aspect' of critical IR theory.[48] This implies that the capacity of the political sphere, and especially of nationalist politics, to acquire in some cases a leading role in the semi-periphery is accepted without qualifications. Third, through critical IR theory, the increased autonomy of politics in the semi-periphery is not considered a cyclical phenomenon corresponding to phases of contraction/crisis in the world economy. Insofar as critical IR theory emphasizes the relative autonomy of states and social forces from the world order, it follows that even in times of global expansion, an upsurge of semi-peripheral nationalism is possible. Although Cox did not examine this question in detail, he did speak of nationalism as a 'typical state policy' in the semi-periphery and, without restricting it to 'downturns' in the world economy, maintained that states in this zone can adopt 'defensive postures' that 'could spark international conflict'.[49]

A key question that is inadequately treated by Wallerstein is the possibility of alliances occurring in the semi-periphery between foreign capital and the comprador bourgeoisie on one hand, and the national bourgeoisie and some lower social strata on the other. Under his conception, in periods of expansion, foreign capital and the comprador bourgeoisie 'intervene illicitly in the state of affairs of each semi-peripheral state', but this intervention, he continues, 'decreases somewhat in moments of downturn', during which the national bourgeoisie gains the upper hand.[50] This proposition, however, limits the role of the national bourgeoisie to complete passivity and overlooks the ability of this class to either resist its marginalization or share power with the comprador bourgeoisie, especially when the entire bourgeois camp faces a common threat (like communism). For example, Wallerstein's thesis fails to see that in cases like the Greek Civil War and its aftermath, US capital and its comprador allies in Greece received substantial support from the country's national bourgeoisie to rescue the entire *Ethnikofron* bloc from the challenge of the Left. In other words, co-opting powerful factions of the national bourgeoisie in a broad (albeit uneasy) alliance is always a possible strategy for the comprador bourgeoisie in times of crisis.

Against this background, for critical IR theory semi-peripheral countries are characterized by an *increased volatility* in comparison to both 'core' and 'peripheral' states. A major source of this propensity is their distinct position in the world system as countries that are both dependent on the core and simultaneously capable of acquiring significant autonomy from it to articulate a confrontational nationalism. This suggests that semi-peripheral countries are marked by a tendency to radically revise their foreign policies from dependence to nationalism and *vise versa* with a frequency that is less common among core or peripheral countries. From the viewpoint of critical IR theory, what influences this irregularity is not their position in the world system alone, but also their distinctive domestic make up as countries whose states can acquire significant autonomy from their social forces. Ultimately, these frequent alterations are not defined solely by shifts in the world order or the domestic environment, but by the volatily of the dialectical relationship between them.

In what follows, a brief outline of how dependence and nationalism affect foreign policy will be provided. In so doing, the aim is to show what forms foreign policy can acquire in the semi-periphery when it shifts from dependence to nationalism and *vice versa*. Dependent and nationalist foreign policies will be presented here as Weberian 'ideal types', that is as contrasting analytical categories whose aim is to accentuate those aspects which are most essential to provide 'the greatest possible conceptual clarity'. Besides enabling a sharper understanding, this exercise aims to illustrate that dependence and nationalism are foreign policy types marked by essentially opposite dynamics and significations. Indeed, Weber himself constructed ideal-typical concepts in a 'dichotomic form' to accentuate 'not the generic similarities between cultural phenomena, but their differences'.[51] Ultimately, a better grasp of the contrasts between dependent and nationalist types should offer a clearer understanding of the tendency towards self-contradiction which semi-peripheral countries exhibit in foreign policy.

Dependence and foreign policy

The concept of dependence has entered the discipline of international relations in the 1970s,[52] but its usage in foreign policy analysis has been hitherto confined to a handful of studies.[53] There is, moreover, a notable lack of consensus over the concept's precise meaning in relation to foreign policy. One area of dispute surrounds the question of whether dependence should be defined in behavioural terms, as a 'psychological condition' affecting policy-makers,[54] or in structural terms, as an economic 'situation' affecting the foreign policies of peripheral and semi-peripheral states.[55] Another question is whether dependence should be conceptualized as an 'external' link[56] or as an 'internal' condition affecting the foreign policy-making elites from within. Following James Caporaso, the concept will be defined here from a composite behavioural-structural perspective as primarily *a relationship* in which the subaltern side (in our case the semi-peripheral state) is characterized by 'the absence of actor autonomy'.[57] Moreover, as Ian Roxborough suggests, dependence will be treated as 'a complex articulation' that is 'both internal and external' or, to be precise, as a link relying on a combination of 'external agency' intervention and 'internal fragmentation'. As Carporaso remarks, the exercise of dependence requires '"transnational" alliances between foreign and domestic groups' that cut across the terrain of the subaltern country.[58]

Dependence typically rests on a powerful comprador bourgeoisie that is allied to global economic and political interests based in the core countries. The comprador class consists of 'middlemen' playing the role of 'a commercial and financial intermediary' who transfer commodities and services at a rate favourable to the latter.[59] Because the comprador bourgeoisie operates chiefly in the commercial and service sectors, it favours liberal trade policies to facilitate its role as a 'transmission belt' linking core and peripheral zones.[60] Costas Vergopoulos has analysed the emergence of a new comprador bourgeoisie in post-war Greece and located its activities in the sectors of shipping, commerce, banking and tourism. To highlight the close ties between this class and the core countries, he cited the example of the sale of 100 *Liberty* freighters by the US Government to Greek ship-owners in the 1940s for less than one sixth of their original value.[61] Similarly, Mouzelis has argued that after 1945, largely 'on borrowed money', the service economy of Greece grew at the expense of 'key manufacturing sectors', while its profits went largely 'to foreign banks or to shipping'.[62]

Image 1 Prime Minister Alexander Papagos and Mrs Maria Papagos with shipowner Stavros Niarchos and wife Evgenia Livanos aboard the tanker S.S. *World Harmony*, Phaleron Bay, September 1954. Photographer: Antonis Patsavos. Antonis Patsavos Collection, ELIA-MIET Photographic Archive.

In ideological terms, dependent foreign policy corresponds to the principles of liberal trade and the values of the hegemonic world order. After 1945, these ideas were embodied in the institutions of the Bretton Woods System and the principles of Atlanticism (or Cold War liberalism). In this context, the notion of Westernization, often referred to in US policy papers as the encouragement of Greece's 'western orientation',[63] took a strong expression after 1945. According to Constantine Svolopoulos, since the Greek Civil War 'accession in the Western world, which was closely linked with the geo-political position of Greece's territory, form[ed] the expression of a vital politico-ideological choice'.[64] From the perspective of underdevelopment theory, Mouzelis stresses the links between

Westernization and evolutionary 'catching up' theory. As he put it, the 'all-pervasive Greek desire to "catch up" with the West', especially after 1945, emanated from the belief that 'the economically backward countries will pass through the same stages as the Western industrialised societies, and eventually will achieve the "marvels" of Western civilisation'.[65]

Dependence is linked to a particular type of state, whose autonomy in relation to both domestic and international social forces is limited. Nicos Poulantzas has argued that we can speak specifically about a 'dependent type of state' as an institution that 'take[s] charge of the interest of the dominant imperialist capital in its development with the "national" social formation'.[66] Cox maintained that dependent states are typically 'constrained by world-order pressures expressed in military and financial forms in the dominant-class links with external classes'.[67] From an instrumentalist theory perspective, Argyris Fatouros has argued that the dependent type of state which emerged in Greece after the Truman Doctrine was specifically linked to 'mechanisms of external penetration'. These, he explains, exist 'where nationals (or representatives) of one state participate directly in another state's processes of value-allocation on an equally authoritative basis as the latter state's nationals'.[68] Fatouros cites the appointment of one British and one American expert on the Greek Currency Committee in 1946 and the employment of other US technocrats on the Foreign Trade Administration and Social Insurance Foundation. After the Truman Doctrine, the United States dispatched sizeable military, economic and intelligence missions to take direct responsibility for guiding the Greek army, the Ministry of Finance and establish the new National Intelligence Agency (KYP).[69]

Dependent foreign policy, finally, corresponds to a particular type of relationship with the prevailing world order. According to James Rosenau, this type of foreign policy falls under the category of 'acquiescent adaptation' in which policy-makers rely on responsive decisions to the demands placed upon them by the external environment.[70] Adaptation embraces both 'high' and 'low politics' and operates as a process of modifying domestic priorities in a manner that facilitates the incorporation of the structures and values of the dominant world order. The process favours membership of all global and regional multilateral institutions in which the world hegemonic power is member. In post-war Greece, this strategy was exercised through the country's enthusiastic membership of the Bretton Woods System, the OEEC, NATO and the US-sponsored regional alliance with Turkey and Yugoslavia, the so-called Balkan Pact. Dependence was also cemented by important bilateral agreements with the United States, including the Aid Agreement of 20 June 1947 (the Truman Doctrine) and the Military Bases Agreement of 12 October 1953.

Nationalism and foreign policy

Despite the renewed scholarly interest in nationalism in recent decades, a notable theoretical gap exists around its influence on foreign policy.[71] The existence of this blind spot is unsurprising given that well-known theorists in the field, like John Breuilly, have put forward the problematic argument that it is supposedly 'difficult to identify specific types of foreign policy which could be called nationalist'.[72] More recent studies, however, like Ilya Prizel's *National Identity and Foreign Policy* (1998), have stressed the close connections between nationalism and specific types of foreign policy.[73] An outline of the main features of nationalist foreign policy should begin with Benedict Anderson's definition of nationalism as a movement aiming to construct 'an imagined political community' which is both 'sovereign' and 'limited', i.e. limited to 'finite, if elastic, boundaries'.[74] From this definition it follows that nationalist foreign policy is marked by a normative outlook that treats external relations as a means of (a) asserting and enhancing the independence and sovereignty of the state in question and (b) completing the construction of 'the imagined community', i.e. the process of nation-building.

While both objectives are central to all nationalist foreign policies, a distinction must be drawn between what Smith calls 'territorial' and 'irredentist' nationalism. The former, he argues, is typical of older European movements and develops as a geographically contained project of integrating state and society. The latter seeks 'to expand by including "kinsmen" outside the present boundaries of the "ethno-nation" and the lands they inhabit, or by forming a much larger "ethno-national" state through the union of culturally and ethnically similar "ethno-national" states'.[75] Although both types of nationalist foreign policy assert sovereignty and independence, they differ over the second objective of completing the nation-building process. While territorial nationalism uses foreign policy as a means of defending national security and enhancing domestic integration, irredentism seeks the expansion of a state's borders to incorporate so-called unredeemed fellow-nationals living under another state. In what follows, nationalist foreign policy will be discussed mainly in relation to the irredentist type.

Smith, Ernest Gellner and others have defined nationalism as both an 'ideology' and a 'political movement'.[76] A cognitive feature of nationalism is its attempt to mobilize broad social alliances that are usually led by the national bourgeoisie and supported by wide segments of the petty bourgeoisie and some rural strata. What marks the socio-cultural composition of nationalist movements is their cross-class character and, by implication, the preponderance of political and cultural over socio-economic factors in their action programme.[77] According to Nikiforos Diamandouros, Greek nationalism since the nineteenth century has found its main articulation in a political subculture which he calls 'underdog culture'. This subculture, he contends, is characterized by 'a defensive perception of the international environment', an 'exaggerated, but also fragile nationalist sentiment' and a 'syndrome of cultural inferiority towards the Western world'. Underdog culture, he maintains, is linked to the protected and less competitive social strata, particularly those engaged in 'subsistence agriculture, petty commodity production not geared to exports, finance, import substitution industries, and the overinflated and unproductive state- and wider-public sector'.[78] After Greece's defeat in the Asia Minor campaign of 1919–22,

Greek nationalism ceased to be primarily articulated around the irredentist and imperialist project of *Megali Idea*, which called for the extension of Greece's borders to include territories from the former Byzantine Empire.[79] However, as Christopher Woodhouse noted, after 1922 'some fragments of the old dream remained vivid', with the Dodecanese, Northern Epirus (southern Albania) and Cyprus usually featuring as the remaining Greek *irredenta*.[80] After the Second World War, claims over Northern Epirus were suppressed because Albania passed to the opposite side of the Iron Curtain, while the Dodecanese returned to Greece in 1947. Therefore, Cyprus began to emerge as the last remaining Greek irredentist claim. A secret Greek government report in 1954 stated that 'no matter how traditionally dear to us it might be, [...] the issue of Northern Epirus is to a large extent hopeless, and the liberation of Cyprus is destined to be the last major milestone for the [...] Greek nation's incorporation within the boundaries of free Greece'.[81]

Historians like Breuilly, Eric Hobsbawm and others have argued that nationalist movements are chiefly constructed 'from above', through political elites working either directly in civil society or in conjunction with the state apparatus. Breuilly questions 'the conventional view that nationalism emerges from a sense of cultural identity' and maintains that 'elites [...] use nationalist appeals [...] to mobilize popular support' in a way that renders nationalism 'a means of creating a sense of identity'.[82] Others, like Paul Brass, have stated laconically that 'ethnicity and nationalism [...] are the creations of elites',[83] while Hobsbawm stressed the role of states in 'mobilizing nationalism among their citizens'. As he put it, states 'use the increasingly powerful machinery for communicating with their inhabitants, above all the primary schools, to spread the image and heritage of the "nation" and to inculcate attachment to it [...] often "inventing traditions" or even nations for this purpose'.[84] Once in power, nationalist movements enhance the autonomy of the state both vis-à-vis domestic social forces and the rest of the world system. According to Cox, the nationalist state corresponds historically to the development of a corporatist power structure which 'obscures' class cleavages and seeks 'to transcend them' through deploying redistributive and other homogenizing mechanisms that favour 'bureaucracies and the middle classes'.[85]

The foreign policy of irredentist nationalist movements corresponds to a particular type of relationship with the dominant world order. This is marked by a revisionist agenda reflecting the territorial aspirations of the nationalist state to redraw its boundaries with the aim of extending sovereignty over the so-called unredeemed fellow nationals. Because of its predisposition towards revising the dominant regional order, nationalist foreign policy tends to favour flexible bilateral alliances known as 'axes'. This preference is linked to the nationalist state's emphasis on safeguarding sovereignty and independence, a policy which rejects the discipline of multilateral hegemonic arrangements and pacts. In the field of foreign economic relations, nationalism tends to adopt neo-mercantilist policies which rely on various forms of trade protectionism, state subsidies and import substitution industrialization (ISI).

The dualism of Greek foreign policy

The co-articulation of dependence and nationalism in the foreign policies of semi-peripheral states is both a structural and a cultural/behavioural phenomenon. The former arises from what development economists, in an adjacent context, call 'structural disarticulations', that is the combination of dissonant components in a way that leads to mutual cancellations and blockages.[86] According to Mouzelis, structural disarticulations are typical of modern Balkan societies. These take the form of 'negative links', initially established because the intrusion of 'Western capital' cannot eradicate 'the traditional sectors in these societies' or integrate them fully with the world economy. As a result, the external/modernized sectors of Balkan society connect with the indigenous/traditional sectors in ways that render 'the growth and dynamism' of one conditional upon the 'drainage of resources from the other'.[87] Structural disarticulations are therefore based on a double dialectic: one negative, whereby growth in a sector requires the depletion of the other sector's resources and *vise versa*; and the second positive, as resources drawn from one sector can also contribute to growth in the other and *vise versa*. Put plainly, structural disarticulations are like a vicious circle whereby societies can neither destroy their traditional sectors nor connect them to their modern sectors in ways that enable them to properly modernize.

In an insightful passage on ideology and politics, Mouzelis argues that structural disarticulations can also occur in the cultural and institutional domains.

> Just as at the economic level [...] so on the superstructural level, imported political and cultural institutions are 'negatively' linked with the indigenous ones [...]. They neither destroy nor integrate positively pre-capitalist superstructural forms [...]. This disarticulation [...] on the level of the superstructure takes the form of political and cultural arrangements which ensure perpetuation of [...] bottlenecks and contradictions.[88]

Besides ideology and politics, disarticulations occur in the sphere of external relations. In contrast to the common view (also implicit in Wallerstein's analysis of the semi-periphery) dependence and nationalism are conflicting phenomena, albeit not mutually exclusive. Despite their sharp opposition at one level, at another level they connect through a mutual attraction that is overlooked in the scholarship. It is precisely because of this mutual attraction that dependence and nationalism do not always alternate in the foreign policies of semi-peripheral states, as suggested by Wallerstein, but can frequently coexist and be co-articulated as forces locked up in a Sisyphean, circular equation.

Prima facie, dependence and nationalism are oppositional notions because the former internalizes the demands of the hegemonic world order, while the latter projects domestic aspirations onto the international system. What this conception overlooks, however, is that during this process, dependence and nationalism produce important side effects that must be later alleviated through compensating rectifications. In particular, dependence sharpens divisions within the semi-peripheral country between the dependent local elites and the subaltern/excluded social strata. The accentuation of these internal divisions can isolate the dependent local elites from their local society and thereby radicalize the subaltern social strata leading them to various forms of popular/national resistance. Therefore, to lessen these side effects (and safeguard dependence in the longer term), the world hegemonic power and the dependent local elites are often obliged to relax the dependence link through an element of self-restraint coupled with efforts to cooperate with sections of the subaltern social strata. Consequently, the dependent local elites, with the tacit approval of the world hegemonic power, often begin to articulate a nationalist or pseudo-nationalist/populist discourse, which can attract wider popular support. In this way, dependence often ends up accommodating an auxiliary degree of nationalism to appease local opposition and secure its long-term survival.

Similarly, irredentist nationalism also incites opposition, both from rival neighbouring states which are directly threatened by it, and from the world hegemonic power which sees it as a challenge to its global order. For instance, in 1950, US Secretary of State Dean Acheson warned the Greek government explicitly 'to formulate all aspects of their foreign policy in terms of their number one problem which is the survival of Greece as a free nation' and give up 'the luxury of a foreign policy directed towards future nationalist goals'.[89] These hegemonic responses, however, force nationalist foreign policy in the semi-periphery to moderate its revisionist plans and show deference towards the world hegemonic power to protect its long-term irredentist aspirations. Sometimes even, nationalism could go as far as to seek the support of the world hegemonic power as a means of gaining strategic advantage over its regional enemies, despite the fact that in so doing it actually challenges the hegemonic order itself. Although the hegemonic power is likely to resist such inducements, nationalism is often compelled to continue seeking this hegemonic support and thus accommodate a certain level of dependence to enhance its long-term prospects of regional expansion.

From the foregoing it follows that effective dependence often requires the adoption of a limited degree of nationalism; and, conversely, an effective nationalist foreign policy is often facilitated through a certain element of dependence on the world hegemonic power. The combinations of these two otherwise conflicting doctrines are the main cause of the structural disarticulations in the foreign policies of semi-peripheral states. What will be called thereafter 'the dualism of Greek foreign policy' principally refers to the co-articulation of dependence and nationalism within a single policy. Foreign policy dualism can take a variety of forms. One is *oscillation*, namely the tendency towards frequent shifts and turns from a dependent to a nationalist foreign policy and *vice versa*, a phenomenon associated with indecisiveness before challenging and/or fluid external or domestic situations.[90] Another form, which constitutes the main focus of this study, is *coarticulation*, that is the tendency to combine elements of dependence and nationalism synchronically, usually because decision-makers perceive that their synthesis is somehow possible and/or desirable. Finally, dualism can take the form of *non-decisions* whereby states either choose or are forced to remain inactive in situations where nationalist forces and the hegemonic world order collide. As we shall see, the Papagos Government occasionally resorted to this form of dualism, especially when the militant organization EOKA began to prepare its armed struggle in Cyprus in 1954–5.

A point worth stressing is that foreign policy dualism in the semi-periphery has clear structural underpinnings. It is a type of foreign policy that is largely affected by the specific socio-economic and historical conditions which render the semi-periphery a zone defined by an equivocal identity as both the 'core of the periphery' and the 'periphery of the core'. Moreover, in its various manifestations, dualism is conditional upon historical and behavioural factors, namely the specific decisions policy-makers make in different junctures and contexts. Much like their counterparts in the core and periphery, semi-peripheral states always have alternative options besides dependence, nationalism and their combination – including the important choice of transforming their foreign policies through various *modernization strategies*.[91] However, in comparison to core states, foreign policy-makers in the semi-periphery are structurally confined to a narrower range of choices which often entrap them in a Sisyphean rotation from dependence to nationalism, and their various combinations. Any attempt to challenge these structural constraints and seek modernization usually requires a long-term effort that is geared towards achieving an historic leap from the semi-periphery of the core of the world system. In the early post-war years, such ambitious plans were never seriously considered by Greek political leaders. The priorities of securing Greece's position in the Western Alliance and reviving the irredentist project of *Megali Idea* stood at the forefront of their agendas and always undermined the prospect of using foreign policy as a vehicle of socio-economic change.

Dependent nationalism in post-Civil War Greece

As noted above, the combination of dependence and nationalism within a single policy corresponds to an historical constellation of forces within and around the semi-peripheral country in question. This can occur because of changes in the world system, the domestic socio-cultural environment or the state. In post-war Greece, the historical context which gave rise to foreign policy dualism resulted from changes at all three levels simultaneously. On the systemic level, the onset of the Cold War and the establishment of US hegemony replaced the volatile interwar European environment which encouraged the growth of semi-autarkic, nationalist regimes like the Metaxas Dictatorship of 1936–41.[92] Moreover, the new post-war order was defined by the process of decolonization which spread across the East Mediterranean and Cyprus and occasioned major shifts in the immediate foreign policy environment of Greece.[93] Meanwhile, British and American intervention in the Greek Civil War of the 1940s was instrumental in bringing back the liberals after their exclusion from the state following their two failed coups in 1933 and 1935.[94] These efforts culminated in the consolidation of a new alliance between the right-wing and liberal forces during the Civil War which replaced the authoritarian/corporatist state of 1936–41 with a restricted democracy that saw non-communist parties alternate in power.[95] Taken together, these sets of changes established a new context which transformed Greece from an isolated semi-fascist dictatorship before the War to a Western-oriented, semi-democracy in the early 1950s.

At the level of social forces, similar changes led to a new alliance between the country's comprador and national bourgeoisies, in a common effort to crush the left. Although historians like David Close have argued that 'a sense of social obligation among the socially privileged' under Metaxas was abandoned after the Second World War for 'an economic system favouring a small group of businessmen',[96] this image is not entirely accurate. More focused analyses have shown that, together with the emergence of a new comprador bourgeoisie, 'many of the prewar elites were equally successful in maintaining or even increasing their wealth'.[97] A case in point was Greece's influential businessman, Prodromos Bodossakis who, according to Morgens Pelt, enjoyed 'close personal relations with [...] the political entourage of Metaxas and with the dictator himself'. Bodossakis operated in both comprador and non-comprador sectors.[98] Another example of the growing synergies between the comprador and national bourgeoisies is that in the 1950s and 1960s, almost half of all Greek banking assets were channelled to local industry.[99] A key factor behind this new social alliance were the determined efforts of Greece's British and American patrons, who encouraged post-war Greek governments to reconcile both class factions in a broad anti-communist social alliance.[100]

Still on the level of social forces, the new context of post-war Greece took an even clearer form in the ideological sphere. From 1944 to 1974, the victors of the Greek Civil War adopted a new discourse which acquired the official name of *Ethnikofrosyni* (national mindedness).[101] *Ethnikofrosyni* was a system of negative myths and stereotypes whose aim was to portray the Greek left as a segment of society that was divested of its 'Greekness' and thereby removed from the body of the nation.[102] As Gonda Van Steen observes, this was 'a vacuous discourse' which aimed 'to fill in for the ideological basis that it otherwise lacked'.[103] Nicos Alivizatos points out that its main function was to enforce 'the separation of citizens on the basis of their political beliefs into "ethnikofrones" and "non-ethnikofrones"', while its content, 'besides denouncing communism and [...] any ideology directed against [...] the existing status quo, presupposed a positive adherence [...] to the values which the Greek ruling classes sought to defend'.[104] As such, *Ethnikofrosyni* operated as an umbrella discourse, capable of veiling and containing the rivalries between the two main interwar ideological currents, right-wing royalism and Venizelist liberalism, which clashed fiercely during the years of the National Schism of 1915–41.[105] Indeed, one of the core aims of this umbrella discourse was to co-articulate the conflicting ideas of right-wing nationalism and liberal Atlanticism in a single framework that posited as intellectually coherent, even though it was superficial and self-contradictory.[106]

Finally, the political context which motivated foreign policy dualism was clearly inscribed at the level of the state. Contemporary politicians and latter-day historians have identified the inner divisions between the formal state institutions and the informal apparatuses of the so-called parastate as a cognitive feature of the Greek political system from 1944 to 1967.[107] In 1961, the Liberal leader Sophocles Venizelos described the parastate as 'the multi-faceted organization that had been ruling our public life in recent years' and named its main elements as: 'the Army General Staff, [...] [the secret service] KYP, the gendarmerie, the [Security Brigades] TEA, and other sinister agents'.[108] According to Alivizatos, a corresponding legal division developed in Greece after 1944, between the official Constitution and what became known as the 'para-constitution', that is a 'varied set of legal texts in th[e] area [of civil liberties] which had been adopted during the Civil War and which were maintained [...] despite their obvious unconstitutionality'. This legal corpus included legislation, often enforced through the military courts, that sought to apply *Ethnikofrosyni* through the dismissal of state employees suspected of communist leanings, the banishment of left-wing citizens and the incarceration of thousands of dissidents in concentration camps.[109]

Most Marxist and *Marxisant* analyses portray the parastate as having played 'the dominant role' in the politics of post-war Greece,[110] whereas ethnocentric historians maintain that 'it was always the governments which prevailed'.[111] Both positions, however, are abstract and empirically unsustainable. Although the latent and authoritarian character of the parastate, as Vernardakis and Mavris have remarked, invested the post-war Greek state with greater 'autonomy',[112] its influence over the official government was varied and never gained the upper hand until the military coup of 1967. Indeed, the survival of the *Ethnikofron* state from 1944 to 1967 rested primarily on the ability of its formal institutions and parastate to accept a flexible regime of power-sharing which, despite their tensions and antagonisms, was able to accommodate both. This alternative assessment was proposed in the 1970s by Poulantzas, whose nuanced analysis on this question has eluded most Marxist and *Marxisant* studies of post-war Greece. As he aptly observed, the '"para-state" apparatus [...] functioned as *an effective dual power parallel with the legal government*' (italics added).[113] This duality was inscribed in the edifice of the post-war Greek state until the parastate eventually dismantled the formal state institutions in April 1967.

Conclusion

Dependent nationalism remains an unexplored phenomenon in both comparative politics and foreign policy analysis. A major factor behind this inattention is the apparent perception that its constituent elements, dependence and nationalism, are essentially oppositional and resistant to any permanent combination. This misconception, in turn, gives rise to the problematic assumption that antithetical (or strikingly unalike) phenomena, such as nationalism and dependence, must be treated as mutually exclusive. This perception is evident in the essentialist view discussed above, which considers that nationalism during the Cold War was not subject to hybridization. As we shall see, however, in many semi-peripheral countries, dependence and nationalism began to acquire a common and often intertwined fate, largely because after the 1940s, both began to face an equally serious challenge from the Left.

In post-war Greece, *dependent nationalism* became established as a type of foreign policy under the Rally Government of 1952–5. Although the historiography is divided between a narrative that overstates the dependent character of the Rally's foreign policy and another which exaggerates its nationalist overtones, there have been a few passing remarks which hint at the existence of a dualism. Victor Papacosmas, for example, has noted that after 1950, Greece attempted to combine an Atlanticist and a nationalist doctrine in a self-contradictory manner:

> The security of Greece's borders against possible aggression was to be maintained by membership in NATO. This new alliance did not, however, preclude the re-emergence of older historical patterns. During the 1950s growing nationalist fervour in Cyprus and in Greece for enosis created problems within NATO.[114]

Similarly, Solon Grigoriadis remarked that Papagos 'had nationalist bents against foreigners [...] and as a ruler displayed contradictory tendencies toward the Americans and the British'. Spyros Linardatos also observed that, at one point, Papagos resorted to a 'double track policy' in the Cyprus question, a view that was later reaffirmed by George Tenikidis:

> The governments of the years 1954–1958 oscillated between directions that were not identical or which cancelled each-other out: on one hand, loyalty to the Western Alliance, identified in the eyes of rulers with the supreme national interest of the country's security and the ruling party's political interests; on the other hand, there was the idea of the national rehabilitation of Cyprus along the traditional lines of Greek 'irredentist' policy.[115]

Even the outlawed Communist Party, in a 1951 statement teeming with Stalinist bombast, pointed out that Papagos was pursuing a self-contradictory agenda, mixing dependence with far-right populism:

> Papagos with his fascist Rally, this most privileged lackey of Americanocracy, has turned into a pole of attraction for the darkest and oligarchic plutocratic reaction. And he has managed, with his anti-plutocratic demagoguery and a particular 'anti-American' and anti-dynastic/anti-royal phraseology, to lead certain popular strata astray, of which the most backward, in their desire to see change, have failed to orient themselves clearly.[116]

These passing remarks, however, do not amount to a systematic analysis of dualism. On the contrary, because they appear as brief, occasional observations, they give the opposite impression, namely that dualism was an aberration or a paradox confined to certain moments or brief periods in Greek foreign policy.[117] As the anthropologist Mary Douglas pointed out, the process of human cognition has a tendency to force complex realities into 'logical categories of non-contradiction'.[118] However, the critical method adopted here is wary of this tendency and places irregularity and contradiction at the heart of its enquiry. As the Frankfurt School philosopher Theodore Adorno observed, 'the dialectical state of facts would be the plain logical contradiction. But the state of facts is not explicable by a hierarchic schema of order'.[119]

A few closing remarks on the concept of dualism are now in order. In her acclaimed book, *Imagining the Balkans* (1997), Maria Todorova critiques the Western discourse about 'the imputed ambiguity' of the Balkans and its stereotypical portrayal as a 'land of contradictions'.[120] This orientalist image, which Todorova appropriately deconstructs, is premised on a conception of duality that differs fundamentally from the concept of dualism adopted here. What Todorova defines as a Western discourse of 'Balkanism' is a Eurocentric notion associated with the evolutionary socioeconomic theories of development. Her critique of that discourse, by contrast, draws on Edward Said's postcolonial theory and other scholarly traditions which apply a core/periphery analysis to the modern world system.[121]

Western Balkanism speaks of a 'duality' arising from the supposed incomplete transition of the Balkans from 'tradition' and 'modernity'.[122] This 'transitional' character has led some development/modernization theorists to refer to 'dual' or even 'dualistic' societies of late developing regions, such as the Balkans. This conception, however, bears little connection to the notion of dualism that is discussed here, which has its roots in core/periphery analyses and postcolonial studies. In core/periphery analysis, the idea of a clear-cut division between 'modern' and 'traditional' sectors is strongly rejected. So-called modern sectors are believed to contain many 'traditional' elements, while so-called traditional sectors are viewed as imbued with equally 'modern' characteristics.[123] A further difference between the two perspectives concerns the linkages between the the so-called modern and traditional sectors. In contrast to Balkanist arguments, these are not considered functional links, i.e. channels whereby 'modern' elements are 'diffused' or 'trickle down' to gradually modernize 'traditional' sectors.[124] Core/periphery analyses, by contrast, underline the disfunctional dialectic linking the two sectors, stressing that growth in one is usually contingent upon the depletion of resources from the other and *vice versa*.[125] As Rodolfo Stavenhagen has argued in relation to Latin America, the fallacy of the 'diffusion' thesis is evident in the fact that after '400 years – and aside from certain dynamic focal points of growth, the continent is still as underdeveloped as ever'.[126] Similar conclusions can be drawn about the Balkans, whether it be the territories formerly colonized by the Venetian and Habsburg empires or those that were under Ottoman rule.

Finally, a key aspect of Balkan dualism relates to what Todorova calls the 'internalization' of Balkanist discourse. This cultural process known as 'self-stigmatization' creates what she calls 'an internal dichotomy' in Balkan societies that is different from the supposed division between 'modern' and 'traditional' sectors. Todorova analyses this internal divide with reference to Aleko Konstantinov's nineteenth-century fictional hero Bay Ganyo Balkanski. Cultural metaphors like

Bay Ganyo, she argues, highlight 'the disharmony' within Balkan societies between 'the superficial mimicry of civilized [Western] behaviour' and 'the crude', 'nouveau riche' anti-Western local residues. As a result, the main sociocultural dichotomy in the Balkans is between a Westernized/dependency subculture and an 'underdog culture' equivalent to Diamandouros's concept discussed above. In stressing this alternative divide, Todorova contrasts the superficial portrayal of Balkan duality 'from the outside', which typifies Balkanist discourse, and the region's 'critique [...] from within', which highlights a totally different category of contradictions.[127] A similar distinction was made by the social anthropologist Michael Herzfeld, who speaks about 'two competing views' of modern Greece: one that is 'externally directed', which shows the Greeks as 'failing to live up to its expectations'; and a second, internal view, that focuses on the 'national shortcomings' of Greek society, 'a self-portrait that does not always flatter'.[128]

The main disparity between the external and internal images of Balkan dualism is that the former is constructed through a Eurocentric behaviourist lens, whereas the latter sees dualism from a non-Eurocentric, historically constituted standpoint. The present study analyses Greek foreign policy from the latter perspective. In so doing, it discusses Greek dualism as an attempt to compromise an internalized world hegemonic order with the intense domestic reactions to it.

2

HEGEMONY, DEPENDENCE AND THE US POLICY REVIEW OF 1952

Although the Truman Doctrine of 12 March 1947 intensified Greece's dependence on the United States, the *Ethnikofron* governments of Athens always retained a limited degree of autonomy vis-à-vis their transatlantic patron. While the precise degree of this autonomy is hard to define, any attempt to do so must begin from an understanding of the domestic and external constraints underlying post-war American hegemony. One of the few areas of agreement between revisionist and post-revisionist historians of the Cold War is the acknowledgement that the architects of the Truman Doctrine had a distinct 'awareness of the limitations, rather than the omnipotence, of American power'.[1] Similar conclusions were drawn at the time by conservative Greek politicians, like Spyros Markezinis, who wrote in 1949 that inadequate funds and imperfect human resources received from the United States posed a major challenge to the Greek political system.[2] In this respect, the limited autonomy of the *Ethnikofron* regime from 1947 to 1952 was less the outcome of its own capacity to resist US power than of Washington's finite capabilities in implementing its hegemony in Europe.

The tendency of some accounts to speak about 'shifts' and 'serious fluctuations' in US policy towards Greece after the start of the Korean War in 1950[3] must be approached with caution. Insofar as any such changes occurred between 1947 and 1952, these were confined to occasional adjustments in Washington's policy to consolidate the framework of US-Greek relations as established under the Truman Doctrine. According to Bruce Kuniholm, 'the invitations to Greece and Turkey in 1951 to join NATO, and their accession to the North Atlantic Treaty in 1952' were 'extensions not so much of the Korean War as of [...] policies outlined in 1946–48'. Similarly, Lawrence Wittner concludes that the decision to admit Greece in NATO in 1951, which 'formally integrated' the Greek army to the defence policy of the United States, was a process already begun in 1949.[4] As we shall see, the first major revision of American policy towards Greece after the Truman Doctrine did not take place until the summer of 1952 and this resulted mainly from several factors, of which the Korean War was the least important. Of greater significance was Yugoslavia's alignment with the West following Tito's break with Moscow in 1948; the admission of Greece and Turkey in NATO in 1951 (decided for reasons other than the Korean War); the termination of Marshall Plan aid; and the expectation of government stability in Greece after the adoption of the majority election system. In contrast to the assumptions of the dependence narrative, which tend to exaggerate the effects of the Korean War on Greece, the US policy review of 1952 did not increase Washington's intervention in the country's affairs. Its aim, rather, was to reduce and consolidate US involvement.

In his book *Entangled Allies* (1992), former US Ambassador Monteagle Stearns described the United States' policy towards Greece after 1945 as 'hegemonic'.[5] While this conclusion is correct, the use of Gramsci's celebrated concept in this context requires some elaboration. Hegemony, which is commonly defined as a combination of power and moral/ideological consent,[6] is not used in international relations simply to describe one state's control over another. Cox, whose contribution in this area is important, explains that

> hegemony at the international level is [...] not merely an order among states. [...] A world hegemony is [...] an outward expansion of the internal (national) hegemony established by a dominant social class. [...] World hegemony can be described as a social structure, an economic structure, and a political structure; and it cannot be simply one of these things but must be all three. World hegemony, furthermore, is expressed in universal norms, institutions, and mechanisms which lay down general rules of behavior for states.[7]

Similar definitions have been provided by scholars who approach the concept from other perspectives. Joseph Keohane, from the standpoint of liberal institutionalism, defines hegemony as 'an international system in which leadership is exercised by a single state', stressing that this state must enjoy both 'enough military power to be able to protect the international political economy' and ideological influence 'to engage in rule-making and rule enforcement'. Wallerstein, from a neo-Marxist perspective, has defined world hegemony as a 'situation in which [...] one power can largely impose its rules and its wishes [...] in the economic, political, military, diplomatic and even cultural arenas'.[8] A further area of consensus across these different perspectives is that from 1945 to the late 1960s/early 1970s, the United States was at the height of its hegemonic power.[9]

From the foregoing it follows that, when we speak about US hegemony in postwar Greece, we are referring primarily to a facet of a wider global phenomenon. At the same time, this conception does not enable a full grasp of the concrete modalities of world hegemony when applied to specific national societies. For example, there are significant variations in the form of US hegemony on states like Canada and France in comparison to Greece. To account for such variations, it is necessary to underline a distinction drawn in the 1930s by the German legal theorist Heinrich Triepel between 'direct' and 'indirect' hegemony.[10] Triepel's concept of 'direct' hegemony refers to a form of unmediated domination by a hegemonic power over a specific state and its society. 'Indirect' hegemony, by contrast, refers to a mediated type of control that is exercised through the hegemonic power's dominance over the world economy, international institutions and the norms governing their operation. In practice, both forms of hegemony may coexist, as they are complementary and mutually reinforcing. However, according to the place and time in which it is exercised, world hegemony blends 'indirect' and 'direct' forms of control through a wide range of combinations.

This chapter will show how US hegemony in post-war Greece took initially a predominantly direct form and how, following the US policy review of 1952, it relied on greater elements of indirect and institutionalized control. In putting forward this proposition, it should be stressed that the transition from a direct to an indirect type was not achieved through a clear-cut shift. The US policy review of August–September 1952, which recommended this change, marked the high point of what was a much longer and more gradual evolution. To be sure, even after its official adoption, Washington continued to exercise its hegemony in Greece often in direct fashion. However, after 1952, the instances of direct intervention ceased to be as common and acquired a supplementary status as corrective mechanisms to an increasingly indirect form of hegemony.[11]

The passage to a predominantly indirect type of hegemony corresponded to a change in the evolution of the *Ethnikofron* regime from crisis to relative stabilization. Although the links between the two processes were close, each retained a relatively distinct dynamic. For this reason, it would be inappropriate to interpret the exit of the *Ethnikofron* regime from crisis in 1952 as a mere adjustment of US hegemony. Although American policy did contribute to the rise of a stable government in Greece in 1952, the fact that this government was led by Papagos rather than Plastiras or that its share of the vote was 49 rather than 39 per cent, were outcomes that were ultimately determined by domestic factors on which Washington's diplomats had limited control. Indeed, world hegemony, whether direct or indirect, cannot be exercised without a degree of active cooperation by the subaltern states themselves – in our case the *Ethnikofron* regime and the social forces supporting it. In addition, hegemony rests on a strategic type of intervention whereby the hegemonic state deliberately refrains from extending power to the point of imposing control in an all-out colonial fashion. At the same time, this self-imposed restriction implies that the subaltern state and its society, no matter how dependent, always retain a limited degree of autonomy over internal affairs and, possibly, over ancillary aspects of foreign policy. The transition from direct to indirect hegemony broadens the scope of this limited autonomy and enables the subaltern actor to exercise greater (albeit far from full) control over its own affairs. How this shift affected the context of Greek foreign policy is the focus of this chapter.

The structures of direct hegemony: US policy in Greece, 1947–52

Since the promulgation of the Truman Doctrine on 12 March 1947,[12] US policy in Greece evolved around two strategic objectives. The first was to protect the local *Ethnikofron* regime from the so-called internal threat of a communist armed rebellion, and the second was to defend the country's 'external security' from the perceived threat of a Soviet-sponsored attack through one of Greece's communist neighbours.[13] To support these objectives, the Truman Doctrine provided Greece with military and economic assistance of $300 million for one year, an amount equivalent to nearly one quarter of the country's GDP. Half of that sum was directed towards the purchase of arms and military materiel and the other half was invested in reconstruction projects to revive the country's war-torn economy.[14] Sizeable teams of US military and economic advisors were despatched to Greece, working as experts under the newly formed American Mission of Assistance to Greece (AMAG). In 1948 AMAG had 1,218 employees, of whom approximately half were American. Of those, 410 were US armed service personnel.[15]

Although both US objectives in Greece were closely intertwined, until the spring of 1951, 'internal security' remained a higher priority. Nine months after the end of the Greek Civil War, on 15 May 1950, the British embassy in Washington noted that 'the State Department emphasised that [...] the dangers confronting Greece were primarily internal than external'.[16] Until the eve of Washington's decision to support Greece's entry in NATO in April 1951, this policy remained unchanged.[17] The primacy accorded to 'internal security' was neither a question of emphasis nor an acknowledgement of the fact that Stalin had offered limited support to the communist-led Democratic Army during the Greek Civil War, a fact unknown to Washington at the time.[18] 'Internal security' was accorded higher priority because the United States could not properly defend the country from outside when it was still likely to turn communist within.[19] In January 1951, the US *chargé d' affaires* in Athens, Charles Yost, reminded Ambassador John Peurifoy that 'the US has no present plans to send troops to Greece in case of war, either general or local'.[20] In February, President Truman approved National Security Council (NSC) decision 103/1 which, on the insistence of the US Joint Chiefs of Staff, removed all references to possible American military involvement in Greece in the event of an external attack.[21]

Because Washington maintained its primary commitment to Greece's 'internal security' until 1951, the bulk of its efforts focused on supporting the country's domestic regime and its economy.[22] This policy, which was sustained through successive extensions of the Truman Doctrine on an annual basis, led to the transfer of substantial military, economic and political resources whose impact was greater than their size. This multiplier effect resulted from the fact that US assistance was always carefully channelled through the nerve centres of the Greek polity and economy. As Fatouros points out, US policy relied on occupying 'key posts of the Greek governmental machinery'.[23] Indeed, the main power centres targeted by the US missions were: (a) the executive branch of the state, including the cabinet, the Palace and the *Ethnikofron* party leaders; (b) the Greek army; (c) the Ministry of Public Order, including the security police and the intelligence service;[24] (d) the Ministry of Economic Co-ordination and the Bank of Greece.[25] The US agencies linked to these four centres were, respectively: (i) the US embassy, which exercised direct influence on the cabinet, the Palace and the party leaders; (ii) AMAG, which supervised the Greek army and, after its dissolution in 1948, was replaced in this task by the Joint United States Military Aid Group (JUSMAG); (iii) the Athens station of the CIA, which was linked to the Ministries of Defence and Public Order and, after this was created in the early 1950s, to the Greek Intelligence Agency

(KYP);²⁶ (iv) AMAG, which initially advised the Ministry of Co-ordination, the Bank of Greece and other economic agencies, but after its dissolution in 1948 was replaced by the Marshall Plan's Economic Cooperation Agency (ECA). In January 1952, ECA was in turn replaced by the Mutual Security Agency (MSA). AMAG's labour affairs experts, together with representatives of the American Federation of Labor (AFL), also took charge of cleansing the General Confederation of Greek Workers (GSEE) of all leftist elements, a task accomplished by 1948.[27]

In the first year of the Truman Doctrine, all US military and economic experts in Greece worked under a centralized structure, AMAG, which soon became an irritant for the US embassy. Several accounts detail the disputes between AMAG's chief, Dwight Griswold, and the US Ambassador in Greece, Lincoln MacVeagh, who claimed, each for their own mission, supreme authority over the implementation of US policy in the country.[28] After an embarrassing crisis, which saw MacVeagh recalled to Washington in October 1947 and Griswold resigning his post in September 1948, the State Department gave overall responsibility for the work of the US missions to the serving ambassador.[29] The embassy's authority over all US personnel in Greece was enhanced in July 1948, following the launch of the Marshall Plan, as AMAG was replaced by two separate missions, JUSMAG in charge of military affairs and ECA in charge of the economy and Marshall Plan aid. When President Truman appointed Henry Grady as his new ambassador in May 1948, he invested him with 'responsibility for all American activities in Greece'.[30] In January 1949, the British embassy reported that Grady was the supreme arbiter to whom the missions 'appealed [...] in case of a serious disagreement with the Greek Government'.[31] This hierarchy reflected the central role of the State Department in overseeing US policy in Greece. As Fatouros remarks, even the dispute between Griswold and MacVeagh in 1947 was an internal dispute within the State Department.[32]

Direct hegemony was not exercised only through the penetration and control of strategic sites in the Greek state and civil society. American policy drew much of its local power from the substantial sums of military and economic aid it provided in the early post-war years. According to State Department estimates, from 1944 to 1951, US economic and military aid reached a cumulative total of $2 billion, approaching, on average, one quarter of Greek GDP per annum.[33] Even after the end of the Civil War, Greece continued to receive substantial sums of economic and military assistance. In 1948–9, US military and economic aid to Greece amounted to $443 million or nearly 25 per cent of GDP, but in 1950–1 this figure still stood at $391 million (although the ratio of economic to military aid was now higher).[34] Moreover, according to the NSC, 'with the exception of the Greek Air Force, all major items of equipment required by the Greek armed forces' were still provided by the American military assistance programme.[35] This state of affairs not only rendered Greece's defence entirely dependent on the United States, but with an army whose soldiers accounted for 9 per cent of the electorate (and whose dependents approached one quarter of the population) US military aid was a vital instrument of exercising direct political patronage over Greek civil society.[36]

Another aspect of US hegemony was Washington's ability to use its political, economic and military capabilities adeptly and shrewdly. This was achieved partly through the appointment of ambassadors possessing what the State Department called 'special qualifications',[37] including extensive international experience. MacVeagh, who served in Athens from 1944 to 1947, was a personal friend to F. D. Roosevelt and had worked closely with Anthony Eden and Vyacheslav Molotov. His successor, Grady (1948–50), had served in the League of Nations and linked his name to the British Deputy Prime Minister, Herbert Morrison, through their 1946 joint partition plan for Palestine.[38] Peurifoy (1950–3), despite being later scorned for having 'no political sense at all',[39] was Deputy Undersecretary of State to Dean Rusk and whilst in Greece was significantly aided by Yost, his politically astute *chargé d' affaires*. In other words, Washington posted to Athens some of its most senior diplomats and experts whose world stage experience could hardly be matched by most leading Greek politicians. For instance, after meeting Markezinis, a rising star of Greek politics with a keen interest in economics, Paul A. Porter, the head of the 1947 American Economic Mission to Greece, noted with astonishment that 'he appeared to ignore important information both in regard to matters concerning the budget and to questions of aid'.[40] It should be stressed, however, that a key objective behind these appointments was Washington's intention to grant its diplomats and technocrats considerable freedom of action which, in turn, enabled them to produce swift, flexible and locally informed decisions.

American policy in Greece drew much capital from its privileged access to knowledge and information which few, if any, Greek politicians could usually acquire. Information was feverishly collected and processed by sizeable teams of US officials, technocrats and spies attached to key positions in the Greek state apparatus, who were supported by large networks of local paid and unpaid informants.[41] Much of this data was rapidly transmitted to and analysed by the US embassy in a manner that the archaic Greek civil service could not possibly match. Such was the dependence of the local administration on US technical knowledge, that when Paul A. Porter arrived in Athens in 1947 to study the Greek economy, Prime Minister Dimitrios Maximos agreed to endorse his report before even reading it.[42] Meanwhile, the US embassy functioned as the headquarters of the local CIA station which operated without any pretence of being a secret mission. In terms of its size, it was thought to be 'the third largest' in the world.[43] According to Alexis Papachelas, CIA employees became 'involved in all sectors of Athenian life', including the Palace itself, where an agent was present almost daily to train the young prince Constantine in badminton and judo.[44] The royal couple were themselves approving of the CIA's activities in Greece and Queen Frederica apparently enjoyed an intimate friendship with the Agency's director, Allen Dulles.[45] Some evidence appears to suggest that tensions developed between the CIA station in Athens and the embassy's diplomatic staff, most notably the vanished Bruce-Lovett Report of 1956, which reportedly stated that the CIA chief in Greece was more powerful than the US ambassador.[46] In the absence of this document, these claims cannot be verified. Alternative evidence, however, suggests that despite antagonisms, the CIA regularly shared information with other US missions in Athens.[47]

A key factor behind the effectiveness of US hegemony in Greece was the high receptiveness of the Greek *Ethnikofron* regime to Washington's heavy-handed intervention. A seeming paradox in Greek-American relations after 1947 was the frequent role reversal between representatives of the hegemonic power and the subaltern local Greek elites. Several US officials reported that, instead of facing local resistance, Greek politicians often invited them to become even more involved in the country's affairs than they already were, thus forcing them, ironically, to start asking Greek leaders to be more independent! One example is the dialogue between Ambassador Grady and Prime Minister Sophocles Venizelos and his Deputy, Panayiotis Kanellopoulos, during the government crisis of March–April 1950. 'They asked me', Grady reported, 'if I wanted [the] government to resign and I have replied that I would ask nothing of [the] government [...]. I kept saying we are giving advice but not dictation'.[48] An almost identical incident was reported by the American *chargé* Harold Minor after his conversation with Prime Minister Plastiras shortly before the latter's resignation in the crisis of August 1950. According to Minor, Plastiras 'asked for American advice and guidance and suggested that I propose some solution to present Government crisis'. Minor, however, said that he 'declined, stating that [the] crisis [was] purely [an] affair of Greek internal politics'.[49] Similar exchanges usually took place before the announcement of any cut in US economic aid. As one ECA report noted, 'from the first rumours of the reduction in aid, the Greek press had been sharply critical of the Mission in particular and, Americans, in general'.[50] In other words, instead of welcoming less dependence on US economic assistance, the *Ethnikofron* press almost invariably treated aid cuts as a curse and calamity signalling American disapproval. Meanwhile, any hint that Greece should increase its exports to become more self-reliant, as the distinguished economist Kyriakos Varvaressos proposed in a famous report in 1952, provoked a barrage of criticisms by economists and politicians who dismissed such ideas as irresponsible and a supposedly unmodern rejection of generous American assistance.[51]

The subservient attitude of post-war Greek elites towards their transatlantic patrons should not be explained only in behavioural terms. Dependence arose also from the fragmented structure of the *Ethnikofron* political system and its economy, which was marked by striking disarticulations, that is to say missing structural links that prevented its effective operation.[52] In post-war Greece, these disarticulations took the form of an ongoing conflict, not only with the left, but also within the *Ethnikofon* camp itself, involving the Palace, the army and the different bourgeois parties over who should control the state and its power centres. Each of the main *Ethnikofron* factions claimed to enjoy US support (real or imagined) in order to gain a political advantage over its domestic rivals. In January 1949, for instance, King Paul maintained that he had ostensibly received approval from Grady and the Director of the Marshall Plan in Europe, Averell Harriman, to dissolve parliament and form an extra-parliamentary government (whose composition he was secretly plotting with Papagos and Markezinis).[53] When

Washington discovered that Harriman and Grady never approved such a plan, it warned the King against appointing a government of that kind and Paul eventually abandoned the idea.[54] Similar invocations of US support (often imaginary) were common among the main party leaders. In a recent account, James Miller remarks that 'politicians of all factions attempted to utilize the U.S. embassy as a tool in their political manoeuvrings'.[55] While this observation is, strictly speaking, correct, it overlooks the significant fact that, in most cases, US officials also succeeded in unveiling and repelling these intrigues, thus enhancing Washington's mastery over the Greek scene.

One of the most telling examples of how these structural disarticulations augmented American hegemony is the government crisis of March–April 1950. After the elections of 5 March 1950 (the first since the end of the Civil War) the three Centre parties (Venizelos's Liberals, Plastiras's EPEK and the Party of George Papandreou) won the majority of seats (Table 1). On 8 March, all three agreed to form a pact under Plastiras. To avert the objections of the Palace (since Plastiras had been a staunch republican before the war) the Centrist pact issued a joint *communiqué* stressing their commitment to the monarchy.[56] Meanwhile, the King, who had avowed never to swear-in or 'shake hands with' Plastiras (because of his anti-royalist past), persuaded Venizelos to break the pact and appointed him prime minister on 23 March at the head of a centre-right coalition.[57] Once again, Paul claimed to be acting in the interests of the United States, and went as far as to disagree with Grady (who favoured a Plastiras-led coalition) over who was a better judge of American interests! As Grady told Secretary Acheson, Paul claimed that the United States 'would become disgusted with the Plastiras regime and withdraw aid'.[58] On 23 March, the US *chargé*, Minor, told Acheson that Paul's appointment of Venizelos was 'contrary to [the] advice given [...] by [the] Ambassador' and added that the 'King thinks' his move 'will be perceived better by foreigners than [a] Plastiras government'.[59] So adamant was the Palace in claiming to enjoy US

Table 1 Results of the Greek legislative elections of 5 March 1950

Party	Votes	Seats	%
Popular Party (Tsaldaris)	317,512	62	18.8
Liberal Party (Venizelos)	291,083	56	17.2
Nat. Progressive Centre Union (EPEK) (Plastiras)	277,739	45	16.4
George Papandreou Party	180,185	35	10.7
Democratic Bloc (Left)	163,824	18	9.7
Independent Political Array (far right)	137,618	16	8.1
United National Party (EEK) (Kanellopoulos)	88,979	7	5.3
National Party of Greece (Zervas)	61.573	7	3.7
Rally of Farmers and Workers	44,308	3	2.6
New Party (Markezinis)	42,157	1	2.5
Others	83,995	0	5.0
Total	1,688,973	250	100.0

Sources: Elias Nikolakopoulos, Η καχεκτική δημοκρατία. Κόμματα και εκλογές, 1946–1967, Athens, Patakis, 2001, p.108; F.R.U.S. 1950, Vol. V. p.341; Linardatos, Από τον Εμφύλιο, vol.1, p.95; Meynaud, *Les forces politiques*, p.82.

approval, that Paul asked the Greek ambassador in Washington to inform the State Department that he was 'very annoyed' and 'found strange' Minor's remark that the Venizelos Government was 'not agreeable' to the United States. Ambassador Vassilios Dendramis also asked the State Department if Minor had indeed been authorized to express his views to the King.

If analyses like Miller's were valid, Washington would have yielded to this pressure. However, after promising to 'see if there has been some misunderstanding', Acheson told Dendramis on 28 March that Grady had full support when he asked Paul to back a 'centrist coalition under Plastiras'.[60] Three days later, Grady waged a fierce counterattack. In a letter to Venizelos which he circulated to the press, he criticized the 'less than satisfactory performance' of the King's new government and announced the suspension of US aid until the country's institutions were allowed to function normally. This is what he said:

> The American people [...] expect that any Greek Government hoping to continue to receive its generously provided aid, should utilise this aid to the maximum possible extent [...]. Only a stable and efficient government, supported by the people and the Parliament, can act with the determination and stability [...] required [...]. Irresponsible talk about adjourning Parliament or of new elections [...] can only create a climate of [...] uncertainty [...]. The Director of ECA and I [...] cannot approve [...] the commitment of American funds [...] until the Greek Government takes important and binding decisions to guarantee the successful use of these funds.[61]

Despite their endeavours, the King, Venizelos, and his right-wing allies could not survive the impact of Grady's intervention. In a pitiful attempt to mirror the US ambassador's action, Venizelos also issued a public letter to Grady. Then he requested the backing of the other Centre parties which was, predictably, denied.[62] A barrage of humiliating criticisms followed from Acheson, the Foreign Office and even Washington's new ally, Tito, while the director of ECA, Paul Hoffman, made implicit threats about suspending a major electrification project. On 14 April, Venizelos resigned.[63] He then returned to his initial position of backing a Centrist coalition under Plastiras, and announced he was leaving Greece 'for health reasons'.[64] The King, who had suffered a major blow, broke his vow and swore in Plastiras.[65]

Besides revealing the degree of American power in Greece, Grady's intervention is instructive in other respects. First, it highlighted the circular relationship between dependence and the internal disarticulations of the Greek economy and political system. The earth-shattering effect of Grady's letter emanated not only from the substantial sums of aid it involved (although this was certainly a major factor), but also from the fact that the Greek economy could not sustain itself if Marshall Plan funds were withheld. Second, the internal fragmentation of the Greek political system was another source of power for the US ambassador. Although Venizelos could perhaps receive a vote of confidence in Parliament, his centre-right Government would have been very fragile.[66] This was so because differences among the right-wing parties supporting it were significant, while the reluctance of the Popular Party to take key ministerial posts left Venizelos exposed.[67] Furthermore, senior politicians within his own Liberals, like George Mavros, opposed his high-handed attitude towards the Centrist pact.[68] When considering all these factors together, it becomes obvious that Grady's intervention was enhanced by the very fact that Greece's post-Civil War regime itself was disjointed and incapable of producing stable governments through its own mechanisms.

At the same time, one must not go as far as to share Grady's own assessment that Venizelos resigned because the US embassy simply refused to support him. On 17 April, Grady told Acheson: 'We got positive results by negative methods [...]. Every effort Venizelos (and the brain trust) made to get American Government blessing failed'.[69] If this assessment were valid, then Grady need not have written and publicized his letter of 31 March; and Acheson, ECA, the British Government and others could have refrained from threatening to suspend economic aid. In reality, Grady's theory of 'negative methods' was a transparent attempt to conceal the semi-colonial character of his intervention and nourish the American myth that in the Cold War the United States supposedly respected the independence and sovereignty of its allies.

Accession in NATO and the rapprochement *with Yugoslavia*

From the end of the Greek Civil War in September 1949,[70] to President Truman's decision to endorse the entry of Greece and Turkey in NATO in April 1951, US strategic thinking underwent considerable reflection. This is apparent in the proliferation of Pentagon, NSC and State Department policy papers titled 'US objectives with respect to Greece', especially after the outbreak of the Korean War on 27 June 1950.[71] However, the most striking feature of all these documents is their inability to produce a new US strategy for Greece, despite their shared conclusion that the old policy required updating. For example, in February 1951, an NSC paper stated that, on one hand, 'the original objective of the military assistance program for Greece, initiated in 1947 [...] was achieved in September 1949', but on the other it recommended that US policy should be 'continued support of the Truman doctrine as applied to Greece'.[72] Most US policy papers on Greece in these twenty months reaffirmed the contents of NSC document 42/1 of 23 March 1949, which extended the application of the Truman Doctrine.[73] This approach was largely justified by the NSC's view that the United States 'has not succeeded in evoking a degree of self-help in Greece' and that the country's 'economic and social structure' was still marked by 'inherent weakness'.[74] Another factor was Washington's continued concern that despite the end of the Civil War in September 1949, there were still 800 communist rebels fighting in various pockets across Greece until early 1950, resulting in 191 deaths and 452 injuries for the National Army of Greece. Indeed, internal order was not considered fully restored until the end of that year.[75] As late as September 1950, the NSC reported that 'the communist internal effort in Greece is meeting with some success'.[76] More importantly still, another factor behind this hesitant US attitude was the absence of a clear alternative to the Truman Doctrine.

Some accounts have argued that between the end of the Greek Civil War and the outbreak of the Korean War, 'Greece's objective strategic importance had declined'.[77] A closer inspection of the evidence, however, suggests otherwise. In November 1949 the State Department opposed any relaxation of US support for Greece on the grounds that this could 'sacrifice [the] hard-won gains of [the] past two years'.[78] Meanwhile, the deepening of the Belgrade-Moscow split and Tito's termination of assistance to the Greek rebels in July 1949 made Yugoslavia a country of utmost strategic importance to the West, with direct effects on Greece. As the historian Elisabeth Barker remarked, US policy-makers viewed the Tito-Stalin split as 'the most significant event which had taken place behind the Iron Curtain since the war'.[79] Conversely, NSC document 18/4 of 17 November 1949, which outlined Washington's position towards the Moscow-Belgrade dispute, justified supporting Tito chiefly in relation to the benefits for the security of Italy and Greece. It said:

> Soviet success in destroying [the] Tito regime [...] and supplanting it by a puppet government [...] would represent a renewal and intensification of threats to the security of Greece and Italy and a serious political reverse for the United States and the Western European nations. [...] In consequence, all the gains we have made in Central and Western Europe and in Greece during the past two years would be jeopardized.[80]

In other words, the high value attributed to Yugoslav security in 1949–50 derived chiefly from the strategic importance of Italy and Greece. This conclusion is further confirmed by NSC report 18/4 of 1949, which emphasized that 'direct control of all Yugoslav territory would have disastrous consequences for Greece. Because of the great blow to Greek morale [...] it would be doubtful whether Greece would be saved from Soviet domination'.[81] This assessment was upheld until the eve of Greece's entry in NATO. In March 1951, a CIA report confirmed that a Soviet-sponsored attack on Yugoslavia 'should be considered a serious possibility' and warned that 'Soviet control of Yugoslavia would greatly facilitate Soviet efforts to dominate the Eastern Mediterranean area' and 'offer an approach for Soviet attacks into Greece or Italy'.[82] In linking Tito's survival to the security of *Ethnikofron* Greece, US policy was placing Greece's strategic importance on a par to that of Yugoslavia, arguably the most important European country for Washington in 1949–51. Contemporary observers, like Leften Stavrianos, noted that the Tito-Stalin split and the defeat of the Greek communists in 1949 'altered the balance of power in southeastern Europe' and led 'certain American army and navy officers' to speak of turning the area 'into a potential offensive – not merely defensive – stronghold'.[83]

Greece's strategic importance for the United States was enhanced by other factors. Months before the outbreak of the Korean War, Washington came to view

Greece not only as a country whose security was linked to Yugoslavia's, but also as the main Western channel for 'keeping Tito afloat'.[84] Since February 1949, the State Department encouraged a diplomatic *rapprochement* between Athens and Belgrade with the aim of 'drawing Tito towards the West'.[85] Greece's role was considered vital, as any hint of direct US involvement in Belgrade could provoke a hostile Soviet reaction.[86] According to Ioannis Stefanidis, this policy was 'warmly' greeted by the Greek Permanent Undersecretary for Foreign Affairs, Panayotis Pipinelis, who saw its benefits for both the Western Alliance and the *Ethnikofron* side, as Washington was intent on forcing Tito to stop assisting the Greek Democratic Army.[87] Secret contacts between Athens and Belgrade began in February 1949, resulting in two early proposals. The first was to reopen the Yugoslav section of the Free Port of Thessaloniki and the railway line connecting it to Belgrade. The second proposal was to start secret talks over a future *entente* between the two states.[88] Meanwhile, Acheson pressed Tito to close the Yugoslav border to the Greek communist rebels as a condition for proceeding with this policy.[89] The attempted *rapprochement* suffered a setback on 31 March 1949, when Greece's Foreign Minister, Constantine Tsaldaris, said in an interview that he predicted Athens will become Tito's ally within a year. As Jože Pirjevec explains, Soviet propaganda used this statement to attack the Yugoslavs, forcing Belgrade to deny all contact with Athens and dismiss what it called 'Tsaldaris's fictions'.[90] Although secret discussions froze for nine months, Tito announced on 10 July at Pula that the Yugoslav border was sealed for the Greek Democratic Army, and this paved the ground for their future revival.[91]

New Greek-Yugoslav contacts were rekindled in January 1950, following a joint US-UK-French initiative.[92] Initially, Washington sought to achieve progress by making economic assistance to Yugoslavia conditional upon reviving the *rapprochement* with Athens. However, on 14 January, Yugoslav Foreign Minister Vladimir Dedijer counterposed 'the democratization of Greece' as a condition for normalizing relations with Athens.[93] A good opportunity therefore arose after the March 1950 Greek elections, when Belgrade told US ambassador George Allen that it was ready to cooperate with a 'progressive' government in Athens led by Plastiras.[94] This position was reaffirmed in April by the official Yugoslav newspaper *Borba*, in what Athens interpreted as external intervention in the crisis surrounding the short-lived Venizelos Government.[95] Although Grady later denied that the improvement of Greek-Yugoslav relations played a part in bringing down the Venizelos Government, Allen's visit to Athens during the crisis suggested otherwise. In a briefing to Acheson, Grady wrote that the prevalent view in Greece was that the United States sided with Plastiras 'to force a Yugoslav alliance on them', adding that these sentiments were encouraged by what he called 'the unfortunate activities of Allen'.[96] Moreover, when Plastiras became prime minister on 15 April, Allen began to mediate between Belgrade and Athens and on 10 May both governments announced their readiness to exchange ministers. To galvanize the new *rapprochement*, Allen obtained Tito's consent to return 1,100 of the children transferred to Yugoslavia during the Greek Civil War, while Plastiras agreed to reopen the Yugoslav Free Zone in Thessaloniki and the railroad to

Belgrade. As a reward to Tito, the United States encouraged 'Gr[ee]k purchases of Yugo[slav] goods with ECA dollars'.⁹⁷

This momentum, however, was again lost when, on 16 May, references were made to the Slavic minority in Greece by the Yugoslav Foreign Minister, Edvard Kardelj, during an otherwise friendly speech on Greek-Yugoslav relations.⁹⁸ On the next day, the Greek Undersecretary for Foreign Affairs, Ioannis Politis, protested against Kardelj's reference to 'the minorities of Aegean Macedonia' and argued that the stirring of this issue 'contradicts the spirit of the revived relations' between the two states. Politis then complained to the US embassy and, on 22 June, submitted a 'long memorandum' presenting Greece's views.⁹⁹ Throughout June, Acheson tried to contain the effects of the incident, asking the US embassy to explain to the Greeks that Kardelj's words were aimed against 'Bulgarian-Cominform propaganda', not Athens,¹⁰⁰ but to no avail. In late June the Yugoslav Minister was recalled from Athens, while his Greek counterpart was prevented from taking up his post in Belgrade. On 28 June, the US embassy in Athens, citing Yugoslav sources, reported that 'the normalization of Yugoslav-Greek relations had reached a stalemate' and predicted that this 'would probably continue for several months'.¹⁰¹

Against this background, the successful third endeavour at fostering a Greek-Yugoslav *rapprochement* in November was a path-dependent evolution arising from the previous two attempts. It was not a response to the Korean War. This is evident, first, in the aforementioned American and Yugoslav predictions in June 1950 that the breakdown of the second *rapprochement* would last 'several months', an assessment suggesting that the resumption of dialogue was viewed as a matter of time before the outbreak of conflict in the Far East.¹⁰² Second, US documents show that after the start of the Korean War in late June, the United States did not judge that the situation necessitated a speedy revival of Greek-Yugoslav relations, but noted that the conflict in the Far East simply 'highlighted' the correctness of its Balkan policy. According to a State Department report on 19 November,

> the Korean events highlight the community of Greek and Yugoslav security interests under the potential threat of similar Cominform military action against either or both states. Tension between the countries which relaxed progressively after Yugoslavia's break with the Cominform, turned into a definite promise of *rapprochement* with the advent of power of the Plastiras Government in Greece in April.¹⁰³

Third, there is no evidence that the outbreak of the Korean conflict changed Washington's view of Greek-Yugoslav relations in any other way. Available documents suggest that Washington continued to view the resumption of the *rapprochement* calmly, as a process defined by its own tempo, which promised a revival within 'a few months'.¹⁰⁴ After an abortive British initiative in August 1950, the State Department patiently concluded that it was 'inopportune at least for the United States to continue to encourage either the Yugoslav or the Greek Government to improve relations'.¹⁰⁵ On 19 September, during informal discussions with the Foreign Office in London, US Undersecretary of State George

McGhee said that 'an active pursuit of this objective [i.e. reviving Greek-Yugoslav relations] should wait until the chances of success appear more auspicious'.[106] This view was reaffirmed in a State Department report proposing that the United States 'shall continue when suitable opportunities occur to endeavour to liquidate the [...] impasse through diplomatic action at Belgrade and Athens'.[107]

Equally, there is no evidence that the admission of Greece and Turkey in NATO, which President Truman approved in April 1951, was decided in response to the Korean War. However, without citing hard evidence, several accounts have assumed that there is a strong causal link between the two developments. Stearns, for instance, maintains that

> when NATO strategists [...] saw hostilities in Korea as the beginning of a coordinated Soviet campaign of world conquest, perhaps to be followed by renewed military pressure on eastern Turkey [...] the immediate need to bolster Greece and Turkey far outweighed other considerations.[108]

Stefanidis also says that 'Greece's admission in NATO was rather left to develop as a function of the changing American policy and the persistent efforts of Turkey'. Pelt argues that 'the decision to admit Greece and Turkey into NATO was conditioned by the outbreak of the Korean War'.[109] These conclusions are not based on any positive evidence and pay little attention to the importance of developments in the Balkans and the East Mediterranean, including the Greek-Yugoslav *rapprochement*, which provide better clues about the causes of Greece and Turkey's accession in NATO. As Ekavi Athanassopoulou aptly remarks, developments in the Balkans were crucial:

> The idea of Greece, Turkey and Yugoslavia becoming the shield to protect western Europe was developing fast in the minds of the American military. In December 1950, the Joint Chiefs of Staff had asserted that Yugoslavia's strategic location had direct importance to the defence of the North Atlantic area.[110]

A careful reading of US records reveals that Greece's entry in NATO was supported by Washington because of several interrelated factors that bear little connection to the Korean War. The most important were (a) the adoption of NATO's first Strategic Concept in early 1951, following General Dwight Eisenhower's appointment as Supreme Allied Commander Europe (SACEUR); (b) Turkey's protests against the absence of sufficient US guarantees to its security; (c) the need to integrate Yugoslavia into the Western security system after its expulsion from the Cominform; (d) the consolidation of Greece's 'internal security' by the end of 1950. Compared to these factors, the Korean War appears to have been of marginal effect, including on NATO's plans to integrate Turkey in the Western security system. It is possible that China's involvement in the Korean conflict in November 1950 played a minor part in encouraging Washington to admit Greece and Turkey in the Alliance. But even if were to accept this, Korea was a factor of limited influence which alone did not tip the balance in favour of Greek and Turkish membership.

2. Hegemony and the US Policy Review of 1952

Turning to the first of these factors, it is important to realize that since NATO's formation in April 1949, US strategists were aware of a security gap between the Alliance's South European Command and the British Middle East Command. This gap, sometimes referred to as 'the Mediterranean problem',[111] raised the issue of how to integrate the Truman Doctrine states (Greece and Turkey) with two nearby Western defence systems (NATO and the Middle East Command). Until early 1951, American strategists contemplated two possible solutions. One was to sign bilateral US-Greek and US-Turkish defence agreements; the other was to create a new Mediterranean Alliance involving the United States, Britain, Greece, Turkey (and possibly Italy and France). Since February 1949, Acheson, together with the Turkish ambassador in Washington, explored 'the possibility of a Mediterranean Pact',[112] and in August 1950, Minor from Athens supported the idea as suitable also for the Greeks.[113] Consensus around this solution was so strong that in April 1951 the State Department produced the text of a draft treaty for a Mediterranean Alliance.[114] The main obstacle to its implementation, however, was its ambiguous relationship to NATO and the British Middle East Command. NATO's Southern Command (headed by Admiral Robert Carney) was already expected to overlap with the British Middle East Command,[115] an issue that rendered the creation of a third Mediterranean Pact a source of greater complications. Consequently, on 14 March 1951, in response to a question by Assistant Secretary of State George Perkins, US admiral Forrest Sherman outlined the problem as follows:

> PERKINS: I am not clear regarding the relationship between Admiral Carney's command and this separate Mediterranean command.
> SHERMAN: No one is clear about it. If the Mediterranean were larger, I could understand the usefulness of a NATO Mediterranean Command and a U.K. line of communications command. However, I do not believe that we can afford two separate commands in the Mediterranean in the event of war. If political considerations did not intrude, the proper way to organize would be to put one man in control of the whole show – including the Aegean and the Balkans.

A major influence behind Sherman's ideas was Eisenhower's new strategic concept developed immediately after he assumed his new role on 19 December 1950 as NATO's first SACEUR. As Sherman told Perkins in March 1951, Eisenhower saw clear military advantages in extending NATO's southern command to include Greece (but apparently not Turkey): 'For the southern flank, General Eisenhower envisages a headquarters in Naples under Admiral Carney. This would include French North Africa and Italy and also Greece, when and if Greece is admitted to NATO'.[116] In other words, the first concrete proposals to include Greece in NATO appear to have come from Eisenhower and these, as we shall see, were linked to his new Strategic Concept for NATO, not to Turkey's security.

Meanwhile, tensions between the United States and Britain over Southeast European security finally led to the abandonment of the Mediterranean Pact. On 14 March 1951, the US Joint Chief of Staffs, General Omar Bradley, remarked that there were 'many irritants in our relationship with the British in recent months' and sardonically suggested having 'a showdown with them' to 'call each other names for a while'.[117] Ten days later, Acheson wrote to Defense Secretary George Marshall to ask what 'security guarantee' the United States could offer Greece and Turkey. After consulting with Bradley's staff, Marshall replied on 14 April to recommend full NATO membership for both states.[118] His letter to Acheson and its two attachments (a memorandum by Bradley and a 'summary of views' from the Chiefs of Staffs) remain classified, but some references to their content can be found in a joint memorandum by McGhee and Perkins.[119] There, we read that the US 'Defense establishment', which included Bradley, Eisenhower and Sherman,[120] supported the inclusion of Greece and Turkey in NATO as the simplest and speediest solution. The memorandum identified the 'principal factors' of this decision as:

a. The views of the Defence establishment;
b. Simplification of political problems connected with command structures;
c. Relative simplicity and speed, from standpoint of US reaction, of extending NATO membership as compared with other forms [...].
d. Turkey and Greece are already associated with the NAT for planning purposes.

McGhee and Perkins also explained why the alternative idea of a Mediterranean Pact was abandoned. The most important reason they gave was the belief that such an option 'would multiply the problems of the major powers by creating overlapping and contending organizations and command structures'.[121] Meanwhile, a CIA report in June 1951 predicted that Moscow would consider the inclusion of Greece and Turkey in NATO 'a potential threat, though a limited and local one' and would therefore react using peaceful means, e.g. intensified propaganda, political and economic pressure, and UN action.[122]

Other evidence shows that the decision to enlarge NATO was also influenced by the revival of the Greek-Yugoslav *rapprochement* in November 1950. In a memorandum on 20 January 1951, Yost proposed the idea of encouraging military cooperation between Greece, Yugoslavia and Turkey, and Peurifoy forwarded the document to the Director of Policy Planning, Paul Nitze, with the notation: 'This memo deserves the Department's careful attention'.[123] The paper, entitled 'The Place of Greece, Yugoslavia and Turkey in Military Planning for the Year 1951', called for 'a reconsideration of [US] military planning' along the following lines:

> When we are desperately endeavoring to organise an army for the defense of Western Europe and are confronted by the inescapable fact that this army cannot attain substantial proportions during 1951, there already exist in South-eastern Europe three large armies of tough fighting quality and high morale, the Yugoslav of over 20 divisions, the Greek of 9 and the Turkish of 19 [...]. Yugoslavia, Greece and Turkey represent the most effective force in being in 1951 on the Soviet periphery of Europe.

2. Hegemony and the US Policy Review of 1952

The paper then proposed sending 'key military equipment' to all three states and arriving at an 'agreement [...] as to what direct assistance in the form of air and ground forces could be supplied' in case of a communist attack.[124]

Yost's paper was discussed at the highest levels in Washington and on 6 February 1951 the NSC recommended consideration 'at an appropriate time, the possibility and desirability of military cooperation between Greece and Yugoslavia'.[125] On 9 March, the paper was considered by the joint Defense and State Department ISAC meeting, but on 16 March Acheson reported that the suggestion of supplying additional equipment was rejected on the grounds that it entailed adoption of an 'advanced line' of defence in Europe.[126] This reluctance, however, must be understood in connection to the ongoing debates at that time regarding the new security commitment the United States should make to Greece and Turkey. A few days later, Acheson raised with Marshall the issue of admitting Greece and Turkey in NATO and explained that this had been 'under continuing study' by his Department.[127] Consequently, initial reservations about Yost's proposal were overcome by the decision to offer NATO membership to Greece and Turkey, which indeed amounted to an 'advanced line' of defence. Meanwhile, the part of Yost's paper which proposed military cooperation between Greece, Turkey and Yugoslavia could now be given utmost priority. Over the next three and a half years, Washington elevated the idea of a tripartite Balkan pact into a centrepiece of its South European policy.

Other sources confirm that Yugoslavia's strategic importance contributed significantly to Greece and Turkey's admission in NATO. In his meeting with the Italian Prime Minister Alcide de Gasperi on 19 January 1951, Eisenhower stressed that

> there was [a] very large Mediterranean population all hostile to Stalin and mentioned Turkey, Greece, Yugoslavia even though its morals may be repugnant [...]. From a purely military view all this could have great influence on defence of Mediterranean where allied naval and air force could assist in defense.[128]

The importance attached by Eisenhower to the military cooperation of these three states emanated from his new Strategic Concept for NATO, which he presented to President Truman and his cabinet on 31 January 1951. During that briefing, Eisenhower likened the geographical shape of Western Europe to 'a long bottleneck' and pointed out that its collective defence required the concentration of 'great air and sea power' on its two sides, the North Sea and the Mediterranean. To achieve this, he stressed,

> I'd make Denmark and Holland a great 'hedgehog' and I'd put 500 or 600 fighters behind them and heavy naval support in the North Sea. I'd do the same sort of thing in the Mediterranean and I'd give arms to Turkey and the 'Jugs'.[129]

These views were reflected in Acheson's letter to Marshall on 24 March, in which he proposed NATO membership for Greece and Turkey. One of the key reasons identified there was the need to develop 'mutual defense arrangements between Turkey and its neighbours', considering that Ankara refused to join any regional pacts unless it was first included in 'a broader security arrangement to which the United States is a party'.[130] On 5 February the State Department's Director of Policy Planning was told by his unit that 'a security commitment from the U.S. would act as [...] an essential prerequisite if we wished to encourage Turkey to enter into mutual, or regional defense arrangements with Greece, Yugoslavia or any other country in the Mediterranean'.[131] Similarly, during the State Department's deliberations over Greek and Turkish security, Peurifoy 'strongly' supported full NATO membership for both states, first, because of the 'important contribution which Greece and Turkey could otherwise make to Western defense', and second, because of the former's importance to the security of Yugoslavia. As he put it, 'an added factor of significance is that the problem of the relationship of Yugoslavia to the Western defense system [...] is rendered even more difficult by the uncertainty as to the position of Greece and Turkey in that system'.[132]

Meanwhile, Turkey's pressure to enter into a formal defence arrangement with the United States provided a further motive behind admitting Greece in NATO. However, Ankara's calls were neither more important than the other two factors (i.e. Eisenhower's new Strategic Concept and Yugoslavia) nor were they linked to the Korean War. Indeed, when referring to Turkey in this context, it must be stressed that since NATO's formation in 1949 (except for a brief period in the summer of 1950) Ankara never asked Washington to join the Alliance. Successive Turkish governments made it plain that they were willing to accept any other defence commitment by Washington, especially the Mediterranean Pact, provided that the United States would also be party to it. As early as 17 February 1949, the Turkish ambassador in Washington, Feridun Erkin, informed the State Department that 'his Government had come to the conclusion that Turkey could not appropriately participate in the North Atlantic arrangement but continued to be interested in the possibility of a Mediterranean pact'.[133] This policy was briefly abandoned when the Democratic Party of Adnan Menderes came to power in May 1950, seeking to exploit the outbreak of the Korean War as an opportunity and formally applied to join NATO on 29 July 1950. Significantly, however, Washington firmly rejected Turkey's application a few weeks later on the grounds that 'under present circumstances it would be unwise' to do so.[134] This setback forced Ankara to revert to its previous position of requesting alternative security commitments. Indeed, on 24 January 1951, Erkin informed McGhee that 'in November 1950 [he had] proposed to his Government in Ankara a Mediterranean formula on a new basis' and that he 'had just received the agreement of his government to make this proposal'.[135] Consequently, the impression that Turkey's incessant calls for a security guarantee were a defining factor behind Washington's decision to enlarge NATO is incorrect, not least because if this pressure were significant, Turkey would not have reverted by early 1951 to its previous position of demanding a Mediterranean Pact. In other words, the fact that a few months later Washington finally favoured NATO membership for Turkey must be attributed to other factors, namely to Eisenhower's new

Strategic Concept, the preference of US strategists for 'simplicity' and the need to anchor Yugoslavia.

Regarding the escalation of the Korean War after China's involvement in the conflict, there is no positive evidence to show that this altered US thinking on Turkey's NATO application.[136] If anything, on 24 January 1951, that is two months after the Chinese attack on the Chingchon River, the Menderes government reconciled itself to the fact that Washington would not consider the Korean War a factor meriting its inclusion in NATO, and expressed favour for the alternative 'Mediterranean formula'.[137] On 12 February 1951, McGhee repeated to Menderes and the Turkish President, Celâl Bayar, that the United States could not support Turkey's entry in NATO because it cannot 'undertake further formal commitments' until the Alliance 'can be given real strength'. In other words, not only did the escalation of the Korean conflict in November 1950 not curb Washington's opposition to Turkey's entry in NATO, but in fact had the opposite effect, as Turkey's accession in the Alliance at that point was viewed in Washington as a policy that could weaken NATO by causing it to overstretch. As McGhee explained to the Turkish leaders on that day, the US Government 'do not consider it wise to undertake obligations beyond our capabilities'.[138] Finally, it should be stressed that when the policy was finally reversed in April 1951, the Korean War was not highlighted as a major factor behind that decision.

Adjusting hegemony: The US policy review of 1952

One of the most important, yet overlooked, changes in US-Greek relations after the Truman Doctrine is the State Department's policy review of August–September 1952. This silenced, yet crucial, adjustment originated in two key documents drafted by Yost.[139] Both were entitled 'Re-Assessment of United States Policy and Tactics toward Greece', and were dated 29 August and 25 September 1952, respectively.[140] Subsequent notations by State Department officials show that many of their recommendations were adopted as official policy,[141] while later developments show that their impact was significant.

The changes proposed by these policy papers were grouped under three clusters. The first recommended that US-Greek relations be established 'on approximately the same basis as [...] relations with other NATO countries'. To this end, it was proposed that the United States should 'continue to exercise guidance and leadership of a very important character but should tend to become increasingly fraternal rather than paternal'. The second set of proposals called for 'the assumption by the Greeks of greater responsibility in the economic and military fields'. The third, in view of impending cuts in economic aid, proposed that the United States keep 'certain key controls' in Greece to safeguard its 'political and financial investments'.[142] All three objectives showed that the new policy intended to limit the level of direct US involvement in Greece and replace it with a greater initiative by the *Ethnikofron* governments. Interestingly, both Yost and the State Department appeared to have a firm grasp of the hegemonic character of US intervention in Greece, which they defined almost in Gramscian terms as the provision of 'guidance and leadership'. Clear differentiation was also made between what Triepel called 'direct' and 'indirect' hegemony, a distinction made through the apt metaphors of 'paternal' versus 'fraternal leadership'.

To effect the transition from one form of hegemony to the other, the 'Policy Re-Assessment' identified practical proposals which, according to Yost, 'have always been comprehended in US policy toward Greece, but [...] may have occasionally, in the heat of the moment, been neglected or forgotten'.[143] Concerning the first cluster, whose aim was to set US-Greek relations on the same footing as other NATO members, the following recommendations were made:

- To the extent possible US influence in Greece should be exercised through NATO, OEEC or other multilateral channels rather than directly by the United States and its representations in Greece.
- Direct expressions of US views in regard to Greek matters should be concentrated on relatively few problems which are vital to our interest.
- Expressions of direct US views [...] should be presented as tactfully as possible [...] as not to wound Greek sensibilities.
- Direct expressions of US views should by and large be private.
- Subordinate officers of US agencies should not be authorized, except when specifically designated [...] to state US policy to the Greek government.[144]

Interestingly, most of these recommendations used the word 'direct' to refer to US hegemony before the policy review. Equally telling is the new emphasis on 'multilateral' channels and international institutions, a view that fully accords with the definition of world hegemony in critical IR theory. As Cox remarked, 'the concept of multilateralism' was the 'principal instrumentality through which the United States shaped the postwar world economic order'.[145]

In the second cluster of objectives relating to military and economic issues, Yost proposed that:

> In view of the fact that our economic aid and hence our economic responsibilities have declined sharply, and that military responsibilities are more and more taken over by NATO organs, [...] our economic and military personnel in Greece could and should be cut very sharply during the current fiscal year.[146]

This recommendation bears the handwritten notation: 'We have this under study. We may be able to avoid cut in embassy personnel on ground that it will assume added econ[omic] rep[resentation] functions if mission is cut'.[147] After Greece's admission in NATO, JUSMAG passed to the American European Command (US EUCOM) and its personnel was slimmed down.

Finally, concerning aid reduction, two recommendations were made. The first defined the amount of $40 million as a floor below which economic aid to Greece should not be cut. The second was to 'lump[...] together all US aid, military and economic, in such a way that it will be impossible or at least difficult to separate out purely economic aid and to label it as another "cut". The paper then proceeded to reaffirm the strategic aims of US economic assistance to Greece as follows: 'a. To preserve the pro-western political orientation of the Greek people through the maintenance of stable economic conditions; and b. to make Greece more self-supporting so that the need for US aid continuously declines'.[148]

To fully comprehend the motives behind this review, both the documents themselves and their specific context should be examined. Concerning the former, Yost was sibylline in presenting his proposals as a response to what he called the 'changing attitudes of the Greek people and Government'.[149] If we were to interpret this sentence against the main developments taking place in Greece at this time, it appears that Yost was referring to the growing anti-American feeling among the Greek people. Although one historian recently claimed that US officials 'overlook[ed] [...] the strong nationalistic undercurrent which crosscut political loyalties in Greece' at the time,[150] both Yost's reference to 'attitudes of the Greek people' and other US embassy evidence clearly suggests the opposite. For example, in March 1952, Peurifoy told Washington that 'we may expect henceforth as memory of civil war fades and Gr[ee]k recovery proceeds that resentment at US controls will increase and accusations of interventions multiply. Emb[assy] is keenly aware of this natural trend'.[151] Two days before Yost drafted the first of the 'Policy Re-Assessment' papers, Peurifoy had expressed his bitterness at the reaction of the Greek press to private remarks he had made about the Greek economy and the need for new elections. A headline from one *Ethikofron* newspaper on 21 August 1952 said that 'Mr Peurifoy interferes in the country's internal affairs', while Prime Minister Plastiras took the unprecedented step of issuing a statement denouncing the press 'attacks against the person' of the US ambassador and urged the country's newspapers to show 'due respect to Mr Peurifoy, a true friend of the country'.[152] Shortly afterwards, Peurifoy told Washington that

> my remarks have [...] produced hysterical howl with Commie overtones from very newspapers which welcomed my pro-government statement upon my return from Paris. While somewhat disheartened [...], I realize that [this] must be expected as our aid and leverage taper away and Greeks feel themselves less dependent on us.[153]

Besides the anti-American rhetoric of the *Ethnikofron* press, declining levels of what Peurifoy himself called Greek 'dependence' on US aid began to show their mark on the 'attitudes of the Greek government'. A major point of friction in August–September 1952 were the repeated threats of Coordination Minister, George Kartalis, to disobey US advice and reduce the Greek defence budget if economic aid for 1952/53 were to be significantly reduced.[154] Some headlines covering the issue read: 'After Mr Kartalis's Speech. Fundamental disagreements with the Americans'; 'Should National Service be Reduced? Greece has the highest percentage: More men and arms than any other NATO country'.[155] Although in Peurifoy's view, this campaign was an attempt by the Centre coalition to 'publicly blam[e] its economic shortcomings on [the] Americans', the truth is that the drastic cut in US economic aid from $182 million in 1951–2 to $80 million in 1952–3 reduced Washington's political clout in Greece. This shift was seized upon by the pro-Rally press, which sought to gain political capital by overstating Kartalis's dispute with the Americans. On 24 August 1952, *Kathimerini* ran the following headline: 'The Government Cultivates Anti-American climate. It Creates Dangerous Situation for National Security'.[156]

The second US 'Policy Re-Assessment' paper attributed the policy review to additional motives. There, Yost discussed the adoption of the majority voting system and the expectation that this would further promote 'political stability' after the impending Greek elections.[157] Another key factor was Greece's entry in NATO and the resulting transfer of military cooperation from a bilateral to a multilateral framework. As Yost put it, 'in view of the fact that our [...] military responsibilities are more and more being taken over by NATO organs, it is believed that our [...] military personnel in Greece could and should be cut very sharply during the current fiscal year'.[158]

Overall, the American policy reassessment of August–September 1952 was a timely response to Greece's changing external and internal environment. Its aim was to substitute what it called 'paternal' with 'fraternal' 'guidance and leadership', thus signalling a conscious attempt on behalf of the United States to bring about a shift from a predominantly 'direct' to a predominantly 'indirect' form of hegemony. Equally important was the source of this change, which was neither the State Department nor the NSC in Washington, but the US embassy in Athens. This case throws into question the image of the supposedly 'conservative' character of the American foreign policy bureaucracy as a slow-moving machine that favours 'set repertoires'.[159] The main driving force behind this change, Yost, was a gifted diplomat with a clear vision of US interests in Greece. In this regard, the widespread tendency across the dependence narrative to identify American policy in Greece in the early 1950s with the brusque and unnuanced style of Peurifoy[160] must be always tempered with the acknowledgement of the key role played by his adept *chargé*, Yost.

Hegemony and relative autonomy

From the Truman Doctrine of 1947 to the US policy review of 1952, the environment of Greek foreign policy underwent profound change. The Civil War, which made the country vulnerable to outside intervention, ended in 1949 with the victory of the *Ethnikofron* forces. Greece's most hostile neighbour, Yugoslavia, suspended its support to the rebel communist army, and after 1950 became one of Athens's most vital allies. Meanwhile, from a relatively isolated country on the southern tip of the Balkans, Greece emerged as one of a dozen states belonging to the world's most powerful alliance, NATO. Although, as a contemporary observer remarked, American policy had 'made no progress in Greece except in a strict military sense',[161] after the economic stabilization programme of 1951–2 the Greek economy regained virtual self-sustainability without requiring large sums of

American aid. In other words, after five years of direct intervention, the United States had largely attained its core objective of rescuing the Greek *Ethnikofron* regime from collapse.

One need not be a Marxist to recognize that US intervention in Greek affairs was instrumental in producing this outcome. Indeed, it was a Republican advisor to the Congressional Committee on Foreign Economic Cooperation, Louis Wyman, who stated publically in April 1949 that 'the only reason the present government remains in power in Greece is United States support'.[162] To carry out what is today known as a process of state-building, that is 'the creation of new government institutions and the strengthening of existing ones',[163] US hegemony in Greece deployed a mixture of heavy-handed interventionism and occasional self-restraint. Of course, US officials typically overstated their supposed self-discipline, claiming that they adhered to a strategy once described by Grady as 'neither laissez faire on one hand nor direct interference on [the] other'.[164] Similarly, a 1950 CIA report noted that 'the Greeks will continue to depend heavily' on the United States, whose missions will contribute 'immeasurably to the survival of Greece', but all that would somehow happen 'without becoming excessively involved in Greek internal affairs'.[165]

These statements, however, were part of a self-delusional American narrative whose aim was to sustain the myth that the United States defended the values of the so-called Free World without violating Greece's sovereignty and parliamentary institutions. Such was the level of awkwardness among US policy-makers that their own reports sometimes referred to American '"intervention"' by placing the word in inverted commas to suggest that their actions, somehow, did not go that far.[166] In other words, in their own eyes, they thought they were both intervening and were not. Still, the US Congress, during a 1950 investigation into the conduct of US officials in Greece, concluded that many behaved in a 'disruptively ostentatious manner'.[167] The Directorate of Protocol at the Greek Ministry of Foreign Affairs is replete with reports on acts of misconduct by US officials in the late 1940s and early 1950s. The most emblematic, perhaps, was the tragicomic incident of an American official in Athens who 'rode on his sports car through the streets' at 5 a.m., 'with his arm extended holding a gun'. According to the police report, the said official 'got off at the house at 49 Raidestos Street, entered the courtyard, and fired his gun', because he 'concluded' that his Greek drinking partner earlier that night 'was a communist' and 'started to search for him to shoot him'!'[168]

The reason for which many US officials in Greece found it difficult to comply with their own government's guidelines was not simply a matter of individual behaviour. Their semi-colonial conduct reflected the nature of their Government's policy itself and specifically the way it was formulated at the very highest levels. This is most evident in the self-contradictory language used by Grady when reporting to Washington his dialogue with Prime Minister Venizelos in March 1950: 'I added that we had thought and still think Plastiras government might offer new hope. I made clear, however, that we are not interfering for or against any government'.[169] The blatant inconsistency between the first and second sentences in this statement never seems to have caused any consternation in Washington.

Similar incongruities can be found in official US policy on economic aid. According to it, Washington was ready to 'cooperat[e] with any Greek Government which enjoys the support of the Greek people [...] and [is] capable of carrying out the objectives of the US aid program'.[170] Again, the second part of the sentence patently contradicts the first, as it makes it clear that Washington would not be cooperating with 'any' democratically elected Greek government if it were deemed incapable of implementing ECA's programme. Judith Jeffery is partly right in saying that 'the [US] administration was cornered by its own rhetoric – caught between its promise of an uncompromising commitment to Greece and the necessity of applying conditions to the receipt of aid'.[171] At the same time, however, there was an important functional necessity for this ambiguity. Its real purpose was to create political space for US officials in Athens to exercise optimum discretion on the ground, whilst keeping the semblance of respecting the sovereignty of Greece and its parliamentary institutions.

Despite the cluttered manner in which it was implemented, US policy remained, overall, committed to the core objectives of the Truman Doctrine.[172] A key factor behind this record was the ability of US officials (despite their tendency to violate their own rules) to operate within a broad framework of determined and well-resourced hegemonic policy whose thrust was to uphold the unity and stability of the Greek *Ethnikofron* regime. In the final analysis, Washington's hegemonic project in Greece was based on a policy of social and political engineering, whereby the dominant local classes and elites would be constantly pressed to form broad coalitions with the aim of consolidating the supremacy of the *Ethnikofron* bloc in the political system. In this sense, high levels of economic and military assistance, the reorganization of the army and security apparatuses, the restructuring of the economy and trade unions and the imposition of the majority voting system, were all key instruments of infusing greater cohesiveness into the post-Civil War Greek regime.

Meanwhile, as a combination of power and consent, hegemony presupposes a degree of relative autonomy for the subaltern actor to enable it to actively contribute to the consolidation of the hegemonic link.[173] In post-war Greece, this limited autonomy was partly acquired through necessity, since the United States always deployed finite resources and its agencies adopted what Poulantzas called 'divergent tactics', representing the 'contradictions within [...] the different American state apparatuses'.[174] At the same time, the limited autonomy of the Greek political system was also partly encouraged by design. As we saw, leading US officials often resisted suggestions by *Ethnikofron* politicians to become more deeply involved in Greek domestic affairs. Similarly, since 1952 Marshall Plan aid was cut sharply regardless of the limited reduction in US influence that this would entail. In this context, the US policy review of that year expanded the relative autonomy of the *Ethnikofron* political system but did so through placing its new remit of authority under an increasingly institutionalized and multilateral framework. What remained unclear, however, was in what way the Greek political system would respond to this hegemonic adjustment.

3

THE DOMESTIC STRUCTURES OF THE POST-CIVIL WAR POLITICAL SYSTEM

One of the main misconceptions about the nature of the Greek post-Civil War political system is the view that after the defeat of the communists in 1949 all power fell in the hands of an omnipotent, monolithic, 'right-wing' state. This perception, which forms a key component of the dependence narrative, has led to the invention of the problematic term 'right-wing state' about the period 1949–67.[1] On closer inspection, however, the post-Civil War state was neither monolithic nor simply 'right-wing'. Despite its excessive authoritarianism towards the Left, the political system established by the victors of the Civil War rested on a power-sharing arrangement in which the 'Right', itself a disjointed and amorphous force, alternated in government with the fragmented parties of the liberal 'Centre'. Moreover, because of their close connections and frequent coalitions, the forces of the Right were not always easily distinguishable from those of the Centre. As Keith Legg aptly remarked, the Greek party system after 1949 was 'characterized by a diverse and fluid membership' which made it 'difficult to describe if only one is limited to the usual labels [...] – republican, royalist, Right, Centre, or Left'.[2]

For example, after the Civil War, the old alignment of the right with the monarchy and the Venizelist Centre with antiroyalist politics had lost much of its significance. Indeed, by the early 1950s, these roles had been almost reversed, with the hero of the Greek right, Papagos, turning into the chief opponent of the Palace and the leader of the Liberals, Sophocles Venizelos, becoming the royals' favourite prime minister.[3] Even the leader of centre-left EPEK, General Plastiras, a former republican whose 1922 coup resulted in the abolition of the monarchy in 1924–35, declared in 1950 that 'the country's interests are now served well by the royal family'.[4] Another blurring of the right/centre divide occurred when two of the three main Centre parties in 1950–1, Venizelos's Liberals and George Papandreou's Democratic Socialists, preferred to enter coalitions with the right instead of teaming up with EPEK to form an ideologically cohesive centrist government. Moreover, on the eve of the 1952 election, both Papandreou and EPEK's co-leader, Emmanuel Tsouderos, abandoned the leadership of their own parties and joined the electoral tickets of Papagos's 'right-wing' Rally. For such reasons, it would be more appropriate to conceptualize the post-Civil War political system in its formative years as a mix of loosely coalesced right-wing and centrist forces which shared power in various combinations that always excluded the left.

From the end of the Civil War in 1949 to the rise of Papagos to power in November 1952, the Greek political system was marked by continuous instability and crises. During these thirty-nine months, three general elections were fought, seven governments rose and fell and two *coups* were attempted, one by the Palace and another by IDEA. Meanwhile, more than half of the deputies who entered Parliament in March 1950 had changed their party affiliation by the end of 1952. In many ways, the victory of the *Ethnikofron* forces in the Civil War brought to the fore a complex web of internal rivalries that proved sometimes more threatening to the survival of the post-Civil War regime than the communist party itself. The main internal conflict was not, as some accounts maintain, between the Right and its Centrist opponents, but between the parliamentary forces on one hand and the authoritarian institutions of the state on the other (i.e. the Palace, the army and the parastate). At the heart of this dispute stood the existential question of whether Greece should remain a 'guided democracy', with Parliament functioning as the main source of authority, or follow the path of other south European states and establish a military dictatorship.

The abortive coup of 30–31 May 1951, carried out by the secret army group Sacred Bond of Greek Officers (IDEA), marked the nadir of this crisis. IDEA was founded on 25 October 1944 as a group of young officers with quasi-fascist ideas codified in their 'Heptalogue', which called for the annihilation of communism, the revival of the foreign policy programme of *Megali Idea* and the cleansing of the army from all Venizelist elements.[5] IDEA's abortive coup in May 1951 was a spontaneous reaction to the sudden news that the organization's idol, Field-Marshal Papagos, had resigned as commander-in-chief, a decision misinterpreted by its leaders as a dismissal by the Venizelos Government and the Palace. Although the coup was quickly averted by Papagos himself, who appeared at dawn in Syntagma Square to tell the mutineers that he had voluntarily resigned, this dramatic reaction revealed how fragile the balance of power was within the *Ethnikofron* camp. More surprising still was the failure of the US embassy to either anticipate these developments or intervene in a timely manner to avert them. Indeed, so clear were the limits of US power on this occasion, that Secretary Acheson later spoke to his officials of 'our conspicuous, unsuccessful effort [to] influence [the] outcome [of the] Papagos affair'.[6] As several contemporary observers remarked, the crisis of the post-Civil War regime reflected the failure of an essentially parochial political system to end the personal rivalries of the past and embark upon a new path of political reconstruction and reform.[7] For some, like Paul A. Porter, these failings were so striking that, at the risk of contradicting his own government's policy of upholding Greece's 'Western orientation', he noted that 'there is really no State here in the Western concept. Rather we have a loose hierarchy of individualistic politicians, some worse than others, who are [...] preoccupied with their own struggle for power'.[8]

As this crisis deepened, an unexpected turn of events occurred in the summer of 1951. After resigning from the army, Papagos went on to found a new party, the Greek Rally, which achieved spectacular electoral results. Five weeks after its formation, on 9 September 1951, the Rally received 36.5 per cent of the vote

3. Structures of Post-Civil War System

Table 2 Results of the Greek legislative elections of 9 September 1951

Party	Number of Votes	Seats	Share of the Vote (%)
Greek Rally	623,297	114	36.5
National Progressive Centre Union (EPEK)	399,529	74	23.5
Liberal Party	324,482	57	19.0
United Democratic Front (EDA)	178,325	10	10.6
Popular Party	113,580	2	6.7
Georgios Papandreou Party	37,033	0	2.1
Rally of Farmers and Workers	23,186	1	1.2
Others	7,469	0	0.3

Sources: Nikolakopoulos, *Η καχεκτική δημοκρατία*, p.139; F.R.U.S. *1951* Vol. V. 781.00/9-1151, p.508, fn1; Linardatos, *Από τον Εμφύλιο*, vol.1, p.290; Meynaud, *Les forces politiques*, p.86.

and returned as the largest party in Parliament, but short of an overall majority. This performance paved the way for its landslide victory in the elections of 16 November 1952, in which the Rally received 49.3 per cent and four-fifths of the parliamentary seats, a performance that made Papagos the first prime minister to lead a one-party government in Greece since Eleftherios Venizelos in 1928–32.[9] The Rally was founded by Papagos and his close associate Markezinis, who cleverly modelled it on General De Gaulle's Rassemblement du Peuple Français.[10] Upon its formation the Rally absorbed Markezinis's New Party and the right-of-centre Popular Unity Party (LEK) of Kanellopoulos and Stefanos Stefanopoulos. Over the next few days, deputies from the traditional and largest party of the right, the Popular Party, began to join its ranks *en masse*.[11] Despite the well-known ties of its founding pair with the right, the Rally's ambiguous ideology and messianic nationalism quickly enabled it to grow into a broad platform capable of absorbing a wide spectrum of *Ethnikofron* forces, including a large portion of the Centre. According to Nikolakopoulos, the party 'managed to attract a significant section of the popular base that was traditionally represented by the Venizelist parties'.[12] In the elections of 16 November 1952, 43 per cent of the Rally's 273 parliamentary candidates came from the Centre parties, including former party leaders and Prime Ministers Papandreou and Tsouderos.[13]

Overall, the Rally's foremost achievement was to reconcile, at least temporarily, the principal dispute within the *Ethnikofron* camp between its authoritarian and parliamentary factions. With a distinguished officer and loyal servant of the Metaxas Dictatorship at its head,[14] and a strategy of winning power through elections, the party emerged as the only political force capable of representing at once both the quasi-fascist elements of IDEA and the overwhelming majority of the *Ethnikofron* parliamentary elites, including a sizeable part of their liberal wing. Under its umbrella, former ministers and leading figures of the Metaxas Dictatorship, like Vassilios Papadakis, Nikolaos Spentzas, Constantine Maniadakis, Andreas Apostolidis, Stavros Polyzogopoulos, Ioannis Diakos, Panayiotis Sfakianakis and Georgios Koronaios, as well as Nazi collaborators like Georgios Pampoukas,[15] shared the same platform with leading liberal parliamentarians, like

Table 3 Results of the Greek legislative elections of 16 November 1952

Party	Number of Votes	Seats	Share of the Vote (%)
Greek Rally	783,541	247	49.3
Union of EPEK-Liberals	544,834	51	34.2
United Democratic Front (EDA)	152,011	0	9.5
Independents	56,679	2	3.5
Others	54,742	0	3.4

Sources: Nikolakopoulos, *Η καχεκτική δημοκρατία*, p.165; Linardatos, *Από τον Εμφύλιο*, vol.1, p.534; Meynaud, *Les forces politiques*, p.88.

Papandreou, Stamatis Merkouris, Tsouderos and others. Also, owing to Papagos's messianic appeal, the Rally quickly began to mobilize support as a party capable of leaving behind the interwar rivalry between Venizelists and anti-Venizelists and opening a new era of *Ethnikofron* unity against the Left. For instance, during the 1952 election campaign, Papagos and his leading candidates, like Constantine Karamanlis, spoke to voters 'with special emphasis', as the latter recalled, about the need to 'remove the divide between anti-Venizelists and Venizelists'.[16] According to Nikolakopoulos, the Rally's emergence marked 'the first conscious, systematic and widely supported effort to place the National Schism below the divisions which arose from the Civil War'.[17]

While the image of a party 'not in the usual sense of the word'[18] was crucial to its appeal, it soon became apparent that the broad coalition of forces which gathered around the Rally was becoming an obstacle against the articulation of a coherent government programme. To maintain the party's character as a broad church of disparate *Ethnikofron* forces, Papagos was obliged to adopt ambiguous policy agendas whose aims were often incoherent and self-contradictory. Therefore, after its initial dynamism, the Rally began to show limits in terms of its capacity to reorganize the *Ethnikofron* camp. Its broad political umbrella turned out to be a thin crust that gave the misleading image of 'a monolith'.[19] Beneath this seemingly solid exterior, the old antagonisms that threatened the unity of the *Ethnikofron* bloc were still intact, waiting for new opportunities to resurface. For example, as late as 1954, the King would tell friends that 'he is still very irked with Papagos and doesn't care much for him'. Meanwhile, in the shadows, IDEA continued to promote its members to key positions in the army to pave the way for a dictatorship.[20] As subsequent developments would show, the Rally's rise did not instil a deeper sense of unity within the *Ethnikofron* bloc. Instead, it simply contained the old factionalism of Greek politics and thus extended the survival of the post-Civil War state by some crucial years.

Conceptualizing the post-Civil War political system as a protective shell

One of the most enigmatic aspects of the post-Civil War political system of Greece is its dual image as both a monolithic structure protected by a police state[21] and as a fragmented patchwork of disjointed political forces.[22] In some ways, the interpretative gap dividing the dependence and ethnocentric perspectives partly reflects the ambiguity surrounding this fractured image. To be sure, it is not easy to analytically reconcile the sharp incongruities between the effective record of the post-Civil War state in suppressing the Left with its astonishing failure to restrain IDEA and the thousands of thugs, gangsters and informants who worked for the parastate.[23] Official data show that in 1949–56 thousands of communists were sent to exile and detained in various concentration camps,[24] whereas the plotters of the May 1951 coup, who were court-martialled and found guilty of 'high treason', were first granted amnesty by the Plastiras Government and then reinstated to their positions by Papagos.[25]

The usual explanation presented by proponents of the dependence narrative is that these striking inconsistencies reflect the identity of the post-Civil War regime, which differed only slightly from IDEA's far-right politics. According to Svoronos,

> after the end of the civil war, the far right sustained the climate of terrorism […] against the [communist] 'insurgents', which now aimed at every dissident […]. This dictatorship was concealed under a bogus parliamentarism founded on the far right.[26]

The image of the post-Civil War political system as a far-right regime masked as a democracy is shared, among others, by Lawrence Wittner, who speaks about the 'conservative, reactionary, and even fascist elements' that the United States brought to power 'in the wartime and postwar era'.[27] This thesis, however, is imbued with reductionist overtones. If the *Ethnikofron* parliamentarians were indeed of the same political ilk as the IDEA officers, why would the latter be constantly plotting to overthrow them and obsessively accuse them of being 'exclusively responsible for Greece's contemporary calamities'?[28] Furthermore, explanations like those of Svoronos and Wittner fail to account for other key factors, such as the nature of Papagos's dispute with the Palace or his opposition to the IDEA coup of 1951 which, as the incumbent Prime Minister Venizelos publicly admitted, 'he, alone at the time, acted against and stopped'.[29]

In the same way, the portrayal of the post-Civil War political system by both Greek ethnocentric historians and US and British observers as a 'maze of personalities', 'clogged by party politics', is equally partial.[30] Such interpretations are linked to a narrative that silences the elaborate system of organized violence against the Left which, besides the well-known executions of Nikos Beloyannis and his comrades on 30 March 1952 and the Makronissos, Ai-Stratis, Yaros, Ikaria and other concentration camps, extended across other aspects of public life.[31] As Alivizatos remarks, the private properties of communists were regularly confiscated, their civil rights violated and the infamous 'certificate of social convictions' was widely used to deny them and their relatives employment.[32] Moreover, an illiberal regime of strict censorship was applied to books, plays and other publications, while radio programmes and the education curriculum disseminated the official discourse of *Ethnikofrosyni*, especially among children and the young.[33] Still, it is almost impossible to find in Greek ethnocentric historiography any detailed discussion of this ubiquitous system of anti-communist repression, the parastate and the extensive record of human rights violations. Such issues are either totally silenced or kept in the distant background to give the misleading impression that they were peripheral to an otherwise functioning parliamentary system in 1949–67.

To overcome this interpretative quandary, it is hereby proposed that the post-Civil War state be conceptualized as a 'protective shell', i.e. as a structure that is solid and well-organized from outside, but pulp and fragmented from within. Such a conception enables us to view the post-Civil War political state in its totality, as it appeared both to its leftist victims and to its supporters in Greece and the West. Moreover, conceptualizing the state as a 'shell' can help capture the mixed character of that system as a blend of authoritarian elements (the Palace, the army, the police, the parastate) and democratic/pluralist institutions (Parliament, political parties and, to some extent, the press). Although a clear-cut division of roles between the two never really existed, broadly speaking, the authoritarian elements were usually charged with the task of marginalizing and purging left-wing opponents, while the democratic/pluralist institutions functioned chiefly as mechanisms of incorporating the *Ethnikofron* masses through clientelistic and, occasionally, populist practices. Viewed from this perspective, it becomes clearer why the successful operation of the post-Civil War regime rested primarily on its ability to maintain a working balance between its authoritarian and democratic structures.

In stressing the dual character of the *Ethnikofron* political system, many of the reductionist conclusions pervading the historiography can be overcome. For example, instead of reducing the post-Civil War political system (following Svoronos and others) to either a dictatorship masked as a democracy or portraying it (following the ethnocentric narrative) as a Western pluralist democracy, viewing it as a 'protective shell' underlines the hybrid character of that system as a variation of 'authoritarian parliamentarism'. This term, which has been deployed to analyse Imperial Germany under Otto von Bismarck and interwar Hungary under Miklós Horty, was also used to describe post-war Greece.[34] Although the concept has not been properly defined, authoritarian parliamentarism refers to a political arrangement whereby a number of non-elected/illiberal institutions share a considerable degree of state power with parliament and other elected bodies. While the frequent tensions between them often attract greater attention, the concept of the 'shell' enables us to focus on the other side of this relationship, namely the mutual interdependence between the authoritarian and parliamentary elements. To put it differently, it does not suffice to say that after 1949 Greece became a 'restricted democracy' or an 'authoritarian parliamentary' system in a manner implying that the democratic institutions were helpless victims of the authoritarian centres of power.[35] It is equally necessary to stress that, despite their antagonisms, *Ethnikofron* parliamentarians consistently tolerated and often encouraged authoritarian practices by the Palace, the army and the parastate. In other words, what made the Greek post-Civil War political system function as a unified whole was the determination of all its *Ethnikofron* forces to work together to keep the Left ostracized.

Through this analytical lens, the key role of intermediary actors becomes more readily understood. In the eighteen years of its existence, the post-Civil War state relied on the ability of its otherwise competing authoritarian and parliamentary structures to maintain a *modus operandi* that enabled them to share power. The attainment of this balance was exceedingly difficult insofar as the authoritarian centres pushed for greater control, while the *Ethnikofron* parliamentarians resisted this incursion to keep a minimum level of democratic legitimacy. In this tense environment, the most influential elements before 1967 were neither the authoritarian centres nor the parliamentary parties, but the few effective arbitrators who were able to mediate between them. This was so mainly because their mediatory role enabled them to bridge the antagonistic strands within the post-Civil War state and posit as saviours of *Ethnikofron* unity. In Gramscian terms, the polarized struggle within the post-Civil War Greek state gave rise to conditions which favoured Caesarist arbitration. According to Gramsci, Caesarism emerges in

> a situation in which the forces in conflict balance each other in a catastrophic manner; that is to say, they balance in such a way that [...] neither A nor B defeats the other – that they bleed each other mutually and then a third force C intervenes from outside, subjugating what is left of both A and B.

Gramsci maintained that Caesarism 'always expresses the particular solution in which a great personality is entrusted with the task of "arbitration".'[36] In the context of post-Civil War Greece, the first to attempt such a mediating role, albeit unsuccessfully, was Sophocles Venizelos, whose favour with the Palace helped him to serve twice as prime minister, despite the fact that his party's popularity never exceeded 19 per cent. As his biographer Grigorios Dafnis remarked, until 1952 Venizelos was 'the key personality of the Greek political scene. Without his participation, support or endorsement it was impossible for any government to stay in power'.[37] However, the first Caesarist type of arbitration after 1949 was that of Papagos, who rallied around him a broad coalition of far-right praetorian elements and centre-right and liberal parliamentarians until his death in 1955. The Rally's heir, the National Radical Union (ERE), also operated as an effective arbitrator between the Palace and the parliamentarians, largely because its leader, Karamanlis, owed his appointment to a politically decisive royal intervention when Papagos was terminally ill.[38] However, throughout his premiership in 1955–63, Karamanlis never grew into an effective Caesarist figure, partly because he lacked Papagos's enormous prestige and bipartisan appeal and partly because his power never became independent from the authoritarian centres, especially the Palace, which ultimately brought him down easily when they clashed in 1963.

The 'Papagos solution' and its misinterpretation in the historiography

According to Mouzelis, whose analysis is the most nuanced from the perspective of the dependence narrative, the choice facing Greece after the Civil War was: 'Either to 'incorporate' the masses by means of parliamentary democracy, or to subordinate them to direct domination [...]. Papagos' electoral successes in 1952 and 1953 [sic] confirmed the military's domination of the parliamentary forces'.³⁹ This assessment, however, rests on a striking confusion between Papagos's civilian role as party leader after 1951 and his previous career as military officer. What Mouzelis's analysis fails to appreciate is that, after his resignation from the army on 28 May 1951, Papagos's authority (both among the officer corps and across the electorate) was drawn directly from his personal prestige as a legendary hero of the *Ethnikofron* camp. In this sense, his authority was not dissimilar to that of General de Gaulle after his resignation in 1946 and, to an extent, General Plastiras, whose political career after 1944 was always treated by the historiography as that of a popular party leader.⁴⁰

More striking still is Mouzelis's assertion that Papagos' 'electoral successes' confirmed 'the military's domination over parliamentary forces'. If anything, 'electoral success' should point, by definition, to the victory of the elected institution, Parliament. Nevertheless, this conclusion appears to be linked to Mouzelis's implicit argument that the 1951 and 1952 elections were somehow rigged. Here is what he says in another study:

> The army was in control of the notorious Battalions of National Defence (TEA) which, headed by right-wing officers, were often terrorising political dissenters in the countryside. And it goes without saying, the army authorities were also monitoring the soldiers' vote. By moving, during elections, whole regiments into marginal constituencies, they could use the 'military vote' in order to help the 'right' candidates to get elected.⁴¹

Unfortunately, every claim in this quoted passage is inaccurate. First, during the 1951 elections, the countryside vote for the Greek Rally was higher than its national average by a mere 1 per cent, while in 1952 it was higher by 3.5 per cent, a common variation, given that in 1951 the (otherwise 'bourgeois') Liberals also did better in the countryside than their national average by 3.7 per cent. Even in 1952, the Liberal-EPEK alliance exceeded its national average in the countryside by 1 per cent.⁴² In other words, the notion that the Rally enjoyed an unusual advantage over its rivals in the countryside is pure fiction, let alone a decisive factor in determining its election victories in 1951-2. Second, an important fact which Mouzelis seems unaware of is that four weeks before the 1951 elections, the Venizelos Government 'ordered the dissolution of the TEA and MEA [...] to secure absolute fairness in the elections', a measure taken in response to the formation of the Greek Rally a week earlier.⁴³ Third, the suggestion that Papagos benefited from a process of gerrymandering associated with the movement of army units to marginal constituencies is equally unfounded. According to an Interior Ministry encyclical on 14 August 1951, soldiers were ordered to vote not in the constituencies where they were located on election-day, but 'using the ballots of the constituencies which they come from'.⁴⁴ This meant that, regardless of where different army units were moved to, the army vote could no longer change the results of marginal constituencies, because the soldiers' vote was now counted as part of their home constituencies. Finally, Mouzelis seems unaware that in 1951 and 1952 the tradition of a separate army vote was abolished, thus leaving many soldiers serving away from their homes without sufficient time to go to their constituencies to cast their ballots. In 1951, Papagos protested strongly against this measure, asking Venizelos sarcastically: 'The Prime Minister is asked, who came up with the plan of denying the vote to the army? Perhaps myself?'[45] It is clear that the Centre Governments did so deliberately to deny Papagos a few more votes.[46]

A variation on Mouzelis's argument has been put forward by Dimitris Charalambis, whose analysis was later adopted with minor adjustments by Vernardakis and Mavris. Although this reading still portrays Papagos's election as a victory of the army over Parliament, the role of the Palace is given greater importance. This is what he says:

> With the assumption of the premiership by Papagos (16.11.52) the reconstruction of bourgeois power in Greece is complete. [...] From 16.11.52 until the death of Papagos (4.10.55) the organization of power became structured around two central poles: the army (IDEA) – government (Papagos) and the pole of the monarchy. They were both nodal points whereby the defining weight fell on the first.[47]

Vernardakis and Mavris, who reproduce this excerpt *verbatim*, add that the so-called army-government pole prevailed over the Palace because it enjoyed 'American support'.[48] A major flaw in both analyses, however, is that they treat elections, voters and Parliament as passive and unimportant factors. Indeed, Charalambis goes as far as to make the absurd claim that, under Papagos, 'we have an effective abolition of Parliament'.[49] A further issue is his flawed argument that 'Papagos [...] was simultaneously the representative of IDEA at the politically legitimate domain'.[50] While Papagos was certainly protective of IDEA, the May 1951 coup clearly demonstrated that it was he who had the upper hand in their relationship, not the opposite. Consequently, the notion that Papagos was an instrument of IDEA and 'represented' their interests in Parliament cannot be treated seriously.

There is ample evidence to show that Papagos enjoyed both autonomy from and considerable authority over IDEA. For example, one of his major opponents inside the army, General Thrasivoulos Tsakalotos, likened his relationship to this organization to that of a father to a 'spoilt child', stressing that IDEA's leaders exhibited 'either real or false dedication to his personality'.[51] Papagos, of course, was always ready to use the organization's loyalty as an asset. As Kanellopoulos, his Defence Minister, later put it, 'the "IDEA" officers were [...] more Papagosites than Papagos', a view echoed by a former leader of the secret organization itself, who wrote that the Field Marshal was 'a National Hero in the hearts of all *ethnikofron* Greeks', including of course IDEA.[52] At the same time, Papagos kept an aloof attitude towards the group, partly because he knew its overzealous dictatorial views and possibly because he saw such distance as a shield of his authority over them. Markezinis, for instance, recalls that in 1948 Papagos advised him 'not to pay attention' to IDEA.[53] Kanellopoulos, who later revealed that, as Defence Minister, he 'extended his confidence also to officers [he] suspected that had once belonged to "IDEA"', spoke about the antagonisms between the organization and the Papagos government of 1952–5. In his view, these disputes influenced the organization's decision not to disband after Papagos became prime minister, an assessment shared by others.[54] Kanellopoulos also noted that IDEA chose to extend its life because it suspected Papagos of making too many 'overtures' and this led it to adopt the role of 'guarding him' 'invisibly'.[55] One of these 'overtures', he says, was his own appointment as Defence Minister, with generals Socratis Dimaratos, Spyridon Georgoulis and Sergios Gyalistras as Deputy-Ministers. All were viewed suspiciously by IDEA, either because they were seen as moderates or potentially disloyal to the prime minister.[56]

Besides overstating IDEA's influence over Papagos, other accounts have argued that the Rally's rise to power resulted from direct US intervention after the outbreak of the Korean War. According to this view, the US embassy set in motion a secret plan, commonly known as 'the Papagos solution', which envisaged the transfer of power from the elected government to the chief of the army in case a parliamentary government proved unable to protect Greece's security. This view was put forward by several influential non-scholarly accounts, like those of Andreas Papandreou, Spyros Linardatos, Tassos Vournas, Potis Paraskevopoulos and others,[57] but it is widely shared among some scholars. John Iatrides, for example, says:

> At first the Papagos 'solution', which Greek rightist elements had been advocating for some time, was resisted by other American officials, including ambassador Henry Grady and initially, his successor, Peurifoy. Although Grady objected to a Papagos government on grounds of both principle and appearance, Peurifoy was concerned with the Palace's indignation over what was seen as Papagos's duplicity regarding his political ambitions [...]. Nevertheless, by 1952 the United States' government was convinced that Papagos offered the best assurance for the successes of American policy in Greece.[58]

Similarly, Van Coufoudakis has argued that:

> It was only with the increasing Cold War tension throughout the world, the frustration of the petty partisan politics of Greece, the growing red scare in the United States, and the outbreak of the Korean War that American officials seriously considered the possibility of an 'evolution to dictatorship' in Greece. The overwhelming conservative victory under Alexander Papagos in the 1952 elections was engineered by the dynamic intervention of Ambassador John Peurifoy.[59]

Similar conclusions have been put forward by Constantine Tsoukalas, Mouzelis, Pelt, Stefanidis and others.[60]

It is worth focusing briefly on Stefanidis's arguments, because his account is based on more recently released American and British archives. According to him, 'Ambassador Peurifoy has been instrumental in bringing the Greek Rally to power', a conclusion which he says is backed by 'a series of verified evidence'.[61] When we turn to this evidence, we find that it boils down to two substantive findings. The first is that 'the environment of Papagos was throughout this period in constant contact with the US embassy and on 26 July [1951] Markezinis informed the embassy about Papagos's plan to attract candidates from both the Right and the Centre'. The second is that 'Peurifoy offered to exert his influence so that the tension between Papagos and the King is diffused'.[62] Although both conclusions are accurate, neither shows that Peurifoy was in any way 'instrumental' in bringing Papagos to power. The first claim reveals that the US embassy learned about Papagos's decision to form a new party only four days before the news was made public. But this indicates neither US support nor active involvement. If anything, it suggests that the US embassy, rather astonishingly, knew nothing about Papagos's decision to stand for election until it was too late for it to act.[63] Moreover, Stefanidis overlooks evidence showing that throughout the months following his resignation from the army, Papagos successfully deceived the US embassy, to the point that Peurifoy seriously believed that he had no intention to enter politics. On 11 June 1951 the US ambassador told Washington that the 'Marshal has repeatedly stated during last two weeks that he will not enter politics and we believe he is wholly sincere'.[64] Subsequent correspondence between Peurifoy and Washington confirms that the US ambassador held on to this impression until late July. As for Stefanidis's second point, that following Papagos's resignation from the army Peurifoy mediated to diffuse the tension between him and the King, it is surprising that the content of this mediation is not discussed. As we shall see, however, Peurifoy's intervention intended to reinstate the Field Marshal as commander-in-chief of the armed forces, not to help him to become prime minister. In other words, far from supporting Papagos's plans to enter politics, the US ambassador's mediation in June 1951 actively aimed to block them.

The failure of the 'Papagos solution'

Some of the accounts discussed above have linked Papagos's rise to power to the enactment of the so-called Papagos solution. This scenario, which began to circulate in 1948, envisaged the formation of an extra-parliamentary government under the premiership of Marshal Papagos.[65] Its implementation brought together a network of diverse actors, which included the US and British embassies, the Palace, IDEA, some parliamentarians, the newspaper owner Dimitris Lambrakis and the shipping tycoon, Bodossakis.[66] Despite several attempts to carry it out, the plan was never implemented. Because of its repeated failures, the Papagos-Markezinis pair ultimately resolved to abandon it in favour of the more viable option of winning power through elections. But let us take things from the start.

The first to speak about a 'Papagos solution' was Markezinis himself.[67] Between November 1948 and August 1950, the Field Marshal's aide was in close contact with the Palace and the British and US embassies to secure support for the appointment of Papagos as head of an extra-parliamentary government.[68] As he later disclosed, Markezinis at that time 'promoted the Papagos solution at all levels'. He appears to have made no distinction between a Papagos dictatorship directly appointed by the Palace and an extra-parliamentary government headed by the Field Marshal that would enjoy the confidence of Parliament – although he appeared to favour the security of the latter option.[69] Either way, the aim of this politician who, according to the British embassy, had a 'thoroughly Machiavellian mind', was to see Papagos in power, so that he could, on his own admission, succeed him as prime minister.[70] Ironically, Markezinis's instrumentalism was met with similar machinations by the Palace, IDEA, and the US and British embassies who, each for their own aims, wanted to use the Papagos-Markezinis pair in different ways. This state of affairs soon led to the rise of at least four competing versions of the 'Papagos solution'.

Besides Markezinis's original plan, the second version was that of the Palace. Since November 1948, the royal couple and the chief of the King's civil bureau, Aristides Metaxas, held discussions with Markezinis about the possibility of appointing Papagos at the head of a transitional government. Everyone hoped that Papagos could receive a vote of confidence in Parliament and rule with an iconic assembly but, if this were to prove impossible, the King was willing to dissolve Parliament and empower Papagos to rule by decree. This plan was first discussed at the Tatoi Palace on 20 November 1948, in Papagos's presence.[71] The royal version of the 'Papagos solution', however, suffered from several defects. First, it met with opposition from Pipinelis, the King's maverick advisor and Permanent Undersecretary for Foreign Affairs, who viewed Markezinis as his *bête noire* in a struggle for royal favour. Pipinelis, who carried sway with the British embassy, persuaded Ambassador Clifford Norton to block the plan on the grounds that Parliament would refuse to grant Papagos a confidence vote. Norton agreed and resolved that 'the King should not nominate a Prime Minister from outside the political parties, unless and until the bankruptcy of those parties is clearly shown'.[72] A more serious defect, however, was Papagos's own reluctance to play the part expected of him. In the eleventh hour, he developed cold feet and proposed Markezinis as a more suitable choice of prime minister. Markezinis, who realized that at that early stage in his career was unsuitable for the role, declined, and the plan was indefinitely postponed. The only tangible outcome was Papagos's appointment to the rank of Field-Marshal in January 1949, with extended powers over the conduct of the Civil War.[73]

The Palace version of the 'Papagos solution' was revived in August 1950, during the crisis that brought down the Plastiras Government. The royal couple, again, proposed to appoint Papagos to the premiership and this time the Field Marshal agreed. However, when he visited the Tatoi Palace on 21 August, he was presented with a cabinet list prepared for him by the royals and their advisors. More surprisingly still, Markezinis's name was missing from the list, although the Palace knew that he was Papagos's closest ally. At that point it became clear that the royals intended to use Papagos as 'puppet prime minister' and, after consulting with Markezinis, the Field Marshal pulled out of the plan.[74] This was the moment when his relations with the Palace became irreparably damaged.[75]

The third version of the 'Papagos solution' was that of the IDEA officers. In April 1949, the secret organization issued an encyclical proclaiming that 'only one solution exists' to end Greece's troubles, and that was 'the Dictatorship of IDEA'. The encyclical gave no clues as to the timing of the dictatorship, but let it be understood that some lengthy preparation was required until the organization's programme was 'propagated to the People'.[76] IDEA always regarded Papagos as their natural leader,[77] a fact that became explicit during the abortive coup of 30–31 May 1951. However, the flaws of their version of the plan were numerous. First, the group never appears to have secured support from either the Palace or the US embassy for an IDEA dictatorship led by Papagos. Second, apart from the newspaper *Ethnikos Kyrix*, which openly backed their views, the organization had no allies in the mainstream press. Judging by the line of *Ethnikos Kyrix*, which was openly 'in favour of Papagos becoming semi-dictator', it appears that IDEA was also hostile to the Palace and the British embassy.[78] Third, it is unlikely that IDEA knew much about Papagos's own plans and although they saw him as their patron, they never appear to have earned his confidence for their adventurist designs. Both their ill-informed response to Papagos's resignation on 30–31 May 1951 and their surprise at hearing his reprimand after launching their coup that night suggest that there was no coordination between them. Indeed, on the morning of 31 May, Papagos arrived to the scene and angrily told the coup leaders: 'Do you realize how much harm you are causing me?'[79] According to another account, Papagos said that 'these gentlemen have caused the greatest mischief both to the country and me personally'.[80] Consequently, IDEA's version of the 'Papagos solution' was ineffectual also because it never secured the Field Marshal's own support.

The fourth version was that of the State Department and the Foreign Office who, as we saw, decided to keep the 'Papagos solution' as an 'extraordinary' plan to be activated only 'in the event that all other means to achieve a more stable Greek government had failed'.[81] As a CIA report explained in 1950, the main drawback of such a scenario was its anticipated harmful effects on the image of the United States inasmuch as it would link its major intervention in Greece with the imposition of a dictatorial government: 'Although a government under Papagos would probably enjoy the support of many Greeks, its authoritarian implications would have unfavourable repercussions on world opinion', it said.[82] While several US documents on this subject are still classified, available records suggest that Washington firmly adhered to this policy until the formation of the Greek Rally in July 1951.[83] Much like Markezinis, Acheson was also undecided over the specific form which the 'Papagos solution' should take – although he marginally favoured the variant which required parliamentary endorsement. To this effect in March 1951 he instructed Peurifoy that 'the Papagos solution should not be encouraged except in the event that all other means to achieve a more stable Greek Government had failed and then such a solution should if possible follow constitutional practices'.[84] However, from January to July 1951, the US and British embassies began to sense a change around the 'Papagos solution'. On 4 January 1951, Yost reported that Markezinis had told him that 'the Marshal continues to be averse to becoming Prime Minister except as the result of elections' and remarked that 'the Court is reported to continue to look with disfavor upon the Markezinis['s] version of the Papagos solution'.[85] In February, Norton reported that the reputed rift between the Palace and the Field Marshal (which had started back in August) was real: 'A tiff [...] I heard recently occurred between the King and Papagos', he said. On 9 March 1951 Peurifoy also wrote that the 'Papagos solution has experienced setback as [a] result [of the] inept behavior [of] his supporters during [the] recent crisis and [the] current coolness between Marshal and palace which undoubtedly exists'.[86] Despite these complications, the US embassy still hoped to mend relations between Papagos and the King to prevent the former from entering parliamentary politics, a prospect that would wreck the 'Papagos solution' as a plan of the last resort. As Peurifoy remarked (well after the outbreak of the Korean War), the US embassy saw 'no reason [to] encourage Papagos'

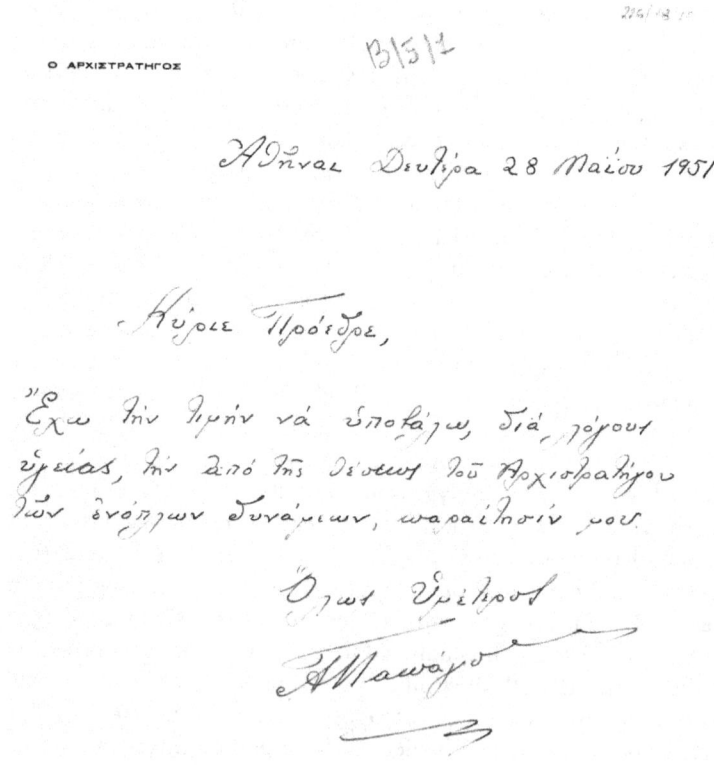

Image 2 Field Marshal Papagos's resignation letter from the leadership of the armed forces, dated 28 May 1951. It says: 'Mr President, I have the honour to submit, for health reasons, my resignation from the post of Field Marshal of the armed forces. All Yours, signature'. Sophocles Venizelos Papers, Benaki Museum Historical Archive.

solution unless international situation worsens or all other means [to] achieve stabler Government fail'.[87] Nevertheless, Papagos's dispute with the Palace was too deep and this led him to resign from the armed forces on 28 May 1951 in order to put an end to the various plots carrying his name.[88] The US embassy was slow to grasp the real motives behind his move and in early June Peurifoy held several one-to-one meetings with the King and Papagos in order to reinstate the latter in the army and keep the 'Papagos solution' alive.[89] After a few days, however, he realized that such an outcome was unlikely and soon all references to the 'Papagos solution' vanished from Peurifoy's correspondence with Washington.

Besides their individual shortcomings, all versions of the 'Papagos solution' shared one common flaw: none, including Markezinis's own, ever received the full endorsement of Papagos himself, the man who was expected to carry them out. In the abortive Palace coup of November 1948, Papagos developed cold feet and proposed Markezinis for the premiership. In August 1950, he initially agreed to lead a royal coup, but then refused when he discovered that the Palace expected him to act as a 'puppet prime minister'. On 31 May 1951, he dismissed IDEA's intervention which required him to resume the leadership of the army and keep the organization's dictatorial plans alive. Finally, in June 1951, he resisted Peurifoy's efforts to reinstate him as commander-in chief to keep the US-British emergency plan intact. Especially after the second setback of August 1950, Papagos appears to have concluded that his only viable route to power was to disassociate himself from all versions of the 'Papagos solution' and make his own independent bid for power through the ballot box.

The role of the US embassy and the Rally's rise to power

To understand the nature of Papagos's venture after his resignation from the army, it is vital to realize that his autonomy grew as soon as he distanced himself from all versions of the 'Papagos solution'. When he founded the Greek Rally party on 30 July 1951, the US embassy, far from lending him support, expressed scepticism towards the prospect of his rise to power. One of several drawbacks it saw in a future Papagos government was the overconcentration of power in the hands of one leader, an outcome that could precipitate a decline of US political influence. These apprehensions were expressed on 24 August 1951 by Acheson, who warned against the consequences of Papagos's 'oft-announced position [of the] necessity [that] Gr[ee]ks conduct their own affairs'.[90] Another fear was the unpredictability of a future Rally Government, a development that could increase the influence of the army in politics and trigger strong reactions by the Palace and the Centre parties. Following a conversation with Yost in early 1952, the Liberal former minister Constantine Tsatsos reported to his party that 'the Americans are seriously worried about the issue of the relationship between the Rally and the Crown. Another reason for which they fear the Rally is the intransigent tone displayed by the Rally vis-à-vis the Crown. They fear complications if it were to come to power alone'.[91] Moreover, an elected government headed by Papagos meant that the United States would be left without an emergency plan in the event of an external attack or a major crisis in Greece. For these reasons, the State Department adopted a strategy of anchoring Papagos onto the rest of the *Ethnikofron* party system to curb his autonomy and influence.

Already before the Field Marshal's resignation from the army, Acheson and Peurifoy (who was in Washington at the time) were trying to merge the Liberals and EPEK, to pave the ground for a new Centre coalition with Plastiras as prime minister. As Acheson and Peurifoy jointly advised the US embassy, their aim was to 'continue [to] encourage Liberal-EPEK merger' and 'point out to King that premiership for Plastiras might well be price worth paying for merger Liberal and EPEK'.[92] Regarding Papagos, who was suspected of planning to stand in the next election, Acheson and Peurifoy instructed the embassy to ask the King to forbid him to do so. 'Palace might be willing [to] suggest that he issue statement disclaiming any intention to participate [in the] forthcoming elections', they wrote.[93] Two weeks later, however, Papagos did the exact opposite. He resigned from the army to stand in the next elections without issuing any public disclaimers.

Upon hearing this news, Peurifoy rushed back to Athens and met Papagos on 1st June. Far from encouraging him to 'enter politics', he requested (and received false assurances to this effect from Kanellopoulos) that the Field-Marshal 'will not enter politics'.[94] For the rest of June and July, Peurifoy focused his efforts on persuading the King and Venizelos to restore Papagos as commander-in-chief.[95] So determined was he in attaining this outcome, that on 6 June 1951 he told the State Department 'it would probably be possible to obtain restoration of Marshal by ultimatum to palace' (because in the meantime the King had assumed the leadership of the armed forces and blocked Papagos's return).[96] Although Peurifoy never issued that ultimatum, he still used threatening language with the King. On 24 August, he told Paul that he 'was gravely concerned by recent partisan polit[ical] activities of Palace which boded ill'. The King replied that he would 'engage no more in such activities'. The US ambassador also threatened to 'issue a statement' denying allegations of US involvement in the so-called Papagos Affair, which the Palace had leaked to the liberal *Eleftheria*. Again, the King replied that 'he sincerely hoped this w[ou]ld not be necessary'.[97] The serialized *Eleftheria* story, entitled 'The Papagos Affair', claimed that in 1948, Marshall Plan director Averell Harriman and ECA's chief Paul Nevin were involved in a plot to make Papagos prime minister. Despite Peurifoy's warnings, *Eleftheria* continued to serialize the story until the US embassy issued a statement on 29 August strongly denying the allegations.[98] Throughout the next four weeks, Peurifoy never appears to have grasped that, apart from the King's and Venizelos's opposition, Papagos also refused to be reinstated as commander-in-chief. Consequently, when elections were proclaimed on 30 July and Papagos announced his candidacy, Norton informed London that the news had come 'as a great surprise to everybody', including the King.[99] Nevertheless, Markezinis, as we saw, had prepared Yost four days earlier, but this did not stop Peurifoy from reporting to Washington on 31 July that Papagos's candidacy introduced an 'entirely new element into [the] political situation'. For this reason, his initial recommendation was for the United States to adopt 'strict impartiality'.[100]

3. Structures of Post-Civil War System

Two days later, in his first thorough assessment of the situation, Peurifoy asked Washington to approve his proposal to 'refrain from intervention or public comment on Papagos entry into politics except as we may wish informally to deny rumors that Americans encouraged his action'. In the same message, he analysed the situation as follows: 'Should Papagos gain control of government, administration would probably become more firm [...] and ECA program would benefit'; but he went on to list the main drawbacks of such an outcome:

> Real disadvantage of Papagos entry into politics is long term one which has hitherto persuaded Dep[artmen]t and Emb[assy] to consider him last card for use in great emergency. Artificial and probably temporary crystallization of political forces around Marshal will interrupt gradual normalization of Greek polit[ical] life.[101]

After the elections of 9 September 1951, which produced another fragile Liberal-EPEK coalition, Papagos, as leader of the largest party in Parliament, immediately demanded new elections. Far from endorsing his calls, Peurifoy wrote to Washington proposing (and obtaining approval for) a policy that would 'put whole weight behind [the] prevention [of] new elections'.[102] The United States then began to encourage the formation of a Liberal-Rally coalition, but Venizelos, who was not entirely opposed to the idea, preferred this time to join a coalition with EPEK. The main stumbling block against this scenario was, again, Papagos, who rejected the notion of any coalition government and continued to demand new elections, despite special pleas from the Palace.[103] Throughout the next six months, the US embassy adhered to the same policy, as both American and Greek sources confirm. In a record of his conversation with Yost, most probably on 4 February, Tsatsos found that 'the Americans do not want elections [...]. They want the solution of a Rally-Liberal coalition for this reason, to avert elections'. This 'solution', he added, was proposed by 'the Americans' because they 'lack confidence in the Rally'.[104] On 7 February 1952, Yost proposed again to Venizelos the 'possibility [of] Rally-Lib coalition without elections', but while the latter was amenable to the idea, once more, during a secret meeting with the King, Papagos 'proposed immediate elections based on a majority system' or short-term support for a transitional Liberal government after which he would consider all options.[105]

At this point, Acheson sought and obtained support from President Truman for an adjustment to US policy to enable 'the inclusion of General Papagos along with Mr. Venizelos in a three-party coalition', possibly followed by new elections to be held 'on a majority voting system'.[106] However, after resisting the previous plan of a two-party Liberal-Rally coalition, Papagos, once again, rejected the new American proposal of a tripartite coalition. On 23 February 1952, following a meeting with Venizelos in Lisbon, Acheson reported that the Greek leader of the Liberals 'had been willing to join in a three-party coalition, but Papagos had shown no disposition to accept this formula. Instead, he was campaigning for new and early elections'.[107] In other words, not only was the US embassy in this period pursuing an agenda that did not envisage a majority Papagos government, but all its plans to tie the Rally in a coalition government were boycotted by Papagos because they ran against his ambitions.

An issue that has attracted much attention in the historiography was Peurifoy's public interventions in 1952 in support of the majority voting system. In March of that year, the US ambassador managed to persuade Plastiras to accept the majority voting system and immediately proceeded to issue a public statement in which he praised the 'patriotic stance' of EPEK's leader. However, because Plastiras's junior coalition partner, the Liberals, were secretly preparing a bill to block the adoption of the majority voting system, Peurifoy issued a further statement using threatening language. This said:

> The re-introduction of proportional representation with the inevitable effect of continuous government instability would have such disastrous implications on the effective use of American aid to Greece, that the American embassy considers itself obliged to proceed with the present statement of support for the prime minister on this particular issue.[108]

There is no question that this statement constituted yet another blatant intervention by Peurifoy in domestic Greek affairs. Even the new British ambassador, Charles Peake, reported to London that the US ambassador's views 'were somewhat bluntly expressed', stressing that this provoked 'a tart rejoinder from the Government and [...] remarkably vicious anti-American articles'.[109] Indeed, Peurifoy himself later felt obliged to defend his actions to the State Department and, in an implicit admission of error, promised to ensure that 'in future our interference is limited to indispensable minimum and carried out as discreetly and inconspicuously as possible'.[110]

Many historians, however, have presented Peurifoy's provocative intervention as the high point of an alleged American plan to promote Papagos to the premiership. Coufoudakis has argued that Papagos's victory in 1952 'was engineered by the dynamic intervention of Ambassador John Peurifoy' and the latter's 'determination of the electoral law utilized in the elections'. Mouzelis asserts that 'under strong American pressure, a new electoral law adopted the principle of majority representation, and with the help of this law the Greek Rally in the November elections secured 49.3 per cent of the total vote'. The same argument has been put forward by Tsoukalas, Linardatos, Paraskevopoulos, Stefanidis, Iatrides and others.[111]

This interpretation, however, seriously confuses Peurifoy's heavy-handed intervention with an alleged secret plan to bring Papagos to power. To understand this crucial distinction, a number of hitherto obscured factors must be brought to light. First, US policy had been consistently pressing for the adoption of majority voting in Greece since the late 1940s, that is long before the Greek Rally was founded. This policy reflected Washington's belief that through this voting system the sequence of fragile coalition governments that threatened the unity of the *Ethnikofron* state would come to an end.[112] Second, in the 1950 elections and prior to the 1951 elections, that is when Papagos was still in the army, the main beneficiary of this electoral system would have been Plastiras's centre-left EPEK. Yet Peurifoy supported the majority system with the same vigour back then, despite objections from the right-wing Popular Party and Venizelos's Liberals.¹¹³ Third, in July 1951, the US embassy used its influence to force electoral law 1878/51, which replaced simple proportional representation with a less proportional variant, in the context of a gradual transition to the majority voting system. According to the psephologist Elias Nikolakopoulos, the electoral system of 1951 was intended to weaken all small parties and strengthen the middle-sized ones, regardless of their ideological orientation, except of course for the Left. As he explains, the voting system was

> specifically adapted to suit the common objective of the right and center parties to exclude the left from the second count, [and to also suit] the objective of the Liberals to deter the Democratic Socialist Party [of Papandreou] and [fulfill] the intention of the Popular Party to prevent the development of LEK.¹¹⁴

The political scientist Jean Meynaud has also argued that the aim of that electoral system was 'to favour large blocs, so that the conditions of more satisfactory government stability are put in place', while another motive, he observed, 'which explains the pressure of the American embassy in favour of this change' was 'concern about the exclusion of EDA from the second count'.¹¹⁵ Despite these analyses, most proponents of the dependence narrative never speak about Peurifoy's bold intervention in 1951 to make the voting system less proportional, but focus only on his intervention in 1952. Even so, what Peurifoy did in 1952 was an extension of his interventions in the previous year. Fourth, with the Rally's massive share of the vote in 1952, which stood at 49.3 per cent, Papagos would still have secured a crushing majority in Parliament even under the previous voting system. This view was shared at the time by the Rally leadership and conveyed by Markezinis to the British embassy.¹¹⁶ For this reason, the Rally, i.e. the party whose hopes of winning supposedly rested on the new electoral law, *voted against* the majority system on the grounds that it was 'unfair'!¹¹⁷ This key fact, however, is completely silenced by proponents of the dependence thesis. Finally, it is worth stressing that the variant of the majority system which was ultimately adopted in 1952 was aptly described by Nikolakopoulos as 'very clearly favouring the Centre parties' and largely based on the system used in 1923 which 'scandalously favoured the Venizelist camp'.¹¹⁸ Naturally, this was yet another reason behind its rejection by the Greek Rally.

One of the key issues which have been systematically confused in the historiography is why Plastiras accepted the majority system. According to some proponents of the dependence narrative, EPEK's leader did so either because he was 'senile' or 'ill' and was therefore easily 'tricked' by Peurifoy. Other accounts have claimed that he was 'enmeshed in the web of "agents"' or that he was 'strongly pressed' by the US ambassador.¹¹⁹ Without citing any sources, Linardatos contends that Plastiras was influenced by 'fortune tellers and mediums, who reassured him of his guaranteed victory'.¹²⁰ All these conclusions, however, are based on the same premise, namely that Plastiras had no rational motive behind accepting the majority system as this was supposedly predestined to drive him to a certain electoral meltdown. This assumption, however, implies that in March 1952, Plastiras could have anticipated the dramatic developments that caused a sharp decline in popularity of the Centre parties in subsequent months. Yet, this postulate has been invented to sustain the notion that Peurifoy's intervention in favour of the majority system was part of a secret policy to make Papagos prime minister.

Nevertheless, on the basis of EPEK's performance six months earlier, which is the baseline most professional politicians would use, Plastiras had good reasons to believe that, through a pact with the Liberals, EPEK could clearly benefit from the majority system. In the 1951 elections, the two Centre parties had jointly received 43.4 per cent against 43.2 per cent for the Rally and Popular Party combined. In contrast to EPEK and the Liberals, who were contemplating a merger, the Rally and Popular Party were caught up in stiff competition, thus making it logical to expect that the latter, no matter how badly it would do, would still deny the Rally crucial votes, giving the EPEK-Liberal alliance the marginal advantage they needed to win. Furthermore, Plastiras clearly believed that an extensive degree of tactical voting would enable him to win additional votes from the Party of George Papandreou and a sizeable portion from EDA, as the version of the majority system which EPEK endorsed was specifically designed to deny both these parties any representation in Parliament at all. In other words, if EPEK could still perform marginally worse than in 1951, the majority system would have returned Plastiras to the premiership with a comfortable majority. This was not an imaginary scenario, but the main prediction of its Machiavellian opponents in the Palace at that time. As late as 27 August 1952, General Constantine Ventiris told Peurifoy that the Palace was concerned that the majority system would weaken the King's allies, Venizelos's Liberals, as it would force them 'to coalesce with EPEK' and believed that 'their support plus that of many Commies might well lead to sweeping EPEK victory'.[121]

The above did not factor in the additional benefits for EPEK arising from the extensive process of gerrymandering that Plastiras's electoral law introduced in September 1952. One example cited by Nikolakopoulos is the conversion of Athens into a single 25-seat super-constituency in which the winning party would win all twenty-five seats. Although in 1951 the three Centre parties had won in Athens a combined total of 40.3 per cent against 40.1 per cent for the Rally and the Popular Party combined, EDA provided an additional pool of 19.5 per cent from which Plastiras expected to attract a substantial share of tactical votes (as the new electoral law denied EDA any representation). Another example was the abolition of the provision enabling soldiers to vote in their barracks under a separate 'military vote', a measure intended to reduce the strong Rally vote within the army (which in 1951 stood at 53.4 per cent compared to 36.5 nationally). Now, soldiers serving in distant places would be discouraged from travelling to their home constituencies to vote.[122] Indeed, as the British embassy noted, the three main reasons which led the Rally to vote against the new electoral law in Parliament were: (a) the 'division of the country into constituencies of widely differing size', (b) the denial of the vote 'to women' and (c) its denial to soldiers 'not residing in their place of registration'.[123] In other words, if the EPEK-Liberal coalition finally lost the November 1952 elections, this had little to do with the majority voting system. As was already shown above, even if the Centre parties had marginally underperformed in relation to 1951, the new voting system would still have enabled them to form a stable government under Plastiras. But Peurifoy's intervention had no effect in making Papagos win 49.3 per cent of the vote.

The real causes of Plastiras's disastrous defeat in 1952, however, must be sought in a chain of dramatic events which have been hitherto understated or silenced in the dependence narrative. A key factor was the Rally's success in securing the backing of eight out of the country's twelve national newspapers. These included the six traditional right-wing newspapers (*Acropolis, Ethnos, Kathimerini, Ethnikos Kiryx, Embros, Estia*) but thanks to Markezinis, the influential liberal papers *To Vima* and *Ta Nea*, both owned by his friend Dimitris Lambrakis, abandoned their historic affiliation to the Centre and switched to Papagos. This was yet another example of how watery the boundaries between the so-called right and centre were. The successful manipulation of the liberal press by the Rally's leaders was considered so important, that when faced with the dilemma, Markezinis sacrificed the support of the Palace for Lambrakis's newspapers. When Queen Frederica demanded explanations, he replied:

> One need not be exceptionally intelligent to understand that one line for the King in 'To Vima' or 'Ta Nea' is worth more than many articles by your friend Vendiris. [...] You advise me to leave Lambrakis. I have no reason to leave him.[124]

In an era when radio was the only other medium of nationwide political communication, the support of the press was vitally important for any political party aspiring to win power. For this reason, a fortnight after the Rally was formed, the Centrist *Eleftheria* named the eight newspapers backing Papagos and publicly challenged them to justify their choice. Five right-wing newspapers immediately replied and defended their position, but Lambrakis's newspapers ignored the call.[125]

An even more important factor behind the Centre's defeat in 1952 was the usually overlooked mass defections of Liberal and EPEK deputies to the Rally in the months preceding the November election. So damaging were these defections, that one historian aptly described them as 'the suicide of the Centre parties'.[126] Already before the scale of this crisis became apparent, the US embassy and the Palace predicted that the party most likely to suffer in the next election was Venizelos's Liberals, who were considered 'so weakened' that they would not obtain 'even 15 per cent' (compared to 19 per cent in 1951).[127] However, after May 1952 the entire ruling coalition began to crumble, seeing its parliamentary majority reduced from two to one seats following the defection of Constantine Venetis from EPEK to the Rally. This development was considered so serious, that Plastiras publicly accused him of having 'lost his sense of honour' and advised him to 'commit suicide'![128] On 31 July 1952, a similar scene reoccurred when Liberal deputy Dionysios Manendis also left the majority benches to sit as an independent, thus reducing the number of government deputies to 129 (out of 258).[129] Although technically the Liberal-EPEK coalition could still govern with support from independents, a major political crisis erupted when George Papandreou, leader of the third Centre party, issued a surprise attack against Plastiras's EPEK for having supposedly 'undermined national security, gotten itself involved in rampant corruption, [...] and caused a deep economic crisis'. Papandreou then called on his former Liberal-EPEK coalition partners 'to resign' from government because they had lost their parliamentary majority after Menendis's defection.[130] At that point, Papandreou was involved in secret talks with Papagos about joining the Rally tickets to rescue his parliamentary seat. His damaging attack against his fellow Centre leaders was the price he had to pay for that seat.

Ten days later, two more Liberal deputies, Stelios Choutas and Dimitris Ioannou, also announced their departure from the government benches. This new setback forced Plastiras to seek support from two non-communist deputies from the left-wing EDA, Michalis Kyrkos and Leonidas Karamaounas, who instantly joined EPEK and restored the government majority to 129 deputies.[131] However, in a confidence vote on 22 August, the EPEK-Liberal coalition received only 127 votes, two short of an absolute majority, because one Liberal deputy was unwell and another, Gerassimos Lychnos, decided not to support it.[132] Despite the result, the Liberal-EPEK government held on to power for a few more weeks, with tacit support from the Palace, until new elections were called for 16 November.[133]

The final act in the drama of the Centre's meltdown came soon after the majority system bill passed through Parliament on 12 September. As already noted, one of its provisions was to deny any parliamentary representation to parties receiving below 17 per cent nationally, a clause that made it impossible for EDA to win any seats. Since Plastiras's aim was to win by forcing some EDA's supporters to tactically vote for him, on 27 September, EPEK's mouthpiece *Allagi* published an article that praised the wartime communist-led resistance organization EAM on the eleventh anniversary of its formation. The article, however, caused a major stir inside EPEK and among the ardently anti-communist Liberals, forcing the latter to issue a *communiqué* 'condemning unreservedly the hymns which were sung in the past few days about EAM'.[134] This reaction forced Plastiras to intervene on 30 September with a front-page article in *Eleftheria* that stressed the difference between 'EAM as the Trojan Horse of KKE', which should stay 'outside the framework of the nation', and the 'individuals associated' with EAM, who should be permitted 'to return to the ranks of the nation'.[135] These explanations, however, satisfied neither the Centre parties nor the left. To rescue their seats, new waves of defections from the Centre to the Rally were unleashed. In what the liberal press called an 'Apostasy' and a 'betrayal', twenty-four Centre politicians, including Tsouderos, joined the Rally tickets on 19 October, while two days later, eleven more Liberal deputies, including some former ministers, followed suit.[136] To add insult to injury, on the same day, the Secretary of the Communist Party in exile, Nikos Zachariadis, issued his well-known statement instructing EDA supporters not to vote for Plastiras because he was 'trying to trick the people'.[137] As a result, EDA's vote in November 1952 was not significantly reduced by any tactical voting towards Plastiras.

As the crisis of the Liberal-EPEK government deepened, the US embassy started to look towards the prospect of a one-party Rally Government as the only available choice. Although official evidence on this period is unavailable, in a little-known book published in 1980, Yost recalled that Papagos 'received the American blessing' before the elections of 1952.[138] By this time, however, Plastiras's defeat looked certain and any prospect of government stability in Greece was unavoidably linked to a Rally victory. However, as late as August 1952, Acheson was issuing instructions to Peurifoy to work with the King to form a tripartite Rally-Liberal-EPEK coalition to introduce currency reform.[139] This US-sponsored plan which, as we saw, was met with the Rally's rejection (because it did not promise immediate elections, but only after '5–6 months'),[140] was still in line with Washington's strategy of tying Papagos to the Centre to limit his autonomy and delay his rise to power. Only when this scenario fell through in August (owing to misgivings by some Centre politicians) did US policy abandon its previous reservations against a one-party Rally Government. In so doing, however, Washington was bowing to the inevitable, as the apostasy of the Liberal-EPEK deputies had already started and Papagos's election victory seemed unavoidable.

The populist character of the Greek Rally

To say that Papagos rose to power neither because of an American plan nor an intervention by the army should not imply that his election to the premiership marked a triumph of democratic politics. As he himself remarked once, the Greek Rally was 'not a party in the usual [...] meaning of the word'. Both its structure and political strategy bore little resemblance to modern parliamentary or bureaucratic parties. By contrast, its highly personalistic character, organization and mode of political communication bore the main hallmarks of a populist movement[141] whose aim was to mobilize diverse masses of *Ethnikofron* voters around the charismatic figure of Field Marshal Papagos. Even its own supporters in the press cared little that the Rally lacked a policy programme and a clear ideological orientation. What they proudly emphasized was the slogan that Papagos is 'the man Greece needs' and appeared to like the fact that he 'has no specific programme'.[142]

Drawing on the body of theory on populism, this section shall argue that the Rally must be conceptualized as the first mass populist party in post-war Greece. Despite the diverse approaches involved in defining populism, there is some consensus in the scholarship regarding the main features of the phenomenon. First, populist parties rely on a centralized, personalistic structure, marked by what Weber has called 'charismatic authority', a type of leadership associated with individuals who are seen as 'extraordinary', 'heroic' and 'endowed with [...] exceptional powers or qualities'. In contrast to 'traditional' or 'bureaucratic' authority, Weber points out that a charismatic leader is someone who 'repudiates the past', a trait which applies to a greater extent to all founders of new movements, like Papagos.[143] Second, as many scholars have remarked, populism relies on 'the vertical relation between the populist leader and his/her followers'. This means that the dominant form of political communication between the leader and his/her supporters takes a direct and informal manner which bypasses traditional intermediary institutions.[144] Third, as Ernesto Laclau pointed out, 'there is no populism without [the] discursive construction of an enemy'. The articulation of a Manichean worldview as a means of constructing 'an internal frontier dividing the social space into two camps', is an essential feature of populism. Often the camp to which the movement belongs consists of the so-called people or nation, whose members are held to be sincere, hardworking, underprivileged and patriotic, while the hostile camp is dismissed as representing 'the *ancient regime*, the oligarchy, the Establishment or whatever'.[145] Fourth, despite some disagreement on this question, much of the scholarship treats populism as a political movement averse to political ideas, stressing its 'loose' or 'thin' ideological character. As Laclau argued, populism deliberately deploys 'imprecise and fluctuating' language and relies on 'the exaltation and intensification of emotions'.[146]

All these characteristics were inscribed in the structure of the Greek Rally. Its leader was never elected but assumed his position before the party was formed. On 30 July 1951, Papagos read a brief message to the press in which he announced his intention to participate in the next election and called on 'the Greeks to invest [him] with their trust, to rid Greece from its lack of governability'.[147] His party still had no name, no formal membership, and when it was called 'Greek Rally' a week later,[148] little followed in terms of defining its formal institutions and programme. So personal was Papagos's political venture that, when asked by a journalist about his planned programme, he replied: 'My programme? Don't you think the Greek people have had enough and are tired of programmes that are announced and never implemented?'[149] In the four years of its life, the Rally never held a founding (or any other) conference, never appears to have had a constitution and never had a central committee. One document claiming to be the party's manifesto mysteriously appeared in 1952, but when asked to defend it, Papagos denounced it as a fake.[150] Although the caucuses of LEK and Markezinis's New Party as well as the Reservist Officers' and War Veterans' clubs[151] formed the pillars of its national network, these associations could not do much in terms of providing a rank-and-file apparatus. LEK and the New Party were themselves recent formations and their combined share of the vote stood roughly at 10 per cent, while the various officers' associations had little experience in electioneering.[152] As Karamanlis, a LEK deputy then, would later remark, 'the newly formed party [LEK] was a failure... We would have certainly sunk had Field Marshal Papagos not decided in the meantime to enter politics'.[153] According to Ambassador Norton, Papagos's 'prestige [was] great enough to ensure widespread support', an assessment shared by his successor, Peake, who attributed the Rally's election victories to its leader's 'own personality'.[154] Already before his resignation from the army, the CIA concluded that Papagos 'enjoys considerable popularity as the result of his military leadership' and reckoned that if he stood for election 'his prestige would win him overwhelming popular support'.[155]

Papagos was never an effective orator. Markezinis later admitted that the Field-Marshal did not 'excel either in oratory or debate' and revealed that he advised him to keep his parliamentary appearances to a minimum because he 'did not possess the necessary preparation and experience for a successful exchange'.[156] Nevertheless, charismatic leadership in the Weberian sense is not defined by rhetorical skill, but by the leader's ability to make followers see them as an heroic figure endowed with extraordinary qualities. In this regard, Papagos enjoyed much greater charisma than any of the masters of parliamentary oratory at the time, like Papandreou and Kanellopoulos who, despite being former prime ministers, were ready to be counted among his followers. Even centrist opponents called Papagos 'a legend', a reputation which he had earned from his so-called two victories, the first in the Greco-Italian War of 1940–1 and the second in the last year of Civil War in 1949.[157] His aloof and epic style as a man destined 'to save' Greece led some observers, like Peake, to remark that he possessed 'something of the mystical quality which once made General de Gaulle so commanding a figure in France'.[158] Witness accounts and photographs show that he was often greeted with banners saying 'You Have Saved Us' and 'Marshal Save Greece', while influential journalists, like Georgios Vlachos, wrote odes about him, declaring that he 'will save Greece for the third time'.[159] As the rival *Eleftheria* remarked, 'messianism was the dominant element of the new "movement"'.[160] This image was so pronounced among friends and critics alike that Peurifoy once remarked that Papagos had been 'obsessed with somewhat Messianic belief that only if free and untrammeled can he save Greece'.[161]

The clout of Papagos's leadership was never confined to his mass appeal. Within the Rally itself his authority was unrestrained, even among his most influential ministers. Far from being, as Mouzelis argues, a *primus inter pares* in a clientelistic party of autonomous party bosses,[162] Papagos's leadership was highly centralized and domineering. For example, in the first days of his government, his future deputy prime minister, Kanellopoulos, refused to be sworn in as Minister of Defence because of doubts over certain cabinet appointments. However, Papagos forced him to assume his post without giving in to his demands.[163] More importantly still, when he was challenged in 1954 by his closest and most powerful minister, Markezinis, Papagos immediately demanded and obtained his resignation and then removed all of Markezinis's friends from the cabinet.[164]

Another aspect of the Rally's populist character was the direct and vertical relationship which Papagos cultivated with his supporters. As Markezinis notes, after the 1951 election, the Rally faced two choices: either 'to return to Parliament and fight a parliamentary battle there or continue its policy of abstention and exercise opposition against the Government from outside the chamber through a direct march to the people'. Of the two, the second strategy was preferred:

> It was concluded that Papagos did not possess the necessary preparation and experience for a successful contest inside Parliament and it was therefore decided to organize long tours across the whole country. The organizational aspects were difficult, particularly since there was no similar precedent.[165]

Besides Markezinis's emphasis on the novelty of this strategy, a view shared by other contemporaries,[166] this choice shows the Rally's difficulty to operate within the formal institutional framework of parliamentary politics. In the fourteen months separating the elections of 1951 and 1952, Papagos appeared in Parliament only a handful of times. Meanwhile, he made several long tours across the countryside, speaking in mass rallies in the Peloponnese, Western Greece, Epirus and Macedonia. His opponents justly accused him of failing to 'conform to the rules of parliamentary government', while Venizelos rebuked him with the words: 'Taking political competition to the balconies and checking the Government through monologues without opponents is incompatible with the principles of a parliamentary polity'.[167] Yet such was Papagos's disregard for institutional accountability, that he opened the parliamentary debate on the Rally's first anniversary in power in November 1953 with the following line: 'If I am addressing you, Messrs deputies, I am doing so not in order to give a detailed account of the Government's record, but to assure the National Assembly and through it the Greek People that our direction is steady'.[168]

There is ample evidence that Papagos's populism was based on a polarized discourse that combined what Margaret Canovan calls 'regular exaltations of and appeals to the "people"' with frequent attacks against various (real or fictitious) 'enemies'.[169] On 25 August 1952, Papagos declared that the choice between the Centrist coalition and his own party amounted to a dilemma between 'the Cominform and Freedom'.[170] A variation on this theme was his earlier declaration that if he had not created the Rally, the Greek people would have turned to communism.[171] In the 1952 election campaign, he developed the theory of the so-called two paths, according to which the dilemma facing the electorate was supposedly a choice between his own party and 'the forces of corruption'.[172] At another rally he spoke about the 'tragic dilemma' facing the Greeks between 'the path leading to freedom [...] to which I shall guide you; [and] the other leading to enslavement to the forces of barbarism'.[173] When he addressed a mass rally in Athens on 12 November 1952, he warned that 'tomorrow, if the others prevail, sooner or later Greece's path will be directed by the communists'.[174]

To portray his leadership as a break with the country's traditional elites, Papagos often turned against another familiar enemy of populism, the 'Establishment'. In several speeches, he, Markezinis and Stefanopoulos, as well as various party *communiqués* attacked the so-called *paleokommatikoi* (the old politicians), who were usually charged with everything the Rally opposed.[175] While only 26 per cent of the party's 114 deputies elected in 1951 were entering Parliament for the first time (compared with EPEK's 62 per cent a year earlier),[176] Papagos still criticized the 'old political world', insisting that his party was a 'movement of political renewal'. He also spoke about his 'passion' to be able one day 'to choose my collaborators among young people at a rate of sixty per cent'.[177] The break with the past was also emphasized in his radio broadcast of 11 August 1951, which made the pro-Rally press print the following headlines: 'Let others talk about the past; you raise the flag of optimism for tomorrow'; 'Let us envision the Greece of tomorrow and not dwell on the Greece of yesterday'.[178] At the Athens rally of 2 September 1951, he claimed that the new dilemma facing Greece was 'either the Rally or old-party-politics'.[179]

Some scholars have suggested that in post-Civil War Greece, the notion of 'the people' was ostracized from the vocabulary of *Ethnikofrosyni*. Alivizatos has even argued that 'the distinction between "the nation" and "the people" formed the

Image 3 Alexander Papagos speaking during an election campaign rally at Klafthmonos Square, Athens, 2 September 1951. To his right (far), Panayiotis Kanellopoulos, and to his left (near) Spyros Markezinis. Karamanlis Foundation Photographic Archive.

quintessence of the dual political order during the first three post-war decades', while Tsoukalas remarks that under 'the new bourgeois elements that emerged after 1949 […] the terms "people" and "populist" were relatively rare'.[180] These unsubstantiated claims are strongly contradicted by the evidence. Papagos's speeches show that, if anything, he overused the word 'the people' and often treated it as synonymous to 'the nation'. During his Athens pre-election rally of 2 September 1951, he used the word 'the people' five times and the word 'nation' only twice.[181] In the parliamentary debate on the first year of the Rally in power, the word 'people' came up ten times in the first fifteen sentences of his speech and whenever it was preceded by the adjective 'the Greek', the official minute takers were apparently instructed to record

Image 4 The Greek Rally enters Parliament for the first time as the official opposition party. Seated in the front row, Alexander Papagos (middle), Stefanos Stefanopoulos (right) and Panayiotis Kanellopoulos (left). First session of the new Parliament, 10 October 1951. Karamanlis Foundation Photographic Archive.

it with a capital initial.[182] The notion of 'the people', however, had greater resonance in the Rally's discourse. At the Athens rally of 2 September 1951, Papagos told thousands of supporters that he decided to enter politics because 'he had to obey the call of the People',[183] while in another rally in Athens before the 1952 election he expressed his 'deep faith in the dynamism of our People'. These quotations from the pro-Rally *Embros* also printed the word 'People' with a capital initial.

To emphasize its anti-elitist and supposedly radical image, the Rally called itself a 'movement', a highly unusual choice for an otherwise bourgeois (not to mention 'right-wing') party in the 1950s. Papagos often spoke of his 'passion of making the Greek Rally a universal movement' and described it as 'a national' or 'pan-hellenic movement'.[184] On other occasions, he claimed that he was heading 'a great peaceful revolution in the interest of the Nation'.[185] The ideological ambiguity surrounding the usage of terms like 'movement' and 'revolution' was of no concern. If anything, the Rally's loose connection to ideology was an issue that Papagos actively sought to cultivate. In an article in *Kathimerini* on 2 September 1951, entitled 'My Sole Ambition', he wrote that a key factor behind his decision to stand for election was 'to abolish the distinction between right-wing and left-wing people and restore the full unity of the Nation'.[186] During the 1952 election campaign, while claiming that Greece's dilemma was between him and the Cominform, he also told a group of centre-left voters that 'if leftist politics is seen as socially progressive, then he, too, is on the left'!¹⁸⁷ A week later, in a rally in Athens, he described his party as a 'broad movement in which the most progressive liberal and conservative elements have their place'.¹⁸⁸

According to Francisco Panizza populism is 'characteristic of times of unsettlement' and grows 'out of the failure of existing social and political institutions to confine [...] political subjects into a relatively stable social order'.¹⁸⁹ Laclau speaks of it equally as 'an aggregation of heterogeneous forces and demands which cannot be organically integrated within the existing differential/institutional system'.¹⁹⁰ These remarks help to clarify why Papagos's political venture in the early post-Civil War years gained strong populist overtones. The prevailing conditions of crisis, his charismatic personality and his Centrist opponents' failure to build a solid coalition were crucial in producing Papagos's landslide victory in 1952. Yet, the most vital element behind his electoral success was his ability to recognize, together with Markezinis, the liminal character of the early post-Civil War years and to respond to it with a broad rallying call that cut across traditional party lines.

Conclusion

With the rise of the Greek Rally to power, the inner divisions which threatened the unity of the *Ethnikofron* regime were temporarily contained. Most IDEA officers returned to their barracks satisfied that their favourite leader had risen to the premiership. The Palace, deeply embittered by its successive failures to appoint its own prime minister, was marginalized by the very man whom it once hoped to use as an instrument to carry out its own dictatorship. For the next three years, the royal couple would focus largely on their ceremonial role, escorting distinguished guests across the Aegean, taking long breaks in Europe, renovating the Tatoi Palace and spending six weeks in the United States on a publicity tour that cost the Greek taxpayer 250 million drachmas ($1.7 million).¹⁹¹ As for the EPEK-Liberal Union, this was reduced to a shadow of its former self, with just fifty-one seats in Parliament and two leadership changes over the next eighteen months.

After Papagos's victory, the long hoped-for stability of the post-Civil War regime was finally achieved, at least in the short to medium term. Compared with the fragile coalitions of the previous six years, the rise of the Rally to power marked a qualitative shift for the *Ethnikofron* camp. Although the opposition press still cried that the Rally 'consists of small factions hating and resenting each other, whose leader [...] is struggling to keep together',¹⁹² such warnings, for the time being, sounded unduly alarmist and premature. Despite sharing similar concerns for the long term, Peurifoy and Yost were gratified that their aim of establishing a stable *Ethnikofron* government was finally realized. The same satisfaction was shared, ironically, by Peake, who wrote to Eden that 'Papagos has a fair opportunity, given his present margin of power, to set Greece on her feet again'.¹⁹³

Still, both Washington and London interpreted the Rally's victory as a temporary solution whose real drawbacks lay in the long term. In August 1951,

Peurifoy had warned that the main disadvantage of Papagos's entry into politics was a 'long term one', namely that the 'temporary crystallization of political forces around Marshal will interrupt [the] gradual normalization of Greek polit[ical] life'.[194] Similar reservations were shared by Norton:

> The sort of Papagos' Government I envisage might (as did Metaxas') begin fairly broad, but would almost certainly soon find its way well into the right of centre. The above will show you how far I should be from welcoming a Papagos government in any but the last resort.[195]

Peake also wondered 'whether the force of [Papagos's] will and the strength of his prestige will prove more powerful than the temptation to intrigue and worse'.[196] Finally, Acheson saw difficulties arising in the Rally's nationalism. In August 1951, he had advised caution 'in view [of] Emb[assy]'s estimate [regarding] Papagos prospects as [a] result [of] coming elections and his oft-announced position [that] Gr[ee]ks [should] conduct [their] own affairs'.[197] Not long after Papagos was sworn in, these misgivings started to appear justified.

Image 5 Swearing-in of the Papagos Government in Parliament, 12 December 1952. Right to left: Alexander Papagos, Emmanuel Tsouderos, Panayiotis Kanellopoulos, Spyros Markezinis, Stefanos Stefanopoulos, Constantine Karamanlis. Karamanlis Foundation Photographic Archive.

4

FROM DEPENDENCE TO DUALISM: CYPRUS ENTERS GREEK FOREIGN POLICY

The rise of the Greek Rally to power in 1952 brought about a revised approach to Greek-American relations. Although the framework of dependence remained largely intact, the new government's foreign policy differed from that of its predecessors in several respects. Save a few exceptions, like Kartalis's threats to introduce defence cuts (which never materialized), under the Rally Government US policy faced a modest degree of resistance that it never encountered since the end of the war. Moreover, after November 1952, for the first time since the Truman Doctrine, US policy-makers had to deal with a Greek government that was not merely responding to their guidance but was determined to initiate policy in line with its own concept of US-Greek relations.

Historians like John Iatrides have contributed significantly towards a different interpretation to the above. According to him, after Papagos became prime minister, 'all key decisions regarding [...] economic and security affairs passed through American hands'.[1] Such sweeping statements, however, constitute an extension of his problematic thesis that Papagos became prime minister because of Peurifoy's interventions. Once the Rally's rise to power is explained in such simplistic terms, there is little scope for presenting its policies as anything other than a record of unmitigated subservience to the United States. Furthermore, historians who subscribe to this narrative have identified two decisions as evidence of Greece's increased dependence on the United States after 1952. The first was the offer of additional troops to Korea, and the second was the acceptance of US military bases on Greek soil.[2]

Despite the misapprehensions surrounding both issues, it should be stressed that the increased autonomy which Papagos claimed in US-Greek relations was a far cry from true independence. More serious than the offer of additional troops to Korea, Greece's continued dependence on the United States was evident in its zealous support for the Balkan Pact, an alliance secretly masterminded by Washington, which Iatrides and others have misguidedly praised as a model of cooperation by independent states 'across ideological boundaries'.[3] However, a more serious flaw in the dependence narrative is the failure of its proponents to explain how a government that was allegedly subservient to the United States could suddenly defy Washington and its NATO allies over a major issue like Cyprus. To circumvent this difficulty, even metaphysical factors were invoked: 'Out of the blue', says Tsoukalas, 'the Cypriot problem successively burst the Balkan Pact [and] threatened the south-eastern flank of NATO'.[4] Another account attributed the issue to Papagos's penchant for drama: 'Overcome by an ultra-nationalism, which often pushed him towards gestures of independence toward both England and the United States [...], he decided to proceed to a solution of the Cyprus question'.[5] A third analysis claims that Papagos resorted to an 'anti-British policy over Cyprus' because he was 'the most consistent follower of American policy'.[6] Behind this assertion, which is implicit in another account,[7] lies the unsustainable hypothesis that Washington supposedly clashed with Britain over the Cyprus question.

The common theme running through all these interpretations, as well as Vournas's more serious argument that Papagos took the Cyprus issue to the UN because he felt 'exposed before public opinion',[8] is the clichéd view that a post-war Greek 'right-wing' government could never have willingly challenged US policy. As a result, the dependence narrative has always maintained that Papagos's Cyprus policy was essentially an aberration which did not represent the bulk of his otherwise subservient foreign policy. For this reason, there has never been an attempt among proponents of this narrative to study his Cyprus policy systematically. Passing remarks, like Linardatos's view that Papagos began to pursue a 'double track policy' over Cyprus,[9] never develop into a full analysis. Ultimately, Linardatos also maintains that subservience to the United States formed the thrust of the Rally's foreign policy and that Cyprus was simply an anomaly.

This interpretation, of course, contrasts with the Greek ethnocentric narrative, which portrays Papagos's policy on Cyprus as the essence of his entire foreign policy. According to Svolopoulos, the Rally's decision to stir the Cyprus question 'was an initiative of crucial importance in the formation of Greek foreign policy in the second half of the [twentieth] century'.[10] Notwithstanding their critique of Papagos's handling of the issue, ethnocentric accounts have presented his policy on Cyprus as an honourably romantic, if unrealistic expression of his nationalism. Historians of this tradition overstate the differences between the foreign policies of the Rally and the Centre governments of 1950–2 and tend to group Papagos's approach, rather misleadingly, with the radical nationalism of Archbishop Makarios, the Panhellenic Committee of the Struggle for Union with Cyprus (PEAEK) and the popular *Enosis* movement. Dimitris Michalopoulos, for instance, argues that 'the governments of the Centre [...] did not want to make the decisive move, that is to take recourse to the UN; the reason must be sought in the[ir] traditional "Anglophile" approach', whereas 'the "crossing of the Rubicon" happened after 1952'.[11] Svolopoulos, in a similar vein, criticized Papagos for upsetting the 'harmony and co-operation with the western allies', but ultimately praises him for upholding 'the just claims of the Cypriot people' and using 'tough language in his successive *demarches* to the leaders of the allies'.[12] Echoing this analysis, Evanthis Hatzivassiliou claims that *Enosis* was the main objective of Greek foreign policy in the 1950s and portrays Papagos as a supposed 'radical', whose approach contrasted with what he calls the 'pragmatic'/'evolutionist' line of the Centre and ERE governments.[13]

This and the next two chapters will provide an alternative reading of Papagos's foreign policy that stresses its dualist character. The aim of this analysis is to offer an holistic approach which reconnects Papagos's Cold War strategy with his Cyprus policy and studies both in the same analytic field. For reasons that will become apparent below, the proposed interpretation holds that, when viewed in its totality, the Rally's foreign policy unfolded like a chain of gradually intensifying contradictions. Using, momentarily, Hatzivassiliou's otherwise flawed binary model of 'radical' versus 'pragmatic' Greek strategies on the Cyprus question, the argument put forward here maintains that Papagos's policy falls in the middle, under a missing third category, which carefully blended elements of both a 'radical' and a 'pragmatic' approach.

Focusing on the first year of the Rally Government, this chapter shows how Papagos attempted a transition from the predominantly Atlanticist approach of the Centre governments to an early form of *dependent nationalism*. During the fourteen months from November 1952 to January 1954, dualism took the form of a contradictory policy whereby greater dependence on the United States was used to support a more vigorously nationalist policy in Cyprus. The next two chapters shall demonstrate how this approach was adapted after January 1954 into a new variant of *dependent nationalism*. During that second stage, the Rally's early attempt to link greater dependence on the United States to a more assertive nationalist policy started to give way to a schizoid variant whereby Greece was increasingly seeking to disassociate its dependence on the United States from its Cyprus policy, as if the two components could be decoupled.

Despite these differences, both forms of *dependent nationalism* were variations of the same self-contradictory doctrine. Both the earlier policy of seeking *Enosis* through dependence and the later policy of seeking *Enosis* alongside dependence were premised on the common, yet arbitrary hypothesis that Greece's loyalty to NATO and the United States could be effectively combined with a vigorous quest for *Enosis*. What differentiated them was, mainly, the tactical handling of the United States. Whereas the earlier version of dualism was premised on *pulling* the United States more deeply into the Cyprus imbroglio as a potential counterweight to Britain, the latter relied on *pushing* the United States towards a 'neutral' stance, in the hope of isolating Britain. In many ways, however, the latter form of *dependent nationalism* was an extension of the former insofar as it constituted a tactical adjustment to Washington's refusal to challenge British colonialism in Cyprus.

Greek-American relations under Papagos

From the early days of his premiership, Papagos approached relations with the United States from a different perspective in comparison to his predecessors. Although he continued to operate within the wider framework he inherited, his policy attempted to redress the balance of Greek-American relations in two ways. First, as some of his early decisions indicate, he sought to expand the competence of the Greek government over certain domestic issues, including some which had clear foreign policy implications. The second included the initiation of decisions aimed at involving the United States more deeply into certain aspects of Greek foreign policy, often to the discomfort of US policy-makers. The basis of this new approach was to restyle Greek-American relations around what Leo Mates called, in a different context, 'voluntary dependence', that is a bilateral relationship that is unequal, but based more on co-operation than subordination.[14] On the surface, the two components of the new policy towards the United States appeared contradictory insofar as one sought to increase Greece's independence whereas the other encouraged its reduction. At a deeper level, however, this apparent contradiction was less acute than it seemed. Ultimately, the two elements of Papagos's new approach towards Washington converged around the objective of strengthening bilateral relations through a strategy that gave Athens greater say within the framework of dependence.

The revision of Greek-American relations in the first months of Papagos's premiership was, to a large extent, successfully implemented. Several factors contributed to this outcome. First, although it seems that neither he nor his ministers knew of its existence, the US policy review of August–September 1952 paved the way for a more positive American response to his actions. Second, the Rally's comfortable parliamentary majority set a limit on the ability of the United States to remove and reinstate prime ministers in the way Grady did when the fragile Centre coalitions were in power. Third, the substantial reduction of Marshall Plan aid since 1952 removed another key instrument from the hands of US diplomats. Meanwhile, Papagos's attempt to redress the balance of Greek-American relations did not challenge the framework of US hegemony. His government never questioned the country's commitment to NATO, the Balkan Pact and the bilateral relationship with Washington as keystones of Greece's foreign policy. If anything, greater zeal was shown in pursuing these objectives. As a result, after their first meeting, Peake reported that 'Papagos has shown his realization that his Government cannot succeed, either in foreign affairs or in the economic reorganization of the country, without the friendship [...] of both the United Kingdom and the United States'.[15] Within these parameters, the Rally began to pursue its approach to relations with Washington.

Enhancing Greece's relative autonomy

One of Papagos's first decisions as prime minister was the dismissal of commander-in-chief, General Tsakalotos, and the chiefs of the three forces, Generals Grigoropoulos, Pentzopoulos and Vassilas. This move, whose aim was to eliminate the influence of the Palace in the army since Papagos's resignation in May 1951,[16] was strongly resisted by the US embassy.[17] Although, as opposition leader, Papagos had accused the dismissed generals of having 'displayed complete idleness' during the IDEA coup of May 1951,[18] his decision to replace them with Generals Kitrilakis, Tsingounis and Ketseas was effectively promoting a new leadership that was, ironically, closer to IDEA.[19] Meanwhile, Papagos had developed a personal hostility towards Tsakalotos (formerly known as one of 'his men')[20] because on 4 August 1951 the latter undermined the Rally's election campaign through a controversial memorandum that recommended the abolition of the separate army vote.²¹ Ever since, Papagos had made it plain to Peurifoy that, should he become prime minister, he would either 'court martial or retire' him.²²

From the perspective of Greek-American relations, the controversy over these military appointments showed that Papagos was both determined and able to defy US policy if he judged this to be expedient. Besides ignoring the US embassy's advice to postpone the new appointments until 'a sufficient period of time' had passed, he ignored Yost's warnings that 'good NATO liaison achieved under the ousted Grigoropoulos might be seriously affected'. The importance attached by Washington to the issue was such that the Chief of JUSMAG, General Hart, was brought in to persuade Papagos to recall them. Hart, however, found that Papagos was 'adamant on ouster of four generals', while Yost, in a subsequent report, conceded defeat: 'Our efforts at least to delay reshuffle in Army High Command have proved fruitless [...]. Nothing short of some sort of US ultimatum and possibly not even that, would prevent him from making these changes and making them immediately'.²³

The same assertion of autonomy was shown during Markezinis's visit to Washington in May 1953. During his discussions with John Foster Dulles, Markezinis asked for additional economic aid to finance an ambitious medium-term development programme. US documents show that when he made this request, he warned explicitly that, if rebuffed, 'Marshal Papagos would declare his intention to maintain Greece's alignment with the West [...] but at the same time would renounce all special connection with the United States terminating the MSA Mission in Greece'.²⁴ These threats continued throughout the visit and Markezinis warned again that if his aid request were not met with approval, Dulles's forthcoming visit to Greece would be 'very adversely affected'. In an atypical manner, Dulles reacted diplomatically, saying that he would study Markezinis's proposal.²⁵ This response was probably influenced by Peurifoy's brief to Dulles prior to the visit, which advised caution because 'Papagos and Markezinis are sensitive individuals with a highly developed sense of their own dignity and of the historical and strategic importance of Greece'.²⁶ Peurifoy's brief also warned that 'if they should get the impression that the US is taking them for granted [...] they might overnight alter, not their basic orientation, but their tactics'.²⁷ Although, as we shall see below, Markezinis never secured the requested aid, he did obtain a face-saving *communiqué* in which the United States promised to 'give prompt consideration' to his proposals.²⁸ What is noteworthy, however, is that Markezinis deployed a bold approach that no Greek government had used with the United States since the proclamation of the Truman Doctrine.

Inviting greater American involvement

Besides requesting economic aid, Markezinis discussed two major security issues in Washington. One was the offer of additional Greek troops to Korea and the second was the granting of US base rights in Greece. Both issues were first raised in a personal letter to Eisenhower by Papagos, which Markezinis hand-delivered to the president on the morning of 7 May 1953.²⁹ Although the text of the letter is classified, from Eisenhower's reply[30] it is clear that both offers were unilateral Greek proposals and not, as often claimed in the historiography, American demands placed on Papagos.[31] Meanwhile (and this might explain part of the confusion in the scholarship), both sides agreed to present the proposals, at least for a while, as American requests. However, on 23 November 1953, Markezinis finally told the Greek Parliament that 'the use of the bases in Greece by the United States [...] resulted from Marshal Papagos's idea which I conveyed to President Eisenhower'.[32] A few days later, Papagos also confirmed that 'immediately after President Eisenhower was elected [...] I extended a personal letter in which I proposed, for safeguarding Greece's defences better [...] to conclude an agreement for the granting of bases'.[33] Nonetheless, only a handful of accounts have taken note of these revelations.[34]

According to American sources, Eisenhower's first reaction upon reading Papagos's letter on 7 May 1953 was to say how 'extremely pleased' he was with its content and 'the spirit' it conveyed.[35] Then, in a more considered response, he expressed reservations about whether 'an additional base in the Greek area was

Image 6 President Dwight Eisenhower inspects a Greek bronze helmet of the fifth century BCE, a gift from Greek Coordination Minister, Spyros Markezinis, centre, and the Greek Ambassador to the United States, Athanase Politis. Other gifts brought by Markezinis and Politis included a gold medal, making the president an honorary citizen of Athens; an eighth-century BCE earthenware wine flask and a necklace of ancient Greek coins for Mamie Eisenhower. White House, Washington, 7 May 1953. Associated Press.

in fact required'. Concerning the extra troops to Korea, he remarked that 'if we felt that to be the case we would be in touch with Marshal Papagos'.[36] Eisenhower finally said that the proposals had to be studied and, in a few weeks, his initial caution gave way to outright acceptance. At the NSC meeting of 4 June 1953, Dulles questioned the desirability of sending additional Greek troops to Korea as the war in the Far East was coming to an end, but Eisenhower disagreed, saying that additional Greek troops 'would relieve American boys and could be maintained cheaper'. Dulles then expressed concern that the offer was linked to increased economic aid to Greece, but Eisenhower argued that these were 'two entirely separate matters'.[37] Consequently, on 5 June 1953, the US President wrote to Papagos accepting the additional troops to Korea without reference to Markezinis's request for economic aid.

In the same letter, Eisenhower expressed interest in the bases proposal, saying that the matter was now 'under study'.[38] By mid-August, he accepted that offer, too, but on condition that the issue was kept secret. As Dulles told the US embassy in Athens, this was required because,

> although there may be some advantages from local point of view in public announcement, [we] believe [...] announcement [is] very likely [to] create Balkan tensions with resulting undesirable effect on Greek political stability and economy. We have in mind such things as propaganda barrage from Free Greek Radio and Bulgarians, as well as possible disruptive communist machinations.

Consequently, the US-Greek Bases Agreement was signed in Athens on 12 October 1953 between the new US Ambassador, Cavendish Cannon, and Foreign Minister Stefanopoulos. On Dulles's request, two annexes were kept secret,[39] and news of the agreement was announced in ambiguous language that simply referred to 'the granting of facilities and rights of joint use of certain navy installations and airports'.[40]

State Department documents show that the secrecy of the Bases Agreement was not a Greek but an American request. On 14 August, when Washington accepted the Greek offer, Papagos started drafting a *communiqué* which began as follows: 'With deep satisfaction, I declare that following a request from the United States Government, the Greek Government, in full agreement with His Majesty the King, have decided to grant air bases for the United States forces.'[41] For reasons that will become apparent below, Papagos's draft *communiqué* misrepresented the bases agreement as an American proposal. In the end, the Greek prime minister was forced to suppress it because the US Undersecretary of State, Walter Bedell Smith, told the US embassy in Athens that

> submission [to the] Greek Parliament [of the prospective bases treaty] would likewise invite UN controversy [...]. Certain aspects [of] these arrangements cannot be made public for military security reasons [...]. Such arrangements would increase East-West tension [...]. Other Governments have insisted on secrecy arrangements for these reasons.[42]

Although Papagos momentarily complied, he continued to object to keeping the agreement secret, explaining to Cannon that if this were not ratified by Parliament, he would be violating the Greek Constitution.[43] Indeed, the Greek prime minister persisted in demanding a public announcement and parliamentary ratification and only reluctantly accepted Washington's request not to alert Congress to the issue. Still, both he and Markezinis informed the Greek Parliament about the treaty on 23 and 25 November, respectively, stressing that this was originally a Greek idea.[44] Even the brief and ambiguous Greek *communiqué* of 12 October 1953, released on the day of the signing of the Agreement, would have not been produced had Papagos not protested strongly to Cannon that 'this [secrecy] can't go on much longer'.[45]

Assessing the Rally's early approach to Greek-American relations

The most important aspect of the Rally's early approach to Greek-American relations was the exclusion of Britain from every crucial development associated with it. This choice contrasted sharply with the old Greek practice of involving Britain over most matters concerning US-Greek relations. Under Papagos, London's influence in Greece declined so sharply that one could almost speak of a British diplomatic debacle. To cite one example, in his report on the Papagos-Dulles meeting in Athens on 27 May 1953, Peake claimed that this amounted to 'nothing more than had been said to Markezinis in Washington, though a good many kind words passed, with assurances that aid of some sort would be continued'.[46] When we look at the State Department record of the meeting, we find that the following issues were discussed: 'a. Personal Letter of Prime Minister to President, b. Soviet Union, c. rhythm of rearmament, d. MEDO, e. British-Egyptian difficulties, f. Balkan Defence, g. Greek military contribution'.[47] Of those, 'MEDO' and 'British-Egyptian talks' were of direct relevance to British interests in the Middle East, including Colonel Gamal Abdel Nasser's successful manipulation of US-British differences to force a British evacuation from Egypt.[48] In other words, while Dulles and Papagos were discussing the failings of British policy in the region, British diplomats were scoffing these talks as being over petty financial squabbles. As if deliberately intended to embarrass Peake, the State Department minute states that 'there was no opportunity to discuss economic questions' at all, because Markezinis had arrived late for the meeting![49]

From a British viewpoint, this incident was not a glitch. Foreign Office documents show that the British embassy in Washington was equally unaware of Papagos's letter to Eisenhower, which Markezinis had delivered on 7 May 1953.[50] Again, the Greek minister's visit was treated light-heartedly as a matter linked to Greece's financial difficulties. Indeed, when the Bases Agreement was announced in October 1953, the British Government was caught by surprise. To make matters worse, Peake naively admitted this much to the new Soviet ambassador, Mikhail Sergeev, during an informal conversation on 23 October 1953. According to Peake, the Soviet Ambassador 'passed to the question of the recent Greek-American agreement about air bases. He said he had been told that the Greeks did not know how to keep secrets, but added a trifle sourly that they had certainly kept this one. I nodded agreement'.[51]

Additional evidence suggests that the Rally's revised approach to Greek-American relations was part of a wider strategy aimed at challenging Britain's position in the East Mediterranean. The main beneficiary would be the United States, but Papagos also envisaged benefits for Greece insofar as this approach would elevate Athens to a regional gatekeeper capable of determining which world power would play a leading role in the Balkans. A clear indication of these intentions was Papagos's response to Yost's request on 14 August that the Greek *communiqué* announcing the US bases agreement had to be supressed. 'The British will be strongly opposed to this agreement and will, as soon as they hear of it, do everything in their power to sabotage and delay', he retorted. Papagos then stressed that 'he wished to confront [the] British and NATO with [a] fait accompli'. Markezinis, who was privy to the exchange, added that Papagos was earnest in his belief that 'the British will do all in their power to obstruct the agreement and may succeed in creating interminable delays'.[52] He also remarked that when the King hears of the bases deal he would inform Admiral Mountbatten, NATO's British Supreme Allied Commander in Europe, with whom he was due to meet in a few days. This dialogue shows that the Rally's leaders sought closer US-Greek relations as a counterweight to Britain's influence in the East Mediterranean. Indeed, they often presented this policy as a major area of difference between them and their domestic opponents, most notably the Palace and the Centre parties, who favoured a more even approach towards Britain and the United States. On 22 August 1953, Markezinis told Yost that 'the strong support which [the] US and NATO are obtaining from Greece in [a] wide variety of fields, including bases, troops to Korea, maintenance of disproportionate army, et cetera, is conceivable only under [a] Rally Government', adding that the alternative would be an 'unstable centre-left coalition [...] which would certainly not carry out these measures'. In his report to Washington, Yost remarked that Markezinis was 'undoubtedly correct'.[53]

As Greek-American relations gathered momentum, Papagos for the first time instructed Stefanopoulos to raise the Cyprus issue with the Americans. At a meeting with Yost on 26 August 1953, the Greek Foreign Minister explained that Papagos was under pressure by the Cypriots to sponsor the issue of the island's self-determination at the UN and requested Washington's help 'to persuade Makarios to drop his appeal "for the time being" on the grounds that [the] time is not ripe'. To this end, he asked Yost to seek Dulles's advice on how to restrain Makarios and added that he [Papagos] was planning to raise the matter with Eden, who was expected in Greece on 30 August. Stefanopoulos explained that Papagos intended to approach Eden

> on personal man-to-man basis alleging that [this] *demarche* is unknown even to his own Cabinet. He intends to propose that [the] British immediately grant to Cypriots constitution which would accord them certain rights of self-government and which would be followed in two or three years by plebiscite in which [the] Cypriots would be given a choice between independence, incorporation into

Greece or some status within [the] commonwealth. For reasons [the] Foreign Minister did not make completely clear he has some hope [that the] British might accept his proposal.⁵⁴

Stefanopoulos admitted that Greek diplomats had advised that, without US backing, any attempt to raise the Cyprus issue at the UN would fail. He said that 'some time ago Kyrou [Greece's representative to the UN] approached Makarios, [and] urged him to abandon [the] appeal to [the] UN on [the] grounds that without US support it would merely invite failure and work to profit of Soviets'.⁵⁵ In saying so, Stefanopoulos was implying that Greece did not intend to go to the UN without US encouragement, but he was also sounding Washington's intentions regarding such a prospect. The Rally Government was obviously seeking to capitalize on its upgraded relationship with Washington and the impending bases agreement to obtain a sympathetic American response to its pro-*Enosis* policy. Indeed, this was how the State Department read Stefanopoulos's *demarche* to Yost.

Two days later, however, Dulles told the US embassy in Athens that he saw no benefits in approaching Makarios and considered Stefanopoulos's initiative as 'another attempt [to] shift responsibility from [the] Greek government and involve [the] US in [the] Cyprus issue'. He stressed Washington's position that the 'US [is] not party to [the Cyprus] problem but does not think useful for Greek Government [to] press [the] matter'.⁵⁶ On 1 September 1953, Yost conveyed Dulles's response to Stefanopoulos who expressed disappointment. The Greek Foreign Minister, however, underlined two factors which he said had forced him to seek US involvement: first, the strong support for *Enosis* among Greeks and, second, his fear that Makarios might ask a communist state to sponsor the Cyprus question at the UN if Greece would not do so itself. During that exchange, Stefanopoulos threatened for the first time that, if the United States refused to get involved in the Cyprus issue and Papagos's meeting with Eden did not produce a breakthrough, the Field Marshal would have no option but to sponsor a UN recourse himself. He said:

> If Papagos['] approach to Eden were unsuccessful and if Makarios' complaint to UN were not withdrawn, he believed Field Marshal would feel obliged to support and even sponsor this complaint. There is no other question, he said, on which Greek people are more united and in which their cause [...] is more just. If Greek Government does not sponsor complaint, some iron curtain or Arab state would, in Kyrou's opinion, probably do so, which would work to [the] advantage of Communists in Cyprus, perhaps increasing their following from 30 to 50 percent.

The meeting with Yost ended with Stefanopoulos's suggestion to revisit the issue after Papagos's impending meeting with Eden.⁵⁷

Seen together, these developments suggest that the strengthening of US-Greek bilateral relations in the first year of the Rally Government was attempted for three reasons. First, to enhance Greece's role in the Balkans and East Mediterranean as a local gatekeeper who determined which Western power could establish a hegemonic presence in the region. In this sense, the bases offer was a decision aimed at weakening Britain's regional influence and strengthening that of the United States. As *Time* magazine noted in November 1953, the boundaries between NATO and the British Middle East Command (Malta, Cyprus and Suez) had become an area where Washington and London were beginning to 'undermine each other'.[58] Papagos's second objective was to secure additional economic aid after the termination of the Marshal Plan, to finance Markezinis's medium-term investments programme. His third objective was to obtain some diplomatic support from Washington to challenge Britain's colonial policy in Cyprus. Because the US Government was expected to be (and indeed was) reluctant to respond positively to Greece's demands, the Rally Government tried to lure it into accepting them in a subtle and gradual manner. Initially, it offered the base rights and additional troops to Korea as unconditional inducements; then, it sought financial assistance; and, finally, it tried to secure some US support over Cyprus.

Although the policy was carried out effectively, the Rally's gamble did not pay off. The United States took up the bases offer, used an additional Greek battalion in Korea and secured Athens's support for the Balkan Pact but in return offered no additional economic aid and made no concessions on Cyprus. The only Greek demand that Washington was willing to fulfil was to risk antagonizing Britain in the East Mediterranean through acquiring military bases in Greece. But even then, the Eisenhower Administration denied Papagos the opportunity to announce the bases agreement early.

The Cyprus question grips Greek foreign policy

Although *Enosis* (union) with Greece was an old demand of the Greek-Cypriots, who made up four-fifths of the island's population,[59] the year 1950 marked the beginning of a new era in the history of the Cyprus question. In that year, several unrelated or loosely connected factors began to rapidly intertwine, giving rise to a mass popular movement, first in Cyprus and then in Greece, which demanded the end of British colonialism and union between the island and Greece. In 1950, *Enosis* grew into a major Greek national issue, but by 1954 it escalated into a complex regional dispute involving Britain, Turkey and the United States. As Lawrence Durrell noted in his dramatized chronicle, *Bitter Lemons of Cyprus* (1957), after that year a 'deepening sense of crisis' started to swathe the East Mediterranean.[60]

A major factor behind this escalation was the adoption of a formal decolonization policy by Britain in the late 1940s. Although by 1947–8 it became clear that London was unwilling to offer Cyprus more than a constitution for self-government within the British Empire, the speeches of Prime Minister Clement Attlee contained confusing pronouncements, including suggestions that his Labour Government had 'no desire to keep any people within the British Empire against their will'.[61] Coupled with other momentous changes, such as the establishment of the UN in 1945, the granting of Independence to India in

1947 and the British withdrawal from Palestine in 1947–8, such statements raised expectations among many Greek-Cypriots that, if they could pose a strong enough claim, Britain might eventually pull out of Cyprus, too. As the Secretary to the Cypriot Ethnarchy, Nicos Kranidiotis, later remarked, these expectations were invigorated by the references of the UN Charter of 1948 to the right of peoples for self-determination, a document that the British Government warmly endorsed.[62]

Another factor contributing to the upsurge of nationalist sentiment in Cyprus was the Cypriot Ethnarchy's initiative to organize a plebiscite on *Enosis* on 15 January 1950. The result was a resounding endorsement of union with Greece by 95.7 per cent.[63] A key influence behind this outcome was the support of the communist Progressive Party of the Working People (AKEL), Cyprus's largest political force, which overcame its previous reservations about supporting union with *Ethnikofron* Greece and reverted to its earlier policy of embracing *Enosis*.[64] A further development adding to this momentum was the election of Makarios III to the throne of the Cypriot Ethnarchy on 18 October 1950. The new Archbishop was a young, educated and charismatic leader who was ready to use radical methods to achieve *Enosis*. Soon, Makarios managed to establish himself as the undisputed representative of the *Enosis* movement in Cyprus and a large and dynamic youth organization started to operate under his guidance.[65] A key issue linked to his leadership was the creation of the National Organization of Cypriot Fighters (EOKA), a militant armed group formed in Athens in 1952, with Colonel Grivas as its future commander, a fierce anti-communist whose wartime paramilitary group 'X' terrorized the Greek left during the Axis Occupation and the Civil War. This time, Grivas was intent on leading an armed struggle against the British authorities in Cyprus.[66]

Shortly after the Cypriot plebiscite of 1950, a nationalist flurry for *Enosis* began to sweep across Greece, causing discomfort to the traditionally Anglophile Centre governments. The main trigger behind this nationalist upsurge was the arrival of a Cypriot Ethnarchy delegation to Athens carrying the plebiscite documents. The disembarkment of the delegation in Piraeus on 20 May 1950 presented the Plastiras Government with a dilemma. On one hand, it would have been embarrassing for any Greek government not to embrace the impassioned pleas of the 'unredeemed' fellow-nationals from Cyprus, but on the other, both Plastiras and Venizelos after him were concerned that any serious support for *Enosis* would be interpreted in London as an unfriendly act of meddling with the affairs of the British Empire. Although Britain had proposed to offer Cyprus to Greece in 1915 (in return for the latter's entry in the First World War) according to the Foreign Office that opportunity had 'lapsed' because Greece embraced neutrality until 1917.[67] In 1941, in reply to a question by Prime Minister Alexander Koryzis, Eden had stated that Cyprus could not be discussed 'until after the War', but in 1947–8 the Attlee Government offered a constitution for self-government without any discussions with Greece.[68] As Robert Holland remarks, the Jewish uprising in Palestine and the Egyptian attacks in the Suez Canal Zone drove the Attlee Government to the conclusion that 'the strategic importance of Cyprus has grown enormously since the Second World War'.[69] Consequently, the renewed British interest in Cyprus since the late 1940s was becoming a serious obstacle against the irredentist ambitions of Greek *Ethnikofron* politicians.

The main concern of the 1950–2 Centre governments regarding this issue was to find a suitable formula to keep the *Enosis* movement under control and avoid a crisis in Anglo-Greek relations. Consequently, although they paid tribute to both the 'patriotic' struggle for *Enosis* and the century-old tradition of 'Anglo-Greek friendship', the Centre Governments gave a clear preference to the second objective. Until October 1952, their policy was committed to supporting *Enosis*, but always within the framework of 'Anglo-Greek friendship'. Seven years later, George Papandreou, who served as deputy prime minister in 1950–1, told the Greek Parliament that this policy was followed because it protected Greece's friendly relations with its Western allies on the eve of Greece's accession to NATO:

> It is a fact that the Governments of the Centre both in 1950 and '51 […] chose diplomatic action […] with the British Government […] because they judged that under the conditions of the years 1950–51, diplomatic action was necessary within the family of our allies.[70]

Despite their efforts to conceal the subordination of *Enosis* to the principles of 'Anglo-Greek friendship', the Centre governments were occasionally forced to make decisions that showed their real priorities. When the Ethnarchy's delegation arrived in Athens on 20 May 1950, Plastiras initially refused to grant it an audience,[71] but he then issued a *communiqué* stating that 'the Government reserves the right to handle the Cyprus Question within the framework of its relations with its powerful friend and ally as soon as conditions for a positive settlement are deemed right'.[72] As a conciliatory gesture, the referendum documents were received by the president of Parliament, Dimitris Gondicas, while Plastiras, after rethinking his position, met the delegates a few days later.[73] At the end of their meeting, he expressed sympathy for the aspirations of the Cypriots, but reaffirmed his position that the Greek Government will not be taking further action 'as it does not judge the present moment opportune'.[74] Meanwhile, Plastiras forbade entry to a second Cypriot delegation representing AKEL on the grounds that communism was outlawed in Greece. Later, as a conciliatory gesture, he met two of its members informally in Paris.[75]

In the face of growing pressure from Cyprus, which culminated in Makarios's visit to Athens in March 1951, the Venizelos government convened an all-party leaders' council. Ironically, the nine party leaders who met on 21 March, instead of overcoming the dilemma between *Enosis* and 'Anglo-Greek friendship', accentuated it further by sanctioning an explicitly dualist policy. Even their joint *communiqué* was drafted in two numbered sections, each expressing support for one side of the Cyprus dilemma. This is what it said:

1. Free Greece cannot remain deaf when the wish is expressed by any section of unredeemed Hellenism, constituting a majority within its geographical space, to unite with the motherland.

2. [...] Greece has old and tested bonds of friendship and gratitude with Great Britain upon which its foreign policy rests, to a large extent, for more than a century. Greece, less than ever before, wishes to depart from this traditional friendship, but neither is it possible to withdraw from the other fundamental principle mentioned above.[76]

While this *communiqué* inaugurated the dualist policy of dependent nationalism later championed by the Rally Government, the Centre coalitions soon reverted to their policy line of supporting *Enosis* strictly within a framework of 'Anglo-Greek friendship'. This should not imply, however, as Vlachos suggested, that their commitment to *Enosis* was merely 'Platonic'.[77] In April, Venizelos instructed Greece's ambassador in London to make a *demarche* to the Foreign Office, which was made on 2 May. This proposed either immediate *Enosis* in return for granting military bases to Britain 'in Cyprus and elsewhere in Greece' or, if this could not be realized, it requested a British statement within a reasonable time frame declaring that a solution of the Cyprus question will be offered in line with the wishes of the Cypriot people.[78]

As pressure from Cyprus and Greek public opinion mounted, the EPEK-Liberal Government of 1951–2 started to explore new ways of addressing the issue. These efforts culminated in a secret meeting between Deputy Foreign Minister Averoff and Eden on 29 November 1951, on the fringes of a NATO Ministers' Council in Rome.[79] Although the meeting came out of a personal initiative by Ambassador Peake, Eden swiftly torpedoed it. According to the Foreign Office record, the British Foreign Secretary warned Averoff from the outset that 'it was much better to leave this topic alone', but the Greek minister asked to present what he described as his 'reasonable' views, starting with the astonishing revelation that he 'did not believe that Enosis was possible'! Eden, however, '*repeated* that the future of Cyprus was not a topic which [he] was prepared to discuss', while in his account Averoff noted that the Foreign Secretary replied in a loud voice: 'A Cyprus question did not exist'. The British record adds that Averoff protested that Eden did not understand the pressure his government was under, both by 'young people' who agitated to the point where 'one or two heads had been broken', and by Makarios, who kept threatening to present the issue to the UN. Eden then retorted that 'all Governments from time to time had to take an unpopular stand' and, sharing the same impression as Averoff, noted that 'this conversation ended coldly'.[80]

Meanwhile, the Centre governments instructed Greek politicians and senior diplomats 'to seize opportunities for declaring in a moderate yet categorical tone that they always expect a solution to the Cyprus Question in accordance with the principle of self-determination'. According to a covering note summarizing the content of some Greek diplomatic reports from that period, the Centre Governments promoted a Greek press campaign to 'enlighten world public opinion'. This offered advice to 'Greek politicians, diplomats and military officers to stress in their private conversations with the British [...] our concerns about the [...] lukewarm views of Greek public opinion [vis-à-vis Britain] because of the Cyprus question'.[81] On 24 November 1951, the Greek Government sent an *aide memoire* to the Foreign Office 'cataloguing the recent manifestations in favour of Enosis and concluding that a change of policy regarding Cyprus might have to be contemplated'.[82] These endeavours should not suggest that the Centre governments ever intended to exert serious pressure on Britain. As one policy paper warned, 'it is in no way in our interest [...] to take a systematic and indiscreet anti-British position' nor to 'allow the British to believe that besides these rhetorical gestures, the issue of Cyprus in any way affects or is going to affect the core of our future foreign policy'.[83] In addition, the Centre governments' policy was underlain with obvious inconsistencies. One paper suggested that if Britain were to offer a constitution for Cypriot self-rule, Greece should discourage 'the Cypriot *ethnikofrones* from participating in any elections'; but another paper proposed that 'the Cypriot Ethnarchy should be persuaded that it is in its interest to recognize' such a constitution and 'fight for *Enosis* within its framework'.[84] Meanwhile, a common position was adopted over the issue of 'internationalization', that is the Cypriot Ethnarchy's support for a UN recourse as the optimal strategy for tackling the Cyprus problem. One report noted that 'it was impossible to expect either from the United Nations or from the Council of Europe a solution to the problem',[85] while another concluded that 'under no circumstances would Britain be placed under obligation by the United Nations to liberate the island'.[86] Two more documents, one by Kyrou in 1951 and another by the diplomat Efstathios Lagakos in 1952, concurred that a 'recourse to the General Assembly [...] would [...] confront difficulties that would make matters highly problematic'.[87] Kyrou, who was chosen to lead the UN recourse three years later, admitted in his 1955 memoir that before Papagos became prime minister he regularly advised against such an option because he feared that the Centre governments were too weak to handle the initiative successfully.[88]

Meanwhile, since the arrival of the Cypriot delegation to Athens in May 1950, a mass movement in support of *Enosis* began to gather momentum. In June, the Head of the Greek Church, Archbishop Spyridon, announced the formation of PEAEK, whose activities started to influence Greek public opinion.[89] PEAEK was jointly founded by the Church of Greece and the General Confederation of Greek Workers (GSEE), which had been cleansed of all leftist elements during the Civil War.[90] Many professional associations, like the unions of Greek industrialists, ship owners, doctors, lawyers, journalists, civil servants, school teachers and others were represented on its 32-member executive.[91] PEAEK's rank-and-file support came largely from university students, who also established their own association, the Students' Committee for the Cypriot Struggle (PEKA), but much support came from churchgoers, workers and schoolchildren, who attended public rallies often at the behest of their teachers. During these rallies, fervent nationalist speeches were given by Archbishop Spyridon, accompanied by anti-British slogans from the crowd, whose obvious aim was to embarrass the Anglophile policy of the Centre governments.[92] At PEAEK's first rally on 21 July 1950, before 100,000 supporters at the Marble Stadium of Athens, Spyridon warned that 'the Greek Church is ready to take its full responsibility with regard to Cyprus if the Greek Government remained hesitant'.[93]

Although formally a pressure group, a large segment of PEAEK's leadership was closely linked to the Greek state, either formally or informally. Besides hosting representatives from the state employees' union (ADEDY), the teachers' union (OLME) and the Confederation of Public Corporations (NPDD),[94] senior army officers, civil servants and establishment academics were active in its committees. According to a record of its early structure, PEAEK had eight 'struggle committees', of which one, the Special Committee on National Defence, recruited members from the army, the police and the gendarmerie. High-ranking officers took part in the secret meetings where PEAEK's so-called clandestine activities were planned. These, *inter alia*, recommended that if a Briton or a Turk committed a 'grave injustice' against a Greek in Cyprus, 'the well-known order "an eye for an eye and a tooth for a tooth"' should be applied 'to maximum degree'.[95] The fact that PEAEK was officially led by a Church that was not separated from the state and a trade union movement that was vertically controlled by the Labour Ministry[96] enhanced its hybrid character as an organization that was quasi-autonomous in relation to the state.

Overall, PEAEK's position in the system of Greek foreign policy defies easy categorization. On one hand, the organization was not a frontage for the Greek government to provide an *alibi* for its nationalist demands towards Britain, as officials in London, Washington and Ankara concluded.[97] Besides the absence of any evidence to support such claims, PEAEK firmly opposed the Centre governments and often antagonized them. Archbishop Spyridon never hesitated to publicly embarrass Venizelos and Plastiras for failing to strenuously campaign for *Enosis*. During a PEAEK rally at Omonia Square on 8 May 1952, before 50,000 supporters, he endorsed a petition expressing 'intense disappointment because successive Greek governments and the country's leadership in general have shown a lukewarm attitude toward [...] *Enosis*'. Correspondingly, the Interior Ministry at that time never failed to use force against the crowds during PEAK's rallies. Even pro-government newspapers, like *Eleftheria*, reported 'episodes', 'injuries' and 'arrests' during police clashes with PEAEK, while Spyridon was often criticized for 'inciting' acts which undermined public order and encouraged aggressive protests outside the British embassy.[98]

On the other hand, the depiction of PEAEK as an essentially independent pressure group supported by some state institutions and right-wing opposition groups is equally problematic. This view, put forward by Stefanidis, reduces PEAEK to a by-product of 'the intimate relationship between the political Right and the leaders of the *Enosis* movement, the Church and the "official" trade unions'. According to this analysis, the Church and the trade unions initially acted 'as a two way transmission belt between public opinion and government', and gradually 'this mechanism tended to develop a momentum of its own'.[99] The main flaws in this interpretation are, first, its exaggeration of PEAEK's autonomy and, second, its portrayal of the 'political Right' as a nationalist monolith. In reality, PEAEK neither enjoyed significant autonomy from the Greek state nor did the opposition

Popular Party (the largest party of the right until September 1951) support its campaign. Indeed, when Rally deputies, like Kanellopoulos and Stefanopoulos, attacked Plastiras on 23 November 1951 for using excessive force against PEAEK, the Popular Party leader Tsaldaris condemned the protest for its 'anti-foreign spirit' and its supposed alignment with the aims of the Cominform. Tsaldaris even criticized the Centre government 'for allowing the gathering to happen'.[100]

A more precise analysis must start by focusing on the intense antagonisms within the *Ethnikofron* political system between the traditional elites whose powerbase lay in Parliament, and the bureaucratic, corporatist and parastatal apparatuses which rose to prominence during the Metaxas Dictatorship, the Axis Occupation and the Civil War. The Popular and Centre parties (despite their differences) embodied the former tradition, while PEAEK emerged as an organization representing the latter which, besides the Church and the unions, was secretly managed by leaders of the parastate, including officers linked to IDEA and retired military leaders like Grivas. One of the core differences between the two factions was the preference of the traditional parties for an institutionalized, elitist and predominantly Atlanticist variant of *Ethnikofrosyni*, which contrasted with the new elites' preference for a populist and pronouncedly nationalist approach that was more militant. Between the two camps, new parties like LEK, the New Party and, ultimately, the Greek Rally opted for a third position which sought to embrace PEAEK's populism, albeit within a firmly Atlanticist framework.

In this context, PEAEK must be conceptualized as one of the corporatist associations of the post-Civil War state originating not in the formal state institutions, but in the informal, semi-autonomous networks connecting its bureaucratic, parastatal and incorporated interest groups (the unions, the Church, officers' clubs, etc.) Therefore, the notion that PEAEK possessed significant autonomy in relation to the Greek state is inaccurate given that it was originally an outgrowth of the state's own incorporative mechanisms with the aim of mobilizing the popular masses in a vertical manner around a vulgar version of *Ethnikofrosyni*. At the same time, because of its origins in the informal bureaucratic, parastatal and corporatist apparatuses, PEAEK also enjoyed some relative autonomy, only in relation to the government and, more so, the governments of the Centre (mirroring a similar tactic by the IDEA officers in the army). For example, when the Rally came to power, PEAEK adopted a lower public profile. After 1952, the organization began supporting the Rally's foreign policy and when Papagos took the Cyprus question to the UN in August 1954, it organized mass rallies in support of the government.[101] This loyalty had shown itself earlier. When Kyrou spoke in New York on 21 September 1953, explaining why the Rally Government was not bringing Cyprus to the UN that year, PEAEK did not organize its usual mass anti-government rallies, even though the Centre press protested that 'The Government has abandoned the Cyprus Question'.[102]

At this point, it is worth examining the evolving policies of Britain, the United States and Turkey regarding the issue. In Britain, despite a change of government in 1951 from Labour to the Conservatives, official policy on Cyprus remained largely unaffected. As Eden noted in his memoirs, successive Greek Governments tried to raise the issue of *Enosis* [...]. The Labour Government in Britain, during its years of office after the war, steadfastly refused to discuss the subject. The Conservative Government which succeeded them maintained the same attitude.[103]

Throughout the early 1950s, British policy was not merely confined to London's refusal to discuss any change of sovereignty in the island but was premised on the rejection of such discussions even in relation to the distant future. For example, during his fruitless meeting with Averoff in Rome in November 1951, Eden repeatedly stressed that 'the future of Cyprus was not a topic which I was prepared to discuss'.[104] The same emphasis was given by Peake in his meeting with Papagos on 25 November 1952. 'Neither now nor in any foreseeable future', he said, 'could my Government contemplate any change of sovereignty'.[105] From a British standpoint, a Cyprus question did not exist. Ahead of his (subsequently cancelled) visit to Greece in April 1953, Eden was advised by the Foreign Office to 'stress as firmly as possible that Her Majesty's Government's attitude is unwavering and that the Greek Government will be well advised not to ventilate the matter at any time or place'.[106]

Although different in both style and substance, US policy was equally unchanged throughout the early 1950s.[107] In July 1952 Acheson stressed that 'our views on Cyprus [are] well known to parties directly concerned. Related briefly, they are that US [is] not party to the problem, but does not believe it useful for [the] Greek Government to press the matter'.[108] In August 1953, Dulles used an almost identical wording in a message to the embassy in Athens: 'Our views continue as previously stated, i.e., that US [is] not party to [the] problem, but does not think [it] useful for Greek Government [to] press the matter'.[109] As Stefanidis remarks, this 'sitting on the fence' originated in Washington's view that 'both Greek national aspirations and British imperial interests' differed from its own strategic objectives, which focused on 'containing Soviet expansion in the region'.[110] In this regard, US policy supported Britain's continued colonial presence in Cyprus chiefly as a deterrent to Soviet expansionism in an island whose largest party was the communist AKEL.[111] Evidently, US policy was marked by contradictions insofar as it sought to combine a neutralist position ('not party to problem') with a strong preference for the colonial *status quo* ('not think useful for Greek Government press the matter'). In other words, Washington's underlying position was to avoid taking sides on the Cyprus issue to prolong British colonialism indefinitely.

Finally, Turkish policy was also consistent, although in contrast to Washington's, it was not marked by inner contradictions.[112] Ankara held long-standing concerns about the future of Cyprus in case British sovereignty were to be withdrawn, but these were not voiced early on.[113] In a meeting with the US ambassador in Ankara on 26 February 1954, Muharrem Nuri Birgi, Director of the Turkish Ministry of Foreign Affairs, stated that his government refrained from 'any action or statement on Cyprus which might inflame public opinion' and avoided formal representations, but 'intimated indirectly several times that [the] Turkish Government hoped [the] Greek Government would not officially support agitation for enosis'.[114]

Birgi repeated these views to the British ambassador in Ankara on 19 March.¹¹⁵ A similar reading of Turkish policy was presented to Papagos on 12 February 1954 by Christoforos Christidis, a Greek advisor who was sent to Istanbul on a secret fact-finding mission. There, Christidis discovered that the Turkish Government 'avoided taking a position over the matter' to protect Greek-Turkish relations.¹¹⁶ In other words, much like London, Ankara refrained from making public statements to avoid turning Cyprus into 'an issue'. As the Turkish ambassador in Washington, Erkin, told the State Department on 10 March,

> although the question of the union of Cyprus with Greece has been controversial for many years, the Turkish Government has taken no note of it and has always attempted to play [it] down... because the *Enosis* issue has never before been supported by the Greek Government.

When Papagos started threatening to take the issue to the UN, Erkin stressed that Turkey saw 'no reason for any change of the *status quo*' in the island. He told US officials that, if British sovereignty were to be withdrawn, his government's position would be the following: 'It is not international custom to decide questions of sovereignty solely on the basis of minority wishes of the population, but there are also equally important geographical considerations which must be taken into account.' Because Cyprus was geographically closer to Turkey, this statement amounted to an implicit territorial claim on the island. To avoid misapprehensions, Erkin stressed that his government believed 'the possession of Cyprus would be of no advantage to Greece' as the island was 'of far greater importance to Turkey'. Nonetheless, the Turkish ambassador reaffirmed that even 'the public airing of the question' was unacceptable to Ankara. Finally, echoing Washington's concerns, he added that 'only the Soviet Union stands to profit' from this issue as the island hosts a large Greek-Cypriot communist party.¹¹⁷

Papagos's early policy on Cyprus and his meeting with Eden

Since his first days in office, Papagos treated the Cyprus question as an issue of high priority. During his new government programme statement on 17 December 1952 he declared that the Rally 'shall address the Cyprus question, which is dear to the hearts and souls of all the Greeks, within the framework of present realities'.¹¹⁸ Although the wording did not signal a major policy shift, the very fact that Cyprus was mentioned at all marked a break with the approach of the Liberal-EPEK coalition, whose leaders omitted all reference to the issue from their own programmatic statement in 1951 for fear of alienating Britain.¹¹⁹

According to Stephen Xydis, while in opposition, Papagos had asked his parliamentary deputy, Stamatis Merkouris, to broach the Cyprus issue with Peake, but the British ambassador 'laughed this message off, saying that all Greek governments raised the Cyprus question'. This response, apparently, 'annoyed' Papagos, who then asked Markezinis to arrange a dinner with Peake where, as

Merkouris later told Xydis, 'he personally sought to impress the British Ambassador about his earnestness'.[120] Although Xydis provided no further details, it should be stressed that Papagos was not alone in holding strong feelings about *Enosis*. His deputy prime minister, Kanellopoulos, was also a PEAEK sympathizer and in November 1951 he strongly protested against the use of force with pro-*Enosis* supporters. Similarly, the Rally's other deputy prime minister, Stefanopoulos, also described the authorities' behaviour on that day as 'barbaric'.[121] Both interventions were unusual, as leading *Ethnikofron* politicians typically refrained from siding with street protesters so soon after of the Civil War.

When the Rally raised the Cyprus issue during its programmatic statement, the British embassy initially misquoted Papagos as having said: 'A faction of the British Island Colony is demanding enosis'. This false report was hailed as good news by the Foreign Office, whose officials described it as 'the first admission by a Greek post-war prime minister' that 'the enosis campaign is really conducted by a vocal minority'.[122] Of course, anyone familiar with Papagos's views, let alone a diplomatic mission charged with the task of closely monitoring his statements, would have questioned the accuracy of this translation. Nevertheless, it took ten days for Peake to resolve the misunderstanding when, after a meeting with Papagos, he reported that the prime minister had expressed the hope that 'one day Greece and the United Kingdom could reach an amicable solution' to the Cyprus question. During that conversation, Peake reaffirmed Britain's position that 'neither now nor in any foreseeable future could [his] Government contemplate any change of sovereignty', but Papagos replied that he 'hoped [the British] should be able to be a little more forthcoming than this in the future'. Still, the Field Marshal conceded that 'it would be wise to give [Peake's] Government an opportunity to see what his could do'. Surprisingly, the Foreign Office still thought that Papagos's 'attitude on Cyprus is quite reassuring', although its officials this time concluded that Greece's new prime minister, 'like his predecessors [...] cannot bring himself to believe that our attitude is final'.[123] Eden seemed more perturbed than his officials by this report and in a handwritten notation asked: 'Should there be any answer?'[124] Eventually, no reply was given, but in January 1953 the Foreign Office requested the State Department 'to make it quite clear to the Greeks, that the U.S. Government would certainly oppose the placing of the Cyprus question on the agenda of the [UN] Assembly'.[125]

Despite these early difficulties, Papagos continued to raise the Cyprus question within the framework of Greece's commitments to NATO. In so doing, he departed from the Centre governments' approach, not only in his resolve to tackle the issue immediately, but also in extracting the Cyprus question from the bilateral context of Greek-British relations and placing it in a triangular framework that also included the United States. His approach also differed from the line of the radical advocates of *Enosis*, like the Cypriot Ethnarchy, who favoured a policy of 'internationalization', i.e. full escalation, including taking the dispute to the UN as a case of colonial occupation. In this regard, Papagos's new policy did not mark, as some historians have argued, a 'crossing of the Rubicon' towards the 'radical' positions of the Cypriot Ethnarchy.[126] In placing the Cyprus question within a trilateral Greek-British-American framework, he was beginning to chart a middle course between the bilateralism of the Centre governments and the line of 'internationalization' favoured by Makarios. As Leontios Ierodiakonou aptly remarks, the Rally Government 'appeared to have positioned itself fairly decisively in support of the *Enosis* struggle, but did not seem willing to follow Makarios's tactics'.[127]

Indeed, the Rally's policy differed from the Cypriot Ethnarchy's approach in several respects.[128] In the course of his own campaign, Makarios wrote on 27 April 1953 to the colonial Governor of Cyprus, Andrew Wright, asking directly for 'the realization of the right of the Cypriot people to self-determination'.[129] On 10 August he complained to the UN Secretary General, Dag Hammarskjold, that 'the UK [was] not respecting the right of the people of Cyprus [for] self-determination'.[130] Makarios then requested the UN Secretary General to submit a draft resolution entitled 'realization of the right of the people of Cyprus to self-determination', while the Ethnarchy's representative in Athens, Savvas Loizidis, submitted similar letters to the 3rd and 4th UN General Assembly Committees.[131] Despite this barrage of initiatives, Stefanopoulos instructed Kyrou at the UN 'to defend of course the issue within the framework of the principles of the UN Charter, but [...] refrain from giving it the character of opposition or provocation towards Great Britain, unless of course provoked'.[132]

On this basis, during his high-profile speech to the Eighth Plenary Session of the UN on 21 September 1953, Kyrou summed up the Greek position as follows:

> The Cyprus question is not to be found among the agenda items of the present session. It is true that on August 10, the spiritual and national Chief of 4/5 of the Cypriot population addressed to the Secretary General [...] a Memorandum requesting the inclusion of that question on the agenda [...]. Normally, no one appeals to a court of law or to an international forum [...] before giving a fair chance to the possibility of direct negotiations. Therefore, my Government do not at this moment contemplate bringing this matter before our Organisation, since they are convinced that the close relations between Greece and the United Kingdom make it incumbent upon us not to underestimate either the resources of diplomacy or the political foresight of our British friends [...]. The door will always be open for us to go before a judge if the ordinary processes of friendly conversations prove to no avail.[133]

After the speech, Kyrou cabled Stefanopoulos to say that his intervention was commended by 'everyone, except the British, the Turks and the Cominformists'. He added that Dulles had looked for him during the reception and congratulated him in the presence of the British Under Secretary for the Colonies, Henry Hopkinson, on 'the moderation and high wisdom' of his intervention.[134] Kyrou also reported that he had had 'a friendly conversation' with Hopkinson and learned that part of his speech 'was sent to the Foreign Office with advice to Mr. Lloyd not to respond to it during his intervention after tomorrow'. He then proudly concluded that 'up to a point, an end has been put to the traditional [British] argument of a "closed issue". Also, a public dispute with Turkey was avoided, as my Turkish colleague did not inscribe his name on the speakers' list'.[135]

Although these conclusions were quite wishful and premature, the Rally Government had other reasons to be hopeful. First, Kyrou's implicit threat at the UN that Greece reserved the right at any time in the future 'to go before a judge' (i.e. the General Assembly) enabled Athens to claim the high moral ground from the Cypriot Ethnarchy as the leading advocate of *Enosis* on the Hellenic side. This became apparent when Loizidis issued a statement supporting what he called Kyrou's 'tactfulness' at the UN.[136] Second, Dulles's complimentary remarks to Kyrou in Hopkinson's presence showed that the Rally's dualist approach could open up a small, but potentially useful gap between the US and British positions. At this point, the US Bases Agreement, which gave Washington a strategic foothold on the boundaries of the British Middle East Command, was being secretly concluded. Against this background, on 22 September 1953, Papagos headed towards his planned secret meeting with Eden at the British embassy.

Eden had been convalescing in Greece throughout the previous three weeks, after a number of gallbladder operations that he had undergone in the United States.[137] It has been suggested that Papagos unwisely tried 'to take advantage' of his courtesy visit to the recovering Foreign Secretary to open the Cyprus issue.[138] However, the same criticism could be made of Eden, as he was the first to raise the subject when Papagos went to see him: 'He had greatly enjoyed his tour, [...] had had a very friendly reception ashore and he had been asked no questions about Cyprus', he said at the outset.[139] These minutes, which were taken by Peake, provide the most detailed record of the conversation. According to this version, after touching on the Field Marshal's forthcoming visit to Italy, the following exchange took place:

> Papagos then raised the subject of Cyprus and said that he felt obliged to mention this question, but that anything that might pass between him and Mr. Eden would be regarded as strictly secret, and that he did not intend to tell his Ministers that he had spoken of it.
>
> Mr. Eden said that he feared no discussion about Cyprus, whether private or no, could be fruitful. His position was that he could not consider, either now or in any predictable future, any change of sovereignty. In reply to a question from the Ambassador, Mr. Eden agreed that the House of Commons would in no circumstances consent to any change in the status of Cyprus. In this matter we, like Greece, had to undergo the discipline of democracy. While in Greece there was a disposition to see Cyprus come to Greece, in the United Kingdom there was an opposite disposition, equally firmly held.
>
> In reply to a question of the Ambassador, Field-Marshal Papagos agreed that the question was one based upon emotion.
>
> Field-Marshal Papagos then briefly developed his arguments in favour of a change of sovereignty. Mr. Eden said that Cyprus had never in fact belonged to Greece and that the only link between the two countries was a common language and hierarchy of the Orthodox Church. After all there was a considerable Greek

population in Alexandria and New York, but he did not suppose that the Greek Government was demanding enosis for them.

Field-Marshal Papagos seemed disappointed and said that, if this was to be our attitude, there hardly seemed any point in going on with the discussion. With this the Secretary of State agreed.[140]

Though broadly similar, Papagos's version of events was presented eighteen months later, in his parliamentary speech of 7 February 1955, most probably based on a minute which, according to Markezinis, he had dictated immediately after his meeting with Eden.[141] The Greek Prime Minister's version revealed details not included in Peake's record, like Eden's invitation to Papagos to visit London and the effect of the Cypriot Ethnarchy's campaign. It also used a braver tone when referring to his own replies, including the heroic crescendo. This is what Papagos recalled:

> At the beginning Eden extended to me an official invitation by the British Government to visit London. Then, turning to the issue, I presented the Cyprus situation to him, how difficult it was for the Greek Government after the Ethnarchy's recourse [to the UN], why we did not back it and insisted that it is necessary to reach a solution to the problem through bilateral friendly relations [...]. Mr. Eden listened to me carefully and replied bluntly that 'I shall repeat what I said before, that for the British Government there exists no Cyprus Question neither in the present nor in the future'. Then I replied that after this categorical statement, the Greek Government will deal with the issue in the way it sees best and most effective and that thereafter it will enjoy complete and total freedom of action.[142]

A third and often quoted account belongs to the former Cypriot diplomat Polys Modinos, who wrote in 1979 that shortly after meeting Eden, Papagos told him in confidence that:

> I considered it to be my duty as prime minister to visit [...] [Eden], who had come to Greece to rest after a serious illness. Following a friendly conversation, before I left, I expressed to him the hope that on another opportunity we should explore the issue of Cyprus which had grown to disappointing proportions. Eden cut me off abruptly and told me forcefully 'I do not see for what reasons Greece should be interested in Cyprus'. Then, for the first time, I felt the size of the gap that separated us.[143]

Although Papagos might have given Modinos this account, after the disclosure of the Foreign Office record, this version of events seems less credible than previously assumed. For example, the claim that Papagos simply said, as he was leaving the room, 'on another opportunity we should explore the issue', understates the importance of the meeting and the mindfulness of all participants that vital policy issues were being discussed.

Another account worth considering is that of the *New York Times* correspondent, Cyrus Sulzberger, whose source was the US ambassador, Cannon. In his diary entry for 19 May 1954, Sulzberger wrote:

> Cannon blames Peake, Eden and Papagos for the Cyprus mess. When Eden was here last autumn, recuperating, Peake could have informally suggested to the Greeks not to raise the matter. But Papagos came to the Embassy and saw Eden. He hauled out a paper outlining the Greek claim to Cyprus. Before he got started Eden arose, almost turning his back and said he would refuse to listen because there was no Cyprus question and he refused to admit its existence. In a cold rage Papagos put his paper back in his pocket. But he will never forget what he terms a personal insult.[144]

In focusing on Peake, Cannon's remarks shed valuable light on a range of important issues that have hitherto eluded the historiography. To begin with, it should be recalled that three weeks earlier, Dulles had forewarned Papagos (via Yost and Stefanopoulos) that raising the Cyprus issue with Eden would be counterproductive.[145] Untypically, Papagos disregarded this warning for reasons that have never been examined. Overlooked evidence, however, suggests that the Greek prime minister did not act arbitrarily, but chose to overlook Dulles's warning because he was advised to do so by someone much closer to Eden, who was none other than Peake himself. A State Department record of a conversation held in April 1954 between Ambassador Politis, US Assistant Secretary of State, Henry Byroade, and the Deputy Director of the Office of Greek, Turkish, and Iranian Affairs, William Baxter, states explicitly that 'last September when Eden was convalescing in Athens, Papagos, *at the personal suggestion of the British Ambassador*, tried to bring up this subject with Eden on a completely informal basis' (italics added).[146]

Seen from this angle, a range of other key points which have hitherto eluded the historiography can be illuminated. If we grasp that Peake was the architect of the Eden-Papagos meeting, we can understand why the encounter took place in such a guarded setting. From the British record of the conversation, it is clear that Papagos walked into a carefully staged meeting, in a room where no one else was present apart from Eden, Peake and, possibly his own *chef de cabinet*, Karatzenis.[147] Unless the British ambassador had known in advance that sensitive policy issues were to be discussed, there would be no reason for such secrecy during a courtesy visit. Moreover, if Peake was the person who advised Papagos to raise the matter, it becomes understandable why the Field Marshal chose to ignore Dulles's warnings, an otherwise uncharacteristic act for a prime minister who seldom disobeyed Washington's advice on foreign policy matters. In this case, only the encouragement of someone as close to Eden as Peake could have persuaded Papagos to cast aside Dulles's warnings.

Meanwhile, there are several contextual factors explaining why Peake proposed this meeting. To begin with, there is hitherto overlooked, yet solid evidence that the British ambassador disagreed with his government's policy on the Cyprus question. Official memoranda by Deputy Foreign Minister Averoff in November 1951 disclose that Peake told him, in strict confidence, that the Cyprus issue

> was serious, that personally he could say it would be definitely resolved, but with patience. That he would be happy, if he could contribute, not to the solution, but to the improvement of the current state of the issue, stressing that this is said at his own initiative and as his personal thoughts, and that he would be happy to discuss the issue as friends to see what could be really done without ignoring wider interests.[148]

In another memorandum, Averoff notes that during a discussion with Peurifoy, the latter revealed in what he asked to be an 'extremely confidential' exchange, that Peake's predecessor, Norton, was 'fully of the view that this issue [Cyprus] was serious and unpleasant, that the British should do something about it, but London did not listen to him'. Peurifoy then added that 'he is under the impression the current British ambassador is starting to embrace these views and thinks he should try to help to bring about some progress'.[149] Another important parameter is that Peake was a close friend of Eden's since their schooldays at Eton and this gave him first-hand access to the Foreign Secretary's thoughts and the liberty to influence policy in ways few other diplomats could. More importantly still, two years earlier, he had encouraged Averoff to go to Rome to raise the Cyprus issue with Eden during a fringe NATO Council meeting. According to Averoff, the British ambassador told him that he 'could freely present [his] views on the Cyprus question, but should not consider this as the beginning of formal talks but as an extremely confidential discussion he was trying, to prepare and explore in the fullest and most effective way, the Cyprus question'. Peake added that 'he would send a personal message to Mr Eden' and gave thorough instructions to Averoff on how to broach the issue: 'The meeting should not appear organised, must take place *a propos* another event, but should offer the chance of a frank ("open hearted") discussion of the Cyprus question'.[150] A very similar approach was used in Papagos's meeting with Eden in 1953.

Other evidence shows that the British ambassador was feeling increasingly frustrated with what he saw as Britain's declining influence in Greece. If he did not write it himself, then he must have known that Eden's briefing ahead of his (subsequently cancelled) visit to Athens in April 1953 spoke of 'a malaise' in Anglo-Greek relations since 1947.[151] Friendly British press reports remarked that 'Anglo-Greek relations [are] seriously strained, at a time when we have lost valuable connections with Greece by the withdrawal of all our forces and practically every mission'.[152] During a reception in Athens in October 1953, the Soviet ambassador Sergeev told Peake derisively that 'it was a pity [British] prestige in Greece was not as high as it had been', while friendly journalists agreed that 'Britain's influence in Greece has sadly declined'.[153] In January 1954, Peake complained to the Foreign Office about the 'formidable Russian and German competition' he was facing in the Greek press.[154] For these reasons, he looked for opportunities to influence British policy in ways that could make it more amenable to a friendly compromise with Greece over Cyprus. These concerns were fully appreciated by a strong opponent of British policy, Alexis Kyrou, who after 'numerous' meetings with him in the tense months preceding the UN recourse of 1954, noted that Peake 'strongly desired the attainment of a friendly compromise over the Cyprus issue between the two countries'.[155]

Another issue that eluded some accounts[156] is that, in opening the subject with Eden, Papagos was not demanding immediate *Enosis*. As Stefanopoulos told Dulles on 26 August 1953, the Field Marshal

> intended to propose that the British immediately grant to Cypriots a constitution which could accord them certain rights of self-government and which would be followed in two or three years by [a] plebiscite in which [the] Cypriots would be given a choice between independence, incorporation into Greece or some status within the Commonwealth.[157]

Although *Enosis* loomed at the end of this plan, Papagos proposed a phased British withdrawal coupled with the reaffirmation of the older offer of granting Britain military bases in Cyprus and Greece.[158] This idea, which belonged to Greek diplomats at the Ministry of Foreign Affairs, was originally proposed by the Venizelos and Plastiras Governments in 1951, and involved, 'besides the bases they would keep in Cyprus, our granting of one or two more in Greek islands [...], e.g. bases in Kefalonia and Melos'.[159] In other words, Papagos's plan aimed at bridging the short-term British solution of self-government with the long-term Greek aspiration of *Enosis*, in return for upgrading Britain's strategic position in the East Mediterranean. Moreover, as we shall see, he was willing to accept a longer transitional period of Cypriot autonomy than three years.[160]

Taken together, the impact of Kyrou's UN speech, Peake's continuous encouragement and the plan of a phased British withdrawal, gave Papagos some hope of making progress during his meeting with Eden. Another motive, which he mentioned on 7 February 1955 in Parliament, was the belief that Eden would appreciate the growing pressure on Athens from the Cypriot Ethnarchy and the *Enosis* movement. Hitherto, Papagos's success in deterring Makarios from seeking a UN sponsor from the Warsaw Pact or the neutral countries was based on his commitment to support a recourse himself, provided he was given time to exhaust the prospects of a bilateral solution with Britain. As it turned out, Papagos's first gambit failed. Still, his meeting with Eden was an option he was obliged to explore, even if the odds of a breakthrough were slim. Anything short of such an approach would have forced him to opt sooner for the more disagreeable option of challenging Britain at the UN; and despite what most historians have claimed since, this was an option he desperately hoped to avoid.

A typically overlooked aspect of Papagos's early foreign policy is that after his meeting with Eden, his immediate response was not to 'internationalize' the issue, but to give the Foreign Secretary a second chance. On 15 October, again on Peake's incitement, Papagos wrote to Eden requesting bilateral talks over the future of Cyprus, as if nothing had gone on between them.[161] Throughout the autumn of 1953, the Greek prime minister had hinged all his hopes on an official visit to London in which he planned to discuss Cyprus with the very man to whom he had, allegedly, taken 'a personal offence', and whose attitude, according to some accounts, had led him to abandon Anglo-Greek friendship.[162] These expectations were inadvertently encouraged by Eden's formal invitation to Papagos, sent on 10 November, in which he avoided replying to the Field Marshal's note of 15 October.[163] This gesture gave Athens the false impression that Eden's invitation did not rule out a discussion of the Cyprus question. Papagos then began to explore a more flexible Cyprus solution plan with the King. On 10 November, Peake reported that, according to Paul, Papagos wondered

> whether a formula could have been devised to the effect that Cyprus be the subject of an exchange between our two Governments and that, after a suitable delay, say two, three, four or even five years, it had been agreed that a plebiscite be held.

Paul added that, so far as he was concerned, 'ten, fifteen or even twenty years might have been mentioned in such a formula'.[164] On this basis, in mid-December Papagos told Peake that during his London visit he was 'minded to raise the Cyprus Question'.[165]

Meanwhile, the Rally Government made every effort to show that its preferred option was to solve the issue through bilateral talks. On 16 November, Kyrou told the US Representative at the UN, Henry Cabot-Lodge, that 'Greece would positively raise the Cyprus question' at the next session, but when asked about Athens's intentions, Kyrou asked if Washington could 'urge the British to show a little spirit of conciliation'.[166] On 25 November, in a *communiqué* stating that 'the Cyprus issue was being handled personally by the Field Marshal', the Greek Government stressed that it was seeking a solution 'by any means deemed necessary', but added its 'clear preference for bilateral talks with the British Government'.[167] Two days later, Stefanopoulos summed up the Greek position as follows:

> We are in favour of an arrangement of the issue based on mutual understanding. However, if against our best intentions, this path [...] is closed, we retain full freedom to resort to all means in our possession for the attainment of a solution.[168]

This time, again, Eden's response was blunt. In December, he told Ambassador Vassilios Mostras that Britain could repel a Greek recourse at the UN and, if necessary, stage a walkout.[169] He then asked Peake to inform Papagos that he 'might as well not come [to London] if he wished to raise Cyprus'. Peake persuaded Eden to moderate his reply and Papagos was finally informed that if he intended to raise the issue again in London, 'he would receive the same answer as last September'.[170] Papagos, who was sent this warning at least twice, waited a few days, and in January cancelled the visit to London. Even then, as the Foreign Office noted, he said 'nothing in public about his refusal to go to the United Kingdom', to avoid escalating the issue.[171] In so doing, he followed Peake's advice, who suggested that he 'better [...] say [...] that the pressure of Government had summoned him back to Greece'.[172]

Conclusion

According to Robert Holland, 'the "Eden-Papagos incident" [...] merits barely a footnote in British diplomatic history, but in Greek political folklore it looms large'.[173] Casting aside how someone unfamiliar with Greek language sources could claim such authority on Greek folklore, this view is factually incorrect. For if, as Holland acknowledges, the episode marked 'the beginning of the end [...] of Anglo-Greek friendship', then one should expect a fallout between two NATO allies at the peak of the Cold War to merit more than just 'a footnote' in the annals of British diplomatic history. Other accounts, which also treat the incident as heralding the end of 'Anglo-Greek friendship', have consistently stressed its importance for both sides.[174]

Strictly speaking, however, the Eden-Papagos episode did not mark a clear-cut break. Although Markezinis recalls that Papagos 'was frustrated' while dictating the minute of that conversation later on that day,[175] his official response was to give the British Foreign Secretary a chance to reconsider. Over the next three months, Papagos prepared his official visit to London with a view to presenting an improved version of his plan for Cypriot self-government followed by a referendum. Until Eden communicated in December 1953 that he was still opposed to discussing Cyprus in London, the depth of his disagreement with Papagos back in September – at least for the Greek side – remained unclear. Only in hindsight did the Greek Government fully realize that Eden's brusque manner in Athens reflected a deeper objection against discussing Cyprus in any form. In this respect, a shift in Anglo-Greek relations occurred when Papagos responded to Eden's second rebuff in January 1954 with a blunt cancellation of his London visit.

In the dominant narrative, the Eden-Papagos incident is considered a turning point in the history of the Cyprus question. Besides its appeal as an encounter befitting the 'great men' view of history, several accounts also suggest that shortly after the episode, the Greek Government announced its intention to 'internationalize' the issue.[176] Brendan O'Malley and Ian Craig argue that the Foreign Secretary's 'bilious outburst enraged Papagos, who resolved to punish Eden's arrogance by bringing the matter before the UN [...] thus internationalising the problem'.[177] James Ker-Lindsay notes that Eden's rebuff 'outraged' Papagos, who 'now adopted a much more hard-line stance'.[178] However, as we saw, Stefanopoulos had already used the UN threat before the Eden-Papagos meeting, when he told Yost on 1 September 1953 that 'if Papagos[']approach to Eden were unsuccessful and if Makarios's complaint to the UN were not withdrawn [...] the Field Marshal would feel obliged to support and even sponsor this complaint'.[179] Moreover, the view that the Rally began to 'internationalize' the issue straight after the meeting also rests on erroneous assumptions. The first is the systematic confusion between the Greek *threats* to 'internationalize' the Cyprus question and the actual adoption of a policy of 'internationalization'. The second is the equally prevalent misconception that 'internationalization' and 'bilateral negotiations' were mutually exclusive strategies.

As we shall see in the next chapter, from Stefanopoulos's exchange with Dulles on 1 September 1953 to the eve of the UN recourse in August 1954, the Rally Government referred to 'internationalization' strictly as *a threat*, with the aim of forcing the British Government to open bilateral negotiations with Athens on the future of Cyprus. Throughout this period, the Greek Government never missed an opportunity to stress that the UN recourse was a warning and not a *fait accompli*. In this regard, the Rally's policy not only rejected the rigid distinction between the strategies of 'internationalization' and 'bi-lateral negotiations' (in a manner contradicting their Manichean separation in the historiography) but was wholly premised on the belief that their combination provided the best method of attaining *Enosis*. For this reason, its public warnings in November 1953 about going to the UN did not constitute a policy shift caused by the Eden-Papagos meeting, but an affirmation of Stefanopoulos's statement to Dulles on 1 September.

A clearer change, however, did occur in January 1954, when Papagos cancelled his planned visit to London. This key decision meant that Greece was now determined to turn Cyprus, from a 'non-existent issue' according to Eden, into the uppermost item on its bilateral agenda with Britain. In cancelling the visit, Papagos was practically freezing all high-level dialogue with London until Eden revised his position on Cyprus. Although the historiography has overlooked the gravity of this reaction, there is no question that after that point Papagos started to place 'Anglo-Greek friendship' under severe strain. Of course, far from seeking to destroy it, his aim was to rescue that friendship through altering British policy.

Meanwhile, this change of tactics at the bilateral level with Britain corresponded to a wider policy revision towards a new version of dualism. While the Rally's early policy was based on drawing the United States more deeply into the dispute with Britain in the hope of gaining Washington's support over Cyprus, around the time of the conclusion of the Bases Agreement the limits of this tactic became apparent. As the exchange between Dulles and Stefanopoulos from 26 August to 1 September 1953 showed, Washington opposed any Greek initiative that could stir a dispute with Britain over Cyprus. In other words, Papagos's attempt to place the Cyprus question in a triangular framework involving Greece, Britain and the United States did not produce significant gains beyond highlighting the existence of a limited gap between the British and US positions. This forced the Rally Government to adjust its policy from seeking greater US involvement to simply securing US 'neutrality'. This adjusted tactics rested on a flexible approach that sought to involve the United States selectively, drawing it into the dispute with Britain when this was deemed capable of undermining London's objectives and holding it at bay when it appeared likely to serve British aims.

5

DEPENDENT NATIONALISM: 'OPERATING BETWEEN TWO NOTIONS'

According to the prevalent view in the historiography, Papagos is thought to have shifted his policy on Cyprus towards the 'radical' line of 'internationalization' after his meeting with Eden in September 1953.[1] This reading, however, is premised on two flawed analytical assumptions. The first is the systematic confusion between Papagos's *threat* to take the Cyprus question to the UN and his *actual decision* to proceed with the recourse itself. One example of this mix-up can be found in Svolopoulos's claim that, on 15 April 1954, Papagos 'took the decision [...] to internationalize the issue', and his later assertion that on 28 July, that is three months later, Papagos was still using 'the recourse to the UN as a threat'.[2] The same inconsistency remerges in Stefanidis' argument that since February 1954 Papagos had 'made up his mind' to go to the UN, even though he later remarks that until August 1954 he was trying 'to exhaust the time limits of direct negotiations'.[3] These positions reveal a serious contradiction over a key aspect of the history of the Cyprus question. For either Papagos was still seeking to 'exhaust the time limits of direct negotiations', which suggests that until August 1954 he was waving the UN recourse strictly as a threat; or, if his mind had been 'made up' in February or April, then he could not have been seeking bilateral negotiations after that point (as he was determined to go to the UN). Yet, in some improbable way, the dominant narrative in the historiography wants Papagos both hesitant and dogmatic over this issue; both seeking bilateral negotiations and having decided to 'internationalize' the Cyprus question; both treating the UN recourse as a threat and as a firmed-up decision.

The second issue in the historiography regarding this period is the blind spot surrounding the timing of Papagos's supposed early decision to proceed with the UN recourse. According to Dimitrios Bitsios, a future Foreign Minister who served at the time as a diplomat in London, 'December 1953' was the moment when Athens supposedly informed his chief, Ambassador Mostras, that 'Greece had exhausted every effort to reach a direct and friendly understanding with Britain' and 'decided to bring the issue to the United Nations'.[4] Such a message, however, was never identified anywhere, including the classified documents disclosed by Ambassador Mostras himself in 1959-60. According to Stefanidis, Papagos 'made up his mind' to go to the UN before Makarios's visit to Athens in February 1954. In saying so, he overlooks the testimony of Makarios's *chef de cabinet*, Kranidiotis, who recalled that during that visit the Greek Government 'was still hesitant' regarding this matter.[5] Stanley Mayes, without citing much evidence, argues that Greece announced it would go to the UN 'in March 1954', but Hatzivassiliou, following Xydis and Svolopoulos, claims that the decision 'was made in April 1954'. Hatzivassiliou notes, however, that this was 'not officially announced', but became self-evident 'in the summer',[6] although Xydis says, '*May 3*: Papagos committed himself publicly to his decision of 15 April to resort to the United Nations',[7] i.e. in the spring. The list is longer,[8] but these examples suffice to illustrate how this narrative, which otherwise claims that Papagos arrived at an early decision to take the Cyprus question to the UN, cannot remotely agree on the simple question of when that historic decision was made.

This chaotic state, however, confirms the speculative basis on which this entire narrative rests, as there is obviously no clear evidence that Papagos chose to go to the UN so long before the eve of the inscription deadline in August 1954. Had this evidence been as reliable as proponents of this narrative suggest, then their accounts should have converged around it. However, the fictional notion of an early Greek decision to 'internationalize' the Cyprus question is essential for the dominant strand in the historiography because it upholds the myth that Papagos was an 'idealist' and a 'radical' who was eager to 'internationalize' the issue and who rejected the supposedly better prospects of a 'pragmatic' bilateral solution. Were proponents of this narrative willing to acknowledge that Papagos decided to proceed at the eleventh hour, i.e. just before the expiry of the General Assembly deadline in August, as he said he would, then they would have to concede that Papagos genuinely wished to avoid a clash with Britain at the UN and truly preferred direct negotiations. But this possibility has been dogmatically ruled out by the historiography.

A more precise and consistent reading of the evidence, however, must start by recovering the nuanced approach of the Rally Government throughout the period January–August 1954. During these eight months, Papagos deployed a consistently intricate language, presenting his policy as a synthesis of two conflicting, yet complementary objectives. He often referred to it as seeking to combine 'openness with determination' or, on other occasions, as a policy blending 'flexibility and firmness'.[9] On 24 April, speaking to *Le Monde*, he stressed that his policy 'had to operate between two notions which at first appear contradictory':

> Le gouvernement est oblige d'agir dans deux sens qui à première vue semblent contradictoires, mais qui ne forment dans le fond qu'une politique parfaitement cohérente. [...] Il considère qu'il est de son devoir de server tant la cause de Chypre que la cause de l'amitié entre la Grèce et la Grande-Bretagne.[10]

On other occasions, his communication strategy (which according to Kyrou, was given utmost attention)[11] portrayed the policy as a conditional approach premised on the pronged formula 'definitely will/unless'. As Papagos told another interviewer at the time, 'the Greek government would definitely bring the dispute before the United Nations in the autumn, unless Great Britain agreed to open talks'. Part of this pronged formula was intended to stress that Greece 'would wait until the last minute' before inscribing the Cyprus issue on the UN agenda, precisely because its preferred option was a solution through bilateral talks.[12] Even an arch critic of the policy, like Ambassador Mostras, whose account was later invoked by several historians to misrepresent Papagos as a dogmatic advocate of 'internationalization', was always careful to frame the Rally's official policy in terms of the split 'either/or' formula. This is how he put it:

> When I assumed my duties in London in September 1953, I knew that the Cyprus issue would be raised directly by the Greek to the British Government, but did not know at that time which method would be followed exactly to this end, until the dilemma was finally posed to the British in February 1954 as: bilateral talks between Governments or recourse to the UN if the outcome of these talks was not satisfactory or if these would not take place.[13]

The liberal opposition press also understood the Rally's policy in this fashion. Following a statement by a Ministry of Foreign Affairs spokesman in April 1954, *Eleftheria* quoted him as saying: 'The Government, in seeking and desiring to conduct bilateral talks, is looking forward to a compromise solution [...] and if until 22 August an understanding is not reached, the Greek Government will take recourse to the UN, as has been decided'.[14] However, all these intricate formulations were later overlooked or subsumed in the scholarship under a reductionist reading that portrayed Papagos as having ostensibly 'simplified a complex issue' and fallen 'hostage to single value: nationalism'.[15]

The alternative interpretation proposed here holds that from January to August 1954, Papagos continued to pursue a dualist foreign policy based on a combination of the conflicting strategies of bilateral negotiations and internationalization. The aim of this approach was to implicate Britain in a game of brinkmanship, i.e. a high-risk confrontation whereby one side threatens to pull the other 'over the brink of disaster' to force it to compromise. As the security theorist Thomas Schelling explains, brinkmanship is

> the tactic of deliberately letting the situation get somewhat out of hand, just because its being out of hand may be intolerable to the [opposite] party and for his accommodation. It means harassing and intimidating an adversary by exposing him to a shared risk.[16]

In Papagos's case, 'the brink of disaster' was to openly clash with Britain at the UN with the aim of exposing it, and the whole NATO Alliance, as powers which, despite their liberal Cold War pronouncements, remained unreconstructed defenders of colonialism. In this game of brinkmanship, internationalization was never his strategic aim.

One of the obvious consequences of this high-risk approach was that, if Britain would persist in refusing to negotiate, Greece would face the major dilemma of either backing down in humiliation or giving substance to its threat and taking the issue to the UN. According to deterrence theory, any act of brinkmanship to succeed must make the opposite side see the threat as credible.[17] For this reason, when referring to the UN threat, the Greek formula often used words like 'definitely will', and Mostras, as we shall see, was instructed to deliver strongly worded messages to the Foreign Office precisely for this reason.[18] This rhetoric, however, does not imply that Papagos had firmed up his mind about going to New York before August. As Mostras found out when he met Papagos in April 1954, in yet another silenced passage from his account, the Greek prime minister 'seemed convinced that the British Government detested so much the discussion of an issue like Cyprus at the UN, that it would back down even in the last moment and accept negotiations between Governments'.[19] In other words, throughout this period the line of internationalization for Papagos had the status of *a threat* whose success, paradoxically, lay in it not being carried out.

As in the earlier variant of his policy, Papagos's revised tactics in January–August 1954 were always based on a dualist approach. The underlying premise of his policy was that the quest for *Enosis* could be most effectively attained through its combination with an Atlanticist policy committed to NATO's interests and the principle of 'Anglo-hellenic friendship'. His loyalty to the Atlantic Alliance and the strategic role of the United States in the Balkans remained so strong, that despite growing discouragement from Washington about his Cyprus plans, he displayed great zeal in furthering US aims in the Balkan Pact and the Trieste dispute. In this context, his early dualism of seeking *Enosis* through dependence gave way to a modified version that sought *Enosis* in tandem with dependence. In practice, this meant that Greece would continue to display full loyalty to the United States, but not with the aim of receiving American support over the Cyprus question. Instead, its new goal was to keep Washington neutral over this issue, in order to isolate Britain as Papagos's brinkmanship game over Cyprus escalated. At no point, however, did the Greek prime minister contemplate, as for example his chief ally-turned-critic, Markezinis, that his unqualified loyalty to the United States could be at odds with his brinkmanship game with Britain over Cyprus. For this reason, when the latter pressed him to revise his Cold War strategy with an opening to Moscow and a postponement of the UN recourse, he first isolated and then dismissed him.

Containing the internal opposition: The marginalization of Markezinis

The departure of Papagos's most powerful minister from cabinet on 29 March 1954 was a major political event, described at the time by *Le Monde* as 'a real bombshell'.[20] Although Markezinis was widely viewed as Papagos's 'chief tactician' and the government's 'most powerful figure',[21] his resignation, rather astonishingly, attracted little attention in the historiography on the Cyprus question. This is more puzzling in view of the fact that his disagreements over foreign policy have been known for a while as the main cause of his dispute with Papagos.

The incident that prompted Markezinis's resignation was a heated argument at the cabinet meeting of 29 March 1954 over the appointment of the Director of the

Controls Council. The Rally's Coordination Minister used provocative language which, according to Linardatos (whose source was probably Markezinis himself), led to the following exchange:

> Papagos: We came here to a meeting. But under these conditions the meeting cannot take place.
> [Markezinis continued to make his points to the other members of the cabinet, ignoring Papagos].
> Papagos: Hear what I say? I demand respect. I am the one who governs.
> Markezinis: Well then, and I am leaving.
> Papagos: We do not keep anyone here against their will. Gentlemen, the meeting is adjourned.[22]

When Papagos met the King on 2 April, he presented Markezinis's resignation as an outcome of the latter's misconduct in cabinet. Peake, who saw the King immediately afterwards, reported that the Field Marshal told Paul that his minister 'had become very excited and had started to wave his arms about and shout at the top of his voice'. Although Markezinis later sent a letter of apology, Papagos stood by his decision and told Peake that he was 'fully determined to have done with [him]'.[23]

Ever since, the ill-mannered style of the Rally's Coordination Minister has been regularly cited as the cause of the most serious split within the Papagos government since its formation. Stefanopoulos remarked that 'Markezinis behaved tactlessly [...] and the dispute was very largely a personal matter'. George Rallis, a junior minister who worked closely with the prime minister, wrote that 'Markezinis used to talk to Papagos in a gruff manner [...] and Papagos would not normally tolerate that sort of thing'.[24] Peake's initial assessment that the incident represented a clash between two individuals in 'a struggle for power' is equally superficial.[25] This conclusion, which could describe any political dispute since the dawn of history, gave no indication either of the kind of power Markezinis was after nor of the ways in which his misconduct in cabinet could have helped him to attain it. The view of another British diplomat in Athens, John Galesworthy, that the clash was motivated by Papagos's refusal to make Markezinis deputy prime minister,[26] was dismissed by the latter, who boldly told Galesworthy that the issue 'had never arisen in any form' since he was 'not interested in being Vice-Premier, but Premier'!'[27] More recent attempts to attribute the dispute to a disagreement over economic policy or Markezinis's alleged 'refusal to move to the Foreign Ministry' are ill-informed.[28]

Forty years after his resignation, Markezinis published his *Modern Political History of Greece* (1994) in which he revealed that his verbal quarrel in cabinet was staged deliberately to conceal what he called 'my deeper dispute with Papagos'. Markezinis described these as consisting of: (a) Papagos's 'refusal to accept the overture towards the Soviet Union'; (b) 'the reversal of the oblivion policy' towards the left and (c) 'above all, the violation of our agreement regarding the Cyprus Question and the Foreign Ministry'.[29] Third-party evidence confirms that this account was not a retrospective invention. Two weeks after his resignation in 1954, in his informal conversation with Galesworthy, Markezinis identified the same issues as the deeper causes of his dispute with Papagos. He began by describing the notorious cabinet scene as 'entirely unimportant' and 'no more the cause of his resignation than the shooting at Serajevo had been the real cause of the first war'. He then turned to what he called – even at the time – the 'real causes underlying his dispute with Papagos', but presented those cautiously, not least because they touched on issues linked to Greece's dispute with Britain over Cyprus. The first issue, he said, was that 'he was not prepared to remain as Minister of Co-ordination without the power which [...] properly belonged to the post', and stressed that he was 'anxious that Greece should be as economically independent as possible from all sides and had striven to achieve this'. The reference here was to the thorny issue of his proposed visit to Moscow, which he discussed explicitly in his 1994 account. Second, Markezinis spoke about 'Papagos' [...] failure to obey the rules of government by Cabinet', explaining that 'it was intolerable that policy on an issue as vital as Cyprus should be known only to Papagos, Stefanopoulos and the Director-General of the Ministry of Foreign Affairs [Kyrou]', adding that 'he shared the views of Papagos and of all Greeks [...] in regard to Cyprus'. The reference here was confined to his own exclusion from the small-knit group in charge of the Cyprus issue, but no mention was made of Papagos's promise to make him Foreign Minister. Finally, without naming the 'oblivion policy' towards the Left, he criticized Papagos's dismissal of the Public Order Minister at the reshuffle of 10 April, his friend Pausanias Lykourezos, a decision he attributed to the Chief of Police, Angelos Evert, who had the prime minister's ear. Although the full background to the Lykourezos-Evert Affair remains unknown, according to Linardatos, the Chief of the Police 'accused Lykourezos of inaction against communist activity'.[30] In this connection Markezinis also added that 'it was a mistake to create an Under-Secretariat of Security and Public Order, since it had a rather unpleasant sound'.[31]

After this exchange, which Galesworthy described as 'sincere' and the Foreign Office found 'remarkably similar to another account',[32] London concluded that Markezinis resigned because he had lost his influence with Papagos. While this reading was more accurate than Peake's initial analysis, Markezinis's loss of influence with Papagos was wrongly attributed by London to the alleged increase in the power of the army and the IDEA group. Other developments, which the Foreign Office could not have known, suggest that IDEA was not a major factor behind the cooling off of relations between the Rally's founding pair. Moreover, Markezinis never mentioned IDEA as an issue, neither to Galesworthy nor in his 1994 account.

Both in his book *Memories 1972–1974* (1979) and his aforementioned *Political History* (1994), Markezinis disclosed that Papagos had agreed to appoint him Foreign Minister ahead of the expected developments in the Cyprus question and that he later reneged on this promise. He stressed that he (Markezinis) was close to Alexis Kyrou and his brothers, Achilleas (who died in 1950) and Kyros, who succeeded his late brother as editor-in-chief of the nationalist *Estia*.[33] Indeed, it was *Estia* that first published Markezinis's articles on the 'national oblivion' policy towards the Left, before they later reappeared in *To Vima*.[34] Kyros was also in contact with the radical elements of the *Enosis* movement, including the group which secretly founded EOKA. In his *Memories*, Markezinis also wrote that he was 'fond of Grivas-Digenis', but added that, together with Kyros, they never forgave him for softening his approach in 1959 and accepting the Zürich Agreement, which they saw as a betrayal of *Enosis*.[35] In 1953, it was Markezinis who persuaded Papagos to recall Alexis Kyrou from New York and appoint him Director of the Ministry of Foreign Affairs, to pave the way for his own arrival at the head of the Foreign Ministry. This story was later confirmed by Kyrou himself.[36] To understand the importance of this appointment, it should be noted that the Turkish Government formally protested to the US Ambassador against it because Kyrou, as Consul in Nicosia in 1931, had supported the *Enosis* riots in Cyprus.[37] Both Ankara and Washington also viewed his appointment as a sign of radicalization in Greek foreign policy.[38]

Another area of disagreement was Papagos's rejection of Markezinis's proposal to visit Moscow. The idea of a trip to the USSR was formally presented as aiming towards an economic opening to the East to ensure, as Markezinis told Galesworthy, that Greece became more 'economically independent'.[39] In his 1994 account, Markezinis added that the proposed visit would also 'contribute toward the consolidation of internal peace' with the Greek Left,[40] an approach which he actively pursued for some time. For example, US archives show that in March 1953 Markezinis met Peurifoy and the local CIA chief, Tom Karamessinis, to alleviate their concerns about his tolerant attitude towards the Left.[41] Markezinis cultivated good relations with the leader of EDA, Yannis Passalidis, and intervened to stop the closure of the party's newspaper *Avgi*.[42] Indeed, it was Passalidis who had advised him 'to go to Moscow and negotiate a trade agreement rather than go to Washington and seek aid'.[43] In his conversation with Peurifoy and Karamessinis, Markezinis claimed that his contacts with EDA were part of a domestic strategy aimed at increasing the power of the left to divide the anti-Rally opposition.[44]

However, there was a deeper dimension to Markezinis's proposed visit to the USSR. In September 1953, four months after the disappointing economic results of his visit to Washington, Greece restored diplomatic relations with the Soviet Union for the first time since 1947.[45] Upon his arrival to Athens, the new Soviet ambassador, Sergeev, met several members of the Rally cabinet and, in the spirit of Moscow's 'new foreign policy', argued that 'there was good scope for a mutually beneficial expansion of trade between Greece and the Soviet Union'.[46] Sergeev also proposed an exchange of 'journalists, scientists and cultural representatives' and recommended the resumption of the old practice of the Russian chartering of Greek ships, a deal that would require the opening of a chartering office with the Soviet red flag waving over the communist stronghold of the Port of Piraeus.[47] Also, on 21 October 1953, the Rally Government agreed to facilitate the visit of thirteen Greek journalists and personalities to Moscow, including two leftists, to attend the celebrations for the anniversary of the October Revolution.[48] This approach contrasted sharply with the previous year's decision in which the Rally forbade its future Minister of Shipping, Lambros Lambrianidis, from accepting a similar invitation.[49]

During his meetings with the Rally ministers, Sergeev proposed the resumption of diplomatic relations between Greece and Bulgaria.[50] On 21 September, the idea was endorsed by cabinet and Markezinis defended it in his conversation with Galesworthy. Although he appeared concerned about what he described as a subtle Soviet ploy 'to break up the Balkan Pact', he added that 'the Russians were [...] sufficiently eager, to be willing to pay the price for it'.[51] A Foreign Office official shared this appraisal and remarked that 'the Soviet "new look" towards Greece was an astute move'.[52] In the same conversation, Markezinis also raised broader questions of East-West relations and expressed the view that 'the cold war had now entered a new phase', arguing that 'the Russians [...] might now be contemplating entirely new tactics'.[53] In saying so, he was clearly not speaking for the government, since Papagos, who discussed the same issue with French Foreign Minister Georges Bidault in Paris in January 1954, thought that 'the Soviet new look was nothing to get excited about'.[54]

Exactly what Markezinis aimed to achieve from the cabinet episode of 29 March 1954 remains unclear. One possibility is that he overreacted in a manner he later regretted. Another, as he always maintained, was that he staged the incident to avoid publicizing the real issues and, by implication, stir a damaging public controversy at a delicate time for the Government's Cyprus policy. In that case, his written apology to Papagos might have been confined only to the verbal quarrel, but not to his decision to resign. A third possibility is that he staged the clash as a last-ditch attempt to change Papagos's mind over the direction of his foreign policy. It is worth stressing that although he controlled a group of deputies, Markezinis continued to sit on the Rally benches for eight more months, until he was forced to leave the party in November 1954, following accusations by his former cabinet colleagues over the 'German credits' scandal.[55] In other words, it is possible that his resignation was not intended as a total break with Papagos, but as a bargaining tool to enable him to return Government on his own terms. In 1994, Markezinis claimed that 'Papagos both expected and desired my return', adding that he refused because he disagreed with the policy on Cyprus.[56] Whatever explanation one adopts, it is clear that Markezinis ultimately caused a rift because Papagos had kept him out of his inner foreign policy group. Even if the Field Marshal had suggested his return, his apparent unwillingness to give him a foreign policy role implies that Papagos still wanted to exclude him from his decision-making team on Cyprus.

Moreover, it is not completely apparent what alternative policy Markezinis envisaged regarding Cyprus. If we collate the fragments from his later accounts, it appears that he favoured a different policy mix, combining a more assertive nationalism (and openness to Moscow) with a more tactful handling of the UN recourse. Markezinis claimed that he 'belonged to the *Enosites* and was the first to support self-determination within a given and sensible time frame, a policy that was abandoned after the death of Papagos'. He was also supportive of EOKA's armed struggle and Grivas's leadership of that organization. At the same time, he disagreed over the timing of the UN recourse, because he feared that Britain would retaliate through encouraging Turkey's involvement and thereby render *Enosis* impossible. In this connection, he recalled Peurifoy's advice 'not to underrate the reaction of the British [...] implying that their reaction would involve raising the minorities' issue', i.e. the rights of the Turkish minority in Cyprus. When he relayed the message to Papagos, he recalled that the latter 'smiled condescendingly' and 'almost called me gutless or so Anglophile as to overstate what Britain wanted and could do'.[57] At any rate, Markezinis's views on the Cyprus question were not that different from those of Kyrou, whom he described as 'my close collaborator on the Cyprus question' for many years to come.[58] In other words, as a leading Rally minister, he favoured a different variant of dualism, whereby a more assertive stand at the level of the Cold War, *Enosis* and EOKA's armed struggle would be combined with greater moderation regarding the UN and Greek-Turkish relations.

In terms of its significance for the Rally's foreign policy, the marginalization of Markezinis was a typical case of what Bachrach and Baratz have termed 'non-decision making'. According to their definition, a 'non-decision' is 'the practice of limiting the scope of actual decision-making to "safe" issues by manipulating the dominant community of values, myths, and political institutions and procedures'.[59] In the case of Markezinis, this was achieved, first, through his quiet exclusion from the small-knit group which formulated the Government's policy on Cyprus and then through indefinitely postponing his appointment as Foreign Minister. Behind this approach stood the prime minister's desire to remove two unwelcome options from the range of decisions which he considered 'unsafe', namely the revision of his firmly Atlanticist framework and the abandonment of the UN threat. The effective use of a series of 'non-decisions' by Papagos was precisely what forced Markezinis to resign. As is often the case, non-decisions are carried out quietly, in ways that are not immediately visible to those outside. In the case of Markezinis, the manipulation of the institutions and government procedures by Papagos was achieved so discretely, that until the publication of the former's semi-autobiographical account in 1994, it was unclear that his resignation forty years earlier was caused by major foreign policy differences.

Upholding dependence: Papagos and the Balkan Pact

On 23 September 1953, Papagos flew with Stefanopoulos to Rome on an official visit. There, he told the Italian Prime Minister, Guiseppe Pella, that Greece's participation in the Treaty of Ankara was a 'military necessity [...] to defend the Balkans from an attack by the Soviet bloc' and expressed his wish that 'Italy should also join this alliance in due course'. Papagos reassured his Italian counterpart that Greece did 'not wish to become involved in the differences between Italy and Yugoslavia' and asked Stefanopoulos to read a telegram from Kyrou saying that, on the behest of the Americans, the Greek Representative at the UN had stopped the Yugoslavs from speaking on the issue of Trieste at the general debate. Stefanopoulos then reassured Pella that far from serving Yugoslav plans, Greece's membership of the Treaty of Ankara served Italian interests in Trieste.[60]

These minor gestures would have mattered little if seven months later a diplomatic crisis had not erupted over the future of the Balkan *rapprochement*. When Tito visited Ankara on 15 April 1954, a joint Turkish-Yugoslav *communiqué* announced that the two governments favoured the evolution of the Treaty of Ankara into a 'military alliance'.[61] Papagos, who was otherwise amenable to such a development,[62] asked the Greek ambassador in Ankara to protest to the Turkish Government on the grounds that 'this step [...] renders Greece a junior partner in the Balkan Alliance'.[63] Ankara then issued a corrective *communiqué* explaining that 'the Yugoslav-Turkish negotiations spoke generally of decisions that would become effective when Greece's consent had been secured'. It also dismissed as 'ridiculous' all reports claiming that 'the Greek Ambassador had left the dinner of our President of the Council or that he protested in the name of the Greek Government'.[64] Most probably, these reports were correct.

In his book *Balkan Triangle*, Iatrides explains Papagos's reaction to the Turkish-Yugoslav *communiqué* as 'most unexpected' and portrayed it as an outcome of poor communication between the three governments.[65] This reading, however, is linked to his broader view that the Balkan Pact was an alliance between three governments which, supposedly, refused to be 'mere pawns in the game of global politics'. As we saw, however, this thesis is flawed insofar as the Balkan *rapprochement* was the outcome of a closely managed American initiative secretly orchestrated from Washington. In this respect, the crisis of April 1954 must be re-assessed in light of new evidence that has come to light since Iatrides's study. A key part of this reassessment is to revise his problematic conclusion that 'the incident was officially considered closed' after the corrective Turkish *communiqué* of 17 April 1954.[66]

Since May 1952, Turkey and Greece had been working under close guidance by the State Department to conclude a political agreement with Yugoslavia which on 28 February produced the tripartite Treaty of Ankara. Initially, Washington requested Greece and Turkey to present the Treaty as an 'initiative belonging to Yugoslavia',[67] while later it instructed them to refrain from direct military talks with Belgrade as these would be 'premature' and supposedly 'incompatible with their positions in NATO'.[68] Washington also added a secret annex to the Treaty of Ankara which appears to have contained five emergency plans involving trilateral cooperation in the naval, reserve and counterattack, communications, information and electronic cooperation fields.[69] Washington finally asked its two NATO allies 'to keep the Italians informed about the political issues' discussed with Yugoslavia,[70] and requested a postponement of the Treaty 'until after the Italian elections [...] to avoid making things difficult for de Gasperi'.[71] Eventually, all but the last of these requests were adhered to, because on 4 February 1953 de Gasperi himself raised 'no objections' to an early signing of the Treaty. Meanwhile, the Yugoslav Foreign Minister, Koča Popović, also protested that the Treaty is 'much too important to be subjected to the Italian elections'.[72]

After its signing, the issue of developing the Treaty of Ankara into a full military pact became a persistent Yugoslav demand. This request was expressed throughout the next fourteen months and, contrary to Iatrides's conclusion, the Soviet 'peace offensive' of 1953 played no part in moderating it.[73] In August 1953, military representatives from Yugoslavia met secretly in Washington with their British, French and American counterparts to share anti-Soviet intelligence and firm up NATO's plans for the defence of Yugoslavia. There, they discussed 'the need to [...] tie up with the Greek and Turkish forces in the South'.[74] In November 1953, during tripartite military talks with Greece and Turkey in Belgrade, the Yugoslavs proposed developing the Treaty of Ankara into a full military pact. These proposals led Dulles to conclude that this 'eagerness' is 'most concrete evidence that [...] Tito [...] feels his future is inextricably linked with the West' and that '"normalisation"' with the Eastern Bloc countries was nothing 'more than just that'.[75] Recent research on the correspondence between Tito and Nikita Khrushchev shows that prior to the conclusion of a military agreement with Greece and Turkey, the Yugoslav leader 'remained deeply distrustful of Soviet intentions' and only after signing the Balkan Pact in August 1954 did he resume relations with Moscow 'with vigour'.[76]

Before 15 April 1954, Washington maintained that, as long as the Trieste dispute remained unresolved, 'there can be no security for Southeastern Europe'. Dulles conveyed this position to Stefanopoulos on 30 October 1953,[77] and on 28 December, Cannon told the Greek Ministry of Foreign Affairs that 'the Question of Trieste will delay the wider integration of Yugoslavia, if not with NATO, at least "under the coordination" of NATO'.[78] This, he explained, meant that full military cooperation between Yugoslavia, Greece and Turkey had to be delayed.[79] On 16 February 1954, Bedell Smith instructed the US embassy in Athens to inform the Greek government that

> political considerations within NATO as concerns Italy and certain North European members [...] make it impossible, (repeat impossible) [to] advance Greek-Yugoslav military planning beyond contingent stage at this time. However, solution [of] Trieste situation would permit thorough re-examination of military situation in Balkans.[80]

When Cannon passed on the message to Stefanopoulos, he stressed that although the United States 'sees with much sympathy the issue of concluding a military pact with Yugoslavia [...] it nonetheless considers that its signing is untimely given that the Question of Trieste remains unresolved'. Athens concurred and confirmed that although 'military talks should continue' Greece will 'promote relations with Yugoslavia, without, simultaneously, neglecting the difficulty created by the Question of Trieste'.[81] Although this approach caused tensions in Greek-Yugoslav relations, Papagos firmly adhered to it. In his meeting with Eisenhower on 18 March 1954, Kanellopoulos expressed 'his embarrassment at the recent request of Marshal Tito to have Greece sign a military agreement with his country', but added that 'Greece was avoiding doing [so] since such an agreement would affront Italy'.[82]

Besides using the Balkan Pact as a pressure lever on Tito over the Trieste issue, the Greek side kept the US embassies in Athens and Rome informed about the content of its discussions with the Yugoslavs. Greek archives contain several reports by Greek officials to the US ambassador in Rome, with extensive references to the Trieste dispute, all in response of his request for any 'information [...] about the discussions of Greek commanding officers with Yugoslav higher or top ranking officers'.[83] There is no evidence that this information was passed on directly from the Greeks to the Italians. It appears that Greek officials gathered intelligence from the Yugoslavs and passed it on to US officials and agents who used it as they saw fit. Therefore, Stefanopoulos's assurances to Popović that Greece hoped 'to see the normalization of your differences with the Italians' and was willing 'to help' both 'toward this end' were not candid.[84] Athens approached relations with Belgrade chiefly with a view to safeguarding its own security and increasing its political capital with Washington as a dependable ally.

Against this background, it becomes clearer why Athens was 'shocked and hurt' by the joint Turkish-Yugoslav *communiqué* of 15 April 1954.[85] After constant US requests to delay discussion of military cooperation with Belgrade until Tito compromised over Trieste, the joint *communiqué* from Ankara marked an unexpected victory for Belgrade and an act of Atlantic disloyalty by Turkey. Although Papagos favoured a speedy evolution of the Ankara Treaty into a military pact, his response shows that he placed Atlantic loyalty above Balkan priorities. Indeed, his first reaction after the issuance of the joint Turkish-Yugoslav *communiqué* was to call Cannon and then cable the Greek embassies in Ankara and Belgrade to say that the agreed policy with Washington had suffered a setback. This is what he wrote:

> You will have learnt about Popović's statement and joint communiqué concerning the decision of the Yugoslav and Turkish governments that the Tripartite Agreement resolves toward its natural development, the signing of a military Pact [...]. You are already aware of our views regarding the conclusion of a military pact, whose desirability we recognised before anyone else, on condition [...] that prior agreement with the members of the Atlantic Treaty is secured. Meanwhile [...] the American government put forward to us and Ankara recommendations about its postponement, which only we obeyed. Officially, the declarations about an agreed decision between Turkey and Yugoslavia, which we made without our knowledge, are an attempt to create a *fait accompli* and shows poor coordination [...] with harmful effects on wider US policy [...]. Our impression is that [...] a more important part was played by the Turkish government, which totally ignored Greek views and American reservations.[86]

Besides clarifying his deeper motives, this document shows that, in contrast to Turkey, Papagos was determined to display, in his own words, full 'obedience' to Washington's 'recommendations'.

However, despite the Turkish corrective *communiqué* of 17 April, the crisis deepened. For some days Papagos expected his loyalty to be reciprocated with

Washington's support, but he was soon to be disappointed. When Birgi extended 'his apologies' to Athens on 20 April 'for not keeping the Greek Ambassador informed',[87] the State Department, surprisingly, seemed to think that there was nothing inappropriate in Ankara's noncompliance. Ambassador Politis in Washington also confirmed that the State Department was taking a lax attitude over the matter:

> The impression of the Americans is that the Turks had been caught unawares by Popović's statement and that they attempted, not wholly successfully, to reduce the negative impression created by suggesting amendments to the joint communiqué. The Americans do not appear settled on a decision regarding how to resolve the situation, but insist on their stated opinion that likely military obligations by Greece and Turkey toward Yugoslavia should not contravene obligations deriving from the North Atlantic Treaty. To my question, the Director of the State Department replied that already, unofficially, surprise was expressed [...] from the Italian Embassy about the unexpected turn of Tito's visit to Ankara.[88]

On 21 April, Politis reported that the State Department was not only unwilling to criticize Turkey, but was now defending its actions:

> Mr Byroade does not think that the Turkish government tried to proceed wishfully toward the signing of a military agreement with Yugoslavia against American recommendations and NATO obligations [...]. Mr Byroade believes that the matter arose rather from the careless phraseology of Mr Popović. He emphasized to me that he has no reason whatever to believe that Turkey will ignore American recommendations.[89]

To confuse matters further, Popović publicly acknowledged that 'his statement was not successful', but blamed Ankara for giving him 'the impression that prior understanding had been arranged *a trois*' and called for 'better coordination – especially by the Turkish side'.[90] Amidst this imbroglio, the only other consistent position besides Papagos's was that of the Italian Government, which told Stefanopoulos on 30 April that they were satisfied 'by the successful [Greek] handling of the situation [...] following the rash Turkish acts'.[91]

In anticipation of Tito's forthcoming visit to Athens in June, Papagos started asking for new guidelines from Washington on how to close the matter. Meanwhile, on 4 May, in a clear proof that Turkey was attempting a deliberate policy shift, Birgi told the Italian Ambassador in Ankara that his government believed 'Trieste must be given second priority, to stop preventing the efforts of developing the Treaty of Ankara [...] into a formal alliance'.[92] On 8 May, the Greek Ambassador in Belgrade reported that 'the absolute silence kept by the Western governments [...] has caused exasperation to officials here' and noted that this was 'owing [...] to tactical reasons dictated by [...] Trieste and [...] other vital [...] international issues'.[93] Meanwhile, Politis from Washington said that his Turkish counterpart was apologetic and that developments over Trieste remain shrouded in mystery: the Yugoslav ambassador was saying that 'the secret talks about Trieste [are] approaching a positive conclusion', but the Italian Ambassador said 'no progress had been achieved at all'![94]

To bring an end to this confusion, Papagos became more persistent in his demands for clearer guidelines from Washington. On 10 May he said that he now 'felt compelled to "match" the Turk-Yugoslav position on a military alliance' during Tito's planned visit to Athens in June, and that 'he no longer felt able to propound the US position on the Balkan Pact'.[95] When he heard nothing back, he wrote angrily to Politis three days later:

> It does not appear that your American contacts have given the least due attention to the wider impending damage if pressure on Belgrade and Ankara were not applied, nor have they adequately understood the delicate and difficult position we are in [...]. Abstract explanations of your contacts are not deemed satisfactory and, in any case, do not agree with clear and consistent position of Mr Dulles on matter nor with strong *demarches* of Mr Cannon here [...]. At no point have we been informed, as we requested, [...] if recommendations to Ankara have been or are about to be made [...] nor do we have other relevant information, although sufficient time has passed.[96]

US policy remained in a state of suspended animation for a few more days. On 15 May, during talks with Menderes in Ankara, Undersecretary Byroade continued to be evasive, saying that 'this issue does not fall under his exclusive responsibility' and that he will 'have to consult about it'. Similar answers were given by the State Department to Politis, whose conversation with Baxter on the same day suggested that Washington had been non-committal because it had supposedly discovered the virtues of non-intervention in the Balkans![97] This is what he told Papagos:

> I reiterated our difficulties in face of Tito's impending visit [...]. Mr Baxter announced that a text is already being drafted to this effect for all three governments [...] adding his personal opinion that he does not see Greece and Turkey signing a military pact with Yugoslavia without the agreement of all NATO members [...]. If hitherto friendly recommendations to the three governments had not been more categorical, this is not due to lack of understanding of the situation, but to the known wish of the American Government to avoid any act of pressure toward friendly governments showing involvement in issues whose initiative it believes rests with them.[98]

This response must have irritated Papagos. Back in May, he had told Peurifoy that he mistrusted Politis and intended to remove him (although he finally took that decision eighteen months later).[99] Meanwhile, Athens had to wait for Baxter's 'friendly recommendations', which were dispatched on 17 May in the form of two identical *demarches* by Dulles to Athens and Belgrade and a notification of their content to Ankara. The *demarches* requested the Greeks and Yugoslavs 'to limit themselves' during Tito's visit to Athens, 'to statements containing specific reservations as to [the] timing' of a military alliance in order to avoid 'a reaction in Italy, which would prejudice the Italian agreement on a basis of Trieste settlement which the US and UK hope shortly to be able to discuss with Italy'. Dulles also recommended that both sides could state in a joint *communiqué* their agreement 'in principle' to the idea of a military pact, but make it clear that this 'would be a proper item for further discussion at the meeting of the *Entente* Foreign Ministers' in July'.[100] Although this formula was a compromise between the previous American position and the new reality emerging on the ground, Papagos continued to press the State Department for clearer guidelines, expressing frustration that his loyalty had not received greater appreciation. To this end, he asked Politis to convey the following response to Dulles's *demarche*:

> We received friendly notice [...] from which it appears [there is] clear commitment by the American Government to hitherto held position not to speed up conclusion of Tripartite Military Alliance [...]. In the above encyclical at least, instructions have not been given [...] to Balkan capitals regarding postponement of military Agreement. It was emphasized to American Embassy [...] that under no conditions would the Greek Government again accept to take the initiative of opposing the Yugoslav urgency to sign a pact. In its vigorous desire to help the United States it did so alone, to the point of appearing before Yugoslavia devoid of 'allied' spirit similar to Turkey's – and a reappearance of this during Tito's visit would inevitably give rise to a cooling of relations with Yugoslavia [...]. We request [...] that you explain that we are justified in expecting an entirely different approach over this very serious issue.[101]

Eventually, Baxter responded to Papagos's calls on 20 May with somewhat clearer guidelines requesting that 'during the forthcoming visit of Marshal Tito to Athens, discussions over the military alliance do not proceed beyond the confirmation of what was said during the visit of Marshal Tito in Ankara'.[102] At that point, Papagos adapted his own policy accordingly, as he concluded that Washington was now amenable to a more conciliatory attitude towards Tito's demands. In a message to the Italian Government, he stated that

> the planned Balkan Military Alliance cannot be postponed indefinitely because of the eternal delay of the Trieste issue, over which the Greek Government, as has been repeatedly stated, takes no position either in favour of Italy or in favour of Yugoslavia, but simply wishes for the speediest resolution of this thorny question.[103]

Predictably, his latest position led the Italian Government to file a friendly protest to Athens.[104] This did not particularly concern Papagos, since his policy towards the Trieste dispute was essentially agnostic. All his previous expressions of support for Italy were motivated mainly by Washington's guidelines. Now that the State Department was adapting its policy to accommodate Turkish-Yugoslav demands,

Papagos seemed perfectly willing to alter his position accordingly. Despite his grand assurances to Pella eight months earlier, his real strategy never went beyond tracking and implementing Washington's recommendations on the Balkan Pact.

After Tito's visit to Athens in June, secret meetings were convened in London between a US-British-French Working Group to set the framework for a tripartite Balkan Pact. As Dulles concluded on 14 June, agreement was quickly reached that a 'Greek-Turk-Yugoslav military alliance [was] inevitable and not likely to be delayed indefinitely'.[105] A week later, the United States, Britain and France made presentations to Greece and Turkey in which they stated that a 'Balkan military alliance is welcomed [...] as [a] step toward closer political and military association of Yugoslavia with [the] west'.[106] On this basis, representatives from the three Balkan states met in Athens in July to draft a new treaty. This was signed officially on 9 August 1954 in Bled, during a ceremony involving Popović, Stefanopoulos and their Turkish counterpart, Mehmet Köprülü.[107]

Brinkmanship over Cyprus: The threat of 'internationalization'

After failing to secure US support over Cyprus, Papagos's new approach on this issue after January 1954 was to seek American neutrality in a game of brinkmanship with Britain. Despite this major tactical adjustment, he never abandoned the two pillars of his earlier strategy. First, he never reneged from his belief that the UN recourse, no matter how far it might go, should not become an end in itself, but remain a means of forcing Britain to open bilateral negotiations. Second, he continued to propose a solution envisaging an initial stage of constitutional autonomy to be followed in a few years by a transfer of sovereignty through a popular referendum. In this connection, he always stressed that a transfer of sovereignty will be reciprocated with an offer of military bases to Britain in both Cyprus and Greece, an idea flaunted since 1951 by the Centre Governments.[108]

After cancelling his visit to London, Papagos was still careful to always keep his policy open to the prospect of Anglo-Greek negotiations. During his meeting with Bidault on 23 January in Paris, the Foreign Office noted with relief that he said little about Cyprus.[109] When the subject came up in his aforementioned *Le Monde* interview, he reiterated the position that his policy combined 'openness with determination'. He stressed that the Cyprus question 'has already been posed and if we wished to draw the definitive conclusion that a bilateral settlement should not be considered likely, Greece will not refrain from using any legitimate means to claim its rights'.[110] This reply was considered so moderate, that the Foreign Office thought he was adopting a 'reasonable line' and did 'not yet feel obliged to take the matter to the United Nations'.[111] Again, during Makarios's visit to Athens on 11 February 1954, Kranidiotis noted that 'the Greek government was still hesitant' about taking the issue to the UN.[112]

This vagueness was consistent with the notion that, in brinkmanship, the optimum chance of obtaining the desired outcome usually occurs near the end, when both

Image 7 Prime Minister Papagos with French Prime Minister, Joseph Laniel, during his official visit to France, 19 January 1954. Karamanlis Foundation Photographic Archive.

sides are about to fall off the brink. As an experienced army commander, Papagos had no reason to harden his position until later, as the General Assembly deadline of 22 August approached.[113] When Eden stated in the Commons on 15 March 1954 that 'Her Majesty's Government cannot agree to discuss the status of Cyprus,'[114] Papagos started using stronger language, but never abandoned his 'either/or' formula. In a personal message to Eden, delivered on 6 April, he wrote:

> I most deeply regret the continued lack of understanding resulting in statements such as that of March 15 which literally pour oil on the flames. Such inflexibility compels me to persist even more in the firm but conciliatory line of policy laid down which is based primarily upon the determination to do or omit [sic] nothing which could give it a character hostile to Great Britain. Should the British Government persist in their inflexible policy the only course left open to Greece would be to bring the matter before the General Assembly of the U.N. as the sole means of forestalling a still further dangerous intensification of anti-British feeling in Greece.[115]

Meanwhile, the Greek Government was doing backstage everything it could to avoid going to the UN. On 5 April, Politis told Baxter and Byroade in Washington that his government was 'dismayed' with Eden's Commons statement and that 'even

British newspapers were suggesting that the British government should adopt a more flexible attitude'. When Byroade reiterated the position that the United States 'could not offer the Greek government any encouragement in expecting support if it brings the question before the United Nations', Politis stressed that this was certainly not what his Government intended. Instead, he said that

> it was the firm desire of his Government *not to put the question to the UN*, but that pressures were so strong that it was hard to see how Greece could resist some positive action in the absence of any modification of the intransigent British stand [...]. If the British would only agree to talk to us in a friendly fashion and admit that there is a problem between us [italics added].

Baxter noted in the minutes of his conversation that such pleas were common and 'repeated what many other Greek officials have frequently said'. Indeed, Politis even revealed that Papagos was ready 'to postpone to some indefinite future time the formal raising of this question' if only 'some public indication of a British willingness to discuss the matter' was given.[116] This was perhaps the most modest demand presented since Papagos came to power. Although lowering the bar to such a point must have given the impression that Athens was beginning to feel entrapped in its own policy, this was certainly not the language of a government burning with desire to 'internationalize' the issue.

Since Greek archives on the Cyprus question remain classified, several historians have relied on two early accounts which claimed insider knowledge of Papagos's diplomacy prior to the UN recourse. The first is a series of articles by Pipinelis, published in 1959 in the newspaper *Kathimerini*, and the second are Xydis's scholarly works from the 1960s, which were based on privileged access to classified documents he received from Averoff.[117] Nevertheless, since the opening of US and British archives in later decades, much of what passed until not long ago as authentic insider information now appears much less reliable than was previously assumed. For instance, in his *Isle of Discord* (1999), Stefanidis correctly remarks that Pipinelis's reference to some allegedly conciliatory proposals by the British embassy in Athens in September 1954 is both 'incompatible with the line of the British government' and without 'any hint' in British and US archives.[118] Still, despite these and many other such inaccuracies, there is a persistent tendency in the historiography on the Cyprus question to treat Pipinelis's 1959 articles as an authentic source and a *tour de force* of realist analysis, while Xydis's studies are cited as timeless classics impervious to criticism.[119]

One of the core arguments shared by both Pipinelis and Xydis is that Papagos ostensibly rejected serious conciliatory proposals by the British Government in March 1954 because his foreign policy was driven by idealist motives that sought a Cyprus solution only through 'the justice of the UN'. Both accounts moreover claim that this historic choice was made at a crucial meeting between Papagos and his Cyprus policy-making team on 15 April 1954. Because these views carry considerable weight on much of the contemporary historiography on the Cyprus question to date,[120] they require in-depth examination.

In his 1959 articles, Pipinelis wrote that in a meeting between Papagos and his aides on 15 April 1954, Ambassador Mostras's views were flatly rejected in favour of the line of internationalization. This is what he said:

> When in April 1954 at a meeting of senior members of the diplomatic corps one of the participants referred to the Turkish reaction and its possible exploitation by the British, another among those present rebutted this view by saying that the Turks and the British are simply threatening politically. And the Prime Minister, having adopted this view, declared – in the presence of his silent Minister of Foreign Affairs – that Greece shall proceed by bringing the issue before the U.N. During the meeting interesting proposals by the British government directly relating to a British-Cypriot solution [...] were mentioned, but were set aside as unworthy of consideration.[121]

With regard to those 'interesting proposals', Pipinelis added:

> As I learnt much later, in March 1954, a most responsible British source stated to our ambassador in London that: 'Under the present state of affairs in Britain, the only suitable line would be the acceptance of a Constitution by the Cypriots, who, through it, after the passage of several years (10 or 15), could manage their own affairs'. The Government to which, naturally [...] our ambassador announced this most important suggestion, replied that it would rather avoid any discussion.[122]

This unsourced account was reproduced a few years later with slight modifications by Xydis, whose scholarly analysis surprisingly provided no citation at all (not even to Pipinelis). Specifically, Xydis wrote that 'the British Government indicated that it was ready to grant self-government to the Cypriots, with the possibility left open to them to decide their own future after a period of ten to fifteen years'. He then added:

> At a conference of April 15 attended by Foreign Minister Stefanopoulos; the Director General of the Foreign Ministry, Kyrou; the Greek Ambassador in London, Mostras; and another high ranking diplomat, Premier Papagos decided to go ahead with the recourse to the United Nations unless bipartite negotiations took place. [...] At this conference of April 15, the Premier, disregarding the views of the British Ambassador in London, seemed convinced that the British feared so much the idea of a public exposure of the Cyprus question in the United Nations that they would in the end agree to enter into bipartite negotiations with the Greek government on the issue. He also expressed optimism in the matter of dealing with the Turkish Government on the Cyprus issue.[123]

Although neither explicitly cited him, the source of these claims was a 1959 dossier compiled by Ambassador Mostras himself (and reproduced with updates in 1960) in which he gave his own first-hand account, providing long excerpts from classified documents. The so-called Mostras File, formally entitled *On the Cyprus Question*, was distributed by the diplomat to a group of influential friends with the aim of highlighting what he called 'the incidents over which I found myself in disagreement with the Government concerning the Cyprus question (1954–1956)'.[124] In this account, Mostras spoke about a telegram he sent to Athens on 1 March 1954 reporting that the British Assistant Undersecretary of State, Geoffrey Harrison, had told him in confidence that

> although London's policy remained unchanged, on the other hand the British government was willing to offer self-government through which the Cypriots could find it possible to determine their own affairs after 10 or 15 years.[125]

Five years later, when the Karamanlis Government signed the Zürich Accords (which granted Cyprus limited independence under protection), Mostras claimed that if Papagos had accepted Harrison's 1954 proposal, the entire history of the Cyprus question would have 'taken a different course'.[126] What he was implying, as Pipinelis later argued, was that *Enosis* rather than qualified 'independence' would have been achieved.[127]

One problem with these claims, however, is that Foreign Office records contain no sign of such a proposal. Instead, they provide clear evidence showing the opposite. Specifically, Harrison's minute of his conversation with Mostras on 1 March 1954 says the following:

> Having asked to see me this morning, [Mostras] made an oral communication in the terms of the attached <u>bout de papier</u>.
>
> 2. [sic] Monsieur Mostras said that, after his interview with the Minister of State on February 23, he had reported to his Government that he could detect no sign of weakening on the part of H.M.G. on this issue. I confirmed that M. Mostras had correctly interpreted the position to his Government.[128]

Now, the said *bout de papier*, which Mostras did not mention in his File, expressed Athens's 'sorrow at Her Majesty's Government's continued inflexible insistence in the matter' and announced that Greece will continue to seek 'friendly negotiations [...] in the spirit of traditional Greco-British friendship' until 'the very last day allowed by the U.N.O. procedure (Sept. 1st 1954)'. A revealing and hitherto overlooked sentence in the *bout de papier* was Athens's assurance that, if the matter came to the UN, the Greek Government will pursue the appeal in 'that same spirit only too sure that the members of this organization, especially those of the democratic world, will appreciate their attitude'. This was a very clear hint of the restrained tactics Athens ultimately adopted at the UN in August–December 1954. Meanwhile, Mostras assured Harrison that his Government 'would take no action *vis-à-vis* the United Nations until "August 25", i.e. one week before' the expected deadline.[129]

Besides this evidence, the usually well-informed State Department also confirmed in a position paper on Cyprus on 14 September 1954 that 'throughout the present year the Greeks have attempted to raise the matter privately with the British but have met with stern rebuffs'.[130] Moreover, as Stefanidis observes, even if Harrison had made the proposal which Mostras claimed he did, this was still too 'vague' to merit serious consideration.[131] Indeed, in a revealing passage from the Mostras File itself, which neither Pipinelis nor Xydis ever mentioned, it is clear that Papagos actually gave the proposal fairly serious 'consideration' and went on to discuss it with the ambassador well beyond the famous meeting of 15 April. According to Mostras, Papagos rebutted that 'the British Undersecretary [sic] had not specified if what he was saying entailed the continued presence of Cyprus inside the Commonwealth [...] and this was sufficient for not exploring the matter further'. Mostras disagreed, insisting that Harrison's phrase 'will determine their own affairs' implied the possibility of independence outside the British Empire. However, as Mostras noted, Papagos continued to doubt that an ambiguous phrase such as 'determine their own affairs' could possibly include the option of leaving the Commonwealth without that being made explicit.[132] Interestingly, when the Labour Party at its Scarborough Conference in September 1954 adopted a clearly worded motion stating that, if returned to power, it would 'introduce a liberal constitution with the prospect, in 15 or possibly 10 years, of the Cypriots being given the opportunity of determining their own future inside *or outside* the Commonwealth' (italics added), Mostras dismissed that position as 'vague'. Also, in another conversation with Harrison on 18 October 1954, Mostras scorned Makarios because he interpreted Labour's motion as equivalent to 'an immediate plebiscite and hand over to Greece'. Three days later, during a British Cabinet meeting, Eden and Harrison praised Mostras's anti-Labour remarks, without suggesting that a similar (albeit more ambiguous) offer was ever made to him by the Conservative Government in March.[133] In reality, Mostras held strong anti-Labour views which seriously clouded his diplomatic judgement. For example, when he defended his view that the Labour motion on Cyprus was 'vague', he stressed that this was supported by 'the same people [...] who always demanded during the bandit war [i.e. the Greek Civil War] the removal of the British brigade in Thessaloniki'. However, the clarity of a motion is a separate matter from the record of some of those who voted for it.[134]

Another misleading statement in Pipinelis's account is the claim that Papagos rejected the idea of a phased transfer of sovereignty supposedly contained in Harrison's proposal. According to Pipinelis, the Rally Government rejected this and two more British offers in the autumn of 1954, because it was 'dragged by its overexcited diplomats' [i.e. Kyrou] to the UN campaign. On these two other occasions, Pipinelis wrote, the British allegedly asked Papagos

> to consider the following plan: a) A liberal democratic constitution approved by the Greek Government would be offered to Cyprus and b) A promise of future self-determination would be then given within a period specified by mutual agreement. [...] It does not take much thinking to see that the realisation of these plans would create in Cyprus a clearly Greek order. [...] The Field Marshal, however, after some vacillation, ultimately refused to pursue these proposals.[135]

Throughout his 1959 analysis, Pipinelis feigned ignorance of the fact that Papagos was not only fully supportive of such proposals himself, but according to all US and British records, he had been the one who repeatedly presented them as the basis for a Cyprus solution. The Greek prime minister made this offer, first, in his previously mentioned message to Dulles on 26 August 1953.[136] Again, on 22 April 1954, Stefanopoulos made Papagos's proposals public, stating that 'we do not ask of British policy anything but the granting of a free constitutional polity to Cyprus, to be used as a basis by the Cypriot people to determine its fate once and for all within a set deadline'.[137] On the next day, a Greek Ministry of Foreign Affairs spokesman confirmed that the Government, 'wishing to conduct bilateral discussions', proposes 'the establishment of constitutional autonomy, under the express condition that [...] a referendum be carried out in two or three years in which the Cypriots will vote over Enosis'.[138] In a memorandum to the British Cabinet on 21 July 1954, Oliver Lyttleton and Selwyn Lloyd appear to have fully understood that the Greeks were proposing bilateral negotiations around a plan envisaging 'representative government in Cyprus for a few years, to be followed by a plebiscite on the issue of union with Greece'. Tellingly, the same Cabinet paper stressed that it was the British Government which 'refused to enter into negotiations with the Greek Government' on this basis, adding that it had given the Greek Government 'no encouragement to believe that this attitude will be changed in the future'.[139] Finally, contrary to Pipinelis's claims, the Mostras File also confirms that Papagos rejected Harrison's purported proposal of 1 March not because it offered a phased transfer of sovereignty, but because it did not state so in a clear and explicit manner. Consequently, the notion that Papagos rejected 'conciliatory British proposals' about a gradual transfer of sovereignty in Cyprus because he was dragged to the UN by Kyrou is based on dubious and uncorroborated claims. To some extent, these criticisms were motivated by complex domestic disputes between Papagos and the Palace, whose maverick advisor, Pipinelis, was known for his personal antipathy towards Kyrou.[140]

Equally implausible, however, is the portrayal of the 15 April 1954 meeting by Pipinelis, Xydis and some other scholars since, as the defining moment of Papagos's decision to take the Cyprus issue to the UN. Pipinelis must have known that Mostras's account was highly subjective and inaccurate, because a second, very different insider account hitherto not mentioned in the historiography appeared three days later in an investigative report by *Eleftheria*'s legendary diplomatic editor, Panos Karavias. According to that report, the meeting of 15 April, which was attended by Papagos, Stefanopolos, Kyrou, Mostras and the Head of Political Directorate A, Georgios Koustas,[141] was never intended to formulate policy, let alone discuss the crucial issue of firming up the decision to go to the UN. Its purpose, rather, was to resolve a dispute regarding the implementation of the already agreed policy and Mostras's widely perceived failure to properly carry out his Government's instructions in his representations to the Foreign Office. In other words, the oft-repeated claim that 'the decision to appeal to the UN was made in April 1954, during a meeting of Papagos and some of his close associates' is totally inaccurate.[142]

5. Dependent Nationalism

To begin with, the established view about this meeting curiously overlooks the fact that Mostras, on his own admission, never belonged to the inner circle of people whom Papagos consulted about the Cyprus question. The ambassador's dossier is replete with complaints about how he was 'kept informed very little about developments relating to the [Cyprus] issue', how his views 'received no attention whatsoever', etc. Mostras, moreover, recounted that when he dined with Papagos in the evening of 15 April, he was snubbed as soon as he started expounding his views on Cyprus. When he tried to raise the subject, he recalled, the Field Marshal 'did not reply. Perhaps he was irritated'.[143] Kyrou in his own account says that since he assumed his duties in Athens on 3 February, he had been meeting Papagos 'every morning' in conferences about the Cyprus question often attended by Stefanopoulos.[144] However, he never mentioned Mostras. Meanwhile, Mostras himself, who was recalled to Athens from 12 to 17 April, mentions attending only one meeting with the Cyprus policy team, that of 15 April (and two one-to-one meetings with Stefanopoulos and Kyrou respectively on 14 April).[145] If he were part of the inner decision-making group, one would expect him to attend more team meetings, since his visit covered five days. Also, when Markezinis discussed his resignation with Galesworthy, he complained that the Cyprus question was 'known only to Papagos, Stefanopoulos and the Director General of the Ministry of Foreign Affairs', but never mentioned Mostras.[146] Consequently, the whole notion that Mostras was member of the privileged group that took the Rally's historic decision to 'internationalize' the Cyprus question is based on a selective reading of one biased source (the Mostras File) while ignoring other accounts. In fairness, Mostras never claimed to have been part of the Cyprus policy-making group. His File emphatically states that he never 'expected Athens to request the view of the London embassy' on matters relating to the Cyprus question.[147]

Furthermore, according to Karavias's overlooked report, Mostras was recalled to Athens to defend himself against allegations that he had failed to carry out the agreed policy:

> Mostras was not invited to provide information about the views of the British, but to settle a conflict which arose between the London embassy and the Foreign Ministry, using Mr Papagos, who is personally handling the Cyprus issue, as an umpire. [...] Regarding the Cyprus issue, the Greek ambassador did not agree to play the part of the simple emissary [...] passing on the views cabled to him by the Foreign Ministry, even when these represented the opinions of the prime minister. Mr Mostras judged that his role was to express these views in a way that enabled discussion with the Foreign Office [...]. Used to British mentality [...] he judged that certain things could be said without altering their content, but in a different form to that conveyed to him from here. This stance of Mr Mostras angered the Director General and the Head of Political Directorate A, who requested the imposition of sanctions to our ambassador in London. Mr Stefanopoulos did not adopt the proposals of his senior aides. However, to prevent a wider difference of opinion, he agreed to call Mr Mostras here to find a mutually agreed way of dealing with the situation.[148]

In other words, the notorious conference of 15 April 1954, which according to the dominant narrative was held to finalize Papagos's historic decision to 'internationalize' the Cyprus question, was not a policy planning meeting but a reprimand hearing concerning Mostras's failure to implement the agreed policy.

The *Eleftheria* report also notes that Kyrou and Koustas were displeased for quite some time with Mostras's reluctance to impress upon the Foreign Office the seriousness of the UN threat. As the newspaper put it, Mostras saw that 'his role was to express [the government's] views in a way enabling discussion [...] not in a manner capable of causing reactions'.[149] Indeed, one of Kyrou's major concerns in the early months of 1954 was to ensure that the Greek threat of going to the UN was not seen by London as a bluff.[150] Moreover, British records confirm that Mostras always toned down his messages to the Foreign Office and sometimes even criticized his own government before British ministers and officials. On 30 March 1954, Eden told Peake that Mostras 'understood' the British position 'and had even asked his Government when they complained that we were rigid, whether they were not open to the same accusation'. Eden then remarked approvingly that the Ambassador 'had taken risks in some of the messages he had sent home'.[151] On another occasion Mostras seemed 'most anxious' to avoid giving the Foreign Office the impression that he had assisted a representative of the Cypriot Ethnarchy who visited London. 'M. Mostras had made it perfectly clear that M. Rossidis could not expect assistance from the Greek embassy beyond the normal courtesies', Harrison noted.[152] In October 1954, when the Greek side had taken the issue to the UN, Harrison reported that 'the Greek Ambassador (who spoke in strict confidence and for obvious reasons should not be quoted) said he was extremely worried about the activities of Archbishop Makarios'.[153] As Stefanidis aptly remarks,

> the records of his contacts at the Foreign Office are replete with references to his 'apologetic manner' in carrying out his representations on Cyprus. On an informal occasion, he appeared to deplore that policy, which he attributed to Kyrou. He would also assure the British that he 'did his utmost' to persuade his government to let a back door open out of the UN recourse – which, of course, he did. The Ambassador was not alone in his sympathies. The Councillor of the Greek embassy, Ioannis Phrantzes, was described by Foreign Office diplomats as a 'die-hard Tory' and a 'good chap [...] absolutely to be trusted'.[154]

Although the Mostras File refers to 'various other issues' raised at the famous 15 April meeting, it never clarifies why Stefanopoulos recalled the ambassador to Athens in the first place. Similarly, it never disclosed that the real purpose of the meeting was to reprimand him. Instead it gives the impression that the whole discussion was about the appropriateness of the policy he was expected to carry out. Naturally, Mostras's seniority and closeness to Papagos, with whom he dined after the meeting, enabled him to turn part of the discussion to a political exchange. It is also clear that neither Papagos nor Stefanopoulos wished to let their disaffection with his representations escalate, since his contacts with the British Government were a valuable asset, especially when the Rally Government was after a friendly negotiation with Britain not a confrontation. As a result, the meeting was confined to a dignified rebuke and the issuing of clearer guidelines to Mostras about how to speak to the Foreign Office.

While the meeting of 15 April might have had a minor impact on Mostras's later representations,[155] in terms of the Greek Government's policy, it changed nothing at all. On the next day, both pro-Rally and opposition newspapers agreed that 'the position of the Greek government over Cyprus remains steady and unchanged'[156] and on 18 April 1954 *Eleftheria* summed up the official line in the familiar 'either/or' formula:

> The Greek government continues to stress that it is ready to abandon the recourse to the United Nations if the British government accepted, only in principle, the possibility of arranging the issue through bilateral talks. It also leaves open the time period until the 22nd of August, the last deadline for submitting the recourse […] to enable the opportunity of a British acceptance of the bilateral talks.[157]

Of course, as the August deadline approached, the language of the Greek Government continued to harden. On 3 May, in response to an intervention by Hopkinson in the Commons, in which he said that if the Greek Government did not obtain bilateral discussions, 'might wish' to bring the matter to the UN, Papagos issued his 'last time' statement.[158] Using the brinkmanship tactic known as 'locking the steering wheel',[159] he used his strongest words yet to underline his determination to go ahead with the recourse if Britain refused to negotiate:

> Following the repeated statements which I myself have made on the firm line which the Greek Government is following on the Cyprus issue, I was entitled to believe that there could be no doubt about this whatsoever in London. […]. I declare for the last time categorically the following: […] The increasing irritation of Greek public feeling and the resentment which is arising against England in a crucial sector of Atlantic Defence constitute a danger which the Greek Government […] cannot overlook. […] Should the negative attitude of the British Government continue, there remains to the Greek Government no alternative to an appeal to the United Nations. Persisting in its policy of moderation, Greece will let the last time limit to expire […] and will on 22nd August next ask for the inclusion of the Cyprus issue in the agenda of the General Assembly.[160]

Behind the scenes, however, Athens continued to appeal to the US Government to urge the British to show some flexibility to avoid a UN showdown. On 24 June, Politis asked the State Department to

> use its good offices during the forthcoming visit of Churchill and Eden to discuss with them the Cyprus question in the hope of convincing the British

to make some conciliatory move which would make it possible for the Greek government not to raise this problem in the UN.

When Byroade replied that the impending British withdrawal from Suez would make it 'impossible to approach Churchill on the basis of any idea that British sovereignty over Cyprus should be relinquished', in his most compromising offer yet, Politis said that Athens was ready to abandon the UN recourse even if British sovereignty in Cyprus were not discussed in the negotiations. According to the State Department, the ambassador reiterated

> his belief that the solution of the problem could be postponed if the British would only agree to recognize the existence of a question of mutual Greek-British interest and to recognize willingness to discuss it. In this connection he was asked whether his Government could agree to conversations which would not take up the sovereignty issue. It was suggested that perhaps the British, if they are willing to institute genuine institutional and internal governmental reforms in Cyprus, might publicly recognize a legitimate Greek interest in the welfare of the Cypriots [...]. This might give an opportunity for British-Greek conversations, thereby meeting the Greek desideratum for bilateral discussions.[161]

In the event, Cyprus was briefly discussed at the Eisenhower-Churchill talks in Washington on 25–29 June and the British prime minister underlined the island's 'value as a military base after [the] British withdrawal from Egypt'.[162] Byroade, however, concealed the news from Politis and confined himself to saying that he informed the British embassy in Washington that the Greek Government was ready 'to talk [...] about British plans for the future welfare of the Cypriot people without any reference to a change in sovereignty'.[163] Yet, even on such a limited basis, London refused to negotiate.

The British constitutional proposals of 28 July 1954

As the UN deadline approached, the British Government made a last-ditch attempt to outmanoeuvre the Greeks. On 21 July, the Churchill Cabinet offered 'self-governing institutions' to Cyprus and secretly conveyed its plans to Washington.[164] Following a joint US-British initiative, at 2 pm on 28 July, Cannon handed Stefanopoulos a letter from Dulles warning that a Greek appeal to the UN would have a 'disruptive effect on free world unity', offer the Soviets 'opportunity for mischief' and 'militate against the best interest of [the Greek] government'. Dulles stressed his belief that the question can be 'resolved by the Cypriots and the United Kingdom [...] in gradual stages' and implied that this would also accommodate the interests of Turkey, which was named as a party 'concerned with the future of Cyprus'.[165] Stefanopoulos's first reaction was to ask for the letter to be kept secret until the British constitutional offer was broadcast. Later in the afternoon, Hopkinson announced to the Commons that his government was ready to start talks with the Cypriots over a Constitution that would offer them self-government. Although he admitted that 'the proposed constitutional arrangements have not yet been worked out in detail', he noted that, in contrast to the constitutional offer of 1948, which the Cypriots had rejected, the legislative assembly which he proposed would be non-electable.

Besides this major regression, whose aim was to block AKEL from controlling a future Cypriot assembly,[166] Hopkinson's offer was strikingly ambiguous over the issue of sovereignty. Initially, in reply to a question by the deputy Labour leader, James Griffiths, he claimed that under his proposals 'there can be no question of any change of sovereignty in Cyprus'.[167] When pressed to clarify this point, he uttered his notorious 'never'. However, in contrast to the decontextualized manner in which his statement was later quoted,[168] Hopkinson's full reply was more confusing than categorical. Here is what he said:

> It has always been understood and agreed that there are certain territories in the Commonwealth which, owing to their particular circumstances, can never expect to be fully independent. [HON. MEMBERS: 'Oh.'] [...] I am not going as far as that this afternoon, but I have said that the question of the abrogation of British sovereignty cannot arise – that British sovereignty will remain.

The overlooked phrase was: 'I am not going as far as that this afternoon'. Indeed, as later developments showed, the use of such ambiguous language by Hopkinson was deliberate as the aim of the constitutional proposal was to disorientate the Greeks and deter them from going to the UN. What had been a rhetorical lapse, however, was his emphatic utterance of the word 'never'. On 19 October, Churchill told the Commons that it was not 'the considered intention of my right hon. Friend [...] to use the word "never". In fact, he was not aware that it had come in his impromptu statement until after he saw it'.[169] Also, the Cyprus official at the Colonial Office later disclosed that Hopkinson on this point 'had gone completely off his prepared brief', which was to adopt a less 'rigid stand'.[170]

From that point on, the Commons' debate turned into a game of words whose aim was to tactfully withdraw Hopkinson's 'never' and restore the equivocal language which he originally intended to use. So, when he was asked to clarify if, by ruling out a change of sovereignty in Cyprus, he was not contradicting the Eisenhower-Churchill declaration of 29 June which supported 'the self-government of peoples',[171] Hopkinson claimed that the two positions were compatible. How so? According to his astonishing reply, his proposals allegedly envisaged Cypriot 'independence', but without a change of sovereignty:

> In regard to the declaration made by my right hon. Friend the Prime Minister and the President of the United States recently, it was made perfectly clear in that statement that independence should be given to those peoples who desire, and are capable of sustaining, an independent existence. What is now proposed in regard to Cyprus entirely conforms with that provision.[172]

The political embarrassment caused by these contradictions became apparent when the resigning Secretary of State, Oliver Lyttelton, was brought in to rescue the situation. Lyttleton used a milder tone, but sounded no more persuasive when he said that 'it is not possible at this stage [...] to give Cyprus full control over her external relations and defence'. The variation between his words and those of Hopkinson was noted by the Labour member Tom Driberg, who remarked that Lyttleton 'used the phrases "at this stage," and "at this moment"' which suggest a 'very important difference between his view and that of the Minister of State for Colonial Affairs'. This forced Lyttleton to distance himself further from Hopkinson's words and claim that, although 'full self-determination' for Cyprus 'is a most unlikely thing in any future we can foresee', 'I never used the term "never" and neither did my right hon. Friend'. The last part of his reply made a parody of the whole debate, as everyone had heard Hopkinson's deafeningly loud 'never'. To add insult to injury, Lyttleton then used what Todorova calls 'Balkanist' stereotypes, to portray Greece as an unstable, insecure and underdeveloped country. 'I can imagine no more disastrous policy for Cyprus than to hand it over to an unstable though friendly Power. It would have the effect of undermining the eastern bastion of N.A.T.O. It would have the effect of depressing the standard of life of everyone in Cyprus'.[173]

This performance could not convince Athens that the British Government was moderating its stance. If anything, the clumsy Hopkinson-Lyttleton double act suggested that London was counter-bluffing, that is, hiding an inflexible policy under a façade of rhetorical fuzziness to deceive Papagos into postponing the UN appeal without offering him anything in return. As a result, on 3 August, Stefanopoulos responded to Dulles with a ten-page text that Cannon described as a 'negative response to [the] Secretary's request that the question not be raised in the UN General Assembly'. The US Ambassador referred to this (hitherto classified) document as a text 'composed at [a] moment of bitter disappointment and resentment caused by [the] recent British parliamentary debate and measures currently being taken by authorities in Cyprus. [...] Message also reveals extreme sensitiveness, and contains angry comment about Turkey's pretentions'.[174] The 'measures' in Cyprus that Cannon spoke about were the anti-sedition laws enacted by the island's Governor, which included press censorship, a ban on demonstrations and the tightening of law and order ahead of the constitutional proposals.[175] These actions, however, made a sham of Dulles's promise to Stefanopoulos on 28 July that London intended to offer 'a mutually accepted' constitution.[176]

According to the established view in the historiography, which goes back again to Pipinelis, Stefanopoulos's reply was supposedly irrational and 'almost hysterical'.[177] In 1959, Pipinelis described it as

> a long drawn out text, composed in the style of an *Estia* article, in which reference was made to the 'impudent' British stance, the 'treachery' of Turkey during the last war, etc., and concluded with the distasteful line that, if the Papagos government had the choice between a solution to the problem in stages

and a 'decisive worsening of its friendly relations with Great Britain and Turkey', it would prefer the latter.[178]

Although Pipinelis appears to be quoting directly, it is doubtful that he had seen Stefanopoulos's letter. Yet, some accounts have embraced his misleading commentary as if it provided an authoritative reading of the original document.[179] To begin with, Pipinelis spoke of a 'personal letter' from Dulles to 'Papagos', but the letter was addressed to Stefanopoulos.[180] Had he seen the document, he would have easily avoided this striking error. Second, according to an extensive British summary of the letter's contents by the British Counsellor in Ankara, David Scott Fox, who was shown the document by his American opposite number, there is no hint that Stefanopoulos ended it, as Pipinelis claimed, by saying that Greece prefers a 'decisive worsening of its friendly relations with Great Britain and Turkey'. According to Scott Fox, 'the reply ends with an appeal to the United States Government to support Greece over the Cyprus issue in the United Nations'. Third, the quoted words 'impudent' and 'treachery' also do not appear in the British summary, although the latter was perhaps implied. The rest of the document, according to Scott Fox, began

> by complaining that H.M.G[overnment], by announcing that they are not going to leave Cyprus and by offering a 'mock constitution' which they themselves admit to be less liberal than that offered in 1948, have betrayed the sacred principles of human rights and the recent Anglo-American declaration at the time of Sir Winston Churchill's U.S. visit. Faced with this situation and the consistent refusal of H.M.G. to discuss the Cyprus question with the Greek Government, the latter had no alternative but to have the question put on the United Nations agenda on the latest date possible [...].

> The Greek Foreign Minister's reply refers to the Turkish aspect of the problem (a point which had been mentioned in Mr. Dulles' message). It says that, most regrettably, the machinations of British policy had succeeded in interesting the Turks in the problem. Greek public opinion (which had not forgotten Turkey's behaviour in the last war, at a time when Greece was engaged in a life-and-death struggle) could however see no justification whatever for Turkey to intervene in the matter, and if she continued to do so, it might have serious effects on the development of the Balkan entente. After all, Turkey had definitely surrendered her rights to Cyprus in the Treaty of Lausanne. It was ridiculous of her to try to make play with the geographical situation of the island, since there were many other Greek islands very much nearer Turkey's coasts [...].

> The reply goes on to claim that if Greece were to go back on her decision to raise the matter in the United Nations, it would have a number of serious ill-effects which would be very welcome to the Russians. The Greek Cypriots would be driven to desperation and fall under communist influence; Anglo-Greek relations would be further strained; and the repercussions on Greek public

opinion would be such that the position of the Greek Government would itself be endangered.[181]

According to this resumé, the letter obviously sounded vexed and assertive, but contained nothing irrational or 'hysterical'.[182] Its content reiterated mostly familiar Greek positions, except for the passage on the recent British constitutional proposals and the section on the Turkish claims. Above all, the letter's political substance contained nothing unexpected. It was a continuation of the Rally's brinkmanship game after it became obvious that its main aim of obtaining bilateral negotiations could not be achieved.

Conclusion

In August 1954, Papagos's dualist foreign policy reached crunch-point. The major dilemma between persisting with his brinkmanship game and retracting the UN threat without having achieved any gains came to a head. Pipinelis's claim, that the Greek Government had a third option, namely the acceptance of Hopkinson's proposals as the only viable path to *Enosis*, is not credible. As Papagos's minister and successor in the premiership, Karamanlis, later remarked,

> all Greek governments until 1954, to avoid opposing Britain, not only sought a friendly settlement of the issue but [...] also offered bases [...]. Yet, Eden obstinately stated that for Britain there is no Cyprus question neither in the present nor in the future.[183]

What Pipinelis's step-by-step approach to *Enosis* failed to explain was why Britain, who never agreed to compromise before the threat of a UN clash was uttered, would suddenly offer Cyprus to Greece on a silver platter when the pressure of a UN recourse had been removed. Moreover, Pipinelis's proposed strategy could not explain why Britain would be more amenable to bypassing Turkey, when its policy constantly encouraged Turkish involvement, even at that stage. In Dulles's letter of 28 July, which Pipinelis invoked, it was made clear that the proposed US solution 'in gradual stages' would also have to accommodate Turkey's interests.[184] Finally, as we shall see, all British records suggest that Athens's retreat from the UN recourse would have been hailed in London as a triumph and a major blow to Greek nationalism, not as a step closer to *Enosis*.

In the event, Stefanopoulos waited until 11 August to announce that the text of the UN appeal was ready – although he added that he would withhold it until 20 August. On the next day, Papagos's office denied that any last-minute American mediation had taken place, stressing that after Hopkinson's Commons statement 'the door to bilateral negotiations was definitely closed by the British side'.[185] As the British embassy remarked, this was the first time in which the Greek Government abandoned the 'either/or' formula that it had faithfully maintained throughout the previous year. The embassy's report spoke of 'a toughening of the Greek line to the extent that they no longer say they will take the Cyprus issue to the United Nations unless we agree to enter into bilateral negotiations and that they are, in any case, filing an appeal'.[186] While as far as the text was concerned, this was indeed correct, in reality not one, but two US-Greek initiatives to cancel the appeal were under way behind the scenes. But as Kyrou noted in his 1955 memoir, 'Mr Hopkinson's "Never!" and the "anti-sedition" laws of the Cypriot Government' forced the Greek Government to proceed with the UN appeal, 'to prevent the outbreak of violent acts on the island'.[187] Besides launching parallel backstage initiatives to withdraw it, the UN recourse, as we shall see, was formally filed also as a means of delaying EOKA's armed campaign, which at that point was almost completely under Makarios's control.

6

THE SEMI-INTERNATIONALIZATION OF THE CYPRUS QUESTION: THE UN APPEAL

The decision of the Papagos Government to give substance to its threats and take the Cyprus question to the UN was a key moment in its foreign policy. In contrast to the prevalent view, this amounted neither to a proper 'internationalization' of the Cyprus question[1] nor to a major break with its previous approach.[2] In taking the issue to the UN, Papagos never set it as a priority to obtain a resolution calling for Cypriot self-determination. Such aspirations were widely shared by his supporters, but not among the group of decision-makers who filed the recourse. For them, this course of action was intended strictly as a means of heightening pressure on Britain to force it to open bilateral talks on Cyprus. In an overlooked passage (which contradicts the rest of his analyses), Xydis has correctly remarked that 'Greek policy makers never […] expected to attain, their ostensible resolutionary goals. For they were well aware that so long as the US opposed the Assembly adoption of any substantive resolution on Cyprus, their draft resolutions had no chance of being adopted'.[3] Consequently, in taking the Cyprus issue to the UN, Papagos made the crucial decision of keeping his previous policy intact – subject of course to some tactical adjustments to align it to a changing situation. This policy was to continue pressing for *Enosis* through bilateral negotiations with Britain outside the framework of the UN.

The filing of the UN appeal was not driven, as several accounts suggest, by an 'optimistic' outlook on the part of the Rally Government. Greek policy-makers resorted to the UN option only because their prior game of brinkmanship had failed. As Mostras remarked during his meetings with Papagos in April 1954, the Field Marshal 'seemed convinced that the British Government detested so much the discussion of an issue like Cyprus, that it would back down in the last moment'.[4] Consequently, when Papagos's brinkmanship miscarried, the option of going to New York was activated as a fallback position with a mixed sense of necessity and despair. Indeed, no sooner had the recourse been publicly announced, than the British embassy in Athens discovered that the Greek Government was 'starting to get a little nervous and to see the shadow of the Sorcerer's Apprentice on the wall'.[5] A few weeks later, President Eisenhower's envoy, Mrs Fleur Cowles, told Hopkinson and the British Minister for Foreign Affairs, Anthony Nutting, that 'the Greek Government now realized that they have been wrong in forcing the pace and were only too anxious to find some face-saving devise which would enable them to withdraw their application'.[6] On 12 September, King Paul told Peake that Papagos 'was much depressed about the effect of the proceedings at the United Nations' and 'would be only too thankful to find some pretext for enabling the Greek Government to withdraw'.[7] Consequently, the unsubstantiated claims that Papagos was supposedly 'overoptimistic' and 'idealist' in filing the recourse[8] contradict a raft of hitherto uncited primary evidence suggesting the opposite. In the historiography, only Professor George Tenekidis seems to have detected that 'the Greek Government, attached to its intra-NATO alliances, never exaggerated internationalization either in enthusiasm or in zeal'.[9]

An important change resulting from the UN appeal was the narrowing of Papagos's room for manoeuvre, as his game of brinkmanship had now touched the brink. Unlike previous months, when failure to obtain a favourable British reaction to his threats would not amount to defeat, after the UN recourse his policy was obliged to yield returns. In game theory terms, brinkmanship is not a 'zero-sum game' because the defeat of one actor (Greece) does not automatically signal victory for the opponent (Britain). In brinkmanship, both sides can 'lose' and that is why weak actors typically favour this game. After the appeal, however, because the dispute was now managed by an arbitrator – the UN – confrontation with Britain turned into a zero-sum game. Thereafter, Athens's failure to obtain a tangible gain (i.e. either a sympathetic UN resolution or a British promise to negotiate) would automatically signify a Greek defeat and a concurrent British victory. To put it plainly, after the recourse, Greece could no longer just rely on empty threats. Now it had to obtain concrete results.

As already noted, Papagos never 'presume[d] overall success' at the UN.[10] For him, the recourse was a tactical retreat in the wake of his failed brinkmanship game in January–August. Although the deeper causes of this choice were never disclosed, an obvious motive was to shield his Government from charges of 'betrayal' and 'defeatism', which supporters of the *Enosis* movement would otherwise level against it. During a surge of nationalist opinion (which was largely of his own making) Papagos and the *Ethnikofron* political system would have suffered a major setback were they to retreat from the threat of taking the issue to the UN. By that stage, even traditional Atlanticists, like the Greek Centre parties, had revised their earlier policy and now favoured dynamic UN action.[11] A further motive was the perception of the appeal by the Rally's policy-makers as the optimal anti-communist strategy. Towards the Greek Left, the recourse was seen as a means of stopping public opinion from sliding towards the anti-NATO/anti-colonial EDA. Internationally, as Stefanopoulos told Washington, the recourse was seen as the only means of stopping Makarios from seeking 'some iron curtain or Arab state' to sponsor the Cyprus question at the UN. Such a development, which Makarios constantly threatened with, would have had explosive effects on the post-Civil War regime.[12] As Savvas Loizidis later disclosed, in 1953 Makarios 'had authorized [him] to contact the delegations of other countries to adopt the Cypriot appeal if Greece were to refuse' and stressed that Papagos understood 'what earthquake would have shaken Greece' if this were to happen.[13] Finally, another motive behind the recourse was Athens's misguided belief that if kept within the bounds of moderation it could function as a pressure lever on Washington and London to force them to accept bilateral talks.

In the four months of the UN venture (August–December 1954), Papagos continued to pursue a dualist policy. This was evident in his consistent offers to either withdraw or postpone the recourse should Britain promise bilateral negotiations. One of a few analyses to grasp the distinctiveness of Papagos's approach was an article by the editor-in-chief of the pro-Rally *Kathimerini*, Emilios Chourmouzios, published shortly after the recourse, on 17 February 1955.[14] Entitled 'Two positions and a third', the article summarized the Greek nationalist and Atlanticist views on the Cyprus question as follows:

> On one hand stand the views which endorse the uncompromising fixation of the Cypriots and the Greek Government to the indivisible quest of immediate self-determination – with an equally immediate pursuit of *Enosis*. On the other hand, are the views of diplomats and paradiplomats who advise a gradual or step-by-step solution of the Cyprus question. [...] The 'diplomatic' approach [...] calls itself pragmatic, because the other position certainly has the beautiful romanticism [...] of *Megali Idea*.

The article then defended a 'third' strategy, which combined a commitment to Anglo-Greek negotiations and sustained pressure on Britain through the UN. This mixed approach, it said, would enable Greece to use the UN appeal in 'good faith, as an ally', and 'pass the burden of a new unrest within the Atlantic community onto Great Britain'. Chourmouzios accurately described this as 'a third position' and stressed that it was 'not new',[15] as it represented the Rally's strategy in the previous year.

The editorial, however, was less eloquent in highlighting the inner contradictions of this 'third position'. A major flaw in the Rally's strategy was its half-hearted commitment to the UN. A reluctance to properly internationalize the Cyprus question at the UN rendered this policy toothless as a means of forcing Britain to negotiate. A further discrepancy was Athens's obvious anxiety to find ways out of the appeal, a tactic that made the Foreign Office interpret Greek policy as hesitant and weak. On 20 September 1954, Hopkinson and the US Representative at the UN, Lodge, remarked that 'the Greeks themselves realized that the matter had gone too far and would like to find a way to extricate themselves'.[16] A further inconsistency was the growing alienation that the recourse was causing in London, even though its ultimate aim was to make Britain accept a friendly bilateral settlement. This conflict of ends and means undermined not only the prospect of direct talks with Britain, but as Mostras, Christidis and others have noted, it led Britain to encourage Turkey's involvement, thus rendering the prospect of any future friendly settlement trilateral, not bilateral.

After the UN recourse, Papagos's dualist approach began to exhaust any potential it might have had to bring Britain to the negotiating table. From that point on, his policy began to turn against itself. The idea of 'forcing a friendly agreement' was premised on a paradox insofar as the pressure applied 'to force' the agreement was harming the very friendship it was supposed to be trying to rescue. In this regard, Papagos's failure to obtain a satisfactory outcome at the UN showed the self-defeating character of his dualist policy. It also highlighted the impossibility of *Enosis* and the depth of the internal divisions within the Atlantic Alliance.

From withdrawal to inscription

On 16 August 1954, Papagos wrote to the UN Secretary General, requesting the inclusion of the item 'Application under the auspices of the United Nations, of the principle of equal rights and self-determination of peoples in the case of the population of the island of Cyprus'. The letter referred to Article 1, par. 2 of the UN Charter, which establishes the right of self-determination of peoples, and Article 14, which gives the UN competence in situations likely to impair friendly relations among states. Regarding the latter, Papagos stressed that he was hoping the UN 'will provide a satisfactory solution to a question which is likely to impair the "friendly relations" [...] between Greece and the United Kingdom'.[17] Back in Athens, under clear guidelines, permission was granted to organize public rallies to endorse the Government's policy.[18] Although later accounts claimed that the Rally was behind the 'excess' and 'verbal bigotry' witnessed in some of these rallies, at the time even the Foreign Office itself recognized that 'the rioting on August 20 seems to have been moderately well controlled by the Greek Government'.[19] In contrast to other assertions,[20] the mood in the street contrasted sharply with that inside the Government, where an atmosphere of sobriety and trepidation appears to have prevailed. A solemn mood also enveloped Cyprus, where Makarios violated the sedition laws and before a large crowd swore the famous oath at Faneromeni Church to defend 'self-determination' even if 'we have to pay the heaviest price'.[21]

On 20 August, Eisenhower wrote to Churchill, expressing willingness 'to be as helpful as possible' on the Cyprus question and requested 'a little briefing'.[22] The US President, meanwhile, had initiated a secret process of backstage mediation.[23] First, he sent the Greek-American magnate, Spyros Skouras, president of 20th Century Fox, to meet the British prime minister. On 18 August, Skouras told Churchill's private secretary, John Colville, that he intended to ask the prime minister to send Papagos a message saying that the Greek Government

> must realise that under present conditions we could not [...] even think of ceding Cyprus to Greece. However, when things were calmer in the world we could certainly be willing to talk the matter over with the Greeks, as friends, and although we could not possibly enter into any advance commitments we should be ready at some indeterminate date in the future to let them present their case to us.

Skouras underlined that such a message 'would have a most soothing effect on the Greek Government and might well result in their not bringing the matter before

Image 8 Clashes between students and police guards during a protest over the Cyprus question, 1954. United Photoreporters Agency-Greece, ELIA-MIET Photographic Archive.

the United Nations'.[24] Ahead of his luncheon with Churchill on 21 August, he wondered how to convey this proposal to the British prime minister, and Lloyd advised him to leave a note saying:

> By virtue of the many difficulties in the international situation today […] it is desirable for Greece to postpone the subject of Cyprus at the present time. When the time is appropriate, the British gov't will discuss it with the Greek govt.[25]

Although Skouras's proposal made no reference to *Enosis*, Eden rejected it outright, saying it would 'be published in Athens and hailed as a British retreat'.[26] At the meeting, as Colville noted, 'Sir Winston told Mr. Skouras flatly that he had no intention of sending such a message to Marshal Papagos' and the cinema magnate 'argued the matter good-humouredly'. The State Department also noted that Churchill 'flatly rejected the whole idea' and Eden informed the British embassy in Washington that 'the UK could not possibly make any public or private statement of the nature suggested since this could only be taken as yielding in the face of Greek pressure'.[27]

A few days later, Eisenhower sent his second envoy to London, Mrs Cowles. In an earlier visit in August, she had spoken to Lloyd and the Colonial Secretary, Henry Lennox-Boyd. This time, she met Hopkinson and Nutting and told them she was looking for 'some means [...] of enabling the Greeks to withdraw their application on the grounds that the matter was the subject of bi-lateral discussions'. She added that the United States would 'abstain from voting on the inscription of Cyprus on the Assembly's agenda' because of pressure from Greek-American circles. As Nutting put it to Eden, her mission intended 'to try and stop' Papagos from

> pursuing the matter in the United Nations, but if such an effort were to succeed, there must be a sweetener. Could we not, she asked, make some gesture, however small, which would go a little way to satisfy Greek requirements?

Eden, who deliberately avoided meeting Cowles, wrote a big 'NO' against Nutting's question.[28] In an earlier conversation, Hopkinson had also told Cowles that he 'could hold out no hope of finding a formula which could accomplish the object which she had in mind'.[29] Although her initiative had failed at that point, on 10 September she flew to Athens, where she was warmly greeted by Papagos.

The Skouras and Cowles missions clearly demonstrate that, from the outset, the Greek Government treated the UN recourse as a bargaining tool to be dropped instantly should London agree to start bilateral discussions at any future time, even without agreeing to discuss *Enosis*. The historiography, however, has either completely silenced these efforts or presented them as purely American initiatives whose failure burdened not the British, but the supposedly UN-obsessed Greeks. The first set of accounts, which take their cue from Pipinelis, fail to mention these mediations at all, even though Cowles's mission later became headline news in Greece.[30] Instead, as we shall see, Xydis and others have reproduced Pipinelis's 1959 narrative that only 'two successive British efforts' were made in September 1954, one through Pipinelis himself and another through the former minister of the Metaxas Dictatorship, Maniadakis, which 'came to nought' because Papagos allegedly 'rejected further contacts for reasons not precisely known'.[31]

Meanwhile, a second group of historians have acknowledged the Skouras and Cowles initiatives, but regularly obscured the fact that both proposed to abandon the recourse not only on Washington's behalf, but always with Athens's prior encouragement and consent. Stefanidis, for example, portrays Skouras as politically inept and appears unaware of his long conversation with Churchill's Private Secretary, in which he comes across as fully briefed by the Greek Government.[32] The same historian overlooks the fact that Skouras sustained his initiative for another week, during which he informed US Undersecretary Bedell Smith that 'the "Greeks would like to be well out of this"'. Indeed, it was Bedell Smith who had recommended Skouras to the British as someone who, far from being politically inexperienced, had 'sometimes been used by the Greek Government as their unofficial Ambassador' and 'proved to be a more reliable guide to Greek Government views than the Greek Ambassador'.[33] Similarly, when referring to Cowles, Stefanidis notes that Papagos proposed nothing except 'to tone down the Greek campaign once the Cyprus item was inscribed on the UN agenda' and, like another account, presents her mission as a purely American initiative.[34] However, in October 1954, *Eleftheria* reported that according to Greek Government sources, Papagos had 'charged Mrs Cowles with the task [...] of trying to restore an Anglo-Greek connection for the conduct of talks, even on an informal basis, which could lead to a compromise solution of the Cyprus question'.[35] This report fully accords with the Foreign Office classified record of Cowles's conversation with Hopkinson, in which she said:

> The Greek Government including Field Marshal Papagos, *with whom she was in close contact*, now realized that they had been wrong in forcing the pace in this matter, and that they were only too anxious to find some face saving device which would enable them to withdraw their application for its discussion in the United Nations [italics added].[36]

This document also agrees with yet another overlooked passage from the Mostras File, which confirms that Cowles 'came to London from Athens with a warm recommendation! – that of the Foreign Minister of Greece'.[37] Consequently, the notion that 'for reasons not precisely known' Papagos was opposed to all conciliatory initiatives, which ostensibly came from the British government, is not only unsubstantiated, but according to an array of strong, yet overlooked British, Greek and US evidence is the opposite of what happened.

Let us now turn to the two supposed *Enosis* offers which Pipinelis, Xydis and others criticized Papagos for turning down. In 1959 Pipinelis wrote in *Kathimerini* that the first supposed 'offer' came in September, through 'a confidential letter from a friend, an eminent journalist', who was told by '"the particular [British] minister in charge of the Cyprus question"' that 'some kind of *Enosis*' could be eventually proposed if the Cypriots accepted self-government. Pipinelis concluded that 'this was obviously an indirect British sounding' and showed the letter to Papagos, via the prime minister's son, Leonidas. A few days later, Leonidas Papagos informed Pipinelis that 'the Field Marshal was extending his thanks for disclosing the letter, but believes he has nothing more to add'. Pipinelis then referred to a second British initiative, soon afterward, through Papagos's *confidante* Maniadakis, in which the Greek side was asked to support Cypriot self-government, again supposedly in return for 'future self-determination'. According to Pipinelis, 'the Field Marshal, after some hesitation, finally refused to follow up this sounding'.[38]

To 'complete' Pipinelis's story – as he himself put it – Maniadakis wrote to *Kathimerini* in March 1959 saying that on 25 September 1954, 'a senior British official' had proposed secret talks around 'a solution that would satisfy the Greeks'. Maniadakis put the suggestion to Papagos, who, he says, 'completely agreed' and instructed him to follow it up, thus launching 'secret negotiations' that lasted 'approximately two-and-a-half months'. These talks were allegedly led by Maniadakis, who sought expert advice from Pipinelis and the chief of the King's Political Bureau, Ambassador Ioannis Koutsalexis. This unusual arrangement, according to Maniadakis, was required to bypass Kyrou, whom the British saw as 'harming the whole issue with his fanaticism'. At the end of the talks, Maniadakis claims that his British interlocutors promised: (a) to 'recognize in principle the right of self-determination of the Cypriots'; (b) to 'grant immediately to Cyprus the most liberal and democratic Constitution approved by the Greek Government'; and (c) to offer self-determination to Cyprus 'within less than eight years' in a bilateral agreement with Greece.[39] Papagos supposedly threw all that away in early December to persist with his ill-fated UN recourse.

For an array of strong reasons, the validity of both stories must be seriously questioned. First, there is no hint in any British or American records that such astonishing proposals were ever made. Instead, there is a plethora of documents only confirming the opposite, namely that Papagos was the one who persistently asked for and supported backstage bilateral discussions while London was the side which flatly rejected them. Second, the letter which Pipinelis interpreted as 'obviously an indirect British sounding', could hardly be viewed as such. But even if it were, the manner in which the approach was made was so unreliable and clumsy, that Papagos had little reason to take it seriously. Third, when the British embassy did make proper contact a few days later with Maniadakis, far from rejecting that initiative, Papagos 'fully agreed' and immediately endorsed secret talks. Unsurprisingly, Pipinelis misrepresented Papagos's positive response to Maniadakis, claiming that the Greek prime minister, 'after some hesitation, finally refused to follow up this sounding'. What Pipinelis did not say was that 'some hesitation' referred to Papagos's engagement in secret discussions for 'two-and-a-half months'! Were Pipinelis to reveal this, he would have had to acknowledge (a) that Papagos was perfectly amenable to bilateral talks with Britain outside the UN, and (b) that his own earlier 'initiative' was rejected not because the Greek prime minister was opposed bilateral talks *per se*, but because the clumsy manner in which he was approached did not merit serious attention. Fourth, although Maniadakis's secret discussions provide further proof that all along Papagos favoured a solution through bilateral talks outside the UN, it is unlikely that his interlocutor was authorized to represent British Government views. This conclusion arises from yet another revealing inconsistency between Maniadakis's and Pipinelis's accounts (which the historiography has naively treated as compatible) whereby the former describes his interlocutor as 'a senior British official of those who monitored and had a view on the Cyprus question', while the latter identifies them as a local 'British embassy official'.[40]

Last, but not least, it is inconceivable that Maniadakis could have agreed with anyone authorized to represent the views of the British Government to have *Enosis* achieved within 'eight years'. Furthermore, it is unthinkable that Papagos would have rejected such an offer. Besides being totally out of kilter with what the Foreign Office and State Department archives show, Maniadakis's testimony, given his long record of duplicitous and arbitrary politics as a fascist sympathizer, cannot be trusted without corroboration.[41] A further source of puzzlement is that Maniadakis in his 1959 article never mentioned that Papagos had himself proposed to the British the same Cyprus solution which he criticized the Field Marshal of rejecting. But as we saw, on 21 July 1954, Lyttleton and Lloyd told the British Cabinet that Papagos had been consistently proposing 'representative government in Cyprus for a few years, to be followed by a plebiscite on the issue of union with Greece'.⁴² Consequently, it is inconceivable that Papagos would have rejected Maniadakis's supposed 'deal', if this offered exactly what he had been presenting to the British as his ideal demand for a whole year. Of course, one should not rule out that some secret contacts involving Maniadakis took place with British embassy officials from September to December. Indeed, in a classified letter to Dulles on 1 December, Papagos might have been referring to these discussions when he spoke of British proposals offering a 'solution confusing self-government with self-determination' as '"delusion"'.⁴³ However, what must be ruled out is that (a) Maniadakis was involved in discussions with officials specifically authorized to negotiate with him by the British Government; (b) these talks produced a deal truly envisaging *Enosis* and (c) that Papagos rejected such an astonishing deal even though it almost matched his own proposed solution.

Meanwhile, on 18 September, Churchill replied to Eisenhower's letter of 20 August, attaching a briefing on Cyprus that was replete with orientalist stereotypes. One sentence, for instance, credited British colonialism for giving Cyprus 'the second lowest death rate in the world'. Churchill's letter warned that 'failure of the United States to support us at U.N.O. would cause deep distress' and threatened with a walkout if the procedural debate would result in the inclusion of the issue in the UN agenda. The letter ended with Churchill's wish 'that we shall not be confronted with American abstention'. Meanwhile, Nutting had already reported that according to Cowles, Lodge would not be voting against inscription, and on 15 September British diplomats were also told the same.⁴⁴

A day earlier, the US Delegation at the UN finalized its negotiating position around four key principles: (a) to discourage any debate in the General Assembly; (b) to oppose the adoption of any resolution; (c) 'to urge the British and Greeks to adopt as reasonable and restrained an attitude as possible'; and (d) to abstain during the procedural vote. The fourth point was presented as a reaffirmation of Washington's usual practice at the UN of supporting 'the principle of freedom of discussion' and a concession to the Greek-Americans ahead of the November congressional elections.⁴⁵ In reality, however, as Dulles informed the US embassies in London, Athens and Ankara, abstention was adopted 'to lessen inter-Allied tension' and give Washington 'greater freedom [to] exert [a] moderating influence' later on.⁴⁶ This position was further encouraged by Lodge's conclusion that 'the UK no longer had any strong feelings about our vote on the Cyprus question'.⁴⁷ When Lodge told Hopkinson on 20 September that he understood the British would not walk out if the United States abstained, the latter protested that 'he could not understand how such an impression had been created'. But when Lodge asked if the UK would actually walk out as Churchill threatened they would, Hopkinson replied: 'Of course not'.⁴⁸ The next day, Dulles wrote to Churchill saying that 'even to abstain stretches our principles', but assured him that he will 'actively oppose the passage of any resolution and will do everything possible to keep any discussion to the absolute minimum'.⁴⁹

On 23 September, the UN General Committee considered the Greek item for a preliminary vote on inscription. Kyrou argued that Greece 'for years endeavoured to bring about a solution by bilateral friendly talks' but failed, and stressed that he was 'resolved' to keep the discussion 'in an atmosphere as conducive as possible to a friendly settlement'. Lloyd rebutted that the item was part of an expansionist Greek plan to acquire 'sovereignty over Cyprus by means of *enosis*'. To this end, he argued, the UN was being asked to interfere in the domestic affairs of Great Britain and invoked Article 2 of the Charter, which forbids the UN from discussing matters of 'domestic jurisdiction' for any state. After speeches by the French, Colombian and Islandic delegates, the General Committee recommended inscription with nine votes in favour, three against (including the UK) and three abstentions (including the United States).[50]

Next day at the General Assembly, a tactical motion was tabled by the Iraqi Representative, Mohammed Al-Jamali, proposing postponement by 'a few more days' to enable a 'more serious study' of the issue.[51] Al-Jamali hoped to buy time to enable Britain to lobby more delegations.[52] His motion, however, failed to obtain a majority, with twenty-four votes in favour, twenty-four against (including the United States) and twelve abstentions (including the UK). Pierson Dixon later wrote that the result partly reflected 'confusion as to the real intent behind

Image 9 Members of the Greek Delegation to the Ninth Session of the UN General Assembly awaiting the opening of proceedings, New York, 30 September 1954. Left to right: Alexis Kyrou, Director General of the Greek Ministry of Foreign Affairs; Constantine Karanikas, Economic Counselor of the Greek Embassy in Washington; and Christian Xanthopoulos-Palamas, Greece's Permanent Representative to the UN. United Nations Photographic Archive.

Jamali's vote',[53] but thought that even if the motion had passed, little would have changed.[54] In the ensuing debate, Lloyd stressed that Greece had recognized British sovereignty over Cyprus in the Treaty of Lausanne and argued that even a discussion constitutes 'interference in a matter of domestic jurisdiction'. Stefanopoulos defended the Greek item's inclusion on the grounds that Greece was not asking for 'a transfer of sovereignty' but 'only requested the right of self-determination' with one purpose, 'the abolition of the colonial regime' in Cyprus. The Turkish delegate, Selim Sarper, remarked that it would have been wiser 'not to have created the so-called question of Cyprus' and agreed with Lloyd that even a debate constituted intervention in British internal affairs. Other delegates spoke and the General Assembly approved the inscription with thirty votes in favour, nineteen against (including Britain and Turkey) and eleven abstentions (including the United States).[55] Although a stronger majority was expected, Dixon later discovered that Lodge had lobbied some Latin American delegates to vote with Britain 'when he was satisfied that inscription was assured'. The same conclusion was drawn by Kyrou.[56]

The restrained Greek campaign

Although the outcome of the inscription vote gave the Greek Government a confidence boost, the main parameters of its policy remained unchanged. From the outset Papagos based the appeal on Article 14 of the Charter, which gives competence to the UN in situations likely to impair 'friendly relations' among states. In doing so, he did not link the issue to Article 73 on non-self-governing territories, which gave the UN competence to 'promote the realization of the right of self-determination of the peoples of Non-Self-Governing and Trust Territories'.[57] Kyrou later claimed that 'it was intentional not to give the recourse an intensely negative character of any kind, whether anti-colonial or other, because of Greece's continuous concern to keep to the end its foremost weapon: moderation'.[58] As a result, the legal basis of the appeal was undermined by the contradiction between the demand to apply Article 1(ii) on self-determination and the presentation of the item as an issue 'likely to impair the "friendly relations"' between Britain and Greece.[59] Kyrou adopted this tactic to avoid alienating the United States, but in terms of the recourse, this was a poor decision since Washington would have opposed any Greek resolution regardless, a fact that Kyrou never fully grasped, as we shall see. Even less convincing was his claim that the loss of India's support was a last-minute decision, unconnected to his choice of legal tactics. British records show that the Indian delegate, Krishna Menon, and Prime Minister Jawaharlal Nehru opposed the Greek appeal from the outset because it avoided presenting Cyprus as a colonial issue.[60]

Moreover, as one British diplomat remarked at the time, the presentation of the Greek item as a dispute 'likely to impair friendly relations' with Britain weakened Athens's case. 'There is one aspect of this which puzzles me', he told the Foreign Office:

> I had always assumed that the main platform for the Greek appeal would be the Assembly's resolutions about self-determination [...]. However, it seems that the Greeks are determined to take the question to either the First or the ad hoc Political Committee. One must assume that they are therefore determined to present this case as an issue between us and them. Quite how they can do this, without putting themselves in the wrong, is not clear. As far as I can see they are making a territorial demand on another member of the United Nations and this could only cause friction or give rise to some situation, of which the United Nations should be seized.[61]

Equally self-contradictory was Athens's diplomatic approach. Twice before (via Skouras and Cowles) and twice after inscription, Papagos offered to withdraw from the UN in return for any British promise to accept future bilateral talks. On 27 September, the Egyptian delegate, Mahmoud 'Azmi, launched an initiative aimed to explore the possibility of a friendly settlement between Britain and Greece outside the UN. During his deliberations with Lloyd and Kyrou, the latter told him confidentially, to his apparent surprise, that the Greek recourse 'had been literally imposed on the Greek Government by London's unbending refusals, until the end, to accept friendly diplomatic negotiations and that this recourse does not constitute Athens's final aim'.[62] This important disclosure was perfectly accurate. Dulles also told his own diplomats that the 'Greeks [are] pressing issue because [of] British refusal [to] negotiate with Greece'.[63] Over the next few days 'Azmi and Kyrou canvassed other delegations to support what they called a 'benign resolution', namely a motion that would abandon all reference to self-determination and simply call for negotiations between Britain and Greece. As Dixon put it,

> the present Greek plan is to work for what Kyrou calls a 'benign' resolution: this might be to the effect that since there is doubt whether the question at issue is one of self determination or territorial transfer, the parties (i.e. the United Kingdom and Greece) should discuss the matter before the Ninth Session. Kyrou is canvassing actively in this sense and has already interested the Egyptian delegation [...]. Kyrou has even put this idea to Sarper (Turkey).[64]

Once again, 'Azmi's initiative fell on its head because London rejected it. The British position was 'to prevent the passage of any resolution on Cyprus' and Dixon was instructed to 'make it clear to delegates that we are firmly opposed to any resolution whatever'. According to the Foreign Office, 'a mild resolution' was 'no improvement', as it would 'concede the Greek point that they have a right to be consulted on the future status of Cyprus'.[65] In early November, a fourth Greek attempt to reach an amicable agreement failed again. This time Papagos had asked his representative in NATO, Ambassador George Exintaris, to meet the British Defence Secretary, Harold Macmillan, during a private visit to London, 'to discuss Cyprus' informally. According to Mostras, who arranged the meeting, Exintaris 'did not manage to obtain one word from his interlocutor on the matter'.[66]

A further example of the Greek campaign's self-restraint was the avoidance of any cooperation with the Eastern Bloc countries. This was not for lack of opportunity, since the Soviet delegate, Andrey Vyshinksy, repeatedly offered Kyrou his support. Kyrou, however, avoided meeting him or the delegates of Poland, Czechoslovakia, Byelorussia and Ukraine for what he called 'understandable reasons'. While these reasons remain unclear, Kyrou argued elsewhere that such contacts would have 'provided British diplomacy with weapons'. Consequently, he only spoke to the Eastern Bloc representatives 'during social events' to confirm their votes during the inscription debate. What is more, when Vyshinsky informed him that he intended to speak on his own accord 'both at the General Committee and the Plenary', Kyrou actively forbade him, asking that he 'did not interfere'.[67] Although Makarios caused some stir in London when he thanked the Soviet and Czech governments for supporting the inscription,[68] Kyrou firmly avoided such gestures. His concern about their exploitation by British propaganda to undermine the recourse is totally unconvincing, since London would be fiercely opposing the Greek item regardless. However, Kyrou was keen not to alienate London further, precisely because Athens's policy was not the success of the recourse but its use as a means of pressure to bring Britain to the negotiating table. This approach was chosen also to avoid alienating the United States.

Some historians have argued that, throughout the recourse, Greek propaganda used 'every course of action', including a 'near obsession with the enlightenment of opinion abroad'.[69] This view, however, overlooks the fact that Athens's international propaganda contrasted sharply with its intense use of populism at home. For instance, a centrepiece of the international campaign, the *Information Bulletin*, was a weekly digest consisting mainly of reprinted articles from the Western press which supported the view of Greece. This edition was cleverly punctuated with quotations like Churchill's 1907 statement: 'It is only natural that the Cypriot people, who are of Greek descent, should regard their incorporation with what may be called their mother country as an ideal'.[70] Greek ambassadors also held professional press conferences in several capitals around the world,[71] while a so-called enlightenment committee toured the United States to raise awareness among Greek-American voters ahead of the November congressional elections.[72] It has been suggested that the dispatch of this mission was 'motivated by domestic considerations',[73] but such views silence the fact that, according to British assessments, 'nine Americans out of ten feel that if the people of Cyprus want to join up with Greece the British should let them go'.[74] Moreover, mirroring the British anti-*Enosis* campaign, articles were planted in various US, European and Latin American newspapers, and when Makarios stopped in London, *en route* to New York, he gave an important interview to the BBC. Moderate diplomats like Mostras, whose views are frequently cited by critics of the Greek recourse, endorsed these initiatives and even proposed the creation of a permanent Bureau of the Cypriot Ethnarchy in London to organize more of them.[75]

At the same time, the Rally Government did stir a nationalist frenzy at home,[76] thus making its entire propaganda campaign oscillate between two conflicting approaches. The tensions between the external and internal campaigns grew to such proportions that they soon became yet another facet of the Rally's dualism which its ministers were anxiously striving to contain. On 15 August, the rector of the University of Athens, Apostolos Daskalakis, told a pro-*Enosis* rally in Greece that 'we will not stop from pouring in the soul of Greek youth the poison of irreconcilable hatred against [Britain]'.[77] Although Stefanidis (citing Christidis) notes that in his 1955 book Kyrou 'praised Daskalakis' conduct as 'a brilliant example', this conclusion is inaccurate. Kyrou in his book did not praise 'Daskalakis's conduct', but 'Athens University during the rectorship of Daskalakis', a fine but significant distinction, as we shall see. Stefanidis moreover remarks that Daskalakis, 'of all others, was selected as member of the committee, which the government sent to the United States in order to "enlighten" American opinion'.[78] British records, however, show that Kyrou's initial response to Daskalakis's speech was to raise the matter immediately with Peake, in what the latter described as 'a somewhat chastened mood', and to stress that the rector 'had been sternly rebuked for his speech' and that 'his term of office which expires next month, would not be renewed'. Kyrou then suggested that Daskalakis 'would not be allowed to be a member of the Greek delegation which was shortly to go to the United States' and condemned the removal of the sign of 'Churchill Street' by some protestors, explaining that Papagos had ordered its restoration.[79] Far from wishing to keep these conciliatory gestures secret, Kyrou asked Peake to issue a joint *communiqué* stressing the Greek government's 'intention to do all in their power to prevent the Cyprus dispute affecting the normal friendly relations between our two countries'. However, it was Peake who sternly refused this conciliatory proposal, and the Foreign Office approved this stance as 'good tactics'.[80] It was in this context that Daskalakis (after having been rebuked) was finally included in the delegation that visited the United States. As Daskalakis later disclosed, he was given firm Government instructions 'not to express any hostility toward Britain' which, on his own admission, he adhered to throughout his two-month mission.[81] Furthermore, as Kyrou promised Peake, Daskalakis's tenure as Rector was not renewed. According to Hatzivassiliou, who researched this case in some depth, the following interesting conclusion must be drawn: 'Self-contradiction constitutes a usual characteristic of Greece's Cyprus policy in 1954'.[82]

Similar friction arose over the inflammatory Athens Radio broadcasts to Cyprus, which attacked British colonial methods in a way interpreted in London as 'incitement to sedition'. After several protests, the broadcasts were toned down, but Peake still found them 'sour, but less offensive'. During a farewell dinner for Admiral Mountbatten on 16 November 1954, the British Ambassador took Papagos aside and spoke to him about the broadcasts in what he described as 'the same language as Minister of State'. Some days later, Stefanopoulos told Peake that a solution could be found, but Peake was totally uninterested, saying that he would soon be calling upon him to 'deliver a very stiff message' about new offensive broadcasts.[83] In their next exchange, Stefanopoulos assured Peake that 'orders had been given [...] not to use any material in their broadcasts to Cyprus which might be offensive or wounding for her Majesty's Government'. In a self-contradictory report to London, Peake said: 'I am not sure that I believe this', but then admitted that 'I trust that the necessary instructions will now be given'.[84] A similar pattern developed over the issue of the planned visit of the British fleet to Greece. Although the Greeks had asked for the visit's postponement to avoid unfriendly public incidents, Churchill called it off completely with an angry notation saying that: the Greeks 'are insulting us so grossly and showing every form of ingratitude'.[85] These tactics notwithstanding, the Foreign Office secretly acknowledged that the Papagos Government was torn in its endeavour to keep its propaganda campaign under control. In one report, Peake informed Churchill that 'the Greek Government were close to creating a monster they could not control'.[86] In saying so, he tacitly admitted that Athens was conflicted and, at least, trying to control its own propaganda.

It has been suggested that the Greek international campaign deployed the energies of Archbishop Makarios to enhance its profile.[87] In reality, the Rally leadership kept a noticeably low profile in its external campaign, while Makarios was never asked to nor did he ever speak as a member of the Greek diplomatic team. He always kept the image of an independent Cypriot leader who would not hesitate to publicly disagree with the Rally Government even at the height of the UN recourse. On one occasion he rebuked Papagos's decision a year earlier to grant military bases to the United States 'without securing guarantees for Cyprus' and reproached Athens's ineffective diplomatic campaign outside the UN. On 11 October, he exposed what he perceptively described as the 'dual handling' of the legal side of the recourse, namely its reliance 'on one hand, on the right of self-determination, and on the other, on the character of the dispute (as a family disagreement) between Greece and Great Britain'.[88] On 5 November, during a press conference at the UN, he deviated from Athens's line and 'attacked the United States Government's attitude' which he called 'disappointing' and inconsistent 'with the principles and general outlook' of the American people.[89] Meanwhile, Papagos had been touring the Iberian Peninsula from 7 October to 2 November. This led even moderate opposition leaders like Kartalis to call on him to stop hiding and 'go to Lake Success to fight the UN diplomatic battle himself'.[90] Similarly, Stefanopoulos spent little time in New York, in sharp contrast to Lloyd, Hopkinson and Nutting, who each stayed much longer at the UN headquarters than him.

Into the blind alley: Dulles's 'non-substantive' motion

After the failure of the American and Greek initiatives to shelve the recourse in the last weeks of the summer, all sides began to prepare for the General Assembly debate in December. When Eden met Dulles in London on 2 October, he rejected a US offer to postpone the recourse, proposing instead tripartite talks (with Turkey and Greece) because he 'could not sit down with [the] Greeks'. At this meeting it was agreed to push the Cyprus item to the end of the December agenda. Washington wanted it deferred until after the congressional elections to avoid alienating the Greek-American vote, but the Foreign Office naively hoped that the issue could 'be forgotten in the desire to get home by Christmas'. US Ambassador Winthrop Aldrich later concluded that, at this stage, Eden 'had no clear plan [...] for handling the matter in the General Assembly'.[91] In mid-November, however, British tactics began to crystalize[92] around two alternative aims: a) to wait for a Greek motion on Cypriot self-determination and 'seek to defeat' it; b) to 'cut the item off' the agenda 'by not reaching it'. Under the former scenario, which was deemed more preferable, Britain would abstain from any discussion and vote against the Greek item at the end of the debate.[93]

Greek tactics also began to crystalize around two alternatives. On 23 October Papagos told Dulles in Paris that 'he hoped [...] the U.S. could either in effect be strictly neutral or else seek to postpone the entire matter for this year'.[94] This meant that the preferred Greek option would be to present a mild motion calling for Cypriot self-determination hoping to secure American abstention (and, perhaps, a General Assembly majority, albeit short of the required two-thirds). Otherwise, Greece could settle for a procedural motion calling for the issue's 'postponement'. It should be noted here that 'postponement' differed from 'withdrawal' as previously proposed by Skouras, Cowles and 'Azmi. Unlike 'withdrawal', 'postponement' was i) not conditional on a British offer to discuss Cyprus outside the UN, but ii) meant that Greece could return with a new recourse in 1955. However, what made the 'postponement' option unacceptable to the British (who often referred to it as 'moratorium') was that it would, first, leave the issue hanging over Britain for a year and, second, confirm the UN's competence to discuss it.[95] Overall, Greek tactics were marked by a self-contradictory logic that reflected the wider antinomies of Papagos's foreign policy. Self-contradiction lay in proposing outcomes that relied on US consent, i.e. 'US neutrality' for a mild resolution or US support for 'postponement'. In other words, the weakness of Papagos's tactics did not lie in their supposed 'idealism', but in the incongruity between his 'realist' attachment to Washington's policy and the 'idealist' aspiration to secure Washington's backing for a resolution that would help the cause of *Enosis*.

Meanwhile, US tactics began to chart a third course, to reconcile the differences between London and Athens. Dulles promised Churchill on 21 September to 'actively oppose the passage of any resolution', a position congruent with Washington's previous warnings to Athens not to expect support if the issue reached the UN. Consequently, Washington's conundrum was to marry its promise to London to 'actively oppose' the Greek item, without completely alienating Athens and, thereby, undermining NATO unity. To this end, the vagueness of the British and Greek tactics offered the State Department some space to find its own mediating role. A key requirement was to inject further fluidity. On 8 October, Dulles asked Lodge 'to try to prevent the matter from ever coming to a head so that we would not have to take a public position'. Lodge agreed, but stressed that 'if it did we should not go on record against the Greeks, both because of the importance of the colonial issue [...] and [...] our own public opinion'. Dulles, by contrast, insisted that 'he wasn't prepared to agree that we should vote with the Greeks', to which Lodge rebutted: 'I was not asking that we should vote with the Greeks, but only that we should not vote against them'.[96] As Stefanidis remarks, besides seeking to reconcile the conflicting positions of its allies, Washington's ambiguous tactics also served to overcome differences among its own policy-makers.[97]

A valid criticism of the Greek handling of the recourse was its misguided ambition to obtain US abstention.[98] In his memoir, Kyrou acknowledged that 'the neutrality of the United States was always considered a precondition for the aforementioned positive conclusion of the Greek efforts'.[99] While this was clearly an unreasonable expectation, it should be noted that it was less utopian than the historiography has hitherto assumed. Although the aim of US 'neutrality' was naive, there was an unacknowledged element of American deception which encouraged this Greek expectation.[100] Although some have questioned Kyrou's claim that on 16 September Baxter told the Greek *chargé* in Washington, Phaidon Kavalieratos, that 'depending on the flexibility of the substantive draft resolution to come, the American delegation would decide if it would give a positive vote',[101] Washington's attitude throughout the recourse, as Dixon remarked, was 'feeble'.[102] To begin with, Lodge, Kyrou's main American interlocutor, clearly disagreed with Dulles and truly favoured abstention. Moreover, despite opposing the Greek appeal, Washington had sent Skouras and Cowles to lobby in favour of Papagos's request for bilateral talks, thus sending mixed signals to Athens. Then, both Dulles and Lodge agreed on 8 October 'to prevent the issue from coming to a head'.[103] Against this background, it was not entirely unreasonable for Papagos to leave his 23 October meeting with Dulles in Paris thinking that the 'US would maintain [a] neutral position'.[104] Although the American record of that conversation reveals that Dulles expressed 'distate' towards the prospect of a 'discussion [of] Cyprus in [the] General Assembly', when Papagos requested that the 'US either maintain strict neutrality or seek [to] postpone [the] discussion', the same document says that the Secretary of State 'made no commitment'.[105]

Furthermore, a closer examination of British and US sources shows that until 16 November, Washington was deliberately sending equivocal messages to London and Athens, partly to defuse tension and partly to enhance its own negotiating position. After receiving an eight-page memorandum from Papagos during their meeting on 23 October, in which the Greek prime minister protested that the United States 'rather than being neutral as promised [...] was assisting the United Kingdom', Dulles made no remarks. Three days later, when Politis called, the US Secretary of State said he had merely 'studied' the paper. Then, when Papagos wrote to Dulles and Eisenhower on 26 October, saying he 'had been perturbed' by Cannon's statement to Kanellopoulos that the United States 'would not maintain its neutrality', Dulles misleadingly told Politis: 'The British had also criticized us, which was perhaps *a pretty good indication of our neutrality*' [italics added].[106] Then, he let three more weeks pass before announcing to Papagos's on 16 November that 'there has been a misunderstanding of our position' and that the United States will 'oppose the passage of any substantive resolution'.[107]

While Dulles's 16 November reply to Papagos reaffirmed Washington's initial position after weeks of ambiguity and evasiveness, it also introduced a new element: the so-called substantive resolution. On 12 November, Dulles finalized US tactics during a senior staff meeting through some combination of the minimum Greek demand of 'postponement' and the minimum British demand of 'cutting off' the item from the agenda. First, he recalled his commitment to Churchill to 'actively oppose the passage of any resolution' and, then noted 'Papagos's mention of "postponement" during their conversation in Paris'. Dulles told his aides that 'his own position had always been that, in assuring the British that we would oppose "any resolution", he meant any "substantive" resolution', and defined this as 'any resolution smacking of action or interference in the affairs of Cyprus'. Dulles then thought that 'the term "postponement" was not a good one' and stressed that what he wanted 'was a way to "adjourn discussion", or have the Assembly decide not to consider the matter further at this time'. In his view, a procedural 'not to discuss further' formula met the minimum British demand of pushing the item off the agenda: 'The British could not logically expect us to oppose a resolution which would result in what we both wanted, namely the adjourning or cutting off of discussion at the current GA session', he said.[108]

On 16 November, as Dulles was informing Papagos that the United States would oppose 'any substantive resolution', Kyrou circulated his first Greek draft resolution which was indeed 'substantive'. Its two operative paragraphs read as follows:

> The General Assembly
> 1. Recommends that the principle of self-determination be applied under the auspices of the United Nations in the case of the population of the island of Cyprus;
> 2. Resolves to include the item 'application under the auspices of the United Nations of the principle of self-determination in the case of the population of the Island of Cyprus' in the provisional agenda of the tenth session of the General Assembly.[109]

Stefanidis portrays this as yet another example of the Greeks' detachment from the realities of the UN.[110] What this criticism discards, however, is that Kyrou's resolution had a good chance of obtaining an absolute majority and this is what both Lodge and Dixon believed. On 24 November, at a meeting with Hopkinson and Nutting, Lodge said 'the furthest [he] was prepared to go in interpreting Dulles' assurances to Churchill on 21 September was to vote against the Greek resolution' but not 'to work actively against' it. This meant that US allies, who carried the balance of votes at the General Assembly, would be left free to support the Greeks and could give Kyrou's resolution a majority. After failing to change Lodge's position, Nutting concluded that the Foreign Office 'must […] accept this disappointing American attitude' and support Dulles's 'not to discuss' motion, because Kyrou's resolution could not be defeated:

> An accurate analysis of probable voting figures on a Greek resolution is very difficult […]. But combination of feeble American attitude and specious attraction which Greek draft would offer to anti-colonials clearly worsen our position. On present form our chances of mobilizing an absolute majority are

pretty slender. On the other hand there is a rather better than even money chance of blocking a two-thirds' majority. Thus taking draft resolution as basis of our forecast we should be able to block passage of operative paragraph 1 but not paragraph 2.[111]

This assessment was not theoretical. It formed the basis on which the British finally abandoned their preferred option of having a substantive Greek motion 'taken up and killed' and accepted Dulles's proposal of a procedural motion. Until that point, Eden and the Foreign Office had dismissed Dulles's 'not to discuss' motion as 'unacceptable' because it carried the danger of being 'transformed into a moratorium'.[112] After his crucial meeting with Lodge, however, Dixon reviewed Britain's options as follows:

a. to seek to defeat the Greek resolution [...];
b. to cut the item off our agenda by not reaching it; and
c. to revert to the 'not to discuss' idea.

His recommendation to London was that the best option now was (c) because this 'would seem to be as good a result as we are likely to get and less objectionable than the passage of all or part of the Greek resolution'.[113] In other words, British records show clearly that Kyrou's draft resolution produced a British retreat which the historiography has never acknowledged. The significance of this retreat to the overall outcome of the UN recourse was limited, but this evidence shows that Kyrou was less detached from the realities of the UN than hitherto assumed.

Until the end of November, London was under the impact of Lodge's refusal to do any 'buttonholing' to defeat Kyrou's first draft resolution. While Dixon, Nutting and Hopkinson saw no alternative to Dulles's 'not to discuss' motion, Eden continued to resist the idea. In a document dated 29 November, which recommended 'to try for a motion not to discuss', Eden noted: 'I [...] do not agree with this telegram as drafted'.[114] For almost a week, as a Foreign Official unwittingly let it be known to the Americans, 'no decision had [...] been taken' by London. On 1 December, while awaiting London's decision, Dixon pulled off a bluff and sent Washington a 'negative reaction to the idea of [...] a procedural resolution'. Although he knew that defeating Kyrou's resolution was impossible given Lodge's categorical refusal to lobby against it, Dixon was testing 'whether the Americans could now be brought to lobby actively for the defeat of the Greek resolution' instead of letting the British suffer a defeat.[115] R.W.L. Wilding in London noted that Dixon was 'right to try this on with the Americans'.[116]

Denouement: Greece votes against itself

By sheer coincidence, it seems, on 1 December the Greek side also pulled off a bluff to test Washington's resolve. Stefanopoulos told Cannon that 'Greece's position now is against postponing issue' and presented a new version of Kyrou's draft resolution.[117] This had one operative paragraph expressing 'the wish that the principle of self-determination be applied under the auspices of the United Nations in the case of the population of the island of Cyprus'.[118] On the same day, Papagos replied to Dulles's letter of 16 November, stressing his earlier point of disagreement with Mostras, namely that any 'solution confusing self-government with self-determination is "delusion"'.[119] It is not clear who proposed such a solution,[120] but despite these manoeuvrings, Athens never really abandoned 'postponement' as its second best option.

After considering other alternatives with the US delegation,[121] Dixon met Lodge on 8 December to reach 'a joint position' on the basis of Dulles's 'procedural motion not to discuss'.[122] Stefanidis's assertion that London's change of heart resulted from the improved 'climate' of US-British relations after the release of the US airmen in China[123] is irrelevant. Foreign Office records show that London compromised because it saw Kyrou's resolution as 'dangerous' and predicted 'complete defeat' should Lodge persist in his refusal to do any 'buttonholing' with Washington's friendly delegations.[124] Finally, on that day, Dixon and Lodge agreed on a joint plan 'to be sprung as a last-minute surprise'.[125] According to it,

> a friendly delegation should, at the outset of the Committee, move a resolution to the effect that the Cyprus item should not be <u>considered further</u>. The Committee should be asked to discuss and vote on this proposal before embarking on the substance of the Greek item. If, as we expect, the proposal is carried, delegations would therefore not have to vote on any Greek draft.[126]

After sounding the US and Norwegian delegations without success, Dixon asked the New Zealand representative, Leslie Munro, to sponsor the Anglo-American motion. The latter agreed and for this he was later knighted by the British queen.[127] Dixon then produced a three-stage scheme which, as he told Lodge, 'should be like a military plan'.[128] It read:

Stage 1

X intervenes at the outset of the proceedings on a point of order concerning the conduct of the debate. He states that he has just handed into the Secretary of the Committee the text of a draft resolution [...].

Stage 2

If this preliminary question is decided against X, the United Kingdom Delegation will have to walk out [...]. If, however, the question is decided in X's favour, debate on his draft resolution will begin [...]. It seems best that X should not himself argue, that his draft can be carried by a simple majority. [...] The Geeks may well claim [...] a two-thirds majority is necessary; presumably on the ground that the draft is tantamount to a reversal of the decision by the

Plenary to inscribe the item [...]. The counter-argument is that a proposal 'not to consider <u>further</u>' is not inconsistent with any decision taken hitherto [...].

Stage 3

If the draft Resolution is carried [...] the Chairman can be asked to rule that the Committee stage of the item has been concluded.

In an 'annexe', the text of a joint Anglo-American counter-resolution was drafted: 'THE General Assembly, DECIDES not to consider further the item entitled "application, under the auspices of the United Nations, of the principle of equal rights and self-determination in the case of the population of the Island of Cyprus"'.[129]

On 11 December, Kyrou moderated his own draft resolution further. He dropped one phrase from the preamble and removed the words 'under the auspices of the United Nations' from the operative paragraph. This now read: '[The General Assembly] Expresses the wish that the principle of self-determination be applied in the case of the population of Cyprus'.[130] Although Kyrou thought that his motion was now 'non-substantive', Dulles told Papagos on 12 December that it was and confirmed that Lodge would be voting against it.[131] In that same message Dulles claimed that Kyrou's resolution 'could not obtain the necessary majority' (but in reality Dixon believed 'many delegations would find it really difficult to vote against such a text'). Dulles then revealed the Anglo-American counterplan, and advised Papagos to vote for it. 'It seems to me', he said, 'that the best outcome from the standpoint of Western unity as well as Greek prestige would be to support a resolution by this Assembly not to discuss the Cyprus question'. To sweeten the pill, he claimed that 'future Assemblies would be unbound' by such a resolution and falsely portrayed it as fulfilling Papagos's request on 23 October to 'postpone' the issue.[132] Meanwhile, Lodge was giving the opposite assurances to Dixon, stressing that 'not to discuss' clearly did not mean 'postponement'.[133]

On 13 December, the eve of the Political Committee debate, the *New York Times* ran a front-page report planted by the State Department. This disclosed that the United States would 'oppose any Greek proposals' to the General Assembly 'that raise the possibility of a change of British sovereignty over Cyprus'. An inside editorial also blamed the Greeks for raising 'another problem of nationalism [...] dividing allies'.[134] Meanwhile, the Greek camp fell in disarray. Before flying to Paris (*en route* to New York), Stefanopoulos confirmed the accuracy of the *New York Times* report but promised that 'other [Greek] drafts would be formulated' which the United States 'would consider more satisfactory'. Meanwhile, Kyrou, who had not yet received Athens's telegram referring to Dulles's 12 December message to Papagos, told journalists in New York the opposite, i.e. that the report was 'inaccurate' and that he had 'no information' that the United States will 'ultimately vote against the Greek recourse'. This made Stefanopoulos issue a corrective statement emphasizing the unity of the Greek policy-making team, but the press did not fail to notice the tangle.[135] Shortly before he started canvassing for the 'not to discuss' motion at 12 noon,[136] Lodge sought Kyrou and told him for the first time about Dulles's message to Papagos. Kyrou then reacted defiantly, pledging to 'fight against this proposal with all [his] power'.[137] Later, as Stefanopoulos promised, a new Greek draft resolution was produced, inviting 'the parties (Great Britain-Greece) to seek a solution in conformity with paragraph 1 of Article 33 of the Charter'. This, too, was rejected by Washington as 'substantive'.[138]

In the evening of 13 December, the Greek side was trapped in a swirl of dilemmas arising from its incurably dualist approach. Papagos still resisted Dulles's advice to 'go along with the [not to discuss] resolution',[139] hoping to extract US neutrality with his latest resolution invoking Article 33. At the same time, he was obviously unwilling to confront the Americans at the UN and that is why he withdrew the last Greek draft resolution when Washington rejected it. This wavering, however, left Kyrou with the earlier draft resolution of 11 December, which Dulles had also rejected, an issue that gave rise to further dilemmas. Upon arriving in Paris, Stefanopoulos made two important phone calls across the Atlantic. First, he called Ambassador Leon Melas, who advised him 'not to insist on a vote over our motion, no matter how mild or harmless, because most member states would turn against us after the US position was made public'. Stefanopoulos then called Kyrou, who told him the opposite: He 'insisted on a debate over our motion'. The Greek Foreign Minister then advised Papagos to 'press for a vote in the Political Committee, where a simple majority is required which, according to [Kyrou], is guaranteed. […] At the General Assembly, where a two-thirds majority is required, seek a way out'.[140] Papagos endorsed this proposal before the start of the debate, but his later instructions to Kyrou during the Political Committee debate remain classified.

Deliberations in the First Committee began at 10.30 am on 14 December. Consistent with the Anglo-American plan, Munro raised a point of order at the start of proceedings and tabled his 'not to consider further' motion. Following a procedural discussion on whether the Greek or New Zealand motion should take precedence, the Committee voted for the latter with twenty-eight votes in favour, fifteen against and sixteen abstentions. In a hitherto crucial but overlooked development, Kyrou called for 'an immediate vote', without a debate, because this would make the New Zealand motion require a two-thirds majority.[141] His attempt, however, failed because Munro asked to speak and the Colombian Chairman, Francisco Urrutia, ruled in favour of a debate, stressing that this meant 'there would be no need for a two-thirds majority'.[142] This incident suggests that Kyrou entered the session, as Stefanopoulos and Papagos had instructed him, trying to contest the Anglo-American motion. However, in his 1955 book, Kyrou misrepresented this Greek setback as a 'successful outcome' and even boasted that, as a result, 'the Cyprus issue was extensively debated'. The same misrepresentation was given later in Parliament by Stefanopoulos.[143] However, the debate, which spanned eleven hours over two days, was precipitated by the British delegation, against Kyrou's wish, because Nutting feared that the New Zealand motion may not obtain a two-thirds majority. Indeed, Nutting criticized Kyrou during the debate for asking 'to vote immediately on the draft resolution itself thus seeking to prevent those who supported it from expressing their views'.[144]

The false portrayal of the procedural discussion by Stefanopoulos and Kyrou as a 'success' aimed to conceal the Greek quantum leap later that afternoon, when Kyrou abandoned his own motion and supported an amended version of the New Zealand counter-resolution. After liaising with five Latin American delegations, he asked the Colombian and El-Salvador representatives to sponsor two amendments to the preamble of the New Zealand counter-resolution. The first stated: 'Considering that, for the time being, it does not appear appropriate to adopt a resolution on the question of Cyprus'. Although this did not turn the resolution into a 'postponement' motion, it opened the possibility for such an interpretation. According to Nutting, the British delegation was consulted beforehand and after discussions with the United States, New Zealand and Turkish delegations, agreed to 'acquiesce'.[145] For this reason, during the formal debate on the second day, Munro and Nutting accepted the amendment without discussion. The second amendment (which was eventually tabled by the Philippines and was rejected by the Political Committee) proposed adding the words: 'Having in mind the Purposes and Principles of the Charter'.

In the vote that followed, the amended New Zealand motion was adopted by forty-nine votes in favour (including Greece, Britain and the United States), none against and eleven abstentions (including Turkey and the Soviet Bloc countries). In their closing statements, Nutting said that the amendment notwithstanding, 'his delegation had not, of course, accepted the principle of the General Assembly's competence' in the matter. Kyrou, in turn, argued that he supported the motion because 'the words "for the time being" [...] implied that the United Nations was prepared to meet any new request' to discuss the issue.[146] On 17 December, the General Assembly adopted Resolution 814 (IX) with fifty votes to none and eight abstentions. The text read as follows:

The General Assembly,

Considering that, for the time being, it does not appear appropriate to adopt a resolution on the question of Cyprus,

Decides not to consider further the item entitled 'Application, under the auspices of the United Nations, of the principle of equal rights and self-determination of peoples in the case of the population of the Island of Cyprus'.[147]

Ever since, Kyrou maintained that 'the amended proposal, together with the preceding thorough debate, constituted, in the event, the most favourable option for us, under the conditions created by the American volte-face of the twelfth [*sic*] hour'.[148] The historiography, which correctly rejects his claim about a supposed last-minute American U-turn, has nonetheless accepted his assessment that once the New Zealand counter-motion prevailed, the Greek delegation had no other choice but to try to mitigate it with an amendment.[149] So firm is this hypothesis, that several older accounts have conjectured that the amendment was an American idea forced upon the British, because Kyrou could not possibly have any leverage left at that point to effect a British retreat.¹⁵⁰ Even Stefanidis, who knows that British records reveal a different story, namely that the British delegation accepted Kyrou's amendment without US pressure because of its continued 'uncertainty about the outcome', still argues that Kyrou abandoned his own motion because he saw 'Greek chances waning'.¹⁵¹ In other words, to make the new evidence fit the traditional view, Stefanidis suggests the improbable thesis that in the afternoon of 14 December the New Zealand motion was both unbeatable and 'uncertain'. This problematic reading is harder to accept given that, on 8 December, Dixon had acquiesced to Dulles's procedural motion on the sole condition that the Anglo-American joint plan would 'ward off any amendments'.¹⁵²

Hitherto uncited evidence, however, makes it abundantly clear that until well into the second day of the UN debate, the British delegation seriously doubted the success of the New Zealand motion, even under a simple majority vote. At the end of the second day, Nutting cabled London the following telling message:

> By midday our position was not too happy. Of the Afro-Asian Group we could count only 3 votes (Pakistan, Iraq, Israel) against [sic] the bald New Zealand draft resolution, while there were at least 3 votes (Indonesia, Philippines, Yemen) against it. It seemed that the rest would all abstain. Everything therefore turned on the Latin-Americans and these began to wobble badly. By this afternoon it was clear that in order to get our resolution through with a good majority it would be necessary to add some extra words.¹⁵³

The fact that the British seriously feared a defeat of the New Zealand motion until the afternoon of the second day meant that Kyrou still retained the option of fighting it with a fair chance of either defeating it or seeing it pass with a slender majority that would politically embarrass Britain and the United States. Indeed, this was Kyrou's accurate forecast when he had spoken to Stefanopoulos on the phone on 13 December.

Consequently, Kyrou's decision to abandon his own motion and cross over to the Anglo-American camp was not forced upon him, as hitherto maintained, by the invincibility of the New Zealand counter-resolution. On the contrary, this was a deliberate Greek choice, apparently originating with Papagos himself, who seems to have decided during the Political Committee debate that the showdown with the Anglo-Americans had to stop there and see that Dulles's recommendation of voting with the allies to preserve 'Western unity' is accepted. This key decision accorded with Papagos's entire approach, whose priority was not to obtain a UN resolution calling for Cypriot self-determination. As the Greek prime minister's advisor Christidis later argued, Kyrou could and should have voted against the New Zealand counter-resolution but failed to do so because his prime minister instructed otherwise. This is what he wrote: 'That the Greek delegation had deemed it expedient, following orders from Athens, to also vote itself for the decision which had essentially rejected the Greek recourse, was considered disgraceful' (by Greek public opinion).¹⁵⁴ The prevalent narrative, however, has overlooked this evidence maintaining that Papagos had no option but to vote for the New Zealand motion to avoid greater humiliation. To acknowledge that he had that choice would imply that the recourse of 1954 was not driven by purely idealist/nationalist motives, but by a more considered approach that never placed *Enosis* above NATO's unity nor the UN above a bilateral settlement with Britain.

The bitter aftermath

Stefanopoulos's dilemma on the eve of the UN debate provides a further insight into the spirit of dualism pervading his Government's foreign policy. On 13 December, the Greek Foreign Minister arrived in Paris, *en route* to New York,[155] with instructions from Papagos to join the General Assembly debate and 'get some delay'. As Dulles was expected in Paris the next day, Stefanopoulos faced a dilemma: either to wait and meet Dulles in the hope of influencing the US position, or fly to New York to join the UN debate, as Papagos had instructed. Unsurprisingly, he chose both. He decided to stay longer in Paris to meet Dulles, and made arrangements to catch the closing stages of the UN debate in New York. Predictably, the meeting with Dulles bore no results and the UN debate ended quickly, leaving Stefanopoulos no time to join it.

Besides its edifying symbolism, the Greek Foreign Minister's quandary in Paris had a wider significance. When Stefanopoulos saw the first reports speaking of what he called 'a total burial of the Cyprus issue',[156] he pleaded with Dulles to issue 'some statement', ostensibly to 'help [the] current U.S. position [...] in Greece, and reduce Leftist demagoguery in Athens'. The State Department realized that his real motive was 'to prove that he has been active at this issue in Paris, even though he did not go to New York'.[157] Still, Dulles agreed to 'make a helpful comment' when the occasion arose. Two days later, the US Secretary of State commented that after their 'friendly discussion of the Cyprus issue' in Paris, he 'communicated personally' with the US delegation in New York and 'late that evening the Resolution under discussion was amended and passed' in a way that 'meets, in a substantial degree, the points which the Foreign Minister raised in his discussion with me'.[158] This was, of course, untrue, and Dixon and Nutting told London this much, stressing that 'the amendment was [...] only agreed to by the US Delegation after we had fallen in' – a further confirmation that the adoption of the New Zealand motion before Kyrou's amendment was not certain. Nevertheless, Eden and Nutting chose not to protest against Dulles's statement and agreed that 'the matter should be allowed to drop'.[159] This silence, however, was misinterpreted by the earlier histography as a tacit acknowledgement that Kyrou's amendment was accepted because of US backstage mediation.

Still, Stefanopoulos decided to submit his resignation. Papagos, however, rejected it to fend off criticisms that the UN recourse was a disaster, especially since Kyrou had also placed himself *en disponsabilité* on 21 December.[160] To justify his return to the government, Stefanopoulos confessed to a third blunder. During the parliamentary debate on the Cyprus question on 7 February 1955, he said he had 'decided to resign before checking with the Greek delegation at the UN the reports' which revealed that 'the debate had not been totally buried'. His chain of gaffes continued, as Stefanopoulos tried to cover all that with a self-aggrandizing crescendo. The real motive behind his resignation, he told Parliament, was not after all the supposedly misleading early reports, but his wish 'to protest against the gross violation of the United Nations' fundamental principles'![161] Vlachos, who knew him well, described Stefanopoulos in his memoirs many years later as 'the embodiment of spinelessness'.[162]

The Greek Foreign Minister's attempted resignation, however, must be placed in the wider context of the Rally's handling of the outcome of the UN recourse. After the outbreak of anti-American protests in Athens on 14 December, the State Department acknowledged that 'Greece has a tremendous public opinion problem on its hands'.[163] To defuse the tension, the Rally Government asked the King to make a radio address to the nation on 20 December, presenting the UN recourse as a qualified success. 'We were expecting more, but it is equally beyond doubt that the Cyprus issue has come out of the obscurity in which it lay', Paul told the Greek people.[164] A day earlier, Papagos promised the Cypriot Ethnarchy that Greece would be 'returning next session to the General Assembly', while on 28 December Makarios criticized the Greek handling of the recourse and threatened to seek 'a group of sponsors' in 1955.[165] These developments culminated in the parliamentary debate of 7 February 1955, whose aim was to defend the Rally's policy on the grounds that it was paying off, albeit modestly. Under these circumstances, Stefanopoulos's resignation had to be withdrawn.

The portrayal of the UN recourse by the Greek Government as a qualified success rested on Kyrou's controversial interpretation of Resolution 814 as an acceptance by the UN of its competence to deal with the issue. On 7 February 1955, Papagos reaffirmed this reading:

> The decision of the General Assembly [...] which confirms the competence of the General Assembly to deal with the matter, but which does not consider it necessary, for the time being, to take any decision over it, is a decision that, even though short of ideal for us, still offers a positive solution.

Then, Papagos told Parliament that, despite the setbacks, he saw no better alternative to his current policy as it provided the best possible synthesis:

> The policy line of the Greek Government on Cyprus is and shall remain unchanged as of its originally declared direction. This policy, combining openness with determination, constitutes the best possible contribution to the consolidation of the Southeast Mediterranean [sic] area, to the unity of the democratic camp and the protection of traditional Greek-British relations, in the belief that the Greek Government, by enacting its policy in Cyprus, shall not do or fall short of doing anything that could in any way constitute an anti-British act.[166]

Two months later, the new Greek ambassador to Washington, Melas, told Dulles that 'his Government would be forced to present [Cyprus] again at the next

General Assembly' and asked the United States to use its influence to moderate London's position.[167]

In contrast to its almost unanimous denunciation in the historiography, Papagos had some reasons to be, at least partially, satisfied with the outcome at the UN venture. First, while falling short of properly internationalizing the issue, the recourse did turn Cyprus from an internal British into a regional issue (involving Greece, Britain, Turkey and the United States). In so doing, it highlighted its significance for the Cold War and the burgeoning Non-Aligned Movement. In that sense, although it failed to force London to negotiate, it inflicted sufficient harm as to make it impossible thereafter for Britain to treat Cyprus as an internal affair. As Ierodiakonou aptly remarks, Resolution 814 became 'a source of pressure on the Government of Britain'.[168] Second, despite criticisms from Makarios and the Greek opposition, the UN debate discharged, in part at least, a subversive wave of Greek nationalism which could have otherwise threatened to destabilize of the *Ethnikofron* regime. In other words, the recourse functioned as a safety valve, since the *Enosis* movement could no longer treat the *Ethnikofron* governments as a barrier to Greek nationalist aspirations, at least until the Cyprus settlement of 1959–60. Third, the myth that the UN was a panacea for *Enosis* was also exposed, thus showing the limits of Makarios's policy to the Greek public. Fourth, despite its ultimate failure, the recourse did provide a legitimizing function that confirmed the Rally's position (and, later, that of its successor, ERE) as the hegemonic force in the *Ethnikofron* camp for the rest of the decade.

At the same time, the UN venture was, on balance, a failure. Its architect, Kyrou, and the Foreign Minister, Stefanopoulos, both tendered their resignations. Such dramatic reactions are usually characteristic of major diplomatic debacles. The rejection of Stefanopoulos's resignation by Papagos could hardly conceal the fact that the Government was embarrassed by the outcome. Second, the recourse failed to achieve any tangible progress with regard to its fundamental aim of bringing Britain closer to a bilateral negotiation with Greece. Third, although the public airing of the issue did not, as some have argued, provoke Turkey's interest,[169] the recourse undermined trust between Athens and Ankara and made it easier for Britain to manipulate Turkish sensitivities against Greece. Fourth, despite the moderate spirit in which it was pursued, the recourse underlined divisions within NATO and made Greece appear both isolated among its allies and incapable of challenging them through a neutralist anti-colonial policy.[170] Bruising remarks were aired in New York, with Kyrou accusing Britain of suppressing 'fundamental freedoms' in Cyprus and Lloyd describing Greece as 'the only place where people have been sent to prison for differing with the political views of the Government'.[171] Fifth, the defeat of the Greek item was undignified. The surprise New Zealand motion left the Greek delegation in disarray, forcing it to respond in a manner that looked like a total capitulation. Greek public opinion and the *Enosis* movement understood that the chief responsibility for that outcome lay, above all, with the United States. Of course, a big share of responsibility also fell on Papagos, whose dualist policy falsely assumed that the United States, even if it could not stay 'neutral', would still refrain from framing a close ally like Greece and inflict upon it a humiliating outcome. Finally, another setback was the deep sense of disillusionment with which the news was received by the Greek press. Headlines such as 'Dramatic Defeat' and 'Humiliation' featured on the front pages of *Ethnikofron* papers, while the pro-Rally *Embros*, printed a front-page cartoon depicting Cyprus in flames and the Nazi swastika flying over the UN headquarters.[172] As a Foreign Office official remarked, 'the indignation of the Greek Press and the riots in Athens and Cyprus [...] show that the result has been similarly interpreted on the other side', i.e. as a British victory.[173] This reception was largely of the Rally's own making, as its populist discourse had raised expectations too high instead of warning the Greek people from the outset about the limits 'UN justice'.

The bifurcation of state power: The Greek Rally and EOKA

If the conclusion of the UN debate exhibited how dualism could drive Greek foreign policy into effective paralysis, the outbreak of EOKA's armed struggle on 31 March 1955 showed how the extension of dualism could erode the unity of the Greek state itself. From 1951 to 1955, EOKA emerged as a paramilitary group enjoying significant autonomy from the Greek Government, even though it was closely connected to the Greek state.[174] Its members, who numbered a few hundred, were mainly Greek-Cypriot,[175] and its first consignment of arms was smuggled to Cyprus from Greece in March 1954.[176] Averoff later disclosed that in 1956, ERE adopted a secret policy of arming EOKA.[177] What remains obscure, however, is what policy the Rally Government adopted towards the organization during EOKA's formative years.

Connections between EOKA and groups linked to the Greek state have been well documented. The founding meetings of the organization were held in Athens on 2 and 21 July 1952 and were chaired by Makarios. These placed EOKA under two committees, one political and one military, both chaired by former Defence Minister, George Stratos.[178] Other committee members included General George Kosmas, Commander of Land Forces and Northern Greece Minister after 1954, retired General Nikolaos Papadopoulos, Colonel Ilias Alexopoulos and Colonel Grivas. Its main civilian members were the Cypriot Loizidis brothers, professors Gerasimos Konidaris and Dimitrios Vezanis, and the lawyer Antonis Avgikos.[179] Outside the committees, several key figures helped EOKA, such as Admiral Alexander Sakellariou, former Defence Minister under Plastiras, *Estia*'s owner, Kyros Kyrou (Alexis's brother) and Archbishop Spyridon, PEAEK's chairman. Although EOKA was formally independent, most of its leaders were linked to the Greek state. Sakellariou, Stratos and Kosmas had recently held ministerial posts, while the latter, who was Papagos's informant about EOKA since May 1951, served directly under him in the army. Sakellariou, who was described by Peurifoy as 'one of [the] Palace inner social circle', informed the royals about EOKA's impending armed campaign since the autumn of 1954.[180]

The obscure relationship between EOKA and the Rally Government has split most of the historiography into two opposing camps.[181] One group claim that

Papagos had no links with the organization and firmly opposed its actions. Vlachos, for example, says that Grivas faced 'intense opposition from the Greek Government' and speaks about an arrest warrant issued by Papagos against the colonel shortly before he left for Cyprus in November 1954. Vlachos also claims that 'the Greek Government was genuinely surprised' by EOKA's first attacks on 31 March–1 April 1955.[182] A similar view is held by Kranidiotis, who argues that 'the armed struggle was imposed on the Greek Governments which, in effect – including the Government of Papagos – wished to avoid it'.[183] Averoff offers a variation on this narrative, saying that Papagos 'originally opposed, [but] later became so ill that he could not become involved in such a daring [...] undertaking'.[184]

The second group of accounts suggest that the Rally Government supported EOKA. Markezinis (then out of the cabinet) contends that Papagos sanctioned a secret policy to this effect and 'delegated to General Kosmas the task of organizing a guerrilla struggle in Cyprus'.[185] Xydis and Panteli maintain that on 11 January the Greek government covertly endorsed the unconventional warfare which Grivas was preparing, while Svolopoulos states that Papagos decided 'to encourage indirectly the assumption of the military struggle'.[186] Similar views were held at the time by Peake and the Foreign Office, based on some intelligence and the intensity of Radio Athens's pro-EOKA broadcasts.[187]

Much of this controversy originates in Grivas's own memoirs. In their initial Greek version, *Apomnimonevmata* (1961), they provide a testimony that contrasts sharply with their subsequent English edition, *Memoirs* (1964). In *Apomnimonevmata*, Grivas states:

> I asked General Kosmas to come to an agreement with Marshal Papagos over the entire issue. He conveyed to me on 3 May 1951 the latter's view: that a liberation movement in Cyprus would be *premature*! [...] Later I troubled General Kosmas and asked him to persuade Papagos to give his support to our movement. In reply, on 14 March 1953, the General reported that once again, Papagos did not wish to become involved and that he did not wish it to be known that he had been informed [...]. I do not believe the Field Marshal, whose tested patriotism remains beyond any doubt, did not genuinely wish to support our movement [...]. His aforementioned reservations and hesitations, I think, stemmed from his fear of finding himself exposed before international public opinion [...]. Later, when he came to power [...] he did not wish, for unknown reasons, to secretly support the movement.

Grivas in *Apomnimonevmata* also refers to an unnamed Rally minister who told him on 28 September 1953 that Papagos knew about his activities and warned him not to attempt anything 'contradicting Government policy'.[188] On 16 May 1954, he says, General Ventiris told him that Papagos thinks 'nothing should be done' to 'disturb our relations with Britain' and that he 'took measures in Cyprus to deter' such action.[189] Finally, in *Apomnimonevmata*, Grivas claimed that after he left Rhodes for Cyprus in November 1954, the Greek authorities tried to arrest him (a story accepted, as we saw, by Vlachos, but dismissed by Averoff).[190]

Whereas Grivas stresses in *Apomnimonevmata* that 'all responsible government representatives [...] tried to deter me' and 'the Greek Government did not wish to offer me any support', these sentences were removed from the English version of his *Memoirs*. So was his claim that EOKA's first attacks 'surprised everyone', including 'those in Greece'.[191] Also, the story of his attempted arrest in Rhodes was omitted, while a new section was added claiming that EOKA's first attacks enjoyed Papagos's full endorsement:

> Archbishop Makarios returned on 10 January 1955, and next day we met in Larnaca Bishopric. He told me of events at the United Nations [...] and said that Marshal Papago was now in full agreement with our activities. I was glad to hear it, for the Greek Premier, up to that date, had offered no support at all, and everything we had done, we had done despite him.[192]

Faced with this contradictory account, the historiography chose that version of events which best suited its narrative, usually without mentioning that Grivas produced two incongruous accounts. When this was rarely acknowledged (as in Averoff's case), readers were told that the conflict between the two versions reflected Grivas's personality and his political disillusionment in the interceding three years, when he tried and failed to lead the Greek Centre parties.[193] While these contextual factors are important, Averoff's account arbitrarily mixes elements from both Grivas's versions (in a manner favouring the former) without explaining the rationale behind this random selection.

The analytical impasse surrounding EOKA's formative years arises mainly from the fact that, until recently, Grivas's memoirs were the only thorough insider's account available on this period. In 2002, however, Andreas Azinas, the link person between Grivas and Makarios, published his own revealing memoir under the fitting title, *50 Years of Silence*. This account sheds light on many obscure points in EOKA's early history. One thing we can now be certain about is that all along Papagos had been kept closely informed about EOKA's activities by none other than Makarios himself. Azinas recalled that the Archbishop had told him:

> I did not want to do anything behind the back of the Greek government and confront them with a dilemma, should anything go wrong [...]. I told him [Papagos] about Grivas as well. He [...] warned me that sooner or later I'll have problems with Grivas.[194]

Another point illuminated by Azinas is that Papagos did not obstruct the preparations for an armed struggle in Cyprus, but through a series of non-decisions (including inaction to block the first consignment of arms from Lavrio in March 1954),[195] treated the matter as though it was an entirely Greek-Cypriot affair (which, of course, it was not). A further revelation is that Papagos's disapproval of Grivas was continuous and mostly caused by his suspicion that the colonel might resort to premature violence, thus undercutting the Greek Government's diplomatic effort. On 25 April 1954, Makarios told Azinas: 'Papagos did not want

Grivas. He is afraid that he may push Cyprus and Greece prematurely towards targets that in fact we may need 2–3 years to reach'.[196]

Azinas also revealed that the distrust was mutual and very soon escalated into a factional dispute between those whom Makarios called 'Grivas's people' and 'Papagos's people'. Admiral Sakellariou also told Azinas: 'I and Giorghis [Grivas] are not on good terms with this government'. Meanwhile Papagos ordered his agents to spy on Grivas, forcing him to seek refuge in remote islands like Tinos and Rhodes. Azinas explained that

> the squeeze applied by the state machinery was due to Grivas's men provoking members of the security forces [...]. This ugly atmosphere permeated the government machinery and Papagos' top executives, resulting in everyone 'tightening up' and Grivas being unable to collect materiel [...]. In these circumstances suspicions arose that others could be used to lead the military wing of the struggle.[197]

This issue divided EOKA's leadership between pro- and anti-government factions, with Stratos and the Loizidis brothers belonging to the former and Sakellariou and Grivas to the latter. Both struggled for EOKA's leadership even after Grivas's arrival in Cyprus on 10 November 1954. This made Grivas avoid getting the Greek Government 'involved in dispatching arms, fearing that such arms might be accompanied by officers siding with Papagos'. Consequently, EOKA's attacks on 31 March/1 April 1955 were carried out with the materiel dispatched by Sakellariou and Azinas in March 1954. As Grivas noted in his memoirs, 'it was with these arms, and these alone, that [EOKA] kept the fight going for almost a year'.[198] Two subsequent shipments, in November 1954 and January 1955, were betrayed. The first was dumped at sea before the British authorities arrived and the second was the highly publicized affair of the caique 'Aghios Georgios', which was caught by the British outside Chloraka on 23 January 1955.[199] Ultimately, what confirmed Grivas as EOKA's leader was Makarios's trust who, despite Papagos's objections, rated his military talents above those of the other two leadership contenders, Socratis Loizidis and a certain Kalianesis.[200] However, until early 1955, Azinas recalled that Grivas feared 'Papagos might in future send officers purportedly to help, while in reality render him powerless with a view to suppressing the movement'.[201]

Thanks to Azinas's account, the self-contradictions in Grivas's memoirs are now easier to unravel. To begin with, this testimony shows that the dual image of Papagos portrayed by Grivas reflected not only the latter's political shifts from 1961 to 1964, but also the Rally's own self-contradictory policy. As we have seen, Azinas stressed that Papagos approved the formation of a paramilitary group in Cyprus, but with the intention of activating it in '2–3 years', i.e. in 1956–7. Moreover, Papagos's detachment from the initiative, to avoid condemnation by the British, denied him the ability to control EOKA, a power he needed if he were to make the organization serve his own rather than Grivas's agenda. Consequently, his opposition to Grivas arose chiefly from his concern that the latter would use EOKA to force his own hard-line nationalist plans on the Greek Government through a premature start of the armed campaign. In other words, the vital distinction that is overlooked in the historiography is that Papagos endorsed EOKA but opposed Grivas.[202] Because EOKA's history was later identified with Grivas's name (Averoff inaccurately called it 'the work of one man')[203] the historiography never contemplated the possibility that Papagos could be simultaneously supportive of EOKA and opposed to its leader. Azinas's memoir, however, reveals that this position was not only possible, but formed the basis of the Rally Government's approach to the armed struggle.

Papagos's opposition to Grivas conformed with his wider policy of suppressing radical nationalist deviations. At the same time, Makarios's determination to keep Grivas as leader of EOKA intensified Papagos's foreign policy dilemmas. After the first consignment of arms and Grivas's arrival in Cyprus, Makarios gained significant control over the organization. Any moment he deemed it expedient, he could order Grivas to launch an attack without having to obtain Athens's approval. A further proof of this influence was that, when Socratis Loizidis made a bid for the co-leadership of EOKA with Grivas, Makarios and Azinas isolated him and arranged for his return to Athens (but in the meantime he was arrested by the British over the 'Aghios Georgios' affair).[204] Although Papagos always retained some influence over EOKA (both through his liaison with Makarios and his capacity to supply the organization with more arms in future) he never really had a major leverage over the organization after March 1954. Consequently, when EOKA launched its first attacks in 1955, it was acting primarily on Makarios's orders. 'You'll start as soon as there is a negative resolution at the UN. Try to avoid bloodshed. Try sabotage only', the Archbishop told Azinas in September 1954. On 11 January and again in mid-March 1955 he reissued the same order.[205]

Even after Azinas's memoirs, however, it remains unclear whether Papagos ever endorsed the launch of EOKA's armed campaign in March–April 1955. Although he clearly encouraged the organization's development, his initial plan did not intend to activate it until 1956–7.[206] If the outcome of the UN debate ultimately changed his mind or not remains unclear. Azinas recalled that Makarios told Papagos on 30 September 1954 about 'the instruction he had given (i.e. if the UN resolution were negative, we should react with a chain of bombings)' but avoided commenting on Papagos's response. After the UN debate, Azinas recounted that on 11 January 1955 Makarios told him and Grivas that Papagos 'was somewhat in a hurry and everyone realized that there was something wrong with his health'. But elsewhere Azinas wrote that Grivas suspected this urgency as a ploy, so that Papagos could 'send officers purportedly to help [...] with a view to suppressing the movement'.[207]

If we assume that Papagos ultimately consented to an early armed campaign in Cyprus, it remains unclear whether he did so out of conviction or out of bowing to the inevitable, namely his loss of control over EOKA. Alternatively, it is conceivable that Papagos continued to oppose an early start to the armed campaign, especially since he never appears to have offered EOKA another consignment of arms, which the organization urgently needed. At any rate, both options are compatible with his dualist foreign policy. The former would suggest a continuation of his previous approach, namely using only the UN as the main form of pressure to make Britain negotiate. The latter would imply that he attempted an escalation of the nationalist leg of his dualist policy by adding EOKA to the UN as an extra pressure lever, always of course with the ultimate aim of forcing Britain to negotiate a bilateral solution. Whatever the case, what is certain is that vital human and military resources were transferred from the Greek state to the Cypriot Ethnarchy, which enabled Makarios to launch an armed struggle on the island regardless of whether Papagos supported it or not. At no point, of course, did EOKA become fully independent from the Greek state, as it always needed more arms and political backing from Athens to uphold an effective struggle. But until Karamanlis sanctioned a secret policy of arming the organization in June 1956, EOKA was operating largely outside the reach of the Greek state, even though it had been originally an extension of it.

Conclusion

The UN recourse of 1954 was not, as the historiography contends, a hoped-for strategy to 'internationalize' the Cyprus question. All reliable evidence shows that this initiative was an unwanted retreat to a fall-back position precipitated by Britain's refusal to submit to Papagos's brinkmanship game and accept bilateral talks with Athens on the future of Cyprus. Without a grasp of this crucial context, any analysis of the Greek handling of the 1954 UN recourse risks falling into reductionist conclusions and a selective treatment of the evidence. That is precisely why the dominant narrative has silenced or misrepresented the successive initiatives by Skouras, Cowles, 'Azmi, Maniadakis and Exintaris, whose common aim was to revoke the recourse in return for some vague British promise to formally discuss Cyprus with Greece in the future. For the same reasons, many accounts have replicated Pipinelis's and Maniadakis's unsubstantiated claims that Papagos ostensibly rejected two British offers of *Enosis* to keep the recourse alive. In trying to portray the UN venture as a policy driven by nationalist idealism, evidence like Skouras's cry that the 'Greeks would like to be well out of this' was suppressed, and unsubstantiated myths about Britain's supposed secret offers of *Enosis* were invented.

Similarly, unless we view the UN recourse of 1954 as a half-hearted attempt, made partly to rescue the domestic authority of the *Ethnikofron* regime and partly to force Britain into negotiations, we cannot understand why the Greek campaign had been reluctant and restrained. In the course of it, the anti-colonial character of the Cyprus question was diluted, and the issue was presented by the Greek Government as a bilateral dispute between friends. Despite several attempts, all offers of assistance by the Soviet Bloc were flatly rejected. Furthermore, the international propaganda campaign was always checked through a back channel of communication with Peake, to avoid hurting British sensitivities. In contrast to the British, who kept three ministers in New York for weeks on end, the Greek side relied on a diplomatic mission that was assisted only for a few days by its Foreign Minister, while the Greek prime minister went on a four-week tour of the Iberian Peninsula. Above all, the final UN debate saw the Greek delegation waver incessantly until it froze in a state of quantum duality, with its own resolution sitting unsupported at one end, and Kyrou voting for a counter-resolution tabled by its opponents at the other end. Against this background, it would be inappropriate to argue that Papagos went to the UN to collide head-on with Britain or to pursue a nationalist campaign of properly internationalizing the issue. Regardless of whether a firmer approach would have yielded better results, a careful reading of the evidence points to the conclusion that the Rally Government's utmost priority at the UN was to avoid clashing with the United States. For this reason, it never approached the recourse as an end in itself.

Apart from friendly observers like Chourmouzios, Papagos's fiercest opponents equally acknowledged at the time that he was charting a midway approach. Wilding, a senior Foreign Office official in charge of the Cyprus question, in a reflective note in January 1955, concluded that there were 'two views about the methods Greece should adopt' over *Enosis*.

> The more moderate party, including King Paul and the Govt (in their public utterances at least), want to pursue their case at the U.N. and work for a change of opinion there and in this country, but in doing so to maintain a fair degree of Anglo-Greek friendship and to confine themselves to legal means. It is probable that this party would be willing to drop the Enosis campaign for the time being if it appeared that its continuation would be a serious danger to Greece's position in NATO or to her internal stability. The other, more extreme, party are prepared to use any means, fair or foul, to get Cyprus, and probably value NATO, the U.N., and the present Grk. Govt, by their ability and willingness to further Enosis alone. The Orthodox Church seem to constitute the backbone of this party, and the Communists no doubt support it.[208]

Because Papagos, as Wilding correctly remarked, was willing to moderate his *Enosis* campaign to uphold Greece's position in NATO, on 14 December Kyrou abandoned his own draft resolution and voted for the Anglo-American (New Zealand) motion. Previously uncited evidence from the British archives shows that, this decision was made, not as hitherto assumed, because Kyrou had no alternative after the Chairman of the Political Committee ruled that the New Zealand motion required a simple majority. Nutting's telegrams to the Foreign Office confirm that, even after that point, the Greek motion was still capable of obtaining, if not a majority, at least enough votes to embarrass the British side. That is precisely why the British delegation retreated for a second time, on this occasion reneging on its categorical condition to Lodge on 8 December to reject 'all amendments' to the New Zealand motion, and accepted the insertion of Kyrou's phrase, 'for the time being'. Furthermore, contrary to the traditional hypothesis that the United States exerted pressure on the British delegation to accept Kyrou's amendment, concrete evidence shows that Nutting and Dixon were adamant that such pressure was never applied. By contrast, what they told London repeatedly was that their delegation accepted Kyrou's amendment because they feared that otherwise the New Zealand motion might be defeated. This, in turn, suggests that Kyrou always retained the option of fighting the New Zealand motion to the end, with some chance of success, but made his last-minute U-turn under instructions from Papagos to protect Atlantic unity.

7

THE DUALIST ASPECTS OF FOREIGN ECONOMIC POLICY

Alongside its articulation at the level of 'high politics', the dualism of the Rally's foreign policy extended to the realm of 'low politics'. Although external economic relations were never integrated with the rest of the government's foreign policy, after 1945 the linkages between them intensified. Historically, this development corresponded to the receipt of unprecedented sums of economic aid, first, from the UN Recovery and Relief Agency (UNRRA), then from the Truman Doctrine and, finally, from the Marshall Plan. This change turned a substantial part of Greek foreign policy towards issues of economic reconstruction and cooperation. Institutionally, it led to a growing role for Directorate 4D in the Ministry of Foreign Affairs, which was charged with the management of foreign economic relations. The overarching responsibility for the government's foreign economic policy, however, still lay with the Ministry of Economic Coordination, although the increased role of Directorate 4D suggests that the institutional boundaries between 'high' and 'low' politics were becoming blurred. For example, when Markezinis travelled to the United States, Canada, Italy, France, Germany and Britain in 1953, his visits were prepared by Directorate 4D in Foreign Affairs and not by his own Ministry of Coordination. Still, in terms of policy formulation, the Ministry of Coordination always retained the upper hand, partly because it had more resources and partly because the US economic agencies were linked to it.

As with the rest of the Rally's foreign policy, external economic relations were marked by a propensity towards self-contradiction. The main inconsistency here arose from Markezinis's commitment to a mixed approach, whereby protectionist and liberal trade principles were combined in a single policy. This mixed approach was acknowledged in official statements, such as Markezinis's warning that his policy did 'not imply that we believe in absolute liberalism' or Trade Minister Panayiotis Papaligouras's declarations that the Rally 'believes in a realistic liberalism, adapted to the modern mission of the state'.[1] Another example can be found in a Ministry of Coordination report, drafted in April 1953 by Vassilios Damalas, a senior advisor, who spoke about a compound policy that feared neither a 'tariff-dependent industry' nor the imposition of 'limits to protection'. According to this report,

> there is a widespread view that industry in Greece is tariff-dependent and that the country's population will be better served through the import of industrial

products. This perception is not merely erroneous, but catastrophic for the country's future. Of course, we shall not deny that tariff protection should be kept within sensible limits, but we cannot accept the generalization of the view about a tariff-dependent industry.[2]

Contrary to the prevalent trend in the scholarship,[3] statements like these suggest that the Rally Government was more critical of the principles of free trade than it was later purported to be. As Vasso Papandreou has argued, the development model Greece embraced in the 1950s was a liberal variant of Import Substitution Industrialization (ISI).[4] However, in contrast to mainstream forms of ISI, which rely on high protectionism and big state intervention, the Rally Government envisaged a more moderate approach, chiefly because it was committed to the liberal institutions of the post-war Bretton Woods system for political and ideological reasons.[5] Consequently, the underlying logic of its moderately protectionist policy was to use Greece's strategic position as a frontline NATO state to finance its ISI programme through American aid. However, as the receipt of US aid was believed to be contingent upon Greece's adjustment to the liberal principles of the Bretton Woods system, its implementation could be envisaged only under limited trade protectionism.

The package of measures which set in motion this mixed strategy was the so-called new economic policy of 1953, whose name was linked thereafter to its political architect, Markezinis himself. The inner contradictions of this policy were many, but its central antinomy lay in the manner in which it sought to reduce the large trade deficit, which was seen at the time as the single most important source of disequilibrium in the Greek economy.[6] On the one hand, Markezinis confronted the issue with a cluster of hidden protectionist measures, chiefly the massive currency devaluation and the imposition of tariff rises across a range of imports; on the other, he introduced a set of liberalizing reforms, including the abolition of quantitative restrictions (quotas) and duties on most imports and incentives to foreign direct investment (FDI). This policy mix ultimately intended to pave the way for financing a medium-term investments programme, including a heavy industry pillar, which the Rally ministers claimed 'will change the entire face of the country'.[7] As George Pagoulatos argues, 'ISI became the most crucial component of the post-1953 outward-looking developmental strategy'.[8] In this regard, what was a contradictory combination of protectionist and liberal measures was promoted as an ideal synthesis that would secure new American aid to finance an ambitious industrialization programme. In the long run, this policy was expected to rapidly modernize Greece and enable it to 'catch-up' with the advanced industrial economies of the West.

Meanwhile, the main assumption underlying Markezinis's 'new economic policy' was that the United States would be persuaded to finance the medium-term investments programme with additional aid, following the official expiry of the Marshall Plan in 1952. This was a major challenge, as ECA's Director, Paul R. Porter, had opposed the notion of an ambitious industrialization programme for Greece in earlier years. In the autumn of 1950, ECA began to revise its strategic assessment for the Greek economy, leading to substantial cuts in US aid from $280 million in 1948–49 and 1949–50, to $231 million in 1950–1 and $182 million in 1951–2 (Table 5).[9] After that point, the question of Greece's economic sustainability became increasingly defined by ECA as a problem of restoring monetary stability rather than accelerating development. This revision was driven largely by ECA's declining confidence in the Greek political and economic elites, whose handling of US aid was deemed scandalously inefficient.[10] For these and other reasons,[11] ECA began to roll over some Marshall Plan funds for Greece beyond the expiry of the programme, i.e. for 1952–4, and to this effect, recommended an early stabilization programme in 1951–2 to curb inflation and increase the capacity of the economy to absorb the remaining investment capital. Regarding the long term, ECA took the view that Greece needed a development model based on agriculture and light industry, not heavy industrialization. Agriculture was preferred, partly because ECA saw that locally produced food could meet the immediate subsistence needs of the economy, saving 30 to 40 per cent of Marshall Plan funds that went towards importing wheat and foodstuffs.[12] It was also favoured because Greece enjoyed comparative advantage in this sector and could therefore use it to reduce its large trade deficit.[13] Light industry was equally favoured by ECA because it was less capital intensive, but more labour intensive, a key factor in reducing Greece's high unemployment. As one ECA report put it, 'Greece needs to look to the development of industries requiring a relatively large amount of employment per $1,000 of product and not to the development of heavy industries requiring large investments per worker'.[14] Consequently, when Kartalis raised the issue of financing large energy and industry projects in 1951, ECA rebuffed his demands as overly ambitious.[15]

Markezinis, was well aware of Washington's objections to any ambitious Greek industrialization plans. When he revived the issue ahead of his official visit to the United States in May 1953, one press report remarked that 'the US Mission holds different views [...] regarding the sector of industrial development'.[16] Although he discounted such criticisms before the visit, upon his return from Washington he publicly admitted that the Americans 'did not want to even hear' about his medium-term investments programme.[17] As with its approach to high politics, in low politics the Rally Government tried to change Washington's policy through an early strategy of 'voluntary dependence'. In the same way as Papagos offered the military bases and extra troops to Korea as incentives for gaining greater US support for *Enosis*, so Markezinis sought additional US economic aid through announcing a unilateral lifting of import quotas at home. From November 1949 to January 1955, the OEEC had asked its member-states to abolish quotas on 90 per cent of imports, but Greece, Iceland and Turkey were exempted because of what the Organization termed 'balance-of-payments difficulties or structural problems'.[18] Shortly after the Rally's rise to power, however, Markezinis unilaterally lifted most import quotas,[19] to present Greece as a champion of free trade and a more robust economy than the OEEC assumed. In this way, he sought to strengthen Greece's case in seeking more American aid.

Greece's post-war economic problem

For many contemporary observers, the central problem of the Greek economy in the early post-war years was its lack of self-sustainability.[20] Between 1944 and 1952, Greece had to rely on substantial sums of overseas aid, which were channelled partly towards 'maintenance' (i.e. immediate consumption needs) and partly towards investment to revive the war-torn economy.[21] According to ECA, from 1945 to 1949, Greece received $1,758 million, of which $560 million in the form of military aid and $1,198 in the form of economic aid (Table 5).[22] Although this ratio later changed, until 1951 foreign economic aid approached one quarter of Greek national income.[23]

Under these circumstances, AMAG saw the attainment of 'a more self-sufficient economy' as its main 'long-term goal' in Greece.[24] Although by 1950 Greek production had returned to its pre-war levels, dependence on US aid was substantial because the recovery of the previous five years had been uneven and fragile. The resulting economic dependence was so acute, that some of Washington's local friends, like Markezinis, publicly cautioned in 1950 against excessive reliance on US aid. 'We must not rely on the unlimited continuation of American economic assistance [...]. If a country's reconstruction cannot arise from within [...] then the loss of that country's independence should be expected', he wrote.[25]

The issue of self-sustainability was not confined to Greece's dependence on US aid nor to its inability to provide subsistence for much of its population. Besides these acute problems, which were highlighted in shocking images of poverty across the Greek countryside, another question was the country's monetary instability, which undermined trust and long-term investment. Until 1950, inflation was high and confidence in the drachma was at such low levels that, according to a

Table 4 Foreign economic and military aid to Greece, January 1945 – July 1949 (in millions of dollars)

Source	Amount
Lend-lease	50
UNRRA	415
British aid	140
Canadian post-UNERA aid	5
Export-Import Bank credit	15
OFLO loans	80
US Maritime Commission credit	45
AMAG	128
ECA	263
Public Law	40
Private relief organizations	17
Military Aid 1945–9	560
Total	1,758

Source: ECA, *European Recovery Program: Greece 1949*, p.11.

Table 5 US economic assistance to Greece, 1948–55 (in millions of current US dollars)

Year	US Economic Aid (Excluding military assistance)
1947/48	240
1948/49	284
1949/50	280
1950/51	231
1951/52	182
1952/53	80
1953/54	75
1954/55	20

Sources: Central Bank of Greece, *Governor's Annual Reports*; *The Varvaressos Report*, 5 January 1952; *F.R.U.S 1949*, Vol. V, p.271, 428–9, 433.

major study in 1952, many government funds channelled to the private sector for investment never made it into production. Instead, these grants were sold for US dollars and gold sovereigns, because of widespread fear that their value would depreciate (due to inflation or a surprise currency devaluation).[26] Writing in 1949, Markezinis noted in astonishment that even the value of gold had been rising sharply in Greece. 'A year ago', he remarked, 'for one gold sovereign you could buy around 30 okes of oil. This year you can buy 10. This means we are [...] a country where inflation fully manifests itself even in gold sovereigns'.[27] Another structural problem was Greece's high unemployment, especially in the countryside. According to a study by Professor Angelos Angelopoulos, in 1950 unemployment stood at 20–25 per cent, while in the farming sector, where half of the population worked, it was estimated at 40 per cent.[28] A higher figure was given by a contemporary British study, which estimated general unemployment in Greece at 30 per cent in 1952.[29]

Table 6 US military aid to Greece, 1947–56 (in millions of US dollars)

Year	Military Aid
1947–8	198
1948–9	159
1949–50	103
1950–1	160
1951–2	171
1952–3	114
1953–4	95
1954–5	59
1955–6	96
1956–7	62

Sources: Theodore Couloumbis, *The United States, Greece, and Turkey: The Troubled Triangle*, New York, Praeger, 1983, p.178; Jeffery, *Ambiguous Commitments*, p.230; Psalidopoulos, *Επιτηρητές σε απόγνωση*, p.44.

Table 7 The Greek balance of trade, 1948–56 (in millions of US dollars)

Year	Exports	Imports	Deficit	Exports/Imports
1948	89.4	390.9	301.5	0.23
1949	83.4	367.6	274.2	0.23
1950	85.1	397.7	314.6	0.21
1951	101.9	431.6	329.7	0.24
1952	114.3	274.7	160.4	0.42
1953	134.1	243.3	109.2	0.55
1954	161.0	328.4	167.4	0.49
1955	206.5	354.2	157.7	0.57
1956	209.6	454.7	255.1	0.45

Sources: George Kottis, *Liberalizing Foreign Trade. The Experience of Greece*, World Bank Comparative Studies, Washington, The World Bank, 1989, p.19; *Economic Surveys by the OECD: Greece*, Paris. OECD, 1962, p.30.

With such gloomy macroeconomic indicators, ECA concluded in February 1949 that 'reconstruction and development in Greece might have to continue beyond 1952', the year of the Marshall Plan's official termination.[30] In February 1951, a NSC policy paper acknowledged that 'the United States has not succeeded in evoking the degree of self-help in Greece which is essential for the ultimate solution of Greece's critical economic problems' and attributed this to the country's unique circumstances, especially the Civil War, which was believed to have delayed reconstruction compared to other OEEC countries by 'three to four years'.[31] The same paper stressed that other factors, such as changing patterns in world trade, the country's political instability, monetary disequilibrium and high inflation, posed further obstacles.[32] Regarding the latter, ECA found that its programme in Greece faced 'the apparently conflicting aims of controlling inflation and at the same time encouraging economic development'.[33]

Despite the long list of mitigating circumstances, which made even ECA's own propaganda describe Greece as 'the most complex problem',[34] Marshall Plan aid to the country, instead of increasing, was being sharply reduced.[35] As Michalis Psalidopoulos remarks, the hitherto prevalent 'developmental' view within ECA started to give way to a 'monetarist' assessment which saw economic stabilization (smaller trade deficit, a balanced budget and lower inflation) as the new primary objectives.[36] According to a contemporary study by the London-based Royal Institute of International Affairs, ECA reduced economic aid to Greece from $280 million to $231 million in 1950–1 chiefly because the Greek Government had failed to pass 'the measures which the mission regarded as essential'. The same study noted that among ECA officials 'there was a growing feeling of exasperation with the failure of the Greeks to take the steps necessary to help themselves and with their increasing tendency to leave everything to the fairy godmother in Washington'.[37]

By contrast, Greek economists who cooperated with ECA, like Professor Leander Nikolaides, maintained that the Agency's views reflected deep-seated prejudices about Greece. ECA's 'objective aim', he argued, was to unsettle the economic foundations of the [Greek reconstruction] programme [...] and as a necessary consequence, to reduce the proposed projects, that is to cut the requested funds for the benefit of other countries [...] This attempt [...] was carried out later throughout the period of the aid allocation [...] The ongoing objections inevitably delayed the implementation of the works. [...] Similar discussions took place in early June [...] when the revised Greek programme for 1949–50 was examined, always with the inclination to reduce aid.[38]

In 1951–2, an even sharper cut, initially to $170 million (which was later adjusted to $182 million) caused consternation even among US embassy staff in Athens. On 29 November 1951, Yost complained that ECA/Washington was too concerned with Greek inflation and applied an overly punitive policy that risked destroying the reconstruction programme. 'We question why [...] it is considered safe to make cut of over 100 million (from 275 actually spent to 170),' he asked. Then he expressed anxiety that ECA/W[ashington], preoccupied with Gr[ee]k aspect of worldwide inflationary problem and with frailty [of] Gr[ee]k political leadership (also as Porter notes [this is] not an exclusively Gr[ee]k phenomenon), may attempt to effect overnight cure by drastic surgical operation which could kill patient.[39] In the end, the allocation was raised to $182 million, but this was still a drastic reduction of 21 per cent from the previous year.

Because ECA judged that Greece's unique circumstances posed limits to its reconstruction programme, some of the withheld sums were rolled over to the period 1952–4, thus effectively extending the Greek programme by two more years. Therefore, while settling the sum at $182 million, ECA withheld approximately $48 million to be disbursed over the next two years, together with some earlier arrears. Although Peurifoy opposed the cut, insisting that '$200 million [...] [should be the] absolute minimum',[40] some historians have mistakenly portrayed his intervention as yet another attempt to undermine Plastiras and facilitate the Rally's ascent to power.[41] This narrative, moreover, seems unaware of the fact that, on 23 September 1951, Papagos himself signed a common note with Venizelos and Plastiras in which all three, in a rare show of *Ethnikofron* unity, protested to the US Government against ECA's proposed cuts. Peurifoy backed the joint initiative with the remark: 'Embassy and US A[gency] [are] substantially in accord with [the] arguments presented'.[42] Ultimately, the figure of $182 million was not revised. On 29 December 1951, Kartalis, wrote a memorandum to the US Government threatening that the cut would affect Greece's defence budget, its financial stability and key investment projects. His warnings, however, fell on deaf ears. For the next ten months, EPEK's Coordination Minister threatened retaliation with massive cuts in defence (which covered 36 per cent of government expenditure) but as we saw above, these were never carried out.[43]

Meanwhile, since October 1951, ECA advised Kartalis to carry out a stabilization programme, which included wage freezes, tax rises, spending cuts, price controls and tighter money circulation.[44] As MSA chief, Roger Lapham, explained on Radio Athens, the programme's aim was to restore monetary stability and, particularly, to curb inflation in order to limit speculation and render the Greek economy self-sustainable.⁴⁵ The underlying aim of the programme, however, was to pave the ground for the termination of Marshall Plan aid (save the small sums rolled over to 1953 and 1954). ECA concluded that Greece needed a currency devaluation to reduce its massive trade deficit ahead of cuts in Marshall Plan dollars and Kartalis's stabilization programme intended to absorb the inflationary pressures of this devaluation. In May 1952, the Deputy Director of MSA-Washington, John Kenney, described its rationale as follows:

a. To institute […] measures necessary to achieve a program which has as its primary emphasis the elimination of inflationary pressures in preparation for a currency reform;

b. To prepare and negotiate, if found necessary, the implementation of a currency reform at the earliest possible time. The anti-inflationary program together with the currency reform shall be designed to restore confidence in the monetary system of Greece, to induce the surrender of hoarded gold and foreign exchange […], to restore an equitable distribution of income […], to reduce Greece's balance-of-payments deficit substantially, and to restore conditions favoring the healthy growth of free enterprise.⁴⁶

MSA-Washington was eager to carry out the currency reform early. To this end, it sent a delegation to Athens in March 1952 with the aim of implementing it within '3 months'.⁴⁷ So determined was the Agency to see an early devaluation that it sent a zealous official, Edward Tenenbaum, to print drachmas in London 'bearing a new name' without even informing the Greek Government! According to Kenney, 'an official or officials of the Bank of Greece had "signed the requisite plate orders" but […] very few people knew about it'. To avoid a scandal, however, the State Department finally blocked the plan on the grounds that such 'action might well be interpreted as intervention of a most blatant nature, and the repercussions could extend considerably beyond Greece'.⁴⁸

Over the next two months, the State Department and the US embassy in Athens persuaded MSA-Washington to take into account the local political situation. As a result, MSA revised its original deadline of '3 months' with the more flexible target of carrying out the currency reform at 'the earliest possible time'.⁴⁹ Under the new framework, Kartalis prepared a plan in June–July 1952, but told the US embassy that the EPEK-Liberal coalition was too weak politically to carry it out, a view endorsed by the Governor of the Bank of Greece, George Mantzavinos. To overcome this obstacle, Acheson instructed Peurifoy on 29 July to work with the King to form a three-party coalition, involving EPEK, the Liberals and the Rally, with a view to introducing the currency reform within a few months and then call an election.⁵⁰ Although the King agreed, and Papagos consented, Kartalis began to raise objections when he learned in early August that US aid for 1952–3 would be massively cut from $182 to $80 million. Although a sharp reduction was expected,⁵¹ the figure was well below the most pessimistic forecasts. Peurifoy, who broke the news to Kartalis, reported the latter's response as follows:

> If figure were announced, he would recommend to [his] government its imm[ediate] resignation. He argued that [the] figure must have been fixed on assumption [that] currency reform would go through, that reform is most uncertain since political prerequisites do not yet exist, that in any case assumption on which aid figure [is] fixed can not be explained to [the] Greek people and that they would believe [the] government carried out [the] stabilization program at [the] behest of [the] Americans merely in order to justify aid cut.[52]

At this point, Kartalis appears to have realized that his stabilization programme was not, as he was led to believe, a corrective interlude to introduce a currency devaluation before resuming the reconstruction programme in 1952–4.[53] Instead, his stabilization programme was now presented as an early wind-up of the Marshall Plan with only limited funds for 1952–4. Meanwhile, the idea of a tripartite government also fell through because, according to Peurifoy, the King 'failed to fol[low it] up and, moreover, revealed [the] plan to Papandreou in spite of explicit warning not to do so'.[54] On 22 August Plastiras also lost the vote of confidence in Parliament and this forced the MSA to postpone the devaluation until after the elections of 17 November 1952.

The foregoing analysis challenges some of the key assumptions in the historiography about Washington's economic policy in Greece. The established view holds that after 1947 the United States was wedded to Greek industrialization. Proponents of the dependence narrative, like Vergopoulos, Close, Margarita Dritsas, George Stathakis and others, have argued that because of geopolitical reasons and the prevalent developmentalist thinking after 1945, Greek industrialization was firmly supported by Washington.[55] Stathakis remarks that 'the West had to provide resources, as Greece was being turned into a bridgehead in the battle against communist expansion. With industrialization, a new field for the expansion of foreign aid was opening up even after the end of the Civil War'.[56] A similar thesis has been put forward by many liberal and non-Marxist economic historians, including Panos Kazakos, Loukas Tsoukalis, Costas Costis and Pagoulatos. The latter, for example, states:

> Corroborated by the verdicts of nearly every international organization of the time as well as the American Mission, 'development via industrialization' was elevated into gospel truth. This broadly held belief in the urgency of industrialization meant other alternative strategies became quickly ostracized.[57]

These analyses, however, are overwhelmingly based on American sources from the late 1940s and overlook ECA's policy revision in 1950 as well as insider Greek accounts, like those of the OEEC delegate, Professor Nikolaides.[58] According to Nikolaides, who was also in the Greek team that negotiated the early Marshall Plan projects in the 1940s, the OEEC had been hostile to the idea of Greek industrialization all along. Speaking in 1954 he recalled:

Both the preliminary talks at Paris in 1947 and the discussions with the American Mission here gave a clear indication that, although the other parts of the reconstruction programme would face a 'normal' response [...] 'industrialization' would be faced with a raging reaction [...] mainly because of its effects on the export trade of the interested countries, and also, for certain big countries, because of the economic autonomy that industrialization would bring about to Greece after a few years. [...] Among most members of the [US] Mission skepticism regarding industrialization was prevalent: 'Greece, they told us, is an agricultural country [...]. It is not possible to establish factories capable of competing with the factories of the industrialized countries, unless they are tariff protected, and this contradicts our general views. Besides, your programme is an autarky programme, and this is also not acceptable. Finally, your consumption does not justify the establishment of more than one big industry unit, which means you will have one refinery, one soda factory, one aluminum factory, one blast furnace; consequently, you are creating monopoly firms and this will be neither acceptable to the US Government nor to American public opinion'.[59]

Ironically, most *Ehnikofron* economists in the early 1950s, firmly believed that, for political reasons, Washington could not possibly block Greece's aspirations to industrialize. This ideological fixation came in full display in early 1952, when a milestone report on the Greek economy was published by the eminent World Bank economist, Professor Kyriakos Varvaressos. Varvaressos had formerly served as deputy prime minister, Governor of the Bank of Greece and delegate at the historic Bretton Woods conference, where he earned the respect of John Maynard Keynes. His controversial *Report* of 1952 was personally commissioned by Prime Minister Plastiras. Besides this context, strong objections were raised against his supposedly heretical views that Greece should expect US aid to be significantly reduced and that the country's only alternative was to finance its development independently.[60] The barrage of criticisms provoked by this argument was probably unprecedented in the history of Greek economic ideas. Later developments, however, showed that Varvaressos had approached this question with much greater realism than his liberal critics.[61]

The Varvaressos Report and its discontents

According to Vergopoulos, the controversy of 1952 between Varvaressos and his critics echoed some of the earlier debates between economic nationalists and liberals in the interwar period.[62] On one side, the elderly professor, practically alone, defended an economic model that resembled the policies that pulled Greece out of depression in the 1930s. On the opposite side, the leading *Ethnikofron* economists, proposed a liberal/ordoliberal model of US-financed industrialization, whose chief proponent, Professor Xenophon Zolotas, had been advocating since the 1920s.[63] Despite their intense disagreements, most of Varvaressos's critics acknowledged

Table 8 Comparison of the projected cuts in US economic aid to Greece in *The Varvaressos Report* and actual reductions, 1950–5 (millions of US dollars)

Year	Varvaressos's Forecasts	Actual reductions
1950–1	230 (known)	230
1951–2	185	182
1952–3	130	80
1953–4	100	75
1954–5	75	20
1955–6	50	-

Sources: *The Varvaressos Report*, p.14; Central Bank of Greece, Governor's Reports; F.R.U.S. 1951, 1952–4, 1955.

that his *Report* offered a comprehensive analysis of the Greek economy and an intellectually challenging, albeit incorrect, vision for the future.

The *Varvaressos Report* identified five problem areas: (a) 'Dependence on American aid'; (b) 'Continuing monetary instability'; (c) 'The serious imbalance' in the country's external accounts; (d) 'The inadequacy of the state administrative machinery'; and, (e) 'The low standards of living of a considerable section of the population'.[64] The bulk of its analysis focused on each of these problems separately and, as Plastiras had requested, specific policy recommendations were provided. Regarding the first area, Varvaressos recommended an end to the country's dependence on US aid, based on his assessment that this was bound to expire soon and Greece should be prepared to face the consequences. The *Report* claimed that its projected cuts in US aid were more pessimistic than widely expected, but defended its cautious approach on the grounds that Greece should resist the temptation of depending on foreign assistance to become self-sustaining. Ironically, although critics castigated the *Report* for its supposedly gloomy forecasts, it soon transpired that even Varvaressos was highly optimistic. For instance, his forecast for 1952–3, was a reduction of US aid to $130 million, but the real figure turned out to be $80 million, an overestimate of 62 per cent (Table 8). Regarding the second area, the *Report* recommended measures to restore monetary stability, including price controls, higher direct taxes (especially on the rich) and tighter credit controls.[65] Third, on trade, Varvaressos proposed restrictions on foreign currency circulation and, in a secret annex, called for a drastic currency devaluation of 40 per cent, from 15,000 to 25,000 drachmas to the dollar.[66] In the fourth area, he outlined measures to improve the efficiency of Greek public administration and, in the fifth, he recommended leniency towards trade union demands for wage increases and better investment opportunities for farmers.[67]

In a final chapter, entitled 'The low standard of living of the population and the possibilities of curing it through economic development', Varvaressos outlined his long-term vision for the Greek economy. He began by examining the difficulties facing 'underdeveloped countries', and listed the main obstacles facing their efforts to industrialize. He argued that the creation of a broad industrial base in underdeveloped economies does not simply require capital, but also technological 'know-how', sophisticated organization and a developed entrepreneurial mentality. This assessment did not rule out the option of channelling capital to industry but stressed that the agricultural sector (especially tobacco and cotton) and light industry (textiles, construction) provided the best opportunities for Greece's long-term development.[68]

There is some truth in Vergopoulos's argument that Varvaressos should be ultimately viewed as a populist who emphasized the benefits of autarky, government regulation and agriculture. In stressing the primacy of small private businesses over large production units, the elderly professor emerged as a spokesman of Greece's petit-bourgeois and farming interests against the powerful Athens bourgeoisie.[69] His critique of the industrial and commercial classes, as well as senior civil servants (whom he blatantly accused of laziness and corruption) was part of an attack on the entire post-war Greek establishment. In several statements, these sentiments were made explicit. One sentence read: 'It is unacceptable that during the present critical period the taxes on thriving industry and prosperous trade should be providing only 7 per cent of Government revenue'; another said: 'I find the recent sharp reduction in taxes on ship-owners' profits extremely difficult to understand'. These ideas often reflected an essentially nationalist rather than Keynesian or socialist outlook, an issue that became apparent in Varvaressos's avoidance of any discussion of the developmental role of the state and his firm commitment to balanced budgets.[70] His analysis was punctuated by occasional nationalist clichés, which seemed to influence some parts of his thinking. One passage read: 'Greece has a history of thousands of centuries [sic] during which she [...] accomplished great things. She is not going to collapse if she does not acquire industrial installations'.[71]

A few weeks after the *Report*'s publication, on 22 February 1952, a group of senior economists and politicians, including members of the very government which had commissioned it, gathered at the Hellenic Association of Economic Science to rip it apart. Participants included the Ministers of Finance and Industry, Christos Evelpides and Yannis Zigdis respectively, former governor of the Bank of Greece and future adviser of the Rally Government, Professor Zolotas, and many others. Evelpides and Zolotas praised the first section of the *Report* as offering a sound analysis of Greece's economic problems, but begged to differ with its second part which contained the recommendations. Zolotas argued that Varvaressos had failed to grasp two major international changes that occurred since 1945:

> First, we are granted and are still being granted free economic aid in large sums to cover our consumer needs and economic development. Second, we have awakened from our fatalism and understood the colossal importance of rational economic development through the systematic exploitation of our natural resources, excess labour force and economic restructuring.

Zolotas was obliged to acknowledge that the track record of the Marshall Plan in Greece was disappointing. But in contrast to Varvaressos, he kept quiet about the corrupt practices of Greece's business elites, and argued instead:

7. Dualist Aspects of Foreign Economic Policy 191

If there have been acts of negligence and more of the capital funds in dollars and drachmas were not used for investment and their distribution has not been sensible [...], this should require measures to fix it. But the recommended reduction in investment to 30 million dollars [...] constitutes, in effect, a total repudiation of economic development.

Then Zolotas turned to the delicate question of the expected termination of US aid, which formed the basis of Varvaressos's argument. To keep the dream of Greek industrialization alive, he resorted to rhetorical questions which, in semi-populist style, aimed to appeal to the raw emotions of his audience:

If substantial production projects which form the basis of economic development are not implemented now that we possess the opportunity of receiving free aid, when will they be? Where will the capital be found for their implementation, when the country will have managed to achieve an equilibrium in its balance of payments?[72]

Throughout his critique, Zolotas displayed precisely the kind of dependent mentality that Varvaressos fiercely criticized. Moreover, Zolotas's second rhetorical question implied that Greece should somehow persist in running large trade deficits to force the United States politically to continue to provide substantial aid.

During the conference, some speakers cited the latest UN reports, stressing the centrality of industrialization for the development of late modernizing economies. They also caricatured Varvaressos's views as a relic of the past. Zigdis, remarked: 'I also grew up with the theory of the non-viability of Greece which was considered the economic orthodoxy in my student years [...]. I am convinced that in ten years Greece will prove to be one of the most affluent corners of Europe'. Zigdis then dismissed the *Report* (which his own prime minister had commissioned) with the remark: 'The Varvaressos Report should be better forgotten as quickly as possible, for if we do not show our capacity for self-development [...] the foreigners will get tired of us'.[73]

In response, Varvaressos wrote to the editor of the *Review of Economic and Political Sciences*, the periodical which published the conference proceedings, stressing that he was not invited to defend his views in a gathering whose sole purpose was to discuss his work. This remark highlighted the political motives of this otherwise supposedly 'scientific' conference,[74] whose obvious aim was to defame the *Report* and stop Plastiras from adopting its recommendations. In the same letter, Varvaressos argued that he did not oppose Greek industrialization and cited several passages which, in fairness, portrayed him more as a sceptic among zealots than a reactionary who opposed industrialization per se. Still, the gulf between him and his critics was so wide, that he did not hesitate to scorn a minister from the government which had commissioned his *Report*: 'Concerning Mr Zigdis's words, I think I should not bother, as I imagine no one could have possibly taken them seriously,' he said.[75]

To some extent, the critics succeeded in undermining *The Varvaressos Report*, but never made it completely irrelevant. In the next few months, the study acquired an equivocal status in government eyes. Officially, the EPEK-Liberal coalition stood by it, but its recommendations were increasingly treated as thought-provoking ideas to be adopted selectively rather than a set of concrete policy proposals. In March 1952, Kartalis kept a tactful distance from it, saying in Parliament that the *Report*

> has been the subject of systematic study by the government [...]. However, the points and issues which Mr Varvaressos inevitably opened and the solutions he recommended belong to the step-by-step and longer-term framework of curing the Greek economy and much less to the handling of immediate problems [...]. The professor's main conclusions and the directions he identified are in agreement with the views and aims of government policy.[76]

On 26 May 1952, Plastiras announced plans for a major overhaul of public administration, stating that these reflected the recommendations of *The Varvaressos Report*. A week later, *Eleftheria* ran a front-page interview with the professor to underline his continued influence.[77] As we shall see, despite their frequent refutations of *The Varvaressos Report*, even the Rally's own economic team quietly accepted some of its ideas.

The 'new economic policy' of 1953

Already before becoming Coordination Minister, Markezinis publicly declared that he stood on the side of Varvaressos's critics. When he took charge of the Rally's economic policy, he appointed Varvaressos's main detractor, Zolotas, at the head of a small team of experts who carried out the currency reform of 1953.[78] As Markezinis later explained, his objections mainly stemmed from his fear that 'with [Varvaressos's] project, industry would pass to the realm of dreams'. When he visited Washington in May 1953, he recalled meeting Varvaressos and saying 'how sorry' he was that he 'did not follow his recommendations'. Markezinis claims that the Professor sounded repentant, but this version of events must be treated with caution, because it contradicts Varvaressos's public statements at the time.[79]

Despite their differences on the question of industrialization, Markezinis appeared more open to other parts of the *Report*, especially its secret annex on currency reform. Although Varvaressos had proposed a sharp devaluation of 40 per cent (from 15,000 to 25,000 drachmas to the dollar) Markezinis finally settled for 50 per cent.[80] In macroeconomic theory, currency devaluation is a hidden protective measure insofar as it increases the price of imports and reduces the price of exports.[81] In this regard, Varvaressos's preference for a devaluation of 40 per cent was consistent with his protectionist views. In Markezinis's case, however, it is difficult to explain why he went further, unless we accept that his alleged 'liberalism' ('eclectic' or non) concealed a substantial element of hitherto unacknowledged protectionism. Of course, in 1952-3, the official rate of the drachma (15,000 to the US dollar) was 28-33 per cent higher than its market rate, estimated between 20,900 and 22,500 drachmas to the dollar.[82] This gap would have led most liberal economists to also recommend some currency devaluation to realign the official to the market rate. Broadly speaking, this was the view of former minister, George Pesmazoglou, who argued (after the Markezinis's devaluation) that 'setting the rate of the dollar at 30,000 drachmas is excessive and this should not have exceeded 23-25,000 drachmas'.[83] Indeed, liberal experts of the Coordination Ministry headed by Zolotas apparently recommended an even smaller devaluation of just 15-20 per cent (perhaps to deliberately keep an ongoing trade deficit to encourage greater American aid, as Zolotas hinted at the Hellenic Association of Economic Sciences conference a year earlier).[84] By contrast, Varvaressos's recommendation of a 40 per cent devaluation, i.e. 7-12 per cent below realignment, was intended to boost Greek exports through a modest level of hidden protectionism. Markezinis not only embraced this approach against other liberal economists, but pushed it to the extreme. As he revealed much later, his preferred option was to devalue by 62.5 per cent, i.e. from 15,000 to 40,000 drachmas to the dollar, but eventually he was forced by the MSA and the US embassy to settle for 50 per cent.[85] Consequently, the famous 'Markezinis devaluation' of 1953, like much of the Rally's foreign economic policy, was half home grown and half directed by American intervention.

Although Markezinis never fully disclosed the motives behind this choice, he still provided some interesting clues.[86] In November 1953, he told Parliament that Kartalis had handed him the secret annex of *The Varvaressos Report*, with handwritten notations, showing that Kartalis disagreed with certain aspects of the proposed devaluation.[87] In the same speech, Markezinis provided the clearest indication yet of his thinking on the issue. After a diatribe, in which he argued that all previous Greek devaluations had failed because they did not go deep enough (a criticism also aimed at Varvaressos's 1945 devaluation),[88] Markezinis stressed that his decision was chiefly influenced by the studies of his experts' team which 'proved through faultless figures' that:

> Had we set the value of the dollar at 23,000 drachmas, again the export of currant, tobacco and many other products would have been difficult. And apart from that, we did not devalue with the intention of doing the same again after four or five years, but to secure once and for all the stability of our currency. To this end, basic precaution dictated that we should keep some safety margins.[89]

The explicit reference to 23,000 drachmas suggests that Markezinis was using these arguments specifically against his liberal critics. Moreover, the reference to currant and tobacco, Greece's foremost export commodities, confirms that he approached the devaluation from a predominantly protectionist standpoint as a means of reducing Greece's balance of trade deficit. Other considerations, like monetary stability and access to cheaper imports, which a liberal outlook would normally prioritize, mattered less to his explanation. For him, these issues could be tackled through the imposition of price controls and other measures requiring government

Image 10 Minister of Economic Coordination, Spyros Markezinis, announces the devaluation of the drachma in his historic radio speech of 9 April 1953. ELIA-MIET Photographic Archive.

intervention. For this reason, the Centre opposition, arguing from a liberal economic standpoint, later dubbed his currency reform as 'the hyperdevaluation'.[90]

A further insight into Markezinis' thinking could be gained through Varvaressos's little-known critique of the devaluation three weeks after its announcement. Before we turn to this critique, it should be stressed that the professor's intervention was provoked by Markezinis himself who, in an ill-fated attempt to outwit his Centrist opponents, disclosed to Parliament that his devaluation was, after all, based on the secret annex of *The Varvaressos Report*, which their own Government had commissioned. While this was the clearest admission yet that Markezinis's views were not as opposed to Varvaressos's as he previously claimed, ironically, it was now the Professor's turn to critique the Rally Government using a range of liberal arguments. The devaluation of 9 April, Varvaressos said, had gone too far because imports were made too expensive and this, he argued, was a major 'sacrifice' for the Greek people. In other words, Markezinis was now being censured by a protectionist for protecting too much! Varvaressos's second objection came from a monetarist perspective, thus confirming his reputation as a central banker at heart who never faltered on questions of sound money. His preference for a 40 per cent devaluation, he stressed, was based on his assessment that anything lower would spiral inflation.[91] After this public rebuke, Markezinis abandoned his tactical manoeuvre of hiding behind *The Varvaressos Report* to defend his devaluation. In his parliamentary speech on 23 November 1953, he returned to the habit of publicly attacking Varvaressos, this time, again, for allegedly 'having learned nothing' from past devaluations.[92]

Nevertheless, the early effects of Markezinis's devaluation began to vindicate Varvaressos's criticisms. Inflation, from 5.1 per cent in 1952, rose to 9 per cent in 1953 and 15.1 per cent in 1954, a cumulative rise of 25 per cent in two years which, as the professor had warned, removed half of the gain of the 50 per cent devaluation to the Greek exporter.[93] Moreover, to prevent inflation from rising further, Markezinis introduced a package of stabilization measures, including subsidies on basic foodstuffs, an import levy on widely consumed agricultural products and a strict regime of price controls, with police patrols monitoring government prices in the marketplace. Even the extra profits which exporters made because of the devaluation were taxed, at 50 per cent for farmers and 100 per cent for all others. Predictably, Kartalis and the liberal opposition press derided Markezinis's supposed 'liberalism' with caustic headlines, such as 'A Police Economy Established as of Yesterday. Intervention is Back'.[94]

Markezinis's 'new economic policy', however, included other measures besides the devaluation. Its most important liberalizing reforms were: (a) the abolition of quantitative restrictions (quotas) and duties on most (but not all) imports, announced during the devaluation speech of 9 April, but these were introduced in July; (b) Law 2687/53, which offered tax concessions and other incentives to overseas investors with the aim of attracting FDI. This was supplemented a year later by law 2681/54, which widened the range of incentives.[95] (c) Tariff reductions, ranging from 4 to 20 per cent over a range of commodities, in accordance with a GATT agreement concluded by the Plastiras Government in June 1952. The 'new economic policy', however, also included several protectionist measures, besides the massive devaluation. There were: (i) tariff increases of up to 50 per cent over a wide range of imports; (ii) the extension of state subsidies for some subsistence commodities, like wheat; (iii) new government incentives (mainly subsidies) to support key export commodities, like currant, tobacco, cotton, rice and olive oil.[96]

Table 9 Comparison of inflation rates in Greece and nine main trading partners, 1952–6

	Greek inflation rate	Average inflation of trading partners*	Difference between Greece and partners
1952	5.1	4.7	0.4
1953	9.2	0.8	8.4
1954	15.0	1.6	13.4
1955	5.7	2.5	3.2
1956	3.7	3.3	0.4
Cumulative 1953–5	29.9	4.9	25.0

* Belgium, France, W. Germany, Denmark, UK, Ireland, Italy, Luxembourg, Netherlands
Sources: Kottis, *Liberalizing Foreign Trade*, p.31, Table 2.11; Candilis, *The Economy of Greece*, p.93, table 33.

Although never officially acknowledged, the second part of Markezinis's package also implemented some proposals from *The Varvaressos Report*, whose short-term aim was to reduce Greece's trade deficit ahead of the termination of the Marshall Plan. The view that Markezinis's reforms contained strong elements of hidden protectionism, like those proposed by Varvaressos, was not considered heretical at the time. An economic study by the Royal Institute of International Affairs noted in 1954 that the Rally's policy 'appeared to be very much on the lines recommended by Professor Varvaressos'. Thomas Anthem, in the British journal *Contemporary Review*, remarked in the same year that 'the Greek Government has so far followed the lines of the report prepared [...] by the noted economist, Professor Varvaressos'.[97] Although these comments overstate the overlap between Markezinis's reforms and the famous *Report* (since there were also notable differences between them on industrialization, the rate of devaluation, etc.) they nevertheless highlight commonalities which the subsequent historiography has seriously overlooked.

Furthermore, according to a 1989 World Bank study on post-war trade liberalization, the effects of Markezinis's reforms were considered very limited. Despite its sympathetic views towards his 'new economic policy', the study found that 'economic openness' (i.e. the ratio of imports plus exports over GDP) increased from 22 per cent in 1953, to 26 per cent in 1954 and 27 per cent in 1955. But in 1952, the year preceding the reforms, the 'openness' of the Greek economy also stood at 26 per cent, the same as 1954. Another clear example of the hidden protectionism accompanying Markezinis's economic reforms are the study's crucial findings that government revenue from import duties and taxes in 1953–4 increased by 36 per cent, even though the total volume of imports fell. If trade had been truly liberalized, these revenues should have been reduced by an even greater proportion than the reduction in the volume of imports. Similarly, from 1953 to 1954 government spending on subsidies linked to exports also rose by 32 per cent, from $19.1 to $25.3 million.[98] In the recent scholarship, Pagoulatos is among a few economists to provide an accurate assessment of the 1953 reforms, as he notes that 'trade opening created the need to counterbalance its effects on domestic production through protectionist policies of ISI'. His analysis pertinently adds that, in relation to the post-war Greek economy, 'the pattern of increased state intervention to offset the dislocating effects of liberalizing trade is familiar in the literature', especially for less developed countries.[99]

Although one seldom finds it mentioned in the historiography,[100] the most important component of Markezinis's 'new economic policy' was neither the currency devaluation nor the trade 'liberalization reforms', but his mammoth medium-term investments programme. In April 1953, the Rally Government unveiled an ambitious 3-/5-year development plan, whose cost was estimated at $237 million. The programme consisted of three components: (i) The irrigation works, estimated at $24 million; (ii) the energy projects, estimated at $96 million; and (iii) the industrial development projects, estimated at $117 million, of which $75 million would go to heavy industry. The industrial development projects included oil refineries, nitrate factories, a caustic soda plant, aluminium factories near Mount Parnassos, salt pits at Messolongi, magnesium and nickel factories and a rail link from Itea to ship the extracted ores to the Gulf of Corinth.[101] Contemporary commentators aptly described it as 'the most ambitious investment programme in the history of Greece'.[102] Nearly all of its projects originated in the Greek Commission's proposals for the Marshall Plan's reconstruction programme in 1948,[103] and were either rejected by ECA as unviable (like the oil refinery) or abandoned when Marshall aid to Greece was drastically cut in 1951.[104] The revival of these projects after the implementation of Kartalis's stabilization programme was not merely a political bid to attract new American aid. It was the basis of a long-term strategy to exploit Greece's Cold War position to achieve rapid economic modernization.

Markezinis's visit to the United States

Soon after his appointment as Coordination Minister, Markezinis informed the US embassy of his wish to meet President Eisenhower and his new administration. An invitation was extended on 7 March 1953 and preparations began for his North America tour in May.[105] As we saw earlier, Markezinis's visit to Washington had important political and security objectives, but a further item on his agenda was the new aid request for his $237 million medium-term investments programme.[106] It is unclear precisely what sum Markezinis requested. Most probably, he asked for either $113 million, a figure quoted in the ten-page memorandum he submitted to the US embassy on 29 April or, as Kartalis later stated, $129 million, a figure quoted from a report by Markezinis to the MSA.[107] Forty years later, Markezinis wrote that he spoke to Dulles about 'nearly two hundred million'. What must be ruled out, however, is Papagos's public claim on 13 June 1953 that Markezinis requested only $73 million, a sum which Greece was already expecting for 1953–4 (lumping together Marshall Plan arrears plus new aid of $20 million).[108]

Upon his arrival in Washington on 6 May 1953, Markezinis dined with Dulles. On the next day he met him again at the State Department, where he made the formal request for extra aid. In his 1994 account, Markezinis recalled that, during dinner, he could not get on with Dulles, adding that 'things did not get better' on the next day. The Greek Coordination Minister recalled that Dulles's initial response was that the Greeks 'did not take into account how much they [the US] were spending' and recalled that 'the conversation basically ended without an outcome'. He then concluded that 'Dulles had absolutely no disposition to understand the problems of Greece'.[109] A similar version of events emerges from the State Department record of the conversation, although the description is more revealing. According to it, Markezinis

> made an impassioned plea for positive American assistance, stressing the gallant nature of the Greek people and in particular the importance of giving concrete evidence of support for the Papagos government. He said that if he returned to Greece and was able to say that the United States Government had been friendly

but not committal, it would have a serious effect on the stability of the Greek Cabinet and on the attitude of Marshal Papagos toward the United States. He was sure that if he (Markezinis) were rebuffed here, Marshal Papagos would declare his intention to maintain Greece's alignment with the West and Greece's armed forces at any cost, but at the same time would renounce all special connection with the United States terminating the MSA Mission to Greece and all MSA aid etc. He would certainly do this if Greece were offered nothing more than a mere $20,000,000 in economic aid for the coming year. Such an attitude would have bad effects for the United States not merely in Greece but throughout the Middle East, where Papagos had great prestige. [He] added that the [US] Secretary's forthcoming visit to Greece would be adversely affected.[110]

Although Dulles did not comment, his officials reported that he was 'unimpressed' by the 45-minute speech to which he had been subjected.[111] Under pressure from Congress, the Secretary of State viewed Markezinis's request unsympathetically and later told his aides: 'Any encouragement [...] would lead the Greeks to think that we were morally committed to financing [a] program of such proportions'.[112]

Two days later, the Greek and US negotiating teams spent hours drafting a joint *communiqué*, as they stumbled over the issue of whether the United States endorsed the idea of 'an' investments programme or 'the' investments programme proposed by Markezinis. Eventually, they settled for the non-committal 'a', but in an act of desperation, as soon as an unauthorized *communiqué* appeared, Markezinis released it to the Greek reporters who escorted him and cabled its content to Papagos.[113] According to the British embassy in Washington, this incident caused a '*scandale*'![114] Dulles, who refused to authorize the leaked draft, continued to amend it to make it more non-committal. Upon discovering this at the railway station, en route to Canada, Markezinis was infuriated and in a voice described by British diplomats as 'hysterical', requested a written explanation from the State Department officials who escorted him. He said that he had never found himself more 'exposed' in his entire career, that he would have to resign and that 'Papagos would in all probability tell the United States to take its money and its mission and go home!'[115] He then cabled Papagos again saying that 'Greece will pay heavily with Foster Dulles as the new Secretary of State of the USA'.[116]

Despite these protests, the final text of the *communiqué* stated, as Dulles wished, that the United States 'welcomes the intention of the Greek Government to develop a long-term investments program' and added that the US Government

> expects to continue, subject to Congressional authorization, economic and military assistance to Greece and the Executive Branch has asked Congress for Mutual Security funds for this purpose at the next fiscal year. Such funds as well as funds previously appropriated for the current fiscal year will, we expect, help in the implementation of the long-term program referred to.

On 15 May, Porter sent an *aide-memoire* to Markezinis saying that the US Government 'is unable at this time to make any firm commitment to the aid which will be available for the fiscal year 1954'.[117] Subsequent correspondence between the State Department and the US embassy in Athens described the funds requested by Markezinis as 'extravagant' and, in the end, it was agreed to offer Greece $75 million for 1953–4. This figure consisted of $55 million in arrears from Marshall Plan funds, plus new aid worth $20 million for 1953–4, a sum which Markezinis had derided as 'trifles' during his meeting with Dulles and as the sort of figure that would make Papagos 'renounce all special connection with the US' and close the MSA mission. Moreover, as Porter proposed on 15 May, the MSA advised Markezinis to seek a loan from the Exports-Imports Bank and the International Bank. In brief, Markezinis's visit to Washington yielded no additional aid to what was originally earmarked for Greece for 1953–4.[118]

When he returned to Athens, with the cabinet's consent, Markezinis concealed the failure of his economic mission, and everyone behaved as though his visit was crowned in spectacular success. Over the next two weeks, in which he fell ill, his fellow ministers engineered a climate of exuberance around the economic results of his North America tour. On 9 June, Kanellopoulos told the press that he was 'deeply satisfied with the outcome of Mr Markezinis's mission to the US' and that his 'success was complete'. On 13 June, Papagos told the Rally's parliamentary group that Markezinis had ostensibly requested only $73 million and that his trip was a success as he brought back $76 million.[119] Finally, on 20 June, the Minister of Coordination himself delivered a radio address in which he claimed that his medium-term investments programme had been approved by the United States and that the age-old dream of Greek industrialization was now within reach for the first time in the country's history:

> The proposed programme has been accepted as sensible and reasonable regarding its fundamentals in all three parts, the irrigation works, energy and the industrial component. [...] In other words, one might say that the Greek view prevailed completely and the dream upon whose realization the Greece of tomorrow depends has entered the realm of reality.[120]

The aim of this propaganda was to conceal not only the political embarrassment that Markezinis had suffered in Washington, but also the colossal setback to the Rally's economic policy resulting from the denial of additional aid. Without new American funds, the entire vision of the *Ethnikofron* economists to extricate Greece from its backwardness and embark on a programme of rapid industrialization would be shattered. However, since Papagos never intended 'to terminate the MSA mission in Greece' and Markezinis was equally unwilling to resign (as he had threatened to do in New York), the only option for the Rally Government was to pretend that the flagship of its 'new economic policy' was supposedly still afloat and hope that, somehow, funds would be raised later.

Meanwhile, Markezinis was obliged to reconcile himself to the development model which *The Varvaressos Report* and the MSA had proposed as the only viable alternative. On 9 May 1953, the Morgan Commission published a report recommending that Greece's development 'should become the responsibility of the Greek government and the Greek people' and went on to propose a reduction of the size of the US missions. The Commission also recommended that the reconstruction projects which had already begun should not be abandoned to become 'monuments of our inefficiency', but made it clear that the United States should not commit itself to funding any new projects.[121] The same conclusions were reaffirmed by the MSA's biannual report to Congress for the second half of 1953. This noted that 'agricultural production reached an all-time high in 1953' and stressed that Greece had achieved 'self-sufficiency' over a range of farming products.[122] However, neither industry nor the reconstruction projects were discussed and Markezinis's medium-term investments programme was not mentioned once. The flagship of the Rally's 'new economic policy' was quietly left to sink.

The misinterpretation of Markezinis's 'new economic policy' in the historiography

One of the best-known textbooks on modern Greece, Richard Clogg's *Short History*, claims that 'under Markezinis's aegis the economy was set on a free enterprise course'.[123] Similar language is used in another popular textbook by Koliopoulos and Veremis: 'Markezinis's views in economic development persisted long after his resignation [...]. Free market economics and importation of foreign investment capital [...] became the conventional wisdom'.[124] The careful reader will have noticed, however, that such statements confuse basic economic concepts in a way that distorts the content of Markezinis's 'new economic policy'. The first error is the use of terms commonly referring to the inner workings of a national economy ('free enterprise', 'free market') to describe reforms relating chiefly to international trade. The second error lies in the implicit claim that 'free market economics' and 'trade liberalization' were ostensibly not 'the conventional wisdom' in Greece until Markezinis arrived. These economic principles, however, constituted the economic orthodoxy in Greece from the nineteenth century to the early 1930s. Indeed, when Markezinis announced his import liberalization measures, he was careful to acknowledge that with these reforms Greece was 'rapidly returning to the good old pre-war days'.[125] Thanos Kapsalis, the Rally's Trade Minister, upon announcing the law lifting import quotas and lowering duties, also stated that this legislation 'marks the termination of the long period of restrictions and state intervention to which the country's economy was subjected for more than 20 years'.[126] Another common fallacy can be found in a recent textbook by Stathis Kalyvas, *Modern Greece: What Everyone Needs to Know*, which states that 'the massive devaluation of the drachma [...] proved highly effective, leading to the containment of inflation'. Others, like Judith Jeffery, equally claim that 'under Prime Minister Papagos, the government managed to control the inflation which had dogged the Greek economy since the end of World War II'.[127] Yet Papagos inherited an inflation rate of 5.1 per cent for 1952 and throughout the three years of his government, inflation was doubled to an average annual rate of 10 per

Table 10 Percentage of annual change in prices in the Greek economy, 1951–5 (Consumer Price Index)

Year	Rate of inflation
1951	12.6
1952	5.1
1953	9.0
1954	15.1
1955	5.8
Cumulative 1953–5	**29.9**
Average 1953–5	**10.0**

Sources: Central Bank of Greece, Xenophon Zolotas, *Monetary Equilibrium and Economic Development*, Princeton, Princeton University Press, 1965, p.39; Pagoulatos, *Greece's New Political Economy*, p.95.

cent in 1953–5 (Table 10). Furthermore, currency devaluations are notoriously inflationary, not the reverse as claimed in the previously quoted passages. For example, a 1954 IMF-Bank of Greece expert study, strongly favouring the currency reform, duly stressed that 'devaluation in itself was an inflationary factor'.[128] Other sympathetic contemporary studies, including one prefaced by Zolotas himself, conceded that 'although special measures were taken to keep inflation under control, the 1953 devaluation caused prices to rise substantially'.[129] In fact, postwar Greek inflation had been curbed to 5.1 per cent because of Kartalis's 1951–2 stabilization programme, but the Rally's devaluation doubled that figure in 1953 and tripled it in 1954.

Besides this confusion, much of the specialist historiography has also treated Markezinis's liberalization measures as the Hellenic equivalent of the repeal of the Corn Laws in Britain, that is, as the country's historic break with protectionism and entry into the free trade era.[130] This simplistic portrayal has been adopted, in varying degrees, by both liberal and structuralist economic historians alike. From a liberal standpoint, Tsoukalis has argued that 'since the end of the civil war all Greek governments have emphasized their strong attachment to liberal economic ideas and the free working of the market mechanism'. Hatzivassiliou describes Markezinis as 'more firmly economically liberal' than any other leading Greek politician in the 1950s.[131] From a *Marxisant* perspective, Tsoucalas observes that 'apart from devaluation and free trade, the Right had no industrial or commercial policy at all', while Sotiris Valden argues:

> The reforms of 1953 correspond to a choice of strategic character for the Greek economy and its external orientation: they correspond to a developmental choice that is founded on deepening Greece's entry into the international division of labour in line with the principles of free trade.[132]

Opinions, of course, diverge when the impact of Markezinis's policy is assessed. While liberal economists emphasize its supposedly modernizing effects, structuralist analyses portray it as leading to a further deepening of Greece's dependence on the US and Western multinational capital.[133] In either case, however, the shared view is that the Rally's 'new economic policy' consolidated Greece's incorporation in the capitalist world system through the adoption of a liberal trade policy.

The myth of the supposedly 'liberal' character of Markezinis's economic policy has its origins in two sources that go back to the time of the reforms themselves. The first is the propaganda campaign deployed by the Rally itself, whose aim was to present its foreign economic policy as a set of bold liberal reforms reflecting Greece's commitment to the doctrine of free trade. Under this guise, the single most important liberalizing reform, the lifting of duties and quotas on most – not all – imports, was deceptively branded as the adoption of 'totally free trade' or 'the total and essential freedom in our import trade'.[134] This discourse engineered the misleading impression that (a) all other restrictions on imports (not just quotas and duties) were removed; and (b) that they were removed on all goods, not on most of them. Consequently, in his devaluation broadcast on 9 April 1953, in which he announced these measures, Markezinis presented them as purportedly bringing about 'a complete and absolute' liberalization of imports. He said: 'I announce to you today another very important measure. All kinds of duties on imports are abolished. And the complete and absolute freedom of import trade is established, except for a few luxury goods'.[135]

To begin with, Markezinis's sentence contained a blatant oxymoron. He spoke of 'complete and absolute' liberalization, while referring to 'exceptions'. Furthermore, his statement claimed that import duties were kept on 'a few luxury goods', but in reality these were not only kept, but extended to second-hand cars, industrial machinery and six key agricultural commodities.[136] Also, the main protective barrier to trade, tariffs, were raised over a wide range of products, chiefly to reverse the balance of trade crisis that was caused by the abolition of most duties. Although initially minor tariff reductions of 4 to 20 per cent were introduced in July 1953, in line with a GATT agreement signed in 1952 under Plastiras,[137] the Rally Government then proceeded to raise tariffs by 50 per cent over a wide range of import categories. On 1 September 1953, the Greek Government informed the GATT that 'the liberalization of Greek trade already involves [...] concessions far exceeding in value all the tariff concessions granted in Annecy and Torquay' and, to safeguard the 'greatly threatened' interests of the Greek economy, it submitted two requests. First, it asked to be permitted to start bilateral negotiations with all interested GATT members 'aimed at securing a reasonable degree of protection for Greek industrial products'; and, second, it asked to take 'immediate measures' in a number of cases 'because the liberalization of trade has resulted in an uncontrollable volume of imports'.[138] A few days later, Finance Minister, Constantine Papayannis, told journalists that he was going to the Eighth GATT Session in Geneva to 'revise the tariff regime with the aim of protecting domestic production and especially industry', stressing that 'with the liberalization of Greek imports there is need to provide protection for certain domestic products'.[139] On 18 September, Papayannis told the GATT Plenary Session that there was an 'unpleasant part' to his speech, namely that he was 'constrained [...] to ask for the sympathetic consideration of the Contracting Parties' in submitting 'a very limited schedule containing a small number of articles for which bound tariffs should be revised or increased'.[140] From March to September 1954, Greece submitted no fewer than four long schedules, raising tariffs by 50 per cent on more than 150 categories of commodities (Table 11, Schedule 1).[141] In November 1954, under the GATT's 'sympathetic considerations' procedure, the Rally also agreed with the United States and Germany to raise tariffs by 50 per cent on four other commodities, while on 5 March 1955, the duty and tax on apples were increased by 35 per cent.[142] Unsurprisingly, this protectionist side of the 'new economic policy' was buried in the back pages of the pro-Rally press and has hardly received any attention in the scholarship.

Besides the gross misuse of adjectives such as 'complete', 'absolute' and 'total', the correct term 'liberalization of imports' was often replaced in the Rally's propaganda by misleading expressions like 'freedom of imports' and 'freedom of trade'. For example, in an interview with Reuters on 18 July 1953, Markezinis stated that his government 'had adopted measures through which free trade was practically established in Greece at a rate of 100 per cent, apart from [sic] a few exception', using again the standard oxymoron. Surprisingly, no journalist wondered how '100 per cent' could possibly leave room for 'a few exceptions'. Similarly, Deputy Trade Minister Papaligouras, shortly before the reforms, spoke about the government's intention to 'move toward the complete freedom of trade'.[143] The obvious aim of these pronouncements was to create the false impression that the lifting of most quotas and a range of duties (at the same time as new protectionist measures were being introduced) did not amount to a limited liberalization, but to a policy that supposedly rendered all imports totally free. Later, Markezinis admitted that he deliberately deployed 'a triumphant tone' in his speech of 9 April 1953, because he thought that 'no reason existed to disappoint public opinion which, on the contrary, should have seen the future with optimism'.[144] Nevertheless, much of the historiography has overlooked these qualifiers and treated his speeches as positive evidence to be read as statement of fact.[145]

The second source of misinterpretation surrounding Markezinis's 'new economic policy' is the traditional economic mentality of the post-war Greek establishment. One example is Papagos's own reaction to the cabinet proposals put forward by Kapsalis. 'Could you explain to me why the import of perfumes from France and flowers from the Netherlands should be allowed?' he asked. This question revealed an old-fashioned concern about the ethics of free trade. Another example is the panic-stricken reaction of some government advisers, like Damalas, whose assessment of the devaluation revealed an astonishing confusion over key macroeconomic principles. The threat to price stability, he argued, was 'greater today if we consider that after the devaluation of the drachma we have also introduced the freedom of imports'.[146] Macroeconomic theory, however, suggests that import liberalization drives prices down, not the opposite.[147] Indeed, in a revealing statement about the context of his policy mix, Markezinis later told Parliament that the abolition of quotas and most duties was an idea proposed to Kapsalis by a US official, mainly to offset the inflationary pressures of the devaluation.[148] Once again, this important disclosure shows

Table 11 First addendum of tariff increases submitted to the GATT by Greece, 26 March 1954 (in metal drachmas)

Tariff Item	Description of Producers	Rate	Rate as of 3 March 1954
2.a.	Hams (general) (100 kg)	30	45
2.b.	Polony sausages (100 kg)	40	60
2.c.	Sausages, Mortedellas (100 kg)	40	60
2.d.	Fois gras (100 kg)	150	225
4	Lobsters, crayfish, tunny-fish and similar (100 kg)	15	22.50
8.a.	Wheat flour	9	13.50
12.b.6.	Dates	15	22.50
15.b.	Aniseed star shaped	80	120
15.c.	Cloves	80	120
35	Caramels	50	75
46	Oak, chestnut, poplar, elm, ash, maple, platane, cypress, cedar, linden, willow and other wood	40	60
46.c.	Boards composed of ply wood or other wood (per m^3)	40	60
47.a.	Furniture wood in pieces or planks (100 kg)	10	15
47.c	Furniture wood in logs (100 kg)	5	7.50
47.d.	Furniture in boards plywood > 2mm thick (100 kg)	8	12
48.b.	Staves for casks: 2 Wrought (100 kg)	2	3
50.i.1	Articles of wood: Spools and bobbins (100 kg)	4	6
50.i.2	Shuttles for weaving looms (100 kg)	8	12
51.f.	Cork in thin sheets (100 kg)		
	1. Unwrought	30	45
	2. Wrought in articles ready for use	60	90
	3. Wrought in articles covered with cloth	150	225
65	Iron manufactures: 1. Radiators (100kg)	13	19.50
100.a.	Machines, apparatus and utensils, etc.		
	5 to 25 kg (100 kg)	30	45
	More than 25 Kg (100 kg)	20	30
120	Bottoms for electric lamps (100 kg)	10	15
123	Aluminium in sheets (100 kg)	20	30
124	Aluminium articles and utensils (100 kg)		
	a. Up to 50 gr.	90	35
	b. From 50 to 250 gr.	70	105
	c. Exceeding 250 gr.	45	67.50
136	Optical instruments		
	d. Eyeglasses and frames (100 kg)	300	450
159	Chemical products:		
	g. Miscellaneous, 1. Glycerine (100 kg)	10	15
161	Drugs and pharmaceuticals:		
	f.3. Bleached cotton up to 45 gr per M2, etc. (100 kg)	120	180
259.b.	Felt for hats: 1. Natural colour	20	30
	2. Dyed	22.5	33.75
260.b.	Hats of animal textile materials (soft) Each	3.80	5.70
288.c.	Pencils with wooden casing	130	195

Source: GATT *Official Documents.* Schedule XXV – Greece: Adjustment of Specific Duties. Addendum, L/184/Add.1 and L/179/ADD.3-L/198/ADD.1, 26 March 1954.

how significant US influence was in setting the parameters of Markezinis's 'new economic policy'.

To be fair, despite presenting their reforms as more liberal than they really were, the Rally ministers never actually claimed to be espousing a doctrine of bold economic liberalism of the kind later ascribed to them by many historians. During his visit to London in July 1953, when asked about the ideological influences on his economic reforms, Markezinis emphasized his preference for ancient Greek 'eclecticism': 'Let me tell you in which deity I believe [...]. I planned, like the Labour Party; and I applied a liberal policy; and I come from a conservative family,' he said.[149] Although this diplomatic reply was influenced by the presence of an all-party audience during the gathering, a few months later Markezinis made a similar statement in the Greek Parliament, this time praising the virtues of political 'pragmatism':

> Personally, I, who has the honour of being in charge of the Greek Rally's economic policy, abhor theory. I am proud to be a politician. And a politician, this is at least what I believe, must not forget that the highest expression of politics is the understanding of reality.[150]

In his radio broadcast on 6 December 1952, Markezinis disassociated himself from orthodox liberal economics. 'This does not mean that we believe in the absolute liberalism of the previous century. We do believe, however, that the state's aim is not to intervene except in cases when nothing else can be done,' he said. Other Rally ministers were keen to underline their commitment to a qualified version of economic liberalism. Speaking at the International Trade Fair in Thessaloniki in September 1953, Papaligouras described his government's views as follows: 'We are not of course liberals in the classical, nineteenth-century sense of liberalism. We believe in a realistic liberalism, adapted to the modern mission of the state and to international technical advances'.[151]

Although these statements stand as a reminder that neither the Rally's economic team nor their reforms were purely 'liberal', they still constituted an idealized self-image. For this reason, a recent attempt by scholars like Kazakos and Hatzivassiliou to dub the 1953 reforms as an example of 'liberal eclecticism'[152] (a term lacking analytical rigour and, first coined, as we saw, by Markezinis himself) reveals a certain confusion between political soundbites and scholarly analysis. The main defect of this label is its failure to acknowledge the substantial elements of hidden protectionism underlying Markezinis's economic reforms. Kazakos, who first imported Markezinis's concept to the scholarship (without acknowledging its ownership), never speaks about the protectionist character of the currency devaluation of 1953, nor does he mention the Rally's successive tariff increases of 1953–5. In his sketchy definition of the term, he argues that 'eclecticism' (as Markezinis himself suggested in 1953) refers only to 'the means' of the policy,[153] thus implying that its ends are still 'liberal'. Such a conception, however, seriously overlooks the fact that the Rally's policy ends, as Kazakos rightly points out elsewhere, converged around a vision of ISI that was marked by strong elements of economic nationalism.

Indeed, back in the 1950s, several reports in Markezinis's own Ministry of Coordination noted that the Rally's policy aimed to 'maintain conditions of protectionism' for industry, regulating prices through 'state intervention' and 'launching the battle' to 'reduce our imports'.[154] Pro-Rally newspapers regularly reported in their back pages that tariffs were being upwardly revised on a range of products, like iron and fabrics, because, 'according to official sources' they were 'originally low and [...] do not provide basic protection for domestic industry'.[155] These reports referred to the previously mentioned addenda submitted to the GATT in October 1953–July 1954, requesting the organization 'to offer the Greek government the option of adjusting its tariff regime to protect its domestic production following the liberalization of imports'. Moreover, as if the tariff rises were not enough, on 3 December 1954, Karamanlis submitted a personal note to Papagos requesting several revisions, including further 'restriction of the freedom of imports regarding luxury goods'.[156] On this basis, a new regime of high tariffs was established by 1955, not only on so-called luxury goods, but also on textiles, to protect the ailing textile industry which covered one quarter of Greece's manufacturing production.[157] Another hidden barrier to trade was the extensive use of 'advance deposits' for imports, a measure described by a 1964 IMF study as 'evidently a departure from the initial content and spirit of the liberalization policy'.[158] Meanwhile, export subsidies also increased. According to the previously mentioned World Bank study on trade liberalization, more hidden barriers to trade were introduced beyond these subsidies. In particular,

> social security contributions paid by employers [in the export trade] were reduced in 1954, payroll taxes were abolished [...] exemption from import charges of materials used for production of exports was extended [...]. Export firms were also allowed to deduct up to 4 per cent of total gross export revenues from taxable profits.

The above was augmented by the massive impact of the devaluation, which erected a further protective wall across the whole of the Greek economy.[159]

Conclusion

Viewed in its totality, the 'new economic policy' of 1953 was a set of reforms defined by the logic of *dependent nationalism*. Its overall conception rested on the self-contradictory notion of a 'liberal ISI', that is a policy of semi-protected industrialization, financed by the United States, that would bring about Greece's rapid post-war modernization. In this regard, the foreign economic policy of the Papagos Government mirrored its approach to 'high politics'. Like the rest of its foreign policy, it sought to exploit Greece's dependence on the United States to further a moderate nationalist economic agenda.

Some scholars, like Pagoulatos, have correctly attributed this approach to such factors as 'the developmentalist orthodoxy of the time that privileged some degree of reliance on ISI' and Greece's 'subjection to US hegemony'.[160] Above all, however, Markezinis's trade liberalization was driven by the need to obtain new US aid for an ambitious medium-term development programme. In the absence of a locally funded public investments programme (and the political will to locally finance it), the only other option for the architects of the 'new economic policy' was to seek more US economic aid. Highlighting the centrality of this choice helps to shed light on a number of key questions. First, it shows that the limited liberalization of Markezinis's reforms arose less from liberal ideological convictions than from Greece's economic dependence on American capital. Second, grasping this fact could explain why Markezinis's so-called liberalism ('eclectic' or non-) cannot be disentangled from his instrumentalist logic of seeking American funds for industrialization instead of raising investment capital locally and supporting it with loans from international institutions. Third, these conclusions demonstrate how the structural disarticulations of Greece's semi-peripheral economy were vital in sustaining the dependence link on American capital. Because of these disarticulations, US hegemony was able to ultimately deny the *Ethnikofron* elites the high-tech development they envisaged to modernize Greece.

Here, a few remarks about the legacy of Markezinis's policy are in order. At the heart of the mythology surrounding the 1953 reforms is the belief that these marked 'a reorientation' of Greek economic policy that set the country on the path of stability and high growth for two decades. With annual inflation averaging 4 per cent and growth averaging 7 per cent, many economic historians have described the period 1953–73 as the Greek 'economic miracle' and 'the "golden age" of the drachma'.[161] In reality, however, Markezinis's reforms contributed little, if at all, to this otherwise impressive record. In terms of monetary stability, his flagship reform, the currency devaluation, fuelled an inflation averaging 10 per cent per annum in 1953–5, that is almost three times above the average of the period 1953–73. Indeed, price stability was not restored until 1955–6, precisely because by then the inflationary effects of the devaluation had evaporated. Similarly, the notion that the devaluation contributed to high growth through boosting exports is equally fictitious. Although the measure gave an initial boom to exports by rendering them cheaper by 50 per cent, the devaluation's inflationary effects, as Varvaressos had warned,[162] reversed six tenths of this gain by the end of 1955 (Table 9). Thereafter, the primary driver for Greek exports until 1973 was overwhelmingly external, namely the surge in consumer demand across the Western economies and the international expansion in the volume of trade. Several econometric studies have shown that Greek exports could have been given a greater boost had their prices been lower.[163] For this reason, Markezinis's devaluation never achieved its primary aim of rendering export trade more competitive as to end Greece's huge balance of trade deficits and chronic crises (Tables 12, 13).

If we now turn to the liberalizing aspects of Markezinis's reforms, again, we find that these had a limited effect on the subsequent performance of the Greek economy. Tariffs, as we saw, were significantly increased in 1953–5 and, after 1958,

Table 12 The trade deficit of Greece, 1951–63 in millions of US dollars

Year	Deficit
1950	314.6
1951	329.7
1952	160.4
1953	109.2
1954	167.4
1955	157.7
1956	255.1
1957	297.0
1958	289.0
1959	252.0
1960	288.5
1961	326.9
1962	365.9
1963	412.5

Sources: *Economic Surveys by the OECD: Greece*, p.30; Kottis, *Liberalizing Foreign Trade*, p.19; Zolotas *Monetary Equilibrium*, p.43.

further restrictions to trade were introduced to tackle a balance of trade crisis and boost falling domestic production. These developments led some sympathetic analysts to stress that 'the 1953–55 liberalization was short-lived' and speak about a 'retreat into limited protectionism during 1955–58'.[164] Other studies, otherwise supportive of the Markezinis reforms, also spoke about an 'almost complete protectionism' prevailing in the Greek economy until 1961:

> Up to the time of the country's association with the EEC, the economy was functioning under a system of almost complete protectionism as far as domestic production was concerned. Tariffs were levied on industrial goods as a protection for the domestic industrial production, and subsidies were paid to farmers [...]. In addition, a plethora of rules and regulations, restraints and restrictions, adulterated to a large extent the free market forces.[165]

Table 13 Agricultural products and ores as a percentage of total Greek exports, 1952–62

Year	Agricultural Products	Ores	Industrial and Handicraft	Other	Percentage of Agricultural Products and Ores
1952	76.8	9.0	7.4	6.8	**85.8**
1954	74.7	5.2	6.5	13.6	**79.9**
1956	69.3	8.4	4.8	17.5	**77.7**
1958	82.0	6.1	4.3	7.6	**88.1**
1960	74.4	8.6	5.7	11.3	**83.0**
1962	74.8	6.4	8.6	10.2	**81.2**

Source: *Hellenic Statistical Authority (ELSTAT), Monthly Bulletin of Greece's Special Trade with Foreign Countries, 1952–62*; Zolotas, *Monetary Equilibrium*, p.139.

7. Dualist Aspects of Foreign Economic Policy

Table 14 Change in the structural composition of Greek GDP, 1950–61

Year	Agriculture	Industry	Services
1950	34%	25%	41%
1956	33%	25%	41%
1961	31%	27%	42%
Change	-3%	+2%	+1%

Sources: Stylianos Geronimakis, 'Post-War Economic Growth in Greece, 1950–61', *Review of Income and Wealth*, 11:1, 1965, p.259; Zolotas, *Monetary Equilibrium*, p.28

In other words, the so-called economic miracle of the years 1953–61 could hardly be attributed to Markezinis's trade liberalization measures, as these were both limited and, subsequently, to a large extent reversed. Instead, the impressive macroeconomic performance of those years must be attributed partly to the hidden protectionism of those years and, partly, to the favourable post-war conditions of international trade. Markezinis's only liberal reform which might have contributed marginally to Greece's post-war growth was his legislation to attract foreign capital. But even then, it is doubtful that laws 2687/53 and 2681/54 played a serious part in the rise of FDI after 1961, since they had practically no impact during the 1950s.[166] Still, it could be argued that this legislation created favourable conditions which contributed, along with many other factors, such as Greece's post-1960 industrialization and the Association Agreement with the EEC, to the sharp increase in FDI in the 1960s.[167] Overall, however, whatever analysis one adopts, the causes of Greece's economic performance in 1953–73 must be sought less in Markezinis's 1953 reforms and more in the policies of later years.

Meanwhile, what must be always remembered when discussing the Rally's 'new economic policy' is that its flagship reform, the $237 million medium-term investments programme, fell flat on its face. As Karamanlis remarked in a letter Papagos on 3 December 1954, the investments programme was back to square one, and a key government priority following Markezinis's departure from the Government was now to lower its ambitious targets to get it off the ground:

> We must formulate a realistic investments programme, corresponding to the means available to the Government. For the success of this programme, we must avoid the distribution of these resources—which, as is known, are limited—to many sectors, so that [we avoid a situation whereby] its completion in any of them is never achieved.[168]

Ultimately, the high growth rates of the 1950s and 1960s did not arise from a radical transformation of Greece's production base. By 1961, agriculture still contributed 31 per cent of GDP, down 3 per cent in relation to 1950, while industry contributed 27 per cent of GDP, up 2 per cent in relation to 1950 (Table 14). For the most part, the high growth rates of this period resulted from the semi-protectionist regime which Markezinis and his successors maintained across the economy to support the traditional, non-competitive sectors of Greek industry. Meanwhile, a more ambitious development policy had to wait for the first five-year plan of the Karamanlis Government in 1959–63, which used public funds to enact several unimplemented projects from the Marshall Plan and Markezinis's medium-term programme.[169] However, by the time of their completion in the late 1960s, valuable time had been lost and their developmental impact was far more limited than envisaged in 1948–53. At any rate, this was a government record for which Markezinis's 'new economic policy' could claim little credit.

CONCLUSION

One who straddles two boats is bound to fall in the water.

Chinese hànyŭ[1]

The adherence of the Papagos Government to a foreign policy combining loyalty to NATO with a firm support for *Enosis* not only failed to achieve its self-assigned objectives but ended up weakening Greece's position in the Cold War and the prospects of Cypriot self-determination. Equally damaging was the policy's impact on Greece's relations with Turkey and the tripartite alliance with Yugoslavia in the Balkan Pact. In the realm of 'low politics', *dependent nationalism* miscarried with regard to Markezinis's medium-term investments programme and the post-war Greek dream of rapid industrialization. In other words, from a macro-historical perspective, the combination of dependence and nationalism after the Civil War bequeathed Greece with all the major foreign and economic policy problems that continue to bedevil it today: a dependent and uneasy relationship with the United States and NATO, an unsolved Cyprus question, ongoing rivalry with Turkey, and a chronic failure to modernize economically and converge with its OECD partners.

The troubled setting of Greek foreign policy over the past seven decades essentially emerged in the few months following the UN recourse. On the eve of the Political Committee debate, on 14 December 1954, an unprecedented wave of anti-American protests broke out in Athens and other major cities causing consternation to the Rally Government and the State Department in Washington. Barely five years since the end of the Civil War, thousands of largely *Ethnikofron* protestors took to the streets holding banners that read: 'Shame on You Americans'; 'We Prefer Obvious Enemies to Friends Like You'; 'Americans, If You Don't Vote with Us You Have No Place in Greece'. In Thessaloniki, protestors stormed the American International Education Library and burnt a portrait of President Eisenhower.[2] Shocked by this outburst of popular discontent, the Rally Government warned its friends in Washington that 'the current US position and prestige in Greece' are under serious threat, while Ambassador Melas apologized and condemned these acts as 'not representative of Greek feeling'. To deescalate the tension, Dulles issued his previously mentioned statement of 18 December 1954 expressing regret that US policy had been 'to some extent misunderstood in Greece', while Cannon, who concluded that anti-American 'public bitterness is general',[3] began to prepare an official visit by Papagos to Washington to rekindle bilateral relations. His efforts persisted until May 1955 but were finally abandoned as Papagos's health continued to deteriorate.[4]

From Greece, the crisis spread over Cyprus, bringing about what Durrell called a 'deathward drift of affairs in the island'.[5] Peake, drawing on local intelligence, had already expressed concern near the end of the UN recourse that 'the next stage in the *Enosis* campaign may be smuggling of arms and explosives into Cyprus'.[6] In January 1955, the 'Aghios Georgios' affair confirmed these fears, fuelling deeper suspicions that Athens might be actively sponsoring a guerrilla campaign in the island.[7] Back in December, Churchill had rejected a State Department proposal to convene the next NATO Ministers' Council in Athens as a show of allied solidarity.[8] But when EOKA launched its first attacks on 31 March, Anglo-Greek relations dipped to a new low. Although no evidence could link EOKA's bombings to the Greek Government, British counterpropaganda accused Radio Athens of inciting violence against the British soldiers in Cyprus.[9] Meanwhile, Churchill's resignation in April 1955 and Macmillan's arrival to the Foreign Office (to replace Eden, who now became prime minister) resulted in subtler British tactics. In July 1955, the Foreign Office extended an invitation to Athens and Ankara to join a Tripartite Conference in London to discuss the 'security implications' of new British proposals for Cypriot autonomy.[10] Although Peake expected a Greek rejection, Vice-Premiers Stefanopoulos and Kanellopoulos, together with Papagos (from his deathbed),

Image 11 Prime Minister Alexander Papagos (middle), with his two Deputy Prime Ministers, Stefanos Stefanopoulos (right) and Panayiotis Kanellopoulos (left). 22 December 1952. Karamanlis Foundation Photographic Archive.

discounted the warnings of Makarios and the Greek opposition leaders regarding Turkey's involvement and joined the Tripartite Conference on 29 August.[11] This was yet another example of the Rally Government's determination to negotiate a Cyprus settlement directly with Britain.

Far from containing the crisis, the London Conference resulted in its further spreading, this time from Greece and Cyprus to Turkey itself. On 6–7 September 1955, violent riots broke out against the Greek minority in Istanbul and Ismir, led by the ultranationalist 'Cyprus is Turkish' group and local members of the ruling Democratic Party. Accounts of the death toll vary from thirteen to fifty-seven, but the British embassy in Ankara reported a material damage equivalent to a full-scale military invasion, with '4,000 houses, 2,000 shops and 80 Christian Orthodox churches' destroyed in two days.[12] Historian John Iatrides, who was serving at the time at the General Staff in Athens, noted that these developments brought Turkey and Greece 'to the brink of war', a testimony later confirmed by Stefanopoulos.[13] In the event, the Greek Government confined itself to a verbal protestation, but the Greek Delegation in London, led by Stefanopoulos, walked out of the Tripartite Talks, bringing the process to an abrupt end. As many have hitherto maintained, the 'September Events' of 1955 ended a period of Greek–Turkish diplomatic friendship inaugurated twenty-five years earlier by Eleftherios Venizelos and Kemal Atatürk.[14]

Reflecting on these developments, the Anglophile former prime minister Tsouderos wrote to his son:

> The atrocities committed by the Turks were unprecedented [...]. The ignominious British provoked Turkish fanaticism over the issue and it is probable that they even organized these acts [...] What saddens and outrages the Greeks is the attitude of the American Government [...]. Everyone in the first days practically demanded that we go to the Russian alliance and send the westerners to hell [...]. Of course, there are also the sensible voices who cried that this would mean total disaster for us! [...] Our friendship with the Americans was seriously damaged.[15]

After the Turkish coup of 27 May 1960, blame for the 'September Events' of 1955 was laid officially on the Turkish government. During the Yasıada Trials, responsibility for these atrocities was among the main charges brought against Menderes and Fatin Zorlu, resulting in their execution.[16] Back in 1955, however, Greek suspicions of British connivance, though never confirmed, were encouraged by Macmillan's mild condemnation of the atrocities in Turkey. This lukewarm response fuelled further anti-Western feeling in Greece which, according to Vlachos, 'took over even the most conservative groups' who started 'calling for the country's exit from NATO'.[17] The same impression was conveyed by the staunchly Atlanticists Queen Frederica in October 1955 in a letter to former US Secretary of State Marshall:

> We feel as if the Western world has given us a hard and undeserved kick and there is desperate bitterness in my country today, not only against the British but

unfortunately this time also against the Americans. The Greek people feel (and I tell you this quite honestly, as I have always been honest in the expression of my feelings to you) that America, the country to whom we looked as giving moral leadership to the world, has for God knows what material and political reasons betrayed her own ideals. [...] The Greeks' opinion of the Western World, the meaning of its ideals and fine words has reached rock bottom in Greece. It just couldn't be worse. [...] There are no demonstrations this time in the streets, but the atmosphere is anti-NATO, anti-Western and pro-neutralism. You can imagine what a wonderful chance this is for the 'new look' of an old Russian policy.[18]

Responsibility for the breakdown of the East Mediterranean order in 1955 cannot be placed solely on the Rally Government. British, Turkish and US policies played an equally decisive part in producing this mischievous outcome. For a variety of reasons, each of these governments supported an indefinite extension of the discredited system of colonialism in Cyprus. While in their speeches, Eisenhower and Churchill portrayed NATO as the bastion of the 'Free World' and stability in Southeast Europe,[19] on the ground they defended an illiberal, and divisive regime of colonial rule in Cyprus. As one British historian has aptly remarked, the Tripartite Conference of 1955 was a 'gambit' of a 'not entirely respectable character' whose aim was to heighten Greek-Turkish differences and justify Britain's 'continued mastery over the island'.[20]

In the intertwined contexts of the Cold War and post-Civil War Greece, the Rally could not have pursued a different foreign policy without upsetting the delicate external and internal balance that its Government relied on. If Papagos were to continue the Centre's policy of subordinating *Enosis* to NATO's collective interests, repressive measures would have to be adopted against his own supporters at home, particularly PEAEK and many powerful elements of the state and the parastate. Moreover, Papagos would have to publicly clash with Makarios, leading the latter to seek a different UN sponsor, a development that would cause what Loizidis called an 'earthquake' at the foundations of *Ethnikofron* Greece. Conversely, if the Rally Government were to adopt an unqualified strategy of internationalization (along the lines proposed by Makarios), Papagos would have to consider a neutralist stance in the Cold War, support an opening to Moscow and provide EOKA with proper support. Such a course, however, would have harmed US-Greek relations, damaged Atlantic unity and sharpened divisions within the *Ethnikofron* camp. Conversely, to claim that Papagos could have somehow resolved his foreign policy dilemmas by simply postponing the UN recourse by 'eight' or '10–15 years' because Britain was supposedly willing to reward him with *Enosis*, is a totally unsubstantiated hypothesis. As earlier chapters have demonstrated, the advocates of this imaginary scenario, Pipinelis, Maniadakis, Xydis, Averoff, Vlachos and others, have all based their claims on flimsy and dubious arguments that are strongly contradicted by British and American evidence.

To be sure, the mythic notion that a different path to *Enosis* was supposedly available, despite its grandiloquent claims to 'realism' and 'rationality',[21] is essentially imbued with greater idealism than the Rally's dualist approach. At the heart of this utopian vision lies a predominantly Atlanticist viewpoint which, in its desire to also appeal to a Greek nationalist audience, contends that, in some magical way, greater dependence on Britain and the United States would have fulfilled Greek irredentist aspirations better. This theory, which forms the backbone of the Greek ethnocentric narrative on the Cyprus question to date, differs from the Atlanticist conception of the Centre governments of 1950–2 in one crucial respect. While the Centre governments also contended that any confrontation with Britain and the United States should be avoided because, as Papandreou claimed in the 1950s, Greece breathed with 'one British and one American lung', they were at least candid enough to recognize that this choice hindered the attainment of *Enosis*. By contrast, the narrative put forward by Pipinelis, Xydis, Averoff, Vlachos and others maintained that, somehow, conformity to British and US demands not only would not hinder but supposedly would make *Enosis* certain. These accounts have also purported that this strategy was the only path to its attainment.

This prevalent narrative, however, together with arguments by some non-ethnocentric accounts which are partially influenced by it, rests on the assumption that the Rally's policy must be judged as a failure because it did not further the cause of *Enosis*. According to one account,

> the Cyprus campaign was ultimately a failure. The outcome did not permit its domestic champions to reap any fruits of victory. The Zürich-London agreements which set up an independent republic under tripartite tutelage and explicitly excluded Enosis in perpetuity, were a far cry from the original Greek objectives.[22]

What this and other similar assessments imply[23] is that *Enosis* was a potentially attainable foreign policy objective in the 1950s and hence, its non-realization must be deemed a foreign policy 'failure'. As we have seen, several accounts have gone as far as to identify Papagos's policy in 1953–4 as the single most important factor behind the decision of the Karamanlis Government to shelve *Enosis* in 1958–9 and accept the solution of 'qualified independence', under foreign 'protection', in the Zürich-London Agreements. In March 1959, a few days after these Agreements were signed, Pipinelis argued that: 'Today, after all that has happened since, I doubt that there are many Greeks who would not recognize that if the then [Papagos] Government had listened to the above suggestions, the situation would have been different'.[24] Mostras, as we saw, made the same point. Moreover, to justify the fixation of this narrative with *Enosis*, historians like Svolopoulos have recently resorted to the problematic assertion that *Enosis* was supposedly not 'a form of nationalism', but an 'existential experience of a nationalist tradition'.[25] Others, too, have used *Enosis* as the primary criterion of assessing the Rally's foreign policy from the perspective of 'rational action' theory. Stefanidis, for instance, has argued that Papagos's policy on Cyprus does not stand up to 'the criteria of rationality' because, among other things, 'the Greek government failed to secure its original aim, that is to expedite a change in British attitude and initiate a process that could lead to *Enosis*'.²⁶ In this regard, Greek historiography has been locked within a traditional narrative that is unable to sever the umbilical cord with the irredentist vision of *Enosis* and the clichéd conception of the Cyprus question as a chain of failed attempts to realize it.

The present analysis has questioned the core assumption of the historiography that *Enosis* could have been ever realized after 1950. As previous chapters have shown, this hypothesis is founded on false and arbitrary claims that are uniformly refuted by all reliable British and American evidence. That is why it would be futile, following Averoff, to continue speaking of 'lost opportunities' in bringing about *Enosis* because, after 1950, such opportunities never presented themselves. For this reason, it is time for the historiography on the Cyprus question to cast aside *Enosis* as a criterion of judging Greek foreign policy after the Civil War. Doing so is akin to criticizing British foreign policy after 1945 for failing to keep the Empire intact or Soviet foreign policy for failing to win the Cold War. Such assessments would be pointless for the simple reason that the basis of any useful analysis cannot be the use of unattainable/utopian criteria. That is why historians of decolonization have approached British foreign policy after 1945 from the perspective of its ability to manage the breakup of the Empire, not its retention. Similarly, analyses of Soviet foreign policy in the Cold War have assessed Moscow's ability to moderate or end that conflict, not to win it.²⁷ By contrast, the historiography on the early years of the Cyprus question has yet to make a paradigmatic shift towards assessing the Greek *Ethnikofron* governments from the perspective of their ability to cast off *Enosis* and focus instead on Cypriot independence.

The foregoing analysis rests on an approach which views the Cyprus question as primarily a question of colonialism.²⁸ Insofar as any criteria of assessing foreign policy success/failure were deployed, these were chiefly linked to Papagos's ability to bring about an end to British colonial rule, not to achieve *Enosis*. In this regard, the preceding discussion has stressed that, in contrast to the dominant ethnocentric narrative, the UN recourse of 1954 was a failure not because it rendered *Enosis* impossible, but because it was undercut by the Rally's self-restrained approach. For the same reasons, the argument highlighted Papagos's self-defeating policies of avoiding an opening to Moscow, delinking progress in the Balkan Pact with developments in Cyprus and failing to reach a common understanding with Turkey. Against another prevalent myth, the foregoing discussion has also argued that Ankara's interest in Cyprus was not triggered by Papagos's decision to 'internationalize' the issue,²⁹ but was strong and alive since 'the autumn of [...] 1953', as the Field Marshal's adviser, Christidis, discovered during his secret mission to Istanbul.³⁰ On this basis, the analysis is critical of Papagos's unwillingness to seek an early understanding with Ankara on the future of Cyprus, a policy that was eventually forced upon Karamanlis, with less spectacular results, after the UN recourse of 1958. At the heart of these conclusions rests the view that, in elevating *Enosis* into one of its two core aims (alongside loyalty to the United States and NATO), Papagos's foreign policy compromised Greece's security without furthering the cause of Cypriot independence.

At the same time, much of the previous discussion has focused on the inner workings (or, rather, malfunctions) of Greek foreign policy. In this context, *Enosis* was sometimes taken as a given objective (much like the Truman Doctrine and NATO membership) only insofar as the Papagos Government itself placed it as the heart of its foreign policy. At no point, however, was it implied that historians today should continue to treat *Enosis* uncritically (or NATO membership, for that matter) or to deploy such objectives as criteria for judging the 'rationality', 'realism' and effectiveness of Greek foreign policy. Critical perspectives differ from positivist approaches in their endeavour to go beyond a mere assessment of ends and means. Critical theory pays as much attention to the choice of policy ends as to the means deployed by governments to attain them. As Cox remarked, a positivist/problem-solving analysis 'takes the world as it finds it', while critical theory questions the order of things and is aware of the historical conditions that produce it.[31] Consequently, the present critique of Papagos's dualism rests on an assessment of both the relationship of ends and means in his foreign policy and his choice of ends. A major contrast with the dominant narrative on the Cyprus issue has been the emphasis given here to the utopian character of *Enosis* as an element of the wider idealist vision of *Megali Idea*.[32] Consequently, throughout the previous discussion an underling assumption has been that whatever policy Greece would have adopted after 1950 to achieve *Enosis* was bound to miscarry. In this regard, Papagos's dualism was criticized not for failing to further the cause of *Enosis* (as this failure was inescapable under his or any other policy) but for weakening the prospects of Cypriot independence and exposing Greek security, especially vis-à-vis Turkey.

To further clarify these points, an argument that has been hitherto implicit must now be brought to light. Papagos's dualist policy was never identified here as the primary reason behind his failure to attain *Enosis*. External factors, independent of Greece's foreign policy choices, especially British and Turkish interests, would never have permitted *Enosis* to take hold irrespectively of what policy Athens would have followed. On this basis, a core theme in the previous discussion (which also explains why Papagos's policy was often defended against simplistic criticisms) is that dualism, despite its self-contradictory character, was probably the less hopeless strategy for seeking to attain *Enosis*. In Camusian terms, if Greek union with Cyprus after 1950 was a Sisyphean task (and this study has firmly maintained that it was), then dualism at that time was probably the policy that could carry the rock of *Enosis* higher up the hill, even though it was still bound to hit the ground. In stressing this point, the aim is not to praise the sterile option of *dependent nationalism*. The object, rather, is to emphasize that this type of foreign policy is highly appealing to policy-makers in semi-peripheral states precisely because it provides substantial false hope that their nationalist agendas could succeed if they could be pursued through policies that are loyal to the world hegemonic power. In this sense, dualist foreign policy is a siren song for all semi-peripheral governments. It promises both heroic nationalist aggrandisement and external security and stability in ways that seem ideal (but in reality are not). For this reason, any proper analysis of dualism must project not only the self-contradictory and self-defeating dynamics of this policy, but also its considerable appeal to policy-makers who often mistake it for a perfect synthesis of their otherwise incompatible objectives.

Insofar as the personality of Field Marshal Papagos played a key part in this process, a few remarks about him are in order. Much like the post-Civil War period, which his leadership helped to define, Papagos's persona in the historiography is bifurcated into two conflicting portrayals. The first depicts him as an ultraconservative, authoritarian leader, whose aloofness concealed an essentially traditional mind that never grasped the complexities of the post-war world. This is the image of the 'reactionary' Papagos, the 1935 coup leader and servant of the Metaxas regime that is usually projected by his opponents. Peake once noted that the anti-Rally opposition painted Papagos 'as a man of straw whose glamour derived from a largely fortuitous association with victories in which he had played a minor role'.[33] This unflattering portrayal emphasized his obsessive anti-communism, subservience to the United States and patronage of 'the extremist domestic faction' of IDEA.[34] A gross caricature of this representation can be found in his description by the KKE as a 'fascist [...] lackey of Americanocracy' or his assimilation by liberal critics to the Spanish dictator (with whom he forged close ties) through dubbing his politics with the (meaningless) label 'parliamentary Francoism'.[35] Milder versions of this sketch were later developed by his former allies-turned-critics, such as Markezinis and, to an extent, Karamanlis.

Opposite this image stands the heroic Papagos, the legendary commander-in-chief of the Greco-Italian War, the Field Marshal who defeated the communists and championed *Enosis*. This is Kanellopoulos's 'man of hegemonic self-dignity', presented by reporters like Sulzberger as 'Greece's only field marshal, national hero and prime minister'.[36] An extreme version of this portrait can be found in the title of his biography by the journalist Takis Papagiannopoulos, *History's Chosen One* (1987) or the posthumous commemorative pamphlets which lauded him as a 'leading figure [...] radiating the magic light of demigods'![37] Averoff's claim that 'all British Governments held Papagos in high esteem' must be qualified by Eden's unflattering remark that he 'told some fibs' in his book *The War of Greece, 1940–1941* (1945).[38] Yet, all British and US ambassadors who knew him referred to him in epic terms. Peake called him 'a legend', Norton found him 'deadly in earnest', and Peurifoy stressed his 'developed sense of own dignity'.[39]

In contrast to both versions, this study has avoided stereotyping Papagos as either 'a straw man' with dictatorial tendencies or a national superhero with mythical powers. Without rejecting the validity of some elements from both portrayals, the alternative view of Papagos presented here focused on a neglected aspect of his political persona, its tragic side. In this book, Papagos was cast as a populist leader who fell victim to his own self-contradictory policies because he tried to combine his critique of the establishment with a dutiful defence of the *status quo*. Like a modern Oedipus, he remained 'blind to the corruption' of the post-Civil War regime which he, above all other Greek politicians, helped to consolidate in 1949–55. And he went on to preside over the gradual corrosion of this order, insisting until the end that his frail Government was 'unshakable'.[40]

From this perspective, the controversy among certain historians over whether his premiership should be assessed as a case of 'strong leadership' or a 'striking [...] failure of leadership' becomes immaterial.[41] The paradox of Papagos's political career after 1949 was that of an exceedingly powerful leader, whose centralizing approach turned into a source of weakness, because he used it to reconcile sociopolitical forces that were essentially irreconcilable.

In his famous analysis of Caesarism, Gramsci describes how charismatic leadership can seize power in an attempt to reconcile conflicting historical forces that are not receptive to dialectical synthesis or historical fusion. In such circumstances, Gramsci argued, 'a great "heroic" personality [...] is entrusted with the task of "arbitration" over a historico-political situation characterized by an equilibrium of [...] conflicting [...] forces heading towards catastrophe'.[42] The tragic element in Papagos's leadership was precisely his inability to realize that his capacity to reconcile the conflicting historical forces operating within the *Ethnikofron* camp was provisional. Gramsci has drawn a key distinction between what he called 'quantitative' and 'qualitative' Caesarism. The former, he argued, is an arbitration that never achieves the 'historical passage from one type of state to another', whereas the latter does.[43] After the end of the Civil War, Papagos treated the Greek Rally as a vehicle for unifying the *Ethnikofron* bloc in the context of what Gramsci called 'quantitative' arbitration, namely through a form of Caesarism that sought 'only "evolution" of the same type' of state, not a transformation.[44]

A key point meriting attention is that neither the Rally's populist character nor Papagos's dualist foreign policy can be properly understood unless we firmly connect them to the sociocultural and political context of *Ethnikofrosyni*. A major area of difference between the present study and the dominant approaches on post-war Greece is the belief that the Greek political system in 1949–67 cannot be purely conceptualized through simplistic models portraying it as a 'rightwing state' (a cliché favoured by the dependence narrative) or an emerging Western democracy (in the romanticized image favoured by Greek ethnocentric historiography). Because of the centrality of the Civil War and its lasting effect on Greek politics, it has been argued throughout that the post-Civil War regime must be conceptualized primarily as an anti-communist order, that is as a power system built on the discursive cultural and institutional practices of *Ethnikofrosyni*. In adopting this perspective, the present study has attempted nothing more than to restore the original meaning of the term 'post-Civil War era', which is increasingly deployed today in the historiography as a hollow concept. However, in reinstating it as a meaningful term, that is as the designation of a period in which the outcome of the Civil War was consolidated and institutionalized, the present analysis seeks to reaffirm a vital, yet often overlooked connection: namely, that the post-Civil War period is the era of *Ethnikofron* hegemony. This perspective takes its cue from the core thesis developed in the 1980s by scholars like Alivizatos, who defined the post-Civil War period as a system whereby the polarization between '*ethnikofrones*' and 'non-*ethnikofrones*' prevailed.[45]

On this basis, the present study has shown that the outbreak of the *Enosis* movement after 1950 and the resulting breakdown of Greek-Turkish relations over the ensuing five years cannot be isolated from the domestic socio-political modalities of *Ethnikofrosyni*. In contrast to the common tendency of separating the end of the Greek Civil War from the revival of irredentist nationalism over Cyprus, the foregoing analysis has underlined the close connections between them. It has argued that the Cyprus question did not come, as some *Marxisant* analyses put it, 'out of the blue' or out of Papagos's penchant for drama.[46] Similarly, it has questioned the reductive view still shared among several historians, which attributes the revival of Greek irredentism in the 1950s to Papagos's poor leadership and failure to keep domestic nationalism at bay.[47] Instead, the previous discussion has shown that the quest for political unity among the *Ethnikofrones* after the Civil War has led them to populist solutions which were historically crucial for their survival as a unified bloc, especially after the abortive coups of the Palace and IDEA in August 1950 and May 1951, respectively. In other words, the espousal of populism by Papagos and its articulation around the quest for *Enosis* (in contrast to the cautious approach of the Centre Governments and the right-wing Popular Party) were not a matter of personal preference or weakness. As a cementing force in the early post-Civil War period, populism was an historical necessity required to contain the sharp inner disputes within the *Ethnikofron* camp in the crisis years 1949–52. At the same time, populism was also inscribed as a latent strand in *Ethnikofrosyni* itself, especially in its Manichean vision which portrayed the world, as Kanellopoulos wrote in a 1951 anti-communist pamphlet, as 'the struggle between humanism and inhumanity', 'freedom' and 'terrorism', 'truth' and 'absolute lies'.[48] To put it starkly, the revival of the *Enosis* movement after the Cypriot referendum of 1950 offered a lifeline to the Greek anti-communist elites insofar as it provided them with a political myth that could rally the popular masses around them after a traumatic civil conflict.

In such a context, it would have been unthinkable for a strong *Ethnikofron* leader, let alone the Field Marshal who linked his name to the defeat of the communists in the Civil War, to miss the opportunity of leading the new wave of nationalism around *Enosis*. Any attempt to ignore or suppress that movement would have unsettled the semi-parliamentary system which the *Ethnikofrones* and their British and American patrons established in 1946–9. This was all the more important in view of the setbacks suffered by Markezinis's 'new economic policy', including Washington's refusal to finance his industrialization programme, which denied the Rally the option of embracing 'economic modernization' as an alternative national project to *Enosis*, in the way Karamanlis would do in 1958–63. For these reasons, there was little choice for the dynamic elements of the *Ethnikofron* bloc after the Civil War than to blend their Atlanticism with a revived nationalist project animated by the Cypriot anti-colonial struggle. Meanwhile, Cold War necessities and the intricacies of US hegemony permitted some politically troubled NATO allies, like *Ethnikofron* Greece, to use this nationalism in a limited fashion as an auxiliary discourse to establish domestic legitimacy and widen popular support. And if such initiatives got out of hand, Washington was always ready to apply its hegemonic power to contain their regional spreading and knock-on effects. The risk, as Papagos's case demonstrated, was that such firefighting interventions could be either badly timed or, as the case of the Military Dictatorship in 1967–74 would show, too cruel and politically embarrassing to achieve their desired ends.

This book has conceptualized the Greek post-Civil-War era as a period in which the victors of the Civil War were eventually defeated by their own selves. In the early morning hours of the IDEA-EENA coup on 21 April 1967, the leaders of the two main *Ethnikofron* parties, Kanellopoulos and Papandreou, who had championed the persecution of thousands of communists as ministers and prime ministers in the 1940s and 1950s, were now themselves put under arrest by their former subordinates in the army and the parastate. This ironic denouement was the predictable outcome of a deeply divided political system, whose restructuring as a loose coalition of antagonistic forces under Papagos was dictated by the need to consolidate the Civil War victory against the Left. Foreign and economic policy issues, like Cyprus and Greece's post-war reconstruction, were never of course detached from the factional struggles of this troubled political system. For the most part, they were closely connected to it and regularly manipulated by competing *Ethnikofron* groups and their conflicting agendas. In this respect, the stirring of the Cyprus question in the early 1950s was inexorably linked to Papagos's venture to unify the *Ethnikofron* bloc around an anti-communist/populist discourse, animated by the old vision of *Megali Idea*. Similarly, Markezinis's 'new economic policy' was equally driven by the belief that Greece could get rid of its socioeconomic backwardness through a semi-protectionist ISI financed by the United States. Both policies formed the pillars of Greece's *dependent nationalism* in the early years of the Cold War and their legacy continues to set the parameters of Greece's foreign and economic policy today. The reasons behind this remarkable endurance are easily discernible. *Dependent nationalism* is an endemic condition of semi-peripheral politics in hegemonic world orders.

NOTES

Introduction

1 David McCrone, *The Sociology of Nationalism*, London, Routledge, 1998, p.1.
2 Mark Mazower, *Dark Continent: Europe's Twentieth Century*, London, Penguin, 1999, p.409.
3 John Mearsheimer, 'Back to the Future. Instability in Europe after the Cold War', *International Security*, 15:1, Summer 1990, p.55; Henry Kissinger, *Diplomacy*, London, Simon and Schuster, 1994, p.618.
4 William Pfaff, *The Wrath of Nations: Civilization and the Furies of Nationalism*, New York, Touchstone, 1993, p.43; Lloyd Kramer, *Nationalism in Europe and America: Politics, Cultures, and Identities since 1775*, Chapel Hill, University of North Carolina Press, 2011, p.177, 189.
5 Alexander Kazamias, 'Antiquity as Cold War Propaganda: The Uses of the Classical Past in Post-Civil War Greece', in Dimitris Tziovas (ed.), *Re-Imagining the Past: Antiquity and Modern Greek Culture*, Oxford, Oxford University Press, 2014, p.131–4, 142.
6 Marina Petrakis, *The Metaxas Myth: Dictatorship and Propaganda in Greece*, London, I.B. Tauris, 2006, p.133; Philip Carabott, 'Monumental Visions: The Past in Metaxas's *Weltanschauung*', in K.S. Brown and Yannis Hamilakis (eds), *The Usable Past: Greek Metahistories*, Lanham, Lexington, 2003, p.25–6; Ioannis Metaxas, *Λόγοι και σκέψεις*, vol.1, Athens, Govostis, 1997, p.53.
7 Antony Smith, *Nationalism in the Twentieth Century*, Oxford, Robertson, 1979, p.152.
8 Nicos Svoronos, *Ανάλεκτα νεοελληνικής Ιστορίας και ιστοριογραφίας*, Athens, Themelio, 1995, p.30–2.
9 This trend must not be confused with the so-called revisionist current in the historiography on the Greek Civil War, which emerged in the late 1990s. The focus of the present study is the post-Civil War period.
10 Evangelos Averoff-Tositsas, *Ιστορία χαμένων ευκαιριών: Κυπριακό 1950–1963*, Second Edition, Athens, Estia, 1982, vol.1, p.120.
11 Angelos Vlachos, *Δέκα χρόνια Κυπριακού*, Athens, Estia, 1981, p.11–12.
12 Constantinos Svolopoulos, *Η ελληνική εξωτερική πολιτική, 1945–1981*, vol.2, Athens, Estia, 2001; Dimitris Michalopoulos, *Ελλάδα και Τουρκία 1950–1959: Η χαμένη προσέγγιση*, Athens, Roes, 1989; Evanthis Hatzivassiliou, *Στρατηγικές του Κυπριακού. Η δεκαετία του 1950*, Athens, Patakis, 2004; id. *Greece and the Cold War: Frontline State, 1952–1967*, London, Routledge, 2006.
13 Couloumbis presented the historiography on post-war Greece as a sequence of 'orthodox', 'revisionist' and 'post-revisionist' narratives; see Theodore Couloumbis, 'Forward', in Hatzivassiliou, *Greece and the Cold War*, p.xii–xiii. This schema, which replicates the labels of US historiography on the Cold War, fails to account for

the distinct developments in the historiography on post-Civil War Greece. What Couloumbis calls 'orthodox' historiography on post-Civil War Greece did not become established until the 1980s, while the Marxist/*Marxisant* historiography of the 1960s and 1970s, which he calls 'revisionist', appeared earlier.

14 Some key works in this body of theory are Robert Cox and Timothy Sinclair, *Approaches to World Order*, Cambridge, Cambridge University Press, 1996; Andrew Linklater, *Beyond Realism and Marxism: Critical Theory and International Relations*, Basingstoke and London, Macmillan, 1990; id. *Critical Theory and World Politics: Citizenship, Sovereignty and Humanity*, Abingdon, Routledge, 2007; Mark Hoffman, 'Critical Theory and the Inter-Paradigm Debate', *Millenium*, 16:2, 1987, p.231–49; Jim George, *Discourses of Global Politics: A Critical (Re) Introduction to International Relations*, Colorado, Lynne Rienner, 1994; Anthony Leysens, *The Critical Theory of Robert W. Cox: Fugitive or Guru?*, Basingstoke, Palgrave Macmillan, 2008; John Moolakkattu, 'Robert W. Cox and Critical Theory of International Relations', *International Studies*, 46:4, 2009, p.439–56; Shannon Brincat (ed.), *From International Relations to World Civilizations: The Contributions of Robert W. Cox*, Abingdon, Routledge, 2017; Richard Devetak, *Critical International Theory: An Intellectual History*, Oxford, Oxford University Press, 2018; Steven Roach (ed.), *Handbook of Critical International Relations*, Cheltenham, Edward Elgar, 2020.

15 Andrew Linklater, 'Neo-realism in Theory and Practice', in Ken Booth and Steve Smith (eds), *International Relations Theory Today*, London, Polity, 1995, p.257.

16 Ralph Pettman, 'Competing Paradigms in International Politics', *Review of International Studies*, 7, 1981, p.46–7.

17 Robert Cox, 'Social Forces, States and World Orders: Beyond International Relations Theory', in Cox and Sinclair, *Approaches to World Order*, p.89.

18 Robert Cox, *Production, Power and World Order: Social Forces in the Making of History*, New York, Columbia University Press, 1987, p.399–400; Leysens, *The Critical Theory of Robert W. Cox*, p.47.

19 Richard Falk, 'The Critical Realist Tradition and the Demystification of Interstate Power: E. H. Carr, Hedley Bull, and Robert W. Cox', in Stephen Gill and James H. Mittelman (eds), *Innovation and Transformation in International Studies*, Cambridge, Cambridge University Press, 1997, p.45; Craig Murphy, 'Understanding IR: Understanding Gramsci', *Review of International Studies*, 24:2, 1998, p.418.

20 Adrian Budd, *Class, States and International Relations: A Critical Appraisal of Robert Cox and Neo-Gramscian Theory*, Abingdon, Routledge, 2013, p.175.

21 Stanley Hoffmann, *Gulliver's Troubles, or the Setting of American Foreign Policy*, New York, McGraw-Hill, 1968, p.177–8.

22 Gabriel Gorodetsky, 'The Formulation of Soviet Foreign Policy – Ideology and Realpolitik', in Gabriel Gorodetsky (ed.), *Soviet Foreign Policy, 1917–1991: A Retrospective*, Frank Cass, London, 1994, p.33.

23 Ibid., p.33.

24 On the differences between realism and nationalism see Edward Morse, *Foreign Policy and Interdependence in Gaullist France*, Princeton, Princeton University Press, 1973, p.141; Kissinger, *Diplomacy*, p.128, 137–8.

25 Reinhold Niebhur, *The Irony of American History*, Chicago, University of Chicago Press, 2008, p.xxiii–xxiv, 1–2.

26 Ibid., p.109–13.

Chapter 1

1. The main works supporting this thesis are Nikos Svoronos, Επισκόπηση της νεοελληνικής Ιστορίας, Athens, Themelio, 1999; Constantine Tsoucalas, *The Greek Tragedy*, London, Penguin, 1969; Nicos Poulantzas, *The Crisis of the Dictatorships*, London, New Left Books, 1976; Nicos Mouzelis, *Modern Greece: Facets of Underdevelopment*, London, Macmillan, 1977; id. *Politics in the Semi-Periphery: Early Parliamentarism and Late Industrialisation in the Balkans and Latin America*, London, Macmillan, 1986; Spyros Linardatos, Από τον Εμφύλιο στη Χούντα, vols 1-5, Athens, Papazisis, 1977; Solon Grigoriadis, Μετά τον Εμφύλιο: Η άνοδος του Παπάγου στην Εξουσία, Athens, Fytrakis, 1979; Lawrence Wittner, *American Intervention in Greece, 1943-1949*, New York, Columbia University Press, 1982; Tassos Vournas, Ιστορία της σύγχρονης Ελλάδας 1940-1967, Athens, Tolidis, undated; Dimitris Charalambis, Στρατός και πολιτική εξουσία, p.67. Η δομή της πολιτικής εξουσίας στη μετεμφυλιακή Ελλάδα, Athens, Exandas, 1985; Potis Paraskevopoulos, Φιλελεύθερα ανοίγματα μετά τον Εμφύλιο, Athens, Fytrakis, 1987; Jon Kofas, *Intervention and Underdevelopment: Greece during the Cold War*, University Park and London, Pennsylvania State University Press, 1989; Christophoros Vernardakis and Yannis Mavris, Κόμματα και κομματικές συμμαχίες στην προδικτατορική Ελλάδα, Athens, Exandas, 1991; Morgens Pelt, *Tying Greece to the West: US-West German-Greek Relations, 1949-1967*, Copenhagen, Museum Tusculanum Press, 2006. The dependence narrative has influenced some liberal works, such as Theodore Couloumbis, *Greek Political Reaction to American and NATO Influences*, New Haven, Yale University Press, 1966; id., Προβλήματα ελληνοαμερικανικών σχέσεων: Πώς αντιμετωπίζεται η εξάρτηση, Athens, Estia, 1978; John Iatrides, *Balkan Triangle: Birth and Decline across Ideological Boundaries*, The Hague, Mouton, 1968; Theodore Couloumbis, Harry Psomiades and John Petropoulos, *Foreign Interference in Greek Politics*, New York, Pella, 1976; Theodore Couloumbis and John Iatrides (eds), *Greek-American Relations: A Critical Review*, New York, Pella, 1980.
2. This narrative is developed in the works Stephen Xydis, *Cyprus: Conflict and Conciliation, 1954-1958*, Columbus, Ohio, 1967; id. 'Toward "Toil and Moil" in Cyprus', *Middle East Journal*, 20:1, 1966; id. 'The UN General Assembly as an Instrument of Greek Policy: Cyprus, 1954-58', *Journal of Conflict Resolution*, 12:2, June 1968; Michalopoulos, Ελλάδα και Τουρκία; Constantine Svolopoulos, Η Ελληνική εξωτερική πολιτική 1900-1945, Athens, Estia, 2001; id. Ελληνική εξωτερική πολιτική, vol. 2; Hatzivassiliou, Στρατηγικές του Κυπριακού; id. Η άνοδος του Κωνσταντίνου Καραμανλή στην εξουσία, 1954-1956, Athens, Patakis, 2000; id. *Greece and the Cold War*. Greek ethnocentric historiography on this period includes key non-scholarly works, such as Averoff-Tositsas, Ιστορία χαμένων ευκαιριών; Vlachos, Δέκα χρόνια Κυπριακού; Spyros Markezinis, Σύγχρονη πολιτική Ιστορία της Ελλάδος 1936-1975, vols 1-3, Athens, Papyros, 1994.
3. Some edited volumes combining both perspectives are: John Iatrides (ed.), *Greece in the 1940s. A Nation in Crisis*, Hanover, University Press of New England, 1981; D.G. Tsaoussis (ed.), Ελληνισμός και ελληνικότητα: Ιδεολογικοί και βιωματικοί άξονες της νεοελληνικής κοινωνίας, Athens, Estia, 1983; Lars Baerentzen, John Iatrides and Ole Smith (eds), *Studies in the History of the Greek Civil War 1945-1949*, Copenhagen, Museum Tusculum, 1987; Richard Clogg (ed.), *Greece in the 1980s*, London, Macmillan, 1983.
4. Hatzivassiliou, Η άνοδος του Καραμανλή, p.38.

5 Svoronos, *Ανάλεκτα*, p.299; Mouzelis, *Modern Greece*, p.40; Poulantzas, *Crisis of the Dictatorships*, p.18; Costas Vergopoulos 'The Emergence of the New Bourgeoisie, 1944–1952', in Iatrides (ed.), *Greece in the 1940s*, p.301; cf Svolopoulos, *Ελληνική εξωτερική πολιτική 1900–1945*, p.322–3; id. *Ελληνική εξωτερική πολιτική*, vol.2, p.13.
6 Vernardakis and Mavris, *Κόμματα*, p.169.
7 Yannis Stefanidis, *Από τον Εμφύλιο στον Ψυχρό Πόλεμο: Η Ελλάδα και ο συμμαχικός παράγοντας, 1949-52*, Athens, Proskinio, 1999, p.138.
8 Richard Jones, *Reductionism and the Fullness of Reality*, Cranbury, Associated University Presses, 2000, p.23; John Hoffman, *A Glossary of Political Theory*, Edinburgh, Edinburgh University Press, 2007, p.40.
9 John M. Hobson, *The State and International Relations*, Cambridge, Cambridge University Press, 2000, p.121.
10 Pelt, *Tying Greece*, p.50–1.
11 Hatzivassiliou, *Στρατηγικές του Κυπριακού*, p.16.
12 Linklater, *Critical Theory and World Politics*, p.45–59; Richard Devetak, 'Critical Theory', in Scott Burchill et al. (eds), *Theories of International Relations*, Fourth Edition, London, Palgrave Macmillan, 2009, p.159–82.
13 Cox and Sinclair, *Approaches to World Order*, p.97–9.
14 Immanuel Wallerstein, *The Modern World System I: Capitalist Agriculture and the Origins of the European World-Economy in the Sixteenth Century*, Berkley and LA, University of California Press, 2011 [1974], p.67; Kenneth Waltz, 'Realist Thought and Neorealist Theory', *Journal of International Affairs*, Spring/Summer 1990, 44:1, p.29.
15 Max Horkheimer, *Critical Theory: Selected Essays*, New York, Continuum, 1972, p.246; Hoffman, 'Critical Theory and the Inter-Paradigm Debate'.
16 Robert Cox, 'Realism, Positivism, and Historicism (1985)', in Cox and Sinclair, *Approaches to World Order*, p.54, italics added.
17 Robert Cox, 'On Thinking about Future World Order (1976)', in Cox and Sinclair, *Approaches to World Order*, p.77.
18 Ibid., p.77; Linklater, *Beyond Realism and Marxism*, p.9; id. *Critical Theory and World Politics*, p.46–7.
19 Steven Roach, *Critical Theory of International Politics: Complementarity, Justice, and Governance*, London, Routledge, 2010, p.1.
20 Valerie M. Hudson, *Foreign Policy Analysis: Classic and Contemporary Theory*, Lanham, Rowman and Littlefeld, 2007, p.191.
21 Elisabetta Brighi, *Foreign Policy, Domestic Politics and International Relations: The Case of Italy*, Abingdon, Routledge, 2013, p.33–4.
22 Robert Cox and Harold Jacobson, 'Decision Making', in Cox and Sinclair, *Approaches to World Order*, p.356, 364.
23 Anthony McGrew and M.J. Wilson (eds), *Decision Making: Approaches and Analysis*, Manchester, Manchester University Press, 1982, p.316–17.
24 Carl Martin Allwood and Marcus Selart (eds), *Decision Making: Social and Creative Dimensions*, Dordrecht, Kluwer Academic Publishers, 2001; Ralph Keeney, *Value-focused Thinking: A Path to Creative Decisionmaking*, Cambridge, MA, Harvard University Press, 1992.
25 Christopher Hill, *The Changing Politics of Foreign Policy*, Basingstoke, Palgrave Macmillan, 2003, p.107–8. Pluralists in the 1960s criticized the concept

of 'non-decisions', largely because it was invented to criticize Robert Dahl's influential pluralist analysis in *Who Governs? Democracy and Power in an American City* (1961).

26 Peter Bachrach and Morton Baratz, *Power and Poverty, Theory and Practice*, New York, Oxford University Press, 1970, p.3–16; Cox and Jacobson, 'Decision Making', p.349.

27 G. Parry and P. Morris, 'When Is a Decision Not a Decision?', in McGrew and Wilson (eds), *Decision Making*, p.19–35.

28 W.E. Jenkins, 'The Case of Non Decisions', in McGrew and Wilson (eds), *Decision Making*, p.318–26.

29 Mark Webber and Michael Smith, *Foreign Policy in a Transformed World*, Harlow, Prentice Hall, 2002, p.30–9.

30 Webber and Smith, *Foreign Policy*, p.39–41, 46; Hill, *Changing Politics of Foreign Policy*, p.165.

31 Cox and Sinclair, *Approaches to World Order*, p.124–43.

32 Mark Rupert, *Producing Hegemony: The Politics of Mass Production and American Global Power*, Cambridge, Cambridge University Press, 1995, p.40–1.

33 Hobson, *The State and International Relations*, p.133.

34 Falk, 'The Critical Realist Tradition', p.46; Budd, *Class, States and International Relations*, p.16.

35 Cox and Jacobson, 'Decision Making', p.356.

36 Immanuel Wallerstein, 'Dependence in an Interdependent World: The Limited Possibilities of Transformation within the Capitalist World Economy', *African Studies Review*, 17:1, April 1974, p.1–26; id. 'Semi-Peripheral Countries and the Contemporary World Crisis', *Theory and Society*, 3:4, Winter 1976, p.461–83.

37 Couloumbis, *Προβλήματα ελληνοαμερικανικών σχέσεων*, p.17.

38 Wallerstein, 'Semi-Peripheral Countries', p.363.

39 Mouzelis, *Politics in the Semi-Periphery*; Kofas, *Intervention and Underdevelopment*; Fatih Tayfur, *Semiperipheral Development and Foreign Policy. The Cases of Greece and Spain*, Aldershot, Ashgate, 2003.

40 Svoronos, *Ανάλεκτα*, p.38; Constantine Vergopoulos, *Το αγροτικό ζήτημα στην Ελλάδα*, Athens, Exantas, 1975, p.37; Mouzelis, *Modern Greece*, p.45; Constantine Tsoukalas, *Εξάρτηση και αναπαραγωγή: Ο κοινωνικός ρόλος των εκπαιδευτικών μηχανισμών στην Ελλάδα (1830–1922)*, Athens, Themelio, p.15; Nikos Psyroukis, *Το νεοελληνικό παροικιακό φαινόμενο*, Athens, Epikairotita, 1974, p.168; Charalambis, *Στρατός και πολιτική εξουσία*, p.67.

41 Mouzelis, *Modern Greece*, p. 45–6.

42 Barry Buzan, 'Introduction: The Changing Security Agenda in Europe', in Ole Wæver et al., *Identity, Migration and the New Security Agenda in Europe*, London, Pinter, 1993, p.12; Mouzelis, *Politics in the Semi-Periphery*, p.xv; for a reading of this work by Mouzelis as 'Weberian', see John Hall, 'Nicos Mouzelis, Politics in the Semi-Periphery: Early Parliamentarism and Late Industrialisation in the Balkans and Latin America', book review, *Sociology*, 21:1, 1987, p.157.

43 Cox and Sinclair, *Approaches to World Order*, p.96–112, 510–19.

44 Christopher Chase-Dunn, 'The Development of Core Capitalism in the Antebellum United States: Tariff Politics and Class Struggle in an Upwardly Mobile Semiperiphery', in A. Bergersen (ed.), *Studies of the Modern World System*, New York: Academic Press, 1980, p.192; Tayfur, *Semiperipheral Development and Foreign Policy*, p.9.

45 Mouzelis, *Politics in the Semi-Periphery*, p.7, 9.

46 Wallerstein, 'Semi-Peripheral Countries', p.472.

47 Ibid., p.462–4; Tayfur, *Semiperipheral Development*, p.51.
48 Hobson, *The State and International Relations*, p.133.
49 Cox and Jacobson, 'Decision Making', p.361.
50 Wallerstein, 'Semi-Peripheral Countries', p.465.
51 Wolfgang Mommsen, *The Political and Social Theory of Max Weber*, Chicago, University of Chicago Press, 1989, p.123–5.
52 Chris Brown, 'Development and Dependency', in Margot Light and A.J.R. Groom (eds), *International Relations*, London, Pinter, 1985, p.63–4.
53 Jacqueline Braveboy-Wagner, 'The English-Speaking Caribbean States: A Triad of Foreign Policies', in Jeanne Hey (ed.), *Small States in World Politics: Explaining Foreign Policy Behavior*, Boulder Co., Lynne Rienner, 2003, p.31–52; Peter McGowan and C.W. Kegley (eds), *Foreign Policy and the Modern World System*, London, Sage, 1983; Marshall Singer, 'The Foreign Policies of Small Developing States', in James Rosenau, Kenneth Thompson and Gavin Boyd (eds), *World Politics: An Introduction*, New York, Free Press, 1976, p.263–90; Couloumbis, *Προβλήματα ελληνοαμερικανικών σχέσεων*; Couloumbis, Psomiades and Petropoulos, *Foreign Interference in Greek Politics*; Couloumbis and Iatrides (eds), *Greek-American Relations*; Tayfur, *Semiperipheral Development*.
54 Marshall Singer, *Weak States in a World of Powers: The Dynamics of International Relationships*, New York, Free Press, 1972, p.51; Peter Baehr, 'Small States: A Tool for Analysis?', *World Politics*, 27:3, April 1975, p.464–5; Randolph Persaud, *Counter-Hegemony and Foreign Policy: The Dialectics of Marginalized and Global Forces in Jamaica*, Albany, State University of New York Press, 2001, p.15–16.
55 Raymond Duvall, 'Dependence and Dependencia Theory: Notes Toward Precision of Concept and Argument', *International Organization*, 32:1, 1978, p.57; McGowan and Kegley (eds), *Foreign Policy and the Modern World System*, p.9; Tayfur, *Semiperipheral Development*, p.1, 8.
56 Couloumbis, 'A New Model for Greek-American Relations: From Dependence to Interdependence', in Couloumbis and Iatrides (eds), *Greek-American Relations*, p.198, 203–5.
57 James Caporaso, 'Dependence, Dependency, and Power in the Global System: A Structure and Behavioural Analysis', *International Organization*, 32:1, 1978, p.18, 23.
58 Ian Roxborough, *Theories of Underdevelopment*, London, Macmillan, 1979, p.76; Caporaso, 'Dependence, Dependency, and Power', p.24.
59 Samir Amin, *Unequal Development: An Essay on the Social Formations of Peripheral Capitalism*, Hassocks, Harvester, 1976, p.339, 380; Poulantzas, *Crisis of the Dictatorships*, p.12, 30, 42–5; Geoffrey Kay, *Development and Underdevelopment*, London, Macmillan, 1975, p.94–5, 119–20.
60 Poulantzas, *Crisis of the Dictatorships*, p.43, 47–8; Mouzelis, *Modern Greece*, p.36–7; Amin, *Unequal Development*, p.297.
61 Vergopoulos, 'The Emergence of the New Bourgoisie', p.298–301, 303–4.
62 Mouzelis, *Modern Greece*, p.27.
63 F.R.U.S. 1951, Vol. V. NSC Draft Policy Statement: The Position of the US with Respect to Greece, [Top Secret], S/S-NSC Files: Lot 63 D 351: NSC 103 Series, 6 February 1951, p.452.
64 Svolopoulos, *Ελληνική εξωτερική πολιτική*, p.321.
65 Mouzelis, *Modern Greece*, p.149.

66 Poulantzas, *Crisis of the Dictatorships*, p.21; id. *Classes in Contemporary Capitalism*, London, New Left Books, 1975, p.73.
67 Cox, *Production, Power and World Order*, p.108.
68 Argyris Fatouros, 'Building Formal Structures of Penetration: The United States in Greece, 1947–1948', in Iatrides (ed.), *Greece in the 1940s*, p.240.
69 Ibid., p.241–2, 245–7.
70 James Rosenau, *The Adaptation of National Societies: A Theory of Political Systems Behavior and Transformation*, New York, McCaleb-Seiler, 1970, p.4; Nikolaj Petersen, 'Adaptation as a Framework for the Analysis of Foreign Policy Behaviour', *Cooperation and Conflict*, 12:4, 1977, p.224.
71 Of little relevance is James Mayall, *Nationalism and International Society*, Cambridge, Cambridge University Press, 1990.
72 John Breuilly, *Nationalism and the State*, Manchester, Manchester University Press, 1982, p.255.
73 Ilya Prizel, *National Identity and Foreign Policy: Nationalism and Leadership in Poland*, Cambridge, Cambridge University Press, 1998, p.19.
74 Benedict Anderson, *Imagined Communities: The Origins and Spread of Nationalism*, London, Verso, 1991, p.5, 7.
75 Antony Smith, *Nationalism and National Identity*, Middlesex, Penguin, 1991, p.81–3.
76 Ernest Gellner, *Nations and Nationalism*, Oxford, Oxford University Press, 1983, p.1; Smith, *Nationalism and National Identity*, p.1; Breuilly, *Nationalism and the State*, 1982, p.365.
77 Breuilly, *Nationalism and the State*, 1982, p.22.
78 Nikiforos Diamandouros, *Cultural Dualism and Political Change in Post-authoritarian Greece*, Madrid, Instituto Juan March de Estudios e Investigaciones, 1994, p.15–16.
79 K.Th. Dimaras, *Ελληνικός Ρωμαντισμός*, Athens, Ermis, 1994, p.417; Michael Llewellyn Smith, *Ionian Vision: Greece in Asia Minor 1919–1922*, London, Hurst, 1973, p.4.
80 C.M. Woodhouse, *Modern Greece. A Short History*, Fifth Edition, London, Faber and Faber, 1998, p.210; Svolopoulos, *Ελληνική εξωτερική πολιτική*, p.187–8; Ioannis Stefanidis, *Stirring the Greek Nation: Political Culture, Irredentism and Anti-Americanism in Post-War Greece, 1945–1967*, Aldershot, Ashgate, 2007, p.19–20, 46, 50.
81 Christoforos Christidis, *Κυπριακό και ελληνοτουρκικά: Πορεία μιας εθνικής χρεωκοπίας, 1953–1967*, Athens, 1967, p.29.
82 John Breuilly, *Nationalism and the State*, Second Edition, Chicago, Chicago University Press, 1993, back cover.
83 Paul Brass, *Ethnicity and Nationalism: Theory and Comparison*, London, Sage, 1991, p.8; Philip Spencer and Howard Wollman, *Nationalism: A Critical Introduction*, London, Sage, 2002, p.48.
84 Eric Hobsbawm, *Nations and Nationalism since 1780: Programme, Myth, Reality*, Second Edition, Cambridge, Cambridge University Press, 1992, p.91–2.
85 Cox, *Production, Power and World Order*, p.187; Nicos Poulantzas, *State, Power, Socialism*, London, Verso, 2000, p.107.
86 Amin, *Unequal Development*, p.236–9; Peter Evans, *Dependent Development: The Alliance of Multinational, State, and Local Capital in Brazil*, Princeton, Princeton University Press, 1979, p.29; Jie Huang 'Structural Disarticulation and Third World Human Development', *International Journal of Comparative Sociology*, 36:3, 1995, p.164–83.

87   Mouzelis, *Modern Greece*, p.29, 42.
88   Ibid., p.138.
89   *F.R.U.S.1950, Vol.V.* Acheson to Athens embassy, [Secret], 781.00/6-2450, p.378.
90   Alexander Kazamias, 'The Greek Variable in EU-Turkish Relations', in Joseph Joseph, *Turkey and the EU: Internal Dynamics and External Challenges*, London, Palgrave Macmillan, 2006, p.146-9.
91   Alexander Kazamias, 'The Modernization of Greek Foreign Policy and Its Limitations', *Mediterranean Politics*, 2:2, 1997, p.87-91.
92   Robin Higham 'The Metaxas Years in Perspective', in Robin Higham and Thanos Veremis (eds), *Aspects of Greece, 1936-40: The Metaxas Dictatorship*, Athens, ELIAMEP, 1993, p.235; David Close, *The Origins of the Greek Civil War*, London, Longman, 1995, p.39-41.
93   Nicos Kranidiotis, Δοκίμια: Προβληματισμοί, σκέψεις και μελέτες γύρω από την πολιτική και πνευματική ζωή της Κύπρου, Athens, Syllogos pros diadosin ofelimon vivlion, 1994, p.24, 31-2.
94   Thanos Veremis, *The Military in Greek Politics*, London, Hurst, 1997, p.132-5.
95   P. Nikiforos Diamandouros and Richard Gunther (eds), *Parties, Politics, and Democracy in the New Southern Europe*, Baltimore and London, Johns Hopkins University Press, 2001, p.5; Constantine Tsoukalas, 'The Ideological Impact of the Civil War', in Iatrides (ed.), *Greece in the 1940s*, p.324; Close, *Origins of Greek Civil War*, p.221.
96   David Close, *Greece since 1945: Politics, Economy and Society*, Abingdon, Routledge, 2014, p.27-8; Vergopoulos, 'The Emergence of the New Bourgoisie, 1944-1952', p.314.
97   Athanasios Lykogiannis, *Britain and the Greek Economic Crisis, 1944-1947: From Liberation to the Truman Doctrine*, Missouri, University of Missouri Press, 2002, p.44-5.
98   Pelt, *Tying Greece*, p.71-80; TNA/FO286/1305/1024. 'Report on the Activities of Bodossakis in Cyprus', [Secret], 21 December 1955.
99   John Lampe and Marvin Jackson, *Balkan Economic History, 1550-1950: From Imperial Borderlands to Developing Nations*, Bloomington, Indiana University Press, 1982, p.588.
100 Heinz Richter, *British Intervention in Greece: From Varkiza to Civil War - February 1945 to August 1946*, London, Hollowbrook, 1985, p.xi.
101 George Alexander, 'The Demobilisation Crisis of November 1944', in Iatrides (ed.), *Greece in the 1940s*, p.159.
102 Nicos Alivizatos, '"Έθνος" κατά "λαού"', in Tsaoussis (ed.), Ελληνισμός - Ελληνικότητα, p.87-8; Constantine Tsoukalas, 'The Ideological Impact', p.329; Despina Papadimitriou, Από τον λαό των νομιμοφρόνων στο έθνος των εθνικοφρόνων. Η συντηρητική σκέψη στην Ελλάδα, 1922-1967, Athens, Savvalas, 2006, p.178, 210, 222.
103 Gonda Van Steen, Gonda, *State of Emergency: Theatre and Public Performance Under the Greek Military Dictatorship of 1967-1974*, Oxford, Oxford University Press, 2015, p.7.
104 Nicos Alivizatos, Οι πολιτικοί θεσμοί σε κρίση, 1922-1974. Όψεις της ελληνικής εμπειρίας, Third Edition, Athens, Themelio, 1983, p.677; id. 'The "Emergency Regime" and Civil Liberties, 1946-1949', in Iatrides (ed.), *Greece in the 1940s*, p.227.

105 Kazamias, 'Antiquity as Cold War Propaganda', p.129-30.
106 Alexander Kazamias, 'Pseudo-Hegelian Contrivances: The Uses of German Idealism in the Discourse of the Post-Civil War Greek State', *Kambos: Cambridge Papers in Modern Greek*, 19, 2012, p.47-50.
107 Heinz Richter, 'The Varkiza Agreement and the Origins of the Civil War', in Iatrides (ed.), *Greece in the 1940s*, p.175; Judith Jeffery, *Ambiguous Commitments and Uncertain Policies: The Truman Doctrine in Greece, 1947-1952*, Lanham MA and Oxford, Lexington, 2000, p.104.
108 Sophocles Venizelos, interview in *Eleftheria*, 26 November 1961; quoted in Linardatos, *Από τον Εμφύλιο*, vol.1, p.101; Takis Pappas, *Making Party Democracy in Greece*, Basingstoke, Macmillan, 1999, p.8.
109 Alivizatos, *Οι πολιτικοί θεσμοί σε κρίση*, 451-523, quote from p.526.
110 Svoronos, *Ανάλεκτα νεοελληνικής Ιστορίας*, p.307, 317; Tsoukalas, 'The Ideological Impact' p.324; Mouzelis, *Modern Greece*, p.117; Charalambis, *Στρατός και πολιτική εξουσία*, p.32, 36; Vernardakis and Mavris, *Κόμματα*, p.138-9; Pappas, *Making Party Democracy,* p.8; Tayfur, *Semiperipheral Development*, p.60, 67; An exception is Poulantzas, *Crisis of the Dictatorships*, p.50.
111 Hatzivassiliou, *Greece and the Cold War*, p.4-5.
112 Vernardakis and Mavris, *Κόμματα*, p.170; despite this pertinent remark, other parts of this study accord the parastate a more dominant role, see p.138-9.
113 Poulantzas, *Crisis of the Dictatorships*, p.50.
114 Victor Papacosmas, 'The Changing Historical Context', in Clogg (ed) *Greece in the 1980s*, p.33.
115 Grigoriadis, *Μετά τον Εμφύλιο*, p.162; Linardatos, *Από τον Εμφύλιο*, vol.2, p.193; George Tenekidis, 'Διεθνοποίηση και αποδιεθνοποίηση του Κυπριακού πριν και μετά την τουρκική εισβολή', in George Tenekidis and Yannos Kranidiotis (eds), *Κύπρος. Ιστορία, προβλήματα και αγώνες του λαού της*, Third Edition, Athens, Estia, 2009, p.207, p.213.
116 Statement by the Second Plenary Session of the Central Committee of the Communist Party of Greece, October 1951, in Communist Party of Greece, *40 Χρόνια αγώνες.1918-1958. Επιλογή ντοκουμέντων*, Athens, KKE, 1964, p.106.
117 The same tentativeness marks the reference to Papagos's 'double track' tactics discussed by Linardatos, *Από τον Εμφύλιο*, vol.2, p.193.
118 Mary Douglas, *Purity and Danger: An Analysis of Concepts of Pollution and Taboo*, vol.2, London, Routledge, 2003, p.163.
119 Theodor Adorno, *Negative Dialectics*, London and New York, Routledge, 2004 [1966], p.140.
120 Maria Todorova, *Imagining the Balkans*, Oxford and New York, Oxford University Press, 1997, p.17-18; see also Mark Mazower, *The Balkans: A Short History*, New York, Modern Library, 2000, p.xxvi-xliii.
121 For Said's use of core/periphery analysis see Edward Said, *Culture and Imperialism*, London, Vintage, 1994, p.59; Edward Shills, *Centre and Periphery: Essays in Macrosociology*, Chicago, University of Chicago Press, 1975, quoted in Todorova, *Imagining the Balkans*, p.40-1.
122 Among these works are George Hoffman, *The Balkans in Transition*, Princeton, Van Nostand, 1963; Lampe and Jackson, *Balkan Economic History, 1550-1950*.
123 J.H. Boeke, *Economics and Economic Policy of Dual Societies*, New York, Institute of Pacific Relations, 1953; Benjamin Higgins, 'The "Dualistic Theory" of

Underdeveloped Areas', *Economic Development and Cultural Change*, January 1956, 4:2, p.99–115; G.E. Meier (ed.), *Leading Issues in Economic Development*, Oxford, Oxford University Press, 1970; Hia Myint, *Economic Theory and the Underdeveloped Countries*, New York, Oxford University Press, 1971, p.315–47; id. 'Organizational Dualism and Economic Development', *Asian Development Review*, 3:1, 1985, p.24–42; on 'dualistic' theories about Greece and the Balkans, see a critical exposition in Mouzelis, *Modern Greece*, p.42–5 and id, *Politics in the Semi-Periphery*, p.119–20, 253, fn81.

124 A functionalist view of dualism can be found in W.W. Rostow, *The Stages of Economic Growth: A Non-Communist Manifesto*, Third Edition, New York, Cambridge University Press, 1990, p.39.

125 Rodolfo Stavenhagen, 'Seven Erroneous Theses About Latin America', in Irving Louis Horowitz, Josu de Castro and John Gerassi (eds), *Latin American Radicalism: A Documentary Report on Left and Nationalist Movements*, London, Jonathan Cape, Boston, New England Free Press, 1969, p. 104–5, 108; Roxborough, *Theories of Underdevelopment*, p.10, 17; Mouzelis, *Modern Greece*, p.42–6, 175, fn46; id, *Politics in the Semi-Periphery*, p.120, fn81; Harold Brookfield, *Interdependent Development*, Abingdon, Routledge, 2011, p.156–7.

126 Stavenhagen, 'Seven Erroneous Theses', p.108.

127 Todorova, *Imagining the Balkans*, p.39–41.

128 Michael Herzfeld, *Ours Once More. Folklore, Ideology, and the Making of Modern Greece*, New York, Pella, 1986, p.vii–ix.

Chapter 2

1 John Lewis Gaddis 'Was the Truman Doctrine a Real Turning Point?' *Foreign Affairs*, 52, January–February. 1974, p.391. Melvyn Leffler, 'The American Conception of National Security and the Beginnings of the Cold War, 1945–48: Reply', *The American Historical Review*, 89:2, April. 1984, p.394.

2 Spyros Markezinis, *Από του πολέμου εις την ειρήνην*, Athens, Pyrsos, 1950, p.40–1.

3 Monteagle Stearns, *Entangled Allies: U.S. Policy towards Greece, Turkey and Cyprus*, New York, Council of Foreign Relations Press, 1992, p.75; Howard Jones,'*A New Kind of War': America's Global Strategy and the Truman Doctrine in Greece*, Oxford, Oxford University Press, 1989, p.234; John Iatrides, 'The United States and Greece in the Twentieth Century', in Theodore Couloumbis, Theodore Kariotis and Fotini Bellou (eds), *Greece in the Twentieth Century*, London, New York, Frank Cass, 2003, p.83–4; Tsoucalas, *Greek Tragedy*, p.122; Grigoriadis, *Μετά τον Εμφύλιο*, p.143; Stefanidis, *Από τον Εμφύλιο*, p.241; Pelt, *Tying Greece*, p.50–1.

4 Bruce Kuniholm, *The Origins of the Cold War in the Near East*, Princeton, Princeton University Press, 1980, p.425; Wittner, *American Intervention*, p.294.

5 Stearns, *Entangled Allies*, p.2.

6 Simon Roger, *Gramsci's Political Thought: An Introduction*, Norfolk, Biddles, 1982, p.24; Benedetto Fontana, *Hegemony and Power: On the Relation between Gramsci and Machiavelli*, Minneapolis, University of Minnesota Press, 1993, p.141; Steve Jones, *Antonio Gramsci*, Abingdon, Routledge, 2006, p.50.

7   Cox, 'Gramsci, Hegemony, and International Relations: An Essay in Method (1983)', in Cox and Sinclair, *Approaches to World Order*, p.135-7.
8   Robert Keohane, *After Hegemony: Cooperation and Discord in the World Political Economy*, Princeton, Princeton University Press, 1984, p.39; Immanuel Wallerstein, 'The Three Instances of Hegemony in the History of the Capitalist World-Economy', *International Journal of Comparative Sociology*, 24:1-2, 1983, p.101.
9   Cox, 'Gramsci, Hegemony', p.136; Keohane, *After Hegemony*, p.15, 135-81; Wallerstein, 'The Three Instances', p.102.
10 Heinrich Triepel, *Die Hegemonie: ein Buch von führenden Staaten*, Aalen, Scientia, 1961, p.218-40; Charles Kruszewski, 'Hegemony and International Law', *The American Political Science Review*, 35:6, 1941, p.1127-44.
11 Charalambis, Στρατός και πολιτική εξουσία, p.61.
12 Dean Acheson, *Present at the Creation*, New York, Norton, 1969, p.217-18.
13 F.R.U.S. 1951 Vol. V. The Position of the US with Respect to Greece – NSC Staff Study, [Top Secret], S/S-NSC 63 D 351: NSC 103 Series, 6 February 1951, p.456-7.
14 Lawrence Wittner, 'American Policy Toward Greece 1944-1949', in Iatrides (ed.), *Greece in the 1940s*, p.234; Stefanidis, Από τον Εμφύλιο, p.14.
15 F.R.U.S. 1949, Vol. VI. NSC to the President, NSC 42/1, 63D 351, [Top Secret], 22 March 1949, p.273; Wittner, *American Intervention*, p.104.
16 TNA/FO371/87692. Barrows to Foreign Office, [Confidential], RG16345/1, 15 May 1950.
17 F.R.U.S. 1951 Vol. V. NSC 103/1, Statement of Policy by NSC, 14 February 1951 (revised 11-24 May 1951), p.465, fn3.
18 U.S.N.A. Intelligence Publication Files, 6924319, ORE 28-48, Current Situation in Greece, [Secret], 17 November 1948; Peter Stavrakis, *Moscow and Greek Communism, 1944-1949*, New York, Ithaca, 1989, p.203, 214-15; Jones, 'A New Kind of War', p.14.
19 TNA/FO371/87692. Barrows to Foreign Office, [Confidential], RG16345/1, 15 May 1950.
20 F.R.U.S. 1951 Vol. V. Yost to Peurifoy, 781.5/1-2051, 20 January 1951, p.448.
21 F.R.U.S. 1951 Vol. V. Jessup to Acheson, [Top Secret], S/S-NSC 63 D 351: NSC 103 Series, 7 February 1951, p.461-2.
22 F.R.U.S. 1951 Vol. V. Position of the United States with Respect to Greece – NSC Staff Study, [Top Secret], S/S-NSC 63 D 351: NSC 103 Series, 6 February 1951, p.452-561; Iatrides, 'The United States and Greece in the Twentieth Century', p.78-82.
23 Fatouros, 'Building Formal Structures', p.250.
24 Alexis Papachelas, Ο βιασμός της ελληνικής Δημοκρατίας, Athens, Estia, 1997, p.23.
25 Jeffery, *Ambiguous Commitments*, p.224.
26 Ibid., p.22, 24-6.
27 TNA/FO371/87692 Bernard to Bart, [Confidential], RG 12645/1, 15 May 1950; Adamandia Polis, 'U.S. Intervention in Greek Trade Unions 1947-1950', in Iatrides (ed.), *Greece in the 1940s*, p.259-74; Theodoros Katsanevas, Το σύγχρονο συνδικαλιστικό κίνημα στην Ελλάδα, Athens, Papazisis, 1996, p.22-3, 31; Wittner, *American Intervention*, p.192-222.
28 Henry Grady and John McNay, *The Memoirs of Ambassador Henry Grady: From the Great War to the Cold War*, Columbia, University of Missouri Press, 2009, p.139-40; Wittner, *American Intervention*, p.117-19; Fatouros, 'Building Formal Structures', p. 248-9; Stefanidis, Από τον Εμφύλιο, p.15-16.
29 F.R.U.S. 1948, Vo. IV, McGhee to Lovett, 868.00/5, 19 May 1948, p.88-9.

30 Letter from Truman to Grady, 11 May 1948, cited in Grady and McNay, *Memoirs*, p.139.
31 TNA/FO371/78341. Norton to Foreign Office, [Secret], R231/1015/19, 8 January 1949.
32 Fatouros, 'Building Formal Structures', p.248–9.
33 *F.R.U.S. 1951 Vol. V.* NSC Staff Study [Top Secret], S/S-NSC 63D 351: NSC 103 Series, 6 February 1951, p.457.
34 Grady and McNay, *Memoirs*, p.149; see Tables 5 and 6.
35 *F.R.U.S. 1951 Vol. V.* NSC Staff Study, [Top Secret], S/S-NSC 63D 351: NSC 103 Series, 6 February 1951, p.455.
36 In the elections of March 1950, the army vote stood at 135,215 in a total of 1,688,923 voters, that is 8 per cent.
37 *F.R.U.S. 1948, Vol.V.* McGhee to Lovett, 868.00/5, 19 May 1948, p.88.
38 John Iatrides, 'Lincoln MacVeagh', in Cathal Nolan (ed.), *Notable U.S. Ambassadors since 1775: A Biographical Dictionary*, Westport, Greenwood, 1997, p.242–3.
39 James Miller, *The United States and the Making of Modern Greece: History and Power, 1950–1974*, Chapel Hill, University of North Carolina Press, 2009, p.25.
40 Paul A. Porter, *Ζητείται: Ένα θαύμα για την Ελλάδα*, Athens, Metamesonykties Ekdoseis, 2006, p.115.
41 Papachelas, *Ο βιασμός*, p.21.
42 Ibid., p.149.
43 Peter Grose, *Allen Dulles: Spymaster. The Life and Times of the First Civilian Dictator of the CIA*, London, André Deutsch, 2006, p.450; id., *Gentleman Spy: The Life of Allen Dulles*, Amherst, University of Massachusetts Press, 1996, p.430.
44 Papachelas, *Ο βιασμός*, p.21–2.
45 Grose, *Gentleman Spy*, p.510; id, *Spymaster*, p.450, 510.
46 Grose, *Spymaster*, p.450; Grose responds to notes taken by Arthur Schlesinger Jr. who found the report in the J.F. Kennedy Papers before it vanished; Peter Grose, *Operation Rollback: America's Secret War behind the Iron Curtain*, New York, Mariner, 2000, p.239, fn17.
47 *F.R.U.S. 1952–1954 Vol. VIII.* Peurifoy to State Department [Secret], 781.00/3-2453, 24 March 1953, p.813.
48 *F.R.U.S. 1950, Vol. V.* Grady to Acheson, [Secret], 781.00/3-3150, 31 March 1950, p.357.
49 *F.R.U.S. 1950, Vol. V.* Minor to Acheson [Confidential], 781.00/8-1850, 18 August 1950, p.399.
50 *F.R.U.S. 1950, Vol. V.* ECA Monthly Report for September 1950, 881.00-102350, 23 October 1950, p.431.
51 For a fuller discussion, see Chapter 7.
52 Amin, *Unequal Development*, p.236–9; Evans, *Dependent Development*, p.29; Huang, 'Structural Disarticulation and Third World Human Development', p.164–83; Caporaso, 'Dependence, Dependency, and Power', p.18, 23; Mouzelis, *Modern Greece*, p.29, 42–3.
53 For more details, see chapter 3.
54 Cyrus Sulzberger, *Long Row of Candles*, 1969, New York, Macmillan, 1969, p.428–31; Anne O'Hare McCormick, *New York Times*, 5 January 1949, p.24; for the views of the palace, see *Eleftheria*, 22 August 1951, p.1, 5; cf Couloumbis and Iatrides (eds), *Greek-American Relations*, p.68, who reproduce *Eleftheria*'s version of events.
55 Miller, *The United States*, p.26.
56 *Kathimerini*, 9 March 1950, p.1, 4; *Eleftheria*, 9 March 1950, p.1; *F.R.U.S. 1950 Vol. V.* Webb to Athens embassy, 781.00/3-1550, 16 March 1950, p.348; *contra* Grigoris Dafnis, *Σοφοκλής Ελευθερίου Βενιζέλος (1894–1964)*, Athens, Ikaros, 1970, p.454–69.

57 Panagiotis Kanellopoulos, *Ιστορικά Δοκίμια. Πώς εφθάσαμεν στην 21ῃ Απριλίου 1967 – 1940-1944 Εθνική Αντίσταση*, Athens, Estia, 1975, p.27; Dafnis, *Σοφοκλής Ελευθερίου Βενιζέλος*, p.461; Linardatos, *Από τον Εμφύλιο*, vol. 1, p.101–2; Sulzberger, *Long Row of Candles*, p.501.
58 *F.R.U.S. 1950 Vol V.* Grady to Acheson, [Secret] 781.00/3-1550, 15 March 1950, p.346.
59 *F.R.U.S. 1950 Vol V.* Minor to Acheson, [Secret] 781.00/3-2350, 23 March 1950, p.352.
60 *F.R.U.S. 1950 Vol V.* Acheson to Athens embassy [Secret], 781.00/3-2350, 24 March 1950, p.353; Acheson to Athens embassy [Secret], 781.00/3-2850, 28 March 1950, p.355.
61 *Kathimerini*, 1 April 1950, p.1; *F.R.U.S. 1950 Vol V.*, p.356; Stefanidis, *Από τον Εμφύλιο*, p.105–18; Linardatos, *Από τον Εμφύλιο*, vol.1, p.97–111; Jeffery, *Ambiguous Commitments*, p.224.
62 *F.R.U.S. 1950 Vol V.* Grady to Acheson, 881.00R/4-350, [Plain], 3 April 1950, p.357–9; *Kathimerini*, 2 April 1950, p.1; Linardatos, *Από τον Εμφύλιο*, vol.1, p.107; Stefanidis, *Από τον Εμφύλιο*, p.115; contra Dafnis, *Σοφοκλής Ελευθερίου Βενιζέλος*, p.467–9.
63 *Kathimerini*, 15 April 1950, p.1; *Eleftheria*, 15 April 1950, p.1.
64 *Eleftheria*, 16 April 1950, p.1; 25 April 1950, p.6; contra Dafnis, *Σοφοκλής Ελευθερίου Βενιζέλος*, p.468–9.
65 Elias Nikolakopoulos, *Κόμματα και βουλευτικές εκλογές στην Ελλάδα, 1946-1967*, Athens, EKKE, 1985, p.126.
66 George Politakis, *The Post-War Reconstruction of Greece. A History of Economic Stabilization and Development, 1944–1952*, Basingstoke, Palgrave Macmillan, 2018, p.230–1.
67 Georgios Dafnis, 'Το νόημα της ψήφου της 5ης Μαρτίου', *Eleftheria*, 20 April 1950, p.1, 6, 21 April 1950, p.1,3, 22 April 1950, p.1, 4.
68 Nikolakopoulos, *Κόμματα και βουλευτικές εκλογές*, p.126.
69 *F.R.U.S. 1950 Vol V.* Grady to Acheson, [Secret], 781.02/4-1750, 17 April 1950, p.365.
70 The Communist Party of Greece officially announced a cease-fire on 16 October 1949.
71 *F.R.U.S. 1950 Vol. V.* First Progress Report on NSC42/1 'US Objectives with Respect to Greece and Turkey to Counter Soviet Threats to US Security', [Top Secret] 63D 351, 6 March 1950, p.342–5; McGhee to Matthews: 'To determine United States action in the event of an attack against Greece by Soviet satellite forces', [Top Secret], 22 July 1950, p.382–6; Jenkins to Joint Chiefs of Staff, 'Policy Review in Greece in Light of Recent World Developments', [Top Secret], 26 July 1950, p.387–90; Webb to Lay: Second Progress Report on NSC42/1, 'US Objectives with Respect to Greece and Turkey to Counter Soviet Threats to US Security', [Top Secret], 19 September 1950, p.410–16; *F.R.U.S. 1950 Vol. I.* 'The Position and Actions of the US with Respect to Possible Further Soviet Moves in the Light of the Korean Situation', 63L 351 [Top Secret], NSC 73/4, 25 August 1950, p.375–90; *F.R.U.S. 1951 Vol. V.* 'NSC Draft Policy Statement on Greece', [Top Secret] S/S-NSC 63D 351: NSC 103 Series, 6 February 1951, p.451–2; 'NSC Staff Study', [Top Secret], S/S-NSC 63D 351: NSC 103 Series, 6 February 1951, p.452–61.
72 *F.R.U.S. 1951 Vol. V.* NSC Staff Study, [Top Secret], S/S-NSC 63D 351, 6 February 1951, p.455; NSC Policy Statement, [Top Secret], NSC 103/1, S/S-NSC 63 D 351, 14 February 1951, p.464.
73 *F.R.U.S. 1949, Vol. VI.* NSC to President, NSC 42/1, 63D 351, [Top Secret], 22 March 1949, p.278.
74 *F.R.U.S. 1951 Vol. V.* NSC Draft Policy Statement on Greece, [Top Secret] S/S-NSC 63D 351: NSC 103 Series, 6 February 1951, p. 454, 455.
75 Grigoriadis, *Μετά τον Εμφύλιο*, p.98.

76 *The Times*, 'Communist Guerrilla Bands in Greece: Plans for Revival', 20 January 1950; Jones, *'A New Kind of War'*, p.221; *F.R.U.S. 1950 Vol. V.* Acting Secretary of State to Secretary of NSC: Second Progress Report on NSC42/1, S/S-NSC: Lot 63D351: NCS42¹, [Top Secret], 19 September 1950, p.415.
77 Miller, *The United States*, p.29; Stefanidis, *Από τον Εμφύλιο*, p.51.
78 *F.R.U.S. 1949, Vol. VI*. MacGhee to Acheson, 868.20/11-3049 [Secret], 30 November 1949, p.464.
79 Elisabeth Barker, 'Yugoslav Policy towards Greece 1947–1949', in Baerentzen, Iatrides and Smith (eds) *Studies in the History of Greek Civil War*, p.280.
80 *F.R.U.S. 1950, Vol. IV*. NSC to President, 63D 351: NSC 18/4 [Top Secret], 17 November 1949, p.1342.
81 Ibid., p.1342.
82 *U.S.N.A.* 263: CIA Records, 7326970, [Secret], ORE 41-49, Probability of an Invasion of Yugoslavia in 1951, 20 March 1951.
83 Leften Stavrianos, *Greece: American Dilemma and Opportunity*, Chicago, Henry Regnery, 1952, p.220.
84 Barker, 'Yugoslav Policy towards Greece', p.283.
85 *F.R.U.S. 1949, Vol.VI*. Drew to Acheson, [Secret], 501.BB Balkans/2-1949, 19 February 1949, p.254–6; Acheson to Athens embassy, [Secret], 501.BB Balkans/2-1949, 25 February 1949, p.257–8.
86 Barker, 'Yugoslav Policy towards Greece', p.283, 285–7; *TNA/FO371/78447*. Peake to Foreign Office, [Secret], R1095/10392/19G, 28 January 1949.
87 Ioannis Stefanidis, 'United States, Great Britain and the Greek-Yugoslav Rapprochement, 1949–1950', *Balkan Studies*, 27:2, 1986, p. 318–19.
88 *F.R.U.S. 1949, Vol.VI*. Grady to Acheson, [Top Secret], 668.0024/3-1849, 18 March 1949, p.267–8; résumé of telegram 668.0024/2-2449, p.267, fn2; Peter Calvocoressi, *Survey of International Affairs 1949–1950*, London, Oxford University Press, RIIA, 1953, p.270; Stefanidis, 'United States, Great Britain', p.327–9.
89 *F.R.U.S. 1949, Vol.V*. Acheson to Belgrade embassy, [Secret], 840.50 Reovery/2-2549, 25 February 1949, p.873–4; Cannon to Acheson [Secret], 860H.005-2649, 26 May 1949, p.895–6; Cannon to Acheson [Secret], 860H.6-949, 9 June 1949, p.897.
90 Jože Pirjevec, 'The Tito-Stalin Split and the End of the Civil War in Greece', in Baerentzen, Iatrides and Smith (eds) *Studies in the History of Greek Civil War*, p.313.
91 *F.R.U.S. 1949, Vol.V*. Cannon to Acheson, [Secret], 760H.00/7-1349, 13 July 1949, p.368–9; Jones, *'A New Kind of War'*, p.214.
92 *F.R.U.S. 1950, Vol.IV*. Memorandum by Campbell, [Secret], 668.81/1-2450, 24 January 1950, p.1356.
93 *F.R.U.S. 1950, Vol.IV*. Cromie to Jernegan, [Confidential], 668.81/2-650, 6 February 1950, p.1364; Stefanidis, 'United States, Great Britain', p.320.
94 *F.R.U.S. 1950, Vol.IV*. Allen to Acheson, [Confidential], 668.81/3-2350, 23 March 1950, p.1394.
95 Calvocoressi, *Survey of International Affairs 1949–1950*, p.271, fn.1; *Borba* 2 April 1950; *Kathimerini*, 4 April 1950, p.6; *F.R.U.S. 1950 Vol V.* Memorandum of Conversations between Allen, Colquitt, Tranos, Patterson, [Secret] 357.AE/3-2250, 22 March 1950, p.349.
96 *F.R.U.S. 1950 Vol V*. Grady to Acheson, [Secret], 781.02/4-1750, 17 April 1950, p.364–5.

97 F.R.U.S. 1950, Vol.IV. Acheson to Belgrade embassy, [Confidential], 881.441/5-550, 5 May 1950, p.1413–14; Athens embassy to State Department, 668.81/5-1050, 10 May 1950, p.1415, fn3; Webb to Belgrade embassy, [Secret], 768.11/4-2850, 15 May 1950, p.1416–17.
98 Kathimerini, 17 May 1950, p.4; Eleftheria, 17 May 1950, p.4; F.R.U.S. 1950, Vol.IV. Webb to Athens embassy, [Confidential], 668.81/5-1950, 23 May 1950, p.1420.
99 Kathimerini, 18 May 1950, p.6; F.R.U.S. 1950, Vol.IV. Summary of telegrams 668.81/5-1950, Athens to State Department, 19 May 1950 and Athens to State Department, 668.81/5-1950, 19 May 1950, p.1426, fn2.
100 F.R.U.S. 1950, Vol.IV. Acheson to Belgrade embassy, [Secret], 768.11/6-2050, 21 June 1950, p.1426; Acheson to embassy in Greece, [Secret], 668.81/6-2450, 24 June 1950, p.1428–9; Acheson to embassy in Yugoslavia, 668.81/6-2650, [Secret], 26 June 1950, p.1430.
101 F.R.U.S. 1950, Vol.IV. Summary of telegrams 668.81/6-2650, Athens to State Department, 26 June 1950, 668.81/6-2750, Belgrade to State Department, 27 June 1950, 668.81/6-2850, 28 June 1950, p.1429, fn6.
102 Ibid., p.1429, fn6.
103 F.R.U.S. 1950 Vol V. Webb to Lay, [Top Secret], S/S-NSC Files: Lot 63D351: NCS42[1], Second Progress Report in NSC 42/1, 19 September 1950, p.413.
104 Ekavi Athanassopoulou, Turkey. Anglo-American Security Interests, 1945–1952: The First Enlargement of NATO, London, Frank Cass, 1999, p.191.
105 F.R.U.S. 1950 Vol IV. Summary of telegram 641.68/8-150 from Belgrade to State Department, p.1440, fn1.
106 F.R.U.S. 1950 Vol V. Webb to NSC Secretary Lay, [Top Secret], S/S-NSC Files: Lot 63D351: NCS42[1], Second Progress Report in NSC 42/1, 19 September 1950, p.413, italics added.
107 F.R.U.S. 1950 Vol V. Memorandum of informal US-UK discussion in connection with McGhee's visit to London, [Secret], 780.00/9-1850, 19 September 1950, p.408–9, italics added.
108 Stearns, Entangled Allies, p.75.
109 Stefanidis, Από τον Εμφύλιο, p.65; Pelt, Tying Greece, p.136.
110 Athanassopoulou, Turkey, p.196.
111 F.R.U.S. 1951 Vol. III. Minutes of State Department-JCS Meeting, [Top Secret], lot 61 D417, January-June 1951, 14 March 1951, p.494.
112 F.R.U.S. 1949, Vol.IV. Conversation between Acheson, Erkin, Jernegan, [Secret], 840.20/2-1749, 17 February 1949, p.117.
113 F.R.U.S. 1950, Vol.III. Acheson to Athens embassy, [Top Secret], 782.5/8-1750, 17 August 1950, p.220; Minor to Acheson, [Top Secret], 740.5/8-2450, 24 August 1950, p.241.
114 F.R.U.S. 1951 Vol. III. McGhee and Perkins to Acheson, [Top Secret], 781.5/5-151, 24 April 1951, p.512.
115 Joel Sokolsky, Sea Power in the Nuclear Age: United States Navy and NATO, 1948–1950, London, Routledge, 1991, p.25.
116 F.R.U.S. 1951 Vol. III. Minutes of Department of State-JCS Meeting, [Top Secret], State-JCS meetings, lot 61 D417, January-June 1951, 14 March 1951, p.491.
117 Ibid., p.493.
118 F.R.U.S. 1951 Vol. III. Acheson to Marshall, [Top Secret], 781.5/5-151, 24 March 1951, p.501-5; McGhee and Perkins to Acheson, [Top Secret], 781.5/5-151, 24 April 1951, p.512.

119 F.R.U.S. *1951 Vol. III*. McGhee and Perkins to Acheson, [Top Secret], 781.5/5-151, 24 April 1951, p.512, fn5.
120 On Bradley's close relations with Eisenhower and Sharman, see Omar Bradley and Clay Blair, *A General's Life*, New York, Simon and Schuster, 1983, p.644-50.
121 F.R.U.S. *1951 Vol. III*. McGhee and Perkins to Acheson, [Top Secret], 781.5/5-151, 24 April 1951, p.513, 514.
122 U.S.N.A. 263: CIA Records, 7326852, [Secret], SE 7, Probable Soviet Reaction to the Inclusion of Greece and Turkey in Western Defense Agreements, 15 June 1951.
123 F.R.U.S. *1951 Vol. V.* Yost to Peurifoy, [Top Secret] 781.5/1-2051, 20 January 1951, p. 446-51, fn1.
124 Ibid., p.449-50.
125 F.R.U.S. *1951 Vol. V.* NSC Staff Study, [Top Secret], S/S-NSC 63D 351: NSC 103 Series, 6 February 1951, p.460.
126 F.R.U.S. *1951 Vol. V.* p.447-8, fn1; Acheson to Athens embassy, 781.5/1-2051, 16 March 1951, p.451.
127 F.R.U.S. *1951 Vol. III*. Acheson to Marshall, [Top Secret], 781.5/5-151, 24 March 1951, p.501. Letter drafted on 19 March.
128 F.R.U.S. *1951 Vol. III*. Mesta to Acheson, [Secret], 740.5/1-1951, 19 January 1951, p.442-3.
129 F.R.U.S. *1951 Vol. III*. Notes on a Meeting at the White House, [Top Secret], Harry S. Truman Library, George M. Elsey Papers, 31 January 1951, p.454.
130 F.R.U.S. *1951 Vol. III*. Acheson to Marshall, [Top Secret], 781.5/5-151, 24 March 1951, p.503.
131 F.R.U.S. *1951 Vol. V.* Villard to Nitze [Secret] PSS Files: Lot 64 D563: Record Copies, January-April 1951, 5 February 1951, p.1118.
132 F.R.U.S. *1951 Vol. III*. Peurifoy to Acheson, [Top Secret], 781.5/4-1351, 13 April 1951, p.508-9.
133 F.R.U.S. *1949, Vol.IV*. Conversation between Acheson, Erkin, Jernegan, [Secret], 840.20/2-1749, 17 February 1949, p.117.
134 F.R.U.S. *1950, Vol.III*. Acheson to Certain Diplomatic Offices, [Top Secret], 700.00 (S)/ 8-250, 2 August 1950, p.175, fn2; State Department Paper 'Security of Greece and Turkey', [Secret], Ankara embassy Files: Lot 58 F33: 320, 11 September 1950, p.279; Webb to Certain Diplomatic Offices, [Top Secret], 700.00 (S)/ 9-1850, 18 September 1950, p.326-7; Conversation between Acheson, Erkin and Anschuetz, [Top Secret], 740.5/9-1950, 19 September 1950, p.333-5.
135 F.R.U.S. *1951, Vol.V.* Conversation between McGhee, Erkin and Moore, [Secret], 740.5/1-2451, 24 January 1951, p.1111.
136 Athanassopoulou, *Turkey*, p.176, 181, 237.
137 F.R.U.S. *1951, Vol.V.* Conversation between McGhee, Erkin and Moore, [Secret], 740.5/1-2451, 24 January 1951, p.1111.
138 F.R.U.S. *1950, Vol.III*. Conversation between Bayar, Köprülü, McGhee, Wadsworth, Rountree, [Top Secret], 782.5/2-1251, 12 February 1951, p.467, fn2, 468.
139 Norman Palmer, 'Charles W. Yost. "History and Memory: A Statesman's Perceptions of the Twentieth Century", p.352. New York: W.W. Norton, 1980', *The Annals of the American Academy of Political and Social Science*, 455:1, 1981, p.176; Markezinis, Σύγχρονη πολιτική Ιστορία, vol.2, p.451; Grigoriadis, Μετά τον Εμφύλιο, p.209. Yost wrote several acclaimed books and articles on world politics.
140 F.R.U.S. *1952-54, Vol. VIII.* Yost to State Department, 611.81/8-2952, 29 August 1952, p.804-6; Peurifoy to State Department, [Secret], 611.81/9-2552, 25 September 1952, p.806-9.

141 Ibid., p.807-8.
142 Ibid.
143 Ibid., p.808.
144 Ibid.
145 Cox and Sinclair, *Approaches to World Order*, p.214.
146 *F.R.U.S. 1952–54, Vol. VIII*. Peurifoy to State Department, [Secret], 611.81/9-2552, 25 September 1952, p.808.
147 Ibid., p.808.
148 Ibid., p.809.
149 Ibid., p.807.
150 Ioannis Stefanidis, *Isle of Discord: Nationalism, Imperialism and the Making of the Cyprus Problem*, London, Hurst, 1999, p.260.
151 *F.R.U.S. 1952–54, Vol. VIII*. Peurifoy to State Department, [Secret], 17 March 1952, 781.00/3-1752, p.789.
152 *Eleftheria*, 21 August 1952, p.1; 26 August 1952, p.1.
153 *F.R.U.S. 1952–54, Vol. VIII*. Peurifoy to State Department [Top Secret], 881.00/8-2752, 27 August 1952, p.804.
154 At this point Kartalis had been secretly informed that US economic aid would be halved for 1952/53, see Chapter 7.
155 Quotes from *Eleftheria*, 24 August 1952, p.1; 18 September 1952, p.1; See also 26 August 1952, p.1; 27 August 1952, p.1; 28 August 1952, p.1; 31 August 1952, p.1; 7 September 1952, p.1; 9 September 1952, p.1; 10 September 1952, p.1; 11 September 1952, p.1; 12 September 1952, p.1; 14 September 1952, p.1; 16 September 1952, p.1; 17 September 1952, p.1; 19 September 1952, p.1; 20 September 1952, p.1; 21 September 1952, p.1; 24 September 1952.
156 *Kathimerini*, 24 August 1952, p.1.
157 *F.R.U.S. 1952–54, Vol. VIII*, Despatch 611.81/9-2552, [Secret], p.807.
158 Ibid., p.807.
159 Graham Allison and Philip Zeliow, *Essence of Decision: Explaining the Cuban Missile Crisis*, Second Edition, New York, Longman, 1999, p.147–60; Morton Halperin, *Priscilla Clapp with Arnold Kanter, Bureaucratic Politics and Foreign Policy*, Second Edition, Washington, The Brookings Institution, 2006, p.357–8; Eugene Wittkopf et al., *American Foreign Policy: Pattern and Process*, Thomson, Belmont, Thomson, 2008, p.476–82.
160 Iatrides, 'The United States and Greece in the Twentieth Century', p.83–4; Tsoucalas, *Greek Tragedy*, p.125–6; Andreas Papandreou, *Democracy at Gunpoint. The Greek Front*, New York, Pelican, 1973, p.90; Grigoriadis, Μετά τον Εμφύλιο, p.15, 36–7; Linardatos, Μετά τον Εμφύλιο, vol.1, p.239–40, 406–8; Pelt, *Tying Greece*, p.52, 62–4.
161 Stavrianos, *Greece: American Dilemma*, p.13.
162 *New York Times*, 10 April 1950, p.25.
163 Francis Fukuyama, *State-Building: Governance and World Order in the 21st Century*, New York, Cornell University Press, 2004, p.ix.
164 *F.R.U.S. 1950 Vol. V.* Grady to Acheson, [Confidential], 781.00-32750, 27 March 1950, p.354.
165 *U.S.N.A. 263*: Intelligence Publication Files: CIA, 6924369, ORE 4-50, [Secret] Current Situation in Greece, 28 February 1950.
166 *F.R.U.S. 1950 Vol. V.* McGhee to Acheson, [Secret], 781.00/4-1850, 18 April 1950, p.367.

167 *New York Times*, 10 April 1950, p.25.
168 G.M.F.A. Deputy Director of General Security, Ministry of Interior to Directorate of Protocol, Ministry of Foreign Affairs, No.32196/322142, 9 August 1953; See also Iatrides, 'The United States and Greece in the Twentieth Century', p.83–4.
169 Ibid., p.354.
170 F.R.U.S. *1950 Vol. V.* Acheson to embassy in Greece, [Secret], 781.00/3-2350, 24 March 1950, p.353; Grady to Acheson, [Confidential], 781.00-32750, 27 March 1950, p.354.
171 Jeffery, *Ambiguous Commitments*, p.125.
172 Cf Jeffery, *Ambiguous Commitments*, p.2–4.
173 Cox, 'Gramsci, Hegemony', p.136–8.
174 Poulantzas, *Crisis of the Dictatorships*, p.38.

Chapter 3

1 Charalambis, Στρατός και πολιτική εξουσία, p.100; Vernardakis and Mavris, Κόμματα, p.168; David Close, 'The Reconstruction of a Right-Wing State' in David Close (ed.), *The Greek Civil War, 1943–1950: Studies of Polarisation*, London, Routledge, 1993, p.156; Pappas, *Making Party Democracy*, p.3–4; Pavlos Petridis, Εξουσία και παραεξουσία στην Ελλάδα, 1957–1967: Απόρρητα ντοκουμέντα, Athens, Proskinio, 2000, p.11; Neovi Karakatsanis, *The Politics of Elite Transformation: The Consolidation of Greek Democracy in Theoretical Perspective*, Westport, Praeger, 2001, p.4; Iatrides, 'The United States and Greece', p.74–5; Pelt, *Tying Greece*, p.46; Jeffery, *Ambiguous Commitments*, p.103; Stan Draenos, *Andreas Papandreou: The Making of a Greek Democrat and a Maverik*, London, I.B. Tauris, 2013, p.227.
2 Keith Legg, *Politics in Modern Greece*, Stanford, Stanford University Press, 1969, p.141.
3 On 27 August 1952, the King's Adjutant, Constantine Ventiris, told the US ambassador that an electoral system which gave Venizelos's Liberals proper representation 'would maintain stabilizing influence of Palace in political life', while a one-party government by Plastiras or Papagos 'would render [the] Palace impotent', F.R.U.S. *1952–1954, Vol.VIII*. Peurifoy to State Department, 881.00/8-2752, [Top Secret], 27 August 1952, p.806; on Venizelos as 'a friend of the royal couple', see Papandreou, *Democracy at Gunpoint*, p.119; Costas Costis, 'Τα κακομαθημένα παιδιά της Ιστορίας': Η διαμόρφωση του νεοελληνικού κράτους, 18^{ος}-21^{ος} αιώνας, Athens, Polis, 2013, p.727.
4 Sulzberger, *A Long Row*, entry '7 March 1950', p.500.
5 Georgios Karayiannis, Το δράμα της Ελλάδος. Εποποιία και αθλιότητες, ΕΕΝΑ, ΙΔΕΑ, 1940–1952, Athens, 1964, p.204–8; Charalambis, Στρατός και πολιτική εξουσία, p.266; *Eleftheria*, 2 September 1951, p.1, 5.
6 F.R.U.S. *1951 Vol. V*. Acheson to Peurifoy, [Secret], 781.00/7-651, 8 June 1951, p.480.
7 *Constantine Karamanlis Archive*, vol. I. 16 November 1950, p.138; *To Vima*, Editorial, 23 February 1951, p.1; F.R.U.S. *1951, Vol. V.* Memminger to State Department, 781.00/3-851, [Confidential], 8 March 1951, p.568–9.
8 F.R.U.S. *1947, Vol. V*. Porter to Clayton, [Top Secret], 868.50/2-1747, 17 February 1947, p.20.

9 *TNA/FO371/101503*. Peake to Eden [Confidential], WG1011/9, 2 December 1952.
10 Markezinis, Σύγχρονη πολιτική Ιστορία, vol.2, p.392; Linardatos, Από τον Εμφύλιο, vol.1, p.269; *TNA/FO371/101503*. Peake to Eden [Confidential], WG1011/9, 2 December 1952.
11 *TNA/FO371/101793*. Annual Report on Greece for 1951; *Kathimerini*, 2 August 1951, p.1; *Embros*, 7 August 1951, p.1.
12 Elias Nikolakopoulos, Κόμματα και βουλευτικές εκλογές στην Ελλάδα, 1946–1967, Athens, EKKE, 1985, p.77.
13 Legg, *Politics in Modern Greece*, p.142, Table 6.3.
14 John Koliopoulos, 'Metaxas and Greek Foreign Relations, 1936–1941', in Robin Higham and Thanos Veremis (eds), *The Metaxas Dictatorship: Aspects of Greece, 1936–1940*, Athens, ELIAMEP, 1993, p.85–110.
15 *Eleftheria*, 1 August 1951, p.1; 15 August 1951, p.1, 6; 29 October 1952, p.1; 5 November 1952, p.1, 3.
16 *Constantine Karamanlis Archive*, vol. I. Elections 1952, 8–9 November 1952, p.151.
17 Nikolakopoulos, Κόμματα και βουλευτικές εκλογές, p.77.
18 The expression was used by Papagos, Interview in *Kathimerini*, 18 November 1951, p.1.
19 *TNA/FO371/101803*. Peake to Eden [Confidential], WG10114/9, 2 December 1952.
20 Sulzberger, *A Long Row*, entry '13 May 1954', p.1009; Hatzivassiliou, Η άνοδος του Κωνσταντίνου Καραμανλή, p.36.
21 Svoronos, Ανάλεκτα, p.307; Mouzelis, *Politics in Semi-Periphery*, p.136–7.
22 Michalopoulos, Ελλάδα και Τουρκία, p.31; Kanellopoulos, Ιστορικά δοκίμια, p.2; Alexis Kyrou, Ελληνική εξωτερική πολιτική, Athens, Estia, 1982 [1955], p.127, 272.
23 The estimated size of the parastate as consisting of 60,000 people is arbitrary and should be viewed with caution, see Close, 'The Legacy', in Close, *The Greek Civil War*, p.216; Pelt, *Tying Greece*, p.44.
24 Alivizatos, Οι πολιτικοί θεσμοί, p.580, table 7.
25 *Official Minutes of Greek Parliament*. Question by Constantine Mitsotakis, Period 3, Synod 1, 50th session, 8 June 1953, p.645.
26 Svoronos, Ανάλεκτα, p.307.
27 Wittner, 'American Policy', p.237; Vernardakis and Mavris, Κόμματα, p.174–5.
28 *General Tsingounis Papers*. 'IDEA, Encyclical Order' [Top Secret], 14 July 1949, copy no.8.
29 *Official Minutes of Greek Parliament*. Sophocles Venizelos during the debate on the appointment of dismissed officers, Period 3, Synod 1, 50th Session, 8 June 1953, p.645.
30 *TNA/FO371/101803*. Peake to Eden, [Confidential], WG10114/9, 2 December 1952; Hatzivassiliou, Η άνοδος του Κωνσταντίνου Καραμανλή, p.44; Miller, *The United States*, p.9.
31 Panourgia, Neni, *Dangerous Citizens: The Greek Left and the Terror of the State*, New York, Fordham University Press, 2009, p.122–3; Michalis Papakonstandinou, Η ταραγμένη εξαετία, Athens, Proskinio, 1997, p.65.
32 Alivizatos, Οι πολιτικοί θεσμοί, p.458–95, 534–6; Richter, 'The Varkiza Agreement and the Origins of the Civil War', p.174; Basil Gounaris, 'Social Dimensions of Anticommunism in Northern Greece, 1945–50', in Philip Carabott and Thanasis Sfikas (eds), *The Greek Civil War: Essays on a Conflict of Exceptionalism and Silences*, Aldershot, Ashgate, 2004, p.180, 183.

33 Tsoukalas, 'The Ideological Impact', p.336-8; Alivizatos, *Οι πολιτικοί θεσμοί*, 529-30, 533-4; Stefanidis, *Stirring the Nation*, p.30-1.
34 Susannah Verney, 'To Be or Not to Be within the European Community: The Party Debate and Democratic Consolidation in Greece', in Geoffrey Pridham (ed.), *Securing Democracy: Political Parties and Democratic Consolidation in Southern Europe*, Abingdon, Routledge, 2016, p.207.
35 Costis, '*Τα κακομαθημένα παιδιά*', p.722-3.
36 Antonio Gramsci, *Selections from the Prison Notebooks*, London, Lawrence and Wishart, 1971, p.219.
37 Dafnis, *Σοφοκλής Ελευθερίου Βενιζέλος*, p.511.
38 Thurston to Baxter, C781.00/9-1255, [Secret], 12 September 1955, p.541-3; Alan Dulles (CIA) to John Foster Dulles (State), Comments of King Paul and Karamanlis, C781.00/9-2255, [Top Secret], 22 September 1955, p.544-5; Linardatos, *Από τον Εμφύλιο*, vol.2, p.364-81; cf Hatzivassiliou, *Η άνοδος του Κωνσταντίνου Καραμανλή*, p.132-47, 160-79, 188-240.
39 Mouzelis, *Modern Greece*, p.116-17; the Rally's election victories were in 1951 and 1952, not 1952 and 1953.
40 Vernardakis and Mavris, *Κόμματα*, p.199; Linardatos, *Από τον Εμφύλιο*, vol.1, p.25; Stefanidis, *Από τον Εμφύλιο*, p.92; Costas Chatziantoniou, *Νικόλαος Πλαστήρας*. *Ιστορική βιογραφία*, Athens, Iolkos, 2006, p.203, 227.
41 Mouzelis, *Politics in Semi-Periphery*, p.137.
42 Nikolakopoulos, *Κόμματα και βουλευτικές εκλογές*, p.143, table 1, p.167, Table 1.
43 *Kathimerini*, 8 August 1951, p.1; *Eleftheria*, 8 August 1951, p.1; 9 August 1951, p.6.
44 *Embros*, 14 August 1951, p.4; *Eleftheria*, 14 August 1951, p.6.
45 *Sophocles Venizelos Papers*. Note by Venizelos on statement by Papagos, 037-009, 226/37/9, dated '1951'.
46 *Kathimerini*, 31 August 1952, p.1; *Embros*, 27 August 1952, p.1.
47 Charalambis, *Στρατός και πολιτική εξουσία*, p.43.
48 Vernardakis and Mavris, *Κόμματα*, p.169.
49 Charalambis, *Στρατός και πολιτική εξουσία*, p.43.
50 Ibid., p.43-4.
51 Thrasivoulos Tsakalotos, *40 Χρόνια Στρατιώτης. Πώς εκερδίσαμε τους αγώνας μας, 1940-1949*, Athens, Acropolis, 1960, vol.2, p.445.
52 Kanellopoulos, *Ιστορικά δοκίμια*, p.28-9; Karayiannis, *Το δράμα*, p.263.
53 Markezinis, *Σύγχρονη πολιτική Ιστορία*, vol.2, p.315.
54 Kanellopoulos, *Ιστορικά δοκίμια*, p.29; Charalambis, *Στρατός και πολιτική εξουσία*, p.46.
55 Kanellopoulos, *Ιστορικά δοκίμια*, p.29.
56 Ibid., p.28-9.
57 Papandreou, *Democracy at Gunpoint*, p.88-90; Linardatos, *Από τον Εμφύλιο*, vol.1, p.445; Vournas, *Ιστορία*, p.11; Paraskevopoulos, *Φιλελεύθερα ανοίγματα*, p.143.
58 John Iatrides, 'American Attitudes Toward the Political System of Postwar Greece', in Couloumbis and Iatrides (eds), *Greek-American Relations*, p.68.
59 Van Coufoudakis, 'The United States, the United Nations, and the Greek Question, 1946-1952', in John Iatrides (ed.), *Greece in the 1940s*, p.293.
60 Mouzelis, *Politics in Semi-Periphery*, p.135; Tsoucalas, *Greek Tragedy*, p.122-3; Tsoukalas, 'The Ideological Impact', p.325; Pelt, *Tying Greece*, p.61; Stefanidis, *Stirring the Nation*, p.178.

61 Stefanidis, *Isle of Discord*, p.260; id. *Από τον Εμφύλιο*, p.150; id. *Stirring the Nation*, p.178.
62 Stefanidis, *Από τον Εμφύλιο*, p.150.
63 *F.R.U.S. 1951, Vol.V.* Peurifoy to State Department, [Secret], 781.00/7-3151, 31 July 1951, p.491, fn1.
64 *F.R.U.S. 1951, Vol.V.* Peurifoy to State Department, [Secret], 781/6-1151, 11 June 1951, p.481.
65 *F.R.U.S. 1949, Vol.VI.* Grady to Acting Secretary of State Department, 868.00/1-549, [Confidential], 5 January 1949, p.234, fn6.
66 *TNA/FO371/95116.* Norton to Noble at Foreign Office, [Confidential], RG10114/2, 31 January 1951; *F.R.U.S. 1951, Vol. V.* Peurifoy to State Department, [Secret], 781.00/7-3151, 31 July 1951, p.491; *Eleftheria*, 31 October 1952, p.1.
67 *TNA/FO371/78341.* From Norton to Foreign Office, [Secret], 11 January 1949; Markezinis, *Σύγχρονη πολιτική Ιστορία*, vol.2, p.314; US sources suggest many American documents on the 'Papagos solution' remain classified, *F.R.U.S. 1950*, vol.V. Minor to Acheson, 781.00/7-1950 [Top Secret], 19 July 1950, p.382.
68 Markezinis, *Σύγχρονη πολιτική Ιστορία*, vol.2, p.314–85.
69 Ibid. p.333, 314.
70 *TNA/FO371/112832.* Minutes of conversation between Markezinis and Galesworthy, WG10112/8, [Confidential], 13 April 1954; *TNA/FO371/107497.* Galesworthy to May at Foreign Office, WG1041/2, [Confidential], 21 October 1953.
71 *TNA/FO371/78341.* Norton to Foreign Office, [Secret], 11 January 1949; Markezinis, *Σύγχρονη πολιτική Ιστορία*, vol.2, p.314.
72 *TNA/FO371/78341.* Norton to Foreign Office, [Secret], 11 January 1949.
73 Markezinis, *Σύγχρονη πολιτική Ιστορία*, vol.2, p.314.
74 Ibid., p.362–3.
75 *Constantine Karamanlis Archive, vol. I.*, 9 September 1951, subsequent narration by Karamanlis p.145; Seferis notes in his diary entry on 5 May 1952 that former British ambassador Reginald Leeper, after a reception at the Palace, referred to 'terrible hatred between the King and Papagos', George Seferis, *Πολιτικό Ημερολόγιο Β΄. 1945–1947, 1949, 1952*, ed. Alexander Xydis, Athens, Ikaros, 1985, p.130.
76 *General Tsingounis Papers.* 'IDEA, Encyclical Order', 14 July 1949.
77 Karayannis, *Το δράμα*, p.263; Kanellopoulos, *Ιστορικά δοκίμια*, p.26–7; Tsakalotos, *40 Χρόνια Στρατιώτης*, vol.2, p.399.
78 *TNA/FO371/95116.* Norton to Noble at Foreign Office, RG10114/8, [Secret/Personal], 28 February 1951.
79 *Official Minutes of Greek Parliament.* Period 3, Synod 1, 50th Session, 8 June 1953; Markezinis, *Σύγχρονη πολιτική Ιστορία*, vol.2, p.389.
80 Tsakalotos, *40 Χρόνια Στρατιώτης*, vol.2, p.402.
81 *F.R.U.S. 1951, Vol.V.* Peurifoy to Acheson, [Secret] 781.00/ 3-951, 9 March 1951, p.470; Acheson to Peurifoy, 3334, p.371; *TNA/FO371/95116.* Norton to Noble at Foreign Office, RG10114/8, [Secret/Personal], 28 February 1951.
82 *U.S.N.A.* 263: Intelligence Publication Files: CIA, 6924369, ORE 4-50, [Secret] Current Situation in Greece, 28 February 1950.
83 *F.R.U.S. 1950, Vol.V.* Minor to Acheson, 781.00/7-1950 [Top Secret], 19 July 1950, p.382; Acheson to embassy in Greece, 781.00/5-1850, [Secret], 19 August 1950, p.401; *F.R.U.S. 1951, Vol.V.* Yost to State Department, 781.00/1-451 [Confidential], 4 January 1951, p.445–6; Peurifoy to Acheson, [Secret] 781.00/ 3-951, 9 March 1951, p.470. Although US documents do not confirm this, Markezinis claims that

on 18 November 1950 the American Chargé, Harold Minor, told him that Peurifoy favoured 'elections with Papagos' by the spring and maintained that he had secured the King's support for the Marshal. Markezinis never explains why this scenario failed to materialise, *Σύγχρονη πολιτική Ιστορία*, vol.2, p.385–6.
84 *F.R.U.S. 1951, Vol.V.* Acheson to Peurifoy, 781.00/3-951, 21 March 1951, p.471.
85 *F.R.U.S. 1951, Vol.V.* Yost to State Department, 781.00/1-451 [Confidential], 4 January 1951, p.445.
86 *TNA/FO371/95116.* Norton to Noble at Foreign Office, RG10114/8, [Secret/Personal], 28 February 1951; *F.R.U.S. 1951, Vol.V.* Peurifoy to Acheson, [Secret] 781.00/ 3-951, 9 March 1951, p.470.
87 Ibid., p.470.
88 *Sophocles Venizelos Papers.* Papagos to Venizelos, resignation letter, 018-017, 226/18/17, 28 May 1951. The justification used for the resignation 'health reasons'.
89 *F.R.U.S. 1951, Vol.V.* Yost to State Department, [Secret], 781.00/6-151, 1 June 1951, p.475–6; Peurifoy to Acheson, 781/6-451, 4 June 1951, p.475; Peurifoy to State Department, [Secret], 781.00/6-551, 5 June 1951, p.476–8; Peurifoy to State Department, [Secret], 781.00/6-651, 6 June 1951, p.478–9; Peurifoy to State Department, [Secret], 781/6-1151, 11 June 1951, p.481–3.
90 *F.R.U.S. 1951, Vol.V.* Acheson to Athens embassy, [Secret], 781.00/8-22-51, 24 August 1951, p.503.
91 *Constantine Tsatsos Papers.* Conversation with Mr Yost, Unit 3:3, Box 53:1, undated, 2.5-2.9. The text dates the conversation '4 current' and notes Peurifoy's lengthy absence from Greece. *F.R.U.S. 1952–1954, Vol.VIII.* shows that 'Peurifoy was in Washington for one month on consultations beginning the latter part of January', p.782, fn4. This makes 4 February 1952 the most likely date.
92 *F.R.U.S. 1951, Vol.V.* Acheson to embassy in Athens, [Secret], 781.00/5-1251, 17 May 1951, p.474.
93 Ibid., p.474.
94 *F.R.U.S. 1951, Vol.V.* Yost to State Department, [Secret], 781.00/6-151, 1 June 1951, p.476. *Eleftheria*, 20 August 1951, p.1 claimed that the meeting took place on 2 June.
95 *F.R.U.S. 1951, Vol.V.* Yost to State Department, [Secret], 781.00/6-151, 1 June 1951, p.475–6; Peurifoy to Acheson, 781/6-451, 4 June 1951, p.475; Peurifoy to State Department, [Secret], 781.00/6-551, 5 June 1951, p.476–78; Peurifoy to State Department, [Secret], 781.00/6-651, 6 June 1951, p.478–9; Acheson to Athens embassy [Secret], 781.00/7-651, 8 June 1951, p.480; Peurifoy to State Department, [Secret], 781/6-1151, 11 June 1951, p.481–3; Yost to Rountree, 781.00/6-1151, 11 June 1951, p.283; Acheson to Athens embassy [Secret], 781.00/6-2551, 25 June 1951, p.283–5.
96 *F.R.U.S. 1951, Vol.V.* Peurifoy to State Department, [Secret], 781.00/6-651, 6 June 1951, p.479.
97 *F.R.U.S. 1951, Vol.V.* Peurifoy to State Department, [Secret], 781.00/8-2451, 24 August 1951, p.499–500.
98 *Eleftheria* 22 August 1951, p.1, 5; negative references to other unnamed US officials, *Eleftheria*, 28 August 1951, p.1, 30 August 1951, p.1, 5; response to the US embassy statement, *Elefhteria*, 30 August 1951, p.1.
99 *TNA/FO371/95117.* Norton to Foreign Office, [Confidential], RG10114/20, 31 July 1951 or *TNA/FO371/95117.* Norton to Foreign Office, [Confidential], RG10114/21, 1 August 1951; *F.R.U.S. 1951, Vol.V.* Peurifoy to State Department, [Secret], 781.00/7-3151, 31 July 1951, 491.

100 F.R.U.S. 1951, vol.V. Peurifoy to State Department, [Secret], 781.00/7-3151, 31 July 1951, p.490-91.
101 F.R.U.S. 1951, vol. V. Peurifoy to State Department, [Secret], 781.00/8-151, 1 August 1951, p.492-3.
102 F.R.U.S. 1951, vol. V. Peurifoy to State Department, [Secret], 781.00/9-1551, 15 September 1951, p.509; Ibid., ftn2, p.509.
103 *Sophocles Venizelos Papers*. Paul to Papagos, 226/24/118, 27 September 1951; Papagos to Paul, 226/24/118, 28 September 1951; Press release publicizing the letters, 226/24/119; Meynaud, Jean, *Les forces politiques en Grèce*, [avec le concours de P. Merlopoulos et G. Notaras], Lausanne, Études de science politique, 1965, p.87.
104 *Constantine Tsatsos Papers*. Conversation with Mr Yost, Unit 3:3, Box 53:1, undated, 2.5-2.9. Most likely date of conversation is 4 February 1952.
105 F.R.U.S. 1952–1954, vol.VIII. Yost to State Department, 781.00/2-752, [Secret], 7 February 1952, p.780; Athens to State Department, 781.00/2-752, 8 February 1952, p.781, fn1.
106 F.R.U.S. 1952–1954, vol.VIII. Acheson to Berry, [Secret], lot 65D 238, 'Memoranda from S&U, 1952', 23 February 1952, p.782.
107 F.R.U.S. 1952–1954, vol.VIII. Conversation between Acheson, Venizelos, Melas and Dorsz, 781.00-2352, [Secret], 23 February 1952, p.785.
108 Translated from *Eleftheria*, 14 March 1952, p.1.
109 TNA/FO371/107479. Report on the Internal Political Situation in Greece during 1952 [Confidential], WG1011/3, 4 February 1953.
110 F.R.U.S. 1952–1954, vol.VIII. Peurifoy to State Department [Secret], 781.00/3-1752, 17 March 1952, p.789.
111 Coufoudakis, 'The United States, the United Nations', p.293; Mouzelis, *Politics in Semi-Periphery*, p.135-6; Tsoucalas, *Greek Tragedy*, p.125; Paraskevopoulos, *Φιλελεύθερα ανοίγματα*, p.183-6; Stefanidis, *Από τον Εμφύλιο*, p.156; Iatrides, 'The United States and Greece in the Twentieth Century', p.83; Pelt, *Tying Greece*, p.91; Michalis Psalidopoulos, *Επιτηρητές σε απόγνωση. Αμερικανοί σύμβουλοι στην Ελλάδα, 1947–53. Από τον Paul A. Porter στον Edward A. Tenenbaum*, Athens, Metamesonykties Ekdoseis, 2013, p.60, 125.
112 TNA/FO371/101803. Galesworthy to Barnes at Foreign Office, [Confidential], WG/10114/3, 17 September 1952.
113 TNA/FO371/107479. Report on the Internal Political Situation in Greece during 1952, [Confidential], WG/1011/3, 4 February 1953.
114 Nikolakopoulos, *Η καχεκτική δημοκρατία*, p.133.
115 Meynaud, *Les forces politiques*, p.85.
116 TNA/FO371/10803. Galesworthy to Barnes at Foreign Office, [Confidential], WG/10114/2, 10 September 1952.
117 TNA/FO371/101803. Galesworthy to Barnes at Foreign Office, [Confidential], WG/10114/4, 8 October 1952.
118 Nikolakopoulos, *Η καχεκτική δημοκρατία*, p.160.
119 Tsoucalas, *Greek Tragedy*, p.125; Papaskevopoulos, *Φιλελεύθερα ανοίγματα*, p.183; Papandreou, *Democracy at Gunpoint*, p.90; Mouzelis, *Politics in Semi-Periphery*, p.135-6.
120 Linardatos, *Από τον Εμφύλιο*, vol.1, p.516; reproduced by Grigoriadis, *Μετά τον Εμφύλιο*, p.95.
121 F.R.U.S. 1952–1954, vol.VIII. Peurifoy to State Department, 881.00/8-2752, [Top Secret], 27 August 1952, p.806.

122 Nikolakopoulos, *Η καχεκτική δημοκρατία*, p.160, 139.
123 *TNA/FO371/10803*. Galesworthy to Barnes at Foreign Office, [Confidential], WG/10114/4, 8 October 1952.
124 Markezinis, *Σύγχρονη πολιτική Ιστορία*, vol.2, p.373-4, 383.
125 'Ο typos', *Eleftheria*, 17 August 1951, p.1; 'Ai efimerides', *Eleftheria*, 22 August 1951, p.1; The eight newspapers were: *Acropolis, Ethnos, Ethnikos Kiryx, Kathimerini, Embros, Estia, Ta Nea, To Vima*. The first four responded to *Eleftheria*'s call, while *Embros* ran a related front-page article on 23 August 1951, titled 'The Marshal's Hour', p.1.
126 Linardatos, *Από τον Εμφύλιο*, vol.1, p.445, 494; Stefanidis, *Από τον Εμφύλιο*, p.177.
127 *F.R.U.S. 1952-1954, Vol.VIII*. Peurifoy to State Department, 781.00/8-2752, [Top Secret], 27 August 1952, p.806.
128 *Kathimerini*, 21 May 1952, p.6; 22 May 1952, p.6; *Eleftheria*, 21 May 1952, p.1; 22 May 1952, p.1, 4; Linardatos, *Από τον Εμφύλιο*, vol.1, p.482.
129 *Embros*, 1 August 1952, p.4; *Eleftheria*, 1 August 1952, p.1; Linardatos, *Από τον Εμφύλιο*, vol.1, p.487.
130 *Embros*, 1 August 1952, p.4.
131 *Kathimerini*, 12 August 1952, p.1; 13 August 1952, p.1; *Eleftheria*, 12 August 1952, p.1; 13 August 1952, p.1; Linardatos, *Από τον Εμφύλιο*, vol.1, p.488-9.
132 *Kathimerini*, 23 August 1952, p.1; *Eleftheria*, 23 August 1952, p.1, 4.
133 Dafnis, *Σοφοκλής Ελευθερίου Βενιζέλος*, p.508-9.
134 Quoted in *Kathimerini*, 30 September 1952, p.1; see also Linardatos, *Από τον Εμφύλιο*, vol.1, p.488-9; *Embros*, 28 September 1952, p.6; 30 September 1952, p.1, 6; *Eleftheria*, 30 September 1952, p.6.
135 Nikolaos Plastiras, 'Το Ε.Α.Μ. και το Έθνος', *Eleftheria*, 30 September 1952, p.1.
136 *Eleftheria*, 22 May 1952, p.1, 4; 24 August 1952, p.1; Stavros Nikolaidis, 'Περί αποστατών', *Eleftheria*, 22 October 1952, p.1; Andreas Birakis, 'Ο λαός της Β. Ελλάδος και οι 24 αποστάται', *Eleftheria*, 23 October 1952, p.1.
137 *Embros*, 22 October 1952, p.1, 4.
138 Charles Yost, *History and Memory*, New York, Norton, 1980, p.228-9.
139 *F.R.U.S. 1952-1954, Vol. VIII*. Byroade to Acheson, [Top Secret], 881.10/7-1952, 28 July 1952, p.799-800; Acheson to Athens embassy, [Top Secret], 881.00/7-2852, 29 July 1952, p.801-2.
140 *F.R.U.S. 1952-1954, Vol. VIII*. 881.00/7-2852, 28 July 1952, p.801, fn3; Peurifoy to State Department [Top Secret], 781.5 MSP/8-752, 7 August 1952, p.802; Peurifoy to State Department [Top Secret], 881.00/8-2752, 27 August 1952, p.804. Initially Papagos requested elections 'within 30-60 days', but then accepted Peurifoy's plan of elections within six months.
141 This view is expressed in passing in Charalambis, *Στρατός και πολιτική εξουσία*, p.58.
142 *Kathimerini*, 'Alexander Clifford "Papagos could be the man Greece needs"', reprint from *The Daily Mail*, 8 September 1951, p.1.
143 Max Weber, *Economy and Society: An Outline of Interpretive Sociology*, Second Edition, vol.1, ed. Guenther Roth and Claus Wittich, Berkley, University of California Press, 1978, p.241, 246, 1130; Mouzelis, *Politics in the Semi-Periphery*, p.88-94; Paul Taggart, 'Populism and the Pathology of Representative Politics', in Yves Mény and Yves Surel (eds), *Democracies and the Populist Challenge*, Basingstoke, Palgrave Macmillan, 2002, p.67; Kurt Weyland, 'Clarifying a Contested Concept: Populism in the Study of Latin American Politics', *Comparative Politics*, 34:1, p.1-22; cf Cas Mudde and Cristobal Rovira Kaltwasser, *Populism: A Very Short*

Introduction, Oxford, New York, Oxford University Press, 2017, p.5–6; Jan-Werner Müller, *What Is Populism?*, London, Penguin, 2017, p.33.

144 Margaret Canovan, *Populism*, London, Junction, 1981, p.183; Mouzelis, *Politics in the Semi-Periphery*, p.89–91; Francisco Panizza, 'Introduction', in Francisco Panizza (ed.), *Populism and the Mirror of Democracy*, London, Verso, 2005, p.29; Kurt Weyland, 'Neoliberal Populism in Latin America and Eastern Europe', *Comparative Politics*, 1999, 31:4, p. 380.

145 Laclau, 'Populism: What's in a Name?', p.39, 43; id. *Politics and Ideology in Marxist Theory: Capitalism, Fascism, Populism*, London, New Left Books, 1977, p.172–5; Roxborough, *Theories of Underdevelopment*, p.108.

146 Ernesto Laclau, *On Populist Reason*, London, Verso, 2018 [2005], p.48, 118–19; Ben Stanley, 'The Thin Ideology of Populism', *Journal of Political Ideologies*, 13:1, February 2008, p.95–110; Daniel Albertazzi and Duncan McDonell, 'Introduction: The Spectre and the Spectre', in Daniel Albertazzi and Duncan McDonell (eds), *Twenty-first Century Populism*, Palgrave New York, Macmillan, 2007, p. 3; Koen Abts and Stefan Rummens, 'Populism versus Democracy', *Political Studies*, 55:2, 2007, p. 420; Yves Mény and Yves Surel, 'The Constitutive Ambiguity of Populism', in Yves Mény and Yves Surel (eds), *Democracies and the Populist Challenge*, p.6; Denis Westlind, *The Politics of Popular Identity: Understanding Recent Populist Movements in Sweden and the United States*, Lund, Lund University Press, 1996, p.54; Peter Wiles, 'A Syndrome, Not a Doctrine: Some Elementary Theses on Populism', in Ghiţa Ionescu and Ernest Gellner (eds), *Populism: Its Meanings and National Characteristics*, London, Weidenfeld and Nicholson, 1969, p. 167; cf Margaret Canovan, 'Taking Politics to the People: Populism as the Ideology of Democracy', in Yves Mény and Yves Surel (eds), *Democracies and the Populist Challenge*, p.33–8.

147 *Kathimerini*, 31 July 1951, p.1; *Embros*, 31 July 1951, p.1; *Eleftheria*, 31 July 1951, p.1; *TNA/FO371/101793*. Annual Report on Greece for 1951; *TNA/FO371/95117*. Norton to Foreign Office, [Confidential], RG10114/21, 1 August 1951.

148 *Kathimerini*, 7 August 1951, p.1; *Eleftheria*, 7 August 1951, p.1.

149 *Eleftheria*, 2 August 1951, p.1.

150 *Eleftheria*, 28 August 1952, p.1 and 5 September 1952, p.1.

151 *Embros*, 8 August 1951, p.4.

152 LEK was formed after the 1950 elections, out of the merger of Kanellopoulos's National Regeneration Party and Stefanopoulos's splinter group from the Popular Party. In the elections of 1950, Kanellopoulos's party received 5.3 per cent of the vote and Markezinis's New Party 2.5 per cent (see Table 1).

153 *Constantine Karamanlis Archive, vol. I*. 16 November 1950, p.138.

154 *TNA/FO371/95117*. Norton to Foreign Office, [Confidential], RG10114/20, 31 July 1951; *TNA/FO371/101803*. Peake to Eden, [Confidential], WG10114/9, 2 December 1952.

155 *U.S.N.A. 263*: Intelligence Publication Files: CIA, 6924369, ORE 4-50, [Secret] Current Situation in Greece, 28 February 1950.

156 Markezinis, *Σύγχρονη πολιτική Ιστορία*, vol.2, p.400–1.

157 *Eleftheria*, 30 July 1952, p.1.

158 *TNA/FO371/101803*. Peake to Eden, [Confidential], WG10114/9, 2 December 1952.

159 Takis Papagiannopoulos, *Στρατάρχης Αλέξανδρος Παπάγος. Ο εκλεκτός της Ιστορίας*, Athens, 1987, p.477–9; *Embros*, 4 September 1951, p.3; photographs from *Embros*, 9 November 1952, p.1; 13 November 1952, p.1; G.A. Vlachos, 'Όλοι μαζί του', *Kathimerini*, 9 September 1951, p.1.

160 *Eleftheria*, 30 July 1952, p.1; 28 September 1952, p.1.
161 *F.R.U.S. 1951, Vol. V.* Peurifoy to State Department, [Secret], 781.00/9-1551, 15 September 1951, p.509.
162 Mouzelis, *Politics in Semi-Periphery*, p.136.
163 *Eleftheria*, 20 November 1952, p.1.
164 Nikolakopoulos, *Η καχεκτική δημοκρατία*, p.185; *Kathimerini*, 11 April 1954, p.1; Markezinis, *Σύγχρονη πολιτική Ιστορία*, vol.3, p.56-7.
165 Markezinis, *Σύγχρονη πολιτική Ιστορία*, vol.2, p.400-1.
166 *TNA/FO371/101803*. Peake to Eden, [Confidential] WG10114/9 2 December 1952.
167 *Eleftheria*, 'Αι περιοδίαι του κ. Παπάγου', 30 July 1952, p.1; *Sophocles Venizelos Papers*. Speech to Parliament, 022-014, 226/22/14, dated '1952'.
168 *Official Minutes of Greek Parliament*. Speech by Papagos on Rally's first year in government, 27 November 1953, Period 3, Synod 2, 9th Session, p.84.
169 Canovan, *Populism*, p.294.
170 *Kathimerini*, 26 August 1952, p.1; *Eleftheria*, 26 August 1952, p.1; 27 August 1952, p.1; 5 September 1952, p.1.
171 *Eleftheria*, 30 July 1952, p.1.
172 *TNA/FO371/101803*. Peake to Eden, [Confidential], WG10114/9, 2 December 1952.
173 *Kathimerini*, 11 November 1952, p.1.
174 *Embros*, 13 November 1952, p.6.
175 *Embros*, 4 September 1951, p.3; 22 January 1952, p.3; 22 June 1952, p.1; 13 November 1952, p.6; 8 September 1951, p.1; 1 August 1951, p.4; 13 September 1951, p.6.
176 Legg, *Politics in Modern Greece*, p.148, Table 6.7.
177 *Kathimerini*, 7 August 1951, p.1; *Eleftheria*, 30 July 1952, p.1; 2 August 1951, p.1.
178 *Embros*, 12 August 1951, p.1; *Kathimerini*, 12 August 1951, p.1.
179 *Embros*, 4 September 1951, p.3.
180 Alivizatos, '"Έθνος" κατά "λαού"', p.81; Tsoukalas, 'The Ideological Impact', p.330.
181 *Embros*, 4 September 1951, p.3.
182 *Official Minutes of Greek Parliament*. Speech by Papagos, Period 3, Synod 2, 9th Session, 27 November 1953, p.84.
183 Papagos's speech in Athens, *Embros*, 4 September 1951, p.3.
184 *Embros*, 13 November 1952, p.6; Papagos interview in *Kathimerini*, 18 November 1951, p.1; *Eleftheria*, 30 July 1952, p.1.
185 *Official Minutes of Greek Parliament*. Speech by Papagos, Period 3, Synod 2, 9th Session, 27 November 1953, p.85.
186 Alexander Papagos, 'Η μόνη φιλοδοξία', *Kathimerini*, 2 September 1951, p.1.
187 *Eleftheria*, 7 November 1952, p.1.
188 *Embros*, 13 November 1952, p. 6.
189 Francisco Panizza, *Populism and the Mirror of Democracy*, London, Verso, 2005, p.9.
190 Laclau, *On Populist Reason*, p.180.
191 *Speeches delivered by H.M. the King of the Hellenes during the State Visit to U.S.A., 28 October-3 December 1953*, Athens, Greek National Institute, 1954, p.1-73; Queen Frederica, *A Measure of Understanding*, London, Macmillan, 1971, 159-81; Markezinis, *Σύγχρονη πολιτική Ιστορία*, vol.3, p.36-8; On the European tour of the royals in September-October 1953, see *Eleftheria*, 20 September 1953, p.6; on the Aegean cruise of the European royals, see *Eleftheria*, 22 August 1954, p.1, 8, 24 August 1954, p.1, 6.
192 *Eleftheria*, 22 October 1952, p.1.
193 *TNA/FO371/101803*. Peake to Eden, [Confidential], WG10114/9, 2 December 1952.

194 F.R.U.S. 1951, Vol. V. Peurifoy to State Department [Secret], 781.00/8-151, 1 August 1951, p.492-3.
195 TNA/FO371/95116. Norton to Noble at Foreign Office, RG10114/2 [Confidential], 31 January 1951.
196 TNA/FO371/101803. Peake to Eden, [Confidential], WG10114/9, 2 December 1952.
197 F.R.U.S. 1951, Vol. V. Acheson to Athens embassy, [Secret], 781.00/8-22-51, 24 August 1951, p.503.

Chapter 4

1 Iatrides, 'American Attitudes'; id., 'The United States and Greece in the Twentieth Century', p.83-4; Couloumbis and Iatrides (eds), *Greek-American Relations*, p.69, 196; John Iatrides, 'Greece and the United States: The Strained Partnership', in Clogg (ed) *Greece in the 1980s*, p.162; Linardatos, Από τον Εμφύλιο, vol.2, p.121-8; Vournas, Ιστορία της σύγχρονης Ελλάδας, p.8; Tsoucalas, *Greek Tragedy*, p.153-5; Papandreou, *Democracy at Gunpoint*, p.88-92; from a different perspective, see Stefanidis, *Isle of Discord*, p.260.
2 Charalambis, Στρατός και πολιτική εξουσία, p.44; Vournas, Ιστορία της σύγχρονης Ελλάδας, p.15-24; Tsoucalas, *Greek Tragedy*, p.142; Tayfur, *Semiperipheral Development*, p.52-3.
3 Iatrides, *Balkan Triangle*, p.3, 161; Theodore Couloumbis, 'Book Review of John Iatrides, Balkan Triangle', *Balkan Studies*, 10:1, 1969, p.198-202.
4 Tsoucalas, *Greek Tragedy*, p.156.
5 Grigoriadis, Μετά τον Εμφύλιο, p.174, italics added.
6 Charalambis, Στρατός και πολιτική εξουσία, p.44.
7 Tsoucalas, *Greek Tragedy*, p.157.
8 Vournas, Ιστορία της σύγχρονης Ελλάδας, p.65.
9 Linardatos, Από τον Εμφύλιο, vol.2, p.193.
10 Svolopoulos, Η ελληνική εξωτερική πολιτική, 1945-1981, p.81-2.
11 Michalopoulos, Ελλάδα και Τουρκία, p.40-1.
12 Svolopoulos, Ελληνική εξωτερική πολιτική, vol.2, p.81-2.
13 Hatzivassiliou, Στρατηγικές του Κυπριακού, p.16, 21-4, 28, 116, 194.
14 Svolopoulos, Ελληνική εξωτερική πολιτική, vol.2, p.81-2.
15 TNA/FO371/101808. Conversation between Peake and Papagos, WG 1052/9, 25 November 1952.
16 Kanellopoulos, Ιστορικά δοκίμια, p.25-6; cf Tsakalotos, 40 Χρόνια Στρατιώτης, vol.2, p.417-18.
17 F.R.U.S. 1952-1954, Vol. VIII. Webb to Athens embassy, [Secret], 781.00/8-2851, 7 September 1951, p.505-6.
18 F.R.U.S. 1951, Vol. V. Yost to State Department, [Secret], 781.00/6-151, 1 June 1951, p.475.
19 *Official Minutes of the Greek Parliament*, Question by Constantine Mitsotakis, Period 3, Synod 2, Session 9, 8 June 1953, p.646-50; Kanellopoulos, Ιστορικά δοκίμια, p.25-6; *General Tsingounis Papers (ELIA)*. The archive contains classified IDEA

documents suggesting close links between General Tsingounis and the organisation; Charalambis, *Στρατός και πολιτική εξουσία*, p.41-2.
20. F.R.U.S. *1951, Vol. V.* Yost to State Department, [Secret], 781.00/6-151, 1 June 1951, p.475; Tsakalotos, *40 Χρόνια Στρατιώτης*, vol.2, p.441.
21. F.R.U.S. *1951, Vol. V.* Peurifoy to State Department, [Secret], 781.00/8-2251, 22 August 1951, p.498, fn.2; Tsakalotos's memorandum was dated 4 August 1951, but was released later, *Eleftheria*, 21 August 1951, p.1, 4; 23 August 1951, p.4; F.R.U.S. *1951, Vol. V.* Peurifoy to State Department, [Secret], 781.00/8-2451, 24 August 1951, p.499-500; Peurifoy to JUSMAG Chief Frederick, [Top Secret], Lot 59, F: 48, 24 August 1951, p.501-2; Peurifoy to State Department, [Secret], 781.00/8-2851, 28 August 1951, p.504; Tsakalotos, *40 Χρόνια Στρατιώτης*, vol.2, p.409-18, 443.
22. F.R.U.S. *1951, Vol. V.* Peurifoy to State Department, [Secret], 781.00/8-2851, 28 August 1951, p.504; Acting Secretary Webb to Athens, [Secret], 781.00/8-2851, 7 September 1951, p.505-6.
23. F.R.U.S. *1952-1954, Vol. VIII.* Yost to State Department, [Top Secret], 781.00/11-1952, 26 August 1953, p.810-11.
24. F.R.U.S. *1952-1954, Vol. VIII.* Memorandum of conversation between Eisenhower, Markezinis, Politis, Jernegan, [Secret], 781.13/5-753, 7 May 1953, p.824-25; in dispatch 781.13/4-1853 Yost informed the State Department of the contents of Papagos' letter to Eisenhower, 18 April 1953, p.822, fn2.
25. Ibid., p.824.
26. F.R.U.S. *1952-1954, Vol. VIII.* Peurifoy to State Department [Secret], 611.81/4-1053, 10 April 1953, p.817.
27. Ibid., p.817.
28. F.R.U.S. *1952-1954, Vol. VIII.* Aide-Memoire by the Chief of MSA Porter to State Department. Transmitted to Markezinis, [Confidential], 881.00/5-1553, 15 May 1953, p.831-2.
29. *Eisenhower Library Documents.* The President's Appointments, Thursday 7 May 1953, 11:30-12:15. Courtesy call, arranged by the Secretary of State. Present: Markezinis, Politis, Byroade. Markezinis presented an antique helmet, supposedly worn by a Greek general at Olympia, a Greek vase, and a necklace of old Greek coins for Mrs Eisenhower.
30. F.R.U.S. *1952-1954, Vol. VIII*, Letter from Eisenhower to Papagos, Athens embassy Files, lot 59 F 48, 53, 5 June 1953, p.839-40; Memorandum of Conversation between Eisenhower, Markezinis, Politis and Byroade, [Secret], 781.13/5-753, 7 May 1953, p.824-5.
31. Tayfur, *Semiperipheral Development*, p.52; Tsoucalas, *Greek Tragedy*, p.155; Vournas, *Ιστορία της σύγχρονης Ελλάδας*, p.17.
32. *Official Minutes of the Greek Parliament.* Speech by Minister Markezinis, Period 3, Synod 2, Session 5, 23 November 1953, p.23.
33. Ibid. Speech by Prime Minister Papagos, 27 November 1953, Period 3, Synod 2, Session 5, p.85.
34. Linardatos, *Από τον Εμφύλιο στη Χούντα*, vol.2, p.123; Svolopoulos, *Ελληνική εξωτερική πολιτική*, vol.2, p.36; Sofianos Chrysostomidis, 'Ελληνοαμερικανικές σχέσεις: Από το δόγμα Τρούμαν και τη ρητορεία του ΠΑΣΟΚ στα σημερινά δεδομένα', *Η Ελλάδα σε Κρίση*, vol.2, Athens, Roes, 1987, p.285-6.

35 F.R.U.S. 1952–1954, Vol. VIII. Memorandum of Conversation between Eisenhower, Markezinis, Politis and Byroade, [Secret], 781.13/5-753, 7 May 1953, p.824–5.
36 Ibid., p.825.
37 F.R.U.S. 1952–1954, Vol. VIII. Memorandum of discussion at the 148th NSC Meeting, [Top Secret – Eyes Only], Eisenhower Papers: Whiteman File: 445, 4 June 1953, p.837–8.
38 F.R.U.S. 1952–1954, Vol. VIII. Letter from Eisenhower to Papagos, Athens embassy Files, lot 59 F 48, 53, 5 June 1953, p.839–40.
39 F.R.U.S. 1952–1954, Vol. VIII. Dulles to Athens, [Top Secret], 711.56381/8-1453, 28 August 1953, p.846–8.
40 Department of State Bulletin, 29:745, 21 December 1953, p.863–4; Svolopoulos, Ελληνική εξωτερική πολιτική, vol.2, p.37.
41 F.R.U.S. 1952–1954, Vol. VIII. Yost to State Department, [Top Secret], 711.56381/8-1453, 14 August 1953, p.842–43.
42 F.R.U.S. 1952–1954, Vol. VIII. Acting Secretary Smith to Athens, [Secret], 711.56381/8-3153, 18 September 1953, p.848–50.
43 F.R.U.S. 1952–1954, Vol. VIII. Memorandum of conversation between Cannon, Papagos, and Schnee, [Secret], 711.56381/-2453, 24 September 1953, p.850–2.
44 Sofianos Chrysostomides, Avgi, 3–4 March 1983; Vournas, Ιστορία της σύγχρονης Ελλάδας, p.32–5. The debate took place on 25 November 1953, but the Secret Annexes of the Treaty did not go through Parliament.
45 F.R.U.S. 1952–1954, Vol. VIII. Memorandum of conversation between Cannon, Papagos, and Schnee, [Secret], 711.56381/-2453, 24 September 1953, p.850–2.
46 TNA/FO371/107495, Peake to Cheetham at Foreign Office, [Confidential], WG10345/1, 4 June 1953.
47 F.R.U.S. 1952–1954, Vol. VIII. Conversation between Dulles, Stassen and Papagos, [Secret], 611.81/5-2853, 28 May 1953, p.835–6.
48 Mohamed Hassanein Heikal, Milaffat Al-Suways: Harb al-thalathīn sana, Third Edition, Cairo, Al-Ahram, 1996, p.240–69; Reem Aboul Fadl, 'Neutralism Made Positive: Egyptian Anti-colonialism on the Road to Bandung', British Journal of Middle Eastern Studies, 42:2, 2015, p.224–5.
49 F.R.U.S. 1952–1954, Vol. VIII. Conversation between Dulles, Stassen and Papagos, [Secret], 611.81/5-2853, 28 May 1953, p.835.
50 TNA/FO371/107505. Chancery in Washington to Foreign Office, [Confidential], WG1102/1, 15 May 1953.
51 TNA/FO371/107497. Peake to Cheetham at Foreign Office, [Confidential], WG1041/3, 29 October 1953.
52 F.R.U.S. 1952–1954, Vol. VIII, Yost to State Department, [Top Secret], 711.56381/8-1453, 14 August 1953, p.843.
53 F.R.U.S. 1952–1954, Vol. VIII, Yost to State Department, [Secret], 711.56381/8-2253, 22 August 1953, p.845–6.
54 F.R.U.S. 1952–1954, Vol. VIII. Yost to State Department, [Top Secret], 747C.00/8-2653, 26 August 1953, p.676–7.
55 Ibid., p.676.
56 F.R.U.S. 1952–1954, Vol. VIII. Dulles to Athens embassy, [Top Secret], 747C.00/8-2853, 28 August 1953, p.677–8.
57 F.R.U.S. 1952–1954, Vol. VIII. Yost to State Department, [Top Secret], 747C.00/9-253, 2 September 1953, p.678, 678, fn3.

58 *Time Magazine*, 'The U.S. and Britain: Allies Undermine Each Other to Foe's Benefit', 16 November 1953.
59 *TNA/FO371/112858*. Cyprus: Its History and Administration, Foreign Office Research Department, May 1950.
60 Lawrence Durrell, *Bitter Lemons of Cyprus*, London, Faber and Faber, 1957, p.189.
61 Thomas Anthem, 'The Cyprus Challenge', *Contemporary Review*, 186, July–December 1954, p.19.
62 Nicos Kranidiotis, *Δύσκολα χρόνια, 1950–1960*, Athens, Estia, 1981, p.44–51.
63 Vlachos, *Δέκα χρόνια Κυπριακού*, p.24.
64 Averoff-Tositsas, *Ιστορία χαμένων ευκαιριών*, vol.1, p.19; Michalopoulos, *Ελλάδα και Τουρκία*, p.19; Andreas Makridis (ed.), *Εθνικιστικά κείμενα του ΑΚΕΛ*, Nicosia, Aegeon, 2010, p.29–53.
65 Stanley Mayes, *Makarios: A Biography*, London, Macmillan, 1981, p.26, 39–40, 42–4; Nancy Crawshaw, *The Cyprus Revolt: An Account of the Struggle for Union with Greece*, London, Allen & Unwin, 1978, p.51; Kranidiotis, *Δύσκολα χρόνια*, p.44–51; cf Vlachos, *Δέκα χρόνια Κυπριακού*, p.39.
66 Georgios Grivas-Digenis, *Απομνημονεύματα ΕΟΚΑ 1955–1959*, Athens, 1961, p.6–15; George Grivas-Dighenis, *The Memoirs of General Grivas*, ed. Charles Foley, London, Longman, 1964, p.12–18.
67 *TNA/FO371/112858*. Wilding to Evans, WG1081/459 [Restricted], 21 September 1954; Memorandum by Headlam-Morley and Childs on Cyprus, [Confidential], C19108/19, p.17.
68 *TNA/FO371/112864*. Foreign Office to UN Delegation, [Confidential], WG1081/649, 24 September 1954; Xydis, *Cyprus*, p.6; Leontios Ierodiakonou, *Το Κυπριακό Πρόβλημα: Πορεία πρός τήν Χρεωκοπία*, Athens, Papazissis, 1970, p.29–30.
69 Robert Holland, *Britain and the Revolt in Cyprus*, Oxford, Clarendon Press, 1998, p.21.
70 *Official Minutes of the Greek Parliament*, Period 5, Synod 1, Session 30, 13 December 1958, p.336.
71 Vlachos, *Δέκα χρόνια Κυπριακού*, p.31–2; Michalopoulos, *Ελλάδα και Τουρκία*, p.30; *Eleftheria*, 20 May 1950, p.4.
72 Quoted in Kranidiotis, *Δύσκολα χρόνια*, p.42.
73 Holland, *Britain and the Revolt*, p.24; Michalopoulos, *Ελλάδα και Τουρκία*, p.31; Stefanidis, *Isle of Discord*, p.12–13; Vlachos, *Δέκα χρόνια Κυπριακού*, p.31, *Eleftheria*, 14 June 1950, p.6.
74 *Eleftheria*, 14 June 1950, p.4.
75 Kranidiotis, *Δύσκολα χρόνια*, p.43; Michalopoulos, *Ελλάδα και Τουρκία*, p.37.
76 All-Party Leaders' Decision on Cyprus, Official Press *Communiqué*, Political Directorate II, 21 March 1951; *Kathimerini*, 22 March 1951, p.4; *Eleftheria*, 22 March 1951, p.4.
77 Vlachos, *Δέκα χρόνια Κυπριακού*, p.34.
78 *Sophocles Venizelos Papers*. Handwritten notation by Venizelos on Cyprus question, 226/11/258, undated, referring to developments in March-May 1951.
79 *Sophocles Venizelos Papers*. Record of Conversation between Averoff and Peake, drafted by Averoff, 226/24/141-2, 8 November 1951; Report by Averoff on the Cyprus question, 226/25/1, 22 November 1951.
80 *TNA/FO800/796*. Eden's Private Papers, Greece 1951–1955: Record of conversation between Eden and Averoff, 29 November 1951, Gr/51/2, 168 (b) Cyprus, p.21–2; Averoff-Tosistas, *Ιστορία χαμένων ευκαιριών*, p.19.

81 G.M.F.A. Note on Cyprus Question, Political Directorate II, [Top Secret], 24 March 1952.
82 *TNA/FO371/95108*. From Athens embassy to Foreign Office, RG1013/26, [Confidential], 28 November 1951.
83 Ibid.
84 G.M.F.A. Cyprus Question: Synopsis of Recommended Measures, [Fully Secret], 27 March 1952.
85 Ibid.
86 G.M.F.A. Note on Cyprus Question, Political Directorate II, [Top Secret], 24 March 1952.
87 G.M.F.A. Possibilities of a Recourse to the UN over the Cyprus Question, Political Directorate II, [Top Secret], by E. Lagakos, 11 April 1952; G.M.F.A. Report by Alexis Kyrou [Top Secret], 8 May 1951, quoted in Lagakos's report supra.
88 Kyrou, *Ελληνική εξωτερική πολιτική*, p.272.
89 *Kathimerini*, 18 June 1950, p.1; *Eleftheria*, 18 June 1950, p.1.
90 *TNA/FO371/87692*. Bernard in Washington to Bart at Foreign Office, [Confidential], RG 12645/1, 15 May 1950; Adamandia Polis, 'U.S. Intervention in Greek Trade Unions 1947–1950', in Iatrides (ed.), *Greece in the 1940s*, p.259–74; Katsanevas, *Το σύγχρονο συνδικαλιστικό κίνημα*. p.22–3, 31.
91 *General Tsingounis Papers*. PEEK Executive Committee Membership List.
92 Vlachos, *Δέκα χρόνια Κυπριακού*, p.34; Stefanidis, *Isle of Discord*, p.15, 28, 30, 74, 95.
93 *Kathimerini*, 22 July 1950, p.1; *Eleftheria*, 22 July 1950, p.1, 3; quoted in Vlachos, *Δέκα χρόνια Κυπριακού*, p. 34.
94 *General Tsingounis Papers (ELIA)*. Panhellenic Committee of Union with Cyprus: Executive Committee Membership List.
95 *General Tsingounis Papers (ELIA)*. Action Plan of PEEK, [later PEAEK], in Four Sections.
96 Sotiris Rizas, *Η Ελληνική πολιτική μετά τον Εμφύλιο Πόλεμο: Κοινοβουλευτισμός και Δικτατορία*, Athens, Kastaniotis, 2008, p.300.
97 *TNA/FO371/112846*, WG1081/13, handwritten notation by R.W.L. Wilding, 11 May 1954; *F.R.U.S. 1952–1954, Vol. VIII*. Memorandum of Conversation between Baxter, Byroade and the Turkish Ambassador in Washington Erkin, [Secret], 747C.00/3-1054, 10 March 1954, p.682.
98 *Eleftheria*, 9 May 1952, p.1, 3.
99 Ioannis Stefanidis, 'Pressure Groups and Greek Foreign Policy, 1945–67', *Hellenic Observatory, LSE*, December 2001, p.19, 26.
100 *Eleftheria*, 24 November 1951, p.1, 4; Linardatos, *Από τον Εμφύλιο*, vol.1, p.358–9; see also *Eleftehria*, 21 July 1950, p.1; on the views of the King, see Sulzberger, *Long Row*, p.1009.
101 *Kathimerini*, 20 August 1954, p.1; *Embros*, 20 August 1954, p.1.
102 *Kathimerini*, 22 September 1953, p.1; *Embros*, 22 September 1953, p.1, 3; Quote from *Eleftheria*, 22 September 1953, p.1.
103 Antony Eden, *Full Circle. Memoirs*, Book 2, London, Cassell, 1960, p.395.
104 *TNA/FO800/796*. Eden's Private Papers, Greece 1951–1955: Record of conversation between Eden and Averoff, 29 November 1951, Gr/51/2, 168 (b) Cyprus, p.22, emphasis added.
105 *TNA/FO371/101808*. Peake to Foreign Office: Conversation with Marshal Papagos, 25 November 1952, italics added.

106 *TNA/FO371/107498*. Main Brief for Visit of the Secretary of State to Greece, [Secret], WG1074, 3 April 1953.
107 On an earlier statement of US views on Cyprus see *F.R.U.S. 1950, Vol.V.* Acheson to Athens embassy, [Secret], 781.00/6-2450, 27 June 1950, p.378.
108 *F.R.U.S. 1952-1954, Vol. VIII*. Acheson to Athens embassy, [Secret], 747C.00/7-1852, 18 July 1952, p.674.
109 *F.R.U.S. 1952-1954, Vol. VIII*. Dulles to Athens embassy, [Top Secret], 747C.00/8-2653, 28 August 1953, p.678.
110 Stefanidis, *Isle of Discord*, p.180, 175.
111 *F.R.U.S. 1951, Vol. V.* Consul in Nicosia to State Department. The Present State of Enosis, [Secret], 747C.00/12-751, 7 December 1951, p.541-2.
112 Xydis, *Cyprus*, p.9-10; Stefanidis, *Isle of Discord*, p.207.
113 Michalopoulos, *Ελλάδα και Τουρκία*, p.17-27.
114 *F.R.U.S. 1952-1954*, vol. VIII, Warren to State Department, [Secret], 747C.00/2-2654, 26 February 1954, p.681.
115 *TNA/FO371/112844*. Embassy in Ankara to Foreign Office, [Confidential], WG1081/52, 19 March 1954.
116 Christidis, *Κυπριακό και ελληνοτουρκικά*, p.17.
117 *F.R.U.S. 1952-1954*, vol. VIII. Memorandum of Conversation between the Turkish Ambassador Erkin, Byroade and Baxter, [Secret], 747C.00/3-1054, 10 March 1954, p.682.
118 *Official Minutes of the Greek Parliament*, Period III, Synod I, 4th Session, 17 December 1952, p.37.
119 *Embros*, 1 November 1951, p.1, 5; *Kathimerini*, 1 November 1951, p.4; Stefanidis, *Isle of Discord*, p.24.
120 Xydis, *Cyprus*, p.8, 594, fn16.
121 cf *TNA/FO371/95108*. From Athens embassy to Foreign Office, RG1013/26, [Confidential], 28 November 1951. According the British embassy the Greek police controlled the situation 'without much trouble'.
122 *TNA/FO371/101808*. Murray on Papagos's parliamentary speech of 17 December 1952, 18 December 1952.
123 *TNA/FO371/101808*. Peake to Foreign Office, Conversation with Papagos, WG1052/9, 25 November 1952; Holland, *Britain and the Revolt*, p.30-1.
124 *TNA/FO371/101808*. Peake to Foreign Office, Conversation with Papagos, WG1052/9, 25 November 1952.
125 *TNA/FO371/112843*. Pearson to Cheetham, [Confidential], 20 January 1953.
126 Michalopoulos, *Ελλάδα και Τουρκία*, p.40; Hatzivassiliou, *Στρατηγικές του Κυπριακού*, p.28, 128, 194.
127 Ierodiakonou, *Το Κυπριακό Πρόβλημα*, p.45; id, 'Το Κυπριακό από τον Β' Παγκόσμιο Πόλεμο ως την Ανεξαρτησία', in Tenekidis and Kranidiotis (eds), *Κύπρος*, 2009, p.172.
128 Stefanidis, *Isle of Discord*, p.262.
129 G.M.F.A. Makarios to Wright, 27 April 1953; Averoff-Tositsas, *Ιστορία χαμένων ευκαιριών*, vol.1, p.36.
130 G.M.F.A. Makarios to Hammarskjold, 10 August 1953; Nikos Kranidiotis, *Η Κύπρος εις τον αγώνα της ελευθερίας*, Athens, Elliniki Ekdotiki Etaireia, 1958, p.83-4.
131 G.M.F.A. Makarios to Hammarskjold, 10 August 1953; Loizidis to Perez, 18 and 21 September 1953.
132 G.M.F.A. Stefanopoulos to Kyrou, no.48246, Political Directorate II, 12 September 1953.

133 G.M.F.A. Kyrou to the Eighth UN General Assembly, 21 September 1953.
134 G.M.F.A. Kyrou to Stefanopoulos, OHE/Z/2 51523, Political Directorate Γ/ΙΙ, no.4589, 21 September 1953.
135 Ibid.
136 *Eleftheria*, 22 September 1953, p.1, 6.
137 David Carlton, *Anthony Eden: A Biography*, London, Allen and Unwin, 1981, p.328; D.R. Thorpe, *Eden: The Life and Times of Anthony Eden First Earl of Avon, 1897–1977*, London, Chatto and Windus, 2003, p.385–9.
138 Averoff-Tositsas, Ιστορία χαμένων ευκαιριών, vol.1, p.42–3; Colin Baker, *Retreat from Empire: Sir Robert Armitage in Africa and Cyprus*, London, I.B. Tauris, 1998, p.111.
139 Holland, *Britain and the Revolt*, p.32.
140 TNA/FO371/107499. Lambert to Foreign Office. Record of conversation between Eden and Papagos, [Confidential], sent on 2 October 1953.
141 This document is either classified or lost, Markezinis, Σύγχρονη Ιστορία της Ελλάδος, p.49.
142 *Official Minutes of the Greek Parliament*. Debate on Cyprus, Period 3, Synod 3, Session 39, 7 February 1955, p.671.
143 Quoted in Vlachos, Δέκα χρόνια Κυπριακού, p.63–4; Michalopoulos, Ελλάδα και Τουρκία, p.41; originally in Polys Modinos, 'Οι πνευματικοί άνθρωποι και το Κυπριακό πρόβλημα', *Efthyni*, 93, September 1979, p.467.
144 Sulzberger, *Long Row*, p.1010–11.
145 *F.R.U.S. 1952–1954, Vol. VIII*. Dulles to Athens, [Top Secret], 747C.00/8-2653, 28 August 1953, p.678.
146 *F.R.U.S. 1952–1954*, vol. VIII. Conversation between Politis, Byroade and Baxter, [Secret], 747C.00/4-554, 5 April 1954, p.685, emphasis added; same point is made by Observer correspondent, Robert Stephens, *Cyprus. A Place of Arms – Power Politics and Ethnic Conflict in the Eastern Mediterranean*, London, Pall Mall, 1966, p.135.
147 Doros Alastos, *Cyprus Guerilla. Grivas, Makarios and the British*, London, Heinemann, 1960, p.41–2.
148 *Sophocles Venizelos Papers*. Record of Conversation between Averoff and Peake, drafted by Averoff, 226/24/141-2, 8 November 1951.
149 *Sophocles Venizelos Papers*. Report by Averoff on the Cyprus question, 226/25/1, 22 November 1951.
150 *Sophocles Venizelos Papers*. Report by Averoff on the Cyprus question, 226/25/1, 22 November 1951; Averoff-Tositsas, Ιστορία χαμένων ευκαιριών, vol.1, p.37.
151 TNA/FO371/107498. Main Brief for Visit of the Secretary of State to Greece, [Secret], WG1074, 3 April 1953.
152 Thomas Anthem, 'Balkan Prospects', *Contemporary Review*, 183, January-June 1953, p.19.
153 TNA/FO371/107487. Peake to Cheetham at Foreign Office, [Confidential], WG1941/3, 29 October 1953; Anthem, 'The Cyprus Challenge', p.21.
154 TNA/FO371/112843. Peake to Cheetham: Minutes of conversation with King Paul, [Confidential], WG 1081/3, 12 January 1954.
155 Kyrou, Ελληνική εξωτερική πολιτική, p.274.
156 Notable exceptions are Stefanidis, *Isle of Discord*, p.46; Hatzivassiliou, Στρατηγικές του Κυπριακού, p339.
157 *F.R.U.S. 1952–1954, Vol. VIII*. Yost to State Department, [Top Secret], 747C.00/8-2653, 26 August 1953, p.676; Stefanidis, *Isle of Discord*, p.46.

158 *TNA/FO371/112864*. Dodds-Parker to Williams, WG1081/633, 24 September 1954; Baker, *Retreat from Empire*, p.111; Brendan O'Malley and Ian Craig, *The Cyprus Conspiracy: America, Espionage and the Turkish Invasion*, London, I.B. Tauris, 2007, p.11–12.
159 *Sophocles Venizelos Papers*. Handwritten notation by Venizelos on Cyprus question, 226/11/258, undated, referring to developments in March-May 1951; quote from Report by Averoff on the Cyprus question, 226/25/1, 22 November 1951.
160 *TNA/FO371/112843*. Peake to Foreign Office, WG1081/56, 10 November 1953.
161 *F.R.U.S. 1952–1954, Vol.VIII*. 781.00/10-2353, not printed, p.685, fn1; Markezinis, Σύγχρονη πολιτική Ιστορία, vol.3, p.49.
162 Stefanidis, *Isle of Discord*, p.262.
163 *F.R.U.S. 1952–1954, Vol.VIII*. Conversation between Baxter, Politis and Byroade, [Secret], 747C.00/4-554, 5 April 1954.
164 *TNA/FO371/112843*. Peake to Foreign Office, WG1081/56, 10 November 1953; *FO371/112843*. Conversation between Peake and King Paul, [Confidential], WG 1081/3, 12 January 1954.
165 *TNA/FO371/112843*. Peake to Harrison at Foreign Office, [Confidential], WG1081/1, 18 December 1953.
166 Stefanidis, *Isle of Discord*, p.49.
167 *TNA/FO371/107502*. Peake to Foreign Office, 1081/62, 26 November 1953; Linardatos, Από τον Εμφύλιο, vol.2, p.136; Stefanidis, *Isle of Discord*, p.49.
168 *Eleftheria*, 28 November 1953, p.4.
169 Xydis, *Cyprus*, p.9; *Official Minutes of the Greek Parliament*. Debate on Cyprus, Period 3, Synod 3, Session 39, 7 February 1955, p.671–2.
170 *TNA/FO371/112843*. Report on Conversation between Peake and King Paul to Cheetham at Foreign Office, [Confidential], WG 1081/3, 12 January 1954; Markezinis, Σύγχρονη πολιτική Ιστορία, vol.3, p.49.
171 *TNA/FO371/112843*. From Peake to Cheetham at Foreign Office, [Confidential], WG1081/6, 23 January 1954.
172 *TNA/FO371/112843*. Report on Conversation between Peake and King Paul to Cheetham at Foreign Office, [Confidential], WG 1081/3, 12 January 1954.
173 Holland, *Britain and the Revolt*, p.31–2.
174 Stanley Mayes, *Cyprus and Makarios*, London, Putnam, 1960, p.112; Stephens, *Cyprus*, p.135; O'Malley and Craig, *The Cyprus Conspiracy*, p.12; James Ker-Lindsay, *Cyprus Problem: What Everyone Needs to Know*, Oxford, New York, Oxford University Press, 2011, p.20; Claude Nicolet, *United States Policy towards Cyprus, 1954–1974: Removing the Greek-Turkish Bone of Contention*, Mannheim, Bibliopolis, 2001, p.44; Thomas Ehrlich, *Cyprus 1958–1967*, New York, Oxford University Press, 1974, p.12; Stefanidis, *Isle of Discord*, p. 262.
175 Markezinis, Σύγχρονη Ιστορία της Ελλάδος, p.49; the Greek record of the meeting remains classified.
176 Tenekidis, 'Διεθνοποίηση και αποδιεθνοποίηση', p.207; Constantine Tsatsos, Λογοδοσία μιας ζωής, vol.1, Athens, Ekdoseis ton filon, 2001, p.350; Stefanidis, *Isle of Discord*, p.48, 129; Baker, *Retreat from Empire*, p.111; contra Averoff-Tositsas, Ιστορία χαμένων ευκαιριών, vol.1, p.45; Frederica, *Measure*, 181.
177 O'Malley and Craig, *The Cyprus Conspiracy*, p.12.
178 Ker-Lindsay, *Cyprus Problem*, p.20; see also Stefanidis, *Isle of Discord*, p.262.
179 *F.R.U.S. 1952–1954, Vol. VIII*. Yost to State Department, [Top Secret], 747C.00/9-253, 2 September 1953, p.678, emphasis added.

Chapter 5

1. Mayes, *Cyprus and Makarios*, p.112; Michalopoulos, *Ελλάδα και Τουρκία*, p.40; Svolopoulos, *Ελληνική εξωτερική πολιτική*, vol.2, p.84; Hatzivassiliou, *Στρατηγικές του Κυπριακού*, p. 28, 106; Holland, *Britain and the Revolt*, p.32; Stefanidis, *Isle of Discord*, p.262.
2. Svolopoulos, *Ελληνική εξωτερική πολιτική*, vol.2, p.84, 83.
3. Stefanidis, *Isle of Discord*, p.262 and p.50.
4. Dimitri Bitsios, *Cyprus: The Vulnerable Republic*, Thessaloniki, Institute for Balkan Studies, 1975, p.20.
5. Stefanidis, *Isle of Discord*, p.50; Kranidiotis, *Δοκίμια*, p.37.
6. Mayes, *Cyprus and Makarios*, p.29; Hatzivassiliou, *Στρατηγικές του Κυπριακού*, p.137.
7. Xydis, *Cyprus*, p.10, italics added.
8. Tenekidis, 'Διεθνοποίηση και αποδιεθνοποίηση', p.207–8.
9. Papagos's statements in *Kathimerini*, 23 January 1954, p.1; 18 March 1954, p.1; *Kathimerini*, 4 May 1954, p.1; *Official Minutes of the Greek Parliament*. Speech by Papagos, 7 February 1955.
10. *Le Monde*, '"La solution de la question de Chypre serait le meilleur moyen de consolider les liens gréco-britanniques", déclare au Monde le maréchal Papagos', interview to André Fontaine, 24 April 1954.
11. Kyrou, *Ελληνική εξωτερική πολιτική*, p.273–4.
12. Anthem, 'The Cyprus Challenge', p.17.
13. Vassilios Mostras, *Επί του Κυπριακού ζητήματος*, Athens, 1960 (henceforth *Mostras File*), p.54, 44.
14. *Eleftheria*, 24 April 1954, p.6.
15. Quote from Stefanidis, *Isle of Discord*, p.299; on a review of the scholarship on this point, see Evanthis Hatzivassiliou, 'British Strategic Priorities and the Cyprus Question, 1954–1958', in Hubert Faustmann and Nicos Peristianis (eds), *Britain in Cyprus: Colonialism and Post-Colonialism, 1878–2006*, Mannheim/Möhnesee, Bibliopolis, 2006, p.200, fn3; cf Ierodiakonou, 'Το Κυπριακό από τον Β΄ Παγκόσμιο', p.173.
16. Thomas Schelling, *The Strategy of Conflict*, New Haven, Harvard University Press, 1980, p.200.
17. Patrick Morgan, *Deterrence Now*, Cambridge, Cambridge University Press, 2003, p.46–58.
18. *Mostras File*, p.66.
19. *Mostras File*, p.44, cf with translation in Xydis, *Cyprus*, p.9.
20. *Le Monde*, 'M. Markezinis donne sa démission', 5 April 1954.
21. TNA/FO371/101803. Peake to Eden, [Confidential], WG10114/9, 2 December 1952; TNA/FO371/107497. Galesworthy to May at Foreign Office, [Confidential], WG1041/2, 21 October 1953; *Constantine Karamanlis Archive*, vol. I. 19 November 1952, p.154.
22. Linardatos, *Από τον Εμφύλιο*, vol.2, p.160–1. Linardatos's named Markezinis as his 'most probable' source, Interview with author, 28 August 1996.
23. TNA/FO371/112382. Peake to Foreign Office, [Confidential], 3 April 1954. Peake met Papagos and the king on 2 April in Corfu immediately after their interview over Markezinis's resignation.
24. TNA/FO371/112832. Wilding at Foreign Office to Tratner in Treasury, 29 April 1954; George Rallis, *Πολιτικές εκμυστηρεύσεις, 1950–1989*, Athens, Proskinio, 1990, p.28.

25 *TNA/FO371/112382*. Peake to Foreign Office, [Confidential], 3 April 1954.
26 This view was shared by *Le Monde*, 'M. Markezinis donne sa démission', 5 April 1954.
27 *TNA/FO371/112832*. Galesworthy's conversation with Markezinis, [Secret], WG10112/8, 13 April 1954.
28 Hatzivassiliou, *Η άνοδος του Κωνσταντίνου Καραμανλή*, p.70, fn12; Psalidopoulos, *Επιτηρητές σε απόγνωση*, p.135.
29 Markezinis, *Σύγχρονη πολιτική Ιστορία*, vol.3, p.54.
30 Linardatos, *Από τον Εμφύλιο*, vol.2, p.164.
31 *TNA/FO371/112832*. Conversation between Galesworthy and Markezinis, [Secret], WG10112/8, 13 April 1954.
32 Ibid., *TNA/FO371/112832*. Lambert to Young at Foreign Office, 9 July 1954; *TNA/FO371/112832*. Note by Wilding on Lambert's letter of 9 July, G10112/9, 16 July 1954. The other account was given by M. Demacos.
33 Spyros Markezinis, *Αναμνήσεις 1972-1974*, Athens, Markezinis, 1979, p.73; id. Markezinis, *Σύγχρονη πολιτική Ιστορία*, vol.2, p.430-3.
34 Markezinis, *Σύγχρονη πολιτική Ιστορία*, vol.3, p.55, fn37; vol.2, p.331-2.
35 Markezinis, *Αναμνήσεις*, p.19.
36 Ibid., p.73; id, Markezinis, *Σύγχρονη πολιτική Ιστορία*, vol.3, p.46; with some variation, Alexis Kyrou, *Όνειρα και πραγματικότης. Χρόνια διπλωματικής ζωής (1923-1953)*, Athens, Kleisiounis, 1972, p.370.
37 *F.R.U.S. 1952-1954, Vol. VIII*. Conversation between Baxter, Byroade and the Turkish Ambassador Erkin, [Secret], 747C.00/3-1054, 10 March 1954, p.682.
38 *F.R.U.S. 1952-1954, Vol. VIII*. Warren in Turkey to State Department, [Secret], 747C00/3-3054, 30 March 1954, p.683.
39 *TNA/FO371/112832*. Minutes of conversation between Galesworthy and Markezinis, [Secret], WG10112/8, 13 April 1954.
40 Markezinis, *Σύγχρονη πολιτική Ιστορία*, vol.3, p.45.
41 *F.R.U.S. 1952-1954, Vol. VIII*. Peurifoy to State Department, [Secret], 781.00/3-2453, 24 March 1953, p.814.
42 Ibid., fn2, unpublished dispatch 781.00/2-2753, Yost to State Department, 25 February 1953, p.813.
43 Ibid., p.813.
44 Ibid., p.813.
45 *Time Magazine*, 'Greece: Good Fellow from the Kremlin', 28 December 1953.
46 *TNA/FO371/107497*. Galesworthy to May at Foreign Office, [Confidential], WG1041/2, 21 October 1953.
47 Ibid.
48 *TNA/FO371/107497*. Peake to Cheetham at Foreign Office, [Confidential], 29 October 1953; *Time*, 'Greece: Good fellow from the Kremlin', 28 December 1953.
49 *TNA/FO371/107497*. Galesworthy to May at Foreign Office, [Confidential], WG1041/2, 21 October 1953.
50 Ibid., Sergeev proposed the idea to Stefanopolulos on 19 September before meeting Markezinis a few days later, *Eleftheria*, 22 September 1953, p.1, 6; 23 September 1953, p.1, 4.
51 Ibid.
52 *TNA/FO371/107497*. Minutes by John Cheetham, WG1041/2, 29 October 1953.
53 Ibid.
54 *TNA/FO371/112834*. Rumbold in Paris to Cheetham in Foreign Office, [Confidential], WG10317/4, 2 February 1954; Markezinis, *Σύγχρονη πολιτική Ιστορία*, vol.3, p.45.

55 *TNA/FO371/112832*. Peake to Foreign Office, [Confidential], WG10112/16, 20 November 1954; Markezinis, Σύγχρονη πολιτική Ιστορία, vol.3, p.60–1.
56 Ibid., p.55–6.
57 Markezinis, Αναμνήσεις, p.302, 17, 300.
58 Markezinis, Σύγχρονη πολιτική Ιστορία, vol.3, p.55, fn37.
59 Peter Bachrach and Morton Baratz, 'Decisions and Nondecisions: An Analytical Framework', *American Political Science Review*, 57:3, 1962, p.632; id, 'Two Faces of Power', *American Political Science Review*, 56:4, 1962, p.948.
60 G.M.F.A. Official Visit by Papagos and Stefanopoulos to Italy, 23–25 September 1953, [Secret], Political Directorate II, no. 52508.
61 *Eleftheria*, 16 April 1954, p.4; *F.R.U.S. 1952–1954*, vol. 781.5 MSP/4-1654, p.642.
62 G.M.F.A. Handwritten telegram from Papagos to Greek embassies in Belgrade and Ankara, undated. The message must have been dispatched shortly after the joint Turkish-Yugoslav *communiqué* of 17 April 1954.
63 Iatrides, *Balkan Triangle*, p.129.
64 G.M.F.A. Démenti du Ministère des Affaires Etrangères, Ankara, 17 April 1954.
65 Iatrides, *Balkan Triangle*, p.129.
66 Ibid., p.87.
67 G.M.F.A. Minutes of conversation between Stefanopoulos and Koprülü, Athens, 27 January 1953.
68 *F.R.U.S. 1952–1954, Vol. VIII*. Acheson to Athens and Ankara embassies, [Top Secret], 681.82/5-652, 7 May 1952, p.591; G.M.F.A. Minutes of conversation between Stefanopoulos and Koprülü, Athens, 27 January 1953; Minutes of conversation between Papagos and Koprülü, Athens, 27 January 1953.
69 G.M.F.A. The existence of a Secret Annex to the Treaty of Ankara can be inferred from two documents. One, titled 'Ratification of Annexes of Tripartite Emergency Defence Plan', [Top Secret, 2 copies], 38060 Α/Γ4, contains five emergency contingency plans: D – Plan of Naval Forces' Activities, E – Use of Reserves and Counterattacks, G – Plan of Coordination of Information, J – Plan of Administrative Supervision, K– Communications and Electronics. This was signed on 1 April 1954 in Ankara and ratified personally by Papagos. The second is titled 'General Chiefs-of Staff Views on Yugoslavia to Colonel Lounderakis, Military Attaché in Rome', [Top Secret], 0210/03. This states that 'contacts have not been hitherto confined to the exchange of each side's general views but extended over points which all Chiefs-of-Staffs consider to be (and are) military secrets. Of course, the announcement of such military secrets takes place under the silent adoption of the principle of mutuality'. Signed by General Kitrilakis, Greek C-o-S, on 2 January 1954.
70 G.M.F.A. Conversation between Popović and Stefanopoulos, Belgrade, 4 February 1953.
71 G.M.F.A. Conversation between Stefanopoulos and Koprülü, Athens, 27 January 1953.
72 G.M.F.A. Conversation between Popović and Stefanopoulos, Belgrade, 4 February 1953.
73 Iatrides *Balkan Triangle*, p.181.
74 *F.R.U.S. 1952–1954, Vol. VIII*. Conversation between Stefanopoulos, Dulles, Kalergis and Baxter, [Top Secret], 611.81/10-3053, 30 October 1953, p.854.
75 *F.R.U.S. 1952–1954, Vol. VIII*, Dulles to Athens embassy, [Top Secret], 760.5/2-1354, 16 February 1954, p.640–1.
76 Svetozar Raia, *Yugoslavia and the Soviet Union in the Early Cold War: Reconciliation, Comradeship, Confrontation, 1953–1957*, Abingdon, Routledge, 2011, p.66–84, quotes from p.66.

77 F.R.U.S. *1952–1954, Vol. VIII*. Conversation between Stefanopoulos, Dulles, Kalergis and Baxter, [Top Secret], 611.81/10-3053, 30 October 1953, p.856–7.
78 G.M.F.A. Joint Staffs Team A/IIB to Political Directorate I, [Top Secret]: Conversation between General Papathanasiades and Cannon, drafted by Dovas, 28 December 1953.
79 Ibid.; *TNA/FO371/112834*. Rumbold to Foreign Office, [Confidential], WG10317/4, 2 February 1954.
80 F.R.U.S. *1952–1954, Vol. VIII*, Smith to Athens embassy, [Top Secret], 760.5/2-1354, 16 February 1954, p.641–2.
81 G.M.F.A. Conversation between Cannon and Stefanopoulos, Athens, 18 February 1954.
82 F.R.U.S. *1952–1954, Vol. VIII*. Conversation between President Eisenhower, Kanellopoulos, Politis and Simmons, 611.81/3-1854, 18 March 1954, p.861–2.
83 G.M.F.A. General C-o-S [Kitrilakis] views on Yugoslavia to Colonel Lounderakis, Military Attaché in Rome [Top Secret], 2 January 1954; Joint Staffs Team A/IIB to Political Directorate I, [Top Secret], Minutes of conversation between General Papathanasiades and Ambassador Cannon, 28 December 1953.
84 G.M.F.A. Conversation between Popović and Stefanopoulos, Belgrade, 4 February 1953.
85 F.R.U.S. *1952–1954, Vol. VIII*. Cannon to State Department, [Secret], 781.5 MSP/4-2054, 20 April 1954, p.642.
86 G.M.F.A. Papagos to embassies in Belgrade and Ankara; handwritten and undated.
87 G.M.F.A. Kalergis to Greek Ministry of Foreign Affairs – Turkey Department, [Secret], A/Γ4 36294, 20 April 1954.
88 G.M.F.A. Politis to Greek Ministry of Foreign Affairs, A/ΓA 35517, 20 April 1954.
89 G.M.F.A. Politis to Greek Ministry of Foreign Affairs, A/Γ4 25517, 21 April 1954.
90 G.M.F.A. Kapetanides in Belgrade to Greek Ministry of Foreign Affairs, A/Γ4 36197, 24 April 1954.
91 G.M.F.A. Matsas to Stefanopoulos, A/Γ4 37009, 30 April 1954; the NAC met in Paris on 23 April 1954, see *Eleftheria*, 24 April 1954, p.1, 6; *Le Monde*, 'Nous ne voyons pas comment le pacte d'Ankara peut devenir une alliance militaire déclare M. Stephanopoulos', 23 April 1954.
92 G.M.F.A. Kalergis to Greek Ministry of Foreign Affairs, NATO Department, A/Γ4 38422, 4 May 1954.
93 G.M.F.A. Kapetanides in Belgrade to Greek Ministry of Foreign Affairs, A/Γ4 38202, 8 May 1954.
94 G.M.F.A. Politis to Greek Ministry of Foreign Affairs, A/Γ4 38375, 8 May 1954.
95 F.R.U.S. *1952–1954, Vol. VIII*. 668.81/5-1054, p.644, fn3.
96 G.M.F.A. Papagos to Politis, A/39344, 13 May 1954.
97 G.M.F.A. Kalergis in Ankara to Greek Ministry of Foreign Affairs, A/Γ4 39629, 15 May 1954.
98 G.M.F.A. Politis to Greek Ministry of Foreign Affairs, [Secret], 2068, 17 May 1954.
99 F.R.U.S. *1952–1954, Vol. VIII*. Peurifoy to State Department, [Top Secret], 123 Peurifoy, John E, 13 July 1953, p.841.
100 F.R.U.S. *1952–1954, Vol. VIII*. Dulles to Athens embassy, [Top Secret], 760.5/5-1754, 17 May 1954, p.645–6.
101 G.M.F.A. Papagos to embassies in Washington, Ankara and Belgrade, cryptographic/handwritten, undated, 18 or 19 May 1954.
102 G.M.F.A. Politis to Greek Ministry of Foreign Affairs, [Top Secret], 2149, 20 May 1954.

103 G.M.F.A. Papagos to embassy in Italy, 39902, 19 May 1954.
104 G.M.F.A. Papagos to embassy in Italy, 39901, 19 May 1954.
105 F.R.U.S. *1952-1954, Vol. VIII*. Dulles to UK embassy, [Top Secret], 760.5/6-1154, 14 June 1954, p.653.
106 F.R.U.S. *1952-1954, Vol. VIII*. Aldrich in UK to State Department, [Top Secret], 760.5/6-1854, 18 June 1954, p.657.
107 Denise Folliot (ed.), *Documents on International Affairs 1954*, London, Oxford University Press, 1957, p.197-200.
108 *TNA/CAB129/69/45*. Memorandum by Lyttelton and Lloyd to Cabinet, C(54)245 [Secret], 21 July 1954; *Sophocles Venizelos Papers*. Report by Averoff on the Cyprus question, 226/25/1, 22 November 1951.
109 *TNA/FO371/112843*. Rambolt (Paris) to Cheetham at Foreign Office, [Confidential], WG10317/4, 2 February 1954.
110 Quoted in *Kathimerini*, 23 January 1954, p.1.
111 *TNA/FO371/112843*. Cheetham to Rambold in Paris, [Confidential], WG10317/2, 29 Janurary 1954.
112 Kranidiotis, Δοκίμια, p.37; contra. Stefanidis, *Isle of Discord*, p.50.
113 Statement by Greek Foreign Minister spokesman in *Eleftheria*, 24 April 1954, p.6.
114 *Hansard: Commons Debates*. 5th Series, vol.525, c.74, 15 March 1954.
115 *Mostras File*, p.66; *Hansard, Vol. 531, c.1597,* 25 October 1954.
116 F.R.U.S. *1952-1954, Vol. VIII*. Memorandum of Conversation – Baxter, Politis and Byroade on Cyprus, [Secret], 747C.00/4-554, 5 April 1954, p.685-7, italics added.
117 Paschalis Kitromilides and Marios Evriviades, *Cyprus (World Bibliographical Series)*, Revised Edition, Oxford, Clio Press, 1995, p.94.
118 Stefanidis, *Isle of Discord*, p.287-8, fn66.
119 Paschalis Kitromilides, 'Milestones in the Historiography on the Cyprus Question', *The Historical Review*, Institute for Neohellenic Research, vol.1, 2004, p.289; Hatzivassiliou, Στρατηγικές του Κυπριακού, p.186-7.
120 Xydis, *Cyprus*, p.9-10; Stavros Panteli, *A New History of Cyprus: From the Earliest Times to the Present Day*, Hounslow, East-West Publications, 1984, p.252; Svolopoulos, Ελληνική εξωτερική πολιτική, vol.2, p.83; Hatzivassiliou, *Greece and the Cold War*, p.50; id. Στρατηγικές του Κυπριακού, p.106, fn2; Stefanidis, *Stirring the Greek Nation*, p.46; Farid Mirbagher, *Historical Dictionary on Cyprus*, Lanham, Scarecrow Press, 2010, p.56.
121 Panayotis Pipinelis, 'Η διαχείρισις του Κυπριακού', *Kathimerini*, 28 February 1959, p.4.
122 Panayotis Pipinelis, 'Η άγνωστος διπλωματική Ιστορία περί την διαχείρησιν του Κυπριακού', *Kathimerini*, 1 March 1959, p.4.
123 Xydis, *Cyprus*, p.9.
124 *Mostras File*, 'Introduction', p.iii.
125 *Mostras File*, p.2, fn2, 45-6; Stefanidis, *Isle of Discord*, p.265-6.
126 *Mostras File*, p.98.
127 Panayotis Pipinelis, 'Η «διεθνοποίησις» του Κυπριακού και αι εξ' αυτού μοιραίαι συνέπειαι', *Kathimerini*, 5 March 1959, p.3-4.
128 *TNA/FO371/112844*. G.W. Harrison: 'Record of Conversation' with Mostras, WG1081/32, 1 March 1954.
129 *TNA/FO371/112844*. Foreign Office Minute by G.W. Harrison, WG1081/33, 1 March 1954; Harrison to Eden, WG1081/33, 1 March 1954; Cheetham to Peake, WG1081/33, 3 March 1954.

130　F.R.U.S. 1952-1954, Vol.VIII. Position Paper, UN Office, SD/A/C.1/448, [Confidential], 14 September 1954, p.706.
131　Stefanidis, *Isle of Discord*, p.266-7, 287, fn60.
132　*Mostras File*, p.47.
133　TNA/CAB 129/71/19. Record of conversation between Harrison and Mostras 18 October 1954, C (54) 319, Annex A, 21 October 1954; *Mostras File*, p.18-20.
134　*Mostras File*, p.21.
135　Pipinelis, 'Η άγνωστος διπλωματική ιστορία', p.4.
136　F.R.U.S. 1952-1954, Vol. VIII. Yost to State Department, [Top Secret], 747C.00/8-2653, 26 August 1953, p.676; Stefanidis, *Isle of Discord*, p.46.
137　*Eleftheria*, 23 April 1954, p.1.
138　*Eleftheria*, 24 April 1954, p.6.
139　TNA/CAB129/69/45. Memorandum by the Minister of State for the Colonies and the Minister of State to Cabinet, C (54) 245 [Secret], 21 July 1954.
140　Markezinis, Σύγχρονη πολιτική Ιστορία, vol.2, p.379-85; Stefanidis, *Isle of Discord*, p.264.
141　*Kathimerini*, 16 April 1954, p.6; *Eleftheria*, 16 April 1954, p.4.
142　Xydis, *Cyprus*, p.9; cf 'Toward "Toil and Moil"', p.11; Svolopoulos, Ελληνική εξωτερική πολιτική, vol.2, p.83; Hatzivassiliou, *Greece and the Cold War*, p.50; id. Στρατηγικές του Κυπριακού, p.106, fn2; Stefanidis, *Stirring the Greek Nation*, p.46, fn113.
143　*Mostras File*, p.68, 21, 69, 4.
144　Kyrou, Όνειρα και πραγματικότης. Χρόνια διπλωματικής ζωής (1923-1953), p.371; *Eleftheria*, 13 February 1954, p.4.
145　*Mostras File*, p.2-3.
146　TNA/FO371/112832. Galesworthy's minutes of conversation with Markezinis, [Secret], WG10112/8, 13 April 1954.
147　*Mostras File*, p.56, 69.
148　*Eleftheria*, 18 April 1954, p.1.
149　Ibid., p.1.
150　Kyrou, Ελληνική εξωτερική πολιτική, p.273-4.
151　TNA/FO800/764. Eden to Peake: Record of Conversation between Eden and Mostras, [Confidential] WG1081/66, 30 March 1954.
152　TNA/FO371/112848. Record of Conversation between Henderson and Mostras, WG1084/182, 9 July 1954.
153　TNA/CAB 129/71/19. Record of conversation between Harrison and Mostras, C (54) 319 [Secret], 18 October 1954.
154　Stefanidis, *Isle of Discord*, p.264.
155　*Mostras File*, p.47.
156　Quoted from *Eleftheria*, 16 April 1954, p.4; *Kathimerini*, 16 April 1954, p.6.
157　*Eleftheria*, 18 April 1954, p.1.
158　*Hansard – Commons Debates*, 28 April 1954, vol.526, cc1593-4.
159　Michael Nicholson, *Rationality and the Analysis of International Conflict*, Cambridge, Cambridge University Press, 1992, p.76.
160　TNA/FO371/112846. Peake to Foreign Office, WG1081/112, 5 May 1954; *Kathimerini*, 4 May 1954, p.1.
161　F.R.U.S. 1952-1954, Vol. VIII, Conversation between Baxter, Politis and Byroade on Cyprus, [Secret], 747C.00/6-2454, 24 June 1954, p.691-2.
162　F.R.U.S. 1952-1954, Vol. VIII, Editorial Note, No. 369, p.690.

163　F.R.U.S. 1952–1954, Vol. VIII, Conversation between Baxter, Politis and Byroade on Cyprus, [Secret], 747C.00/7-254, 2 July 1954, p.692–3.
164　TNA/CAB129/69/45. Memorandum by SoS for the Colonies and MoS to Cabinet, [Secret], C (54) 245, 21 July 1954.
165　F.R.U.S. 1952–1954, Vol. VIII. Personal message from Dulles to Stefanopoulos, Athens embassy files, lot 60, F16, 350 Cyprus 1954, [Secret], delivered 28 July 1954, p.697–8; Stefanidis, Isle of Discord, p.61–2.
166　TNA/FO371/112848. Harrison to Makins in Washington, [Secret], WG1081/179, 8 July 1954; Anthem, 'The Cyprus Challenge', p.17.
167　Hansard, HC Deb 28 July 1954, 5th Series, vol.531, col.504–8.
168　Kranidiotis, Η Κύπρος εις τον αγώνα; id. Δοκίμια, p.38; Averoff-Tositsas, Ιστορία χαμένων ευκαιριών, vol.1, p.46.
169　Hansard, HC Deb, 19 October 1954, 5th Series, vol.531, col.1034; Stefanidis, Isle of Discord, p.83; Vlachos, Δέκα χρόνια Κυπριακού, p.74; Ierodiakonou, Το Κυπριακό πρόβλημα, p.49, fn10.
170　Robert Holland, 'Never, Never Land: British Colonial Policy and the Roots of Violence in Cyprus, 1950–1954', The Journal of Imperial Commonwealth History, 21:3, 1993, p.167–9; Stefanidis, Isle of Discord, p.142.
171　F.R.U.S. 1952–1954, Vol. VI. Declaration by President Eisenhower and Prime Minister Churchill, Conference files, lot 60, D627, CF337, 29 June 1954, p.1130.
172　Hansard, HC Deb, 28 July 1954, 5th Series, vol.531, col.509.
173　Hansard, HC Deb, 28 July 1954, 5th Series, vol.531, col.550, 552; Stefanidis, Isle of Discord, p.63.
174　F.R.U.S. 1952–1954, Vol. VIII. Cannon to State Department [Secret], 747C.00/8-454, 4 August 1952, p.703.
175　Kranidiotis, Δοκίμια, p.38.
176　F.R.U.S. 1952–1954, Vol. VIII. Personal message from Dulles to Stefanopoulos, Athens embassy files, lot 60, F16, 350 Cyprus 1954, [Secret], delivered 28 July 1954, p.698.
177　Stefanidis, Isle of Discord, p.223, fn1, 274–5; Hatzivassiliou, Στρατηγικές του Κυπριακού, p.231.
178　Panayotis Pipinelis, 'Τα διπλωματικά παρασκήνια της διαχειρήσεως του Κυπριακού', Kathimerini, 4 March 1959, p.3.
179　Stefanidis, Isle of Discord, p.290–1, fn132.
180　Pipinelis, 'Τα διπλωματικά παρασκήνια', Kathimerini, 4 March 1959, p.3; F.R.U.S. 1952–1954, Vol. VIII. Personal message from Dulles to Stefanopoulos, Athens embassy files, lot 60, F16, 350 Cyprus 1954, [Secret], delivered 28 July 1954, p.697–9.
181　TNA/FO371/112852. Scott-Fox in Ankara to Young at Foreign Office, WG1081/188, [Secret – Guard], 12 August 1954.
182　Stefanidis, Isle of Discord, p.272, 274–5.
183　Constantine Karamanlis Archive, vol. I. Commentary by Karamanlis, 16 August 1954, p.208.
184　F.R.U.S. 1952–1954, Vol. VIII. Personal message from Dulles to Stefanopoulos, Athens embassy files, lot 60, F16, 350 Cyprus 1954, [Secret], delivered 28 July 1954, p.698.
185　TNA/FO371/112852. Extract from Daily News Bulletin, [Confidential], WG1081/189, 12 August 1954.
186　TNA/FO371/112852. Royce in Athens to Young in Foreign Office, [Confidential], WG1081/189, 13 August 1954.
187　Kyrou, Ελληνική εξωτερική πολιτική, p.278.

Chapter 6

1. Pipinelis, 'Η «διεθνοποίησις» του Κυπριακού', p.3; Xydis, *Cyprus*, p.26; id., 'The UN General Assembly as an Instrument of Greek Policy: Cyprus, 1954–58', *Journal of Conflict Resolution*, 12:2, 1968, p.142; Linardatos, *Από τον Εμφύλιο*, vol.2, p.205; Kranidiotis, *Δύσκολα Χρόνια*, p.65; Mayes, *Makarios*, p.60; Vlachos, *Δέκα χρόνια Κυπριακού*, p.68; Averoff-Tositsas, *Ιστορία χαμένων ευκαιριών*, vol.1, p.28; Menelaos Alexandrakis, Vyron Theodoropoulos, Efstathios Lagakos, *Το Κυπριακό 1950-1974. Μια ενδοσκόπηση*, Athens, Evroekdotiki, 1987, p.24; Panteli, *New History of Cyprus*, p.254; Stefanidis, *Isle of Discord*, p.1; Svolopoulos, *Ελληνική εξωτερική πολιτική*, vol.2, p.81; Evanthis Hatzivassiliou, 'Κύπρος και Κυπριακό Ζήτημα', *Ιστορία του Ελληνικού Έθνους*, vol.16, Athens, Ekdotiki Athinon, 2000, p.435.
2. As Tenekidis remarks, 'the terms "internationalization" and "de-internationalization" cover Protean and constantly shifting situations'. In this sense, the half-hearted UN recourse of 1954 falls between the two concepts, but closer to 'internationalization'. Hence the reference here to 'semi-internationalization'. Meanwhile, Tenekidis's definition of 'internationalization' as a 'systematic and in-depth information campaign across world public opinion' and a 'recourse to international bodies', is limited and formulaic, Tenekidis, 'Διεθνοποίηση και αποδιεθνοποίηση', p.296, 305. Internationalization is, above all, a process of politically and diplomatically involving the international community (states, international bodies, world public opinion) in an issue in a *multilateral* (as opposed to bilateral/trilateral) framework.
3. Xydis, 'The UN General Assembly', p.155.
4. *Mostras File*, p.44; Edward Johnson, 'Keeping Cyprus off the Agenda: British and American Relations at the United Nations, 1954–58', *Diplomacy and Statecraft*, 11:3, 2000, p.228–9, 230.
5. *TNA/FO371/112852*. Lambert to Harrison, WD1081/287, 12 August 1954.
6. *TNA/FO371/112861*. Foreign Office to Athens embassy, GW1081/559, [Secret], 10 September 1954.
7. *TNA/FO371/112861*. Nutting to Eden, WG1081/559G, 9 September 1954.
8. *Mostras File*, p.50–1; Panayotis Pipinelis, 'The Greco-Turkish Feud Revived', *Foreign Affairs*, 37:1, January 1959, p.313; Xydis, *Cyprus*, p.12; id. 'Toward "Toil and Moil"', p.17; Christidis, *Κυπριακό και ελληνοτουρκικά*, p.38, 88–9; Bitsios, *Cyprus*, p.42; Averoff-Tositsas, *Ιστορία χαμένων ευκαιριών*, vol.1, p.49; Panteli, *New History of Cyprus*, p.254; Stefanidis, *Stirring the Nation*, p.156; Hatzivassiliou, *Στρατηγικές του Κυπριακού*, p.114, 117–18, 124, 127–8.
9. Tenekidis, 'Διεθνοποίηση και αποδιεθνοποίηση', p.213–14.
10. *Mostras File*, p.51; Pipinelis, 'The Greco-Turkish Feud', p.313; Xydis, *Cyprus*, p.12; id. 'Toward "Toil and Moil"', p.17; Christidis, *Κυπριακό και ελληνοτουρκικά*, p.84; Bitsios, *Cyprus*, p.42; Averoff-Tositsas, *Ιστορία χαμένων ευκαιριών*, vol.1, p.45; Panteli, *New History of Cyprus*, p.254; Stefanidis, *Stirring the Nation*, p.275–6; Hatzivassiliou, *Στρατηγικές του Κυπριακού*, p.117–18, 128; contra. Tenekidis, 'Διεθνοποίηση και αποδιεθνοποίηση', p.208.
11. *Official Minutes of the Greek Parliament*. Intervention by Venizelos, Period 3, Synod 3, Session 39, 7 February 1955, p.689.
12. *F.R.U.S. 1952-1954, Vol.VIII*. Yost to State Department, [Top Secret], 747C.00/8-2653, 26 August 1953, p.676; Yost to State Department, [Top Secret], 747C.00/9-253, 2 September 1953, p.678.

13 Savvas Loizidis, *Άτυχη Κύπρος. Πώς έζησα τους πόθους και τους καημούς της, 1910-1980*, Athens, Bergadis, 1980, p.91.
14 Hatzivassiliou misinterprets this article as supposedly not articulating a 'third' view. This reductionist reading is driven by his attempt to make Chourmouzios's nuanced position fit his simplistic binary model of pragmatist vs radical Greek strategies on the Cyprus question in the 1950s, *Στρατηγικές του Κυπριακού*, p.188.
15 Emilios Chourmouzios, 'Αι δύο θέσεις και η τρίτη... (Συμβολή στις συζητήσεις περί του Κυπριακού)', *Kathimerini*, 17 February 1955, p.1-2.
16 *F.R.U.S. 1952-1954, Vol.VIII*. Lodge to State Department, 747C.00/9-2054, [Confidential], 20 September 1954, p.713; Memorandum of conversation between Papagos and Dulles, [Confidential], USUN files, 23 October 1954, p.720.
17 *UN: Official Records of the General Assembly*. Ninth Session, Annexes, Item 62, Document A/2703, 20 August 1954, New York, 1954, p.1-3.
18 *Hellenic National Audio-Visual Archive*, Newsreel, Popular Rally in Athens for the Union of Cyprus with Greece, D2528, T15424, 2:25 minutes, 20 August 1954.
19 Hatzivassiliou, *Στρατηγικές του Κυπριακού*, p.132-3; *TNA/FO371/112852*. Notation by R.L. Wilding, WG1081/307, 23 August 1954.
20 Panteli, *New History of Cyprus*, p.258; Stefanidis, *Stirring the Nation*, p.275-8; Hatzivassiliou, *Στρατηγικές του Κυπριακού*, p.170-1, 178-9.
21 Kranidiotis, *Η Κύπρος εις τον αγώνα*, p.91; *Kathimerini*, 21 August 1954, p.1, 5, 6; *Eleftheria*, 21 August 1954, p.1, 5, 6.
22 *F.R.U.S. 1952-1954, Vol. VIII*. Eisenhower to Churchill, Eisenhower Papers, Whitman file, p.709-10, fn3.
23 *TNA/FO371/112852*. Lambert to Harrison, WG1081/287, 12 August 1954.
24 *TNA/FO371/112852*. Colville to Churchill, WG1081/298, 18 August 1954.
25 *TNA/FO371/112852*. Notation by Sykes, WG1081/298, 21 August 1954.
26 *TNA/FO371/112852*. Notation by Eden, WG1081/298, 21 August 1954.
27 *TNA/FO371/112854*. Colville to Stark, WG1081/363, 21 August 1954; *TNA/FO371/112854*. Foreign Office to Washington embassy, [Confidential], WG1081/359, 30 August 1954; *TNA/FO800/764*. Foreign Office to Washington embassy, Cy/54/4, 30 August 1954; *F.R.U.S. 1952-1954, Vol.VIII*. Key to Lodge, USUN files, Cyprus-1950-August 1955, 16 September 1954, p.714, fn2.
28 *TNA/FO371/112861*. Nutting to Eden, WG1081/559G, 9 September 1954; Foreign Office to Athens embassy [Secret], 10 September 1954.
29 *TNA/FO371/112860*. Record of conversation between Hopkinson and Cowles, Lennox-Boyd to Eden, [Top Secret and Personal], WG1081/534G, 2 September 1954; Nutting to Eden, WG1081/534G, 2 September 1954.
30 *Eleftheria*, 9 October 1954, p.1.
31 Pipinelis, 'Η άγνωστος διπλωματική ιστορία', p.4; Constantine Maniadakis, 'Αι μυστικαί διαπραγματεύσεις Παπάγου και Άγγλων δια το Κυπριακόν', *Kathimerini*, 8 March 1959, p.1-2; Xydis, *Cyprus*, p.16; id, 'Toward "Toil and Moil"', p.16; id. 'The UN General Assembly', p.144; id. *Cyprus*, p.42; Panteli, *New History of Cyprus*, p.252; Alexandrakis, Theodoropoulos and Lagakos, *Το Κυπριακό 1950-1974*, p.22; Pantelis Terlexis, *Πολιτική και διπλωματία του Κυπριακού. Ανατομία ενός λάθους*, Athens, Kedros, 2004, p.131-3.
32 *TNA/FO371/112852*. Colville to Churchill, WG1081/298, 18 August 1954; cf Stefanidis, *Isle of Discord*, p.75-6.
33 *TNA/FO371/112854*. Scott to Foreign Office, [Secret], WG1081/359, 27 August 1954; *TNA/FO800/764*. Scott to Foreign Office, [Secret], Cy/54/3, 27 August 1954.

34 Stefanidis, *Isle of Discord*, p.76; Johnson, 'Keeping Cyprus off the Agenda', p.232–3.
35 *Eleftheria*, 9 October 1954, p.1.
36 *TNA/FO371/112860*. Record of conversation between Hopkinson and Cowles, Lennox-Boyd to Eden, [Top Secret and Personal], WG1081/534G, 2 September 1954.
37 *Mostras File*, p.47, fn2. Ironically, Mostras claims that he boycotted Cowles's mission, even though it enjoyed Stefanopoulos's personal backing. 'She operated in a manner likely to generate doubts as to the Greek direction', he says. Meanwhile he, after his reprimand in April, started to 'close the path for conciliatory plans', including those backed by his own Minister! In so doing, Mostras was undermining Athens's policy (which now looked for a conciliatory way out of the UN). His approach was practically helping Eden, who was the one determined to torpido Cowles's mission.
38 Pipinelis, 'Η άγνωστος διπλωματική ιστορία', p.3–4.
39 Maniadakis, 'Αι μυστικαί διαπραγματεύσεις', *Kathimerini*, 8 March 1959, p.1–2.
40 Pipinelis, 'Η άγνωστος διπλωματική ιστορία', p.4; Maniadakis, 'Αι μυστικαί διαπραγματεύσεις', *Kathimerini*, 8 March 1959, p.1.
41 According to the Nobel Laureate poet and diplomat, George Seferis, Maniadakis used to say that the Metaxas Dictatorship (of which he was a member) fought the 1940–1 war against Mussolini 'only to be seen to be doing so', a statement which according to Seferis captured 'the conscience' of the man and his circle, George Seferis, Πολιτικό Ημερολόγιο Α', *1935–1944*, Athens, Ikaros, 1973, p.51. In 1941, Maniadakis left for Argentina, where he spent the wartime years, even though he was an army officer who could have helped the war effort, Christoforos Christidis, Χρόνια Κατοχής, *1941–1944. Μαρτυρίες Ημερολογίου*, Athens, 1971, p.571; Panourgia, *Dangerous Citizens*, p.40–5.
42 *TNA/CAB129/69/45*. Memorandum by the Minister of State for the Colonies and the Minister of State to Cabinet, C (54) 245 [Secret], 21 July 1954.
43 *F.R.U.S. 1952–1954, Vol. VIII*. Cannon to State Department, [Secret], 747C.00/12-154, 1 December 1954, p.733.
44 *F.R.U.S. 1952–1954, Vol. VIII*. Churchill to Eisenhower, [Top Secret], Eisenhower Papers, Whitman file, 18 September 1954, p.709–12; *TNA/FO800/764*. Churchill to Eisenhower, [Top Secret], Cy/54/6, 18 September 1954; *TNA/FO371/112860*, Nutting to Eden, WG1081/534G, 2 September 1954; *F.R.U.S. 1952–1954, Vol. VIII*. Dulles to Athens embassy, [Secret], 747C.00/9-1554, 15 September 1954, p.708; *TNA/FO371/112861*. Harrison to Eden, WG1081/543B, 17 September 1954.
45 *F.R.U.S. 1952–1954, Vol. VIII*. Position Paper USUN 'The Cyprus Problem', [Confidential], 747C.00/9-1415, 14 September 1954, p.704.
46 *F.R.U.S. 1952–1954, Vol. VIII*. Dulles to embassies in Athens, London and Ankara, [Secret], 747C.00/9-1554, 15 September 1954, p.708–9.
47 *F.R.U.S. 1952–1954, Vol. VIII*. Position Paper USUN 'The Cyprus Problem', [Confidential], 747C.00/9-1415, 14 September 1954, p.704.
48 *F.R.U.S. 1952–1954, Vol. VIII*. Lodge to State Department, [Confidential], 747C.00/9-2054, 20 September 1954, p.713–14.
49 *F.R.U.S. 1952–1954, Vol. VIII*. Dulles to Churchill, [Secret], 747C.00/12-154, 21 September 1954, p.715–16; *TNA/FO371/112865*. Dulles to Churchill, [Secret], WG1081/682, 22 September 1954.
50 *United Nations: General Assembly Official Records*, General Committee, 9th Session, 93rd Meeting, 23 September 1954, par.6, 18–24, 29–31, 32, 48, 49, p.7–11.

51 *United Nations: General Assembly Official Records*, Plenary Meetings (IX) 477, 24 September 1954, par.95, p.51.
52 *TNA/FO371/112866*. Commonwealth Office to various High Commissions, WG1081/702, 25 September 1954.
53 *TNA/FO371/112865*. New York to Foreign Office [Confidential], WG1081/677, 26 September 1954.
54 *TNA/FO371/112862*. Dixon to Foreign Office, [Confidential], WG1081/692, 28 September 1954.
55 *United Nations: General Assembly Official Records*, Plenary Meetings (IX) 477, 24 September 1954, par.119–20, 161m 183–8, 209, p.52–62.
56 *TNA/FO371/112865*. New York to Foreign Office [Confidential], WG1081/674, 25 September 1954; Kyrou, Ελληνική εξωτερική πολιτική, p.285–6, 290–1.
57 *United Nations: General Assembly Resolutions.* Seventh Session, Supplement 20, vol.1, A/RES/637 (VII) A, A/PV.403, 16 December 1952, p.26.
58 Kyrou, Ελληνική εξωτερική πολιτική, p.280–1.
59 *UN: Official Records of the General Assembly.* Ninth Session, Annexes, Item 62, Document A/2703, 20 August 1954, New York, 1954, p.1–3; Christidis, Κυπριακό και ελληνοτουρκικά, p.85–7.
60 Kyrou, Ελληνική εξωτερική πολιτική, p.280–2; *TNA/FO371/112858*. Hopkinson to Nutting, [Confidential], WG1081/468, 6 September 1954.
61 *TNA/FO371/112852*. Royce to Young, [Confidential], WG1081/289, 13 August 1954.
62 Kyrou, Ελληνική εξωτερική πολιτική, p.294–5; *Eleftheria*, 29 September 1954, p.6.
63 *F.R.U.S. 1952–1954, Vol.VIII*. Dulles to Athens, [Secret], 747C.00/12-1354, 14 December 1954, p.739.
64 *TNA/FO371/112866*. Dixon to Foreign Office, [Confidential], WG1081/716, 30 September 1954.
65 *TNA/FO371/112866*. Harrison to Ankara, 1 October 1954; Foreign Office to New York, [Confidential], 2 October 1954.
66 *Mostras File*, p.32, 57, fn1, 69.
67 Kyrou, Ελληνική εξωτερική πολιτική, p.283, 277.
68 *TNA/FO371/112875*. Barton to Muirhead, WG1081/1008, 5 November 1954; *Daily Telegraph*, 'Russia Thanked for Cyprus Vote', 25 September 1954.
69 Vlachos, Δέκα χρόνια Κυπριακού, p.79; Panteli, *New History of Cyprus*, p.258–9; Stefanidis, *Isle of Discord*, p.83, 276–9; Hatzivassiliou, Στρατηγικές του Κυπριακού, p.131 fn1; Stefanidis, *Stirring the Nation*, p.95.
70 Greek Press and Information Service, *Information Bulletin, The Cyprus Question*, No.12, Athens.
71 *TNA/FO371/112852*. Fordham to Eden, WG1081/297, 11 August 1954.
72 *TNA/FO371/112860*. Record of conversation between Hopkinson and Cowles, Lennox-Boyd to Eden, [Top Secret and Personal], WG1081/534G, 2 September 1954.
73 Stefanidis, *Isle of Discord*, p.277.
74 *TNA/FO371/112874*. Russell to Makins at Foreign Office, WG1081/998, 10 November 1954.
75 *Mostras File*, p.41.
76 This intended to deny EDA a monopoly on Greek anti-colonial discourse, but Peake believed it served to justify the Rally's claim that the UN recourse was driven by 'the weight of public opinion', *TNA/FO371/112853*. Peake to Churchill, WG1081/327, [Confidential] 21 August 1954.

77 *Hellenic National Audio-Visual Archive*, Newsreel, Student protests in Athens for the Union of Cyprus with Greece, D2528, T15425, 2:09 minutes, 15 August 1954; *TNA/ FO371/112852.* Peake to Foreign Office, [Confidential], WG1081/297, 19 August 1954.
78 Christidis, *Κυπριακό και ελληνοτουρκικά*, p.44; Stefanidis, *Isle of Discord*, p.277, 292; id. *Stirring the Nation*, p.172; Kyrou, *Ελληνική εξωτερική πολιτική*, p.437, fn1.
79 *TNA/FO371/112852.* Peake to Foreign Office, [Confidential] WG1081/303, 19 August 1954; Peake to Foreign Office, WG1081/311, 21 August 1954; *TNA/FO371/112853.* Peake to Churchill, WG1081/327, [Confidential] 21 August 1954.
80 *TNA/FO371/112852.* Peake to Foreign Office, [Confidential] WG1081/303, 19 August 1954; notation by Wilding, WG1081/307, 23 August 1954.
81 *University of Athens Senate Secretariat Archive*, Minutes of Senate Meetings, vol.66, 1954-5, 7 December 1954, p.2-7.
82 Hatzivassiliou, *Στρατηγικές του Κυπριακού*, p.173.
83 *TNA/FO371/112875.* Peake to Foreign Office, WG1081/1015, 19 November 1954; Peake to Foreign Office, G1081/1016, [Confidential] 20 November 1954.
84 *TNA/FO371/112876.* Peake to Foreign Office, WG1081/1043 [Confidential], 26 November 1954.
85 *TNA/FO371/112853.* Churchill, personal minute, WG1081/330A, 25 August 1954.
86 *TNA/FO371/112853.* Peake to Churchill, [Confidential], WG1081/327, 21 August 1954.
87 Stefanidis, *Isle of Discord*, p.83.
88 *Eleftheria*, 12 October 1954, p.1, 6.
89 *TNA/FO371/112874.* Hesmondhalgh at UN to Selby at Foreign Office. Statement by Makarios at the UN [Confidential], WG1081/993, 10 November 1954.
90 *Eleftheria*, 8 October 1954, p.6; Linardatos, *Από τον Εμφύλιο*, vol.2, p.214, 220.
91 *F.R.U.S. 1952-1954, Vol. VIII.* Aldrich to State Department, 747C.00/10-254, [Secret], 2 October 1954, p.717-18.
92 On fluidity of British tactics see *TNA/FO371/112854.* Mathieson to Young, WG1081/992, 11 November 1954; Mathieson to Young [Secret], WG1081/1003, 17 November 1954.
93 *TNA/FO371/112875.* Dixon to Foreign Office, G1081/1033, [Secret], 25 November 1954.
94 *F.R.U.S. 1952-1954, Vol.VIII.* Conversation between Dulles and Papagos, [Confidential], USUN files, Cyprus, 1950-August-1955, Paris, 23 October 1954, p.720.
95 *TNA/FO371/112875.* Foreign Office to UN Delegation, WG1081/1021 [Secret], 20 November 1954; *F.R.U.S. 1952-1954, Vol.VIII.* Memorandum of conversation by Mangano, [Secret], 747C.00/11-1654, 12 November 1954, p.726; *TNA/FO371/112880.* Dixon to Foreign Office, WG1081/1165, 13 December 1954.
96 *F.R.U.S. 1952-1954, Vol.VIII.* Memorandum of conversation between Dulles and Lodge, USUN files, Cyprus-1950-August 1955, [Confidential], 8 October 1954, p.719.
97 Stefanidis, *Isle of Discord*, p.192-3.
98 *Mostras File*, p.37-40; Pipinelis, 'Τα διπλωματικά παρασκήνια', *Kathimerini*, 4 March 1959, p.3; Xydis, 'Toward "Toil and Moil"', p.16-17; Stefanidis, *Isle of Discourse*, p.86; Hatzivassiliou, *Στρατηγικές του Κυπριακού*, p.125;
99 Kyrou, *Ελληνική εξωτερική πολιτική*, p.278.

100 Pipinelis, 'Τα διπλωματικά παρασκήνια', *Kathimerini*, 4 March 1959, p.3; Xydis, 'Toward "Toil and Moil"', p.16-17; Stefanidis, *Isle of Discourse*, 85-6; Hatzivassiliou, *Στρατηγικές του Κυπριακού*, p.125.
101 Kyrou, *Ελληνική εξωτερική πολιτική*, p.278; cf *Motras File*, p.35-7.
102 *TNA/FO371/112875*. Dixon to Foreign Office, G1081/1032, [Secret], 25 November 1954.
103 *F.R.U.S. 1952-1954, Vol. VIII*. Memorandum of conversation between Dulles and Lodge, USUN files, Cyprus-1950-August 1955, [Confidential], 8 October 1954, p.719.
104 *F.R.U.S. 1952-1954, Vol. VIII*. Cannon to State Department, 747C.00/11-954, [Secret], 9 November 1954, p.723.
105 *F.R.U.S. 1952-1954, Vol. VIII*. Merchant to Hughes, 747C.00/10-2753, 27 October 1954, p.720, fn3 (supra).
106 *F.R.U.S. 1952-1954, Vol. VIII*. 747C.00/10-2354, 23 October 1954, p.720, fn3 (infra); Memorandum of Conversation between Dulles, Politis and Wood, 747C.00/10-2654 [Secret], 26 October 1954, p.720-1, italics added.
107 *F.R.U.S. 1952-1954, Vol. VIII*. Dulles to Papagos [Secret], 747C.00/11-1654, 16 November 1954, p.727.
108 *F.R.U.S. 1952-1954, Vol. VIII*. Memorandum of conversation by Mangano, [Secret], 747C.00/11-1654, 12 November 1954, p.724-5.
109 *TNA/FO371/112875*. Dixon to Foreign Office, WG1081/1034, 25 November 1954; *TNA/FO371/112876*. Commonwealth Office to High Commissions of Commonwealth states, WG1081/1051, 29 November 1954.
110 Stefanidis, *Isle of Discord*, p.281.
111 *TNA/FO371/112875*. Dixon to Foreign Office, G1081/1032, [Secret], 25 November 1954.
112 *TNA/FO371/112875*. Foreign Office to UN Delegation, authorized by Eden, WG1081/1021 [Secret], 20 November 1954; *TNA/FO371/112875*. Makins to Foreign Office, WG1081/1028 [Secret], 23 November 1954.
113 *TNA/FO371/112875*. Dixon to Foreign Office, G1081/1033, [Secret], 25 November 1954.
114 *TNA/FO371/112876*. Minute by Speaight, WG1081/1060, 29 November 1954.
115 *TNA/FO371/112876*. Dixon to Foreign Office, WG1081/1064, 1 December 1954; *F.R.U.S. 1952-1954, Vol. VIII*. Key to Dulles, [Secret], 747C.00/12-154, 1 December 1954, p.733-4.
116 *TNA/FO371/112876*. Minute by Selby, WG1081/1054, 2 December 1954; Minute by Wilding, 2 December 1954.
117 *F.R.U.S. 1952-1954, Vol. VIII*. Cannon to State Department, [Confidential], 747C.00/12-154, 1 December 1954, p.731.
118 *TNA/FO371/112879*. High Commissioner in Canada to Commonwealth Office, WG1081/1113, 7-8 December 1954.
119 *F.R.U.S. 1952-1954, Vol. VIII*. Cannon to State Department, [Secret], 747C.00/12-154, 1 December 1954, p.733; it is unclear who proposed such a solution at that point. Compare with Maniadakis's account discussed in the previous chapter.
120 See earlier reference to possible connection to Maniadakis's secret negotiations.
121 *TNA/FO371/112876*. Dixon to Foreign Office, WG1081/1067, 4 December 1954.
122 *F.R.U.S. 1952-1954, Vol. VIII*. Lodge to State Department, [Secret], 747C.00/12-854, 8 December 1954, p.735; *TNA/FO371/112878*. Dixon to Foreign Office, WG1081/1094, 8 December 1954.
123 Stefanidis, *Isle of Discord*, p.87, 196.

124 *TNA/FO371/112876*. Foreign Office minute 'Cyprus and the United Nations', Speaight, WG1081/1050, 29 November 1954; *TNA/FO371/112879*. Notation by Wilding, WG1081/1130, 13 December 1954; *TNA/FO371/112881*. UN Delegation New York to High Commission in Canada and Australia, WG1081/1176, 11 December 1954; *TNA/FO371/112882*. UN Delegation New York to High Commission in New Zealand, WG1081/1208, 13 December 1954; *TNA/FO371/112881*. Dixon on behalf of Nutting to Foreign Office, WG1081/1193, 15 December 1954.
125 *TNA/FO371/112878*. Dixon to Foreign Office, WG1081/1094, 8 December 1954.
126 *TNA/FO371/112880*. Dixon to Foreign Office, WG1081/1158, 13 December 1954.
127 *TNA/FO371/112879*. Dixon to Foreign Office, WG1081/1123, 10 December 1954; *F.R.U.S. 1952-1954, Vol. VIII*. Dulles to UN Delegation, [Secret], 747C.00/12-854, 9 December 1954, p.737; *New York Times*, 'Sir Leslie Munro, Diplomat, Dies, 72', 14 February 1972, p.44; Kyrou, *Ελληνική εξωτερική πολιτική*, p.303.
128 *F.R.U.S. 1952-1954, Vol. VIII*. Lodge to State Department, [Secret], 747C.00/12-854, 8 December 1954, p.736.
129 *TNA/FO371/112880*. UN Delegation to Foreign Office, WG1081/1163, 11 December 1954.
130 *F.R.U.S. 1952-1954, Vol. VIII*. Cannon to Papagos, Lot 60, F16, 350 Cyprus 1954, [Secret], 12 December 1954, p.738, fn5; *TNA/FO371/112879*. Notation by Wilding, WG1081/1130, 13 December 1954.
131 Kyrou, *Ελληνική εξωτερική πολιτική*, p.300; *F.R.U.S. 1952-1954, Vol. VIII*. Cannon to Papagos, Lot 60, F16, 350 Cyprus 1954, [Secret], 12 December 1954, p.738.
132 *F.R.U.S. 1952-1954, Vol. VIII*. Cannon to Papagos, Lot 60, F16, 350 Cyprus 1954, [Secret], 12 December 1954, p.738; *TNA/FO371/112880*. Dixon to Foreign Office, WG1081/1165, 13 December 1954; Stefanidis, *Isle of Discord*, p.150, 196.
133 *TNA/FO371/112880*. Dixon to Foreign Office, WG1081/1165, 13 December 1954.
134 *New York Times*, 'U.S. Opposes Plea of Greece in U. N. for Cyprus Union; Challenge to British Control of Island Inopportune Now, Washington Decides. U. S. Due to Oppose Greece on Cyprus', by Sydney Gruson, 13 December 1954, p.1; 'Cyprus and the U.N.', 13 December 1954, p.26.
135 *Eleftheria*, 14 December 1954, p.1, 6; *TNA/FO371/112882*. Statements by Stefanopoulos on Cyprus, WG1081/1207, 13 December 1954; Kyrou, *Ελληνική εξωτερική πολιτική*, p.300-2; *Official Minutes of the Greek Parliament*. Speech by Stefanopoulos, Period 3, Synod 3, Session 39, 7 February 1955, p.676.
136 *TNA/FO371/112879*. Dixon to Foreign Office, WG1081/1132, 12 December 1954.
137 Kyrou, *Ελληνική εξωτερική πολιτική*, p.301-2; Xydis, *Cyprus*, p.22.
138 *F.R.U.S. 1952-1954, Vol. VIII*. 747C.00/12-1354, 13 December 1954, p.739, fn2; Dulles to Athens, 747C.00/12-1354, 14 December 1954, p.739.
139 *TNA/FO371/112880*. Makins to Foreign Office, WG1081/1167, 13 December 1954; Dixon to Foreign Office, WG1081/1165, 13 December 1954.
140 *Official Minutes of the Greek Parliament*. Speech by Stefanopoulos, Period 3, Synod 3, Session 39, 7 February 1955, p.676.
141 *United Nations Documents*. General Assembly Ninth Session Official Records, First Committee, 749 Meeting, A/C.1/SR.749, 14 December 1954, p.543-4, par.1-16.
142 *United Nations Documents*. General Assembly Ninth Session Official Records, First Committee, 749 Meeting, A/C.1/SR.749, 14 December 1954, p.543, par.17-18, p.545, par.28, 34; 'New Zealand Saves the Day for Britain', *Reuters - Manchester Guardian*, 15 December 1954, p.1.

143 Kyrou, *Ελληνική εξωτερική πολιτική*, p.307; *Official Minutes of the Greek Parliament*. Speech by Stefanopoulos, Period 3, Synod 3, Session 39, 7 February 1955, p.676.
144 *United Nations Documents*. General Assembly Ninth Session Official Records, First Committee, 749 Meeting, A/C.1/SR.749, 14 December 1954, p.545, par.28; in a jumbled paragraph, Kyrou confirms that he called 'twice' for an immediate vote, but says he did so "for basic tactical reasons" which he never explained, *Ελληνική εξωτερική πολιτική*, p.307.
145 TNA/FO371/112881. Dixon on behalf of Nutting to Foreign Office [Confidential], WG1081/1193, 15 December 1954.
146 *United Nations Documents*. General Assembly Ninth Session Official Records, First Committee, 752 Meeting, A/C.1/SR.752, 15 December 1954, p.566-8, par.62-120; Kyrou, *Ελληνική εξωτερική πολιτική*, p.307-9.
147 *United Nations Resolutions*. General Assembly, Ninth Session, Supplement 21 (A/2890), RES/814 IX, 17 December 1954, General Assembly Official Records, New York, p.5.
148 Kyrou, *Ελληνική εξωτερική πολιτική*, p.313.
149 Xydis, 'Toward "Toil and Moil"', p.17; Linardatos, *Από τον Εμφύλιο*, vol.2, p.254; Vlachos, *Δέκα χρόνια Κυπριακού*, p.79-80; Averoff-Tositsas, *Ιστορία χαμένων ευκαιριών*, vol.1, p.51-2; Stefanidis, *Isle of Discord*, p.281-2; Svolopoulos, *Ελληνική εξωτερική πολιτική*, vol.2, p.134.
150 Xydis, *Cyprus*, 13; Vlachos, *Δέκα χρόνια Κυπριακού*, p.79-80; Averoff-Tositsas, *Ιστορία χαμένων ευκαιριών*, vol.1, p.51-2; Svolopoulos, *Ελληνική εξωτερική πολιτική*, vol.2, p.134.
151 Stefanidis, *Isle of Discord*, p.90.
152 *F.R.U.S. 1952-1954, Vol. VIII*. Dulles to UN Delegation, [Secret], 747C.00/12-854, 9 December 1954, p.737; *TNA/FO371/112882*. UN Delegation to High Commission in New Zealand, WG1081/1208, 13 December 1954.
153 TNA/FO371/112881. Dixon on behalf of Nutting to Foreign Office [Confidential], WG1081/1193, 15 December 1954. The first 'against' in the message should read 'for'.
154 Christidis, *Κυπριακό και ελληνοτουρκικά*, p.90.
155 TNA/FO371/112882. Statement by Stefanopoulos to Radio Athens from Paris announcing his departure to New York, WG1081/1204, 13, December 1954.
156 *F.R.U.S. 1952-1954, Vol. VIII*. Dulles to State Department, [Secret], 747C.00/12-1554, Paris, 15 December 1954, p.740; *Official Minutes of the Greek Parliament*. Speech by Stefanopoulos, Period 3, Synod 3, Session 39, 7 February 1955, p.677; Stefanidis, *Isle of Discord*, p.92.
157 *F.R.U.S. 1952-1954, Vol. VIII*. Brewster to Merchant, [Secret], 747C.00/12-1654, 16 December 1954, p.741.
158 *F.R.U.S. 1952-1954, Vol. VIII*. Merchant to Greek Delegation at NATO, [Secret], 747C.00/12-1654, Paris, 16 December 1954, p.742; *TNA/FO371/112883*. Makins to Foreign Office [Priority], WG1081/1260, 20 December 1954.
159 TNA/FO371/112883. Dixon to Foreign Office, WG1081/1244, 20 December 1954; embassy in Washington to Foreign Office, WG1081/1250, 20 December 1954; notation by Wilding, WG1081/1243, 22 December 1954; Johnson, 'Keeping Cyprus off the Agenda', p.235.
160 *Eleftheria*, 22 December 1954, p.1; cf *TNA/FO371/117620*. Peake to Foreign Office, RG1081/2, 31 December 1954. This states that 'relations between Stefanopoulos [...] and Kyrou were already strained to breaking point and, since the Prime Minister could hardly dispense with Stefanopoulos, Kyrou's fate was already sealed'.

161 *Official Minutes of the Greek Parliament*. Speech by Stefanopoulos, Period 3, Synod 3, Session 39, 7 February 1955, p.677.
162 Angelos Vlachos, *Μια φορά κι έναν καιρό, ένας διπλωμάτης...*, Fourth Edition, vol.3, Athens, Estia, 1998, p.221.
163 'Demonstrations in Athens. Protests against U.S.', *Manchester Guardian*, 15 December 1954, p.1; *Eleftheria*, 15 December 1954, p.1; *F.R.U.S. 1952-1954, Vol. VIII*. Brewster to Merchant, 747C.00/12-1654, [Secret], 16 December 1954, p.741.
164 *Kathimerini*, 21 December 1954, p.1; *TNA/FO371/112883*. BBC, WG1081/1273, 20 December 1954.
165 *The Times*, 20 December 1954.
166 *Official Minutes of the Greek Parliament*. Speech by Papagos, Period 3, Synod 3, Session 39, 7 February 1955, p.672-3.
167 *F.R.U.S. 1955-1957, Vol. XXIV*. Memorandum of conversation between Melas and Dulles, [Secret], Lot 64, D199, 6 April 1955, p.533-4.
168 Ierodiakonou, 'Το Κυπριακό από τον Β΄ Παγκόσμιο', p.176.
169 Pipinelis, 'Η «διεθνοποίησις» του Κυπριακού', p.3; id., 'Η «διεθνοποίησις» του Κυπριακού', *Kathimerini*, 5 March 1959, p.4; Vlachos, *Δέκα Χρόνια Κυπριακού*, p.69; Averoff-Tositsas, *Ιστορία χαμένων ευκαιριών*, vol.1, p.53; Hatzivassiliou, *Ιστορία του Ελληνικού Έθνους*, vol.16, p.440; Vryonis, *The Mechanism of Catastrophe*, p.31; cf Christidis, *Κυπριακό και ελληνοτουρκικά*, p.4-5, 17-18, 30-3.
170 *Mostras File*, p.33.
171 *United Nations: General Assembly Official Records*, Plenary Meetings (IX) 477, 24 September 1954, par.104, 109, 136, p.52, 54.
172 *Eleftheria*, 16 December 1954, p.1; *Embros*, 18 December 1954, p.1.
173 *TNA/FO371/112882*. Wilding, written notation, G1081/1219, 20 December 1954.
174 Grivas, *Απομνημονεύματα*, p.15; Loizidis, *Άτυχη Κύπρος*, p.96.
175 François Crouzet, *Le Conflit de Chypre, 1946-1959*, Brussels, Emile Bruylant, 1973, vol.2, p.486-7; Holland, *Britain and the Revolt*, p.53; Crawshaw, *The Cyprus Revolt*, p.52.
176 Andreas Azinas, 50.
177 Averoff-Tositsas, *Ιστορία χαμένων ευκαιριών*, vol.1, p.69.
178 Socratis Loizidis, 'Η αλήθεια δια την Ε.Ο.Κ.Α. Πώς εδημιουργήθη και πώς παρασκεύασε τον κυπριακόν αγώνα', *Eleftheria*, 27 September 1960, p.1; Loizidis, *Άτυχη Κύπρος*, p.99-100.
179 Gerasimos Konidaris, *Ιστορικαί αναμνήσεις από την προετοιμασία του αγώνος δια την ελευθερίαν της Κύπρου και η 7ⁿ Μαρτίου 1953*, Athens, 1964, p.11.
180 Grivas, *Απομνημονεύματα*, p.19-21; Foley (ed.), *Memoirs of General Grivas*, p.17-18; Azinas, *50 Years of Silence*, p.294-5; Makarios had apparently informed the King of this since September 1954, p.265-6; *F.R.U.S. 1951, Vol.V*. Peurifoy to State Department, 781.13/10-3051, 30 October 1951, p.517.
181 A notable exception is Clement Dodd, *The History and Politics of the Cyprus Conflict*, London, Palgrave Macmillan, 2010, p.20.
182 Vlachos, *Δέκα χρόνια Κυπριακού*, p.84-6, 89.
183 Kranidiotis, *Δύσκολα χρόνια*, p.81-2.
184 Averoff-Tositsas, *Ιστορία χαμένων ευκαιριών*, vol.1, p. 63-4, 67-8. For a similar view, see Hatzivassiliou, *Ιστορία του Ελληνικού Έθνους*, 16, p.442; id., *Στρατηγικές του Κυπριακού*, p.266, 340.

185 Markezinis, Σύγχρονη πολιτική Ιστορία, p.64.
186 Xydis, 'The UN General Assembly', p.144; id. *Cyprus*, 24; Panteli, *New History of Cyprus*, p.241; Svolopoulos, Ελληνική εξωτερική πολιτική, vol.2, p.81–2.
187 *TNA/FO286/1305/1024, Pt. I.* Mischief in the Air. A Selection of Extracts from Athens Radio Broadcasts to Cyprus, Cyprus Government Printing Office, March–August 1955; *TNA/FO371/112880*. Peake to Eden, WG1081/1172, 10 December 1954; Peake to Ward, WG1081/1174, 10 December 1954; Peake to Eden, 5 January 1955.
188 Grivas, Απομνημονεύματα, p.17–18, 21.
189 Ibid. p.18; Foley (ed.), *Memoirs of General Grivas*, p.22.
190 Grivas, Απομνημονεύματα, p.18; Averoff-Tositsas, Ιστορία χαμένων ευκαιριών, vol.1, p.64.
191 Grivas, Απομνημονεύματα, p.18, 20, 35.
192 Foley (ed.), *Memoirs of General Grivas*, p.29.
193 Averoff-Tositsas, Ιστορία χαμένων ευκαιριών, vol.1, p.64.
194 Azinas, *50 Years of Silence*, vol.1, p.216–17; On 30 September Makarios also informed the King about the preparations for an armed struggle, pp.265–6.
195 Ibid., p. 217–32; Grivas, Απομνημονεύματα, p.23; Foley (ed.), *Memoirs of General Grivas*, p.21–2; cf Averoff, Ιστορία χαμένων ευκαιριών, vol.1, p.226.
196 Azinas, *50 Years of Silence*, vol.1, p.234.
197 Ibid., p.234, 223, 240, 265–6.
198 Grivas, Απομνημονεύματα, p.23; Foley (ed.), *Memoirs of General Grivas*, p.22.
199 Grivas, Απομνημονεύματα, p.31–2; Foley (ed.), *Memoirs of General Grivas*, p.29–30; Loizidis, 'Η αλήθεια δια την Ε.Ο.Κ.Α.', p.6; Loizidis, Άτυχη Κύπρος, p.105–9; Azinas, *50 Years of Silence*, vol.1, p.327–54.
200 Azinas, *50 Years of Silence*, vol.1, p.258–64, 309, 316; Hatzivassiliou, Στρατηγικές του Κυπριακού, p.82.
201 Azinas, *50 Years of Silence*, vol.1, p.262, 320.
202 A more nuanced position is adopted by Hatzivassiliou, Στρατηγικές του Κυπριακού, p.266; id. Ιστορία του Ελληνικού Έθνους, vol.16, Athens, Ekdotiki Athinon, 2000, p.442.
203 Averoff-Tositsas, Ιστορία χαμένων ευκαιριών, vol.1, p.63, 224–5; Xydis, 'Toward "Toil and Moil"', p.18.
204 Ibid., p.223–4; cf Loizidis, 'Η αλήθεια δια την Ε.Ο.Κ.Α.', p.6.
205 Azinas, *50 Years of Silence*, vol.1, p.264; cf Loizidis, Άτυχη Κύπρος, p.105.
206 Azinas, *50 Years of Silence*, vol.1, p.234.
207 Ibid., p.314.
208 *TNA/FO371/117620*. Note by Wilding, RG1081/18, 10 January 1955.

Chapter 7

1 Spyros Markezinis, Radio Broadcast on the New Government's Economic Policy, *Embros*, 7 December 1952, p.6; Panayiotis Papaligouras, Speech at the Thessaloniki International Trade Fair, *Embros*, 9 September 1953, p.3.
2 G.M.F.A. Vassilios Damalas, 'Preliminary Report on the Evolution of the Greek Economy' (henceforth 'The Damalas Report') Directorate of Foreign Economic Affairs, Δ/4 5548, 25 April 1953, p.21, 19.

3   This is discussed extensively at the end of the present chapter.
4   Vasso Papandreou, *Πολυεθνικές επιχειρήσεις και αναπτυσσόμενες χώρες. Η περίπτωση της Ελλάδας*, Athens, Gutenberg, 1986, p.283.
5   George Pagoulatos, *Greece's New Political Economy: State, Finance, and Growth from Postwar to EMU*, Basingstoke, Palgrave Macmillan, 2003, p.25, 39, 41.
6   G.M.F.A. The Damalas Report, D/4 5548, 16 May 1953, p.28.
7   Anthem Thomas, 'The U.S.-Greek Agreement', *Contemporary Review*, 185, January-June 1954, p.88, 83.
8   Pagoulatos, *Greece's New Political Economy*, p.25.
9   Jeffery, *Ambiguous Commitments*, p.208, 215–22, 247.
10 Politakis, *The Post-War Reconstruction of Greece*, p.223, 229, 241–3; Apostolos Vetsopoulos, *The Economic Dimensions of the Marshall Plan in Greece, 1947–1952: The Origins of the Greek Economic Miracle*, PhD thesis, London, UCL, 2002, p.20–1, 351; Michalis Psalidopoulos, *Πολιτική οικονομία και Έλληνες διανοούμενοι. Μελέτες για την Ιστορία της οικονομικής σκέψης στη σύγχρονη Ελλάδα*, Athens, Typothito, 1999, p.193.
11 The view that the Korean War supposedly shifted US funds to Greece from economic to military aid, thus undermining the country's reconstruction is unconvincing. See Politakis, *The Post-War Reconstruction of Greece*, p.236–48, 266. There is no firm evidence that the decline in US economic aid to Greece in 1949–50 and 1950–1 from $280 and $231 was caused by the rise of military aid for the same period from $23 to $83 million. By contrast, there is evidence that the misuse of US economic aid was the main cause. Also, it is unclear how much the conflict in the Far East affected US military aid to Greece. In 1951–2, US military aid to Greece fell, but the Korean War escalated, while in 1952–3 it rose even though the War was coming to an end (see Table 6).
12 ECA, *European Recovery Program: Greece, Country Study*, Washington, US Government Printing Office, 1949, p.18.
13 F.R.U.S. *1952–1954, Vol. VIII*. Peurifoy to State Department, [Secret], 611.81/9-2552, 25 September 1952, p.809.
14 ECA, *European Recovery Program: Greece 1949*, p.28.
15 Vetsopoulos, *The Economic Dimensions of the Marshall Plan in Greece*, p.325–6.
16 *Eleftheria*, 8 April 1953, p.4.
17 Markezinis's speech quoted in *Nea Economia*, 7, June–July 1953, p.292.
18 *GATT Official Documents*. Developments in OEEC Trade Liberalization. Note by the Executive Secretary, [Restricted], L/542, 9 October 1956; Leander Nikolaides, 'Το ελληνικόν πρόγραμμα ανασυγκροτήσεως και η προβολή του εις το εξωτερικόν', *Spoudai*, March–April 1954, p.267.
19 Andreas Gerakis and Haskell Wald, 'Economic Stabilization and Progress in Greece, 1953–61: Contribution of Foreign Exchange and Trade Reforms', *IMF Staff Papers*, 11:1, March 1964, p.128.
20 William McNeill, *The Greek Dilemma: War and Aftermath*, Philadelphia and New York, Lippincott, 1947, p.272–8; Evangelos Eliades, 'Stabilization of the Greek Economy and the 1953 Devaluation of the Drachma', *IMF Staff Papers*, 4:1, September 1954, p.23; G.M.F.A. The Damalas Report, p.18.
21 ECA, *European Recovery Program: Greece 1949*, p.6; Vergopoulos, 'The Emergence of the New Bourgeoisie', p.298.
22 ECA, *European Recovery Program: Greece 1949*, p.11.
23 Psalidopoulos, *Επιτηρητές σε απόγνωση*, p.45.
24 Porter, *Ζητείται: Ένα θαύμα για την Ελλάδα*, p.234.

25 Markezinis, *Από του πολέμου*, p.74.
26 *Archive of the Central Bank of Greece*. The Varvaressos Report, No.75325, 5 January 1952, p.18–43; Vergopoulos, 'The Emergence of the New Bourgeoisie', p.302.
27 Markezinis, *Από του πολέμου*, p.34.
28 Angelos Angelopoulos, 'Απόψεις περί του οικονομικού προβλήματος της Ελλάδος', *Nea Economia*, 7, Athens, March 1953, p.100.
29 Axel Heyst, 'Greece in 1954', *Contemporary Review*, 187, January–June 1955, p.17.
30 ECA, *European Recovery Program: Greece*, 1949, p.1, 34, 48.
31 F.R.U.S. 1951, Vol. V. Peurifoy to State Department, 781.00/9-1251, 12 September 1951, p.507.
32 F.R.U.S. 1951, Vol. V. NSC Staff Study: The Position of the United States with Respect to Greece, [Top Secret], NSC 103 Series, Lot 351, 6 February 1951, p.454.
33 ECA, *European Recovery Program: Greece*, 1949, p.49.
34 ECA, *Three Years of the Marshal Plan*, Washington, 1951, p.9.
35 George Mantzavinos, 'Annual Report of Governor of the Bank of Greece George Mantzavinos for 1952', *Nea Economia*, 7 March 1953, p.180.
36 Psalidopoulos, *Επιτηρητές σε απόγνωση*, p.140–1.
37 Bickham Sweet-Escott, *Greece: A Political and Economic Survey, 1939–1953*, London and New York, RIIA, 1954, p.113–14.
38 Nikolaides, 'Το ελληνικόν πρόγραμμα', p.265–6.
39 F.R.U.S. 1951, Vol. V. Yost to State Department, 881.00/R11-2951, 29 November 1951, p.524, fn2.
40 F.R.U.S. 1951, Vol. V. Peurifoy to State Department, 781.00/9-1251, 12 September 1951, p.506–7; Peurifoy to State Department, 881.00 R/11-2051, 20 November 1951, p.520–1; Peurifoy to State Department, 781.5 MSP/12-2151, 21 December 1951, p.526.
41 Tsoucalas, *Greek Tragedy*, p.124; Linardatos, *Από τον Εμφύλιο*, vol.1, p.346; cf George Stathakis, *Το Δόγμα Τρούμαν και το Σχέδιο Μάρσαλ: Η ιστορία της αμερικανικής βοήθειας στην Ελλάδα*, Athens, Vivliorama, 2004, p.24.
42 F.R.U.S. 1951, Vol. V. Peurifoy to State Department, 781.00/9-2451, 24 September 1951, p.510–11.
43 F.R.U.S. 1951, Vol. V. Turkel to State Department, 881.00/11-1051, [Confidential], 10 November 1951, p.518–19. Kartalis claimed the figures were 43 per cent of the state budget and 10 per cent of GDP, but he included the budget on internal security forces.
44 F.R.U.S. 1951, Vol. V. Turkel to State Department, 881.00/11-1051, 10 November 1951, p.518–19.
45 Excerpts from Roger Lapham's radio speech, *Eleftheria*, 15 June 1952, p.1.
46 F.R.U.S. 1952–1954, Vol. VIII. Kenney to Peurifoy, [Top Secret/Personal], embassy files, lot 59 F48, 49–57, 29 May 1952, p.794–5.
47 F.R.U.S. 1952–1954, Vol. VIII. Locker to Rountree, 881.10/3-2052, 20 March 1952, p.791, fn4.
48 F.R.U.S. 1952–1954, Vol. VIII. Acting Assistant Secretary Berry to Acheson, [Top Secret, Special Handling], 881.10-3-3152, 31 March 1952, p.791; Psalidopoulos, *Επιτηρητές σε απόγνωση*, p.118–21.
49 F.R.U.S. 1952–1954, Vol. VIII. Kenney to Peurifoy, [Top Secret/Personal], Athens embassy files, lot 59, F48, 49–57, 29 May 1952, p.795; Peurifoy to Kenney, Athens embassy files, lot 59 F48, 49–57, p.791, fn4.
50 F.R.U.S. 1952–1954, Vol. VIII. Byroade to Acheson, [Top Secret], 881.10/7-1952, 28 July 1952, p.799–800; Acheson to Athens embassy, [Top Secret], 881.00/7-2852, 29 July 1952, p.801–2.

51 Xenophon Zolotas, 'Εν όψει μειωμένης βοηθείας. Η ελληνική οικονομία εις κρίσιμον καμπήν', *Eleftheria*, 17 May 1952, p.1.
52 F.R.U.S. *1952-1954, Vol. VIII*. Peurifoy to State Department, [Top Secret], 781.5 MSP/8-752, 7 August 1952, p.802.
53 In June–July, Kartalis asked Washington for an extension of the Greek recovery programme and announced a 'new stabilization and reconstruction programme' for 1952-5, *Eleftheria*, 27 June 1952, p.1, 12 July 1952, p.1.
54 F.R.U.S. *1952-1954, Vol. VIII*. Peurifoy to State Department, [Top Secret], 881.00/8-2752, 27 August 1952, p.805-6.
55 Vergopoulos, 'The Emergence of the New Bourgeoisie', p.305-6; Close, *Greece since 1945*, p.44; Margarita Dritsas, 'National Integration and Economic Change in Greece during the Twentieth Century', in Alice Teichova, Herbert Matis, Jaroslav Pátek (eds), *Economic Change and the National Question in Twentieth-Century Europe*, Cambridge, Cambridge University Press, 2000, p.220.
56 Stathakis, *Το Δόγμα Τρούμαν και το Σχέδιο Μάρσαλ*, p.23.
57 Loukas Tsoukalis, *The European Community and its Mediterranean Enlargement*, London, Allen and Unwin, 1981, p.34; Panos Kazakos, 'Assessment', in Σπυρίδων Μαρκεζίνης, *Στρατηγικές οικονομικής ανάπτυξης και η υποτίμηση της δραχμής (1953)*, Athens, Greek Parliament Foundation, 2013, p.102; Costis, *'Τα κακομαθημένα παιδιά'*, p.716-20; Politakis, *The Post-War Reconstruction of Greece*, p.266; quote from Pagoulatos, *Greece's New Political Economy*, p.29.
58 Among the notable exceptions are Tsoukalas 1969, p.129; Stefanidis, *Από τον Εμφύλιο*, p.232-3; Psalidopoulos, *Επιτηρητές σε απόγνωση*, p.61.
59 Nikolaides, 'Το ελληνικόν πρόγραμμα', p.261, 263, 265.
60 *Archive of the Central Bank of Greece*. The Varvaressos Report, p.9-16, 66, 117, 142, 199.
61 Stefanidis, *Από τον Εμφύλιο*, p.232-3.
62 Vergopoulos, 'The Emergence of the New Bourgeoisie', p.308.
63 Xenophon Zolotas, *Η Ελλάς εις το στάδιον της εκβιομηχανίσεως*, Athens, Eleftheroudakis, 1926; Pagoulatos, *Greece's New Political Economy*, p.29; Michalis Psalidopoulos, *Ο Ξενοφών Ζολώτας και η ελληνική οικονομία*, Athens, Metamesonykties Ekdoseis, 2008, p.16-17.
64 *Archive of the Central Bank of Greece*. The Varvaressos Report, p.7-16.
65 Ibid., p.17-141.
66 Ibid., p.141-200. The Secret Annex to *The Varvaressos Report* was published by the Rally Government after the devaluation of 9 April 1953, see *Nea Economia*, 7 May 1953, p.13-14, 238.
67 *Archive of the Central Bank of Greece*. The Varvaressos Report, p.201-32.
68 Ibid., p.233, 236.
69 Vergopoulos, 'The Emergence of the New Bourgeoisie', p.305-6.
70 Panos Kazakos, *Ανάμεσα σε κράτος και αγορά. Οικονομία και οικονομική πολιτική στη μεταπολεμική Ελλάδα, 1944-2000*, Athens, Patakis, 2010, p.158.
71 *Archive of the Central Bank of Greece*. The Varvaressos Report, p.42-3, 53, 58, 80, quotation p.4; On Varvaressos's earlier opposition to the Athenian bourgeoisie, see Athanasios Lykoyannis, *Britain and the Greek Economic Crisis, 1944-1947*, Columbia, University of Missouri Press, 2002, p.118.
72 Xenophon Zolotas, 'Η έκθεσις του κ. Βαρβαρέσσου και η οικονομική ανάπτυξις', *Epitheorisis Economikon kai Politikon Epistimon*, January-March 1952, p.1-24; Christos Evelpides, 'Σκέψεις τινές επί της εκθέσεως του κ. Βαρβαρέσσου', *Epitheorisis*

Economikon kai Politikon Epistimon, January–March 1952, p.24–5; cf Psalidopoulos, *Ο Ξενοφών Ζολώτας*, p.55-7.
73 Yannis Zigdis, quoted in *Epitheorisis Economikon kai Politikon Epistimon*, January–March 1952, p.27–8.
74 On the supposedly 'strictly scientific' character of this journal, cf Psalidopoulos, *Πολιτική οικονομία*, p.180.
75 Kyriakos Varvaressos, Letter to the editor, *Epitheorisis Economikon kai Politikon Epistimon*, 24 June 1952, p.205-9.
76 Quoted in *Eleftheria*, 22 March 1952, p.1; cf Psalidopoulos, *Πολιτική οικονομία*, p.198.
77 *Eleftheria*, 27 May 1952, p.1; 3 June 1952, p.1.
78 *Official Minutes of the Greek Parliament*, Speech by Markezinis, 23 November 1953, Session 5, p.14.
79 Report, see *Eleftheria*, 30 April 1953, p.1, 6. Markezinis, *Σύγχρονη πολιτική Ιστορία*, vol.3, p.18.
80 Markezinis, *Σύγχρονη πολιτική Ιστορία*, vol.3, p.30; On the declassification of the Secret Annex of the Varvaressos Report, see *Eleftheria*, 30 April 1953, p.1, 6.
81 Bradley Schiller, *Essentials of Economics*, New York, McGraw-Hill, 1999, p.382; Pagoulatos, *Greece's New Political Economy*, p.43.
82 Eliades, 'Stabilization of the Greek Economy and the 1953 Devaluation of the Drachma', p.51; Gerakis and Wald, 'Economic Stabilization and Progress in Greece, 1953-61', p.126-7.
83 *Eleftheria*, 11 April 1953, p.4.
84 Kottis, *Liberalizing Foreign Trade*, p.40, fn8; cf George Stathakis, 'US Economic Policies in Post Civil-War Greece, 1949-1953: Stabilisation and Monetary Reform', *Journal of European Economic History*, 24:2, 1995, p.401.
85 Markezinis, *Σύγχρονη πολιτική Ιστορία*, vol.3, p.12.
86 Ibid., p.12.
87 *Official Minutes of the Greek Parliament*, Speech by the Minister of Coordination Spyros Markezinis, Session 5, 23 November 1953 p.14; Markezinis, *Σύγχρονη πολιτική Ιστορία*, vol.3, p.11.
88 Gail Makinen, 'The Greek Stabilization of 1944-46', *The American Economic Review*, 74:5, December 1984, p.1069.
89 Ibid., p.14-15.
90 Linardatos, *Από τον Εμφύλιο*, vol.2, p.61; Vournas, *Ιστορία*, p.13.
91 *Eleftheria*, 30 April 1953, p.1, 6; Varvaressos expressed similar views before the devaluation, see Psalidopoulos, *Επιτηρητές σε απόγνωση*, p.123-5.
92 *Official Minutes of the Greek Parliament*, Speech by the Minister of Coordination Spyros Markezinis, Session 5, 23 November 1953, p.14.
93 See table 9.
94 Eliades, 'Stabilization of the Greek Economy and the 1953 Devaluation of the Drachma', p.54, fn19; Kottis, *Liberalizing Foreign Trade*, p.25-6; *Eleftheria*, 14 April 1953, p.1, 4; 15 April 1953, p.4.
95 Papandreou, *Πολυεθνικές επιχειρήσεις*, p.167-72.
96 George Mantzavinos, 'Annual Report of the Governor of the Bank of Greece George Mantzavinos for 1953', *Nea Economia*, 8, April 1954, p.215-25; Sotiris Valden, *Ελλάδα και Ανατολικές Χώρες: Οικονομικές Σχέσεις και Πολιτική*, Athens, Odysseas, 1991, p.4.
97 Sweet-Escott, *Greece: A Political and Economic Survey*, p.88; Thomas, 'The U.S.-Greek Agreement', p.88.
98 Kottis, *Liberalizing Foreign Trade*, p.28, table 2.9, p.35, table 2.17.

99   Pagoulatos, *Greece's New Political Economy*, p.39.
100 This omission is acknowledged by Kazakos, see 'Assessment', p.102.
101 Spyros Markezinis, Radio Broadcast, 20 June 1953, see *Embros*, 21 June 1953, p.5.
102 Heyst, 'Greece in 1954', p.16.
103 Nikolaides, 'Το ελληνικόν πρόγραμμα', p.260.
104 Ibid., p.264; Vetsopoulos, *The Economic Dimensions of the Marshall Plan*, p.105, 108, 268.
105 *Eleftheria*, 8 March 1953, p.4.
106 *Eleftheria*, 7 April 1953, p.4; 8 April 1953, p.4.
107 *F.R.U.S. 1952-1954, Vol. VIII*. Memorandum of Conversation between Dulles, Markezinis, Politis, Jernegan, [Confidential], 781.5 MSP/5-753, 7 May 1953, p.823, fn3; Statement by Kartalis, *Eleftheria*, 23 June 1953, p.4; Markezinis, *Σύγχρονη πολιτική Ιστορία*, vol.3, p.16; Psalidopoulos, *Επιτηρητές σε απόγνωση*, p.134 speaks of '$100 million' without identifying his source. This figure is not contained in the source he cites.
108 *Eleftheria*, 14 June 1953, p.1.
109 Markezinis, *Σύγχρονη πολιτική Ιστορία*, vol.3, p.16.
110 *F.R.U.S. 1952-1954, Vol. VIII*. Memorandum of Conversation between Dulles, Markezinis, Politis, Jernegan, [Confidential], 781.5 MSP/5-753, 7 May 1953, 824.
111 Ibid., p.824; *F.R.U.S. 1952-1954, Vol. VIII*. From Baxter to Peurifoy, [Secret-Personal/Official-Informal], Athens Embassy Files, Lot 60, F16, '500 Greece 1953', 12 May 1953, p.827.
112 Ibid., p.827.
113 Ibid., p.826, 827-8.
114 *TNA/FO371/107505*. Salt in Washington to Foreign Office, [Confidential], WG1102/1, 15 May 1953.
115 *F.R.U.S. 1952-1954, Vol. VIII*. From Baxter to Peurifoy, [Secret-Personal/Official-Informal], Athens Embassy Files, Lot 60, F16, '500 Greece 1953', 12 May 1953, p.827; *TNA/FO371/107505*. Salt in Washington to Foreign Office, [Confidential], WG1102/1, 15 May 1953.
116 Markezinis, *Σύγχρονη πολιτική Ιστορία*, vol.3, p.17.
117 *F.R.U.S. 1952-1954, Vol. VIII*. Aide-Memoire by MSA (Porter) to Markezinis, [Confidential], 881.00/5-1553, 15 May 1953, p.831-2.
118 Pelt, *Tying Greece*, p.75-6; Psalidopoulos, *Επιτηρητές σε απόγνωση*, p.133-5.
119 *Kathimerini*, 10 June 1953, p.4; *Eleftheria*, 14 June 1953, p.1.
120 Spyros Markezinis, Radio Broadcast, 20 June 1953, *Embros*, 21 June 1953, p.5.
121 'The Morgan Commission Report' *Nea Economia*, 7, June-July 1953, p.291.
122 MSA, *Report to Congress on the Mutual Security Program for the Six Months Ended 31 December 1953*, p.33.
123 Richard Clogg, *A Short History of Modern Greece*, Second Edition, Cambridge, Cambridge University Press, 1986, p.169.
124 John Koliopoulos and Thanos Veremis, *Modern Greece: A History Since 1821*, London, Blackwell, 2010, p.130-1.
125 Spyros Markezinis, Radio Broadcast: 9 April 1953, *Embros*, 10 April 1953, p.3.
126 Quoted in *Embros*, 7 July 1953, p.1.
127 Stathis Kalyvas, *Modern Greece: What Everyone Needs to Know*, Oxford, Oxford University Press, 2015, p.105; Jeffery, *Ambiguous Commitments*, p.250.
128 Eliades, 'Stabilization of the Greek Economy and the 1953 Devaluation of the Drachma', p.53.

129 Wray Candilis, *The Economy of Greece, 1944–66: Efforts for Stability and Development*, New York, Praeger, 1968, p.164; Evanthis Hatzivassiliou, *Ελληνικός Φιλελευθερισμός. Το ριζοσπαστικό ρεύμα 1932–1979*, Athens, Patakis, 2010, p.277; quote from Kottis, *Liberalizing Foreign Trade*, p.30.
130 Stathakis, 'Approaches to the Early Post-War Evanthis Greek Economy', p.163; Psalidopoulos, *Πολιτική οικονομία*, p.191.
131 Evanthis Hatzivassiliou, 'Ο Ψυχρός Πόλεμος ως κρίση εκσυγχρονισμού: υπέρβαση κρίσεων και ελληνική εμπειρία, 1932–1959', in Constantina Botsiou and Yannis Sakkas (eds), *Η Ελλάδα, η Δύση και η Μεσόγειος, 1945-62. Νέες ερευνητικές προσεγγίσεις*, Thessaloniki, University of Macedonia, 2015, p.27; id. *Ελληνικός Φιλελευθερισμός*, p.274–6; Tsoukalis, *The European Community*, p.33; Kazakos, *Ανάμεσα σε κράτος και αγορά*, p.32, 167.
132 Tsoucalas, *Greek Tragedy*, p.131; Valden, *Ελλάδα και Ανατολικές Χώρες*, vol.1, p.59.
133 Kottis, *Liberalizing Foreign Trade*, p.24; Hatzivassiliou, 'Ο Ψυχρός Πόλεμος ως κρίση εκσυγχρονισμού', p.31, 34; Kofas, *Intervention and Underdevelopment*, p.133–5.
134 Spyros Markezinis, Radio Broadcast: 9 April 1953, *Embros*, 10 April 1953, p.3; Thanos Kapsalis, quoted in *Embros*, 7 July 1953, p.1.
135 Spyros Markezinis, Devaluation Speech, *Embros*, 10 April 1953, p.3, italics added.
136 For a full text of the law for liberalising imports, see *Embros*, 7 July 1953, p.1, 3; Gerakis and Wald, 'Economic Stabilization and Progress in Greece, 1953–61', p.128.
137 *GATT Official Documents*. Special Import Taxes Instituted by the Government of Greece and Increase of Import Duties on Products Specified in Schedule XXV, L/88, 1 May 1953; Increase of Import Duties in Schedule XXV – Greece (G/27 and SR.7/13) – Restoration of Pre-war Coefficients, G/51, 5 August 1953; *Embros*, 21 July 1953, p.4.
138 *GATT Official Documents*. Article XXVIII – Application of the Schedules – Views of the Government of Greece, L/117, 1 September 1953.
139 *Embros*, 10 September 1953, p.6.
140 *GATT Official Documents*. European Office of the United Nations, Geneva, GATT Eighth Session of the Contracting Parties – Speech by C. Papayannis to the Plenary Session, 18 September 1953.
141 *GATT Official Documents*. Schedule XXV – Greece: Adjustment of Specific Duties. Addendum, L/184/Add.1 and L/179/ADD.3-L/198/ADD.1, 26 March 1954; Schedule XXV – Greece: Adjustment of Specific Duties. Addendum, L/184/Add.2 and L/179/ADD.3-L/198/ADD.1, 11 June 1954; Greece: Adjustment of Specific Duties. Addendum, L/184/Add.3 and L/179/ADD.3-L/198/ADD.1, 28 October 1954; Greece: Adjustment of Specific Duties. Addendum, L/387 and L/379-L/392/REV.1, 18 August 1955.
142 *GATT Official Documents*. Schedule XXV – Greece: Results of Renegotiations, L/391 and L/379-L/392/REV.1, August 18, 1955; Schedule XXV – Greece: Modification of Concessions on Item 12 a) 1) under the Procedures of Article XIX, L/346 and L/337-L/351/ADD.2, 5 March 1955.
143 Quoted in *Embros*, 19 July 1953, p.6; 15 July 1953, p.4.
144 Markezinis, *Σύγχρονη πολιτική Ιστορία*, vol.3, p.13.
145 A notable exception is Close, *Greece since 1945*, p.45.
146 G.M.F.A. The Damalas Report, p.25; Later Damalas argued that the devaluation stabilized the drachma but protested that it did not balance the country's foreign accounts. Presumably, he would have favoured a deeper devaluation, cf Vasilios

Damalas, *Σύντομος ιστορία της δραχμής (από του 1833 μέχρι του 1953)*, Athens, Spoudai, 1959, p.44–5.
147 C.H. Kirkpatrick and F.I. Nixson, 'The Origins of Inflation in Less Developed Countries: A Selective View', in Michael Parkin and Goerge Zis (eds), *Inflation in Open Economies*, Manchester, Manchester University Press, 1976, p.155.
148 *Official Minutes of the Greek Parliament*, Speech by Spyros Markezinis, 23 November 1953, Session 5, p.17.
149 Markezinis, *Σύγχρονη πολιτική Ιστορία*, vol.3, p.23.
150 *Official Minutes of the Greek Parliament*, Speech by Spyros Markezinis, 23 November 1953, 5th Session, p.22.
151 Spyros Markezinis, Radio Broadcast on the New Government's Economic Policy, *Embros*, 7 December 1952, p.6; Panayiotis Papaligouras, Speech at the Thessaloniki International Trade Fair, *Embros*, 9 September 1953, p.3; Psalidopoulos, *Πολιτική οικονομία*, p.203–4.
152 Kazakos, *Ανάμεσα σε κράτος και αγορά*, p.171–2; Hatzivassiliou, *Ελληνικός Φιλελευθερισμός*, p.274, 288; Hatzivassiliou, 'Greek Liberalism in the Twentieth Century: Dilemmas for Research', in Constantine Arvanitopoulos and Konstantina Botsiou (eds), *The Constantinos Karamanlis Yearbook for Democracy 2010*, Heidelberg, Springer, 2010, p.123.
153 Kazakos, *Ανάμεσα σε κράτος και αγορά*, p.163–9, 172.
154 G.M.F.A. The Damalas Report, p.21, 22, 28.
155 *Kathimerini*, 11 September 1953, p.4; quote from *Embros*, 11 September 1953, p.4.
156 *Constantine Karamanlis Archive, vol. I*. Letter by Karamanlis to Papagos, 3 December 1954, p.214.
157 *Embros*, 29 August 1953, p.4; Kottis, *Liberalizing Foreign Trade*, p.26, 36.
158 Gerakis and Wald, 'Economic Stabilization and Progress in Greece,1953–61', p.140, fn20.
159 Kottis, *Liberalizing Foreign Trade*, p.26–7.
160 Pagoulatos, *Greece's New Political Economy*, p.21, 24. It should be noted that, in contrast to the present analysis, Pagoulatos does not consider this mixed policy as self-contradictory or dualist.
161 Kazakos, *Ανάμεσα σε κράτος και αγορά*, p.41–2, 168–9; Sophia Lazaretou, *Greek Monetary Economics in Retrospect: The Adventures of the Drachma*, Athens, Bank of Greece, Working Paper, 2 April 2003, p.26; Hatzivassiliou, *Ελληνικός Φιλελευθερισμός*, p.274–5, 278; Tsoukalis, *The European Community*, p.17, 28; Politakis, *The Post-War Reconstruction of Greece*, p.1.
162 Psalidopoulos, *Επιτηρητές σε απόγνωση*, p.137.
163 K.P. Prodromidis, *Foreign Trade of Greece: A Quantitative Analysis at Sectoral Level*, Athens, Centre of Planning and Economic Research, 1976, p.27, 154–6; Evangelos Voloudakis and Panayotis Fylaktos, *Greek Exports: Determinants and Policies, 1960–1979*, Report to the World Bank, unpublished, 1982, quoted in Kottis, *Liberalizing Foreign Trade*, p.82–9; cf Gerakis and Wald, 'Economic Stabilization and Progress in Greece, 1953–61', p.128.
164 Kottis, *Liberalizing Foreign Trade*, p.36; Pagoulatos, *Greece's New Political Economy*, p.25.
165 Candilis, *The Economy of Greece*, p.164.
166 Ibid., p.139–40, table 53; Gerakis and Wald, 'Economic Stabilization and Progress in Greece,1953–61', p.137; Poulantzas, *Crisis of the Dictatorships*, p.17; cf Kazakos, 'Assessment', p.104; id. *Ανάμεσα σε κράτος και αγορά*, p.189.

167 Tasos Giannitsis, 'Οικονομική ολοκλήρωση της Ελλάδας στην ΕΟΚ και άμεσες επενδύσεις', in Marios Nikolinakos, *ΕΟΚ-Ελλάδα-Μεσόγειος*, Athens, Livanis, 1978, p.45-8; Poulantzas, *Crisis of the Dictatorships*, p.17-18.
168 *Constantine Karamanlis Archive, vol. I*. Letter by Karamanlis to Papagos, 3 December 1954, p.214.
169 Kazakos, *Ανάμεσα σε κράτος και αγορά*, p.182-9; Hatzivassiliou, *Ελληνικός Φιλελευθερισμός*, p.355-7; Stathakis, 'US Economic Policies in Post Civil-War Greece', p.401.

Conclusion

1 John Rohsenow (ed.), *ABC Dictionary of Chinese Proverbs (Yanhu)*, Hawai'i, University of Hawai'i Press, 2003, p.67.
2 Thomas Anthem, 'Prospects in Cyprus', *Contemporary Review*, 187, January-June 1955, p.157; *Eleftheria*, 15 December 1954, p.1; *F.R.U.S. 1952-1954*, vol.VIII. Memorandum of Conversation between Acting Secretary Hoover, Baxter and Ambassador Melas, [Confidential], 611.81/12-1654, 16 December 1954, p.743.
3 *F.R.U.S. 1952-1954*, vol.VIII. Dulles to State Department, [Confidential], 747C.00/12-1854, 18 December 1954, p.750; Cannon to State Department, [Confidential] 781/12-1754, 17 December 1954, p.746; Memorandum by Brewster in France to Assistant Secretary Merchant, [Secret], 747C.00/12-1654, 16 December 1954, p.741; Memorandum of Conversation between Acting Secretary Hoover, Baxter and Melas, [Confidential], 611.81/12-1654, 16 December 1954, p.743.
4 *F.R.U.S. 1955-1957*, vol.XXIV. Cannon to Dulles, C.781.5-MSP/5-2055 [Confidential], 20 May 1955, p.537.
5 Durrell, *Bitter Lemons*, p.189.
6 *TNA/FO371/112880*. Peake to Eden, WG1081/1172, 10 December 1954; Peake to Ward, WG1081/1174, 10 December 1954; Peake to Eden, 5 January 1955.
7 Grivas, *Απομνημονεύματα*, p.31.
8 *F.R.U.S. 1952-1954*, vol.VIII. Dulles to State Department, [Confidential], 747C.00/12-1854, 18 December 1954, p.750, fn6.
9 *TNA/FO286/1305/1024 Pt.III*. 'Mischief in the Air: A Selection of Extracts from Athens Radio Broadcasts to Cyprus – March to August 1955', Cyprus Government Printing Office, September 1955.
10 *TNA/FO800/667*. Foreign Office to embassy in Istanbul [Top Secret], 21 June 1955; Istanbul to Foreign Office [Top Secret], 23 June 1955; Macmillan to Eden, 10 August 1955; Eden to Macmillan, M(E)56/55, 19 August 1955.
11 *TNA/FO800/667*. Macmillan to Eden, PM/55/14 [Confidential], 31 August 1955; Holland, *Britain and the Revolt*, p.64-75; *Sophocles Venizelos Papers*. Venizelos's views on the British invitation to discuss the Cyprus issue, 018-017, 226/11/101, 1 July 1955; on the reactions of party leaders, see Vlachos, *Δέκα χρόνια Κυπριακού*, p.104-14.
12 *TNA/FO371/117721*. Embassy in Ankara to Turkish Ministry of Foreign Affairs, [Confidential], RK 10110/12A, 9 November 1955; Helsinki Watch, *Denying Human Rights and Ethnic Identity: The Greeks of Turkey*, New York, Washington, LA, London, Human Rights Watch, 1992, p.10; Vryonis, *The Mechanism of Catastrophe*, p.213, fn35, 581-2.

13 Iatrides, *Balkan Triangle*, p.170.
14 Thanos Veremis, *Ιστορία των ελληνοτουρκικών σχέσεων 1453–1998*, Athens, Sideris/ELIAMEP, 1998, p.113.
15 Quoted in Linardatos, *Apo ton Emphylio*, vol.2, p.346–8.
16 Helsinki Watch, *Denying Human Rights*, p.10; Vryonis, *The Mechanism of Catastrophe*, p.42.
17 Vlachos, *Deka Chronia Kypriakou*, p.121.
18 Frederica, *Measure*, p.182.
19 *Eisenhower Library Documents*. Annual Message to the Congress on the State of the Union, H. Doc, 251, *83rd Congress*, 2nd Session, 7 January 1954; Annual Message to the Congress on the State of the Union, H. Doc, 251, *84th Congress*, 1st Session, 6 January 1955; Winston Churchill, *Hansard*, HC Debates, vol.538, c.969, 14 March 1955.
20 Holland, *Britain and the Revolt*, p.65, 74.
21 Pipinelis, 'Το Κυπριακόν εις το μέλλον', *Kathimerini*, 5 February 1955, p.1; Xydis, *Cyprus*, p.23, 31–5; Averoff-Tositsas, *Ιστορία χαμένων ευκαιριών*, vol.1, p.50; Vlachos, *Δέκα Χρόνια Κυπριακού*, p.76; Alexandrakis, Theodoropoulos, Lagakos, *Το Κυπριακό*, p.23; Stefanidis, *Isle of Discord*, p.x, 295; Svolopoulos, *Ελληνική εξωτερική πολιτική*, vol.2, p.85–6; Hatzivassiliou, *Στρατηγικές του Κυπριακού*, p.124–7, 230–1.
22 Stefanidis, *Stirring the Nation*, p.107.
23 Averoff-Tositsas, *Ιστορία χαμένων ευκαιριών*, vol.1, p.53; Vlachos, *Δέκα Χρόνια Κυπριακού*, p.68; Svolopoulos, *Ελληνική εξωτερική πολιτική*, vol.2, p.86–7; Stefanidis, *Isle of Discord*, p.295, 297; Hatzivassiliou, *Στρατηγικές του Κυπριακού*, p.126, 303.
24 Pipinelis, 'Η «διεθνοποίησις» του Κυπριακού', p.3; *Mostras File*, p.98; Hatzivassiliou, *Στρατηγικές του Κυπριακού*, p.322–4.
25 Svolopoulos, *Ελληνική εξωτερική πολιτική*, vol.2, p.75.
26 Stefanidis, *Isle of Discord*, p.295, 297; id., *Stirring the Nation*, p.107.
27 William Roger Louis, *Ends of British Imperialism: The Scramble for Empire, Suez, and Decolonization*, London, I.B. Tauris, 2010, p.958–63; Robert Miller, *Soviet Foreign Policy Today: Gorbachev and the New Political Thinking*, Hoboken, Taylor and Francis, 2012, p.167–8.
28 The reader should note the difference between the critique of Papagos's Cyprus policy and the critique of his foreign policy, of which Cyprus was one (albeit pivotal) component.
29 Pipinelis, 'Η άγνωστος διπλωματική ιστορία', p.3; id., 'Τα διπλωματικά παρασκήνια', *Kathimerini*, 3 March 1959, p.3; id., 'Η «διεθνοποίησις» του Κυπριακού', p.3; Vlachos, *Δέκα Χρόνια Κυπριακού*, p.69; Panteli, *New History of Cyprus*, p.263; Hatzivassiliou, *Ιστορία του Ελληνικού Έθνους*, 16, p.440; Vryonis, *The Mechanism of Catastrophe*, p.31.
30 Christidis, *Κυπριακό και ελληνοτουρκικά*, p.4–5, 17–18.
31 Cox and Sinclair, *Approaches to World Order*, p.88.
32 Anastasia Stouraiti and Alexander Kazamias, 'The Imaginary Topographies of the Megali Idea: National Territory as Utopia', in Nikiforos Diamandouros, Thalia Dragonas and Çağlar Keyder (eds), *Spatial Conceptions of the Nation: Modernizing Geographies in Greece and Turkey*, London, I.B. Tauris, 2010, p.13–21.
33 TNA/FO371/101803. Peake to Eden, [Confidential], WG10114/9, 2 December 1952.
34 Tsoucalas, 'The Ideological Impact of the Civil War', p.325.
35 Quoted in Vernardakis and Mavris, *Κόμματα*, p.71; Nikolakopoulos, *Κόμματα και βουλευτικές εκλογές*, p.80.

36 Panagiotis Kanellopoulos, *Η ζωή μου*, Athens, Yallelis, 1985, p.110-11; Sulzberger, *Long Row of Candles*, p.1011.
37 Papagiannopoulos, *Στρατάρχης Παπάγος*, p.1; Nikolaos Depastas, *Αλέξανδρος Παπάγος (1883-1955): Ο στρατιώτης, ο πολιτικός, ο άνθρωπος*, Athens, Armed Forces General Command, 1980, p.30; Anonymous, *Στρατάρχης Αλέξανδρος Παπάγος*, Centaur Magazine, Special Issue, Athens, December 1955, p.5.
38 Averoff-Tositsas, *Ιστορία χαμένων ευκαιριών*, vol.1, p.42; *TNA/FO371/101808*. Peake to Eden, handwritten notation, [Confidential], WG1052/9, 25 November 1952; Alexander Papagos, *Ο πόλεμος της Ελλάδος, 1940-1941*, Athens, Goulandris-Horn Foundation, 1995.
39 *TNA/FO371/101803*. Peake to Eden, [Confidential], WG10114/9, 2 December 1952; *TNA/FO371/95117*. Norton to FO, [Confidential], RG10114, 1 August 1951; *F.R.U.S. 1952-1954*, vol.VIII. Peurifoy to State Department, [Secret] 611.81/4-1053, 10 April 1953, p.817.
40 Alexander Papagos, interview to Takis Papagiannopoulos, *Kathimerini*, 13 February 1955, p.1.
41 Coufoudakis, 'United States, United Nations, and Greek Question', p.239; Stefanidis, *Isle of Discord*, p.295.
42 Gramsci, *Selections*, p.219, 222.
43 Gramsci, *Selections*, p.222.
44 Ibid., p.222.
45 Alivizatos, *Οι πολιτικοί θεσμοί σε κρίση*, p.677.
46 Tsoucalas, *Greek Tragedy*, p.156; Grigoriadis, *Μετά τον Εμφύλιο*, p.174; Charalambis, *Στρατός και πολιτική εξουσία*, p.44; Vournas, *Ιστορία της σύγχρονης Ελλάδας*, p.65.
47 Xydis, *Cyprus*, p.23; Stefanidis, *Isle of Discord*, p.295, 299; id. *Stirring the Nation*, p.84-5.
48 Panayiotis Kanellopoulos, *Εικοστός Αιώνας. Η πάλη μεταξύ ανθρωπισμού και απανθρωπίας*, Athens, Pyrsos, 1951, p.i, 177, 209, 227.

BIBLIOGRAPHY

Unpublished Primary Sources

British National Archives, FO Series, CAB Series, London.
Central Bank of Greece Archive, Athens.
Constantine Tsatsos Papers, American School of Classical Studies, Athens.
Dwight D. Eisenhower Presidential Library Documents, Abilene, Kansas.
General Agreement on Tariffs and Trade, Official Documents, Stanford University Library, Stanford.
General Tsingounis Papers, Hellenic Historical and Literary Archive (ELIA), Athens.
Greek Ministry of Foreign Affairs Historical Archive (G.M.F.A.), Athens.
Hellenic National Audio-Visual Archive, Online Collection, Athens. http://www.avarchive.gr/portal/
Official Minutes of the Greek Parliament, 1950–1958, Athens.
Sophocles Venizelos Archive, Benaki Museum, Athens.
United States National Archives (U.S.N.A.)
University of Athens Senate Secretariat Archive, Athens.
Vassilios Mostras, *Επί του Κυπριακού ζητήματος*, Athens, 1960, p.i-iii+1-99 (Mostras File), Hellenic Historical and Literary Archive (ELIA), Athens.

Published Primary Sources

Constantine Karamanlis Archive, vols 1–12, Ed. Constantine Svolopoulos, Athens, Constantine Karamanlis Foundation-Ekdotiki Athinon, 1992.
The Department of State *Bulletin*, 1953, 29:745, Washington D.C., US Government Printing Office.
Documents on International Affairs *1954*, Folliot, Denise (ed.), London, Oxford University Press, 1957.
Economic Cooperation Administration, *Three Years of the Marshal Plan*, Washington, ECA, 1951.
Economic Cooperation Agency, *European Recovery Program: Greece, Country Study*, Washington, US Government Printing Office, 1949.
Foreign Relations of the United States (F.R.U.S.), 1947–55, Washington, Department of State: United States Government Printing Office, 1971–92.
Greek Press and Information Service, *Information Bulletin: The Cyprus Question*, No.12, Athens, Press and Information Service, 1954.
Hansard, House of Commons Debates, London.
Hellenic Statistical Authority (ELSTAT), Monthly Bulletin of Greece's Special Trade with Foreign Countries, Athens, 1952–62.
Helsinki Watch, *Denying Human Rights and Ethnic Identity: The Greeks of Turkey*, New York, Washington, LA, London, Human Rights Watch, 1992.

Mutual Security Agency, *Report to Congress on the Mutual Security Program for the Six Months Ended 31 December 1953.*
North Atlantic Treaty Organization, *NATO's First Enlargement: Greece and Turkey 1952. A Commemorative Exhibition - Premier élargissement de l'OTAN. Une exposition commémorative*, Brussels, NATO, 2012.
United Nations Documents.
United Nations: General Assembly Official Records.
United Nations: General Assembly Resolutions.
United Nations: General Assembly Resolutions and Decisions.

Newspapers and Periodicals

Contemporary Review
Daily Telegraph
Eleftheria
Embros
Epitheorisis Economikon kai Politikon Epistimon
Kathimerini
Le Monde
Manchester Guardian
Nea Economia
New York Times
The Times
Time Magazine
To Vima

Articles/Book Chapters

Aboul Fadl, Reem, 'Neutralism Made Positive: Egyptian Anti-colonialism on the Road to Bandung', *British Journal of Middle Eastern Studies*, 42:2, 2015, p.219–40.
Abts, Koen and Stefan Rummens, 'Populism versus Democracy', *Political Studies*, 2007, 55:2, p.405–24.
Albertazzi, Daniel and Duncan McDonell, 'Introduction: The Scepter and the Specter', in Daniel Albertazzi and Duncan McDonell (eds), *Twenty-first Century Populism*, New York, Palgrave Macmillan, 2007, p.1–13.
Alexander, George, 'The Demobilisation Crisis of November 1944', in John Iatrides (ed.), *Greece in the 1940s. A Nation in Crisis*, Hanover, University Press of New England, 1981, p.156–66.
Alivizatos, Nicos, '"Εθνος" κατά "λαού"' in D.G. Tsaoussis (ed.), *Ελληνισμός - Ελληνικότητα. Ιδεολογικοί και βιωματικοί άξονες της νεοελληνικής κοινωνίας*, Athens, Estia, 1983, p.79–90.
Alivizatos, Nicos, 'The "Emergency Regime" and Civil Liberties, 1946-1949', in John Iatrides (ed.), *Greece in the 1940s. A Nation in Crisis*, Hanover, University Press of New England, 1981, p.220–8.
Angelopoulos, Angelos, 'Απόψεις περί του οικονομικού προβλήματος της Ελλάδος', *Nea Economia*, 7, Athens, March 1953, p.99–110.

Anthem, Thomas, 'Balkan Prospects', *Contemporary Review*, 183, January–June 1953, p.15–21.
Anthem, Thomas, 'Prospects in Cyprus', *Contemporary Review*, 187, January–June 1955, p.155–9.
Anthem, Thomas, 'The Cyprus Challenge', *Contemporary Review*, 186, July–December 1954, p.16–21.
Anthem, Thomas, 'The U.S.-Greek Agreement', *Contemporary Review*, 185, January–June 1954, p.83–9.
Bachrach, Peter and Morton Baratz, 'Decisions and Nondecisions: An Analytical Framework', *American Political Science Review*, 57: 3, 1962, p.632–42.
Bachrach, Peter and Morton Baratz, 'Two Faces of Power', *American Political Science Review*, 56: 4, 1962, p.947–52.
Baehr, Peter, 'Small States: A Tool for Analysis?', *World Politics*, 27:3, April 1975, p.456–66.
Barker, Elisabeth, 'Yugoslav Policy towards Greece 1947–1949' in Baerentzen et al. (eds), *Studies in the History of the Greek Civil War, 1945–1949*, Copehagen, Museum Tusculanum Press, 1987, p.263–95.
Braveboy-Wagner, Jacqueline, 'The English-Speaking Caribbean States: A Triad of Foreign Policies', in Jeanne Hey (ed.), *Small States in World Politics: Explaining Foreign Policy Behavior*, Boulder Co., Lynne Rienner, 2003, p.31–52.
Brown, Chris, 'Development and Dependency', in Margot Light and A.J.R. Groom (eds), *International Relations*, London, Pinter, 1985, p.60–73.
Buzan, Barry, 'Introduction: The Changing Security Agenda in Europe', in Ole Wæver et al., *Identity, Migration and the New Security Agenda in Europe*, London, Pinter, 1993, p.1–14.
Canovan, Margaret, 'Taking Politics to the People: Populism as the Ideology of Democracy', Yves Mény and Yves Surel (eds), *Democracies and the Populist Challenge*, Basingstoke, Palgrave Macmillan, 2002, p.25–44.
Caporaso, James, 'Dependence, Dependency, and Power in the Global System: A Structure and Behavioural Analysis', *International Organization*, 32:1, 1978, p.13–43.
Carabott, Phillip, 'Monumental Visions: The Past in Metaxas's *Weltanschauung*', in K.S. Brown and Yannis Hamilakis (eds), *The Usable Past: Greek Metahistories*, Lanham, Lexington, 2003, p.23–37.
Chase-Dunn, Christopher, 'The Development of Core Capitalism in the Antebellum United States: Tariff Politics and Class Struggle in an Upwardly Mobile Semiperiphery', in A. Bergersen (ed.), *Studies of the Modern World System*, New York: Academic Press, 1980, p.189–230.
Chourmouzios, Emilios, 'Αι δύο θέσεις και η Τρίτη… (Συμβολή στις συζητήσεις περί του Κυπριακού)', *Kathimerini*, 17 February 1955, p.1–2.
Chrysostomidis, Sofianos, 'Ελληνοαμερικανικές σχέσεις: Από το δόγμα Τρούμαν και τη ρητορία του ΠΑΣΟΚ στα σημερινά δεδομένα', *Η Ελλάδα σε Κρίση*, vol.2, Athens, Roes, 1987, p.255–323.
Close, David, 'The Reconstruction of a Right-Wing State' in David Close (ed.), *The Greek Civil War, 1943–1950: Studies of Polarisation*, London, Routledge, 1993, p.156–89.
Coufoudakis, Van, 'The United States, the United Nations, and the Greek Question, 1946–1952', in John Iatrides (ed.), *Greece in the 1940s. A Nation in Crisis*, Hanover, University Press of New England, 1981 p.275–97.
Couloumbis, Theodore, Book Review of John Iatrides, Balkan Triangle, *Balkan Studies*, 10:1, 1969, p.198–202.

Devetak, Richard, 'Critical Theory', Scott Burchill et al. (eds), *Theories of International Relations*, Fourth Edition, London, Palgrave Macmillan, 2009, p.159-82.

Dritsas, Margarita, 'National Integration and Economic Change in Greece during the Twentieth Century', in Alice Teichova, Herbert Matis, Jaroslav Pátek (eds), *Economic Change and the National Question in Twentieth-Century Europe*, Cambridge, Cambridge University Press, 2000, p.196-228.

Duvall, Raymond, 'Dependence and Dependencia Theory: Notes toward Precision of Concept and Argument', *International Organization*, 32:1, 1978, p.51-78.

Eliades, Evangelos, 'Stabilization of the Greek Economy and the 1953 Devaluation of the Drachma', *IMF Staff Papers*, 4:1, September 1954, p.22-72.

Evelpides, Christos, 'Σκέψεις τινές επί της εκθέσεως του κ. Βαρβαρέσσου', *Epitheorisis Economikon kai Politikon Epistimon*, January-March 1952, p.24-5.

Falk, Richard, 'The Critical Realist Tradition and the Demystification of Interstate Power: E. H. Carr, Hedley Bull and Robert W. Cox', in Stephen Gill and James Mittelman (eds), *Innovation and Transformation in International Studies*, Cambridge, Cambridge University Press, p.39-55.

Fatouros, Argyris, 'Building Formal Structures of Penetration: The United States in Greece, 1947-1948', in John Iatrides (ed.), *Greece in the 1940s. A Nation in Crisis*, Hanover, University Press of New England, 1981, p.239-58.

Gaddis, John Lewis 'Was the Truman Doctrine a Real Turning Point?', *Foreign Affairs*, vol. 52: January-February. 1974, p.386-402.

Gerakis, Andreas and Haskell Wald, 'Economic Stabilization and Progress in Greece, 1953-61: Contribution of Foreign Exchange and Trade Reforms', *IMF Staff Papers*, 11:1, March 1964, p.125-38.

Geronimakis, Stylianos, 'Post-War Economic Growth in Greece, 1950-61', *Review of Income and Wealth*, 11:1, 1965, p.257-80.

Giannitsis, Tasos, 'Οικονομική ολοκλήρωση της Ελλάδας στην ΕΟΚ και άμεσες επενδύσεις', in Marios Nikolinakos, *ΕΟΚ-Ελλάδα-Μεσόγειος*, Athens, Livanis, 1978.

Gorodetsky, Gabriel, 'The Formulation of Soviet Foreign Policy – Ideology and *Realpolitik*', in Gabriel Gorodetsky (ed.), *Soviet Foreign Policy, 1917-1991: A Retrospective*, Frank Cass, London, 1994, p.30-44.

Gounaris, Basil, 'Social Dimensions of Anticommunism in Northern Greece, 1945-50', in Philip Carabott and Thanasis Sfikas (eds), *The Greek Civil War: Essays on a Conflict of Exceptionalism and Silences*, Aldershot, Ashgate, 2004, p.175-86.

Hall, John, 'Nicos Mouzelis, Politics in the Semi-Periphery: Early Parliamentarism and Late Industrialisation in the Balkans and Latin America', book review, *Sociology*, 21:1, 1987, p.155-7.

Hatzivassiliou, Evanthis, 'Κύπρος και Κυπριακό Ζήτημα', *Ιστορία του Ελληνικού Έθνους*, vol.16, Athens, Ekdotiki Athinon, 2000, pp.429-63.

Hatzivassiliou, Evanthis, 'British Strategic Priorities and the Cyprus Question, 1954-1958', in Hubert Faustmann and Nicos Peristianis (eds), *Britain in Cyprus: Colonialism and Post-Colonialism, 1878-2006*, Mannheim und Möhnesee, Bibliopolis, 2006, p.199-210.

Hatzivassiliou, Evanthis, 'Greek Liberalism in the Twentieth Century: Dilemmas for Research', in Constantine Arvanitopoulos and Konstantina Botsiou (eds), *The Constantinos Karamanlis Yearbook for Democracy 2010*, Heidelberg, Springer, 2010, p.119-28.

Hatzivassiliou, Evanthis, 'Ο Ψυχρός Πόλεμος ως κρίση εκσυγχρονισμού: υπέρβαση κρίσεων και ελληνική εμπειρία, 1932-1959', in Constantina Botsiou and Yannis Sakkas (eds), *Η Ελλάδα, η Δύση και η Μεσόγειος, 1945-62. Νέες ερευνητικές προσεγγίσεις*, Thessaloniki, University of Macedonia, 2015, p.17-34.

Heyst, Axel, 'Greece in 1954', *Contemporary Review*, 187, January-June 1955, p.15–18.
Higgins, Benjamin Higgins, 'The "Dualistic Theory" of Underdeveloped Areas', *Economic Development and Cultural Change*, January 1956, 4:2, p.99–115.
Hoffman, Mark, 'Critical Theory and the Inter-Paradigm Debate', *Millenium*, 16:2, 1987, p.231–49.
Holland, Robert, 'Never, Never Land: British Colonial Policy and the Roots of Violence in Cyprus, 1950-1954', *The Journal of Imperial Commonwealth History*, 21:3, 1993, p.167–9.
Huang, Jie, 'Structural Disarticulation and Third World Human Development', *International Journal of Comparative Sociology*, 36:3, 1995, p.164–83.
Iatrides, John, 'Greece and the United States: The Strained Partnership', in Richard Clogg (ed.), *Greece in the 1980s*, London and Basingstoke, Macmillan, 1983, p.150–72.
Iatrides, John, 'Lincoln MacVeagh', in Cathal Nolan (ed.), *Notable U.S. Ambassadors since 1775: A Biographical Dictionary*, Westport, Greenwood, 1997, p.241–9.
Iatrides, John, 'The United States and Greece in the Twentieth Century' in Theodore Couloumbis, Theodore Kariotis and Fotini Bellou (eds), *Greece in the Twentieth Century*, London and New York, Frank Cass, 2003, p.69–110.
Ierodiakonou, Leontios, 'Το Κυπριακό από τον Β΄ Παγκόσμιο Πόλεμο ως την Ανεξαρτησία', in George Tenekidis and Yannos Kranidiotis (eds), *Κύπρος. Ιστορία, προβλήματα και αγώνες του λαού της*, Third Edition, Athens, Estia, 2009 [1981], p.169–89.
Jenkins, W.E., 'The Case of Non Decisions', in Anthony McGrew and M.J. Wilson (eds), *Decision Making: Approaches and Analysis*, Manchester, Manchester University Press, 1982, p.318–26.
Johnson, Edward, 'Keeping Cyprus off the Agenda: British and American Relations at the United Nations, 1954-58', *Diplomacy and Statecraft*, 11:3, 2000, p.227–55.
Kazamias, Alexander, 'Antiquity as Cold War Propaganda: The Uses of the Classical Past in post-Civil War Greece', in Dimitris Tziovas (ed.), *Re-Imagining the Past: Antiquity and Modern Greek Culture*, Oxford, Oxford University Press, 2014, p. 128–46.
Kazamias, Alexander, 'Pseudo-Hegelian Contrivances: The Uses of German Idealism in the Discourse of the post-Civil War Greek State', *Kambos: Cambridge Papers in Modern Greek*, 19, 2012, p.47–73.
Kazamias, Alexander, 'The Greek Variable in EU-Turkish Relations', in Joseph Joseph (ed.), *Turkey and the EU: Internal Dynamics and External Challenges*, London, Palgrave Macmillan, 2006, p.138–60.
Kazamias, Alexander, 'The Modernization of Greek Foreign Policy and Its Limitations', *Mediterranean Politics*, 2:2, 1997, p.71–94.
Kirkpatrick, C.H. and F.I. Nixson, 'The Origins of Inflation in Less Developed Countries: A Selective View', in Michael Parkin and Goerge Zis (eds), *Inflation in Open Economies*, Manchester, Manchester University Press, 1976, p.126–174.
Kitromilides, Paschalis, 'Milestones in the Historiography on the Cyprus Question', *The Historical Review*, Institute for Neohellenic Research, 1, 2004, p.287–92.
Koliopoulos, John, 'Metaxas and Greek Foreign Relations, 1936-1941', in Robin Higham and Thanos Veremis (eds), *The Metaxas Dictatorship: Aspects of Greece, 1936-1940*, Athens, ELIAMEP, 1993, p.85–110.
Kruszewski, Charles, 'Hegemony and International Law', *The American Political Science Review*, 35:6, 1941, p.1127–44.
Laclau, Ernesto, 'Populism: What's in a Name?', Francisco Panizza (ed.), *Populism and the Mirror of Democracy*, London, Verso, 2005, p.32–49.

Leffler, Melvyn, '[The American Conception of National Security and the Beginnings of the Cold War, 1945-48]: Reply', *The American Historical Review*, 89:2, April 1984, p.391-400.

Linklater, Andrew, 'Neo-realism in Theory and Practice', in Ken Booth and Steve Smith (eds), *International Relations Theory Today*, London, Polity, 1995, p.241-262.

Loizidis, Socratis, 'Η αλήθεια δια την Ε.Ο.Κ.Α. Πώς εδημιουργήθη και πώς παρασκεύασε τον κυπριακόν αγώνα', *Eleftheria*, 27 September 1960, p.1.

Makinen, Gail, 'The Greek Stabilization of 1944-46', *The American Economic Review*, 74:5, December 1984, p.1067-74.

Maniadakis, Constantine 'Αι μυστικαί διαπραγματεύσεις Παπάγου και Άγγλων δια το Κυπριακόν', *Kathimerini*, 8 March 1959, p.1-2.

Mearsheimer, John, 'Back to the Future. Instability in Europe after the Cold War', *International Security*, 15:1, Summer 1990, p.5-56.

Mény, Yves and Yves Surel, 'The Constitutive Ambiguity of Populism', Yves Mény and Yves Surel (eds), *Democracies and the Populist Challenge*, Basingstoke, Palgrave Macmillan, 2002, p.1-21.

Modinos, Polys, 'Οι πνευματικοί άνθρωποι και το Κυπριακό πρόβλημα', *Efthyni*, 93, September 1979, p.467.

Moolakkattu, John, 'Robert W. Cox and Critical Theory of International Relations', *International Studies*, 46:4, 2009, p.439-456.

Murphy, Craig, 'Understanding IR: Understanding Gramsci', *Review of International Studies*, 24:2, 1998, p.417-25.

Myint, Hia, 'Organizational Dualism and Economic Development', *Asian Development Review*, 3:1, 1985, p.24-42.

Nikolaides, Leander, 'Το ελληνικόν πρόγραμμα ανασυγκροτήσεως και η προβολή του εις το εξωτερικόν', *Spoudai*, March-April 1954, p.257-69.

Palmer, Norman, 'Charles W. Yost. "History and Memory: A Statesman's Perceptions of the Twentieth Century", p.352. New York: W.W. Norton, 1980.', *The Annals of the American Academy of Political and Social Science*, 455:1, 1981, p.176.

Panizza, Francisco, 'Introduction', in Francisco Panizza (ed.), *Populism and the Mirror of Democracy*, London, Verso, 2005, p.1-31.

Parry, G. and P. Morris, 'When Is a Decision Not a Decision?', in Anthony McGrew and M.J. Wilson (eds), *Decision Making: Approaches and Analysis*, Manchester, Manchester University Press, 1982, p.19-35.

Petersen, Nikolaj, 'Adaptation as a Framework for the Analysis of Foreign Policy Behaviour', *Cooperation and Conflict*, 12:4, 1977, p.221-50.

Pettman, Ralph, 'Competing Paradigms in International Politics', *Review of International Studies*, 7, 1981, p.39-49.

Pfaff, William, *The Wrath of Nations: Civilization and the Furies of Nationalism*, New York, Touchstone, 1993.

Pipinelis, Panayotis, 'The Greco-Turkish Feud Revived', *Foreign Affairs*, 37:1, January 1959, p.306-16.

Pipinelis, Panayotis, Η «διεθνοποίησις» του Κυπριακού και αι εξ' αυτού μοιραίαι συνέπειαι', *Kathimerini*, 5 March 1959, p.3-4.

Pipinelis, Panayotis, Η άγνωστος διπλωματική Ιστορία περί την διαχείρησιν του Κυπριακού', *Kathimerini*, 1 March 1959, p.3-4.

Pipinelis, Panayotis, Η διαχείρισις του Κυπριακού', *Kathimerini*, 28 February 1959, p.3-4.

Pipinelis, Panayotis, 'Τα διπλωματικά παρασκήνια της διαχειρήσεως του Κυπριακού', *Kathimerini*, 3 March 1959, p.3, 6.

Pipinelis, Panayotis, 'Τα διπλωματικά παρασκήνια της διαχειρήσεως του Κυπριακού', *Kathimerini*, 4 March 1959, p.3.
Pipinelis, Panayotis, 'Το Κυπριακόν, εις το μέλλον. Από της αυτοδιοικήσεως εις την αυτοδιάθεσιν', *Kathimerini*, 5 February 1955, p.1, 4.
Pipinelis, Panayotis, 'Το Κυπριακόν, εις το μέλλον. Πρώτος σταθμός η αυτοδιοίκησις', *Kathimerini*, 5 February 1955, p.1-2.
Pirjevec, Jože, 'The Tito-Stalin Split and the End of the Civil War in Greece', Baerentzen, Lars, John Iatrides and Ole Smith (eds), *Studies in the History of the Greek Civil War 1945-1949*, Copenhagen, Museum Tusculum, 1987, p.309-15.
Polis, Adamandia, 'U.S. Intervention in Greek Trade Unions 1947-1950', in John Iatrides (ed.), *Greece in the 1940s. A Nation in Crisis*, Hanover, University Press of New England, 1981, p.259-74.
Richter, Heinz, 'The Varkiza Agreement and the Origins of the Civil War', in John Iatrides (ed.), *Greece in the 1940s. A Nation in Crisis*, Hanover, University Press of New England, 1981, p.167-80.
Singer, Marshall, 'The Foreign Policies of Small Developing States', in James Rosenau, Kenneth Thompson and Gavin Boyd (eds), *World Politics: An Introduction*, New York, Free Press, 1976, p.263-90.
Stanley, Ben, 'The Thin Ideology of Populism', *Journal of Political Ideologies*, 13:1, February 2008, p.95-110.
Stathakis, George, 'Approaches to the Early Post-War Greek Economy: A Survey', *Journal of Modern Hellenism*, 7, p.163-90.
Stathakis, George, 'US Economic Policies in Post Civil-War Greece, 1949-1953: Stabilisation and Monetary Reform', *Journal of European Economic History*, 24:2, 1995, p.375-404.
Stavenhagen, Rodolfo, 'Seven Erroneous Theses About Latin America', in Irving Louis Horowitz, Josu de Castro and John Gerassi (eds), *Latin American Radicalism: A Documentary Report on Left and Nationalist Movements*, London, Jonathan Cape, Boston, New England Free Press, 1969, p.102-17.
Stefanidis, Ioannis, 'Pressure Groups and Greek Foreign Policy, 1945-67', *Hellenic Observatory, LSE*, December 2001, p.1-45.
Stefanidis, Ioannis, 'United States, Great Britain and the Greek-Yugoslav Rapprochement, 1949-1950', *Balkan Studies*, 27: 2, 1986, p.315-43.
Stouraiti, Anastasia and Alexander Kazamias, 'The Imaginary Topographies of the Megali Idea: National Territory as Utopia', in Nikiforos Diamandouros, Thalia Dragonas and Çağlar Keyder (eds), *Spatial Conceptions of the Nation: Modernizing Geographies in Greece and Turkey*, London, I.B. Tauris, 2010, p.11-34.
Taggart, Paul, 'Populism and the Pathology of Representative Politics', Yves Mény and Yves Surel (eds), *Democracies and the Populist Challenge*, Basingstoke, Palgrave Macmillan, 2002, p.62-80.
Tenekidis, George, 'Διεθνοποίηση και αποδιεθνοποίηση του Κυπριακού πριν και μετά την τουρκική εισβολή', in George Tenekidis and Yannos Kranidiotis (eds), *Κύπρος. Ιστορία, προβλήματα και αγώνες του λαού της*, Third Edition, Athens, Estia, 2009 [1981], p.195-323.
Tsoukalas, Constantine, 'The Ideological Impact of the Civil War', in John Iatrides (ed.), *Greece in the 1940s. A Nation in Crisis*, Hanover, University Press of New England, 1981 p.319-43.
Varvaressos, Kyriakos, Letter to the editor, *Epitheorisis Economikon kai Politikon Epistimon*, 24 June 1952, pp.205-9.

Vergopoulos, Costas, 'The Emergence of the New Bourgeoisie, 1944–1952', in John Iatrides (ed.), *Greece in the 1940s. A Nation in Crisis*, Hanover, University Press of New England, 1981, p.298–317.

Verney, Susannah, 'To Be or Not to Be within the European Community: The Party Debate and Democratic Consolidation in Greece', in Geoffrey Pridham (ed.), *Securing Democracy: Political Parties and Democratic Consolidation in Southern Europe*, Abingdon, Routledge, 2016 [1990], p.203–23.

Wallerstein, Immanuel, 'Dependence in an Interdependent World: The Limited Possibilities of Transformation within the Capitalist World Economy', *African Studies Review*, 17:1, April 1974, p.1–26.

Wallerstein, Immanuel, 'Semi-Peripheral Countries and the Contemporary World Crisis', *Theory and Society*, 3:4, Winter 1976, p.461–83.

Wallerstein, Immanuel, 'The Three Instances of Hegemony in the History of the Capitalist World-Economy', *International Journal of Comparative Sociology*, 24:1–2, 1983, p.100–8.

Waltz, Kenneth, 'Realist Thought and Neorealist Theory', *Journal of International Affairs*, Spring/Summer 1990, 44:1, p.21–37.

Weyland, Kurt, 'Clarifying a Contested Concept: Populism in the Study of Latin American Politics', *Comparative Politics*, 34:1, 2001, p.1–22.

Weyland, Kurt, 'Neoliberal Populism in Latin America and Eastern Europe', *Comparative Politics*, 1999, 31:4, p.279–401.

Wiles, Peter, 'A Syndrome, Not a Doctrine: Some Elementary Theses on Populism', in Ghiţa Ionescu and Ernest Gellner (eds), *Populism: Its Meanings and National Characteristics*, London, Weidenfeld and Nicholson, 1969, p.166–79.

Wittner, Lawrence, 'American Policy toward Greece 1944–1949', in John Iatrides (ed.), *Greece in the 1940s. A Nation in Crisis*, Hanover, University Press of New England, 1981, p.229–38.

Xydis, Stephen, 'The UN General Assembly as an Instrument of Greek Policy: Cyprus, 1954–58', *Journal of Conflict Resolution*, 12:2, June 1968, p.141–58.

Xydis, Stephen, 'Toward "Toil and Moil" in Cyprus', *Middle East Journal*, 20:1, 1966, p.1–19.

Zolotas, Xenophon, 'Εν όψει μειωμένης βοηθείας. Η ελληνική οικονομία εις κρίσιμον καμπήν', *Eleftheria*, 17 May 1952, p.1.

Zolotas, Xenophon, 'Η έκθεσις του κ. Βαρβαρέσσου και η οικονομική ανάπτυξις', *Epitheorisis Economikon kai Politikon Epistimon*, January–March 1952, p.1–24.

Books

Acheson, Dean, *Present at the Creation: My Years at the State Department*, New York, Norton, 1969.

Adorno, Theodor, *Negative Dialectics*, London and New York, Routledge, 2004 [1966].

Alastos, Doros, *Cyprus Guerilla. Grivas, Makarios and the British*, London, Heinemann, 1960.

Alexandrakis, Menelaos, Vyron Theodoropoulos, Efstathios Lagakos, *Το Κυπριακό 1950–1974. Μια ενδοσκόπηση*, Athens, Evroekdotiki, 1987.

Alivizatos, Nicos, *Οι πολιτικοί θεσμοί σε κρίση, 1922–1974. Όψεις της ελληνικής εμπειρίας*, Third Edition, Athens, Themelio, 1996 [1983].

Allison, Graham and Philip Zeliow, *Essence of Decision: Explaining the Cuban Missile Crisis*, Second Edition, New York, Longman, 1999.
Allwood, Car Martinl and Marcus Selart (eds), *Decision Making: Social and Creative Dimensions*, Dordrecht, Kluwer Academic Publishers, 2001.
Amin, Samir, *Unequal Development: An Essay on the Social Formations of Peripheral Capitalism*, Hassocks, Harvester, 1976.
Anderson, Benedict, *Imagined Communities: The Origins and Spread of Nationalism*, Second Edition, London, Verso, 1991 [1983].
Anonymous, *Στρατάρχης Αλέξανδρος Παπάγος*, Centaur Magazine, Special Issue, Athens, December 1955.
Athanassopoulou, Ekavi, *Turkey. Anglo-American Security Interests, 1945–1952: The First Enlargement of NATO*, London, Frank Cass, 1999.
Averoff-Tositsas, Evangelos, *Ιστορία χαμένων ευκαιριών: Κυπριακό 1950–1963*, vols 1–2, Second Edition, Athens, Estia, 1982 [1981].
Azinas, Andreas, *50 Years of Silence. Cyprus' Struggle for Freedom – My EOKA Secret File*, vols 1–2, Nicosia, Airwaves, 2002.
Bachrach, Peter and Morton Baratz, *Power and Poverty, Theory and Practice*, New York, Oxford University Press, 1970.
Baerentzen, Lars, John Iatrides and Ole Smith (eds), *Studies in the History of the Greek Civil War 1945–1949*, Copenhagen, Museum Tusculum, 1987.
Baker, Colin, *Retreat from Empire: Sir Robert Armitage in Africa and Cyprus*, London, I.B. Tauris, 1998.
Bitsios, Dimitri, *Cyprus: The Vulnerable Republic*, Thessaloniki, Institute for Balkan Studies, 1975.
Boeke, J.H., *Economics and Economic Policy of Dual Societies*, New York, Institute of Pacific Relations, 1953.
Bradley, Omar and Clay Blair, *A General's Life*, New York, Simon and Schuster, 1983.
Brass, Paul, *Ethnicity and Nationalism: Theory and Comparison*, London, Sage, 1991.
Breuilly, John, *Nationalism and the State*, Second Edition, Chicago, Chicago University Press, 1993 [1982].
Brighi, Elisabetta, *Foreign Policy, Domestic Politics and International Relations: The Case of Italy*, Abingdon, Routledge, 2013.
Brincat, Shannon (ed.), *From International Relations to World Civilizations: The Contributions of Robert W. Cox*, Abingdon, Routledge, 2017.
Brookfield, Harold, *Interdependent Development*, Abingdon, Routledge, 2011 [1975].
Budd, Adrian, *Class, States and International Relations: A Critical Appraisal of Robert Cox and neo-Gramscian Theory*, Abingdon, Routledge, 2013.
Calvocoressi, Peter, *Survey of International Affairs 1949–1950*, London, Oxford University Press, for the Royal Institute of International Affairs, 1953.
Candilis, Wray, *The Economy of Greece, 1944–66: Efforts for Stability and Development*, New York, Praeger, 1968.
Canovan, Margaret, *Populism*, London, Junction, 1981.
Carlton, David, *Anthony Eden: A Biography*, London, Allen and Unwin, 1981.
Charalambis, Dimitris, *Στρατός και πολιτική εξουσία. Η δομή της πολιτικής εξουσίας στη μετεμφυλιακή Ελλάδα*, Athens, Exandas, 1985.
Chatziantoniou, Costas, *Νικόλαος Πλαστήρας. Ιστορική βιογραφία*, Athens, Iolkos, 2006.
Christidis, Christoforos, *Κυπριακό και ελληνοτουρκικά: Πορεία μιας εθνικής χρεωκοπείας, 1953–1967*, Athens, 1967.

Christidis, Christoforos, *Χρόνια Κατοχής, 1941–1944. Μαρτυρίες Ημερολογίου*, Athens, 1971.
Clogg, Richard, *A Short History of Modern Greece*, Second Edition, Cambridge, Cambridge University Press, 1986.
Clogg, Richard (ed.), *Greece in the 1980s*, London, Macmillan, 1983.
Close, David, *Greece since 1945: Politics, Economy and Society*, Abingdon, Routledge, 2014 [2002].
Close, David, *The Origins of the Greek Civil War*, London, Longman, 1995.
Communist Party of Greece, *40 Χρόνια αγώνες.1918–1958. Επιλογή ντοκουμέντων*, Athens, KKE, 1964.
Costis, Costas, '*Τα κακομαθημένα παιδιά της Ιστορίας*': *Η διαμόρφωση του νεοελληνικού κράτους, 18ος-21ος αιώνας*, Athens, Polis, 2013.
Couloumbis, Theodore, *Greek Political Reaction to American and NATO Influences*, New Haven, Yale University Press, 1966.
Couloumbis, Theodore, *The United States, Greece, and Turkey: The Troubled Triangle*, New York, Praeger, 1983.
Couloumbis, Theodore, *Προβλήματα ελληνοαμερικανικών σχέσεων: Πώς αντιμετωπίζεται η εξάρτηση*, Athens, Estia, 1978.
Couloumbis, Theodore, and John Iatrides (eds), *Greek-American Relations: A Critical Review*, New York, Pella, 1980.
Couloumbis, Theodore, Harry Psomiades, John Petropoulos, *Foreign Interference in Greek Politics*, New York, Pella, 1976.
Cox, Robert, *Production, Power and World Order: Social Forces in the Making of History*, New York, Columbia University Press, 1987.
Cox, Robert and Timothy Sinclair, *Approaches to World Order*, Cambridge, Cambridge University Press, 1996.
Crawshaw, Nancy, *The Cyprus Revolt: An Account of the Struggle for Union with Greece*, London, Allen & Unwin, 1978.
Crouzet, François, *Le Conflit de Chypre, 1946–1959*, vols 1–2, Brussels, Emile Bruylant, 1973.
Dafnis, Grigoris, *Σοφοκλής Ελευθερίου Βενιζέλος (1894–1964)*, Athens, Ikaros, 1970.
Damalas, Vassilios, *Σύντομος ιστορία της δραχμής (από του 1833 μέχρι του 1953)*, Athens, Spoudai, 1959.
Depastas, Nikolaos, *Αλέξανδρος Παπάγος (1883–1955): Ο στρατιώτης, ο πολιτικός, ο άνθρωπος*, Athens, Armed Forces General Command, 1980.
Devetak, Richard, *Critical International Theory: An Intellectual History*, Oxford, Oxford University Press, 2018.
Diamandouros, Nikiforos, *Cultural Dualism and Political Change in Post-authoritarian Greece*, Madrid, Instituto Juan March de Estudios e Investigaciones, 1994.
Diamandouros, Nikiforos and Richard Gunther (eds), *Parties, Politics, and Democracy in the New Southern Europe*, Baltimore and London, Johns Hopkins University Press, 2001.
Dimaras, K.Th., *Ελληνικός Ρωμαντισμός*, Athens, Ermis, 1994.
Dodd, Clement, *The History and Politics of the Cyprus Conflict*, London, Palgrave Macmillan, 2010.
Douglas, Mary, *Purity and Danger: An Analysis of Concepts of Pollution and Taboo*, vol.2, London, Routledge, 2003 [1966].
Draenos, Stan, *Andreas Papandreou: The Making of a Greek Democrat and a Maverik*, London, I.B. Tauris, 2013.

Durrell, Lawrence, *Bitter Lemons*, London, Faber and Faber, 1957.
Eden, Antony, *Full Circle. Memoirs*, Book 2, London, Cassell, 1960.
Ehrlich, Thomas, *Cyprus 1958-1967*, New York, Oxford University Press, 1974.
Evans, Peter, *Dependent Development: The Alliance of Multinational, State, and Local Capital in Brazil*, Princeton, Princeton University Press, 1979.
Fontana, Benedetto, *Hegemony and Power: On the Relation between Gramsci and Machiavelli*, Minneapolis, University of Minnesota Press, 1993.
Frederica, *A Measure of Understanding*, London, St Martin's Press, 1971.
Fukuyama, Francis, *State-Building: Governance and World Order in the 21st Century*, New York, Cornell University Press, 2004.
Gellner, Ernest, *Nations and Nationalism*, Oxford, Oxford University Press, 1983.
George, Jim, *Discourses of Global Politics: A Critical (Re) Introduction to International Relations*, Colorado, Lynne Rienner, 1994.
Grady, Henry and John McNay, *The Memoirs of Ambassador Henry Grady: From the Great War to the Cold War*, Columbia, University of Missouri Press, 2009.
Gramsci, Antonio, *Selections from the Prison Notebooks*, London, Lawrence and Wishart, 1992 [1971].
Grigoriadis, Solon, *Μετά τον Εμφύλιο: Η άνοδος του Παπάγου στην Εξουσία*, Athens, Fytrakis, 1979.
Grivas-Digenis, Georgios, *Απομνημονεύματα ΕΟΚΑ 1955-1959*, Athens, 1961.
Grivas-Dighenis, George, *The Memoirs of General Grivas*, ed. Charles Foley, London, Longman, 1964.
Grose, Peter, *Allen Dulles: Spymaster. The Life and Times of the First Civilian Director of the CIA*, London, André Deutsch, 2006.
Grose, Peter, *Gentleman Spy: The Life of Allen Dulles*, Amherst, University of Massachusetts Press, 1996.
Grose, Peter, *Operation Rollback: America's Secret War Behind the Iron Curtain*, New York, Mariner, 2000.
Halperin, Morton, Priscilla Clapp with Arnold Kanter, *Bureaucratic Politics and Foreign Policy*, Second Edition, Washington, The Brookings Institution, 2006.
Hatzivassiliou, Evanthis, *Ελληνικός Φιλελευθερισμός. Το ριζοσπαστικό ρεύμα 1932-1979*, Athens, Patakis, 2010.
Hatzivassiliou, Evanthis, *Greece and the Cold War: Frontline State, 1952-1967*, London, Routledge, 2006.
Hatzivassiliou, Evanthis, *Στρατηγικές του Κυπριακού. Η δεκαετία του 1950*, Athens, Patakis, 2004.
Hatzivassiliou, Evanthis, *Η άνοδος του Κωνσταντίνου Καραμανλή στην εξουσία, 1954-1956*, Athens, Patakis, 2000.
Heikal, Mohamed Hassanein, *Milaffat Al-Suways: Harb al-thalathīn sana*, Third Edition, Cairo, Al-Ahram, 1996.
Herzfeld, Michael, *Ours Once More: Folklore, Ideology, and the Making of Modern Greece*, Austin, University of Texas Press, 1982.
Higham, Robin, 'The Metaxas Years in Perspective', in Robin Higham and Thanos Veremis (eds), *Aspects of Greece, 1936-40: The Metaxas Dictatorship*, Athens, ELIAMEP, 1993.
Hill, Christopher, *The Changing Politics of Foreign Policy*, Basingstoke, Palgrave Macmillan, 2003.
Hobsbawm, Eric, *Nations and Nationalism since 1780: Programme, Myth, Reality*, Second Edition, Cambridge, Cambridge University Press, 1992 [1983].

Hobson, John, *The State and International Relations*, Cambridge, Cambridge University Press, 2000.
Hoffman, George, *The Balkans in Transition*, Princeton, Van Nostrand, 1963.
Hoffman, John, *A Glossary of Political Theory*, Edinburgh, Edinburgh University Press, 2007.
Hoffmann, Stanley, *Gulliver's Troubles, or the Setting of American Foreign Policy*, New York, McGraw-Hill, 1968.
Holland, Robert, *Britain and the Revolt in Cyprus, 1954–1959*, Oxford, Clarendon Press, 1998.
Horkheimer, Max, *Critical Theory: Selected Essays*, New York, Continuum, 1972.
Hudson, Valerie, *Foreign Policy Analysis: Classic and Contemporary Theory*, Lanham, Rowman and Littlefeld, 2007.
Iatrides, John (ed.), *Greece in the 1940s. A Nation in Crisis*, Hanover, University Press of New England, 1981.
Iatrides, John, *Balkan Triangle: Birth and Decline Across Ideological Boundaries*, The Hague, Mouton, 1968.
Ierodiakonou, Leontios, *Το Κυπριακό Πρόβλημα: Πορεία πρός τήν Χρεωκοπία*, Athens, Papazissis, 1970.
Jeffery, Judith, *Ambiguous Commitments and Uncertain Policies: The Truman Doctrine in Greece, 1947–1952*, Lanham MA and Oxford, Lexington, 2000.
Jones, Howard, *'A new kind of war': America's Global Strategy and the Truman Doctrine in Greece*, Oxford, Oxford University Press, 1989.
Jones, Richard, *Reductionism and the Fullness of Reality*, Cranbury, Associated University Presses, 2000.
Jones, Steve, *Antonio Gramsci*, Abingdon, Routledge, 2006.
Kalyvas, Stathis, *Modern Greece: What Everyone Needs to Know*, Oxford, Oxford University Press, 2015.
Kanellopoulos, Panayiotis, *Εικοστός Αιώνας. Η πάλη μεταξύ ανθρωπισμού και απανθρωπίας*, Athens, Pyrsos, 1951.
Kanellopoulos, Panayiotis, *Η ζωή μου*, Athens, Yallelis, 1985.
Kanellopoulos, Panayiotis, *Ιστορικά Δοκίμια. Πώς εφθάσαμεν στην 21ῃ Απριλίου 1967– 1940–1944 Εθνική Αντίσταση*, Athens, Estia, 1975.
Karagiannis, Georgios, *Το δράμα της Ελλάδος. Εποποιία και αθλιότητες, ΕΕΝΑ, ΙΔΕΑ, 1940–1952*, Athens, 1964.
Karakatsanis, Neovi, *The Politics of Elite Transformation: The Consolidation of Greek Democracy in Theoretical Perspective*, Westport, Praeger, 2001.
Katsanevas, Theodoros, *Το σύγχρονο συνδικαλιστικό κίνημα στην Ελλάδα*, Athens, Papazisis, 1996.
Kay, Geoffrey, *Development and Underdevelopment*, London, Macmillan, 1975.
Kazakos, Panos (ed.), *Σπυρίδων Μαρκεζίνης. Στρατηγικές οικονομικής ανάπτυξης και η υποτίμηση της δραχμής (1953)*, Athens, Greek Parliament Foundation, 2013.
Kazakos, Panos, *Ανάμεσα σε κράτος και αγορά. Οικονομία και οικονομική πολιτική στη μεταπολεμική Ελλάδα, 1944-2000*, Athens, Patakis, 2010.
Keeney, Ralph, *Value-focused Thinking: A Path to Creative Decisionmaking*, Cambridge Ma., Harvard University Press, 1992.
Kentauros Magazine, *Στρατάρχης Αλέξανδρος Παπάγος*, Athens, General Army Command, December 1955.
Keohane, Robert, *After Hegemony: Cooperation and Discord in the World Political Economy*, Princeton, Princeton University Press, 1984.

Ker-Lindsay, James, *Cyprus Problem: What Everyone Needs to Know*, Oxford, New York, Oxford University Press, 2011.
Kissinger, Henry, *Diplomacy*, London, Simon and Schuster, 1994.
Kitromilides, Paschalis and Marios Evriviades, *Cyprus (World Bibliographical Series)*, Revised Edition, Oxford, Clio Press, 1995.
Kofas, Jon, *Intervention and Underdevelopment: Greece during the Cold War*, University Park and London, Pennsylvania State University Press, 1989.
Koliopoulos, John and Thanos Veremis, *Modern Greece: A History since 1821*, London, Blackwell, 2010.
Konidaris, Gerasimos, *Ιστορικαί αναμνήσεις από την προετοιμασία του αγώνος δια την ελευθερίαν της Κύπρου και η 7η Μαρτίου 1953*, Athens, 1964.
Kottis, George, *Liberalizing Foreign Trade. The Experience of Greece*, World Bank Comparative Studies, Washington, The World Bank, 1989.
Kousoulas, George, *The Price of Freedom: Greece in World Affairs, 1939–1953*, Syracuse, New York, 1953.
Kramer, Lloyd, *Nationalism in Europe and America: Politics, Cultures, and Identities since 1775*, Chapel Hill, University of North Carolina Press, 2011.
Kranidiotis, Nikos, *Δοκίμια: Προβληματισμοί, σκέψεις και μελέτες γύρω από την πολιτική και πνευματική ζωή της Κύπρου*, Athens, Syllogos pros diadosin ofelimon vivlion, 1994.
Kranidiotis, Nikos, *Δύσκολα χρόνια, 1950–1960*, Athens, Estia, 1981.
Kranidiotis, Nikos, *Η Κύπρος εις τον αγώνα της ελευθερίας*, Athens, Elliniki Ekdotiki Etairia, 1958.
Kuniholm, Bruce, *The Origins of the Cold War in the Near East*, Princeton, Princeton University Press, 1980.
Kyrou, Alexis, *Ελληνική εξωτερική πολιτική*, Athens, Estia, 1982 [1955].
Kyrou, Alexis, *Όνειρα και πραγματικότης. Χρόνια διπλωματικής ζωής (1923–1953)*, Athens, Kleisiounis, 1972.
Laclau, Ernesto, *On Populist Reason*, London, Verso, 2018 [2005].
Laclau, Ernesto, *Politics and Ideology in Marxist Theory: Capitalism, Fascism, Populism*, London, New Left Books, 1977.
Lampe, John and Marvin Jackson, *Balkan Economic History, 1550–1950: From Imperial Borderlands to Developing Countries*, Bloomington, Indiana University Press, 1982.
Lazaretou, Sophia, *Greek Monetary Economics in Retrospect: The Adventures of the Drachma*, Athens, Bank of Greece, Working Paper, 2, April 2003.
Legg, Keith, *Politics in Modern Greece*, Stanford, Stanford University Press, 1969.
Leysens, Anthony, *The Critical Theory of Robert W. Cox: Fugitive or Guru?* Basingstoke, Palgrave Macmillan, 2008.
Linardatos, Spyros, *Από τον Εμφύλιο στη Χούντα*, vols 1–5, Athens, Papazisis, 1977.
Linklater, Andrew, *Beyond Realism and Marxism: Critical Theory and International Relations*; Basingstoke and London, Macmillan, 1990.
Linklater, Andrew, *Critical Theory and World Politics: Citizenship, sovereignty and humanity*, Abingdon, Routledge, 2007.
Llewellyn Smith, Michael, *Ionian Vision: Greece in Asia Minor 1919–1922*, London, Hurst, 1973.
Loizidis, Savvas, *Άτυχη Κύπρος. Πώς έζησα τους πόθους και τους καημούς της, 1910–1980*, Athens, Bergadis, 1980.
Louis, William, *Ends of British Imperialism: The Scramble for Empire, Suez, and Decolonization*, London, I.B. Tauris, 2010.

Lykogiannis, Athanasios, *Britain and the Greek Economic Crisis, 1944–1947: From Liberation to the Truman Doctrine*, Missouri, University of Missouri Press, 2002.
Makridis, Andreas (ed.), *Εθνικιστικά κείμενα του ΑΚΕΛ*, Nicosia, Aegeon, 2010.
Markezinis, Spyros, *Σύγχρονη πολιτική Ιστορία της Ελλάδος 1936–1975*, vols 1–3, Athens, Papyros, 1994.
Markezinis, Spyros, *Αναμνήσεις 1972–1974*, Athens, Markezinis, 1979.
Markezinis, Spyros, *Από του Πολέμου εις την Ειρήνην*, Athens, Pyrsos, 1950.
Mates, Leo, *Non-Alignment Theory and Current Policy*, Belgrade, Oceana, 1972.
Mayall, James, *Nationalism and International Society*, Cambridge, Cambridge University Press, 1990.
Mayes, Stanley, *Cyprus and Makarios*, London, Putnam, 1960.
Mayes, Stanley, *Makarios: A Biography*, London, Macmillan, 1981.
Mazower, Mark, *Dark Continent: Europe's Twentieth Century*, London, Penguin, 1999.
Mazower, Mark, *The Balkans: A Short History*, New York, Modern Library, 2000.
McCrone, David, *The Sociology of Nationalism*, London, Routledge, 1998.
McGowan, Peter and C.W. Kegley (eds), *Foreign Policy and the Modern World System*, London, Sage, 1983.
McGrew, Anthony and M.J. Wilson (eds), *Decision Making: Approaches and Analysis*, Manchester, Manchester University Press, 1982.
McNeill, William, *The Greek Dilemma: War and Aftermath*, Philadelphia and New York, Lippincott, 1947.
Meier, G.E. (ed.), *Leading Issues in Economic Development*, Oxford, Oxford University Press, 1970.
Metaxas, Ioannis, *Λόγοι και σκέψεις*, vol.1, Athens, Govostis, 1997.
Meynaud, Jean, *Les forces politiques en Grèce*, [avec le concours de P. Merlopoulos et G. Notaras], Lausanne, Études de science politique, 1965.
Michalopoulos, Dimitris, *Ελλάδα και Τουρκία 1950–1959: Η χαμένη προσέγγιση*, Athens, Roes, 1989.
Miller, James, *The United States and the Making of Modern Greece: History and Power, 1950–1974*, Chapel Hill, University of North Carolina Press, 2009.
Miller, Robert, *Soviet Foreign Policy Today: Gorbachev and the New Political Thinking*, Hoboken, Taylor and Francis, 2012.
Mirbagher, Farid, *Historical Dictionary on Cyprus*, Lanham, Scarecrow Press, 2010.
Miscellaneous, *Ιστορία του Ελληνικού Έθνους*, 16, Athens, Ekdotiki Athinon, 2000.
Mommsen, Wolfgang, *The Political and Social Theory of Max Weber*, Chicago, University of Chicago Press, 1989.
Morgan, Patrick, *Deterrence Now*, Cambridge, Cambridge University Press, 2003.
Morse, Edward, *Foreign Policy and Interdependence in Gaullist France*, Princeton, Princeton University Press, 1973.
Mouzelis, Nicos, *Modern Greece: Facets of Underdevelopment*, London, Macmillan, 1977.
Mouzelis, Nicos, *Politics in the Semi-Periphery: Early Parliamentarism and Late Industrialisation in the Balkans and Latin America*, London, Macmillan, 1986.
Mudde, Cas and Cristobal Rovira Kaltwasser, *Populism: A Very Short Introduction*, Oxford, New York, Oxford University Press, 2017.
Müller, Jan-Werner, *What Is Populism?*, London, Penguin, 2017.
Myint, Hia, *Economic Theory and the Underdeveloped Countries*, New York, Oxford University Press, 1971.
Nicholson, Michael, *Rationality and the Analysis of International Conflict*, Cambridge, Cambridge University Press, 1992.

Nicolet, Claude, *United States Policy towards Cyprus, 1954–1974: Removing the Greek-Turkish Bone of Contention*, Mannheim, Bibliopolis, 2001.
Niebhur, Reinhold, *The Irony of American History*, Chicago, University of Chicago Press, 2008 [1952].
Nikolakopoulos, Elias, *Η καχεκτική δημοκρατία. Κόμματα και εκλογές, 1946–1967*, Athens, Patakis, 2001.
OECD, *Economic Surveys by the OECD: Greece*, Paris, Organization for Economic Co-Operation and Development, April 1962.
O'Malley, Brendan and Ian Craig, *The Cyprus Conspiracy: America, Espionage and the Turkish Invasion*, London, I.B. Tauris, 2007.
Pagoulatos, George, *Greece's New Political Economy: State, Finance, and Growth from Postwar to EMU*, Basingstoke, Palgrave Macmillan, 2003.
Panizza, Francisco, *Populism and the Mirror of Democracy*, London, Verso, 2005.
Panourgia, Neni, *Dangerous Citizens: The Greek Left and the Terror of the State*, New York, Fordham University Press, 2009.
Panteli, Stavros, *A New History of Cyprus: From the Earliest Times to the Present Day*, East-West Publications, Hounslow, 1984.
Papachelas, Alexis, *Ο βιασμός της ελληνικής Δημοκρατίας*, Athens, Estia, 1997.
Papadimitriou, Despina, *Από τον λαό των νομιμοφρόνων στο έθνος των εθνικοφρόνων. Η συντηρητική σκέψη στην Ελλάδα, 1922–1967*, Athens, Savvalas, 2006.
Papagiannopoulos, Takis, *Στρατάρχης Αλέξανδρος Παπάγος. Ο εκλεκτός της Ιστορίας*, Athens, 1987.
Papagos, Alexander, *Ο πόλεμος της Ελλάδος, 1940–1941*, Athens, Goulandris-Horn Foundation, 1995.
Papakonstandinou, Michalis, *Η ταραγμένη εξαετία*, Athens, Proskinio, 1997.
Papandreou, Andreas, *Democracy at Gunpoint. The Greek Front*, New York, Pelican, 1973 [1970].
Papandreou, Vasso, *Πολυεθνικές επιχειρήσεις και αναπτυσσόμενες χώρες. Η περίπτωση της Ελλάδας*, Athens, Gutenberg, 1986.
Pappas, Takis, *Making Party Democracy in Greece*, Basingstoke, Macmillan, 1999.
Paraskevopoulos, Potis, *Φιλελεύθερα ανοίγματα μετά τον Εμφύλιο*, Athens, Fytrakis, 1987.
Pelt, Morgens, *Tying Greece to the West: US-West German-Greek Relations, 1949–1967*, Copenhagen, Museum Tusculanum Press, 2006.
Persaud, Randolph, *Counter-Hegemony and Foreign Policy: The Dialectics of Marginalized and Global Forces in Jamaica*, Albany, State University of New York Press, 2001.
Petrakis, Marina, *The Metaxas Myth: Dictatorship and Propaganda in Greece*, London, I.B. Tauris, 2006.
Petridis, Pavlos, *Εξουσία και παραεξουσία στην Ελλάδα, 1957–1967: Απόρρητα ντοκουμέντα*, Athens, Proskinio, 2000.
Politakis, George, *The Post-War Reconstruction of Greece. A History of Economic Stabilization and Development, 1944–1952*, Basingtoke, Palgrave Macmillan, 2018.
Porter, Paul A., *Ζητείται: Ένα θαύμα για την Ελλάδα. Ημερολόγιο ενός προεδρικού απεσταλμένου, 20 Ιανουαρίου – 27 Φεβρουαρίου 1947*, ed. Michalis Psalidopoulos, Athens, Metamesonykties Ekdoseis, 2006.
Poulantzas, Nicos, *Classes in Contemporary Capitalism*, London, New Left Books, 1975 [1974].
Poulantzas, Nicos, *The Crisis of the Dictatorships*, London, New Left Books, 1976 [1975].
Poulantzas, Nicos, *State, Power, Socialism*, London, Verso, 2000 [1978].

Prizel, Ilya, *National Identity and Foreign Policy: Nationalism and Leadership in Poland*, Cambridge, Cambridge University Press, 1998.
Prodromidis, K.P., *Foreign Trade of Greece: A Quantitative Analysis at Sectoral Level*, Athens, Centre of Planning and Economic Research, 1976.
Psalidopoulos, Michalis, *Επιτηρητές σε απόγνωση. Αμερικανοί σύμβουλοι στην Ελλάδα, 1947–53. Από τον Paul A. Porter στον Edward A. Tenenbaum*, Athens, Metamesonykties Ekdoseis, 2013.
Psalidopoulos, Michalis, *Ο Ξενοφών Ζολώτας και η ελληνική οικονομία*, Athens, Metamesonykties Ekdoseis, 2008.
Psalidopoulos, Michalis, *Οικονομολόγοι και οικονομική πολιτική στη σύγχρονη Ελλάδα*, Athens, Metamesonykties Ekdoseis, 2010.
Psalidopoulos, Michalis, *Πολιτική οικονομία και Έλληνες διανοούμενοι. Μελέτες για την Ιστορία της οικονομικής σκέψης στη σύγχρονη Ελλάδα*, Athens, Typothito, 1999.
Psyroukis, Nikos, *Το νεοελληνικό παροικιακό φαινόμενο*, Athens, Epikairotita, 1974.
Raia, Svetozar, *Yugoslavia and the Soviet Union in the Early Cold War: Reconciliation, Comradeship, Confrontation, 1953–1957*, Abingdon, Routledge, 2011.
Rallis, George, *Πολιτικές εκμυστηρεύσεις, 1950–1989*, Athens, Proskinio, 1990.
Richter, Heinz, *British Intervention in Greece: From Varkiza to Civil War–February 1945 to August 1946*, London, Hollowbrook, 1985.
Rizas, Sotiris, *Η Ελληνική πολιτική μετά τον Εμφύλιο Πόλεμο: Κοινοβουλευτισμός και Δικτατορία*, Athens, Kastaniotis, 2008.
Roach, Steven, *Critical Theory of International Politics: Complementarity, justice, and governance*, London, Routledge, 2010.
Roach, Steven (ed.), *Handbook of Critical International Relations*, Cheltenham, Edward Elgar, 2020.
Roger, Simon, *Gramsci's Political Thought: An Introduction*, Norfolk, Biddles, 1982.
Rohsenow, John (ed.), *ABC Dictionary of Chinese Proverbs (Yanhu)*, Hawai'i, University of Hawai'i Press, 2003.
Rosenau, James, *The Adaptation of National Societies: A Theory of Political Systems Behavior and Transformation*, New York, McCaleb-Seiler, 1970.
Rostow, W.W., *The Stages of Economic Growth: A Non-Communist Manifesto*, Third Edition, New York, Cambridge University Press, 1990 [1960].
Roxborough, Ian, *Theories of Underdevelopment*, London, Macmillan, 1979.
Rupert, Mark, *Producing Hegemony: The Politics of Mass Production and American Global Power*, Cambridge, Cambridge University Press, 1995.
Said, Edward, *Culture and Imperialism*, London, Vintage, 1994.
Schelling, Thomas, *The Strategy of Conflict*, New Haven, Harvard University Press, 1980.
Schiller, Bradley, *Essentials of Economics*, New York, McGraw-Hill, 1999.
Seferis, George, *Πολιτικό Ημερολόγιο Α΄, 1935–1944*, ed. Alexander Xydis Athens, Ikaros, 1979.
Seferis, George, *Πολιτικό Ημερολόγιο Β΄, 1945–1947, 1949, 1952*, ed. Alexander Xydis, Athens, Ikaros, 1985.
Shills, Edward, *Centre and Periphery: Essays in Macrosociology*, Chicago, University of Chicago Press, 1975.
Singer, Marshall, *Weak States in a World of Powers: The Dynamics of International Relationships*, New York, Free Press, 1972.
Smith, Anthony, *Nationalism in the Twentieth Century*, Oxford, Robertson, 1979.
Smith, Anthony, *Nationalism and National Identity*, Middlesex, Penguin, 1991.

Sokolsky, Joel, *Sea Power in the Nuclear Age: United States Navy and NATO, 1948-1950*, London, Routledge, 1991.
Speeches Delivered by H.M. The King of the Hellenes During the State Visit to U.S.A., 28 Oct.-3 Dec. 1953, Athens, The Greek National Institute, 1954.
Spencer, Philip and Howard Wollman, *Nationalism: A Critical Introduction*, London, Sage, 2002.
Stathakis, George, *Το Δόγμα Τρούμαν και το Σχέδιο Μάρσαλ: Η ιστορία της αμερικανικής βοήθειας στην Ελλάδα*, Athens, Vivliorama, 2004.
Stavrakis, Peter, *Moscow and Greek Communism, 1944-1949*, New York, Ithaca, 1989.
Stavrianos, Leften, *Greece: American Dilemma and Opportunity*, Chicago, Henry Regnery, 1952.
Stearns, Monteagle, *Entangled Allies: U.S. Policy towards Greece, Turkey and Cyprus*, New York, Council of Foreign Relations Press, 1992.
Stefanidis, Ioannis, *Isle of Discord: Nationalism, Imperialism and the Making of the Cyprus Problem*, London, Hurst, 1999.
Stefanidis, Ioannis, *Stirring the Greek Nation: Political Culture, Irredentism and Anti-Americanism in Post-War Greece, 1945-1967*, Aldershot, Ashgate, 2007.
Stefanidis, Yannis, *Από τον Εμφύλιο στον Ψυχρό Πόλεμο: Η Ελλάδα και ο συμμαχικός παράγοντας, 1949-52*, Athens, Proskinio, 1999.
Sulzberger, Cyrus, *Long Row of Candles*, New York, Macmillan, 1969.
Svolopoulos, Constantine, *Ελληνική εξωτερική πολιτική 1900-1945*, vol.1, Athens, Estia, 2001.
Svolopoulos, Constantine, *Η ελληνική εξωτερική πολιτική, 1945-1981*, vol.2, Athens, Estia, 2001.
Svoronos, Nicos, *Ανάλεκτα νεοελληνικής Ιστορίας και ιστοριογραφίας*, Athens, Themelio, 1995.
Svoronos, Nicos, *Επισκόπηση της νεοελληνικής Ιστορίας*, Athens, Themelio, 1999.
Sweet-Escott, Bickham, *Greece: A Political and Economic Survey, 1939-1953*, London and New York, RIIA, 1954.
Tayfur, Fatih, *Semiperipheral Development and Foreign Policy. The Cases of Greece and Spain*, Aldershot, Ashgate, 2003.
Tenekidis, George and Yannos Kranidiotis (eds), *Κύπρος. Ιστορία, προβλήματα και αγώνες του λαού της*, Athens, Estia, 2009.
Terlexis, Pantelis, *Πολιτική και διπλωματία του Κυπριακού. Ανατομία ενός λάθους*, Athens, Kedros, 2004.
Thorpe, D.R., *Eden: The Life and Times of Anthony Eden First Earl of Avon, 1897-1977*, London, Chatto and Windus, 2003.
Todorova, Maria, *Imagining the Balkans*, Oxford and New York, Oxford University Press, 1997.
Triepel, Heinrich, *Die Hegemonie: ein Buch von führenden Staaten*, Aalen, Scientia, 1961.
Tsakalotos, Thrasivoulos, *40 Χρόνια Στρατιώτης. Πώς εκερδίσαμε τους αγώνας μας, 1940-1949*, vols 1-2, Athens, Acropolis, 1960.
Tsaoussis, D.G. (ed.), *Ελληνισμός και ελληνικότητα: Ιδεολογικοί και βιωματικοί άξονες της νεοελληνικής κοινωνίας*, Athens, Estia, 1983.
Tsatsos, Constantine, *Λογοδοσία μιας ζωής*, vol.1, Fourth Edition, Athens, Ekdoseis ton filon, 2001.
Tsoucalas, Constantine, *The Greek Tragedy*, London, Penguin, 1969.
Tsoukalas, Constantine, *Εξάρτηση και αναπαραγωγή: Ο κοινωνικός ρόλος των εκπαιδευτικών μηχανισμών στην Ελλάδα (1830-1922)*, Athens, Themelio, 1987 [1977].

Tsoukalis, Loukas, *The European Community and Its Mediterranean Enlargement*, London, Allen and Unwin, 1981.
Valden, Sotiris, *Ελλάδα και Ανατολικές Χώρες: Οικονομικές Σχέσεις και Πολιτική*, Athens, Odysseas, 1991.
Van Steen, Gonda, *State of Emergency: Theatre and Public Performance under the Greek Military Dictatorship of 1967–1974*, Oxford, Oxford University Press, 2015.
Veremis, Thanos, *The Military in Greek Politics*, London, Hurst, 1997.
Veremis, Thanos, *Ιστορία των ελληνοτουρκικών σχέσεων 1453–1998*, Athens, Sideris/ ELIAMEP, 1998.
Vergopoulos, Constantine, *Το αγροτικό ζήτημα στην Ελλάδα*, Athens, Exantas, 1975.
Vernardakis, Christophoros and Yannis Mavris, *Κόμματα και κομματικές συμμαχίες στην προδικτατορική Ελλάδα*, Athens, Exandas, 1991.
Vlachos, Angelos, *Δέκα χρόνια Κυπριακού*, Athens, Estia, 1981.
Vlachos, Angelos, *Μια φορά κι έναν καιρό, ένας διπλωμάτης...*, vol.3, Fourth Edition, Athens, Estia, 1998 [1986].
Vournas, Tassos, *Ιστορία της σύγχρονης Ελλάδας 1940–1967*, Athens, Tolidis, undated.
Vryonis, Speros, *The Mechanism of Catastrophe: The Turkish Pogrom of September 6–7, 1955, and the Destruction of the Greek Community of Istanbul*. New York: Greekworks.com, 2005.
Wallerstein, Immanuel, *The Modern World System I: Capitalist Agriculture and the Origins of the European World-Economy in the Sixteenth Century*, Berkley and LA, University of California Press, 2011 [1974].
Webber, Mark and Michael Smith, *Foreign Policy in a Transformed World*, Harlow, Prentice Hall, 2002.
Weber, Max, *Economy and Society: An outline of interpretive sociology*, vol.1, ed. Guenther Roth and Claus Wittich, Berkley, Second Edition, Berkeley, University of California Press, 1978.
Westlind, Denis, *The Politics of Popular Identity: Understanding Recent Populist Movements in Sweden and the United States*, Lund, Lund University Press, 1996.
Wittkopf, Eugene et al., *American Foreign Policy: Pattern and Process*, Thomson, Belmont, Thomson, 2008.
Wittner, Lawrence, *American Intervention in Greece, 1943–1949*, New York, Columbia University Press, 1982.
Woodhouse, C.M., *Modern Greece. A Short History*, Fifth Edition, London, Faber and Faber, 1998 [1991].
Xydis, Stephen, *Cyprus: Conflict and Conciliation, 1954–1958*, Columbus, Ohio, 1967.
Yannakopoulos, Nikolaos, Manos Kountouris, Michalis Psalidopoulos, *Ξενοφών Ζολώτας. Φιλελευθερισμός στην πράξη*, Athens, Metamesonykties Ekdoseis, 2009.
Yost, Charles, *History and Memory*, New York, Norton, 1980.
Zolotas, Xenophon, *Η Ελλάς εις το στάδιον της εκβιομηχανίσεως*, Athens, Eleftheroudakis, 1926.
Zolotas, Xenophon, *Monetary Equilibrium and Economic Development*, Princeton, Princeton University Press, 1965.

INDEX

Abdel Nasser, Gamal 90
Acheson, Dean 22, 36–8, 40–1, 43–5, 54, 65, 67–9, 75, 82, 100, 186
　see also, State Department, US embassy in Greece
Acropolis, newspaper 73
Adorno, Theodor 27
'Aghios Georgios' Affair 175–6, 212
　see also, National Organization of Cypriot Fighters
agriculture, in Greece 19, 181, 190, 209
Aldrich, Winthrop 160
Alexopoulos, Ilias 172
Alivizatos, Nicos 24–5, 57, 78, 219
Al-Jamali, Mohammed 154
Allagi, newspaper 74
Allen, George 40
American bases in Greece 18, 83, 88–93, 104, 111, 159, 181
American Economic Mission to Greece 34
　see also, Economic Cooperation Administration, Mutual Security Agency
American European Command, US EUCOM 48
American Federation of Labor, AFL 33
American hegemony, *See* hegemony
American intervention 8, 23, 30–1, 35, 37–8, 40, 47, 51, 62–3, 65, 69–73, 75, 126, 185–6, 193
　see also, hegemony, Central Intelligence Agency, Peurifoy, Truman Doctrine, US embassy,
American Mission of Assistance to Greece, AMAG 32–3, 182
Anderson, Benedict 19
Angelopoulos, Angelos 183
Anglo-Greek
　friendship 95–6, 109–11, 116, 178
　negotiations on Cyprus 102–3, 105, 108–9, 111, 113–15, 128, 134, 137–8, 142–3, 145, 147, 150, 152–3, 156, 161, 169, 171, 177, 263 fn2
　relations 95, 102, 105, 107–8, 110, 141, 151, 212
　see also, Britain
Anglophile approach, Greek, re: Cyprus question 84, 94, 97, 121, 213
anti-American
　discourse 26, 49, 70
　protests 170, 211
　sentiment 49–50, 211
anti-colonial
　character of UN recourse 155, 177
　discourse 266 fn76
　policy 171
　states 162
　struggle 146, 220
anti-communism 24, 58, 74, 94, 146, 218–21
　see also, *Ethnikofrosyni*
anti-*Enosis* campaign 157
anti-sedition laws, Cyprus 140, 143
Apostolidis, Andreas 55
armed forces, Greek 7–8, 18, 25, 29, 32–3, 35, 42–5, 47–8, 50, 52, 54, 56, 58, 60–3, 67–8, 70, 72, 75–6, 86–7, 89–91, 98–9, 118, 129, 172, 177, 182–3, 198, 221
　Balkan military cooperation 42–5, 90, 121–8
　US policy review of 1952 47–8, 50
　see also, army vote, American military bases, National Organization of Cypriot Fighters, Sacred Bond of Greek Officers, US military aid to Greece
army vote 60–1, 72, 233 fn36
Atatürk, Kemal 213
Athanassopoulou, Ekavi 42
Atlanticism 1–2, 5, 17, 24, 26, 85, 99, 116, 121, 146–7, 215, 220
Attlee, Clement 93–4
　see also, Labour Party
authoritarian
　elements/power-centres 55, 58–9
　institutions/structures 54, 58–9

leadership/practices 58, 218
parastate 25, 35
parliamentarism 58
state 8, 24, 53
see also, guided democracy
Averoff-Tositsas, Evangelos 3, 96, 100, 107, 130, 172–4, 176, 214–16, 218
Avgi, newspaper 119
Avgikos, Antonis 172
Axis occupation 94, 99
Azinas, Andreas 174–6
'Azmi, Mahmoud 156, 160, 177

Bachrach and Baratz 11, 121
see also, non-decisions
balance of trade 184, 193, 202, 207–8
balance of payments 181, 186, 191
crisis of 202, 208
deficit 193, 207
Balkan Pact, also *entente* 18, 45, 83–4, 86, 93, 116, 120–4, 126, 128, 141, 211, 216
see also, Treaty of Bled, Treaty of Ankara
Balkan *rapprochement* 38, 40–2, 44, 122
Balkanism, discourse 27–8, 140
Balkans 1–2, 13, 27–8, 42–3, 50, 91–2, 116, 121, 123, 126
Bank of Greece 32–3, 183, 186, 188–90, 201
Barker, Elisabeth 39
Battalions of National Defence, TEA 60
Baxter, William 106, 126–7, 129–30, 161
see also, State Department
Bayar, Celâl 47
Beloyannis, Nikos 57
benign resolution 156
see also, 'Azmi, Mahmoud
Bidault, Georges 120, 128
Birgi, Muharrem Nuri 100–1, 125
Bismarck, Otto von 58
Bitsios, Dimitrios 113
Bodossakis, Prodromos 24, 63
Bradley, Omar 43–4, 237 fn120
Brass, Paul 20
Bretton Woods System 17–18, 180, 188
see also, liberalism
Breuilly, John 19–20
brinkmanship

deterrence theory 116
failure of 142, 145–6, 177
over Cyprus 115–16, 128, 137, 142, 145–6, 177
Papagos' initial confidence in 116, 145
zero-sum-game 146
see also, game theory, Schelling
Britain 8, 18, 23–4, 26, 32, 38, 41, 43–4, 57, 63, 67, 84–5, 90–111, 113–16, 118, 121, 123, 128–42, 145–7, 149–73, 175–9, 182–3, 196, 198, 201, 212–18, 220
see also, Anglo-Greek, colonialism, British embassy, Churchill, Eden, Middle East, United Nations
British embassy 8, 33, 63–6, 71–2, 90, 98, 102, 104, 130, 138, 142, 145, 149, 152–3, 198, 213, 253 fn121
see also, Norton, Peake
British military bases
Greek offer of 96, 108, 128, 142
Budd, Adrian 4
Bulgaria 41, 89, 120
Buzan, Barry 13
Byroade, Henry 106, 125–6, 129–30, 138
see also, State Department

Cabot-Lodge, Henry 109, 147, 153, 155, 160–6, 178
see also, Dixon, Dulles, John Foster, United Nations
Caesarism 59, 219
see also, Gramsci, hegemony
Canada 30, 179, 198
Cannon, Cavendish 89–90, 106, 123–4, 126, 138, 140, 161, 163, 211
see also, US embassy, Peake
Canovan, Margaret 78
Carney, Robert 43
Carporaso, James 16
Central Intelligence Agency, CIA 34–5, 39, 44, 51, 65, 76, 119
see also, Dulles, Allen, Karamessinis
Centre 53, 55, 63, 72–5, 194, 214
centre-right coalition 36–7, 68
centre/right divide, ambiguity of 53, 73
coalition government(s) 49, 86, 61, 68, 84–6, 91, 94–9, 102–3, 128, 215, 220

electoral meltdown 73–4
parties 36–7, 53, 55, 67, 71–4, 91, 99, 146, 174
press 73, 99
see also, Liberal Party, National Progressive Centre Union, Papandreou, George Plastiras, Venizelists, Venizelos, Sophocles
Certificate of social convictions 57
see also, anti-communism, *Ethnikofrosyni*
Charalambis, Dimitris 61
charismatic authority 75, 77, 81, 94, 219
China 42, 47, 164
see also, Korean War
Chourmouzios, Emilios 147, 178, 264 fn14
Choutas, Stelios 74
Christidis, Christoforos 101, 147, 158, 168, 216
Churchill, Winston 137–9, 141, 148–50, 153, 157–60, 162, 212, 214
see also, Colville, Eden, Eisenhower, Hopkinson
civil society 7, 20, 33
Civil War, Greek 2, 15, 17, 23–5, 32–3, 36, 38–40, 49–50, 53–4, 56–7, 59, 64, 77, 94, 97, 99, 102, 133, 184, 187, 201, 211, 216, 219–21
clientelism 58, 77
Clogg, Richard 200
Close, David 24, 187
Cold War 1–5, 7–8, 23, 25, 29, 38, 62, 85, 110, 116, 120–1, 171, 197, 211, 214, 216, 220–1
East-West tension 89, 120
see also, Atlanticism, Cold War liberalism, Eastern Bloc, North Atlantic Treaty Organization, Western World
Cold War liberalism 2, 17, 115
see also, anticommunism, Atlanticism
collaborators, Nazi 55
Colombia, UN Representation 154, 166–7
colonialism 5, 115, 216
British 85, 93, 100, 153
in Cyprus 85, 93, 100, 153, 214, 216
see also, anti-colonialism, decolonization

Colville, John 148–9
see also, Churchill, Skouras
Cominform 41–2, 78, 80, 99, 103
communism 1, 5, 9, 15, 24–6, 31–2, 38–40, 45, 50–1, 54, 57, 74, 78, 89, 92, 94, 100–1, 118–19, 141, 178, 187, 218
see also, Cominform, Communist Party of Greece, Progressive Party of the Working People, Soviet Union, communist threat
communist threat 15, 31, 39, 41, 54
Communist Party of Greece, KKE 26, 54, 74, 218
Free Greek Radio 89
see also, Zachariadis, Democratic Army
comprador bourgeoisie 15–16, 24
concentration camps, for communists 25, 57
Confederation of Public Corporations, NPDD 98
Constantine, crown prince 34
constitutional offer to Cyprus, British 91, 93–4, 97, 108, 128, 131, 133–4, 138–42, 152
see also, 'liberal' constitution for Cyprus
constructivism, IR theory 11
core/periphery analysis 13–16, 23, 27
corporatist state mechanisms 20, 24, 58–9, 99
Costis, Costas 187
Coufoudakis, Van 62, 70
coup d' etat, See military coup, royal couple
Cowles, Fleur 145, 149–51, 153, 156, 160–1, 177, 265 fn37
Cox, Robert 4, 9–12, 15, 18, 20, 30, 48, 217
see also, critical theory
Critical Foreign Policy Analysis, Critical FPA 10–12
critical theory 4, 9–13, 217
Cyprus Question 3, 7, 26, 84–5, 92–3, 95–7, 99–103, 105–7, 109–11, 113–14, 116–18, 121, 128, 130–2, 135–7, 141–2, 145–9, 151–3, 165, 169, 177–8, 211, 215–16, 220–1

Dafnis, Grigorios 59
Damalas, Vassilios 179, 203
Daskalakis, Apostolos 158
De Gasperi, Alcide 45, 122
De Gaulle, Charles 1, 55, 60, 77
decision-making, process/groups 4,
    10–11, 22, 120–1, 135, 145
decolonization 23, 93, 216
Dedijer, Vladimir 40
defections, apostasy of 1952 73–5
    see also, Centre parties, Liberal Party,
    National Progressive Centre Union,
    Plastiras
Democratic Army, in Greek Civil War 32,
    40, 50
Dendramis, Vassilios 37
dependence 1, 4–5, 7, 13–16, 18, 21–3,
    25–6, 29–30, 33–5, 37, 49, 83, 85–6,
    116, 121, 181–2, 189, 202, 206–7,
    211, 215
    dependent mentality, Greek/Balkan
        elites 22, 28, 35, 191
    dependent state 18
    economic dependence 16, 35, 37, 49,
        182, 189, 202, 206–7
    and foreign policy 16–18, 26, 206
    and limited autonomy 8, 12, 18, 29, 31,
        49–52, 83, 86–7
    and nationalism 21–3, 25–6, 85–6, 116,
        211
    voluntary dependence 86, 181, 248 fn14
    see also, structural disarticulations,
        Varvaressos Report
dependence narrative, in Greek
    historiography 7–8, 30, 50, 53, 57,
    59, 71, 73, 83–4, 187, 219, 224 fn1
dependence(y) theory 8–9, 13
dependent nationalism 2, 4–5, 23, 25–6,
    85, 96, 113, 206, 211, 217, 221
devaluation, of drachma 180, 183, 186–7,
    189, 192–6, 200–3, 205–7
    ECA/MSA's proposal 186–7
    hyperdevaluation 194
    inflationary effects of 186, 194–5,
        200–1, 203, 207
    Varvaressos' critique of 189, 192–6
    see also, inflation, Markezinis, Mutual
        Security Agency
Diakos, Ioannis 55

Diamandouros, Nikiforos 19, 28
    see also, underdog culture
Dictatorship, See Metaxas Dictatorship,
    Military Dictatorship,
Dimaratos, Socratis 62
diplomatic history 1–2, 12, 110
Dixon, Pierson 154–6, 161–5, 168–9, 178
Douglas, Mary 26
Driberg, Tom 140
Dritsas, Margarita 187
dual/duality 2, 25, 27–8, 56, 58, 79, 159, 175
dualism
    foreign economic policy 179
    foreign policy 4–5, 7, 21–4, 26–8, 83–5,
        95–6, 104, 111, 115–16, 121, 142,
        147–8, 158, 166, 169, 171–2, 176–7,
        179, 215, 217, 219
dualistic models
    Foreign Policy Analysis 10
    societies 27
Dulles, Allen 34
    see also, Central Intelligence Agency
Dulles, John Foster 87, 89–92, 100, 103–4,
    106, 108, 111, 123, 126–8, 134, 138,
    140–2, 153, 156, 159–66, 168–70,
    197–9, 211
    see also, State Department
Dunn, Christopher 13
Durrell, Lawrence 93, 212

East Mediterranean 23, 39, 42, 91–3, 108,
    170, 214
    see also Southeastern Europe
Eastern Bloc 108, 121, 123, 157, 167, 177
    see also, Poland, Czechoslovakia,
        Byelorussia, Ukraine
economic liberalism, See liberalism
economic reconstruction 32, 179, 182,
    184–5, 187–8, 197, 200, 221,
    273 fn11, 275 fn53
    see also, Marshall Plan
Eden, Anthony 34, 81, 91–2, 94, 96,
    99–100, 101–2, 104–11, 113, 129,
    133, 136–7, 142, 149–50, 159–60,
    163, 169, 218
    Prime Minister 212
    Eden-Papagos incident 91–2, 101,
        104–8, 110–11, 113
    meeting with Averoff 96, 100, 107

Index

Egypt 90, 94, 138, 156
   see also, 'Azmi, Nasser
Eisenhower, Dwight 145, 211, 214
   Administration 87–90, 93, 123, 197
   Cyprus question mediation 145, 148–9, 153, 161
   discussions with Churchill 138–9
   NATO's new strategic concept 43–7
   SACEUR 42–6, 237 fn120
   supports Greek accession in NATO 45–6
Eisenhower, Mamie 88
'either/or' formula ('definitely will/unless') 114–16, 128–9, 131, 137, 142–3, 170
   see also, third strategy
elections 37, 49–50, 53–5, 60–3, 66, 68–70, 74, 76, 80, 186, 243 fn83, 245 fn140, 246 fn152
   Cyprus 94, 97
   Greece, 1950 36, 40, 70, 233 fn36, 246 fn152
   Greece, 1951 55, 60, 68–70, 72, 76–7, 79, 82, 86
   Greece, 1952 7, 50, 53, 55–6, 60–2, 70, 73–5, 77–8, 80, 187
   Italy, 7 June 1953 122
   see also, majority voting system, army vote, US Congress
Eleftheria, newspaper 68, 73–4, 77, 98, 115, 134, 136–7, 151, 192
El-Salvador, UN Representation 167
Embros, newspaper 73, 80, 172
Enosis, Union of Cyprus with Greece 3, 9, 26, 84–5, 92–105, 108, 111, 116, 119, 121, 132, 134, 142, 147–54, 160, 171, 177–8, 211–12, 214–18, 220
   impossibility of 96, 121, 148, 215–18
   movement 4, 84, 94–5, 97–8, 108, 119, 146, 156, 158, 171, 178, 219–20
   policy 85, 92, 94–6, 108, 111, 116, 134, 145, 169, 178, 181, 211, 214–18
   see also, anti-*Enosis* campaign, irredentist nationalism, plebiscite on, Panhellenic Committee of the Struggle for Union with Cyprus
EPEK, *See* National Progressive Centre Union
Erkin, Faridun 46, 101

essentialism 3, 4, 25
Estia, newspaper 73, 118–19, 140, 172
Ethnarchy, Cypriot 94–5, 97, 102–5, 108, 136, 157, 170
   see also Makarios, Kranidiotis, Loizidis, Savas
Ethnikofron(es) 2, 24, 211, 219–20
   economists 188, 199
   governments 29, 47, 81, 171, 216, 220
   Greek-Cypriot 97
   parties/forces/bloc 15, 32, 35, 40, 50, 52, 54–61, 68, 75, 81, 95 102, 171, 207, 214, 219–21
   press 35, 49, 172
   state/regime 25, 29, 31, 35, 39, 51–2, 70, 81, 94, 171, 177, 207, 214, 219–20
   unity of 56, 59, 185
Ethnikofrosyni
   discourse 2, 24–5, 57, 78, 219–20
   elite and vulgar 99
   political system of 35, 52, 58, 68, 94, 99, 146, 214, 219–20
   see also, anticommunism
Ethnikos Kyrix, newspaper 65, 73
Ethnocentric, Greek historiography 3–4, 7–8, 25, 57–8, 84, 219, 224 fn2
   narrative/perspective 7–8, 57–8, 84, 215–16
Ethnos, newspaper 73
European Cooperation Administration, ECA 33, 35, 37–8, 41, 52, 69, 180–2, 184–6, 197
   see also, devaluation, Hoffman, industrialization, Nevin, Nikolaides, Porter, Paul R.
Evelpides, Christos 190
Evert, Angelos 118
Exintaris, George 156, 177

fascist 26, 57, 152, 218
   quasi-fascist 24, 54–5
Fatouros, Argyris 18, 32–3
foreign direct investment, FDI 180, 195, 209
foreign economic policy 179, 193, 202, 206
foreign economic relations 20, 179
Foreign Office 37, 41, 65, 90, 94, 96–7, 100, 102–3, 105, 107, 109, 116, 118, 120, 128, 132, 134–7, 147–8, 151–2, 155–6, 158–9, 162–4, 172–3, 178, 212

Foreign Policy Analysis, FPA 2, 10–13, 16, 25
Foreign Trade Administration 18
France 1, 30, 40, 43, 77, 120, 123, 128–9, 154, 179, 195, 203
Francoism, 'parliamentary Francoism' 218
Frankfurt School 9, 27
   see also, Horkheimer, Max and Adorno, Theodor
Frederica, queen 34, 73, 213
   see also, royal couple, Paul, Palace, Constantine
'Free World' 5, 51, 138, 214
   see also, Western world

Galesworthy, John 117–20, 135
game theory 146
   see also, brinkmanship
Gellner, Ernest 19
General Agreement on Tariffs and Trade, GATT 195, 202–4, 206
General Confederation of Greek Workers, GSEE 33, 97
Georgoulis, Spyridon 62
Gondicas, Dimitris 95
Gorodetsky, Gabriel 5
Grady, Henry 33–8, 40, 51, 62, 86
Gramsci, Antonio 4, 30, 59, 219
   Gramscian 12, 48, 59
   see also, Caesarism, hegemony
Greek Currency Committee 18
Greek 'enlightenment committee', on Cyprus 157
   see also, propaganda
Greek Orthodox Church 104, 178
Greek Rally
   government 26, 67, 74–5, 79, 81, 83–6, 90–3, 96, 99, 101–4, 109–11, 114–5, 117–21, 133, 135, 137, 142, 145–8, 157–9, 170–3, 176, 178–81, 186, 190, 194, 196, 199 202–3, 205, 211, 213–14, 219–20
   party 53–6, 59–60, 62–3, 65, 67, 69–78, 80–3, 86, 99, 219
   pro-Rally press 50, 73, 78–9, 137, 147, 172, 203, 206
   see also, Papagos, Papagos Government, Markezinis
Greek-American relations, *See* US-Greek relations
Griffiths, James 139

Grigoropoulos, Theodoros 86–7
Griswold, Dwight 33
   see also, American Mission of Assistance to Greece
Grivas, George 94, 99, 119–20, 172–6
   see also, National Organization of Cypriot Fighters, 'X' paramilitary group
Grogoriadis, Solon 26
growth, economic 21, 27, 207, 209
guided (or restricted) democracy 24, 54, 58
   see also, authoritarian parliamentarism
Gyalistras, Sergios 62

Hammarskjold, Dag 103
   see also, United Nations
Harriman, Averell 35–6, 68
   see also, Marshall Plan
Harrison, Geoffrey 132–4, 136
   see also, Foreign Office
Hart, Charles 87
Hatzivassiliou, Evanthis 84, 114, 158, 201, 205
heavy industry 180–1, 196
hegemonic world order 4, 12, 14, 17–18, 21–3, 28, 30–1, 48, 217, 221
hegemony 14, 18, 20, 22, 28–9, 30–1, 47, 50, 52, 93, 248 fn14
   American 4–5, 23, 29–31, 34–6, 47–8, 50–2, 86, 207, 217, 220
   direct 30–1, 33, 48, 50
   global 1, 12, 14, 17–18, 21–3, 28, 30–1, 48, 50, 217, 221
   indirect 30–1, 48
   national hegemonic bloc 12, 171, 219
   see also, Cox, Gramsci, subaltern
Herzfeld, Michael 28
high and low politics 4, 18, 179, 181, 211
Hobsbawm, Eric 20
Hobson, John M. 12, 14
Hoffman, Paul 37
Hoffmann, Stanley 4
Holland, Robert 94, 110
Hopkinson, Henry 103–4, 137–40, 142–3, 145, 147, 149–51, 153, 159, 162–3
   'Never' 139–40, 143
   see also, Churchill, House of Commons, Lyttleton
Horkheimer, Max 9
   see also, critical theory

Horty, Miklós 58
House of Commons 104, 129, 137, 139, 142
Hudson, Valerie 10

Iatrides, John 7, 62, 70, 83, 122–3, 213
Iberian Peninsula, Papagos' tour of 159, 177
Iceland 181
IDEA, *See* Sacred Bond of Greek Officers
ideal types, Weberian 15–16
  see also, Weber, Max
Ierodiakonou, Leontios 103, 171
import quotas 180–1, 195, 200, 202–3
Import Substitution Industrialization, ISI 20, 180, 196, 206–7, 221
independence
  Greece's alleged 7–8, 38, 83
  Greek, efforts to become 3, 35, 83–4, 86, 118–19, 182, 188
  in foreign policy 19–20, 83
Independence of Cyprus 5, 91, 108, 133, 159, 216–17
  denied 139
  qualified 132, 215
  see also Zürich-London agreements
India 93, 155
industrialization 13, 20, 180–1, 187–9, 191–2, 196, 199, 206–7, 209, 211, 220
  Industrialists 97
  Varvaressos Report 188–9, 191–2, 196
  see also Import Substitution Industrialization, Economic Cooperation Administration
inflation 181–6, 194–5, 200–1, 203, 207
  see also, devaluation
inscription of Greek item, UN 114, 148
interdependence 13, 58
internal security, *See* security
internationalization 97, 102–3, 108, 110–11, 113–16, 128, 130–1, 135–6, 145–7, 171, 177–8, 214, 216, 263 fn2
  see also semi-internationalization
Ioannou, Dimitris 74
irredentist nationalism, *See* nationalism
Italy 1, 39, 43, 77, 104, 121–2, 123, 125–7, 179, 195, 218
  Papagos' visit 104, 121–2
  security of Greece 39, 43, 121, 123, 127
  Trieste dispute 1, 121, 123, 127
  see also, de Gasperi, Pella

Jacobson, Harold 10–12
Jeffery, Judith 52, 183, 200
Joint United States Military Aid Group, JUSMAG 32–3, 48, 87

Kalyvas, Stathis 200
Kanellopoulos, Panayiotis 35–6, 55, 61–2, 68, 77, 79–80, 82, 99, 102, 123, 161, 199, 212, 218, 220–1
Kapsalis, Thanos 200, 203
Karamanlis, Constantine 56, 59, 76, 82, 142, 177, 206, 209, 218, 220
  Government 59, 84, 132, 177, 210, 215–16, 220
  see also, National Radical Union
Karamaounas, Leonidas 74
Karamessinis, Tom 119
  see also, Central Intelligence Agency
Karanikas, Constantine 154
Karatzenis, Christos 106
Karavias, Panos 134–5
Kardelj, Edvard 41
Kartalis, George 49–50, 83, 159, 181, 185–7, 192–3, 195, 197, 201, 238 fn154, 274 fn43, 275 fn53
Kathimerini, newspaper 50, 73, 80, 130, 147, 151
Kavalieratos, Phaidon 161
Kazakos, Panos 187, 205
Kenney, John 186
Keohane, Joseph 30
Ker-Lindsay, James 110
Ketseas, Themistocles 86
Kitrilakis, Stylianos 86, 258 fn69
Koliopoulos, John 200
Konidaris, Gerasimos 172
Konstantinov, Aleko 27
Köprülü, Mehmet 128
Korean War 29–30, 38–9, 41–2, 46–7, 62, 66, 83, 87, 89, 91, 93, 181, 273 fn11
Koronaios, Georgios 55
Koryzis, Alexander 94
Kosmas, George 172–3
Koustas, Georgios 134, 136
Koutsalexis, Ioannis 151
Kranidiotis, Nicos 94, 114, 128, 173
Kuniholm, Bruce 29
Kyrkos, Michalis 74
Kyrou, Achilleas 118

Kyrou, Alexis 92, 97, 99, 103–4, 108–9, 114, 118–19, 121, 131, 133–6, 143, 151, 154–8, 161–3, 165–9, 171–2, 177–8, 270 fn144, 160
Kyrou, Kyros 118–19, 172

Labour Party 133, 139–40, 205
   Government, 1945–51 93, 99–100
   see also, Attlee
Laclau, Ernesto 76, 81
Lagakos, Efstathios 97
Lambrakis, Dimitris 63, 73
Lambrianidis, Lambros 120
Laniel, Joseph 129
Lapham, Roger 185
Latin America 13, 27, 155, 157, 167
Le Monde, newspaper 114, 116, 128
Legg, Keith 53
Lennox-Boyd, Henry 149
'liberal' constitution for Cyprus 91, 133–4, 139, 141, 152
   see also constitutional offer
liberal eclecticism 192, 205, 207
liberal (free) trade policies 16–17, 179–81, 196, 200–8, 278 fn136
   see also, liberalizing reforms, liberalism, liberal eclecticism
liberal institutionalism, IR theory 30
Liberal Party, also Liberals 25, 36, 38, 55–6, 60, 67–75, 81, 96, 101, 186, 192, 239 fn3
   and anti-communism of 74
   Liberal-EPEK alliance/coalition 56, 60, 68–70, 72–5, 81, 96, 101, 186, 192
   see also Centre parties, defections of 1952, National Progressive Centre Union, Venizelos, Sophocles
liberalism 1, 24, 179–80, 188, 192, 195–6, 200–1, 205, 207
   alleged 192, 195, 200–8
   Atlanticism 1, 24
   economic 179–80, 188, 192, 195–6, 200–1, 205, 207–8
   realistic 179, 205
   Venizelist 24, 55
   see also, liberal, liberals, Liberal Party, Cold War liberalism
liberalizing reforms 180, 195–6, 202–3, 205–9, 278 fn136

liberals 23–4, 55, 59, 67, 81, 115, 188, 193–5, 200–1, 205, 218, 224 fn1
   Centre 24, 53, 55, 59, 115, 194–5
   economists 187–8, 193, 200–1, 205
   press 68, 73–4, 195, 218
   see also liberal, liberalism, Liberal Party, Venizelists, liberal eclecticism
liminal character, of post-Civil War period 81
Linardatos, Spyros 26, 36, 55–6, 62, 70–1, 84, 117–18
Linklater, Andrew 3, 10
Livanos, Evgenia 17
Lloyd, Selwyn 103, 134, 149, 152, 154–6, 159, 171
Loizidis, Savas 103–4, 146, 172, 175, 214
Loizidis, Socratis 172, 175–6
Lychnos, Gerassimos 74
Lykourezos, Pausanias 118
Lyttleton, Oliver 134, 140, 152

McGhee, George 41–2, 44, 46–7
Macmillan, Harold 156, 212–13
MacVeagh, Lincoln 33–4
majority voting system 50, 52, 69–71, 73
   see also, Peurifoy, Plastiras, Papagos
Makarios III, Archbishop 84, 91–2, 94–6, 103, 108, 110, 113, 128, 133, 136, 143, 146, 148, 157, 159, 170–2, 174–7, 213–14, 271 fn180, 272 fn194
   see also, charismatic authority, Ethnarchy, National Organization of Cypriot Fighters, Grivas
Manendis, Dionysios 73
Maniadakis, Constantine 55, 150–3, 177, 214, 265 fn41, 268 fn119
Mantzavinos, George 186
Markezinis, Spyros 29, 34–6, 55, 62–8, 71, 73, 76–9, 81–2, 90–1, 101, 105, 110, 173, 179–82, 192–203, 205–11, 218, 220–1, 242 fn83, 256 fn22
   hidden protectionism 193–4, 196, 206–8
   medium-term investments programme 87, 93, 180–1, 196–200, 207, 209–11
New Party 36, 55, 76, 99, 246 fn152
oblivion policy 117–19
resignation 77, 116–21, 135, 256 fn22

visit to the US 87–8, 90, 181, 197–9
  see also, devaluation, eclectic liberalism, Greek Rally, import quotas, liberalism, new economic policy, Papagos solution
Marshall, George 44–5, 213
Marshall Plan 29, 33, 35, 37, 52, 68, 86, 180–1, 184, 186–7, 190, 196–7, 199, 210
Marxisant historiography 3–4, 8, 13, 25, 201, 220, 222–3 fn13
Marxist, neo-Marxist approaches 3–4, 8–9, 13–14, 25, 30, 51, 222–3 fn13
  see also dependence(y) theory
Mates, Leo 86, 248 fn14
Mavris, Yannis 25, 61
Mavros, George 38
Maximos, Dimitrios 34
Mayes, Stanley 114
Mazower, Mark 1
Mearsheimer, John 1
Mediterranean Pact 43–4, 46–7
  see also, Turkey
Megali Idea 20, 23, 54, 147, 217, 221
Melas, Leon 166, 170, 211
Menderes, Adnan 46–7, 126, 213
Menon, Krishna 155
Merkouris, Stamatis 56, 101–2
Metaxas, Aristides 64
Metaxas, Ioannis 2, 24, 82
Metaxas Dictatorship 1936–41 2, 23–4, 55, 99, 150, 218
Meynaud, Jean 36, 55–6, 71
Michalopoulos, Dimitris 84
Middle East ii, 90, 93, 198
  British Middle East Command 43, 93, 104
  Middle East Defence Organization, MEDO 90
military coup, Greece
  coup of 1922 53
  coup of 1933 23
  coup of 1935 23, 218
  coup of 21 April 1967 25, 221
  IDEA abortive coup, 30–31 May 1951 54, 57, 61, 65, 86, 220
  see also, royal couple, Turkey
Military Dictatorship, 1967–74 221
Miller, James 36–7
Minor, Harold 35–7, 43

mix of liberalism-protectionism 179–80, 203, 279 fn160
  see also, new economic policy, dualism, liberalism, protectionism
modernized sectors 21, 27
  see also, traditional sectors
modernization
  foreign policy 23
  Greek economy 180, 191, 197, 201, 206–7, 211, 220
  theory 27
Modinos, Polys 105
Molotov, Vyacheslav 34
Morrison, Herbert 34
Mostras, Vassilios 109, 113, 115–16, 131–7, 145, 147, 156–7, 164, 215
  File 113, 132–6, 151, 265 fn37
Mountbatten, Louis 91, 158
Mouzelis, Nicos 13, 16–17, 21, 59–62, 70, 77
Munro, Leslie 164, 166–7
  see also, New Zealand motion
Mutual Security Agency, MSA 33, 185–7, 193, 197–200
  devaluation of drachma 186–7, 193
  MSA-Washington 186

national bourgeoisie 15, 19, 24
  see also, comprador bourgeoisie
National Intelligence Service, KYP 7, 18, 25, 33
  see also, Central Intelligence Agency
National Organization of Cypriot Fighters, EOKA 23, 94, 119–21, 143, 172–7, 212, 214
  see also, Grivas, Makarios, Azinas
National Progressive Centre Union, EPEK 36, 53, 55–6, 60, 68–75, 78, 81, 96, 101, 185–6, 192
  EPEK-Liberal Union 81
  tripartite EPEK-Liberal-Rally coalition, US plan of 69, 74–5, 186–7
  see also, Centre, Liberal Party, Plastiras
National Radical Union, ERE 59, 84, 171–2
National Schism 24, 56
nationalism 1–5, 14–16, 18–26, 49, 55, 82, 84–5, 94, 96–9, 113, 115, 118, 120, 142, 146–7, 157, 165, 169, 171, 175–8, 188, 190, 206, 211, 213, 215, 217, 220–1

economic 14, 20, 188, 190, 206
  in foreign policy 18–20
  irredentist 19–20, 22–3, 26, 95, 215–16, 220
  semi-peripheral 14–16
  see also, dependent nationalism, Enosis
Nehru, Jawaharlal 155
neutralism 94, 108, 171, 214
  see also, Non-Aligned Movement
Nevin, Paul 68
new economic policy, 1953 180, 192, 195–6, 199, 200, 210
  legacy 207–9
  misinterpretation 200–3, 205–6
  see also, Markezinis
New Party, See Markezinis
New York Times 106, 165
  see also, Sulzberger
New Zealand
  motion 166–9, 171, 178
  UN Delegation 164, 167
  see also, Munro
Niarchos, Stavros 17
Niebuhr, Reinhold 5
Nikolaides, Leander 184, 187
Nikolakopoulos, Elias 36, 55–6, 71–2
Nitze, Paul 44
Non-Aligned Movement 171
  see also, neutralism
non-decisions 10–11, 23, 121, 174, 225–6 fn25
  see also, Bachrash and Baratz
non-substantive resolution, See substantive resolution
North Atlantic Treaty Organization, NATO 3, 5, 7–9, 18, 23, 26, 83–7, 91, 93, 95–7, 107, 110, 115–16, 122–6, 137, 146, 147–8, 156, 160, 169, 171, 178, 180, 211–14, 216–17, 220
  Greek accession in 29, 32, 38–9, 42–50
  First Strategic Concept 42–3, 45–7
  see also, Atlanticism, Eisenhower, Mediterranean Pact
Norton, Clifford 64, 66, 68, 76, 82, 107, 218
  see also, British embassy, Peake
'not to discuss' motion, or procedural resolution 162–6
Nutting, Anthony 145, 149–50, 153, 159, 162–3, 166–9, 178
  see also, Foreign Office, Dixon, Lloyd

O'Malley, Brendan and Ian Craig 110
Organization of European Economic Cooperation, OEEC 8, 18, 48, 181, 184, 187
orientalism 27, 153
  see also, Said
Orthodox Church, Greek 97–9, 104, 178
Pagoulatos, George 180, 187, 196, 201, 207
Palace (also Crown) 32, 34–6, 53–4, 57–9, 61–9, 72–4, 81, 86, 91, 134, 172, 220, 233 fn54, 239 fn3, 242 fn75
  see also, Paul, Frederica, Constantine, royal, royalism
Palestine 34, 94
Pampoukas, Georgios 55
Panhellenic Committee of the Struggle for Union with Cyprus, PEAEK 84, 97–9, 102, 172, 214
  Students' Committee for the Cypriot Struggle, PEKA 97
  see also, Greek Orthodox Church, Spyridon
Panizza, Francisco 81
Papachelas, Alexis 34
Papacosmas, Victor 26
Papadakis, Vassilios 55
Papadopoulos, Nikolaos 172
Papagiannopoulos, Takis 218
Papagos, Alexander 17, 26, 35, 53–7, 59–93, 99–111, 113–37, 140–2, 145–53, 155–6, 158–62, 164–6, 168–78, 181, 185–6, 197–200, 203, 206, 209, 211–21
  Civil War 64, 77, 218, 221
  Cyprus policy 83–5, 91–3, 99, 101–11, 113–16, 118–21, 128–37, 140–2, 145–53, 155–6, 158–62, 164–6, 168–78, 211, 219–21
  dispute with Palace 55–6, 63–8
  EOKA 172–7
  Field Marshal 7, 54, 61, 63–6, 68, 75–6, 92, 102, 104, 106, 108–10, 117, 120, 133, 135, 145, 151–2, 173, 216, 218, 220
  and IDEA 61–2, 65
  ill health 59, 212
  letter to Eisenhower 87–90
  meeting with Dulles 90, 160–1
  persona in historiography 218–19

Index

resignation from army 60, 65–8, 86
rise to power 7–8, 54, 59–82
see also, American military bases, Balkan Pact, brinkmanship, charismatic authority, dualism, Eden-Papagos incident, Greek Rally, Markezinis, military coup, non-decisions, Papagos Government, Papagos, Leonidas, Papagos, Maria, Papagos solution, Peurifoy, populism, Sacred Bond of Greek Officers, US embassy
Papagos Government 23, 26, 31, 55, 61–2, 67, 69, 74–5, 83, 85, 91–3, 96, 99–100, 103–4, 109, 111, 114, 117, 119, 133, 137, 145, 157, 159, 170, 172, 176, 178, 180–1, 190, 194, 196, 199, 202, 211, 213–14, 217
Papagos, Leonidas 151
Papagos, Maria 17
Papagos solution 8, 59, 62–7, 242 fn67
Papaligouras, Panayiotis 179, 203, 205
Papandreou, Andreas 62
Papandreou, George 53, 55–6, 71, 74, 77, 95, 187, 215, 221
 anti-communism 221
 Democratic Socialist Party 53, 71
 Greek Rally candidate 53, 55, 74, 77
 George Papandreou Party 36, 54–5, 72
 see also, Centre parties, defections of 1952
Papandreou, Vasso 180
Papayannis, Constantine 202
para-constitution 25
Paraskevopoulos, Potis 62, 70
parastate 7, 25, 54, 57–8, 99, 214, 221, 240 fn23
Passalidis, Yannis 119
 see also, United Democratic Left
path-dependence 41
Paul, king 35–7, 68, 109, 117, 146, 170, 178
 see also, Palace, royal couple, Frederica
Peake, Charles 70, 76–7, 81–2, 86, 90, 96, 100–2, 104–10, 117–18, 136, 146, 158–9, 173, 177, 212, 218
 see also, British embassy
Pella, Guiseppe 121–2, 128
Pelt, Morgens 24, 42, 62
Pentzopoulos, Thomas 86
Perkins, George 43–4

Peurifoy, John 32, 34, 44, 46, 75, 78, 81–2, 119, 126, 172, 185–7, 218, 242–3 fn84, 91, 245 fn140
 Cyprus question 107, 121
 intervention in Greek affairs 49–50, 62, 70–3
 majority voting system 70–3
 Papagos' rise to power 62–3, 67–70, 72–3, 77, 83, 87
 and Papagos solution 65–7
 US policy review (1952) 49
Pfaff, William 1
Philippines, UN Representation 167–8
Phrantzes, Ioannis 136
Pipinelis, Panayiotis 40, 64, 130–4, 140–2, 150–2, 177, 214–15
Pirjevec, Jože 40
Plastiras, Nikolaos 31, 35–7, 40–1, 49, 51, 53, 57, 60, 64, 68, 70–5, 94–5, 98–9, 108, 172, 185, 187–9, 191–2, 195, 202, 239 fn3
 and Cyprus question 94–5, 98–9, 108, 172
 defections of 1952 73–4
 majority voting system 70–3, 239 fn3
 see also, National Progressive Centre Union, Plastiras Governments, Varvaressos Report
Plastiras Government 35, 37, 40–1, 49, 51, 57, 64, 70–5, 94–5, 98–9, 108, 172, 185, 187–9, 191–2, 195, 202
plebiscite, on *Enosis*, 1950 94–5, 220
 proposed plebiscite for Cyprus solution 91, 108–10, 128, 133–4, 152, 226 fn25
pluralism, theory 4, 8, 11, 58, 225 fn25
policy makers 10, 16, 18, 23, 161, 217–18
 Greek 120, 130, 135, 145–6, 159, 165
 US 39, 51, 83, 86, 161
Politis, Athanase 88, 106, 125–7, 129–30, 137–8, 161
Politis, Ioannis 41
Polyzogopoulos, Stavros 55
Popović, Koča 122, 124–5, 128
Popular Party 36, 38, 55, 71–2, 99, 220, 246 fn152
 see also, Tsaldaris, Constantine
Popular Unity Party, LEK 55, 71, 76, 99, 246 fn152
 see also, Kanellopoulos, Stefanopoulos

populism 22, 26, 58, 75–9, 81, 99, 157, 172, 190–1, 218–21
  see also, Greek Rally
Porter, Paul A. 34, 54
Porter, Paul R. 180, 185, 198–9
  see also, Economic Cooperation Administration
positivist approaches, to International Relations 3, 9, 217
  see also, realism
post-civil war 3, 5, 59, 78, 81, 214, 218–21
  period 81, 218–20
  political system 53, 56, 58, 219
  regime 38, 52, 54, 57–8, 81, 146, 218–19
  state 8, 53, 56–9, 99, 219
postponement
  Greek UN recourse (withdrawal) 116, 130, 138, 140, 147, 149, 159–60, 214
  Iraqi delay tactic 154
  UN motion ('moratorium') 160–5, 167
Poulantzas, Nicos 25, 52
poverty, in Greece 182
  low living standards 189
  socioeconomic backwardness 199, 221
power centres 8, 32, 35, 58–9
Prizel, Ilya 19
Progressive Party of the Working People, AKEL 94–5, 100, 139
propaganda
  British 157
  Cominform 40–1, 44, 89
  counterpropaganda, British 212
  ECA 184
  Greek, re: Cyprus question 96, 150, 157–9, 177
  Greek Rally, economic 199, 202–3
proportional representation 70–1
  see also, majority voting system, Peurifoy
protectionism 20, 180
  ERE 208–9
  Rally 179–80, 192–6, 201–3, 205–6, 209
  semi-protectionism 209, 221
  see also, tariff increases, Markezinis
Psalidopoulos, Michalis 183–4
Public opinion
  Greek 84, 96–8, 141–2, 146, 168, 170–1, 203, 214, 266 fn76
  Turkish 100
  United States 158, 160, 188
  world 65, 96, 157, 173, 273 fn2

qualified independence, See Independence of Cyprus
quantitative restrictions, See import quotas

radio, Greece 57, 158, 170, 173, 185, 194, 199, 205, 212, 279 fn155
Rallis, George 117
rational action theory 215
rationality 71, 190, 214–15, 217
  irrationality 140, 142
realism 188
realism, IR theory 1, 3–4, 8–9, 13, 130, 160, 214, 217, 223 fn24
realistic liberalism, See liberalism
reductionism 7–8, 57–8, 115, 177, 264 fn14
Right, Greek 53, 201
  post-Civil War right-wing state 53, 84
Roach, Steven 10
Roosevelt, Franklin D. 34
Rosenau, James 18
Roxborough, Ian 16
royal couple 34, 53–4, 63–5, 81, 172, 239 fn3
  anti-royal(ism) 26, 36, 53
  attempted coups 54, 64–5, 67, 220
  favouritism 53, 59, 64, 172
  royalism 24, 53
  see also, Frederica, Palace, Papagos, Paul
Rusk, Dean 34

Sacred Bond of Greek Officers, IDEA 54–7, 61, 81, 86, 118, 220–1
  and Papagos 61–2, 218
  and Papagos solution 63–5, 67
  and PEAEK 99
  see also, armed forces, fascism, military coup, Military Dictatorship, Papagos
Said, Edward 27
  see also, orientalism

Sakellariou, Alexander 172, 175
Sarper, Selim 155–6
Schelling, Thomas 115
Scott Fox, David 141
Security 12, 19, 115
  external, Greek 26, 31–2, 39–46, 87–9, 197
  internal, Greek 31–2, 42
  national, Greek 26, 39–41, 50, 62, 74, 83, 124, 216–17
  Western 12, 39–46, 87–9, 123, 197, 212, 218
  Western 'security gap' 43
  see also, American military bases, East Mediterranean security, North Atlantic Treaty Organization, Southeastern Europe
Security Brigades 25
Security Police, Greece 7, 32, 52, 175, 274 fn43
self-sustainability, economic 50, 182, 186, 189
  lack of 182
semi-internationalization, of Cyprus question 145, 177, 263 fn2
  see also, internationalization
semi-periphery 13–16, 21–3, 25, 207, 217–18, 221
  Greece as part of 13, 22–3, 207, 217–18
semi-protectionist, See protectionism
September Events, Turkey 213–14
Sergeev, Mikhail 90, 107, 119–20, 257 fn50
  see also, Soviet Union
Sfakianakis, Panayiotis 55
Sherman, Forrest 43–4
Sisyphean, process 21, 23, 217
Skouras, Spyros 148–50, 156, 160–1, 177
Smith, Anthony D. 2, 19
Smith, Walter Bedell 89, 123, 150
Southeastern Europe 39, 43–4, 84, 123, 214
Soviet Union 1, 5, 29, 31, 39–40, 42, 44, 90, 92, 100–1, 107, 116–21, 123, 138, 157, 167, 177, 214, 216
  New Foreign Policy, 'new look' 119–20, 123, 214
  see also, Eastern Bloc, communism, Stalin, Cominform, Sergeev, Vyshinsky

Spentzas, Nikolaos 55
Spyridon, Archbishop 97–8, 172
  see also, Orthodox Church, Panhellenic Committee of the Struggle for Union with Cyprus
stabilization, economic 184
  Kartalis' programme, 1951–2 50, 181, 185–7, 197, 201
  Markezinis' measures 195
Stalin, Joseph 32, 45
  split with Tito 39
  Stalinist language 26
  see also, Soviet Union, Tito, Yugoslavia
State Department 32–4, 37–43, 45–7, 50, 65, 68, 70, 92, 101–2, 122, 125–7, 132, 137–8, 149, 160, 165, 169–70, 186, 197–9, 211–12
  records/archives 89–90, 106, 152, 197, 199
  see also, Acheson, Dulles, John Foster, Foreign Office
State Employees' Union, ADEDY 98
Stathakis, George 187
Stavrianos, Leften 39
Stearns, Monteagle 30, 42, 299
Stefanidis, Ioannis 40, 42, 62–3, 70, 98, 100, 113, 130, 133, 136, 150, 158, 160, 162, 164, 168, 215
Stefanopoulos, Stefanos 78, 80, 82, 89, 117
  attempted resignation 169–71
  Balkan Pact 121–5, 128
  Cyprus question 91–2, 99, 102–3, 106, 108–11, 118, 131, 134–6, 138, 140–2, 146, 155, 158–9, 163, 165–9, 212–13
  Popular Unity Party, LEK 55, 246 fn152
step-by-step, Cyprus solution 134, 138, 140, 142, 147
  Stavenhagen, Rodolfo 27
Stratos, George 172, 175
structural disarticulations 21–2, 35–7, 207
subaltern
  actor 31, 52
  social strata 22
  state 16, 31, 248 fn14
  local elites 35
  see also, hegemony
substantive resolution 145, 161–3, 166

non-substantive resolution 159, 161–2, 165
  see also, Dulles, John Foster
Suez, Canal Zone 93–4, 138
Sulzberger, Cyrus 106, 218
  see also, New York Times
Svolopoulos, Constantine 17, 84, 113–14, 173, 215
Svoronos, Nicos 2, 57–8

Ta Nea, newspaper 73
tariffs, commercial
  increases 180, 195, 202–8
  reductions 195, 202
  tariff-dependent industry 179, 188
  see also, protectionism
Tenekidis, George 146
third strategy, of Rally re: Cyprus question 85, 99, 147
  see also, dualism, dependent nationalism
Tito, Josip Bros 37, 39–41, 122–3
  Balkan Pact 122–8
  break with Moscow, also Tito-Stalin Split 29, 39
  Democratic Army of Greece 39–40
  visit to Athens, 1954 125–8
To Vima, newspaper 73, 119
Todorova, Maria 27–8, 140
traditional
  authority 75, 218
  economic mentality 203
  Greek elites 78, 99
  sectors, socioeconomic 21, 27, 210
Treaty of Ankara, 1953 121–5
  see also, Balkan Pact
Treaty of Bled 1954 128
  see also, Balkan Pact
Treaty of Lausanne, 1923 141, 155
Triepel, Heinrich 30, 48
Trieste dispute 1, 116, 121–7
  see also, Italy, Yugoslavia
Tripartite Cyprus talks 159
  London Conference, 1955 212–14
Truman Doctrine 3, 8, 18, 29, 31–3, 38–9, 43, 47, 50, 52, 83, 87, 179, 217
Truman, Harry S 32, 38, 42, 45, 69
Tsakalotos, Thrasyvoulos 61, 86
Tsaldaris, Constantine 36, 40, 99
  see also, Popular Party

Tsatsos, Constantine 67, 69
Tsingounis, Alexander 86
Tsouderos, Emmanuel 53, 55–6, 74, 82, 213
Tsoukalas, Constantine (also Tsoucalas) 62, 70, 79, 84, 201
Tsoukalis, Loukas 187, 201
Turkey 121, 181, 183, 211, 214, 217
  accession to NATO 29, 38, 42–7
  Balkan Pact 18, 44, 121–8
  Cyprus question 93, 98–9, 100–1, 104, 119, 121, 131, 138, 140–2, 147, 155–6, 159, 167, 171, 212–14, 216–17, 219
  September Events, 1955 213–14
  see also, Mediterranean Pact, Truman Doctrine, Menderes

underdevelopment 8, 27, 140, 189–90
  theory 17
underdog culture 19, 28
unemployment 181, 183
United Democratic Left, EDA 55–6, 71–2, 74, 119, 146, 266 fn76
United Nations 44, 54, 89, 93–4, 121, 179, 191
  British tactics 96, 103, 108–9, 137–40, 142–3, 145, 147–50, 152–6, 158–60, 162–9, 171, 178
  Cypriot Ethnarchy 97, 102–5, 108, 115, 136, 146, 148, 176, 214
  Greek recourse to 84, 91–2, 96–7, 99, 101–5, 108–11, 113–16, 120–1, 128–43, 145–60, 162–72, 174–8, 211–12, 214, 216
  Political Committee debate 156, 165–8, 178, 211
  Resolution 814 (IX) 165, 167, 170–1
  Turkish position 101, 104, 155
  US tactics 102–3, 138, 145–50, 153–5, 159–69, 178
  see also, Dixon, Dulles, Hammarskjold, inscription of Greek item, Kyrou, Munro, Nutting, Political Committee debate, Sarper, Urrutia
UN Recovery and Relief Agency (UNRRA) 179, 182
Under-Secretariat of Security and Public Order, Greece 118
Urrutia, Francisco 166
US Congress 51, 90, 198, 200

Congressional Committee on Foreign Economic Cooperation 51
congressional elections, 1954 153, 157, 159
US economic aid, to Greece 32–3, 35, 38, 47–50, 52, 179–84, 186, 188–90, 238 fn154, 273 fn11
  Markezinis' request for more 87, 89, 93, 181, 198, 207
  see also, US military aid
US embassy in Greece 7–8, 32–4, 38, 41, 49–50, 54, 62–71, 73–4, 86–7, 89, 92–4, 100, 123–4, 127, 153, 185–6, 193, 197, 199
  see also, Cannon, Peurifoy, Yost
US military aid to Greece 32–3, 38, 52, 182–3, 198, 273 fn11
US military bases, See American military bases
US National Security Council, NSC 32–3, 38–9, 45, 50, 89, 184
US 'neutrality', in UN debate 85, 100, 111, 116, 128, 160–1, 166, 171
US-Greek relations 29, 35, 43, 47–8, 83, 85–7, 90–2, 143, 214
USSR, See Soviet Union

Valden, Sotiris 201
Varvaressos, Kyriakos 35, 188–96, 207, 276 fn91
  1952 Report 35, 183, 188–94, 196, 199
  and devaluation 189, 192–6, 207
Vassilas, Efthymios 86
Venetis, Constantine 73
Venizelists 24, 53–6, 71
  anti-Venizelists 56
  see also, Centre parties, Venizelos, Eleftherios
Venizelos, Eleftherios 55, 213
  see also, Venizelists, Centre parties
Venizelos, Sophocles 25, 35–8, 40, 51, 53–5, 57, 59–61, 66, 68–9, 71–3, 78, 94–6, 98, 108, 185, 239 fn3
  see also, Liberal Party, Centre parties
Ventiris, Constantine 72, 173, 239 fn3
Veremis, Thanos 200
Vergopoulos, Costas 16, 187–8, 190
Vernardakis, Christophoros 25, 61
Vezanis, Dimitrios 172
Vlachos, Angelos 3, 96, 170, 173, 213–15

Vlachos, Georgios 77
Vournas, Tassos 62, 64, 84
Vyshinsky, Andrey 157

Wallerstein, Immanuel 13–15, 21, 30
Weber, Max 13, 15–16, 75, 77
  Weberian ideal types 15–16
Western
  allies/Alliance 7, 23, 26, 29, 39–40, 42–6, 84, 87, 89, 95, 120, 123, 128, 198
  anti-Western feeling 213–14
  capital 21, 187, 202
  economies 180, 207
  as 'Free World' 5, 51, 138, 214
  governments 5, 39, 42, 93, 125
  institutions/political systems 2, 8, 13, 18, 58, 219
  unity 165, 167
  world 1, 17–19, 58, 123, 128, 213–14
  see also, Balkanism, Westernization, North Atlantic Treaty Organization
Westernization, of Greece 17–18, 24, 28, 49, 54
Wilding, R.W.L. 163, 178
Wittner, Lawrence 29, 57
Woodhouse, Christopher 20
Wright, Andrew 103
Wyman, Louis 51

'X', wartime paramilitary group 94
  see also, Grivas
Xanthopoulos-Palamas, Christian 154
Xydis, Stephen 101–2, 114, 130–1, 133–4, 145, 150–1, 173, 214–15

Yost, Charles 32, 34, 44–5, 47–50, 66–9, 75, 81, 87, 91–2, 106, 110, 185
  see also, Peurifoy
Yugoslavia 18, 29, 38–42, 44–7, 50, 121–8, 211

Zachariadis, Nikos 74
Zigdis, Yannis 190–1
Zolotas, Xenophon 188, 190–3, 201, 208–9
Zürich-London Accords/Agreements 119, 132, 215
  see also, qualified Independence for Cyprus

www.ingramcontent.com/pod-product-compliance
Lightning Source LLC
Chambersburg PA
CBHW052148300426
44115CB00011B/1577